CW00706513

THE SERIOUS JOKE BOOK

George Coote

THE SERIOUS JOKE COLLECTION
© G. COOTE 1996

First published in 1996 by
Gap Publications
44 Wendell St
Norman Park
Queensland 4170 Australia

The Serious Joke Book
First published 1994
Reprinted 1994, twice
reprinted 1995, twice

The Seriously Rude Joke Book
First published in 1995
Reprinted 1995 (twice)
Reprinted 1996 (twice)
Reprinted 1997

Printed in Australia by
McPherson's Printing Group
Maryborough, Victoria

ISBN 0 947163 29 8

DEDICATION

To Bonny, my first wife.

ACKNOWLEDGEMENTS

WHO told the first joke? Who makes them up?

Are there really any new ones, or are they the same old yarns adapted and re-cycled through generations with only the names changed, not to defend the innocent, but to ensure we dob in the guilty.

I make no claim to the yarns in this book, indeed, I have heard most of them over the years in so many forms and versions it would be impossible to source their origin.

Most have been gathered from fellow travel writers during delays at airports, long flights and longer train rides. Swapping yarns is an affliction of the profession. (I was destined to be a travel writer. My first job was a proof reader for a sky-writing firm. And I hope that didn't go over your head).

I pay tribute to those fellow journos who could always see the funny side of lost luggage, or missing the last flight out of Mozambique, and to those who could still swap eye-watering belly laughs when broke and far from home in dire straits.

Contents

INTRODUCTION

EVEN a baby smiles at its father, which is proof that human beings are quick to recognise a joke. From then on, throughout life, any gathering of good folk is better off if it raises a laugh.

A life of journalism and travelling has meant listening to hundreds of speeches, most of them dull. But the speakers remembered were those who had a sense of humour and those who included a few gags. I always remembered the wisecracks and usually forgot the earth-shattering theme of the speech, and if the gags were good I wrote them down. Be it parliament, a municipal council meeting, a court case, a dinner party, a family reunion, a wedding, or even a funeral, these events are all the more memorable, if someone cracks a joke and creates a smile.

The purpose of this book is to make sure there is plenty of ammunition for those who find themselves having to "say a few words" at the rostrum, standing beside the wedding cake, bidding farewell to a retiring colleague at the office, or leaning on the bar holding court at the local.

Given a free choice most people would rather be amused than be on the receiving end of a lecture, and no matter how informative the speech may be it can be improved if peppered with a few gags. It will keep the audience alert, waiting for the next one.

The aim of this book is not to turn speeches into an entire comedy routine. Too many jokes will detract from the purpose of the address, and there are important things to be said at weddings, 21st birthdays or an election speech for local council. The art of public speaking is to select a few anecdotes central to the theme and select a few gags that can be tailored to the topic.

1

KEEPING THEM CLEAN

JOKES are known by the company they keep and their tendency to slip below the belt doesn't necessarily rule them out of order. Rude need not be crude, and some of the roughest can be salvaged with different wording to retain the same punchline in an acceptable form. What we are saying here is best illustrated by the limerick, those compact rhymes so often concerned with the bawdy;

> The limerick packs laughs anatomical
> Into space that is quite economical
> But the good ones we've seen
> So rarely are clean
> And the clean ones so seldom are comical.

In this volume we give readers the option;

> If you are ultra-fastidious by far
> And never tell yarns to your Ma
> Here are jokes by the mile
> That will sustain a wide smile
> But don't read any marked (R).

NOTES ARE ESSENTIAL

PUBLIC speaking is a comparatively simple business if you are properly prepared, but notes are essential. Unless you are an orator of the calibre of Winston Churchill, or have a phenomenal memory, don't try to deliver a speech without notes. Prime ministers don't.

One of the funniest speeches delivered recently was Michael Palin's tribute to George Harrison at a dinner to honour Harrison's financial backing of Handmade Films. Palin, of Monty Python fame, made sure he didn't miss one point of his hilarious monologue by shuffling a sheaf of foolscap notes, held at arm's length because of his long-sightedness. His note-reading was central to his delivery.

Most talks are delivered from completely written speeches, delivered word for word with few, if any, ad-lib departures. With a little practice it can appear to be friendlier and be appreciated as more spontaneous with note cards in one hand and several wisecracks up your sleeve.

The art is delivery and timing. If you have the advantages of a rostrum where your notes can be laid out on the lectern, then it is a comparatively simple matter to prepare well in advance and control the presentation with confidence, especially with a microphone.

Everybody tests a microphone, so turn yours to advantage to gain composure:

"Can you hear me over in that far side? Last time I asked if anybody could hear me in that far corner a bloke stood up and said indeed he could. And he offered to change places with somebody who couldn't!"

Standing before your contemporaries at a less formal office farewell, with no microphone, is a little more difficult but there is usually a semblance of order at these functions and there is at least the expectation of an address. Small prompt cards that can be shuffled in your hand is the most practical way to tackle this gathering.

The third, and most difficult arena for "public speaking" is the club, the pub, or around the dinner table where there is no order, and where contributing rather than dominating the conversation is a fine art. It takes a certain amount of confidence to embark on a lengthy yarn and expect to hold attention while you construct the plot to the punchline. Interjections, distractions and the waiter bringing the soup can cripple a good story unless the teller can cope with the interruption, anticipate the waiter's arrival, or suddenly stop the yarn at a high point of the teller's choosing. When the waiter leaves he shouldn't have to say, "Now where was I?" It is much more satisfying to have his listeners chase him for the rest of the yarn with someone eagerly asking "C'mon, what happened next?"

One-liners are the ideal tin-openers to tap the conversation with strangers around the table. Just raise your glass and say: "You can tell the happy motorcyclists by the insects on their teeth." And just leave it at that. Listen for the appropriate break in the conversation and say: "Oh I heartily agree. I was only saying the same thing to my wife in the bath last night." These are throw-away lines to test the water, and there are two pages of these profound statements in this volume. Your kind of humour will either be quickly embraced, or totally ignored.

A trick to hold attention in the rough and tumble of the bar or dinner table is to introduce your story with an off-beat opening line that will grab their attention.

"Did you hear about the one-armed Irish publican called Jock McTavish who took his first holiday abroad after pulling right-handed beers for 30 years?"

This story about the publican's trip to the Canary Islands is a top yarn and appears in the Travel section of this book. The "one-armed publican called Jock" has nothing to do with the thrust of the yarn but the introduction enables the construction of the story to continue. The listeners wait for the relevance of an Irishman called Jock and are led down a different trail to the punchline.

SALTING THE TALE

THE art of making an implausible story believable is to salt it along the way.

For example, did you hear about the woman who complained that passing trains rocked her bed so much she couldn't sleep?

"Unbelievable," is what the estate agent said, too, but the woman, who had just taken a lease on the flat near the railway line, insisted it was true and demanded the estate agent come around.

As he was shown in he noticed a mouse trap with a fish in it. "What's that?" he enquired.

"Oh, I'll talk to you about the rising damp later. Right now there is a train due and I want you to experience the vibrations."

They entered the bedroom. It was quiet. "I can't believe passing trains rock the bed," he said.

"Shakes the living daylights out of it," she persisted, looking at her watch. She heard a distant train whistle.

"Here's the five-thirty-five. Quick, lie down on the bed yourself," she said, and she climbed on to the other side.

That's when her husband came in. "What do you think you are doing?" he roared, glaring at the estate agent stretched out on the eiderdown.

"Would you believe, waiting for a train?" he ventured.

Remember, this book provides the raw material presented here in cold type. A little acting, timing and delivery will greatly enhance their reception to your audience. Delivering the appropriate gag at the right time is what it is all about, and when one joke follows another on the same topic, then it's a double-whammy. A series of yarns on the same theme raises those belly laughs that are good for the soul.

So if these cold pages make you smile, then imagine the effect when they are delivered as repartee.

The categories are designed to cover every occasion from births to funerals, including bonking (which actually comes before births).

If it is your responsibility to farewell a retiring office colleague, toast the happy couple, propose the toast at the coming of age party or make a presentation, there are anecdotes in this book suitable for adapting to your guest of honour ... or the victim of your address.

Select some, tinker with them and enjoy them yourself, and before taking centre stage remember the ABC and the XYZ of public speaking. ABC is Always Be Cheerful, and XYZ is Examine Your Zipper.

A WEDDING

LET'S take a wedding anniversary as an example. It depends on how formal the function is, and how well everybody knows each other, but if you have drawn the short straw to "say a few words" then do some serious research on the couple for the proper tribute which needs to be said, and cobble in as many of these one-liners you judge the gathering will appreciate.

Ladies and gentlemen, in-laws and outlaws, friends and foe ... it has befallen my lot to say a few words on behalf of you all and to toast Bill and Mabel who have been married 30 years today.

Mabel tells me that includes ten years of wedded bliss. And Bill reminds us all that the sentence for manslaughter is only 25 years. But they both agree, that the reason they have stuck together so long is that neither will take custody of the kids. I can well remember the day they had to get ... sorry, the day they got married. Bill has always remembered it too. Unlike most husbands who forget these anniversaries, their wedding day never slipped Bill's memory. It was the day Arsenal thrashed Liverpool.

And of course Mabel was not the street-wise matron she is today. Bill says she was so naive when he married her she thought intercourse was a ticket to the races.

Although it was a big wedding with family and friends from both sides, I am reliably informed that Bill and Mabel still sat up all night waiting for their sexual relations to arrive. It was also the night Bill exploded the myth about oysters. He tells me he had a dozen on his wedding night but only eleven of them worked.

Marriage is a marvellous institution. No family should be without it. (Or, marriage is a marvellous institution, but who wants to live in an institution?) Bill tells me that marriage is a matter of give and take, and that he gives and Mabel takes. And Mabel says they have stopped giving each other anniversary presents long ago, now they shake hands each year and call it quits.

Those who miss out on marriage miss a great deal in life. It reminds me of a bishop I know, right in this very town, who was touched with compassion when he saw an elderly couple standing together in the queue at the Op Shop sale. He thought to himself, "They have shared a lifetime together, through thick and thin, and now here they are, fallen upon hard times, in their twilight years." He went up to them and asked if they would like to spend a week's holiday at Bishop's Retreat in the mountains and packed them off in his chauffeured limousine before they could express their thanks. It was a month later when the bishop saw the old man in the Op Shop again, standing alone this time.

"Did you enjoy the holiday? Did you enjoy the food?" he asked.

"Oh, everything was tops," said the old-timer. "But tell me yer grace, who was that old-boiler I had to share the room with?"

And so, ladies and gentlemen, back to the topic in hand. Could we have two minutes silence … oops, sorry. Could we all raise our glasses and drink to the long and happy health of our dear friends, Bill and Mabel.

THE ANNUAL MEETING

ANOTHER example is the reunion, the annual general meeting, the yearly bunfight or social gathering. Whether

7

it is pompously formal or loosely ad hoc, somebody has to say a few words:

Gentlemen. Excellent to see such a roll-up tonight. It has befallen my lot to give you a short address. Here it is: 29 Bay Street.

Since last we met we've passed a lot of water under the bridge. We have an apology. Smithers can't get bail.

New members will be delighted to know that our president is a man of substance, a pillar of society who needs no introduction. So he won't get one.

We have the treasurer's report from Sticky Fingers Smithers who has cooked the books to show we have a healthy bank balance. As already stated, Sticky can't be here tonight. He is helping the police with some enquiries.

We should move a vote of thanks to our honorary president who slaves all day over a hot secretary on behalf of us all. And it should be said that his dedication to the club is such that in pursuit of its well-being he never leaves a turn unstoned.

And let's pay tribute to our committee. As you all know, half the members of most committees are hopeless layabouts while the other half do all the work, but with our committee it is completely the reverse.

GET THE PUNCHLINE STRAIGHT

MANY people who enjoy a good joke lament that they cannot remember them. Those that can remember them, vaguely, lose the plot and lack the confidence to relate them.

The key to it all is to remember the punchline, get it straight, and store it in your mind with a recall word.

A stock of jokes, as this book sets out to supply, will provide the flexibility to match the repartee around the table, especially when you are halfway into the yarn and the resident smart alec (every function has one) interjects with: "Don't tell me its the white horse joke!"

"Wrong, again," you lie, and change direction for horse joke number two, three or four. Style is important.

HOW TO USE THIS BOOK

MOST jokes can be reconstructed and adapted to suit all occasions.

Take this bland example of three politicians who died on the same day and arrived at the Devil's reception centre simultaneously.

"Ah, a Tory MP," said the Devil. "We've been waiting for you," and he took him to a dungeon where a terrible witch was the only occupant. The MP was pushed into the dingy cell and as the door clanged behind him the Devil's voice over the PA system boomed: "Tory MP, this is your punishment!"

Next was a Labor MP. "We've been waiting for you, too," and taking him to another dungeon which contained yet another horrible witch, he was given a push and, as the door clanged behind him, the Devil's voice over the PA system boomed: "Labor MP, this is your punishment!"

The third polly was the prime minister. "Ah, we have certainly been waiting for you," said the Devil and he was led to another dungeon. Inside, through soft lights, the PM could see Miss Lottzabazooma reclining naked on a satin couch. He was given a shove and, as the door clanged shut behind him, the Devil's voice over the PA system boomed: "Miss Lottzabazooma, this is your punishment!"

Consider how much better that story would be if you used the names of well-known politicians who fitted the bill.

Better still, personalise the same story by including

those around your table; Tom, Dick and Harry. And set up the guest of honour (Harry in this case) by saving him for the last dungeon.

First, Tom gets berated by the Devil over the sins for which he is notorious: "being late for your own wedding, never arriving at a golf match on time, and for collecting parking tickets."

Dick gets thrown into his cell for "telling those boring jokes, ad nauseum and for giving worthless racing tips to close friends" and Harry gets a similar drubbing listing his "in-house" personality traits that your listeners readily recognise. Involving your friends in the joke makes it far more humourous.

So run an astute eye over the "raw material" listed here and consider their modification to different professions and new situations.

A

IN a Serious Joke Book the funniest jokes are not necessarily upfront. In alphabetical order we are obliged to start, like we all began, with accidents.

ACCIDENTS
See CARS, MOTORING, DRIVERS.

THE young woman was giving details of the accident to the police and denied she was speeding.

"What gear were you in?" asked the cop.

"An apricot yellow two-piece with chartreuse picture hat," she said.

*　　*　　*

TEN per cent of all accidents are caused by drivers affected by alcohol. Which is another way of saying that 90 per cent of accidents are caused by non-drinkers.

*　　*　　*

THERE was a knock on the door and Fred found himself being asked to become a Jehovah's Witness.

"I didn't even see the bloomin' accident," he said.

*　　*　　*

THE woman at the cocktail party was intent on making the acquaintance of the young medical officer.

"Do you deal with many accidents?" she asked.

"I really don't know," he replied.

"But you are a doctor, what do you mean you don't know?"

"How could I," he said, "My field is obstetrics."

* * *

WHEN Harry arrived at the pub his mates noticed he was on crutches, his face was bruised and there was plaster over his eye. "I must have had one too many when I left here last night," he explained.

His mates said they thought he had been quite sober. "As maybe," said Harry, "but after I left the pub, I turned up High Street, did the roundabout on the corner three times, came back on the wrong side of the road, crossed the median strip and crashed right into the front door of this pub.

"Lucky I wasn't in my bloomin' car!"

* * *

"HOW did this accident happen, sir?"

"My wife fell asleep in the back seat."

* * *

"HOW did this accident happen, sir?"

"Well, the sign said, STOP, LOOK AND LISTEN, and while I was doing that a bloody train ran over me."

* * *

SAID the cop: "Have you ever had an accident, Missus?"

"Well, I met my husband at a service station."

* * *

THE wife told the police that although she had broken the umbrella over her husband's head it was an accident. "If I had known the umbrella would break I would have used a golf club," she said.

* * *

FRED had just parked his old car when a cop came and asked him if he had reported the accident.

* * *

FIVE Hells Angels walked into the bar, ordered their drinks and suggested the lone drinker at the end of the bar should pay. When he refused they punched him up and threw him out of the pub.

"He wasn't much of a fighter," said one of the bikies to the barman.

"He is not much of a driver either," said the barman, "He has just had an accident and driven his truck over five motorbikes."

*　　*　　*

AFTER a terrible accident at the factory, where Fred fell into the upholstery machine, he is now fully recovered.

*　　*　　*

THE cop pushed through the crowd at the scene of the accident to see a blonde and a young man having passionate sex on the nature strip.

He quickly put a stop to it and demanded to know what was going on.

"It's all my fault," she said. "He was thrown from his car in the accident and I was giving him mouth to mouth resuscitation, and, well, we both got carried away."

*　　*　　*

HE was sitting at the bar knocking back double Scotches. As fast as the barman could place them in front of him he scoffed them down in one gulp.

"It's the only way I've been able to drink them since my accident," he explained to a friendly enquirer.

"What sort of accident?" asked his new friend.

"Shocking," he replied. "I knocked one over with my elbow."

ACCOUNTANTS
See FINANCE

MY old Dad said I'd never make an accountant.

"There are three kinds of people in this world, son," he said. "Those who can count, and those who can't!"

A CHARTERED accountant is an undertaker who has had a charisma bypass.

*   *   *

THE chartered accountant went into the pub after work and ordered a pot of beer. As the publican pushed it across the bar the accountant said: "Do you think you could get a nip of whisky in that?"

"Certainly, sir," said the publican.

"In that case," said the accountant, "perhaps you'd just top it up with beer!"

*   *   *

THEY say Adam was the first accountant, after he turned a leaf and made an entry.

*   *   *

HE thought the new office girl was as beautiful as an Income Tax Refund.

*   *   *

HE told his wife he was changing their accountant.

"He's too shy and retiring," he explained.

"Is that a reason to sack him?" she asked

"Yes. He's $200,000 shy and that's why he's retiring."

*   *   *

ON his retirement after 35 years as Chief Accountant the company presented him with a silver-bound ledger book, framed and mounted on a little pedestal.

He looked at the trophy and said, "Well at least it has finally settled a concern of mine. I almost chose a career as a gynaecologist."

*   *   *

THE executive director visited the company's accountant who was sick in hospital. "John," he said, "the board decided to send you a Get Well Card and I would like you to know it was a majority decision."

*   *   *

THE partners in the accountancy firm crossed the road to their local bar for their usual afterwork drink.

"Oh, I forgot to lock the safe," said one.

"It's okay," said his partner. "We're both here aren't we?"

ADVERTISEMENTS

PLACED in the personal column: "Fred, please do not come home. All is forgiven."

* * *

GIRL wanted for petrol pump attendant.

* * *

MAN wanted to wash dishes, and two waitresses.

* * *

ACCOMMODATION, suit two girls willing to share room or young man.

* * *

ACCOMMODATION: Honeymoon suite, sleeps three.

* * *

STRADIVARIUS violin for sale. Almost new.

* * *

"PHOTOGRAPHER setting up own business needs model, as sleeping or active partner."

* * *

LOST dog. Has three legs, blind in left eye, right ear missing, broken tail, no teeth, recently castrated. Answers to Lucky.

* * *

A SALESMAN was staying overnight in a country town where the only excitement was watching the spin-dry in the laundromat. Out of sheer boredom he opened the Gideon Bible provided in all motel rooms. On the fly-leaf was a message: If thou art bored and lonely and desireth some warm comfort, ring Susie, 58-6683.

* * *

WONDERFUL opportunity for woman to join fishing partners. Must have own boat. Must be able to cook, wash and gut fish. Please send photo of boat.

ALCOHOLICS

ALCOHOLICS Anonymous is a place where you drink in secret.

*   *   *

THERE is a new organisation called AAAA.
It is for people being driven to drink.

*   *   *

THE vicar was invited to address the Alcoholics Anonymous meeting. "I have lived in this town all my life," he said sternly. "There are 95 hotels and I can honestly say I have never been in one of them."
"Which one is that?" said a voice from the rear.

*   *   *

HE bought one of those audio tapes that help you to stop drinking while you're sleeping. It worked. He hasn't had a drink in his sleep since.

*   *   *

"ALCOHOL is your trouble," said the judge. "Alcohol alone is responsible for your present predicament."
"Thank you, judge," said the drunk. "Everyone else says it's my fault."

*   *   *

THE wife sought some advice from the doctor about her alcoholic husband.
"Has he tried Alcoholics Anonymous?" asked the Doc.
"I expect so. He'll drink anything," she replied.

*   *   *

CHAP was walking home when an alcoholic stepped in front of him with a gun in one hand and a bottle in the other. Pointing the gun at his victim the drunk thrust the bottle forward and said, "Take a drink of this."
The unfortunate man took a swig then spat it out. "It's awful," he gasped.
"I know," said the drunk. "Now you hold the gun on me while I take a swallow."

THEY were in the Mexican army on curfew duty. "You patrol this side of the street, and I will patrol the other," said Pedro to his mate.

They hadn't gone very far when a shot rang out and Pedro ran across the street to discover his mate with a smoking gun and a dead man on the footpath.

"Why did you shoot him?" demanded Pedro. "The curfew is not in force for another half hour?"

"I know that," said his mate. "But I know where this hombre lives and there is no way he would have got home in time."

* * *

THE difference between being a drunk and being an alcoholic is that the drunk doesn't have to bother attending all those boring meetings.

* * *

AN alcoholic is somebody you don't like, but drinks as much as you.

* * *

AN alcoholic believes a teetotaller is someone who practices moderation to excess, and abstinence is okay provided you do it in moderation.

* * *

FRED joined Alcoholics Unanimous. "There are no arguments," he explained.

* * *

THE drunk asked a passer-by if he knew the way to Alcoholics Anonymous.

"Why," he said, "do you want to join?"

"No, I want to resign."

* * *

FRED stumbled into the AA meeting and knocked over a few chairs.

The secretary frowned: "Oh, we were so happy last night when you turned up sober."

"Well, tonight it's my turn to be happy," said Fred.

THE doctor noticed that the chronic alcoholic could not hold his hands out straight. They shook violently.

"How much have you been drinking lately?" he asked.

"Hardly any," said the drunk. "I spill most of it!"

* * *

SHE answered a knock on the door. "I am collecting for the Home for Alcoholics," said the caller.

"Well come back around nine o'clock," she said. "My husband will be home then, and you can have him."

* * *

HE preached moderation in all things. "First, I never drink whisky without water. Second. I never drink water without whisky."

ANIMALS

THERE is a big difference between buffaloes and bisons.

For a start, you can't wash your hands in a buffalo.

* * *

WHERE would you find a turtle with no legs?

Exactly where you left him.

* * *

THE bi-sexual donkey had a hee in the morning and a haw at night.

* * *

THE suicidal seal flip-flopped into the pub and asked for a Canadian Club on the rocks.

* * *

A BLOKE went to the pub with a giraffe. They drank all afternoon. By six o'clock the giraffe collapsed in an ungainly heap on the floor and his drinking partner staggered towards the door.

"Hey," said the barman, "Don't go and leave that lyin' on the floor."

The man turned and said, "It's not a lion. It's a giraffe!"

LEO the Lion was swaggering down the jungle path confronting each animal in turn: "Who's the king of the jungle?" he asked Gerald the giraffe.

"You are, of course," said Gerald.

"Who's the king of the jungle?" he asked Harold the hyena.

"You are, of course."

The answers were the same until he confronted Jumbo the elephant. "Who's the king of the jungle?" he asked, blocking Jumbo's path.

With a blast from his trumpet the elephant picked the lion up in his trunk, threw him in the air, caught him, dashed him against a tree then flung him over his shoulder.

"Alright," said Leo dusting himself off. "You don't have to get nasty just because you don't know the answer!"

* * *

LEO the lion was drinking from a stream with his bottom in the air, just as a big chimp was passing. From the chimp's viewpoint it looked like Lily the lion so he crept up for a quiet slap and tickle.

The lion let out a mighty roar and the chimp, realising his mistake, took off like greased lightning. He sped through the jungle with the lion in hot pursuit.

The chimp dashed into a hunter's camp, quickly donned a safari suit, slapped on a pith helmet, dived into a chair, grabbed a copy of The Times and hid behind it as if was reading. The lion screeched into the clearing and as soon as the dust settled asked the "hunter", "Have you seen a chimp dash past here?"

"Not the chimp that dated the lion down by the stream?"

"Hell," said the lion, "don't tell me it's in the papers already."

* * *

THE visitor was admiring the family's pet pig.

"Yes, he's an amazing animal," said the farmer. "Once

he raised the alarm and saved the house from burning down. Another time he saved young Johnny from drowning and pulled him out of the dam ..."

"That's incredible," said the visitor, "but tell me, why does he have one leg missing?"

"Well," said the proud farmer, "you don't eat a pig like that all at once!"

* * *

ONE zebra got to thinking. "Hey, Zeke," he said to his mate, "are we white with black stripes, or black with white stripes?"

Zeke didn't know and they pondered this problem for a week before asking the king of the jungle.

"Hey Leo, are we white with black stripes, or black with white stripes?"

Leo didn't know but he directed them up to the top of a mountain. "Ask God," he said.

They spent a day sitting on top of the mountain shouting: "Hey God. Are we white with black stripes or black with white stripes?"

It wasn't until sunset that the booming voice of God bellowed out: "You are what you are."

Next day Leo asked them the result. "You are what you are. That's what God said. What the heck does that mean?"

Leo thought this over for a while and then gave his verdict: "It means you are white with black stripes. Otherwise he would have said 'Yo is what yo is'."

ANNIVERSARIES

ON their golden anniversary he said there was nothing he wouldn't do for his wife and there was nothing she wouldn't do for him.

"And that's how it's been for the past 50 years," he added. "We've done nothing for each other."

* * *

"I'M afraid I can't make the darts match tomorrow night,

20

Fred. I promised to take Thingummy out for our silver anniversary."

* * *

FOR 22 years Harry and his wife were deliriously happy. Then they met each other.

* * *

HE asked how they should celebrate their 25th anniversary.

She suggested two minutes' silence.

* * *

HE was telling his mate how he and his wife spent their 25th anniversary. "We left town on the same train, went to the same hotel, managed to get the same room. But this time it was me who went to the bathroom and cried!"

* * *

ON quiet nights, when he is alone, Fred runs their wedding video backwards, just to watch himself walk out of the church a free man.

* * *

IT was their 40th wedding anniversary and Rachael took Izzi to an upmarket part of town and proudly showed him a block of flats. "It's ours, Izzi, we own it," she said.

"But how?" he asked.

"You remember all these years how I charged you $10 each time we made love?" said Rachael. "Well, I saved all that money and bought this block of flats."

"Oh, Rachael, if only I had known, I would have given you all my business."

* * *

THERE'S not much difference between a toilet seat and an anniversary. Men usually miss them both.

ARMY

THE old diggers were renewing old acquaintances at the Anzac reunion. "Was it you or your brother who got killed in New Guinea?"

A SIGNAL from HQ circulated along the front line declared that there was a $10 bounty for anyone who shot one of the enemy.

Next day at a forward observation post Paddy whispered to Mick, "Psst. There's two hunnerd t'ousand dollars creeping up my side of the hill!"

* * *

THE new rookie looked a trifle uncomfortable when the brigadier stopped in front of him.

"Aren't you happy, man?" asked the officer.

The rookie nervously agreed he was happy.

"And what were you in civvy street?"

"A bloody sight happier," said the rooky.

* * *

CALLED up for national service the young man was being examined by an army doctor.

"Just give me a gun, I'll show 'em," said the lad. "If they shoot off my hands I'll work the trigger with my arms. If they shoot off my arms then I'll do it with my legs. If they shoot off my legs, then b'jeezus I'll pull the trigger with my teeth."

"Good show, that's the spirit," said the doctor.

"Hang on," said the lad. "Don't you think I'm a little crazy?"

* * *

A TOUGH drill sergeant ordered his men to hold up their left legs. One recruit mistakenly held up his right leg, thus placing it beside his neighbour's left.

"Alright, alright," roared the sergeant. "Who's the wise guy holding up both legs?"

* * *

THE sergeant major had been lecturing the new recruits on their duties for the past two hours and suddenly noticed that Private Murphy was dozing.

"Now then, Murphy!" he roared. "Why should a soldier be ready to die for his country?"

Paddy scratched his head for a moment. "You're damned right sir. Why should he?"

* * *

THE court martial decreed that the deserter be taken to Boot Hill where he would be shot. It was a grim and rainy day and at dawn the firing squad arrived to escort the condemned man a mile or more to his execution.

He grumbled all the way. "Fancy having to march all this way in this terrible weather just to be shot," he lamented.

"Yeah, but think of us," said one of his guards. "We've got to march back again."

* * *

THE tough sergeant major knew that he was unpopular with the ranks and while carpeting a soldier who was due for discharge said: "I've heard it said that when I die some of you blokes are coming back to piddle on my grave. I suppose you will be among them?"

"Not me, sarge," said the soldier. "Once I get out of this army I've promised myself I will never stand in long queues again."

* * *

AS the sergeant major approached the camp he was challenged by the new recruit on sentry duty.

"That's not bad Private Smithers," said the officer, "but the expression is 'Friend or Foe' not 'Goodies or Baddies'!"

* * *

A PARTICULARLY unpopular sergeant major popped his head up above the trench and a sniper's bullet whizzed within one centimetre of his ear.

"Paddy! Get out and get that sniper," he roared to private Kelly.

Kelly was the regiment's best scout and within ten minutes he was back, the enemy sniper, with raised hands, walking before him.

Then Paddy began to punch hell out of his prisoner.

"Hey go easy," said his mates. "What's that for?"

"It's for missing the bloody sar'major," said Paddy.

*   *   *

THE navy recruiting officer looked the applicant up and down. "Can you swim?" he said.

"Why," said the prospective sailor, "don't you have any boats?"

*   *   *

THE visitor breasted the Returned Servicemen's Bar and asked for a double Scotch.

"That'll be eight-dollars-fifty," said the bartender.

"Hell," said the visitor. "If you had have charged like that at Gallipoli we would have won."

*   *   *

THERE was once a discreet brigadier
Fond of his ten thousand a year
But when he heard the guns rattle
Said: "Sounds like a battle!"
And quietly slipped to the rear.

*   *   *

THE C.O. had just welcomed the young army officer, shown him around the camp and was outlining the recreational facilities.

"On Mondays we have a snooker tournament, a jolly good show with the winner taking the jackpot."

"I'm afraid I don't play snooker sir," said the officer.

"Well, on Tuesdays we have a darts match," continued the C.O., "and first to make 301 wins the drinks."

"I'm afraid I don't like gambling or playing darts, sir."

"Really?" said the C.O. "Well, on Wednesday nights a few girls come up from the village for a dance and a bit of hanky panky and…"

"Sorry sir," said the officer. "I have no time for women."

"Good God, man," said the C.O. "You're not gay are you?"

"Certainly not sir," said the officer.

"Oh dear," said the C.O., "then you are not going to like Thursday and Friday nights much either."

24

ARTS

FRED is a bit of an artist. He doesn't understand women, but he knows what he likes.

* * *

SALVADOR Dali took Picasso aside and said, "Excuse me friend, could I have a word in your eyeball?"

* * *

AN artist's model is a girl who shows the painter where to draw the line.

* * *

THE model got off the couch and came to inspect the painting. She blushed and said, "Oh Mr Renaldo. You've been looking."

* * *

AN artist and his model were smooching on the sofa when they heard a car arrive. "Quick, it's my wife," cried the artist. "Get your clothes off and pretend we're working."

* * *

THE mayor had officially opened the one-man art show and was browsing along the paintings when he stopped with a start in front of a picture of a woman reclining nude on a couch.

"That's my wife," he cried. "You scoundrel. You have had my wife up here posing nude in your studio."

The artist, a little terrified, said it wasn't the case at all. "I painted it from memory," he said.

* * *

A SOCIALITE approached a prominent portrait artist and asked if he would paint her in the nude.

"Sure," he said, "but I'll have to keep my socks on otherwise I'll have nowhere to stick my brushes."

* * *

THE artist said: "I only paint what I see."

The critic said: "Then you should never paint in that condition."

FRED's Dad was an artist. He was always drawing corks.

* * *

"MY art is becoming internationally acclaimed. One of these days I will be immoral."

"Don't you mean immortal?"

"I know what I mean."

* * *

"DID you sell any of your paintings at the art show?"

"No, but I am encouraged," he replied. "Somebody stole one."

* * *

"MUM, what is pop-art?"

"Why do you ask, son?"

"Well, it's what Dad says when he's going to pop-art for a quickie down the pub."

* * *

A BLOKE cleaning out his attic discovered an old violin and an oil painting. Thinking they might be valuable he took them to an art dealer.

"Well, that's a Stradivarius," mused the dealer, "and this here is a Rembrandt."

"Then, are they valuable?" he asked hopefully.

"Not really," said the dealer. "Stradivarius was a hopeless painter, and look at Rembrandt's violin. You'd never get a tune out of it."

* * *

SALVADOR Dali was robbed while on a visit to New York, but he managed to get a good look at the offender and was able to provide the police with a rough sketch of the felon.

For the next two weeks New York police searched for a man with a head like a horse, a fried egg on his forehead and a sword in his mouth.

ASTROLOGY

A FAMOUS astrologer was quite entranced by the baby in the pram. "Beautiful," she said, "absolutely beautiful," and beaming at the proud mother she said, "Do you happen to know what sign she was conceived under?"

"Yes," blushed the young mum. "It said 'Keep off the Grass'!"

* * *

IT has got to the stage where people who introduce themselves now add their birthsigns.

"Hi, I'm Bill Moloney, Sagittarius."

"Hi, I'm John Spriggs, Cancer."

"Hi, I'm Joe Bloggs, bladder infection."

* * *

"WHAT sign were you born under?"

"I think it was a red and green flashing Neon.

ATHEISTS

AN atheist is a man with no invisible means of support.

* * *

FRED was an atheist, but he gave it up. He said there were no holidays.

* * *

GRAFFITI. "Thank God I'm an Atheist."

* * *

IF God is good
  Why do his peoples
  Put lightning rods
  On top of steeples?

* * *

ROSES are red
  Violets are bluish
  If it wasn't for Jesus
  We'd all be Jewish

B

BACHELORS

A BACHELOR is a man who comes to work every morning, from a different direction.

*　　*　　*

AFTER his check-up the doctor told Barry the bachelor he was getting on in years and his lifestyle of wine, women and song would have to change.

"In fact, you will have to give up the first two," said the doc, "but you can sing as much as you like."

*　　*　　*

THE bachelor finished his meal and placed his tip on the table. The waiter took one look at the 15 cents and said: "Thank you for your generosity. You can always tell the character of a diner by the way he tips."

"Oh, really," he said. "What do these five-cent coins tell you about me?"

"Well, you put the three coins in a row," said the waiter. "That tells me you are tidy for starters. The first coin tells me you are frugal and the second coin tells me you are a bachelor."

"That's true," said the diner, impressed. "And what does the third coin tell you?"

"That tells me your father was a bachelor too."

28

FRED is safe now that he has joined Bachelors Anonymous.

Each time he feels like getting married the club sends round a woman in hair-curlers to nag him for a while.

* * *

MANY a poor husband was once a rich bachelor.

* * *

HE had so much fun at the bachelor party he postponed the wedding.

BARBERS

THE sign on the barber shop read: Haircuts, while you wait!

* * *

HIS hair was neatly departed in the middle.

* * *

HE asked the barber if he had something to stop falling hair. The barber sold him a net.

* * *

WHEN one barber cuts another's hair, which one does the talking?

* * *

"HOW do you like your hair cut, sir?"
"Off."

* * *

"JUST a shave please, I haven't time to listen to a haircut."

* * *

"DO you shave yourself all the time?"
"No. I often stop for food."

* * *

THE barber was late for work. While shaving that morning he talked himself into a shampoo and hair tint.

* * *

EVERY time the nation's economic recession gets worse,

the local barber puts up his prices. He says longer faces take more time to shave.

*   *   *

THE customer noticed the barber's dirty hands and complained about it.

"Can't help it if nobody has been in for a shampoo yet," he replied.

*   *   *

THE boss demanded to know where he had been.

"I've been for a haircut."

"You can't have your hair cut in office time?"

"Why not? It grows in office time."

"Not all of it," said the boss.

"So I didn't get it all cut off," he replied.

*   *   *

THE sign said: "Beatles' Style Cut Here."

So he went in and was aghast to be shorn almost bald.

"That's not how the Beatles have their hair cut," he protested.

"It will be if they come here," said the barber.

*   *   *

TWO business acquaintances were seated side by side in the hairdresser's. One barber asked his client if he would like some French toilet water on his hair.

The man declined. "No way, the wife would think I'd been in a French brothel."

The second barber asked the same question to his client who responded: "Sure, I'll have some. My wife has never been in a French brothel."

*   *   *

FRED had just retired and was about to go on a world trip. He popped in to Bob the Barber's for a short back and sides on the eve of his departure.

"Be sure to come and tell me all about it when you come home," said Bob after he had finished the cut.

Two months later Fred was back in the chair again

30

relating the highlights. "I even went to see the **Pope at St Peter's**" he said.

"Wow," said Bob.

"And what's more, the Pope came over and spoke to me."

"That's unbelievable," said Bob, still clipping away. "What did the Pope say?"

"He said, 'Where the hell did you get a haircut like that'!"

* * *

FLIRTY Fred popped into the hotel's barber shop for a haircut and while waiting for the barber to strop his razor he was enjoying a manicure from the very shapely blonde assistant and took the chance to chat her up.

"What time do you knock off," he leered out the side of his mouth.

"About six," she said.

"What about coming up for a drink?"

"I'm married," she said. "What would I say to my husband?"

"Just tell him straight. Tell him you are going out tonight," said Fred.

"You tell him," she said. "That's him stropping the razor."

* * *

A MAN entered the barber's saloon and asked, "How long will you be?"

"About an hour," replied the barber.

"Okay, I'll come back," said the man who then left.

He didn't return until the next day when he entered the doorway again and asked, "How long will you be?"

The barber had six customers waiting and said, about an hour or more.

"Okay, I'll come back."

When the prospective customer did this every day of the week and never returned as he always promised the barber became intrigued and asked his apprentice to follow him.

"Tell me where he goes," he said.

The apprentice was back in five minutes. "He goes straight round to your place," he told the barber.

* * *

THE bald man was astounded to be charged $15 for a cut and trim.

"That's more than you charge for people with a full head of hair," he complained.

"Yeah," said the barber. "A treasure hunt costs more."

* * *

IF barristers can be de-barred, and ministers be de-frocked, can a barber be dis-tressed?

* * *

HARRY Cox was looking for his brother Bob. He couldn't find him in his usual haunts or in the pub. Thinking he might be having a haircut Harry went to the barber's shop.

"Bob Cox in here?" he asked.

"Sorry sir," said the barber. "We only do shaves and haircuts."

* * *

(R) THE barber broke his leg in a skiing accident.

Now he can only cut hair on crutches.

BEAUTY

HIS wife used to have a nice firm chin. But now the firm has taken on a couple of partners.

* * *

SHE said: "Will you love me when I'm old and grey?"

"Why not," he said. "I've loved you when you were blonde, henna, brunette and blue."

* * *

IT'S no use making your mind up to stay in if your wife has made her face up to go out.

* * *

SHE was wearing a faint perfume. One sniff and you fainted.

WHEN she came down the stairs he said: "My word, you look lovely. That must have taken quite some time."

* * *

BEAUTY comes from within ... from within bottles, jars, tubes, phials, compacts...

* * *

"DOES your sister still make up jokes?"
  "Yes, she still works at the beauty parlour."

* * *

SHE approached the hairdresser.
  "What do you have for grey hair?"
  "The greatest respect, madam."

* * *

THE better a woman looks, the longer a man does.

BEDS

MORE than one-third of our lives are spent in bed. Most of us were begotten in a bed, and born in a bed and we will probably die in a bed. In between these important events the bed is an essential accessory for play and rest; and no joke book should be without a bed section, and no bed should be without a joke section.

* * *

A BED is where one good turn can get all the blankets.

* * *

BEDS cause hangovers. Statistics prove that drunks will go to bed happy, and wake up feeling terrible.

* * *

WHEN he was in bed he was terrified that somebody might be underneath it. When he got underneath it he was terrified that somebody might be on top of the bed.

  The psychiatrist told him he had bed phobia and was treating him at $100 a visit.

  After a year of treatment, and the loss of a small

fortune, he told the psychiatrist he wasn't coming back again.

"I had a talk to the barman and he solved my problem," he said.

"Oh, and what did he do?" enquired the psychiatrist.

"He came round and sawed the legs off my bed!"

BETS

"REMEMBER I bet a tenner I'd beat my drink problem?"

"Yeah."

"Well now I've got a gambling problem."

* * *

CARRYING his bat nervously he walked on to the ground for his first match with the seniors. A spectator called to him: "I've got a bet on you."

"That's nice of you," he said modestly, "I'll probably get a duck."

"That's what I bet."

* * *

THE argument at the bar was on religion.

"And I betcha a tenner you don't know the Lord's Prayer."

"You're on."

"Okay, say it"

"Now I lay me down to sleep..."

"Gawd. Here's the money. I didn't think you knew it."

* * *

THE Elderly Citizens' Club now has a community bus and each Sunday they go off on a mystery tour. To make it interesting the oldies dob in 50 cents in a sweep to guess the mystery destination. Bert the driver has won it three times in a row.

* * *

A PUNTER would bank $500 every Monday morning so regularly that finally the bank manager's curiosity got the better of him. Where did he get the money?

"I am a punter," explained the customer, "but I only bet on sure things."

Intrigued, the banker pressed him for an example of a sure thing.

"No worries," said the punter. "I'll bet you $500 that you've got red jocks. That's a sure bet for a start."

The banker could hardly believe his ears, and slapping the money on the counter he said "You're on."

"Okay, drop your trousers so I can check," said the punter.

"Not here," said the banker, "come into my office."

Once inside the banker said, "There you are, they are definitely not red."

"Not good enough," said the punter, "they look red to me, but I'm colour-blind. D'yer mind if your accountant checks the colour?"

The accountant was called in and immediately fainted.

"What's up with him?" asked the manager.

"Oh, I bet him $1000 I'd get you to drop your dacks before 10 this morning."

BIRDS

MY wife does bird imitations. She watches me like a hawk.

* * *

A BIRD in the hand is better than two in a photograph.

* * *

A BIRD in the hand is useless when you have to blow your nose.

* * *

HE was responsible for feeding the pelicans at the zoo. It wasn't much of a job but it filled the bill.

* * *

AT the Stork Club. "Do any deliveries today?"

"No, but I frightened hell out of a few secretaries."

* * *

"NEXT!" roared the theatrical agent, and when Bert

shuffled in self-consciously before him he muttered, "Well, what do you do?"

"I do bird impressions," said Bert.

"Not another one," said the agent without raising his eyes from documents on his desk. "Get on with it then."

So Bert flapped his arms, dropped a deposit on the window ledge and flew off into the blue sky yonder.

BIRTHS and BIRTHDAYS

SHE'S just turned 32, but the way she's turned it, makes her 23.

* * *

A husband who forgets his wife's birthday will get something to remember her by.

* * *

WHEN a man has a birthday he takes a day off. When a woman has a birthday she takes a year off.

* * *

SHE was born in the year of our lord only knows.

* * *

I WAS so surprised by my birth, I was speechless for a year and a half.

* * *

IN what State were you born?
  In the nude.

* * *

SHE was looking forward to her 30th birthday. But she was looking in the wrong direction.

* * *

"HAVE you known your wife long?"
  "Yes. Ever since we were the same age."

* * *

LIFE is full of complications. Even when you are born there is a string attached.

"MY mother was disappointed when I was born."
   "Why, did she want a girl?"
   "No. She wanted a divorce."

* * *

"THE stork brought a little peach,"
   The nurse said with an air.
   "I'm bloomin' glad," the father said,
   "He didn't bring a pear!"

* * *

ANOTHER candle on the cake
   Well that's no cause to pout
   Be glad you still have wind enough
   To blow the damn thing out

* * *

THE best way to remember your wife's birthday is to forget it once.

* * *

SHE: "I hate to think about my 30th birthday."
   He: "Why? What happened?"

* * *

IT'S terrible to grow old alone. My wife hasn't had a birthday for three years.

* * *

SHE'S celebrating the second anniversary of her 16th birthday.

* * *

YOU'RE getting old when the only thing you don't want for your birthday is to be reminded of it.

* * *

IT was a brave husband who whispered to his mate, "I'm so glad she was born in winter. The birthday candles heat up the house. If it was in summer she'd need a fire permit."

* * *

IT was one of those cruises so well patronised by the elderly when a sprightly old geezer approached a spinster reclining on a deck chair.

"Guess how old I am," he said.

She looked him up and down for a moment, then put her hand up the leg of his shorts. She grabbed his crown jewels, felt their weight, moved them gently from side to side and then declared with authority: "You are 83 and seven months."

"That's amazing," said the old codger, "how do you know?"

"Because you told me yesterday you silly old fool," she replied.

BOASTERS

WHEN the sliding door opened in the confessional box he started: "Father, I had sex with a pair of lovely 18-year-old nymphomaniac twins five times last week."

"What kind of Catholic are you?" demanded the priest.

"I am not a Catholic," he replied.

"Then why are you telling me this?"

"I am telling everyone!"

*　　*　　*

"DO you think I am conceited?" he asked his girlfriend.

"No. What makes you ask, darling?" she said.

"Well, most blokes as handsome as me usually are."

*　　*　　*

HE had told her how he won the best and fairest award in his football club, all the details of his life, his training and the goals he scored and his philosophy on life.

Finally he said, "But that's enough about me. Let's talk about you. Tell me, what did you think of my performance in Saturday's game?"

*　　*　　*

THE old gent was getting sick and tired of Young Turk boasting of his sexual conquests.

"Listen," he said. "I am 87 and I make love nearly every night of the week."

The young bloke said he didn't believe him.

"True," said the old geezer. "I nearly made it Monday, I nearly made it Tuesday, ... "

* * *

YOUNG Father Murphy phoned the bishop to say he was ill and couldn't celebrate mass. As soon as he heard the bishop say he could get a replacement the young priest grabbed his golf clubs and was one of the first on the course.

St Peter saw this and nudged God. "Look at Father Murphy. Lied to say he was ill, and look at him down there. He has got to be punished."

"Okay," said God, and they watched as the priest pulled out a number one wood, swung a mighty stroke and belted the ball straight up the fairway, narrowly between two bunkers onto the green to roll slowly in for one.

St Peter was aghast. "I thought you were going to punish him."

"I have," said God. "Who can he boast to?"

BONKS
(R)...

LET's face it, there is a lot of bonking going on. It is the reason we all got here, so we can hardly avoid it as a classification for jokes, especially when most jokes are about pre-bonking, trying to get a bonk, actual bonking and post bonking.

* * *

HE'S bi-sexual, which means if he can't get it, he buys it.

* * *

CHARLIE said he once went without sex for 12 years. "Wasn't even bothered by it," he said. "Then I had my 13th birthday."

* * *

FRED said he gave up sex and booze at the same time once. "It was the worst half hour of my life!" he said.

WHEN Paddy walked into the pub it caused a snigger among his mates at the bar. "Boy, the joke was on you last night, Paddy," they said. "You left your bedroom light on and the blind was up. You put on a great show with your missus."

"Well, the joke's on you lot," countered Paddy. "I wasn't home last night."

* * *

A HOUSEWIFE was asked by her neighbour how she happened to have so many home appliances around the house.

"Bonking," she replied. "I charge my husband $10 for a bonk. In fact, I have a scale of charges. It costs him 50 cents for a fondle."

Her neighbour thought this was a wonderful proposition and said she would introduce the same scale of fees.

A month later they met again. "By the way, are you making any money," asked the first housewife.

"Afraid not," said the neighbour. "I charge him 50 cents for a fondle and pretty soon I have to get out of bed to lend him another 50 cents, and by then I don't mind paying him ten."

* * *

FRED was complaining to his doctor that his wife had lost interest in sex. The doc explained that it was a matter of preparation. "Next time you come home from work, bring a bunch of flowers, give her a big kiss, then sweep her off her feet and carry her to the bedroom. You will be surprised."

On Fred's next visit he asked if it worked. "Yes, she was indeed surprised. And so were all the members of her bridge club."

* * *

FRED was leaning on the bar recounting the most recent tragedy in the neighbourhood. "Ernie came home and found his wife in bed with the bloke next door. He got his gun and shot them both."

"Well, it could of been worse," said his listener.

"What d'yer mean," said Fred, "what could be worse than that?"

"Well, if Ernie had come home early the night before I'd be dead by now."

* * *

THE pretty fraulein approached the Aussie tourist in the Munich beer hall and invited him home. She gave him a nice meal and took him to bed.

In the morning, after a hearty breakfast, he was about to leave and made a little speech about the outstanding hospitality he had received.

"Ja, the speech is nice, but what about marks," she said.

"Bloody oath, nine out of ten I reckon," he said.

* * *

IT was their 50th wedding anniversary and Rachael took Izzi to the city and proudly showed him a block of flats. "It's ours, Izzi, we own it," she said.

"But how did you?" he said.

"You remember all these years I used to charge you $10 for a tumble in bed," said Rachael. "Well I saved all that money and bought that block of flats."

"Oh Rachael. If only I had known, I would have given you all my business!"

* * *

DAVE and Mable checked over their meagre finances and realised times were tough. "I've got an idea," said Dave. "Every time we have a bit of nookie in bed I will pay you a dollar. It will be a means of saving with pleasure."

Two months later they needed some extra funds and busted open the cash box. Dave was amazed to see the bundle of notes which included fives, tens and twenties.

"Mabel, where did you get all this money. Each time we did it I only gave you a dollar."

"Listen Dave," she said, "not everyone is as stingy as you."

*　　*　　*

OLD Dad and Mum overheard the above episode with Dave and Mabel. Convinced there was money to be made he suggested Mum should try her luck on the street.

Mum returned that evening, emptied her handbag on the kitchen table and out tumbled the cash which included fives, tens and twenties. It added up to $75 and 50 cents.

"What lousy cheapskate gave you the 50 cents?" demanded Dad.

"They all did," said Mum.

*　　*　　*

"MRS Smith," queried the doctor. "Do you smoke after intercourse?"

"I've never looked," she replied.

*　　*　　*

THE couple were laying on the bed naked, smoking a post coital cigarette.

After a while she said, "Mother always told me to be good. Was I?"

*　　*　　*

MRS Murphy, the young mother of triplets, was being congratulated by her neighbour, Mrs Kelly.

"Yes, 'tis a wonderful thing indade," said the proud Mum, "and you know the doctor says it only happens once in a hundred t'ousand times."

"Heavens," said Mrs Kelly in astonishment, "whinever did yer foind time to do yer housework?"

*　　*　　*

CHAP suffering from laringitis could hardly talk with his sore throat, so he went to the clinic after hours.

The door was opened by the doctor's pretty young wife.

"Is the doctor in," he whispered.

"No," she whispered. "Come on in."

42

CHAP walking along the beach one evening in the dark stepped on a bloke's bottom. And a girl's voice said "Thank you!"

* * *

HE was telling his mate that he and his wife had discovered a new way of making love; back to back.

"That would be nigh impossible wouldn't it?"

"Oh we have another couple in to help us," he explained.

* * *

BOB, Jane, Mary and Bill had been friends for years. The two couples went on a camping trip and pitched their tents close together. While sitting around the camp fire they got to talking about the current trend of swinging couples and ventured far enough to suggest they try it.

"Haven't had so much fun for years," said Bob later. "Do you think the girls are having as much fun as we are?"

* * *

ONE night the husband came home early from afternoon shift and found the lodger in bed with his wife.

"What's the meaning of this?" he cried. "It's a fine way to repay our hospitality. After all we've done for you... and stop doing that while I'm talking to you!"

* * *

HE came home from the pub fairly late and his wife met him at the front door. "We've had a burglar," she sobbed.

"Did he get anything?" he said in alarm.

"He sure did," she said. "I thought it was you!"

* * *

IT was Friday night and Barbie had just finished preparing the evening meal for her husband John when there was a knock on the door. She opened it and was surprised to see her husband's best mate, Freddie.

"John's scored some overtime," said Fred. "He told me to tell you he won't be home until eleven-thirty."

A long chat on the doorstep resulted in Barbie inviting Freddie inside. "In fact, you might as well eat some of this food I have prepared."

Freddie was in like Flynn. And after the food, and half a bottle of good red, began chatting up Barbie about the good old days when they used to go together, before she was married. In fact, he soon got to the point. "Give us a kiss for old time's sake?" he said.

"No, I'm an honest married woman," she said.

"Okay," said Fred. "Give us a kiss for old time's sake... and twenty dollars," and with that he slammed the note on the table.

Barbie looked at the money. Well, she used to kiss him for nothing once. No harm in a kiss. So she gave him a quick peck and scooped up the cash.

Freddie had another drink and began praising Barbie's figure. "You're still in great shape," he said looking at her blouse. "Give us a quick look ... for fifty dollars."

And with that he dropped fifty on the table.

He used to do more than looking once, for nothing, thought Barbie. A quick flash shouldn't hurt anybody. So a quick flash it was, and again she scooped up the money.

To cut a long story short there was a bit more chit-chat and $200 dropped on the table, followed by a quick adjournment to the bedroom.

Indeed it was eleven-thirty when John arrived home that night and Barbie got out of bed to make him a cup of tea.

"Did Freddie call round?" he asked.

Barbie nodded.

"Did he bring my pay?"

*   *   *

A PLUMBER one night feeling free
Was plumbing his girl by the sea

Said the maid, "Quick, stop plumbing,
I fear someone's coming."
Said the plumber, still plumbing, "It's me."

BOOBS

THE old man was the only other occupant of the train compartment and he looked like a kindly grandfather so the young mother had no qualms about breast-feeding her baby.

"What a lovely child," said the old man. "What do you feed him on?"

"Just milk and orange juice," she said.

The old man thought about this for a moment. "Which one is the orange juice?" he said.

*　　*　　*

AFTER three years in a seminary three priests were assigned to parishes in Tottenham. At the railway station the clerk in the ticket box proved to be a buxom young woman with a deep cleavage. It brought the three of them out in a sweat.

"Three tickets to Titterton," stammered the first before retiring in embarrassment.

"Here, I'll have a go," said the second, and approaching the window stuttered: "Three titties to Tockerton."

"You are making a shocking mess of it," said the third, snatching the money and getting a grip on himself. He sternly approached the buxom wench and said: "Three tickets to Tottenham, Miss, and unless you dress more demurely St Finger will point his Peter at you."

*　　*　　*

THE two gossips noticed young Mrs Lottzabazooma in the park.

"Is that hussy breast-feeding again, right out in public?"

"It's her right enough," said the other sticky-nose. "And look, the boy's at least 16, and not even her son.

45

WORRIED about her daughter's cough her mother took her to the doctor who proceeded to examine her chest.

"Big breaths," he said.

"Yeath," she replied. "And I'm only thixteen."

*   *   *

THE long legged blonde arrived at the wedding in a topless frock.

"You can't come in," declared the verger.

"I've got a divine right," she said.

"Your left's not bad either, but you can't come in this church without a hat."

*   *   *

A MOUSE dashed up a girl's leg, under her frock and came to rest in the crevice of two ample bosoms.

"You are obviously a Titmouse," she said.

"No I'm not," he replied. "I'm a Mickey Mouse, but I overshot the mark."

*   *   *

A BUXOM young Miss from Valetta
Loved to parade in a sweater
Three reasons she had
To keep warm was not bad
But the other two reasons were better.

*   *   *

ON a maiden a man once begat
Fine triplets named Mat, Pat and Tat
It was fun in the breeding
But when came time for feeding
She found she had no tit for Tat.

BOOKS

"EXCUSE me Miss," he said. "I'm writing a phone book. Could I have your number?"

*   *   *

THERE'S a new dictionary published for the showbiz

world listing all the actors and actesses. It's called "Who's Whose."

*   *   *

A BLOKE lent me a book on memory training last week. I want to return it, but I can't remember his name.

*   *   *

BY the time a man learns to read women like a book, he's too old to start a library.

*   *   *

HE said to the librarian, "I'd like a book. Something very deep."

"What about 20,000 Leagues Under the Sea?"

*   *   *

MY wife's preference is chequebooks. Once she starts one she can't put it down until its finished.

*   *   *

"I READ your new book," said the snobbish critic to the author. "Who wrote it for you?"

"Who read it for you?" he replied.

*   *   *

CRITIC: "What do you consider your best work of fiction?"

Author: "My last Income Tax Return."

*   *   *

DOOR to door salesman was selling leather bound dictionaries for a mere $5.

"What's the catch?" asked the householder.

"Oh, it's got all the words alright, but they are not in alphabetical order."

*   *   *

A BLOKE who was run over by the mobile library began to groan and moan. The librarian jumped out of the vehicle, bent down and said, "SSShhhhh!"

*   *   *

HAVE you noticed how every prominent politician, even former prime ministers, decide to write books when they retire? It would have been better for the country if they had read one.

BROTHELS
(R)...

"IT'S a business doing pleasure with you," said the hooker accepting her fee.

*　　　*　　　*

THE old chap toddled into the house of ill repute and the madam told him it would cost $100. He was quite surprised. "You're putting me on," he said.

"That will be an extra $10," said the madam.

*　　　*　　　*

THE old bloke made it shakily into the Blue Light Brothel. The receptionist looked him over and noting his age said, "Just a moment, Pops, I had better call the Madam."

After a whispered conference the Madam nodded agreement and said to the old gent, "Sorry love, we think you've had it."

"Oh, then how much do I owe you?" he said reaching for his wallet.

*　　　*　　　*

WHILE playing in the street two young boys noticed that only men were calling at the house with the red light and that after a short conversation which appeared to consist of "$30 for a short time," these men would disappear inside, only to emerge later looking satisfied and contented.

The boys decided to give it a go and pooling their resources they knocked on the door.

"We've only got $3," they said to the madam, "so can we just have a short time?"

The madam took them in, took their money, knocked their heads together, kicked them in the backside and threw them back on to the street.

As the lads got to their feet one said, "Gee, I'm glad we only had three dollars. I couldn't stand thirty dollars' worth of that!"

*   *   *

IZZY Cohen had just taken his trousers off and was about to get into bed with Tiger Lil when there was a hell of a commotion downstairs. The cops had raided the house.

He just managed to grab his clothes, climb through the window, slide down the drain pipe and dash into the bar next door where he met his friend Sam.

He related his narrow escape, which had effectively dampened his ardour. "But listen Sam," he said. "As soon as the cops disappear, whip up to the first floor and give Tiger Lil a bang. It's paid for."

BUSES

CONDUCTOR: "Full fare for the kid, he's five."

Mother: "How could he be five, I've only been married three years!"

Conductor: "Look lady, I take fares, not confessions."

*   *   *

A WOMAN rushed into the hardware store and said: "A mousetrap please, and hurry because I have a bus to catch."

"Sorry, lady," said the shop-keeper. "None of the mousetraps we've got are big enough."

*   *   *

THE bus was so crowded even the young men couldn't get seats.

*   *   *

THE busline has a timetable, but it is against the rules to leave on time. It would upset the entire schedule.

*   *   *

THE arrogant bus driver was always telling people where to get off.

THE drunk on the bus told the ticket inspector that he had bought a ticket, but couldn't find it.

"It's okay," said the inspector, "I'm sure you have paid."

"It's not okay at all," insisted the drunk, still searching his pockets. "Without my ticket I don't know where I'm going."

* * *

A COPPER arrested a bloke for smoking on a bus.

"Can't you see that sign which says No Smoking?" said the cop.

"No, and I can't read anyway," said the bloke, who appeared to have three too many.

"What's your name?" demanded the cop, but all he got was a mumbled reply.

"Write it down," said the cop handing him his notebook. The drunk scribbled something illegible.

"What's that?" said the cop.

"I don't know," said the bloke, "I told you I can't read!"

* * *

PADDY, his wife and their seven kids were waiting at the bus-stop when they were joined by a blind man. When the bus arrived it was almost full and the conductor said only eight could board.

"Okay Teresa," said Paddy to his wife, "you take the kids on board and me and the blind man will walk."

Without giving the blind man an option in the matter Paddy helped his family scramble aboard and the bus took off.

He and the blind man then set off walking down the road and all went well until the constant tap-tap-tap of the blind man's cane began to irritate Paddy.

"Tap-tap-tap, that damned tapping is driving me crazy. Can't you put a bit of rubber on the end of it," he complained irritably.

The blindman was quick to respond. "If you had've

stuck a bit of rubber on your own stick we would be on that bloomin' bus."

BUSINESS

"HOW'S business?"
   "Looking up."
   "You mean it's flat on its back."

* * *

"PRICES subject to change, according to customer's attitude."

* * *

AT the board meeting: "All those in favour say Aye. All those against, resign."

* * *

YOUNG Moishe was learning economics and asked his father about the ethics of business.

   "Ethics?" repeated his father. "You ask me about ethics? Well, my lovely boy, let me put it this way. A lady comes in and buys a garment for $95 and she pays with a $100 note. She is very excited about the garment and as she leaves with the parcel under her arm I notice she has left her $5 change on the counter.

   "Now here my son comes in the big question of ethics. Do I tell my partner or not?"

* * *

AN art critic interviewing the famous contemporary artist asked why he tolerated the sexual escapades of his young wife.

   "I would rather a 20% interest in a going concern, than 100% in a bankruptcy," he said.

* * *

PLOTKIN met Rozenbloom on the street and said, "Tell me, Mr Rozenbloom, we bump into each other often on this street, we meet at the synagogue and we meet at the market. So why is it you never ask me how's business?"

"Okay Plotkin. How's business?"

"Oi voi, don't ask!"

* * *

IN a small school in Dublin the teacher told the class she would give 50 pence to whoever could name the holiest man in history.

One hand went up like a shot, that of little Izzie Cohen. "That would be St Patrick, Miss."

Teacher handed over the money and said, "Izzy, how come the only boy to know the answer is Jewish?"

To which Izzy replied, "In my heart of hearts I know it was Moses, but business is business."

* * *

THE landlord of a pub in Carlton was a fanatical Blues supporter and even had a large sign in the bar which read: "No Collingwood supporters served in this pub."

One day a bloke wearing a black and white scarf breasted the bar. "I know you don't serve Collingwood supporters, but I'm desperate for a drink and I'll pay $5 for a pot."

The publican thought this over, then decided to serve the beer.

It was gulped down in one draught.

"Same again," said the Magpie fan, "in fact I'll have two," and he slapped a tenner on the bar.

When he asked for a third the barman said tentatively, "That's another fiver?"

"That's okay," he said, pushing $20 across the bar, "I'll have a couple for the road." When the drinker had gone the publican put up a new sign: "Only Collingwood fans served here."

(N.B. Use your own local football teams and colours.)

* * *

WHEN the wife went on a dirty week-end and her rich lover bought her a fur coat worth $10,000, the problem was, how to bring it home.

After lengthy thought she pawned it. She then told

her husband that while driving to the airport, on the trip to see her mother, a woman had hailed her cab and begged a ride. She said the young woman only had minutes to catch a plane that would take her to a betrothed wedding in Istanbul which would make her rich. She had no money, except a pawn ticket which she insisted should be payment for the ride.

With this tale the wife urged her husband to redeem the ticket for her.

He did so and presented his wife with a pair of binoculars, which were ideal for viewing the new fur coat her husband's secretary was wearing at the races next day.

* * *

MOISHE had started in the second-hand trade but was now one of the richest businessmen in the city. As his Rolls Royce stopped in front of the Ritz one night an old school mate who had fallen on hard times was waiting for him.

"Hey Moishe, remember me?"

"Eddie Rozenbloom, of course I do. Haven't seen you in years. How's business?"

"Moishe," says Eddie. "I've hit a bad patch. In fact I was wondering if you could let me have five dollars for a bed."

"Sure Eddie. Bring it around in the morning!"

* * *

TWO Jewish gentlemen were seated together on a plane. They had been in the air for 30 minutes when the younger man asked the other if he had the time.

There was no answer. "Can you tell me the time please?"

Again there was no answer and the younger man detected some kind of deliberate resistance.

The aircraft was on its descent path when the older man quickly looked at his watch and said it was ten past three.

There was silence for a while before the young man said. "Why didn't you tell me the time earlier?"

"Well, you know what it is like on flights. People get talking to each other. We could become friendly, especially when we are both Jewish. I would be obliged to invite you home. I have a lovely daughter and you are a young man, quite handsome. Romance could blossom and before long you could be asking for her hand in marriage. And to put it bluntly, I don't want no son-in-law who hasn't got a watch."

*   *   *

WHEN Abe met Isaac he said: "I hear your store was robbed last night. Lose much?"

Isaac replied: "A little, but it could have been much worse. Yesterday I just marked down the entire stock by 20 per cent."

*   *   *

"SO your opening sale has just closed, what now?"

"So now we open the closing sale."

*   *   *

HE walked into the pawnbroker's shop in Russell St, Melbourne and asked for the loan of $20. "Where's your collateral?" asked the pawnbroker.

He indicated the Rolls Royce parked out front. "Right there," he said, "and here are the keys and ownership documents."

He got his $20 and was off. Three days later he returned to claim the car with a crisp $20 in his hand. He received the keys and was charged $5 interest.

He was about to leave when curiosity got the better of the pawnbroker. "Pardon me, but why should a man like you need the loan of $20?"

The businessman replied, "Oh I don't really. I'm down from *Sydney* to do some business, and where else can you park a car for a few days for $5?"

(N.B. You can replace 'Melbourne' and 'Sydney' with cities relevant to your situation.)

IT was three in the morning and the worried husband was pacing up and down the bedroom floor to the consternation of his wife who found it very difficult to sleep.

"What's wrong?" she asked.

"I'm sick to death with worry," he said. "We owe a thousand dollars on the mortgage tomorrow and we haven't got a cent," he said.

The wife got out of bed, looked up the phone book and dialed a number. When the bank manager answered, obviously still dazed from a deep sleep she said. "There is no way my husband can pay, so you will be a thousand dollars short tomorrow."

She hung up and said, "Now come to bed and let him worry about it."

*   *   *

IT was three in the morning when a busker began playing his banjo outside the bedroom window of a wealthy tycoon.

Eventually the window was opened. "What do you think you are doing waking me up in the middle of the night?"

"Listen, mate," said the busker. "I don't tell you how to run your business, so don't tell me how to run mine!"

C

CAMELS

ANGUS was delighted to find himself a girl at the pub who appeared to be no drain on the pocket. When he asked could he get her a glass of wine she said no, she didn't drink.

When he asked if she would like a cigarette she said no, she didn't smoke.

"What about a packet of crisps?"

"No, I'm not hungry," she said.

"A game of pool?"

"No, I don't play," she said.

"Then can I take you home?" asked Angus, who was delighted when she said yes.

When they arrived at her house she opened the front door, and there, lying in the hallway was a dead camel.

"Well," said the young woman, "I didn't say I was tidy, did I?"

CARS
See ACCIDENTS, MOTORING, DRIVERS

WHEN it comes to used cars, it's hard to drive a bargain.

* * *

USED cars are alright, as far as they go.

SHE was trying to get a new car for her husband, but nobody would swap.

* * *

HE had a stereo system in his car for years. His wife in the front and her mother in the back.

* * *

FRED got behind in his car payments and, in an effort to shame him into paying the hire-purchase company wrote: "What would your neighbours think if we came and repossessed your car?"

He wrote back: "Dear Sirs. I took the matter up with my neighbours and they all reckon it would be a lousy trick."

* * *

"THIS car," said the salesman, "runs so smoothly you can't feel it, so quietly you can't hear it, so perfectly you can't smell it and so fast you can't see it."

Fred considered this for a moment. "Then how the hell do we know it's there?"

* * *

FRED listened to all the motoring advertisements and is now having a terrible time with his car. He bought a carburettor which saved 30% on petrol, an exhaust system which saved 50% on fuel and a set of spark plugs which saved 25%. Now every time he goes for a drive his fuel tank overflows.

* * *

WHEN it comes to petrol consumption some cars perform better than others. "But Fred's car is the best I've ever heard of," said Barney.

He explained: "Fred told me he met a blonde at the pub on Friday night and drove her home, hours and hours away. And he said he went all that way for nothing!"

* * *

FRED phoned the car yard and asked for the dealer who had sold him the car just two days before.

"You said this car had only one owner, a little old lady who drove it to church each Sunday?"

"That's right," said the salesman.

"Well, can I have her address," said Fred. "I have just cleaned out the glove box and there is a bottle of whisky, a packet of condoms and a bikini top she might be looking for."

CATS

THEIR cat was called Ben Hur.

It had originally been called Ben, until it had kittens.

* * *

THE music professor entered the spinster's home to hear the strains of classical music delicately performed on the piano, but he got the shock of his life when he entered the drawing room and saw that it was a large black tom cat at the keyboard.

"Taught himself," said Miss Haversham proudly.

"That's amazing," said the professor.

"Wrote that particular piece himself, too," she said.

"Astounding," marvelled the prof listening to the chords and nuances of the minuette.

"Marvellous," he said. "Have you had it orchestrated?"

The cat dived out the window and hasn't been seen since.

* * *

WHEN he saw a lovely gold watch as the centrepiece of a window display, set on a velvet cushion with gold chain around it, he decided immediately it was to be the ideal present for his wife's 50th birthday.

"I'd like to buy that watch in the window," he told the shopkeeper.

"It's not for sale," was the reply.

And against the man's pleading to sell him the watch the shopkeeper said, "Look mate, I don't sell watches. I de-sex tomcats."

"Well, what are the watches in the window for?"

"What would you want me to put in the window?" replied the shopkeeper.

*　　*　　*

THE youngster ran to his mum crying. "Dad just drowned our cat," he blubbered.

"Maybe he had to do it," she said.

"No he didn't. He promised me I could."

*　　*　　*

"STOP pulling the cat's tail, Johnny."

"I'm not. "I'm just holding it. It's the cat that's doing the pulling."

*　　*　　*

THE elderly spinster had called the vet because her cat seemed to be off her food. He made a quick examination and pronounced that the cat was pregnant.

"Impossible," said the spinster. "Moggie never goes out. I feed her in here. She has had no contact with stray cats of any kind."

Just then a battered old Ginger Tom wandered out from behind the couch.

"There's the culprit," said the vet.

"Preposterous," said the spinster, "That's Moggie's brother."

*　　*　　*

HER tom cat was out every night ranting, wailing and impregnating all the other cats in the neighbourhood. It never spent a night at home.

So she took him to the vet and had him fixed.

Now he is still out every night, acting as a consultant.

*　　*　　*

WHEN Paddy's cat died he asked the priest to say requiem mass. "No way. What d'yer think the church is coming to?" said the priest.

Paddy asked the Anglican vicar to bury his cat and got the same response.

The priest met Paddy next day. "Are you still fussing about that cat?" he said.

"Yes," said Paddy. "I even asked the Jewish Rabbi if he would bury him for $500, but he refused too."

The priest's face lit up. "Why didn't you say he was a Catholic cat?" he said.

CENSUS

A COW-COCKY was filling in the census form. In answer to the question, "Length of residence in Australia," he wrote: "Thirty feet, ten inches, with a verandah front and two sides."

* * *

THE census taker told the mayor of the little bush town that he was puzzled about the town's population. For the past five years he had been on the job the population was the same, 1,503. "Must be something wrong."

"No," said the mayor. "It's always been 1,503."

"But don't you have babies?"

"Yep," said the mayor, "and everytime we do some bloke has to leave town."

* * *

A CENSUS official was assisting a farmer's wife to fill in her forms. "How many children have you got?" he asked.

"Six," she replied. "Three sets of twins."

"How very extraordinary," said the census man. "Twins every time."

"Oh no," she said with a blush. "Not every time. Hundreds of times, nothing."

* * *

SHE told the census taker she had five children, and he was astounded to learn that they were all born two years apart, and all on August 12.

"What's your husband's profession?" he asked.

"Precision grinder," she replied.

YOUNG woman answered the door for the census taker and told him her husband had died five years ago.

The official noted this down, then asked if she had any children.

"Yes, three," she said. "Aged one, two and five."

The official queried this. "Didn't you say your husband was dead?"

"Yes. He is but I'm not!"

* * *

CENSUS taker went next door where the woman told him she had four children. "But I am definitely not having any more."

"Why?" said the official.

"Because I read in a magazine that every fifth child born in the world is Chinese."

CHOOKS

CHOOKS are the only things you can eat before they are born and after they are dead.

* * *

WAITER: "Those are the best eggs we've had for years."

Diner: "Well, bring me some you haven't had for so long."

* * *

PADDY crept around the back of the country parish presbytery and stole one of the priest's chooks, then promptly went to confession.

"I stole a chook, father," he began. "I know it was wrong and I am sorry. Can I give it to you for penance?"

"Certainly not," said the priest. "Return it to the person you stole it from."

"I've offered it to him, but he says he doesn't want it," said Paddy.

"In that case you might as well keep it and say ten Hail Marys," said the priest.

THE young wife wanted to impress her husband that she was a good cook, so she rang him to ask if he could bring home a live chicken.

He bought the chook at the market and then realised his car was being serviced and would not be available for another two hours.

He decided to pass the time by going to a movie, and hid the chook by stuffing it down the front of his trousers.

Once in the theatre he became absorbed in the movie and was oblivious to the fact that the chook had stuck its head out of his fly.

Two women were sitting next to him and one nudged the other. "You should see what's sticking out of this bloke's pants."

Her friend was blase, "Seen one, seen 'em all", she said, not bothering to take her eyes off the screen.

"Yeah, but this one is eating my pop corn!"

*　　*　　*

FEELING guilty about running over what appeared to be a prize rooster, the travelling salesman stopped his car and approached the nearby farmhouse and knocked on the door.

He told the farmer's wife he would like to replace it.

"Please yourself, luv," she said. "The chooks are around the back!"

*　　*　　*

"TWO of our chooks have stopped layin'," said the farmer to his wife.

"How do yer know?"

"Cos I just run over them with the tractor."

*　　*　　*

SHE was stocking up for her hobby farm and ordered a dozen chooks, and a dozen roosters.

"Madam, you only need one rooster," he pointed out.

She gave him a stern look. "Evidently you don't know what it is like to be overlooked."

A FARMER was having his lunch on the front porch when a squawking chicken dashed around the corner with a rooster in hot pursuit. As the chooks dashed down the porch a few crumbs of bread fell from the farmer's sandwich and the rooster stopped to gobble them up while the hen got away.

"Strewth!" exclaimed the farmer, "I hope I never get that hungry."

* * *

WHEN the shire president arrived at the country town all the neighbouring chooks gathered in the main street. They heard he was to lay a foundation stone and they didn't want to miss it.

* * *

THE local vet was in the middle of a complicated operation when the phone rang. It was Farmer Brown's wife who wanted to know how long she should leave a rooster with her chooks.

"Just a minute," said the vet turning back to his operation. The woman thanked him and hung up.

* * *

THE old rooster had been king of the chook house for years and he intended to keep it that way, so when yet another young cock was tossed into the yard by Farmer Brown it was time for some quick negotiation.

"There are 40 hens here, buster, and I am not going to fight you for them. We will need all our strength. So let's decide it with a race. Three times around the perimeter of the yard gets the lot."

The young rooster looked at the stringy old geezer. "I don't think you could make it twice around, Pops."

"Then give me a start," said the old rooster and he was off and running with a three metre break. The old farmer was sitting on his porch when the roosters came in sight; the old one in front desperately hanging on to his lead, the young one flat-out and gaining slowly.

The farmer reached for his shotgun, took aim and shot the young rooster dead.

"Y'know, Martha," he said to his wife, "it's funny, but that's the third queer rooster I have had to shoot this month!"

CHRISTMAS

GO to church this Sunday and avoid the Christmas rush.

*　　*　　*

A COUPLE of fattened turkeys were chatting in the chook house.

"Tell me, Cyril," said one, "do you believe in Santa Claus?"

*　　*　　*

ONLY 25 shoplifting days to Christmas!

*　　*　　*

WHY wasn't Christ born in Australia?

Well, where would you find three wise men, or a virgin?

*　　*　　*

ACTUALLY there were four wise men. On the way to Bethlehem one of them said he knew a short cut.

*　　*　　*

THE rich kid kept pestering his father that he wanted a Mickey Mouse outfit for Christmas.

So his old man bought him the NSW State Cabinet.

(N.B. Change 'NSW State Cabinet' to any political institution in the news.)

*　　*　　*

DON'T give me a watch for Christmas. I've already got one. And I can assure you a man with one watch knows what time it is, while a man with two watches would never be sure.

*　　*　　*

IN the department store at Christmas the little boy had been waiting patiently in the queue to meet Santa. When his turn came Santa picked him up, sat him on his knee and said: "Ho, ho, ho, little boy. And what would you like for Christmas?"

The little tyke jumped down and kicked Santa fair in the shins. "I just told you yesterday you silly old goat."

* * *

THE kid said: "What's Christmas, Dad?"

So Dad took him to a department store where he met Santa Claus and saw the toy department. "That's Christmas, son!"

Little Isaac said to his father, Moishe, "What's Christmas, Dad?"

Moishe took the lad to a vast and empty warehouse. "That's Christmas, son!"

CLAIRVOYANTS
(AND THINGS SUPERNATURAL)

THE annual general meeting of the Clairvoyants' Society is postponed, due to unforeseen circumstances?

* * *

DURING World War Two, Adolph Hitler consulted his clairvoyant to find out how long he would live and on what day he would die.

The clairvoyant looked into the crystal ball and said "Mein Fuhrer, I have a vision that you will die on a Jewish holiday."

Hitler flew into a rage. "Which Jewish holiday?" he screamed.

"Mein Fuhrer, any day you die will be a Jewish holiday."

* * *

A MAN visited the fortune teller at the circus and sat down in front of her crystal ball. He was a sceptic.

"I see you are the father of two children," she began.

"Ha! That's what you think," replied the man, "I'm the father of three children."

"That's what you think," smiled the fortune teller.

FRED sat silently while she looked into the crystal ball. Suddenly she threw her head back and began roaring with laughter. She shook with mirth until Fred leaned across and punched her in the nose.

It was the first time he had struck a happy medium.

* * *

"WHY do you call your father-in-law the Exorcist?"

"Because every visit he rids our house of spirits."

* * *

THE two drunks at the bar were having a philosophical discussion on reincarnation.

"And how long have you believed in reincarnation?" said one.

"Ever since I was a frog," said the other.

* * *

THE Olde English Pub was called the Black Cat. Legend had it that it was named after the favourite moggy of the first innkeeper on that site. The cat had met its death when a runaway stage coach had run over it, cutting off its tail.

And for the past two hundred years its ghost appeared each time the pub changed hands.

Thus it was that the new licencee, up late cooking the books, was confronted by the ghostly apparition of the cat, carrying its tail in its paw.

"My soul won't rest until my tail is restored," moaned the ghost. "Can you help me?"

The publican put down his pen. "I'm afraid it can't be done," he said, "I am not allowed to retail spirits after ten-thirty."

CLUBS

IT was Groucho Marx who declared: "Any club which would admit me as a member isn't worth joining."

* * *

THE club president was delivering his annual report and

66

was praising the committee. "Unlike other clubs where half the committee does all the work and the other half are hopeless, here, it is completely the reverse!"

*   *   *

HE heard the club was looking for a treasurer.

"But didn't they take on a new treasurer just a month ago?"

"Yes. That's the one they are looking for!"

*   *   *

"I SAY, old chap, who is Fonsonby talking to?"

"He is talking to himself."

"Then why is he shouting?"

"He's deaf!"

*   *   *

THE oldtimers were lamenting that the club had gone to the pack. "Noisy lot, all on the make," said one. "All corduroy trousers, thin moustaches and crew-cut hair. And the women are just as bad."

*   *   *

THE doorman to the swank club saw a limousine stop at the kerb. In his haste to get out and open the door he tripped on the step and went head-first into the gutter.

The manager rushed out and picked him up. "That's enough of that, James. People will think you're a member."

*   *   *

WHEN Sam walked into his poker club it caused a snigger among his mates at the bar. "Boy, the joke was on you last night, Sam," they said. "You left your bedroom light on and the blind was up. You put on a great show with your missus."

"Well, the joke happens to be on you lot," Sam retorted. "I wasn't home last night!"

CONMEN

HE took a young lady home to his flat, offered her a Scotch and sofa, and she reclined.

67

THE judge fixed him with a beady eye: "How could you take money from people who trusted you?"

"Because it just doesn't work with people who don't trust you," the conman replied.

* * *

"GOOD Evening," said the barman. "What's your pleasure?"

"A Scotch and a box of matches," said Con.

He sinks the drink and puts ten cents on the counter, explaining that the money is for the matches. "I didn't really want a drink, but when you invited me so nicely, well..."

The barman said he was only being polite and when Con refuses to pay he is ordered out and barred from the pub.

A week later Con returns and the barman shouts: "Hey you. I told you last week you were barred from this hotel."

"I've never been here before," said Con. "You must have me mixed up with somebody else."

"Then you must have a double," said the barman.

"Thanks," said Con, "and a box of matches."

* * *

AS Con walked into the pub he asked his friend: "What's your great ambition in life?"

"To own a pub," said his mate. "What's yours?"

"A double brandy, thanks," said Con.

* * *

TWO conmen in an English pub called the publican over and asked him to settle an argument. "Are there two pints in a quart, or four?" asked one.

"There are two pints in a quart," confirmed the publican.

They moved back along the bar to where they had been drinking and soon the barmaid asked for their order.

"Two pints please Miss, and they are on the house."

When the barmaid appeared to doubt her boss would dispense free beer, one of the lads called out to the publican at the other end of the bar: "You did say two pints, didn't you?"

"That's right," shouted the publican. "Two pints."

* * *

THE blind man had his hand out. "Can you spare a dollar?"

She looked at him suspiciously. "Why, I'm sure you can see out of one eye."

"Well, fifty cents then?"

* * *

SHE stopped at the next blind man and dropped all her small change into his cup with a clunk.

"God bless you lady," he said. "I knew you was kind hearted the moment I saw you turn the corner."

* * *

SHE intended the 50-cent piece to drop into his hat, but she missed and it clinked on to the pavement. In a swift movement the blindman scooped it up.

"How did you see that?" she said. "I thought you were blind."

"No, I'm not blind," he said. "It's my mate that's blind, and I am filling in for him while he's at the movies."

* * *

HE was propped up against *Young & Jacksons* on crutches with his head bandaged and one arm in a sling. In the other hand he held his hat outstretched.

"You poor man," she said, dropping a fiver in the hat. "But think how much worse it would be if you were blind."

"You're dead right, lady" he said. "When I was blind I kept getting foreign coins."

* * *

WHILE leaning on the bar, Ron the Con said, "D'yer want to buy a watch, Fred?"

"Let's see it," said Fred.

"Shh," said Ron, "the bloke next to you is wearing it."

* * *

THE gangling lad from the bush was amazed to learn that his new friend, Larry the Lounge Lizard was 100 years old.

"I'm surprised. You look very healthy," said the lad.

Old Larry gritted his teeth bravely, "Trouble is," he said, pushing his glass forward, "thirst doesn't show on the outside."

* * *

BACK on the farm from his first visit to the city, Dave proudly showed the family a large, sparkling diamond ring.

"Is it the real thing?" they gasped in amazement.

"It had better be," mumbled Dave, "otherwise I've been done out of a tenner."

* * *

RON the Con walked into the pub and ordered a pie and sauce. As it was served to him he told the barman he had changed his mind. He pushed the pie back and said he would have a beer instead.

When it came to payment Ron said he owed nothing. He had swapped the pie for the beer.

"But you didn't pay for the pie," argued the barman.

"And I didn't eat the pie. You've still got it," said Ron.

A little bamboozled, the barman said, "Here is a dollar. Go over the road to the pub opposite and pull the same stunt."

Ron pocketed the money. As he reached the door he said, "I might as well tell you. The publican over the road gave me $2 to pull the same stunt here."

* * *

THEY had dined well and after the wine Con reminded Ron it was his turn to take care of the bill. Ron called the manager and asked for an interview in his office.

"We have been doing a survey on the prevalence of those people who order large meals and then declare they have no money. What do you do?"

The manager said there was nothing much that could be done. "It only means notoriety, bad publicity and costly litigation if we prosecute. We usually bring them into this office and give them a good kick in the backside."

Ron bent over and said: "In that case can you take for two?"

* * *

AS the train left the station the conman sized up the old prospector sitting opposite. When they got to talking the conman proposed they play a game to pass the time.

"What kind of game?"

"General knowledge quiz. You look like a man of the world," said the conman. "We each ask the other a question, and if one can't answer he pays the other a dollar."

The old geezer thought this over for a minute. "Yeah, I like a quiz. But I don't like the even money bit."

"What do you mean?"

"Well, I've spent most of my life in the bush. I'm just a simple man, whereas you look like a city-slicker to me. So I suggest that if you can't answer my questions, then it costs you a dollar, but if I can't answer yours, then you should let me off with 50 cents."

The conman was sure he was on a winner. "Okay, I pay 50 cents to your dollar."

"Then here's the first question," said the old geezer. "What's got five legs and flies backwards?"

"Don't know," said the conman slapping down a dollar.

"My question now, and I'm interested to know exactly what does have five legs and flies backwards?"

"Blowed if I know. Here's your 50 cents," said the old man.

CONUNDRUMS

IF you weigh a whale at a weigh-weigh station, where do you weigh a pie? Somewhere over the rainbow, weigh up pie!

* * *

FRED was a keen one for conundrums, so when the barman presented one he listened intently.

The barman said: "My mother had a child. It wasn't my brother and it wasn't my sister. Who was it?"

Fred scratched his head and admitted he was beat.

"It was me," declared the barman triumphantly.

Fred thought it was a good one and couldn't wait to relate it to his wife. In fact he woke her up to tell it.

"My mother had a child. It wasn't my brother and it wasn't my sister. Who was it?"

His sleepy wife said she didn't have a clue.

"Easy," said Fred. "It was Harry the barman down at the pub."

* * *

"WHAT'S the difference between a tram and a taxi?" he said.

"I give in, I don't know," she said.

"Good, then we'll take the tram."

* * *

WHAT did Mrs Quasimodo give Quasi for Christmas?

A Wok! She thought it would help her iron his shirts.

COURTING
See ENGAGEMENTS

"I DON'T believe we've met. I'm Mr Right."

* * *

"I AM writing a phone book. Could I have your number Miss?"

"LET'S get married, or something."

"Let's get married, or nothing."

* * *

OUT on her first date her mother's words were ringing in her ears: "Say no to everything he suggests."

So after dinner and a couple of drinks he said: "Do you mind if we fool around in bed?"

* * *

IT was their second date and after a few drinks in the cocktail lounge he thought the time was right. He leaned over and whispered in her ear, "How about coming away with me for the week-end to a little cabin I have in the snow?"

She replied: "I suspect my anticipation of your proclivities in the esoteric aspects of sexual behaviour preclude such an erotic confrontation."

He scratched his head, "I don't get it."

"Exactly," she replied.

* * *

"I WILL go to the end of the world for you," he said.

"Yes, but will you stay there," she yawned.

* * *

HE said it was love at first sight.

Then why didn't he marry her?

Because he took a second look.

* * *

FRED'S been turned down so many times he is like the hot page in a naughty novel.

* * *

"I'VE heard plenty about your love-making."

* * *

"AM I the first man you've ever made love to, dearest?" he asked.

She studied him for a moment. "You could be," she said, "there is something familiar about your face."

* * *

THE ardent suitor was urging his girlfriend to live with

him. "It will be exactly like the real thing only we won't have the expense of getting married. And then if we find later that we have made a mistake, then we won't have the cost of the divorce."

"Yes," she said. "But what do we do with the mistake?"

* * *

HE had been watching the blonde at the other end of the bar for some time before he got sufficient courage to approach her.

"Would you like a Harvey Wallbanger?" he asked.

"Love one," she said. "But let's have a drink first."

* * *

HE snuggled up to her and said: "I'm yours for the asking."

She snuggled back and said: "I'm asking fifty bucks!"

* * *

IT was love at first sight and they had taken the big step and slept together for the first time. They were still in bed when the phone rang next morning.

He reached out and picked up the receiver, listened for a moment, then gave her a shake.

"It's for a Miss Sheila Kelly," he said. "Is that you?"

* * *

THE stern father took the lad aside when he had brought his daughter home. "I'd like a word," he said.

"If you are going to see our Ethel regularly I hope you know the difference between right and wrong."

The young man gulped. "But surely you yourself have brought her up to know what's right?"

"Indeed we have," said the father.

"Well, I've taken care of the other side, so everything's fine."

* * *

WHEN Myrtle finally brought a bloke home her parents were relieved that this might be the Mr Right that would take her off their hands. But when they took a closer look they took Myrtle aside.

"He's not exactly a young man," whispered Mum to her daughter. "He's fat, he's bald and he's pretty old isn't he?"

"There's no need to whisper, Mum," said Myrtle, "he's stone deaf too."

CROCODILES

PADDY O'Reilly was walking up High St with a crocodile on a lead when a concerned policeman stopped him.

"Where are you going with that beast?" asked the cop.

"I am taking him to the zoo," replied Paddy, which satisfied the cop.

Next day the same cop saw the same Paddy with the same crocodile on the same lead.

"I thought you were taking that thing to the zoo?" said the cop.

"Aye, I did, and he liked it. Today I'm taking him to the pictures."

* * *

PADDY took his crocodile into a pub and said: "Do you serve Catholics?"

The barman said he did.

"Well, Oi'l be having a pot of stout, and two catholics for my crocodile!"

* * *

TARZAN was coming home after a hard day's work and turned the bend in the river just in time to see a crocodile taking one of his kids.

He rushed in and told Jane, but she was more intent on taking Tarzan to bed. "Don't worry about it," she said. "We've got plenty of kids. Let's go to bed and make another one."

The following evening after a hard day's work Tarzan staggered home just in time to see a crocodile taking another kid.

75

"Oh, don't worry," said Jane. "Come to bed and we'll make another one."

"Listen," said an angry Tarzan, "I'm not working all day and making love all night just to feed the damned crocodiles!"

CRICKET

IT was the club's social dance and the young debutante had trouble dancing with her awkward partner.

"Sorry," he said, "I'm a little stiff from bowling."

"I don't care where you come from," she said, "just keep off my feet."

* * *

FRED'S wife rang the cricket club.

"Sorry, he has just walked to the crease. He is about to bat. Shall I ask him to ring you back?"

"No. I'll hang on," she said.

* * *

THE club's best batsman was on the phone to his captain trying to explain why he couldn't play next day.

"No, I can't let you off the game," said the captain who was made of stern stuff. "If I did, then I would have to do the same for any other player whose wife dies."

* * *

THE famous test player began his career with the Werribbee Wanderers so the social committee sent him a telegram asking if he would make a guest appearance for $100.

The cricketer sent back a telegram: "Will accept, but double the offer or count me out."

The committee's immediate reply was: "1, 2, 3, 4, 5, 6, 7, 8, 9, 10."

* * *

EVENTUALLY they got Allan Border as guest player at the Werribbee Wanderers testimonial fund raiser and indeed there was a large crowd at the ground.

Ned, the club's fast bowler, had never faced a test cricketer before and he felt the tension as he hurled down his first ball.

To Ned's surprise the off stump went flying. Clean bowled. "No ball," roared the umpire, and then took Ned aside. "Slow down you idiot. They've come to see Border bat, not you bowl."

*   *   *

TWO fans settled down at the MCG when one realised he had left his wallet in his mate's Mercedes. He returned from the car park 15 minutes later, pale and shaken.

"I've got bad news, Bob. A truck has crashed into your car and the impact set it on fire. It's totally destroyed."

"And have I got some bad news for you," said Bob to his mate. "Border is out for a duck."

*   *   *

FRED's wife snuggled up beside him in bed and whispered: "Remember the Saturday you proposed to me. My word you were bold then."

"No way," said Fred. "I was caught."

*   *   *

"SO, you had a hard time trying to explain the test match to your wife?"

"Yes, especially when she found out I wasn't there."

*   *   *

THE cricketer was getting a medical. "I dunno, Doc," he said. "My fielding is very bad lately. I can't bowl like I used to and everytime I go in to bat I get a duck lately."

"Why don't you try some other sport?" said the doctor.

"I can't," he said. "I'm captain of the Australian Eleven."

*   *   *

THE cricket fan was trying to interest his girlfriend in the game and took her to the Saturday match.

Pointing out a promising batsman he said, "It won't be long before that bloke will be our best man."

"Oh Frederick," she gushed, "this is so sudden."

THE visiting church team was surprised to see no scoring facilities at the sports ground. "Don't worry about that," said the bush captain, a well-muscled shearer, "we keep the scores in our heads, and if there is any dispute we settle the argument behind the shearing shed after the game."

* * *

"THAT was very sporting of you to cheer our team for winning the match," said the church captain to the Patchywollock host. "By the way, where's the umpire?"

"He's in the dam," was the reply.

* * *

THE Devil challenged St Peter to a cricket match. "Remember," said St Peter, "we have all the good cricketers up here." "Yes," said the Devil, "but we've got all the umpires down here."

* * *

THEY take their cricket seriously in the bush. A stranger at the Patchywollock v. Wonga Creek game was cheering the batsman's play and at the same time applauding the bowler and fieldsmen.

This bothered one local shearer.

"Do you come from Patchywollock?"

"No," said the stranger.

"From Wonga Creek then?"

"No," said the stranger.

"Well in that case mind you own bloody business and keep your trap shut."

* * *

THE batsman was describing his big hit.

"I gave it everything I had. The ball went into the sky and hit a passing duck."

"Hit a duck? Was it wild?"

"It was ruddy-well livid."

* * *

THE boys were playing cricket in the backyard with a shiny new ball. It attracted the interest of their father.

"Where did you get the ball?" he asked.

"We found it," chorused the kids.

"Are you sure it was lost?"

"Of course it was lost. We watched them looking for it."

*　　*　　*

THE bush town's cricket match was stopped when the ball was hit clear over the fence. While players from both sides searched in the long grass they were watched by an idle lad sitting against the fence.

"Did you see a cricket ball come over?" one of the cricketers asked him.

"No I didn't," said the lad, "but I have brought this fairly new one from home that I could sell you."

*　　*　　*

FRED was always bragging. "I walked out of the Gabba last Saturday," he said, "and a crowd of 30 or more clamoured around me for my autograph."

"Come off it, Fred."

"Fair dinkum. If you don't believe me, ask Allan Border. He was standing right beside me."

*　　*　　*

FRED was trying to join the local team.

"Have you had any experience?" asked the captain.

"Well, I think I once played with Don Bradman."

"Really?"

"Yes," said Fred, "he told me after the game who he was. He said if I was a batsman, he was Don Bradman."

*　　*　　*

THERE is a man in Wycheproof who has devised a game that in some aspects is similar to cricket.

What he doesn't know, is that the Australian Eleven has been playing it for years.

*　　*　　*

TWO old boys were bragging in the bar at Lords.

"What was your highest score," said one.

"One hundred and fifty," said the other.

"Well, mine was one hundred and fifty-five," said the first smuggly. "And what was the highest number of wickets you got?" he continued.

"Oh no. You go first this time."

* * *

NED was building up record averages as the club's fast bowler, but he was a little worried when he learned that his father-in-law was to umpire the day's match.

Ned hurled the first ball down at terrific pace and caught the batsman LBW.

"Owzat!" he yelled.

"Not out," said the umpire.

The second ball came down like a missile, snicked the bat and was caught by the wicket-keeper.

"Owzat!" roared Ned.

"Not out," said the umpire.

With the wildest fury he could muster the third ball screamed down the wicket, hit the middle stump and snapped it in half, sending wickets and bails in the air.

"Ruddy-well nearly got him that time," said Ned.

* * *

AFTER a series of bad decisions from the umpire, Ned approached him and said: "If I called you a stupid old goat who didn't know the first thing about cricket what would you do?"

"I would report you and you would be fined," said the umpire.

"What if I didn't say it, and just thought it?"

"Well, nothing could be done about it."

"Okay," said Ned, "then we'll just leave it at that, then, eh?"

* * *

ON the train Fred couldn't keep his eyes off the old codger sitting in the opposite corner with one of his boots glued to his ear. He was listening with intense concentration.

Fred's curiosity finally got the better of him. He leaned across and said: "What's going on?"

The old man motioned him to be silent and continued listening until Fred pulled the boot away and asked again.

"If you must know," grunted the old man, "I'm listening to the test match."

"Here, give me a go," said Fred snatching the boot and putting it to his ear.

He listened for a while. "I can't hear a thing," he said.

"No, and you won't either," grinned the old man. "They just stopped for tea."

*   *   *

THE big shearer's cook was batting in the annual bush grudge match and had survived three appeals for obvious LBW.

The next delivery hit the middle stump and sent the bails flying.

"Owzat?" they roared.

"Not out," said the umpire.

"What kind of a damned decision is that?" cried the bowler. "He's been out four times already."

The umpire was adamant. "I say he stays. We've only got a nine-gallon keg and he's the best guzzler in the whole district"

*   *   *

AN expectant father rang the hospital to see how his wife was progressing. By mistake he was connected to the cricket ground.

"How's it going?" he asked.

"Going well," came the answer. "We've got three out and hope to get the rest out before lunch. The last one was a duck!"

CRICKET INSULTS

"WHY are you looking so down-hearted?"
  "The doctor says I can't play cricket."
  "When did he see you play?"

*　　*　　*

CAPTAIN: "It's a pity you didn't take up the game sooner."
  "You mean I'd be better now?"
  "No, you would have given the game up long ago."

*　　*　　*

OUT for a duck the angry batsman marched into the pavilion and said, "I've never played so badly before."
  The captain appeared surprised: "You mean, you've played before?"

*　　*　　*

"THAT was the best innings I've ever played."
  "Well, you mustn't let that discourage you."

*　　*　　*

"ARE your team members good losers?"
  "Good? They're perfect!"

CRIMINALS

THE prisoner said to the social worker: "Women have been my downfall."
  "What kind of women?"
  "Those who carry handbags."

*　　*　　*

HE said his Dad gave him three words of advice on being financially solvent.
  "What were they?"
  "Stick 'em up!"

*　　*　　*

A TRAVELLER was walking down a dark street one night when he was stopped by a tramp who said: "Excuse me, Guv. Would you be so kind as to help a poor unfortunate who is hungry and out of work, with no money and no worldly possessions, except for this sawn off shot gun...!"

* * *

THEY were walking arm in arm down High St when she saw a diamond ring in the showcase window. "Oh, it's lovely," she said.

So he heaved a brick through the glass and grabbed it.

A little further on she saw a fur coat on display and implored him to get it for her.

He heaved another brick through the window and snatched it.

Around the corner she stopped at the show window which featured a beautiful Jaguar sports car. "Oh, I'd love that," she said.

"Enough, Myrtle," he said. "Do you think I'm made of bricks?"

CUSTOMS AGENTS

CUSTOMS officer was inspecting a sweet young thing's suitcase and discovered six pair of French knickers. "What are these for?" he asked.

"Sunday, Monday, Tuesday, Wednesday, Thursday and Friday," she replied.

"And what about Saturday?" he asked.

She replied with a smile and a wink and minced by.

Next was a big German frau who flung her suitcase onto the counter.

"And what are these for?" said the customs officer discovering 12 pair of thick flannel bloomers.

She replied: "January, February, March, April..........."

* * *

CUSTOMS officer at the airport asked Paddy if he had anything to declare.

"No, only this bottle of holy water from Lourdes."

The officer was interested and asked to see it. When

Paddy produced it the officer removed the cork and put his nose to the bottle.

"That's not water," he said grimly. "That's whisky."

"Mother of God!" exclaimed Paddy, "It's another bloomin' miracle!"

*   *   *

A MARRIED couple, Freda and Fred, had been successfully smuggling native birds out of Australia to the United States for years.

Freda suggested they could double their earnings by smuggling some American wildlife on the return trips.

"For example," she said. "I've got a squirrel here and I am going to hide it by stuffing it down the front of my pants."

"And this is for you, Fred," she said, handing him a skunk. "That will bring big money in Australia. Stuff it down the front of your trousers."

Fred protested: "What about the smell?"

Freda shrugged her shoulders. "If it dies ... it dies."

D

DANCING

DANCING is the perpendicular expression of horizontal desire.

*   *   *

"I DON'T dance, but I'd love to hold you while you do."

*   *   *

DANCING is a physical contact sport.

*   *   *

DON'T miss our next show. Six dancing girls and five beautiful costumes.

*   *   *

"COULD I have the last dance?"
    "You've just had it."

*   *   *

HE: "Doesn't this dance make you long for another?"
    She: "Yes, but he couldn't come tonight."

*   *   *

A GIRL is something you look damned silly dancing without.

*   *   *

THE clergyman had delivered a fiery sermon against the evils of dancing and made it clear that he was opposed to any kind of dancing. After the congregation had filed out he was approached by a young dancing enthusiast. "Just what's wrong with dancing?" he asked.

"Well, for one thing," said the minister, "it's the close touching of the bodies."

"Not so," protested the parishioner, "it is all in the mind of those who look at it with the wrong attitude."

"Then let's suppose," argued the minister, "that you came home from work and found me holding your wife in that manner. What would you think?"

"I'd think that you'd better be dancing," was the reply.

* * *

AT a country dance a young couple were pressed together, dancing cheek to cheek. She whispered in his ear, "Come out to the car."

He declined, saying the tune being played was one of his favourite numbers, but she persisted and pleaded for him to come out to the car.

He finally agreed. When they left the hall it was pitch black outside so he produced a torch from his pocket to light the way to the car.

She said: "Did you have that torch in your pocket all night?"

"Yes," he said.

"Well let's go back to the dance," she said.

* * *

FRED was asked how he got his black eye.

"I was teaching my girlfriend the tango when her father came in. How was I to know he was stone deaf?"

* * *

THE debutante at the country ball
   Knows that pride goes before a fall
   So when she trips the light fantastic
   She always wears good strong elastic.

DEATH
See FUNERALS

DEATH is nature's way of telling you to slow down.

"SO Old Smithy is dead. Did he leave his wife much?"

"Nearly every night."

* * *

"WHAT's the death rate around here?"

"Same as any place. One death per person."

* * *

AS Woody Allen said: "It is not that I'm afraid to die. I just don't want to be around when it happens."

* * *

WHILE on holiday, Fred bought the local paper, and browsing through the death notices he was intrigued to see that everyone had died in alphabetical order.

* * *

HE died a natural death. He was hit by a car.

* * *

"DOC, I'm afraid I'm going to die."

"Nonsense! That's the last thing you'll do."

* * *

THE clock and watchmaker millionaire died recently. They reckon it will take years to wind up his estate.

* * *

"HEY Mum, how did Dad know the exact date he was going to die?"

"The judge told him."

* * *

THE relatives gathered around to hear the solicitor read Fred's short will:

"Being of sound mind I spent the lot before I carked it."

* * *

SHE was complaining to her neighbour. She had made constant trips to the city, three times to the insurance office, twice to the probate office, hundreds of papers and documents to sort through. "I sometimes wish Fred hadn't died," she said.

SHE was ebbing fast and she raised herself on one elbow and beckoned her John to come closer. "On the day of the funeral," she gasped, "it would please me if you would ride in the same coach as mother."

"Okay" he said grudgingly, "but you know it will completely spoil my day."

*　　*　　*

OLD Jake was on his death bed. He raised himself on one elbow and beckoned his wife closer.

"Emily," he gasped. "You were with me through the Great Depression."

She nodded.

"Emily, you were with me through the worst droughts in the fifties."

She nodded.

"And you were with me when we lost the farm in the bush fires. Now here you are again, by my side when I'm about to cark it."

She nodded.

"You know Emily," he said, "I'm beginning to think you've been bringing me bad luck."

*　　*　　*

DYING at sea can have its complications. The captain informed the first mate that the passenger in Cabin 25 had died and ordered him to arrange for a burial at sea.

An hour later the mate came onto the bridge and reported that the matter relating to Cabin 27 had been attended to.

"What," said the captain aghast. "I said Cabin 25. Didn't the man tell you he wasn't dead?"

"Yes, Cap'n," said the mate, "but he was a Pommie and you know what lying bastards they are."

*　　*　　*

HERE snug in her grave
　　My wife do lie

Now she's at rest
And so am I.

∗   ∗   ∗

UNDERNEATH this pile of stones
  Lies the remains of Harry Jones
  His name was Smith
  It was not Jones
  But Jones was put
  To rhyme with stones.

DEFINITIONS

AUTOMATIC SHIFT: When the driver moves closer to his girlfriend.

AUTOBIOGRAPHY: The car's logbook.

APEX: The female of the gorilla species.

ADVERTISEMENT: Something that makes you think you've longed for it for years, but never heard of it before.

ALIMONY: A mistake by two people paid for by one.

ABSENTEE: A missing golfing accessory.

ANTI-FREEZE: When you don't talk to your uncle's wife.

ADAMANT: The very first insect.

ADIEU: Hymie Finklestein.

ADORN: What comes after the darkest hour.

AROMATIC: An automatic longbow.

ARTFUL: A painting exhibition.

AWE-STRUCK: Being hit with a paddle.

AVAIL: Helpful for ugly women.

ALPHABET: Not quite the complete wager.

ABUNDANCE: A local hop usually staged in a barn.

ACME: Pimples on the face running towards the top.

BURLESQUE SHOW: Where attendance falls off if nothing else does.

BADMINTON: The reason the lamb tasted off.

BORN EXECUTIVE: A bloke whose father owns the company.

BRAZIER: Something to warm your hands on.

BALANCE: Something you lose if the bank pushes you.

BARBARIAN: The man who cuts your hair.

BOOKCASE: Litigation about a novel which ensures wide sales.

BRUSSELS SPROUTS: A world famous statue found in that city.

BOXER: A bloke who stands up for the other fellow's rights.

CLIMATE: The best thing to do with a ladder.

CONDESCENDING: A Greek parachutist.

CONSCIENCE: The thing that aches when everything else feels good.

COWARD: A man who thinks with his legs.

CABBAGE: The fare you pay a taxi driver.

DETEST: The West Indies playing India (cricket).

ELECTRICIAN: A switch doctor.

FASTIDIOUS: A girl who is fast and hideous.

FAUCET: What you have to do if the tap won't turn.

FETE: A boring picnic worse than death.

FLOOSIE: A sweet girl with the gift of the grab.

GRANARY: A home for senior female citizens.

GALLERY: A hostel for young women.

HUMBUG: A singing cockroach.

HYACINTH: A yank greeting a gal called Cynthia.

IDOLISE: Eyes that refuse to look at anything.

INCOME: What you have to make first, because you can't make it last.

JEALOUSY: The friendship one woman shares with another.

LACTIC: A grandfather clock which doesn't work.

MONOLOGUE: A discussion between man and wife.

MARCONI: The first man to send a message through a length of spaghetti without it touching the sides.

NONDESCRIPT: A television play.

ODIOUS: Not very good poetry.

PARENTS: Couples who practise the Rhythm Method.

PEDESTRIAN: A motorist with teenage sons.

RACIAL DISPUTE: When the course judge calls for a photo.

REFLECTION: What a girl looks at, but is not given to.

SAGE: A bloke who knows his onions.

STALEMATE: A husband who has lost his ardour.

SNUFF: Sufficient unto the day.

SONATA: A song sung by Frank.

DENTISTS

A MAN and his wife rushed into the dentist's surgery and offered double the going rate if he would pull a tooth immediately.

"We are in a hurry to get to the airport," explained the husband. "We are running late and there is not time for that anaesthetic stuff. Just rip it out."

The dentist said it would be painful.

"To hell with the pain. Just rip it out," he insisted.

"Very well," said the dentist. "You certainly have courage. Now which tooth is it?"

The man turned to his wife. "Hop up into the chair, Myrtle and show him."

*　　*　　*

"GOOD grief, you've got the biggest cavity I've ever seen," said the dentist. "You've got the biggest cavity I've ever seen."

"Okay," said the patient, "you don't have to repeat it."

"I didn't" said the dentist, "that was the echo!"

*　　*　　*

SHE thought the Tooth Fairy was a Gay Dentist.

*　　*　　*

"I DON'T know which is worse," said the sweet young thing settling into the dentist's chair, "having a tooth pulled, or having a baby."

"Well make up your mind," said the dentist, "so that I can fix the chair in the appropriate position!"

* * *

"SATISFACTION Guaranteed, or your teeth refunded."

* * *

THE wharfie was built like the proverbial outhouse and as he settled in the chair he gripped the dentist by his short and curlies.

"We're not going to hurt each other, are we?" he said.

* * *

"WHY are you screaming?" said the dentist. "I haven't started drilling yet."

"I know, but you're standing on my feet," said the patient.

* * *

A DESPERATE looking gangster settled into the chair after telling the dentist he needed a tooth pulled out.

"Which one is it?"

"That's for you to find out," growled the tough guy. "I ain't no stool pigeon."

* * *

A FARMER who had an abiding fear of dentists asked his neighbour what the new bloke was like. "Did that new dentist stop the pain in your tooth?" he asked.

"Well put it this way," said his mate. "You remember last week when I stepped on that rake, got cracked on the head by the handle, fell backwards, and sat on that rabbit trap?"

"Yeah."

"Well that was the first time since I visited that new dentist that the pain in my jaw didn't bother me."

* * *

NERVOUS patient: "This will be the first tooth I've lost."

Nervous Dentist: "That's a co-incidence. This will be the first tooth I've pulled."

"WHAT was it like having all your teeth out?"

"Terrible. I'll never do it again."

DESERT ISLANDS

"THE most important thing we have in common," he said as they staggered ashore on the desert island, "is that I'm a man and you're a woman."

* * *

A FOOTBALL star fell overboard from a cruise ship and finally drifted ashore on a tropical island. He was eventually revived by a beautiful native girl.

She took him to her hut where she supplied him with food.

Then she produced a bottle of Scotch from a crate which had also drifted onto the beach.

Then she said: "Would you like to play with me?"

The footballer was frankly astonished. "Don't tell me you've got a football too?"

* * *

AN Englishman, an Australian and an Irishman had been marooned on a desert island for 15 years. One day the Aussie saw a bottle floating past and waded in to the sea to retrieve it. When he pulled the cork a Geni appeared.

"Oh what a relief to get out," he said. "I've been stuck in there for a thousand years, and the rules say you three blokes have got one wish each."

The three mates could not believe their eyes, but the genie insisted he was real, and so were the wishes. "But remember, it's just one each."

The Englishman was sceptical, but said he would give it a try. "I wish I was back on the Old Kent Road in London town," he laughed. In a blinding flash he disappeared.

"I wish I was back in the Members' Stand at Flemington Races," said the Aussie quickly. Another flash and he was gone.

The Irishman thought hard, screwed his face in thought but couldn't make up his mind. "Oh, I wish my mates were back here to help me!"

DIPLOMACY

DIPLOMACY is when you make your in-laws feel at home, when you wish they were.

*　　*　　*

YOUNG bloke had just become engaged and met his fiancee's mother for the first time. "How old do you think I am?" she asked the lad.

"Well," he said after a moment's thought, "I am wondering whether to make you ten years younger to fit with your looks and figure, or ten years older on account of your wise intelligence."

*　　*　　*

"LOOK at that ugly old bag over there," said one drinker to his mate, "got a face like the back of a bus."

"That's my wife," replied the other cooly.

"Got great legs," said the first.

*　　*　　*

THE white missionary had lived with the Bullabukanki tribe for 18 months when the chief took him aside and said the reverend was in big heaps of trouble.

"Yesterday a white baby was born to my sister, and you are the only white man in this village," said the chief sharpening his axe.

The missionary broke out in a sweat. "Look, old man, I know it looks bad, but see your flock of sheep down by the river?"

"Yeah, I see them," said the chief.

"Well can you see the black sheep in the flock. There is only one and ... "

"Okay, okay," said the chief, "I'll keep quiet if you'll keep quiet."

DIVORCE

SHE told the lawyer: "I want a divorce."

"On what grounds?" he said.

"Bigamy," she replied. "He can't have his Kate and Edith too."

* * *

HARRY mumbled a few words in church and found himself married. A few years later he mumbled a few words in his sleep and found himself divorced.

* * *

SHE was given a divorce because the judge found her husband had flat feet. They were always in the wrong flat.

* * *

SHE says maintenance is the best policy. That's a man's cash surrender value.

* * *

THEY had to admit she was a great housekeeper. Divorced three husbands and kept the house each time.

* * *

SHE was suing for divorce. She told the judge that every time she and her husband drove past one of his girl-friends, he made her duck her head.

* * *

HE left his wife because of another woman. Her mother.

* * *

JUDGE: "I have taken all factors into account and decided to award your wife $150 a week."

Defendant: "That's real decent of you, yer honour. Why, I might throw in a few dollars myself."

* * *

FRED was leaning on the bar and confided in Bill that he was going to get a divorce.

"The wife hasn't spoken to me in five months. Not a word," he said.

Bill pondered this and said "Don't be too hasty, Fred. Wives like that are damned hard to find."

* * *

HE said his father was very disappointed when he was born.

"Why, did he want a girl?"

"No, he wanted a divorce."

* * *

THE pretty young wife was suing for divorce.

"On what grounds?" asked her solicitor. "You've got to have grounds".

"But we do," she assured him. "Yes, we have large grounds, a 20 hectare block."

"No, no," he said. "Do you have a grudge?"

"Yes, we have a double garage because we have two cars."

"No, no," said the solicitor, near exasperation. "Does he beat you up?"

"Never," she said. "I'm always up at six, and he sleeps in till ten sometimes."

The solicitor finally grabbed her by the shoulders. "Reasons!" he shouted. "What are your reasons?"

"Oh, we don't seem to be able to communicate," she said.

* * *

FREE at last, ain't life grand
  I've just divorced my old man.
  I laughed til I cried at the judge's decision
  He gave him the kids
  And none were his'n.

DOCTORS
See HOSPITAL

THE doctor felt the patient's thin purse and admitted there was nothing he could do.

96

MOST doctors can decide on the treatment you need just by feeling your wallet, but throughout history the medical profession has never ceased to produce an endless supply of doctor jokes. Here are but a few:

*   *   *

DOCTOR to new patient: "First I need to study your medical history. Do you pay your medical bills promptly?"

*   *   *

"I WILL examine you for twenty dollars."
   "Go ahead, Doc. If you find it you can have it."

*   *   *

WHAT'S the use of consulting a doctor about a cold when he gives you a heart attack with the bill?

*   *   *

"I THINK I've got amnesia, Doc."
   "Okay, then I will ask for my fee in advance."

*   *   *

THE doctor finally discovered a cure for amnesia, but forgot what it was.

*   *   *

"DOCTOR, I have a small, embarrassing wart."
   "Divorce him."

*   *   *

PATIENT: "Aren't these pills habit-forming?"
   Doctor: "Rubbish, I've been taking them for years."

*   *   *

"DOCTOR, I've got Parkinson's disease, and I think he's got mine."

*   *   *

"ARE you taking the medicine regularly?"
   "No, Doc. I tasted it and decided I'd rather keep coughing."

*   *   *

"WELL Doc, how do I stand?"
   "I don't know. It's a damned miracle."

PATIENT: "I'm having trouble breathing, Doc."

Doctor: "Well I'll soon put a stop to that."

*   *   *

THE woman marched into the doctor's surgery dragging her young son along by the ear. "Doc. I just want to ask you one question. Can a a boy of twelve take out his own appendix?"

"Most certainly not madam," said the surgeon.

She belted her son across the head. "Hear that, Nigel. Now put it back at once."

*   *   *

AFTER a lengthy examination the doctor came out of the surgery and said to the patient's wife, "I don't like the look of your husband."

"Neither do I, but he's nice to the kids," she said.

*   *   *

THE doctor told his patient he had better sit down. He had two items of bad news. "First, I am sorry to say you have a sexually transmitted disease," said the doc.

"Oh, that's terrible," said his patient. "How will I explain it to the family?"

"And you also have Alzheimer's Disease," added the doc. "Oh, no! A double calamity, what a shock," lamented the patient. "Er, what was that first thing you said I had?"

*   *   *

HE parked his sportscar outside the clinic and bounced in without an appointment. "I just want to thank the doctor for his treatment," he said.

"But, you're not a patient of mine are you?" said the Doc.

"No, but my late Uncle Harry was."

*   *   *

"THE doctor told me to take these pills for the rest of my life."

"So, what's the problem?"

"He only gave me half a dozen."

"THE doctor gave me two weeks to live."

"Goodness, what did you say?"

"I told him I'd take the first two weeks in December."

*   *   *

MURPHY was given two weeks to live. He decided to take one week in January and the other in March.

*   *   *

O'REILLY was given six months to live. But when he said he couldn't pay his bill the doctor gave him another six months.

*   *   *

A BUSINESSMAN went for his annual medical. The grim-faced doctor said he had better sit down because he had some bad news. "To put it bluntly, you've got ten hours to live," he said.

"No, I can't believe it," said the businessman, "I want a second opinion."

"Well, you've got a nasty disposition, too," said the Doc (no, that's not the joke).

The businessman hurried to another clinic and was given the same distressing diagnosis. "You have nine hours to live."

Finally accepting the inevitable he got into his car and drove home. "Edna my darling," he said looking at his watch, "I have about eight hours to live."

As soon as his wife grasped the gravity of the situation she said, "Ralph, your slightest wish is my command. What would you like?"

He thought for a moment and said: "To bed!"

They were at it for an hour, and after a short rest she said, "What now, Ralph?"

He thought for a second. "Let's do it again!"

She compliantly agreed and after another hour she asked if he would like anything else.

Ralph said he was ready for a third.

"Oh for goodness sake," she cried. "It's okay for you, but I've got to get up in the morning!"

* * *

THE doctor had given Fred the dreadful news that he had contracted cancer and only had six months to live, so why was Fred telling everyone he was dying from AIDS.

"It's like this Doc," he explained. "I don't want anyone fooling around with my wife after I'm gone."

* * *

THE doctor told him he had good news and bad news. Which did he want first. The patient opted for the bad news first and the doc told him he had three weeks to live. "Hell, what's the good news then?" he asked.

The doctor leaned close and whispered, "See that blonde nurse there. I'm taking her out tonight!"

* * *

THE Doc told his patient he had some bad news, and some very bad news.

"What's the bad news?"

"You've only got two weeks to live."

"What news can be worse than that?" cried the patient.

"I should have told you a fortnight ago."

* * *

THE doctor had finished his examination and with a smile on his face said: "Mrs Jones, I have some very good news for you."

"Miss Jones," she corrected.

The doctor wiped the smile off his face. "Miss Jones, I have some very bad news for you!"

* * *

"IT'S my nerves," she said. "Please doctor you have to give me something for my nerves."

The doctor reached for a packet of pills. "Take these, they are $10 a packet."

She said: "I'll give you $7 for them."

Doctor: "There's nothing wrong with your nerve, lady."

THE farmer's wife, the mother of ten kids, called in to tell the doctor cheerfully that she won't be coming back as an expectant mother any more now that she had her birth control appliance.

The doctor was puzzled because she indicated that her "appliance" was an ordinary hearing aid.

"Before I had it," she explained, "we would get into bed at night and my husband would say "Will we put out the light and go to sleep, or what?"

"And I would say 'What'?"

* * *

OLD Fred was having his annual check-up.

"Well, old man," said the doctor tactfully, "you are getting on in years and I suggest you play it safe and give up half your sex life."

Fred thought this over for a moment, then asked which half he was supposed to give up. "Talking about it? Or thinking about it?"

* * *

THE doctor checked his patient over and with a puzzled frown said: "I can't really tell what the trouble is. I think it must be due to drinking."

"I understand Doc. I'll come back when you're sober!"

* * *

THE doctor was explaining to Paddy O'Leary how nature adjusted some physical disabilities. "For example, if a man is blind he develops a keen sense of hearing and touch. If he is stone deaf, then he develops his other senses..."

"Oi know what you mean," said Paddy. "Oi've noticed that if a bloke has one short leg, then the other one is always a bit longer."

* * *

THE doctor answered the phone to hear an excited voice say: "Quick, send an ambulance. My wife Bridget is about to have a baby!"

"Calm down," said the Doc. "Is this her first baby?"

"No, this is her husband, Pat speaking!"

*   *   *

THE doctor examined the young woman and said with a smile: "You can go home and tell your husband he is going to become a Daddy."

"But doctor, I'm not married."

"Well, you can tell your boyfriend."

"But doctor," she said. "I haven't got a boyfriend. I have never been out with a man."

The doctor walked over to the window and looked into the night sky. "Last time this happened there was a big star in the east," he said.

*   *   *

FRED complained to his doctor that his wife had lost interest in sex. The doc counselled him that it was a matter of preparation.

"Next time you come home from the office, bring a bunch of flowers, greet her with a big kiss, sweep her off her feet and carry her upstairs to the bedroom. You will be surprised."

On Fred's next visit he asked if it had worked. "Yes, indeed she was surprised," said Fred, "and so were all the members of her bridge club."

*   *   *

PADDY went to the doctor. He had two burnt ears.

"The phone rang when I was ironing, didn't it," said Paddy explaining.

"But what about the other ear?" asked the doctor.

"Well I had to phone you for an appointment, didn't I!"

*   *   *

A MARRIED couple visited the doctor who specialised in sex therapy. Romance had gone out of their lives, they said. Sex wasn't interesting anymore.

The doc listened to their nightly routine of evening meal, television and the same old missionary position.

"No wonder it's dull," he said. "You have made it monotonous, even the same time every night. What you have got to do is make it spontaneous. Do it when the mood takes you." And he gave them a pep talk on spontaneity.

A week later they came back, all smiles.

"We did what you suggested," said the husband. "Half way through a candle-lit dinner I felt randy. Ethel said she did too, so I leant over and ripped off her blouse, then pulled her down to the floor and we made love under the table. It was ecstatic spontaneity," he said.

And Ethel added, "But they said we could never go back to that restaurant again!"

*　　*　　*

"MY brother swallowed a box of fire crackers."

"Is he alright?"

"Don't know. We haven't heard the last report."

*　　*　　*

THE aging playboy was having his annual medical check.

"Sex?" asked the doctor.

"Infrequently," came the reply.

"Hmmm," said the doctor, "is that one word or two?"

*　　*　　*

FEELING run-down and listless, Fred visited the doctor for advice. The medic examined him and solemnly announced: "The remedy is simple. Whatever it is you are doing, stop it!"

*　　*　　*

THE notorious casanova went to the doctor to complain of impotence.

The medic was astonished. "You of all people," he said. "Why, you have a reputation as long as my arm."

The patient replied, "What's the good of a reputation if it won't stand up?"

*　　*　　*

PENSIONER couple wanted the doctor to check the way

103

they make love. He watched and said it is the way most people did it. They came back next day and asked him to check again. Doc approved.

When they arrived the third day the doctor asked what the heck was going on.

The old man finally explained: "I can't take her to the old men's home. We can't go to her place. We can't afford a motel room on the pension. So we do it here and get a 75% rebate on Medicare."

* * *

PADDY was angry, and his wife was obviously pregnant, when the doctor finally called.

"Look at this," said Paddy indicating his wife's condition. "I've been away at sea for a year and look at this. How do yer explain it?"

"Simple," said the doctor. "That's a vindictive pregnancy. Somebody has had it in for you while you have been away!"

DO-GOODERS

THE social welfare officer was making an annual inspection of the asylum when he noticed a chap out in the garden who seemed to enjoy a contented composure.

"Oh no, I'm not like that lot in there," said the gardener. "They have all lost their marbles."

Indeed the official couldn't help notice the garden neatly divided into rows of vegetables and flowers and in further conversation learned that the gardener had not only built his own shed but the aerial on the roof was part of his short-wave radio system he had also built. "I write books on that computer, and I paint in oils in my spare time," he told the inspector.

The official was amazed. "You shouldn't be here in this institution," he said, "it's a crime."

"That's what I've been telling them for years," said

the gardener. "My papers were lost in a complicated change of solicitors and I have been unable to get a proper legal clearance," he said.

"Well I am going to do something about this first thing tomorrow morning," said the official turning to leave.

He had taken three steps when the gardener stooped, picked up a red brick, threw it and hit the official square on the back of his head knocking him to the ground.

"You won't forget, will you?" he asked.

DOGS

THE dog entered the bar, sat up on a stool and ordered a gin and tonic. The barman served him, the dog swallowed the drink, left some money on the bar and left.

"That's extraordinary," said a drinker who had watched the whole thing.

"Yes," said the barman. "He usually has a brandy."

*　　*　　*

"LOST Dog," said the newspaper notice, "Has three legs, blind in left eye, large scar on throat, right ear missing, tail broken in two places, no teeth, recently castrated, answers to Lucky."

*　　*　　*

FRED said his dog Deefer could read.

He said he proved it the other day when the dog walked up to a "Wet Paint" sign, inspected it carefully, then followed the instructions.

*　　*　　*

MY dog's so obedient
　He does as he's bid
　The park bench said "Wet Paint"
　And that's what he did!

*　　*　　*

FRED put some Spot remover on his dog. Now he's gone.

"IS that an obedient dog, Fred?"

"Too right. I only have to say 'attack', and he has one."

* * *

SID the Spiv said his greyhound could run like greased lightning. "He is so fast on the track that on every third lap he has to jump over himself."

* * *

ONE drover was surprised to see his mate playing poker with his sheepdog. "I know kelpies are intelligent," he said, "but that one's a ripper."

"Ar, he's not that good," drawled his mate, throwing down another card. "Every time he gets a good hand he wags his tail!"

* * *

LEANING on the bar the drover said: "I am a man of simple tastes. I'm happy with a bottle of whisky, a tin of biscuits and a dog."

"Why the dog?" asked a listener.

"Hell, somebody has got to eat the biscuits!"

* * *

WHEN the publican spotted the little dog being brought into the pub he loudly declared it was not allowed.

"But you don't understand," said the drinker, "I'm blind and that's my guide dog."

"What?" roared the publican. "That's a Chihuahua."

"Well I'll be blowed," said the drinker, "they told me it was a Labrador."

* * *

MERV took his mongrel dog to a flea circus and the clever mutt stole the show.

* * *

WHEN drover Bill retired he set about fulfilling his dream of riding with the gentry at the hunt club. He was told that his scruffy horse barely met the equestrian standards, and not to come back until he had his own hound.

Not to be deterred, Bill fronted up for the Saturday

hunt with his trusty mount and his faithful greyhound. He was grudgingly accepted, but he failed to tell the officials that his greyhound bitch was on heat. Ten minutes after the chase started the Master of Foxhounds turned to his companion and said: "Which way are they headed?"

"West," was the reply.

"And where's the fox?"

"At the moment he's running seventh but gaining ground rapidly!"

* * *

"DID you say your dog's bark was worse than his bite?"

"Yes."

"Well for goodness sake don't let him bark. He's just bitten me."

* * *

THE salesman was bailed up by a ferocious dog. Finally its mistress came out and said: "It's okay. You know the old saying, a barking dog never bites."

The worried salesman replied: "I know it, you know it, but does that bloomin' dog know it?"

* * *

WHEN Mrs Moloney met Mrs Murphy at the market she noticed that her friend had a puppy under her arm.

"That's a nice pup," said Mrs Moloney.

"Yes, I got it for Murphy," said her friend.

"Lucky you. I wish I could swap Moloney for one!"

* * *

A MAN was sitting on the bank of the river having his lunch when a lady of 'the blue rinse set' came along the path with her pet poodle.

The yapping dog showed a lot of interest in the man's sandwich.

"Shall I throw him a bit?"

She nodded her approval.

So the man picked up the dog and threw it in the river.

IT was during the Great Depression and the drover had hit on hard times. Not to put too fine a point on it, he was starving. He looked at his faithful kelpie, Rufus, and with a tear in his eye said, "Sorry old-timer, it's you or me." And with that painful decision, Rufus ended up in the camp pot.

It was the first meal the drover had had for three weeks. And as he leant back against a stringybark, licking his lips after the satisfying meal he looked at the bones piled up on his plate.

"Pity Rufus is not here," he mused. "He would have loved those scraps!"

*   *   *

"SORRY, Sir, dogs are not allowed in this restaurant," said the waiter.

"But this is a talking dog," said its owner.

"If that dog can talk I will give you both a free meal," said the sceptical waiter.

"Right then Rover," said the owner to his pooch, "what's on the top of this building?"

Rover growled: "R-r-r-roof!"

"Now I'll ask one," said the waiter."Who is the greatest footballer in the league?"

"R-r-r-roof," repeated Rover.

The waiter kicked them both out on the footpath, and as they walked away Rover said: "Who should I have said?"

*   *   *

WORD had got around, and at the next pub the barman said, "Is it true that your dog can talk?"

"No," said the old man, "and if he tells you he can, he's a bloomin' liar."

*   *   *

THE old-timer wandered into the pub with his dog and a tame goanna which he placed on top of the piano. The dog climbed up on the seat and began to play the piano while the goanna sang a number of popular songs.

The drinkers were amazed and the publican rewarded the old-timer with a beer and said, "That's a great act. You are wasting your time travelling around the Outback pubs."

"They are not as good as you think," confessed the old-timer. "The goanna is tone deaf and can't sing a note. The dog is a ventriloquist."

*   *   *

"I THINK your dog likes me Gladys. He hasn't taken his eyes off me all night."

"That's because you are eating off his plate!"

*   *   *

WE have a fine watch dog. So far he has watched somebody steal our car, watched the garage burn down and watched a bloke pinch the lawn mower.

*   *   *

THE Buddhist knocked on the vicar's door with the sad news: "My carma has just run over your dogma."

*   *   *

"I DON'T want you to bring your dog into the house. It's full of fleas," she said.

"Fido, stay out of the house. It's full of fleas."

*   *   *

I HAD a dog called Carpenter. He used to do little jobs around the house.

I had a dog called Mechanic. Give him a kick in the nuts and he would make a bolt for the door.

But I rue the day I called my third dog Sex. It got me into a lot of trouble. When I went to the town hall to register him I said to the clerk, "I would like a licence for Sex."

He said, "I wouldn't mind one myself."

When I got married I asked the vicar if we could have Sex at the wedding. He said okay as long as it didn't interrupt the ceremony.

When I booked into the hotel for our honeymoon I asked the receptionist if he had a room for Sex. "They all are," he said.

My wife and I were always fighting over Sex. Finally it caused our divorce. I told the judge I had Sex before marriage. "Didn't we all," he said. One night he slipped his lead and ran off. I was in the park when a cop asked me what I was doing. "I am looking for Sex," I said. My case comes up next Monday.

* * *

"I HAD to shoot my dog yesterday."

"Was he mad?"

"Well, he wasn't too pleased about it."

* * *

IT was winter and the regulars in the country pub were gathered around the fireplace when Pete the Punter entered the bar with a mongrel dog called Ralph.

He loudly announced to one and all that this dog understood every command he could give it. "Never gets it wrong," he said.

There were drovers who owned top dogs around the bar and they looked askance at the mangy dog which was supposed to be so obedient.

Pete said he wasn't talking about simple commands like "sit," "stay," and "all that rubbish."

"I'm talking about a five-word sentence, and instant obedience," said Pete.

This was too much for the sceptics and they soon collected $100 to prove him wrong. Pete matched it, put the money on the bar, picked up the dog, threw it on the blazing fire and roared: "Ralph, get off that fire!"

* * *

A COUPLE of dogs met on the street. "What's your name?" said one.

"I'm not sure. I think it's Down Boy."

"HOW much did that terrier set you back, Fred?"

"Six hundred dollars ... he's half bull and half foxie."

"Which half is bull?"

"The part about the six hundred dollars."

* * *

THE grocer was alarmed to learn that Mrs Jones' weekly order of a dozen cans of pet food was being fed to her husband. "Oh he doesn't know the difference," she said. "He even likes it."

"But it could kill him," protested the grocer.

Mrs Jones took no heed, but a month later she entered the shop wearing a black armband.

"I told you so," said the grocer. "I told you that dog food would kill him."

"Oh no, it wasn't the dog food," she said. "We were going home the other evening when he sat on the tramline to scratch himself and got bowled over!"

* * *

A FLEA had spent the evening in the pub. At closing time he hopped out and landed flat on his face.

"Who the hell moved my dog," he said.

* * *

THE spectators at the local cricket match were surprised to see that the next batsman was a fox terrier. The dog shaped up at the crease and began hitting balls for sixers.

"That's amazing," said one of the spectators.

"Yes, he's good, but he is still a disappointment to his parents. They wanted him to play football."

* * *

THE movie buff settled into his seat and was surprised to see a man in front with his arm around a large dog which seemed to be enjoying the movie. The dog was growling at the villain and giving excited yelps each time the hero escaped.

The movie buff was fascinated. "Excuse me," he said,

tapping the chap on the shoulder. "Your dog is amazing. I just can't get over it."

"Frankly, he has surprised me too," said the owner. "He hated the book."

* * *

"DOES your dog bite?" enquired the friendly chap of the bulldog sitting beside Paddy.

"No," said Paddy.

The friendly chap extended a hand to pat the dog and nearly had it bitten off.

"I thought you said your dog didn't bite," the man said in alarm.

"That's not my dog," said Paddy.

* * *

AN expensive poodle fell into a river and was having difficulty staying afloat. In fact it was drowning. Isaac Goldstein dived in, brought the dog to shore, gave it mouth to mouth resuscitation and revived it.

"That was wonderful," said the grateful owner. "Are you a vet?"

"Of course I'm a vet," replied Goldstein. "I'm a bloody soaking."

DRIVERS
See ACCIDENTS, MOTORING, CARS

THE model driver, of course, is the one who has just seen the car in front pulled up by the police.

* * *

IF your wife insists on learning to drive, don't stand in her way.

* * *

"HAS your wife learned to drive yet, Fred?"

"Only in an advisory capacity."

* * *

"HOW's the wife's driving lessons going, Fred?"

"Improving. The roads are starting to turn when she does."

*   *   *

REMEMBER when the police didn't hide behind trees on the side of busy roads with radar guns, but took their chances out in the traffic like everybody else?

*   *   *

WHEN she drove the car up to the toll gate the keeper said: "That will be $5 for the car and $2.50 for the passenger."

Martha replied: "The car's yours for a fiver, but I won't take less than three dollars for my old man."

*   *   *

TWO men struggled into the pub dragging their mate between them. When they reached the bar they let him go and he collapsed in a heap on the floor.

"Two beers please," said one of those still on their feet.

The barman looked down at the crumpled heap on the floor. "What about him?"

"Oh, no more for him. He's driving."

*   *   *

FOLLOWING the sound advice to take a rest when sleepy, a motorist pulled over, stopped the car on the side of the road, settled down and closed his eyes.

He was just drifting off when a jogger rapped on the window and asked for the time. Bleary-eyed he reached for his watch and announced that it was 6 am.

Sleeping at last he was soon awakened by another jogger rapping on the window asking if he had the time.

"It's six-fifteen," he said grumpily. At this rate he wasn't to get any sleep so he wrote a note and stuck it on the window for all passing joggers to see. It read "I do not have the time."

Again he settled down for his badly needed nap, but only for a few minutes before there was another rap on the window.

"Hey mate," said yet another jogger, "it's seven o'clock!"

113

DROVERS

DROVERS are the strong silent type and don't usually waste words. One night at the camp fire beside the river, Frank said: "There's a bloke down near the river bank."

"Getting fish is he?" said his mate.

"No."

"Gettin' rabbits then?"

"No."

"Well what's he gettin?"

"He's gettin' drowned," said Frank.

* * *

IT was the time of the great drought thoughout Australia and Dan the drover decided to move his mob south. He had them grazing in the Derwent Valley when a Tasmanian farmer asked where he had come from.

"Three thousand kilometres from the back o' Bourke," drawled Dan. "We were on the road for three months."

"Crikey," said the local. "How did you get that mob across Bass Strait?"

"Ah, we didn't come that way," Dan explained.

DRINKERS

DRINKERS' Motto: Conserve water, always dilute it.

* * *

HE drinks to forget, but he has forgotten why.

* * *

HE believed the best way to pull himself out of trouble was with a corkscrew.

* * *

SHE said one glass was enough
   Or two at the most
   "Three and you're under the table
   Four and you're under the host."

DRUNKS
See ALCOHOLICS

ABSTINENCE is a good thing, but it should always be practised in moderation.

*   *   *

THE difference between an Australian wedding and an Australian funeral, is one less drunk.

*   *   *

"AFTER three whiskies my husband turns into a most disgusting beast, but after the fourth I pass out altogether."

*   *   *

DRUNK, to barman: "Has Paddy been in tonight?"
    "Yes, he popped in about an hour ago."
    Drunk: "Was I with him?"

*   *   *

"TELL me, why do you swig your drinks so fast?"
    "Because I once had one stolen."

*   *   *

"THE doctor told me I would have to limit my drinking to one each day. I'm now up to April 10, 2005."

"TERRIBLE beer they serve in this pub."
    "Yes, I'll be glad when I've had enough."

*   *   *

BRUCE the Boozer has finally given up drink, for the sake of his wife and kidneys.

*   *   *

"I'VE got no sympathy for a man who spends every night drinking," she said sternly.
    "If I could spend every night drinking I wouldn't need your sympathy," he replied.

*   *   *

"I JUST got twenty bucks off Merv."
    "Off Merv? I always thought he was tight."
    "He was."

THE barman looked up to see a green rat, a pink elephant and a yellow snake wander into the pub together.

"You're too early fellas. He hasn't had his third pot yet."

*   *   *

HE suffers from alcoholic constipation. He can't pass a pub!

*   *   *

HE suffers from alcholic rheumatism.

He gets stiff in most joints.

*   *   *

A LARGE woman at a social function was startled to find herself seized and embraced by a man who was slightly under the weather. But the man quickly released her and apologised.

"Excuse me. I'm so sorry," he mumbled, "I thought for a moment you were my wife." The woman quickly recovered from her surprise and snarled: "Fancy having a drunken slob like you for a husband, you clumsy, gross disgusting beast."

"Crickey," he slurred, "you not only look like her, you sound like her too!"

*   *   *

DENIS went to the doctor because his hands kept shaking.

The doctor checked him over and said, "Do you drink much?"

"No," said Denis, "I spill most of it."

*   *   *

THE town drunk received an inheritance and was able to fulfill his dream and build a houseboat and retire. He named his boat Cirrhosis of the River.

*   *   *

"I THOUGHT you said you get drunk after one whisky."

"Yes, and I do. Usually it's the fifteenth."

"THEN what will we drink to?"

"What about three in the morning?"

* * *

HE said the reason he likes whisky is because it makes you see double and feel single. "But I always know when I've had enough. That's when I fall over."

* * *

"THERE is indeed an evil worsht than drink."

"Whatsh that then?"

"Thirsht, that's what."

* * *

THE drunk approached the policeman.

"Offisher, can you tell me where I am?"

"You are on the corner of Main St and Chester Avenue."

"Forget the details. What town is it?"

* * *

PASSING a cemetery late at night a drunk saw a sign: "Ring the bell for caretaker."

He did, and a sleepy voice growled: "What do yer want?"

"I want ter know why you can't ring the bloomin' bell yerself?"

* * *

"DRINKING makes you look beautiful, darling."

"But I haven't been drinking."

"No, but I have."

* * *

WOMAN looking under the table in a hotel saw Fred lying there. "Oh, I'm sorry," she said. "I was looking for a lady's husband."

"Well I'm one, luv," said Fred. "Crawl under."

* * *

IF your friend has had too much to drink, never fill him with coffee or you will have a wide-awake drunk on your hands.

PAT and Mick staggered out of the pub together but soon lost each other. Pat approached a policeman.

"Offisher," he said, "have you seen a fella wandering about without me?"

* * *

BRUCE went to the doctor for a check-up.

"It's quite obvious to me," said the Doc, "that alcohol is entirely responsible for your poor physical shape."

"Well I'm glad to hear that," said Bruce. "The wife keeps insisting it's my fault."

* * *

"WHY do you keep coming home three parts sloshed?" demanded his wife.

"Because I keep running out of money!"

* * *

FRED had been celebrating for most of the night before he staggered to the bar and loudly proclaimed: "Drinks for everybody, and have one yourself, barman."

There was a rush to the bar and after everybody was served the barman said to Fred, "That will be $57.80."

"But I haven't any money," said Fred quietly.

With that the barman grabbed him by the shirtfront, punched him several times and threw him out on the street.

A few minutes later Fred returned through the swinging doors, staggered up to the bar and loudly proclaimed: "Drinks for everybody, except you, barman, you get bloomin' nasty when you drink!"

* * *

THEY were leaning on the bar in a deep philosophical discussion. "Do you know that ten per cent of all road accidents are caused by drinking drivers?"

"Which means," said his mate, "that the other 90 per cent are caused by teetotallers."

* * *

AN old Scot on his death bed called his best friend, Jock,

118

to his side. "I bin saving a bottle of whisky, and when I'm gone I want you to sprinkle it on my grave. Will you do that, Jock?"

"Och Aye, but would ye mind if I pass it through my kidneys first?"

*　　*　　*

THE pub had just closed and Paddy was taking a short cut through the cemetery when he fell into a newly-dug hole which the grave-diggers had left uncovered. Paddy made a valiant attempt to get out but couldn't make it. He gave up, pulled a bottle from his hip pocket and decided to settle in the corner until morning.

Half an hour later another drunk fell into the hole.

"You'll never get out, lad," said Paddy.

But he did, in one mighty leap.

*　　*　　*

WHISKY kills more people than bullets.

That's because bullets don't drink.

*　　*　　*

FRED was having trouble with a drinking problem and swore that he would correct it with willpower. He had decided to walk straight past the pub without going in.

As he approached it he kept repeating to himself, "You can do it. You can do it."

The pressure was tough, but Fred persevered, right past he went.

Fifty metres past and he congratulated himself, "I knew you could do it. You were great. Let's go back and I'll buy you a drink."

*　　*　　*

PADDY entered the pub at lunchtime. "Was I in here last night?" he asked the barman.

"Yes," was the reply.

"Was I drunk?"

"Yes, very drunk."

"And did I spend much money," pressed Paddy.

"Yes, about twenty dollars," said the barman.

"Thank goodness. I thought I lost it!"

* * *

IRISH publican: "I'm sorry gents, but the bar won't be open for another hour. But would you loike a drink while you are waiting?"

* * *

TWO drunks were about to board the train when they saw the sign: "Dogs must be carried."

"Hold it," said one. "Where are we gonna get a dog at this time of night?"

* * *

WIFE: "Why do you drink liquor?"

Husband: "What do you suggest I do with it?"

* * *

THE sergeant answered the phone in the police station. The voice at the other end was slow and slurred.

"I wanna report a theft, offisher. I've been robbed. Shum dirty crook has shtolen things from my car."

"What kind of things?" asked the sergeant.

"My shteering wheel, brakes, dashboard, accellerator... the bloody lot's gone."

The sergeant humored him for a moment, and said he would investigate. "Bloody drunks," he said when he hung up.

Five minutes later the phone rang again.

"Cancel that report. It's all right. Yers can stop lookin," said the same voice. "My mishtake. I got inter the back seat!"

* * *

THE cops had been instructed to clean up the neighbourhood so it was dead easy when one drunk staggered towards a constable and said: "Excuse me offisher, what time is it?"

The cop replied, "One o'clock," and hit him once over the head with his baton.

120

"Crikey," said the drunk, "I'm glad I didn't ask you an hour ago."

*   *   *

THE drinker was sobbing into his beer. "What's up, mate?" asked the barman.

"I can't remember the name of the girl I am trying to forget."

*   *   *

SAID the drunk as he staggered into the kitchen. "Am I home darling?"

DUMB

SHE thought an aperitif was a set of dentures.

HE thought alter ego was a conceited priest.

SHE thought intercourse was a ticket to the races.

HE thought VAT 69 was the Pope's phone number.

SHE thought a bigamist was a thick Italian fog.

HE thought fidelity was unadulterated boredom.

SHE thought Good Friday did Robinson Crusoe's housework.

HE thought Robinson Crusoe was a world famous tenor.

SHE thought a Norwegian fjord was a Scandinavian car.

HE thought manual labour was a Spanish waiter.

SHE thought Chou En-lai was Chinese for breakfast in bed.

HE thought a brassiere was something you warm your hands on.

SHE thought Au Pair was a living bra.

HE thought polyunsaturated was a parrot in a raincoat.

SHE thought awe-struck was being hit by a paddle.

HE thought a bulletin was a can of pressed beef.

SHE thought climate was the only thing you could do with a ladder.

thought hyacinth was a greeting for anybody called .thia.

SHE thought an optimist was a hope addict.

HE thought odious was not very good poetry.

SHE thought an operetta was a girl who works at the telephone exchange.

HE thought Yoko Ono was Japanese for one egg please.

SHE thought a transistor was a nun in men's clothes.

HE thought grammar was the woman who married grandpa.

SHE thought Joan of Arc was Noah's wife.

HE thought a lieutenant commander was the lieutenant's wife.

SHE thought pregnant was the past tense of virgin.

HE thought a polygon was a dead parrot.

SHE thought the tooth fairy was a gay dentist.

HE thought the landed gentry were tricked into marriage.

SHE thought blue serge was a sad Russian.

HE thought a cross section of the public were taxpayers.

SHE thought a crowbar was where the girls hung out for a drink.

HE thought Badminton was why the lamb tasted awful.

SHE thought good housekeeping was the name of a magazine.

SHE thought a penal colony was an all-male nudist camp.

HE thought Karl Marx was the brother of Chico and Harpo.

SHE thought Columbine is the wife of the guy who discovered America.

HE thought that where there is life there's opium.

SHE thought Kosher is Jewish bacon.

HE thought myxomatosis was wiping out Rabbis.

SHE thought a meadow lark was a party in a paddock.

HE thought the Union Jack was something you got at the Trades Hall.

SHE thought hypocrisy was a Greek philosopher.

HE thought vice-versa was a rude poem.

SHE thought a teetotaller was the scorekeeper at golf.

*   *   *

DUMB Doris said she was thin, and her friend Wendy was thin, but there was a girl in the office who was as thin as the two of them, put together.

*   *   *

SOME blokes are three bricks short of a load, not the full two-bob, or two sandwiches short of a picnic.

*   *   *

THE small outback community was getting a lecture on first aid and how to stop bleeding.

"Of course you all know what a corpuscle is," said the instructor.

"Most of us do," said the chairman, "but you'd better explain it for the sake of those who have never been in one."

E

ECONOMY

IT is a recession when your friend loses his job. It is a depression when you lose yours. And it is a recovery when Paul Keating loses his. (Or substitute the politician of your choice).

* * *

THERE are two types of people. Those with swimming pools and those who can't keep their heads above water.

* * *

THE owner of a small business was telling his bank manager that the recession was tough: "Things are so bad that even people who don't pay have stopped buying."

EDUCATION
See SCHOOLS, TEACHERS

EDUCATION is what you get from reading the fine print. Experience is what you get from not reading it.

* * *

"EDUCATION has failed the younger generation," said the businessman. "Our survey shows that as many as 40 per cent can't read, another 40 per cent can't write and the other 30 per cent can't add up."

THE teacher pointed to little Solly Cohen and said, "Solly, what's three per cent?"

"You're right, teacher," said Solly shrugging his shoulders, "what is three per cent!"

* * *

LITTLE Nigel's mother had been away for a week and asked her son about events during her absence.

"There was a big thunderstorm on Wednesday and I was so scared me and Daddy snuggled up in the same bed."

"Nigel," said the boy's pretty nurse, "you mean Daddy and I."

"No," said the kid. "That was last night. I'm talking about Wednesday."

* * *

TWO Australians in London down on their luck saw an advertisement for two footmen. "References essential," it said. "That's okay," said Bruce, "I'll write yours and you can write one for me." Thus they arrived on the estate and offered the duchess two glowing references. "First things first," she said. "Formal wear here means wearing kilts, so drop your trousers while I check your knees."

The lads were a little surprised but they did so. The duchess gave the knees the nod of approval and said, "Okay, now let me see those testimonials."

After they were thrown off the property Bruce said: "With a little more education we would have got that job."

EGO

THE human body is an interesting phenomenon. A pat on the back can result in a swollen head.

* * *

HIS ego was bigger than the Outback.

MOST actors are all ham and ego.

*   *   *

HE was the kind of chap who had plenty to be modest about.

*   *   *

HE makes so many enemies, he really needs an enemy agent.

*   *   *

THERE were so many famous egos at the theatrical awards, I was the only person in the room I'd never heard of.

ELEPHANTS

WHY have Elephants got Big Ears?
Because Noddy won't pay the ransom.

*   *   *

ONE reason elephants drink so much water is that nobody ever offers them anything else.

*   *   *

AN elephant was drinking from the Zambesi when he noticed a turtle asleep on a log. He ambled over and kicked it clear across the river.

"What did you do that for?" asked a passing giraffe.

"Because I recognised it as the same turtle which took a nip out of my trunk 53 years ago."

"What a memory," exclaimed the giraffe.

"Yes," said the elephant, "turtle recall."

*   *   *

"WHO'S the king of the jungle?" called the lion swaggering down the bush trail.

"Oh, you are," replied the tiger with its tail between its legs.

"Who's the king of the jungle?" said the lion to the leopard.

"Oh you are," said the leopard cowering in the grass.

126

"Who's the king of the jungle?" said the lion to a huge elephant which blocked the jungle path.

Without answering the elephant gathered the lion in his trunk, hurled him in the air, caught him and smashed him against a tree.

"Look," said the lion. "Don't get mad just because you don't know the answer!"

*　　*　　*

AN elephant escaped from a circus and no trace had been found until a lady who had never seen an elephant before rang the police. She was panic-stricken.

"There is a weird monster in my back yard," she said. "It is pulling up the cabbages with its tail. But what is worse... I cannot describe what it is doing with them!"

ENGAGEMENTS
See WEDDINGS, NEWLY-WEDS, MARRIAGE and MARRIEDS

THE suitor had been shown into the lounge room to wait for his date while she got ready, when her little brother came in.

"Is Jean your oldest sister?" he said to make small talk.

"Yep," said the kid.

"And who comes after her?"

"You and two other blokes."

*　　*　　*

THE lad has just asked Paddy O'Leary for his daughter's hand in marriage. "Can you support our Teresa in the manner to which she is accustomed?"

"Indeed, sir I can."

"Have you ever seen her eat?" said Paddy.

"Indeed sir, I have."

"But have you ever seen her eat when there's nobody looking?"

I HAVE come to ask for your daughter's hand."

"Okay, take the one that's always in my pocket."

* * *

"SIR, I would like to marry your daughter."

"Okay, leave your name and address and if nothing better turns up we will contact you."

* * *

"SIR, I wish to marry your daughter."

"Do you drink alcohol young man?"

"Thanks all the same, but let's settle this business first."

* * *

"SIR, I wish to marry your daughter."

"Can you support a family?" enquired the prospective father-in-law.

"Yes sir, I can."

"There are eight of us."

* * *

"SIR, I want your daughter for my wife."

"Well I'm not swapping until I've seen your wife."

* * *

THE young man was so nervous when he approached his highly formal prospective father-in-law that he blurted out the words: "I am asking for your daughter's hole in handy matrimony!"

* * *

"IF we did become engaged," she said, "would you give me a ring?"

"Certainly, what's your number?"

* * *

WHEN he proposed she got so excited she insisted on showing the ring to her workmates in the office. She soon returned and threw it at him. Three of her girlfriends had recognised it.

* * *

"YOU have broken it off with Milicent?"

"Yes. She was just a passing fiancée."

"I HAVE been asked to get married hundreds of times," she pouted.

"By whom?"

"My mum and dad," she said.

* * *

"I WONDER if my fiancée loves me?"

"Of course she does. Why should she make you an exception?"

* * *

"NO," she said. "I don't love you, so I won't marry you. But I will be a sister to you."

"That's okay," he said. "How much do you think our father will leave us?"

* * *

"DO you believe in free love, Jack?" she asked.

"Well, I've never sent you an invoice, have I?"

* * *

"FRED," she said, "when we are married I want to share all your worries and troubles and help lighten your burden."

"Forget it, Madge, I've got no worries or troubles."

"But we're not married yet, darling."

ESTATE AGENTS

A YOUNG Swedish woman was thinking of buying the house. The estate agent was showing her the property. They inspected the lower floor then he said "Now we'll go upstairs and I will show you the bedroom and den."

She looked at him sideways: "And den what?"

* * *

AN auctioneer has no friends. Only nodding acquaintances.

* * *

AFTER I got married I said to my mother-in-law, "My house is your house."

"Three days later she sold it."

SIGN outside a big home: COSTA PLENTI.

* * *

HE said Swindle & Wrun had the best salesmen in the business. "They sold me a block of land and when I went to see it I discovered it was five metres under water."

"Well, didn't you go back and complain?"

"Yes, that's the trouble. They then sold me a boat."

* * *

HE breasted the bar and announced: "The drinks are on me. I've just sold the house for $100,000."

And as they all placed their orders he added: "Mind you, the council might go bananas when they find out."

* * *

TWO country land agents were leaning on the pub's verandah rail looking at the dust storm going by.

"All that country changing hands, and we're not getting a cent commission," grumbled one.

* * *

A WOMAN who had just taken a lease on a unit near the railway line rang the estate agent to complain that passing trains rocked her bed so much she was in fear of falling out of it.

The agent came around. "But it's so quiet," he said, "I can't believe that passing trains rock the bed."

"Shakes the living daylights out of it," she persisted, looking at her watch.

She heard a distant train whistle. "Here's the five thirty-five. Lie down on the bed yourself," and she climbed on to the other side.

That's when her husband came in.

"What do you think you are doing?" he roared, glaring at the estate agent.

"Would you believe waiting for a train?" he ventured.

130

FAIRYTALES

TWO young women were walking along a country lane when a large green frog jumped out before them and said: "Please dear maidens. One of you kiss me and I will turn into a handsome prince."

One girl quickly scooped up the frog and put it in her handbag.

"Aren't you going to restore him to a prince?" asked her friend.

"No. Princes are a dime a dozen. But a talking frog, now there is potential for making a dollar."

FAMILIES

FRED can trace his family tree right back to the time when it was his ancestor's address.

* * *

I AM not saying my brothers were fast eaters, but ours was the only house with racing colours on our knives and forks.

* * *

CECIL got in after midnight and his mother wanted to know where he had been.

"I've been out with a boy I know."

"You mean a girl, don't you?" she said.

"Boy or girl, what's the difference?" he said.

"If you don't know the difference, then I guess it's alright," said his relieved mother.

* * *

THE teenage girl got home very late and explained to her mother: "You know how it is, Mum ... "

"Yes, I certainly do. And what is his name?"

* * *

BERT got interested in his ancestors. He looked up his family tree and found most of them still swinging in the branches.

* * *

THE family had gathered around because old Grandpa was dying.

"Is there anything I can do for you?" said his wife.

The old man raised himself on one elbow and peered at a jug of beer on the table.

"I wouldn't mind a swig of that," he gasped.

"Well you can't," snapped his wife. "That's for the wake."

* * *

"MUM, how do lions make love?"

"Don't know, son. All your father's friends are Rotarians."

* * *

"MUM, Dad's going out again.

"Well pour some more petrol on him."

* * *

JUST when your children get old enough, so that you can stand them, they can't stand you.

* * *

CHILDREN should be seen and not had.

* * *

EVERY family should have at least three children. Then if one is a genius the other two can support him.

THEY say children brighten the home. That's because they never turn off the bloody lights.

* * *

SHE took after the mother, who took after the father, who took after the maid.

* * *

ANY one of your friends can become an enemy, given time. But a relative is one from the start.

* * *

SUCCESS is relative. The more success the more relatives.

FARMS

AT the National Agricultural Conference it was easy to pick the dairy milking champion. He was the bloke who shook hands with everybody, one finger at a time.

* * *

BATTLING Bill had brought his family down from the farm to attend the Royal Show. A prize winning bull was the major exhibit, with an entrance fee of one dollar. Bill asked the attendant if he could get a concession for his family; himself, his wife and 13 kids.

"Hang on a minute," said the attendant, "I'll bring the bloomin' bull out and give him a gawk at you."

* * *

IT was the night of the school concert and all the kids had their poems, songs and recitations at the ready; except little Charlie who had just come down from the country and had started school that day.

"C'mon Charlie," said the teacher. "Surely you can do something for the concert."

It took much cajolling, but finally Charlie agreed to do some farmyard impressions.

The instant applause gave Charlie a boost of confidence and he strode to centre stage. "Farmyard noises," he announced.

Then cupping his hands to his face like a megaphone he yelled at the top of his voice: "Get off that blasted tractor. Shut that blasted gate. Get that blankety bull out of that yard ...!"

* * *

YOUNG Johnny was late for school again. "And what kept you this time, Johnny?" asked the young mistress in despair for yet another yarn.

"It's the breeding season, Miss, and I had to put the bull to the cows," he said.

"Couldn't your father do that?" she said.

"No," said Johnny, "it's gotta be a bull!"

* * *

FARMER Murphy met Farmer O'Leary in town. "What did you give to your ailing bull when it had colic?" asked Murphy.

"A good dose of phenyl," said Murphy.

A week later they met in the pub. "What did you say you gave your sick bull?" said O'Leary.

"Phenyl," said Murphy.

"Well I gave phenyl to my bull and it died," said O'Leary.

"So did mine," said Murphy.

* * *

THE farmer's sons were sent home from the bush school with a note from the teacher complaining that they swore too much. Their father gave them a lecture, a thump in the ear and sent them to bed without dinner.

Next morning when they sat at the table they were asked what they wanted for breakfast.

"I'll have some of those bloody cornflakes," said one, and immediately received a thrashing from his father.

"And what would you like," said the angry father to his second son.

"I don't know. But it won't be those bloody cornflakes, that's for sure."

TWO city slickers attended the Royal Agricultural Show and were impressed with the fine examples of life on the farm. They got absorbed in watching Paddy grooming a large fearsome bull, until he sat quietly on a stool beside it.

"Gee it must be late, what's the time?" said one of the city slickers. Paddy put two hands under the testicles of the bull and lifted them gently. "It's ten past six," he said.

The men were about to leave when the significance of Paddy's uncanny country skill sunk through.

"Did you see that?" said one.

"Amazing," said the other.

They couldn't believe it, and talked it over for awhile before gingerly approaching Paddy again.

"Er, can you tell us the time again, please?"

Paddy, still seated on his stool, gently lifted the bull's balls once more. "It's a quarter-past six," he said.

The city slickers could contain themselves no longer.

"How do you do that?" they asked.

Paddy told them to climb through the rail and bend down near him. "Look, when I lift the bull's balls you can see the town hall clock from here!"

*   *   *

FARMER and his son were on a train headed for their first visit to the city when a priest hobbled into their compartment on crutches, with his foot in plaster.

"Slipped in the bathtub," he explained.

When the priest got out at the next station the son said: "What's a bathtub, Dad?"

"I dunno son, I'm not a Catholic."

*   *   *

DAVE had come down from the farm for his first visit to the city and was enjoying a beer in a pub when a character sidled up to him and whispered: "How would you like to buy some pornographic material?"

135

"No use to me, mate," replied Dave. "We haven't got a pornograph."

* * *

A CENSUS official was assisting a farmer's wife to fill in her forms.

"How many children have you got?" he asked.

"Six," she replied. "Three sets of twins."

"How very extraordinary," said the census man. "Twins every time."

"Oh no," said the farmer's wife. "Not every time. Hundreds of times, nothing!"

* * *

THE union rep was checking on the farmer who was suspected of underpaying his employees and was being introduced to the farmhands.

"This is Harry," said the farmer, "he milks the cows, and looks after the dairy and gets $200 a week with room and board."

"And this is Mary. She cooks and does the housework and gets $130 a week with room and board."

"Fair enough so far," said the union rep. "Is there anyone else?"

"Yes," said the farmer. "There's the half-wit. He works fifty hours a week and gets around $15 a week with room and board."

"Ah," said the rep. "I'd like to speak to him."

"You're talking to him right now," said the farmer.

FARTS

NO less a literary giant than Chaucer gave recognition to the humble fart in his 13th century writing of "The Miller's Tale." Then Jonathan Swift, author of "Gulliver's Travels," wrote in 1731 that the odd fart was notorious for its stifling effect on romance.

Farts are an undeniable part of life. They are often

tried to be denied with euphemisms like flatulence or breaking wind but it never disguises the reality that a fart is a fart.

Rich men, poor men, beggars and thieves, even politicians and bishops pay homage to the old adage: Better to have an empty house than a grumbling tenant.

It can be said that the sign of a consolidated marriage is when either partner can fart without the need to say "excuse me."

* * *

IT's a sign of wedded security
A marriage that's reached its maturity
When neither accuses
Nor offers excuses
For farts that fly with impunity.

* * *

THE Queen was showing the Archbishop of Canterbury around the Royal Stables when one of the stallions close by broke wind in such a loud and gusty manner it couldn't be ignored.

"Oh dear," said the Queen blushing, "how embarassing. I'm frightfully sorry about that."

"It's quite understandable," said the archbishop, and after a moment added, "as a matter of fact, I thought it was the horse."

* * *

THE chubby matron was consulting her doctor and explaining her problem in a timid manner. "What can you do for me, doctor, I have a lot of wind."

The doctor gave her a kite.

* * *

A BUSINESSWOMAN explained to her doctor that she had an unusual complaint. She was always breaking wind, at board meetings, during interviews, in lifts, on the tram. It was impossible to control.

"But at least I am fortunate in two respects," she told

the doctor, "they neither smell nor make a noise. In fact you will be surprised to know it's happened twice since I've been talking to you Doctor."

The doctor reached for his notebook, scribbled a prescription and handed it to her.

She read it. "What? Nasal drops?" she queried.

"Yes," said the Doc. "We'll fix your nose first then we'll have a go at your hearing."

* * *

SECOND businesswoman tells the doctor she is suffering from the same problem. The Doc listens to a few extraordinary blow-offs that register 6.2 on the Richter scale then asks her to lower her bloomers and hop up on the couch.

She is alarmed when he reaches for a long pole with a hook on the end of it.

"Goodness, what are you going to do with that," she said.

"First it's necessary to open some of these skylights," he replied.

* * *

THE feuding neighbours had decided to patch up their differences over a few drinks. All was going well until one of the blokes broke wind.

"How dare you fart in front of my wife," roared the husband.

"How was I to know it was her turn," replied the other.

* * *

LADY Fotheringham suffered from flatulence a great deal and was prone to make certain noises when she got excited while entertaining friends at the manor. She was fortunate in having in her employ a very loyal and discreet butler called James.

Upon hearing these subdued explosions James would instantly say "Excuse me," and promptly leave the room taking the blame with him and saving her ladyship great embarrassment.

But one day James fell ill and was replaced by a butler from the employment service to help out on an important tea party.

In the middle of a conversation with the vicar Lady Fotheringham suffered one of her attacks accompanied by the usual sound effects.

She turned to the new butler and said: "James, stop that!"

"Certainly madam," said the new James, "which way did it go?"

* * *

THERE was a young girl from Jakarta
Who was widely renowned as a farta
Her deafening reports
At athletics and sports
Made her much in demand as a starta.

* * *

OVER the years Fred had never attempted to control his bad habit of breaking wind. It sounded like a gale ripping a spinnaker to shreds and often registered 7.3 on the Richter scale. Constant pleas from his wife, Myrtle, to control these thunder claps failed to have effect until one day she threatened to leave him.

"Okay, I'll do my best," he said.

"Not good enough," said Myrtle. "Prove it by refraining from that terrible practice for one whole month," she insisted.

Fred promised. And despite times when he gripped the armchair until his knuckles went white, crossed his legs and grimaced in pain, he never let one go for weeks.

One night he arrived home from the office to find the dining table set with flowers and candles. "What's all this?" he asked.

"It's a month tonight and you've been so good I have cooked one of your favourite dishes as a reward." She then placed a blindfold over his eyes. "I want it to be a surprise," she said.

Fred sat there in silence, and while listening to Myrtle rattling pots in the kitchen he felt a king-sized fart gathering force. He crossed his legs, clenched his fists and the sweat gathered on his brow.

"What the hell," he thought, "the month is up, I've gone the distance and I'm sitting here like a fool with a blindfold on while I can still hear her out in the kitchen. It would be safe to let one rip."

With that he leant to one side, lifted one rump off the chair and with a grin of great relief let it rumble free.

It was just in time for he heard Myrtle's footsteps coming and felt her fumble with the blindfold before ripping it off.

That was the signal for a chorus of "Happy Birthday" from Fred's family all seated around him at the birthday table.

FASHION

FASHION is something that goes in one era and out the other.

* * *

MY ol' Dad was dedicated to fashion. When we were kids he would say: "If you must polish your boots while you are still wearing them, take your socks off. Then if you get some black nugget on your ankles you simply put your socks back on and nobody knows."

* * *

AND if it is a formal occasion, do your best to get two matching thongs.

* * *

THE tall blonde told the attendant in the fashion store that she wanted a pair of low heels.

"To wear with what, madam?"

"A short, plump, rich stock-broker," she replied.

* * *

"HOW do you like the fit, madam?"

"Fit? It's a convulsion."

* * *

IT'S not the cost of a strapless gown, it's the upkeep.

* * *

THE bride wore a beautiful gownless evening strap.

* * *

HER dress looked pretty good considering the shape it was on.

* * *

WHEN he criticised the scantiness of her swim suit, she laughed it off.

OR... When he complained that her strapless dress was too daring, she laughed it off.

* * *

THE outfit made her look like a million dollars; all wrinkled and green.

* * *

"I WANT the dress in the window."

"Well it's in the window."

* * *

A TIGHT skirt has never yet stopped a girl's circulation.

* * *

"I'D like to see something cheap in a straw hat."

"Here, try this. And the mirror is over there."

* * *

"I'D like to buy that hat in the window."

"It's not necessary. We can sell it here over the counter."

* * *

SHE said she was a physical education instructor and she wanted a pair of bloomers to wear around her gymnasium.

"How big is your gymnasium," enquired the attendant.

SHOPPER: "I'd like to see something in silk stockings."
   Attendant: "You men are all alike."

*   *   *

WHEN he heard that Parisian women would not be wearing dresses much longer this season he decided to go there for his holidays.

*   *   *

HE chooses his own suits, but his wife picks his pockets.

*   *   *

THE latest thing in men's clothing is women.

*   *   *

FATHER: "Why are you wearing my raincoat?"
   Son: "Well you don't want your best suit to get wet, do you?"

*   *   *

SHE was ecstatic over the bargain. "Look at this dress," she said, "I bought it for a ridiculous figure."
   "Yeah, I know," said her husband, "but how much did you pay for it?"

*   *   *

"HOW many shirts does your husband wear a week?" she asked.
   "You mean how many weeks does he wear his shirts," she replied.

*   *   *

ACCORDING to the latest fashion magazine, women will be wearing their legs longer this summer.

*   *   *

HE asked what Mabel's new evening dress looked like.
   He was told: "In a lot of places it looks like Mabel."

*   *   *

"WHENEVER I am down in the dumps, I treat myself to a new hat."
   "We wondered where you got them."

*   *   *

"NO one knows," complained Miss Cox

"The pain that it engenders
"Keeping up my bobby-sox
"With ord'nary suspenders."

* * *

HE was a bit old-fashioned and it upset him to see the outrageous dress of some young people in the street.

"Just look at that one?" he barked at a bystander. "Is it a boy or a girl?"

"It's a girl, and she's my daughter," came the reply.

"Oh, I'm sorry," apologised the grump, "I didn't know you were her mother."

"I'm not," snapped the bystander, "I'm her father!"

* * *

MODERN fashions are crazy. Fish-net stockings and forcing feet into those high heel shoes is ridiculous. I've told my father to stop wearing them.

* * *

SOME dresses worn by women
  Are like fences at the zoo
  They safeguard lovely bodies
  But don't obstruct the view.

FATHERS-IN-LAW
See MOTHERS-IN-LAW

THE old codger was hogging the fireplace, monopolising the telly and stinking the lounge room with his pipe. Finally, it got too much for the young couple and she whispered to her husband, "Look dear, fair's fair. He's been here ever since we were married. It's time your father went home."

"My father. My father," he gasped. "I thought he was yours!"

* * *

"WHEN I see your father coming up the front path," she said to her husband, "I sometimes wish I had loved and lost."

143

WHEN he arrived home his wife had a smug look. "There was a door-knock collection today," she said. "People were collecting for the Old People's Home. So I gave them your father."

*   *   *

MADGE: "I've just got a bottle of whisky for my father-in-law."
MARY: "That's a good bargain!"

*   *   *

MADGE: "I stuck up for Pops the other night."
MARY: "Yeah?"
MADGE: "They said he wasn't fit to eat with pigs. I said he was."

*   *   *

IT took time, but Madge eventually developed an attachment for her father-in-law. It fitted over his mouth.

*   *   *

HER father-in-law once got a job on a farm. He left it after a few weeks. He got tired of standing out in a wheat field with his arms outstretched scaring the crows away. He not only chased the birds off, they even brought back the grain they stole the previous year.

FATHERS AND SONS

HE was a young father, wheeling the pram through the gardens while the baby was screaming its head off. "Take it easy Jason," he said calmly, "there's nothing to fuss about."

A middle-aged woman noticed his soothing manner and marvelled at the new breed of young husbands.

When the baby screamed even louder she heard him say: "Cool it, Jason, don't get excited, lad, cool it son."

Touched by his gentle manner the woman leaned into the pram and cooed: "There, there Jason, what's bothering you?"

144

"Excuse me, lady," said the father, "that's Jeremy, I'm Jason."

* * *

FATHER and son were posing for a picture to mark the son's graduation from university. "Stand closer," said the photographer to the father, "and put your hand on his shoulder."

"Wouldn't it be more appropriate," replied the father, "if he put his hand in my pocket?"

* * *

TWO fathers were at the bar of their club sharing their problems. "My son is at college and is always writing home for money. I don't know what he does with it," lamented one.

"My daughter is at college and never asks for money. I wonder where she is getting it," lamented the other.

* * *

HE came home from the office to find his lay-about son asleep in the garden hammock once more. It was time he had a lesson about life.

He shook him awake and said: "You've been out of school for three years, you haven't tried looking for a job. Isn't it time you smartened yourself and studied for a profession?"

"Why?" said the son sleepily.

"So that you can become a businessman like me."

"Why?" persisted the son.

"So you can make a lot of money."

"Why?"

"So you can have enough in the bank."

"Why?"

"So that you can retire and not go to work."

"But I don't go to work now," said the son.

* * *

"WHAT'S a monologue, Dad?"

"That's a conversation with your mother, son."

"WHEN I was your age," said the father to his teenage son, "I would be up at dawn, run ten miles across frosty ground, dive into the sea, run another mile along the beach and sprint all the way home. I would do all that before breakfast and think nothing of it."

The son yawned and said, "I don't think much of it myself."

* * *

IN many fields of endeavour the cleverness or fame of the father often proves the stumbling block for the son.

"Well thank goodness," said Mum, "our Johnny has nothing to fall over."

* * *

TWO fathers were discussing the trials and tribulations of bringing up teenage sons. "I insist on discipline," said one. "I have always insisted on discipline from the day he started to walk."

Just then the boy under discussion entered the room waving a set of car keys in his hand. "Hi Dad. I'm taking the car. I've pulled a bird and I have just raided one of your bottles of Scotch to make sure I'm on a winner. I won't be back tonight."

The visiting father's jaw dropped. "I thought you said you had disciplined him?"

"Of course I have," said the first. "He didn't have to come and tell me, did he?"

* * *

HIS father was sternly insisting that he continue his education to ensure he gained a profession. "Digging holes is the only job you can get where you start at the top," he said.

* * *

TWO old boys met at the club after years apart. "How's your son making out in life?" asked one.

"Oh he's the top car salesman of a nation-wide franchise. Going so well he topped the sales chart and they gave him a brand new Mercedes," said the proud father. "But he gave it away. Can you imagine that, gave it away."

"That's amazing," said the other old chap. "My son's in real estate and development. Clinched the biggest deal this year and they gave him a penthouse, but he gave it away. Can you imagine that?"

Right then a third old boy came in. "How's your son?" they asked him.

"Bit disappointing really," he said. "He's turned out to be a raving homosexual. But still, he's managing quite well. One of his best friends gave him a Mercedes last week, and another gave him a penthouse."

FEMINISTS

MARRIAGE: It begins as you sink in his arms, and ends with your arms in the sink.

* * *

EQUALITY is a myth; women are superior.

* * *

WHAT do you call a man who has lost 90 per cent of his brain?

A widower!

* * *

IF a woman does household chores for $200 a week, that's domestic science. If she does it for nothing, that's marriage.

* * *

COMMON sense would save a significant number of marriages. If women used it, there wouldn't be any.

* * *

THE feminists are hailing a miracle birth.

The baby has a dick AND a brain.

* * *

SHE said she wouldn't mind having a baby, but unfortunately you have to marry one to get one.

THERE are three kinds of men; the handsome, the caring, and the majority.

*　　*　　*

A WOMAN who strives to be like a man lacks ambition.

*　　*　　*

THE only problem with women, is men. And the worst thing about men is that all the nice ones are gay.

*　　*　　*

SHE said we all have to live with our disappointments. "But why do I have to live with mine?"

*　　*　　*

WHEN the boss put the hard word on the lively new girl she had the answer: "No way, bozzo, you've got the words 'liberated' and 'free' mixed up."

*　　*　　*

LOVE is the delusion that one man is different from the rest.

*　　*　　*

WHEN a woman makes a fool of a man it's usually an improvement.

*　　*　　*

IT is said that the wisest of men can become foolish over women; and the most foolish of women is wise to men.

*　　*　　*

THE only difference between men and pigs is that when pigs drink they don't make men of themselves.

*　　*　　*

MEN are like pigeons. They should never be looked up to.

*　　*　　*

THE only thing wives have in common with their husbands is that they were married on the same day.

*　　*　　*

SHE wanted a husband and put an advertisement in the personal column. She got a hundred replies saying: "You can have mine!"

WOMEN are called birds because of all the worms they pick up.

* * *

FRED was a window cleaner and he couldn't believe his eyes when he saw a young woman get out of the bath and start drying off, right in front of him.

She was a feminist, and instead of screaming she stared straight back at him in an effort to shame him.

Their eyes locked in confrontation for an interminable minute. Neither would budge.

Finally Fred roared: "What are ya staring at? Haven't ya ever seen a window cleaner before?"

* * *

TWO unattached office girls decided it would make economic sense if they teamed up to take advantage of the twin-share prices on their next holiday. After they booked in to their first hotel room one turned to the other and rested her hand on her shoulder. "There's something I haven't told you about myself," she said. "I'll be frank…"

"Oh no you won't," interrupted her friend, "I'll be Frank."

* * *

THE young couple had a knee-trembler against a paling fence and got so excited they knocked it down.

The commotion aroused the house-holder who grabbed the young man and collected $100 on the spot for repairs to the fence.

Later the young bloke said: "Listen Mabel. You are a feminist and you are always shouting about equal rights. Here's your chance. You owe me $50 for half cost of the fence."

"No way," she said. "It was you who did all the pushing."

FINANCE
See ACCOUNTANTS

"I WOULD go through anything for you."

"Good. Let's start with your bank account."

THE ship's purser asked the sailor how he had spent his month's pay on shore leave.

"Some went on drink, some on women. And I guess I squandered the rest," was the reply.

*   *   *

EVERY day a ragged old man with a tray of shoe laces would take up a position at the entrance to a city skyscrapper, and every morning and executive entering the building would drop a dollar in his tray, without taking any laces.

One day the executive dropped his usual dollar and was about to walk away when the old man tapped him on the shoulder. "Excuse me, sir. I don't like to complain, but laces are now $1.50."

*   *   *

THRIFT is the most admirable virtue of any ancestor.

*   *   *

COP to bank manager: "Can you describe the missing teller?"

"Yes, he's six foot tall and $100,000 short."

*   *   *

A YOUNG Jewish lad was learning arithmetic. "What's two-and-two, Father?"

Dad: "Are we buying or selling?"

*   *   *

WITH the new world order, the USA will, from now on, be known as the IOUSA.

*   *   *

ALWAYS borrow money from a pessimist. He doesn't expect to get it back.

*   *   *

MONEY, money, money.
  If a man is always chasing it, he's mercenary.
  If he doesn't chase it, he lacks ambition.
  If he hoards it, he's stingy.

If he spends it, he's a spendthrift.

If he gets it without working, he's a parasite.

If he scrimps and saves, he is wasting his life.

* * *

TREASURER'S report: "Last year we were poised on the edge of a precipice. This year we have made a great leap forward!"

* * *

I HAVE always tried to pay my bills with a smile. But invariably they want money.

* * *

REMEMBER, the darkest hour is just before the pawn.

* * *

"WHAT is your major worry?"

"Money."

"I didn't know you had any."

"I haven't."

* * *

"HEY Fred, lend us twenty bucks until pay day to buy a round of drinks."

"Okay, but when's pay day."

"How should I know. You're the one who's working!"

* * *

"HEY Fred, remember last time when I was broke and you helped me out with twenty bucks and I said I'd never forget you?"

"Yes."

"Well, I'm broke again!"

* * *

MONEY won't help you make friends. But you'll have a better class of enemy.

* * *

THE wealthy financier took a tumble for a blonde and lost his balance at the bank.

* * *

SHE told her banker: "I haven't got much collateral, but will you take one of those promiscuity notes?"

THE manager told the new clerk to count a package of one thousand single dollar notes. He noticed the clerk laboriously counting and heard him reach, "502, 503, 504, 505." Then the clerk threw the package into the drawer and remarked: "If it's right that far, it's probably right all the way."

* * *

THE Prime Minister was on the dais as the parade of military might passed by. First squadrons of jets flew overhead, then lines of tanks, heavy artillery and columns of infantry armed to the teeth. Finally, a group of men in pin-striped suits, awkwardly marching out of step brought up the rear of the parade.

"Is that your Secret Service Mr Minister?" asked a foreign diplomat.

"Hell no. They are our economists. They can cause more damage than the rest put together!"

* * *

THE Chinese businessman pressed the teller to explain why his interest rate had increased two points from the previous day.

"Fluctuations," said the teller.

"And the same to you, ya bloomin' ocker," said the Chinaman.

* * *

A YOUNG accountant was overjoyed to learn that he had won a million dollars in Lotto. He lived with his Mum and Dad and they were equally excited when he broke the news.

"Naturally I want to share my good fortune so I am going to make you a present of $100 each," he told his parents.

There was silence for a moment before the old man spoke.

"Well son, we've done a lot for you," he began. "It was a struggle during the depression, and we never had much money. In fact, we didn't have enough to get legally married."

"What," said the shocked son, "you mean … I am…"

"Yes, son, and a damned miserable one at that."

* * *

THEY had been down-and-outers all their life, but Bill and Jacko had always managed to share a Lotto ticket, and of course, one day their dream came true. They celebrated with a beer in their local pub and agreed that a million dollars would not change their nature, except for the flash car they had always wanted.

Bill paid for the beers and off they went to the car sales showroom where they shocked the salesman by buying a Rolls Royce each.

Bill produced his cheque book with a flourish and reached for his pen when Jacko said: "No, no, Bill. Fair go. You paid for the beers."

* * *

THE man who writes the bank's advertising is not the same man who makes the loans.

* * *

WHEN Jock McTavish received a letter from the electricity board threatening to cut off the electricity if he didn't pay his long-overdue account he stormed down to the office.

"Look here," he told the manager. "Each month I put all the bills in my hat, give them a good stir, then pull one out and pay it. But if you don't stop hounding me with threatening letters your bill won't even go in the hat next month."

* * *

"DEAR Bank Manager. Stop sending me letters, just because my account is in the red. I didn't pester you with letters when my account was in the black."

* * *

THE owner of the corner shop was adamant. She told Paddy: "I'm sorry, but you can have no more credit. Your bill's already bigger than it should be."

"I know that," retorted Paddy. "As soon as you cut it to the proper amount I'll pay it!"

FIREFIGHTERS

THERE was a fire at the nurses home. It took the firemen 15 minutes to put it out. It took the nurses three hours to put the firemen out.

* * *

THE phone rang at the fire station and a frantic voice said: "I have just had the front yard landscaped, and there is a new rock-garden which cost me heaps and a flower bed down the side..."

"What's this got to do with the fire station?" yelled the officer.

"Plenty," continued the caller. "The house next door is on fire and I don't want you blokes trampling all over my new garden."

* * *

STATION officer Jones took the call. "There's a house on fire in Centre Rd," said the frantic voice.

"We're right in the middle of a poker game at the moment and I've got a winning hand. Can you throw a bucket of petrol on it and keep it going till we get there?"

* * *

THE Mexican fireman was the proud father of twin boys. He called one Jose and the other Hose B.

* * *

THERE's a bloke who sells Immitation Fire Insurance to people with imitation fireplaces.

* * *

AND we all know why firemen have bigger balls than policemen. They sell more tickets.

* * *

THE firefighter answered the phone to hear Paddy in a panic.

"Quick, there's a fire! There's a fire!"

"Where is it?"

"At my place of course."

"I mean what's the location?"

"It's in the kitchen."

"But how do we get there?"

"Crikey. Haven't you got a fire engine?"

FISHERMEN

PADDY said that he once cleaned 500 fish in one day.

"Now that takes guts."

* * *

"I WISH I could afford the time to go fishing."

"But you are always fishing."

"Yes, but I wish I could afford it!"

* * *

HE went off for a week's fishing and didn't catch anything until he got home.

* * *

AGAINST his wife's wishes he set off for another week-end. "What's that Dad's carrying?" said their young son.

"It is called a fishing rod, dear, and it has a worm at both ends."

* * *

ONE dedicated fisherman told his fellow angler that he had a marvellous dream the previous night. "I dreamt I was alone in a boat with Raquel Welch and we were both nude."

"Well what was good about it," asked his mate.

"We caught 50 bream and a record sized salmon," he said.

* * *

THE angler from the city settled down on the banks of the river with all his sophisticated gear and tried to make conversation with an old local seated on a nearby log with a line in his hand.

"Do you fish with flies here?"

"Fish with them? I've fished with them, camped with them, and tried to sleep with them," said the old timer.

* * *

TWO fishermen were out in their boat one Sunday morning when they heard the church bells ring in the distance. One said contritely, "You know, we really ought to be in church."

Baiting his hook the second chap replied: "I couldn't have gone today anyway. I've got the wife sick in bed."

* * *

TWO lads from went fishing and got caught in a terrible storm. Night fell and things began to look bad as they were blown to sea at the mercy of the wind. One began to sob and pray: "Oh Lord. I have not been very good in my life. I have drunk to excess, gambled my wages, cheated on my wife. But if you spare my life now I promise faithfully I will ..."

"Hang on a minute, Bert," interrupted his friend. "Don't go too far, I think I see a light."

* * *

AN angler's wife asked him for some money. He gave her two fifties, two twenties, three tenners and a fiver. She threw the small one back.

* * *

IT was the worst trout season New Zealand had experienced for years and the disgruntled American tourist held up his single fish.

"I've come half way round the world to catch this one darn fish so I reckon it has cost me at least $10,000."

"Bloomin' lucky you only caught one then," said his guide.

* * *

AT the waterside bar the young fisherman was describing

the crayfish he had pulled to the surface. "It was at least a metre long," he said.

His listeners were amazed. "Well, where is it?" they asked.

"Oh, it busted the top of the pot and got away," he said.

An old salt who had been leaning on the bar during this revelation said "I was fishing and my line hooked onto an old ship's lantern on Shipwreck Reef. When I hauled it up the lantern was still burning."

The young man eyed the old salt with suspicion. "Fair go mate, you don't expect us to believe that."

"Well," said the old man, "if you chop half a metre off your crayfish, I will blow the bloomin' candle out!"

*   *   *

OH give me the luck to catch a fish
   So big that even I
   When talking of it afterwards
   May have no need to lie.

FLASHERS

THREE old maids were sitting on a seat in the park when a member of the raincoat brigade flashed at them. Two of the old ladies had a stroke. The third was too slow.

*   *   *

IT was so cold the other day that the local flasher was seen describing himself to a woman.

*   *   *

FRED the Flasher had been working the riverbank for 30 years and Pete the Perv asked him when he was retiring.

"I have been thinking about it seriously," said Fred. "But I think I will stick it out for another year."

157

FLOOSIES

SHE has an impediment in her speech. She can't say no.

* * *

SHE had always been a gold-digger, so when her husband's partner died she was quick off the mark to arrange a replacement she had groomed for the job.

"Darling," she said, "I have just the right candidate to replace your partner who died yesterday."

"That's alright with me," he replied, "provided you can arrange it with the undertaker."

* * *

THE sugar daddy presented his floosy with a beautiful skunk coat. "Amazing," she said, "that such a beautiful coat could come from such a smelly little beast."

"Look," he said, "I don't expect gratitude, but there's no need to get personal."

* * *

LIL went out with many men
    And accepted all they gave her
    But she married a man with a will of his own
    Made out in her favour.

* * *

FLOOSIE'S toast:
    Here's to the men I've loved
    And here's to the men I've kissed.
    And here's my profound apologies
    To all the men I've missed.

FOOD AND WINE

EAT, drink and be merry, for tomorrow we diet.

* * *

HERE'S a toast to Mum's cooking. And may my wife never know how bad it was.

PEOPLE who like home cooking should stay home.

* * *

WINE improves with age. I like it more the older I get.

* * *

HOW do you make Liviewitz wine?
Leave without paying.

FOOTBALL
See FOOTBALL FANS

THE team was facing defeat. At the final change the coach roared some fight into them. "And you Murphy, it's about time you got ferocious."
"What's his number?" said Murph.

* * *

THE woman reporter asked him: "Are all the champion football players conceited?"
"I don't really know, but I'm not."

* * *

"WHERE does your football team play, Grandpa?"
"What football team? What are you talking about?"
"Oh, Dad says that when you kick off we can get a new house!"

* * *

THE game was so close that the two football fans would not leave the stand, despite their hunger. "Send that kid for some pies," suggested one. They were $2 each so they gave the kid $6 and told him to get one for himself.
The kid came back five minutes later and handed back $4. "They only had one pie left," he said.

* * *

THE star recruit who had just been transferred for an enormous sum was being interviewed on telly.
"You appear to be earning more money than the prime minister," said the interviewer.

159

"Only fair," said the football star, "I play a lot better than he does."

*　　*　　*

YOUNG man looking for a job travelled to the country and approached the general store in a small town. The man behind the counter was also the president of the country football league and offered the lad a job immediately. "We need a centre-half forward with courage and a strong set of hands," he said.

"Sorry sir," said the lad. "I don't know a thing about football."

"No worries. We need umpires too."

*　　*　　*

THE player was dashing through with the ball when he was brought down with a blatant trip.

"Free kick," roared the umpire.

"Who to?" shouted one of the players.

"Us," said the Ump.

*　　*　　*

A PSYCHIATRIST has a thriving practice, particularly in the football season. He tried an idea-association test on a patient one day and asked him what came to mind when he thought of something brown, firm and had smooth curves.

"A football," said the patiently immediately.

"Good. And what do you think of when two arms slide around your waist?"

"An illegal tackle," was the instant reply.

"Now picture a pair of firm thighs..."

"A fullback."

"Top marks," said the psychiatrist. "Your reactions are quite normal. You would be surprised at some of the stupid answers I get."

*　　*　　*

IT was the jungle's soccer classic of the year, the annual grudge match between the animals and the insects, and by half time the elephants, zebras and cheetahs had proved too much for the grasshoppers, beetles and ants with a convincing score of 58 goals to nil.

However, when the match resumed the animals noted a substitute player run onto the field with the insects. It was a shiny black centipede.

From then on the centipede became the star of the game peppering the goals from all angles. Indeed, the animals failed to score another goal and the insects ran out winners, 59 goals to 58.

At the bar after the game the animals' captain, a tough looking elephant, said to the insects' skipper, a wily grasshopper, "Great game, but you were damned lucky that centipede arrived at half time."

"You're wrong," said the grasshopper. "He was here for the start of the game, but it took him until half time to put his boots on!"

*   *   *

THE champ from the bush was not all he was cracked up to be so the runner was sent out with a message.

"The coach says he will pull you off at half time."

"Great," said the country lad, "we only get oranges at Snake Gully."

FOOTBALL FANS
See FOOTBALL

FOOTBALL fans are quite a different species from the rest of the human race. The average footy fan buys his final series tickets three months in advance, and waits until December 24 to do the Christmas shopping.

*   *   *

"I HEAR you had a difficult time explaining the grand final to your wife."

"Yes. She found out I didn't go."

AT the turnstiles it was being explained to McTavish that there were seats at $20, $15 and $10 and that programs were 50 cents.

"Okay," said McTavish, "I'll sit on a program."

* * *

CLASSIFIED Ad: "Young football supporter of good appearance and sound health offers hand in marriage to any young lady with two tickets to the grand final next Saturday. Please send photograph of the tickets."

* * *

THE two mates were down at the front fence for the rugby league match when the beer cans started to fly. One was so concerned about being hit he kept looking over his shoulder and couldn't concentrate on the game.

"Don't worry," said his mate, "as they say in the war, if there's one with your name on it ..."

"That's just it. My name is Foster!"

* * *

ON a crowded train going to the football game the fan resplendent in black and white colours had a large duck tucked under his arm.

Sitting directly opposite, at face level with the duck, was an old codger flaunting a scarf in the opposing team's colours. "They won't let you take a pig into the ground ya know," he said loudly.

"It's not a pig, it's a duck ya burk," said the fan in the black and white scarf.

"I wasn't talking to you," said the old codger.

* * *

"I BELIEVE you are a member of the school's football team," said the proud grandfather to his 13-year-old grandson. "What position do you play?"

"I'm not sure Gramps," said the lad, "but I heard the sports teacher say that I was the team's main drawback."

ONE-eyed supporter arrived at the ground. "How much to get in," he said.

"Sixteen dollars," said the ticket-seller.

"Well here's eight," said the fan, "I only watch one side."

*　　*　　*

IT was the day of the grand final when the officials took a call from the gatekeeper. "There are two life-members here. They are close friends of the umpire and they have lost their tickets."

"Throw them out," said the executive. "They are liars. Whoever heard of an umpire having two friends!"

*　　*　　*

WE all know that soccer is taken seriously in the United Kingdom, so when Ireland and Scotland clashed at Wembly a fan wearing the colours of neither side and cheering the goals of both teams was a thorn in the side of a Scot and an Irishman standing either side of him.

"Are ye from Scotland?" enquired the Scot.

"Or are ya from Ireland?" joined the Irishman.

"I'm neither. I'm English really," came the answer.

"Well then," said the Scot and Irishman together as they thumped him, "mind your own flaming business."

*　　*　　*

IT was a mid-winter Saturday. The two footy fans were huddled together in the wind and rain. Their team was being thrashed, their feet were soaked and they were both beginning to shiver. Fred turned to his mate and said: "Harry, tell me how much fun we are having here today. I keep forgetting."

*　　*　　*

A BLOKE took his black and white fox terrier in to the pub and was enjoying a few drinks until the footy scores appeared on telly. When it was announced that his team had lost the dog went mad, knocking over tables and snapping at customers.

"What's got into your dog?" asked the barman.

"He just can't take it when our team is beaten," explained the owner.

"Heck. What does he do when they win?"

"Don't know. I've only had him two years!"

* * *

A BLOKE went into the pub with his dog. Both were supporters of the local team and they watched the match on TV with great interest. Every time their team kicked a goal the dog yelped with delight.

The barman was impressed. "What does he do when the other side scores?" he asked.

"Somersaults" said the owner.

"How many?" asked the barman.

"Depends on how hard I kick him!"

FUNERALS
See DEATH

IF you don't go to your friends' funerals... they won't come to yours.

* * *

THE difference between an Australian wedding and an Australian funeral is one less drunk.

* * *

AN Irish funeral is merrier than an English holiday.

* * *

A LARGE crowd had gathered at a funeral. A passer-by asked who had died.

"Dunno," he replied. "I'm only here for the beer."

* * *

IT was an overcast and threatening sky the day Fred buried his mother-in-law. In fact, just as the funeral party left the cemetery there was a loud clap of thunder and flash of lightning.

"Crikey," said Fred. "She's there already."

AFTER the funeral she took her husband's suits to the Op Shop. The manager noted the thin material and the holes in the trousers. "My goodness," she said, "your old man died just in time."

* * *

BRIDGET took one look at her late husband, lying in his coffin with a smile on his face.

"Look at him now," she said.

"He's smiling because he died in his sleep and he doesn't know he's dead yet. He is dreaming he is still alive, so when he wakes up and finds that he is dead, begorrah, the shock will kill him."

* * *

HE had died a very rich man, and at the funeral service Paddy was beating his breast and wailing louder than any of the other mourners.

One of the relatives comforted him. "We didn't know you knew him."

"That's the trouble. I didn't," wailed Paddy.

* * *

LOUIE had been a big time gambler and all his race-track friends had assembled in the small church for his funeral.

With heads bowed they heard the priest solemnly intone: "Our friend Louie is not dead. He merely sleeps," when a voice from the back of the church said, "I've got a hundred to say he won't wake up."

* * *

AFTER three weeks during which her husband had been slowly dying in bed the doctor came downstairs and told Mrs Murphy he had good news. He said her husband had made a remarkable recovery.

Mrs Murphy burst out crying. "What am I going to do now? I've sold all his clothes to pay for the funeral."

A LAWYER was merely fulfilling a duty by being present at the funeral service of a millionaire when a colleague arrived, a little late, and stood in the pew beside him.

"How far has he got?" said the newcomer referring to the vicar's eulogy.

"He's just opened the defence," replied the lawyer.

* * *

DID you know there is a law which prohibits anybody living south of the river being buried in the cemetery? It's on account of them being not dead yet.

* * *

HARRY had been a workaholic journo all his life and his friends at the office took up a collection for a head-stone, which read: "Erected in memory of Harry Bloggs, drowned in the river, by his relatives and friends."

The headstone had been installed hastily before the ground over the grave had settled. On inspecting the work next day the cemetery attendant found that it was tilting sideways. As a temporary measure he looped a wire around it and tied it to a nearby tree.

Harry's mates took the opportunity that afternoon to visit the grave for the first time. "Gawd, that's our Harry," said one, noting the wire. "He's still working. Now he's got the phone on!"

* * *

AT the funeral service the vicar and the undertaker had never seen a husband so grieved. Fred was sobbing his heart out and beating his breast. He was so distraught that the vicar took him aside in a bid to comfort him.

"It's tough, I know," said the vicar, "but believe me you will eventually get over it. And dare I say it," he paused, "in three or six months you might well meet another woman and ..."

"Yeah!" wailed Fred, "but what am I gonna do tonight?"

G

GAMBLERS

"DO you play cards for money?"

"No. But the blokes I play with do."

*   *   *

WHEN the little old lady fronted up to the bookie for yet another payout he was perplexed.

"You must study the form," he said.

"Oh, no," she said, "I just stick a pin in the paper."

"But how have you managed to pick four winners in one afternoon?"

"Oh, today I used a fork," she explained.

*   *   *

SLICK Sam was always winning at cards, and always losing at the races. "Why is that?" asked his mate Pete.

"Simple. They won't let me shuffle the horses."

*   *   *

DID you hear how Slick Sam lost $100 on the Melbourne Cup, and another $100 on the replay?

*   *   *

"WHAT'S the meaning of the three balls over the pawnshop?"

"It's two-to-one you won't get it back."

*   *   *

AFTER the last race a bloke who stuttered slightly approached a bookmaker who had a winning day.

"Excuse me, I b-b-backed a five-tt..."

The bookie was sharp. "There was no five-to-one winners, mate, nick off."

The bloke persisted. "I b-b-backed a five-tt."

"Look," said the bookie, "I've had a good day. Here's a fifty-note. Now nick off."

The punter shrugged his shoulders with resignation, accepted the note, walked over to his mate and said. "That bookie's a nice bloke. I tried to tell him I backed a five-ton truck into his Rolls Royce, and he gave me fifty dollars."

* * *

THE lads had arranged to go fishing on Sunday morning. All turned up on time except Fred. He finally arrived ten minutes late. "What kept you?" they asked.

"It was a toss-up if I went to church or joined you blokes fishing."

"Well, that shouldn't have taken you long."

"I had to toss up 23 times."

* * *

WHEN he got to the tote window a little voice in his ear said: "Put it all on number six."

He did, and it came in at 100 to one.

When he fronted the window for the second race a little voice in his ear said: "Put the lot on number 13."

He did and it romped home by a street.

When he pushed ten thousand over the counter at the tote window for the third race a little voice said: "Put it all on number nine."

He did and it ran stone motherless last, and the little voice in his ear said: "Oh well. Win some, lose some."

* * *

THE gambler who had just won the $100,000 jackpot on the Melbourne Cup was asked by reporters how he would spend the money.

"Oh, I've got it all figured out," he said. "First I'll spend

$25,000 on whisky and beer, $25,000 on horses, dogs and cards, and $25,000 on women and wild living."

"Wow, and what of the other $25,000?"

"I will probably just squander that," he said.

* * *

ONCE again he had to explain his bad luck to his wife. "As I walked into the racecourse a sudden gust of wind blew my hat off. It was a sure sign," he said. "So I put it all on a horse called Gone with the Wind."

"And it didn't win?"

"No. Some foreign horse called Mon Chapeau won by a mile."

* * *

PETE the Punter was at the pub early and got a few under his belt before he noticed a large sign on the wall: Lunch 12 to 1.

"Bloody good odds," he said to himself. He called the barman over and said he wanted to put down a hundred for a win.

"No gambling here," said the barman, and ordered him out. Pete wandered down to the next pub where he saw another sign: Lunch 11 to 2.

"The odds are down already," he muttered. "It must be a good thing." He went straight in to the bar and said he wanted to place a bet.

He was immediately thrown out for a second time.

Pete wandered around the corner where a third pub displayed the sign: Lunch 1 to 2.

"That's blown it. It's odds on now." But he decided to go in and listen to the result. As he entered the pub the chef delivered a plate on the bar and called "Sausages one!"

Pete the Punter breathed a sigh of relief. "Just as well I didn't back that bloody Lunch!"

* * *

WHEN the well-dressed gambler left the club he was

accosted by a down-and-outer who asked him for a few dollars for a meal.

The gambler took pity. "Come inside and I'll buy you a beer."

"No, I don't drink," said the man.

"Well, how about a cigar?"

"No, I don't smoke."

"Well, I know a certainty tomorrow. I'll put a $100 on it for you."

"No. Just a few dollars for food," insisted the man.

"Then come home with me for a meal. I want my wife to see what happens to a man who doesn't drink, smoke or gamble."

*　*　*

"HOW come you always come back from the races with a small fortune?"

"Cos I always go there with a bigger one."

*　*　*

AFTER six months at Gamblers Anonymous, Fred believed he was cured. "I'd like to thank you all for helping me kick the habit," he said.

"I'll never gamble again. I'll wager a fortune on it."

*　*　*

THEY had been gambling mates for years and finally it came to Fred's attention that his poker playing mate was having an affair with his wife.

"Let's settle this in a civilised way," said Fred. "We will play a hand of poker for her. And just to make it interesting how about a $50 wager on the side?"

*　*　*

TWO London gamblers were on holiday in Italy and visited the Vatican. They were the last to leave the Cistene Chapel and happened to see a white robed figure fall down some stairs. They recognised him as the Pope and he was stone dead.

The first Vatican authorities on the scene begged them

170

not to say anything for 24 hours. There were world-wide implications. The two gamblers agreed. After all, they were flying home that night.

On the plane one of them had a brilliant idea. "As soon as we land I am going straight to Ladbrokes and getting great odds on the life of the Pope."

"Sounds like a great idea," said Paddy, his mate.

It was two days before the Pope's death was announced and the first gambler made a clean up.

"And what about you, Paddy?" he asked.

"Nothing at all," admitted Paddy. "I took the Pope in a double with the Archbishop of Canterbury."

GARDENERS

A GARDENER is a bloke who calls a spade a spade; until he falls over one.

* * *

NOW is the time of the year when the bulbs you forgot to plant last autumn will fail to bloom.

* * *

FRED'S specialty was growing vegetables and he eventually won the Nobel Peas Prize, for being outstanding in his field.

* * *

WE know a bonsai tree grower who has been so successful he is now looking for a house with a smaller garden.

* * *

SHE talked to the trees. That's why they took her away.

* * *

"DO you really think talking to plants makes them grow?" confided one keen gardener to the other.

"Nah," said Fred. "My Missus hasn't stopped talking to me for the last 25 years, and I haven't grown one iota."

MY wife talks to the rhododendrons for hours on end. One day I asked them how the heck they could stand it.

"Who listens?" they replied.

* * *

"I CAN'T find anything to say to my plants," she said while laying newspaper on the garden beds, "so I'm giving them something to read instead."

* * *

IT was such a serious drought the government placed a ban on sprinkler hoses. Then suddenly the drought broke and the heavens opened up with a downpour that flooded everybody's garden. "If this rain keeps up," said Fred, "we will be able to use our hoses again."

* * *

PHIL, the philsophical gardener, was asked how he remained so tranquil in such a frustrating hobby. "I learned long ago," he said, "that when it wants to rain the best thing to do is just sit back and let it."

* * *

"WHAT causes rain?" asked the horticultural student.

"Weekends," was the unanimous answer.

* * *

"MY husband is an invertebrate gardener," she said.

"Don't you mean inveterate?"

"No. Invertebrate. He's got no backbone for it."

* * *

THE customer in the nursery was spending such a long time looking at two wheelbarrows an attendant eventually asked if he wanted assistance.

"Yes," he replied. "I can't decide between the red one or the green wheelbarrow. It is a present for my wife's birthday."

"Will it be a surprise?" asked the attendant.

"I predict it will. She is expecting a diamond ring."

* * *

THE nurseryman was running a special on ferns this

week and filled his shop with fronds of every species. But the customer insisted he wanted an anemone.

"With fronds like these who needs anemones?" said the nurseryman.

* * *

THE vicar was delighted to see Fred working up a sweat in his front garden. He leaned over the fence and gushed: "Your garden is looking lovely. Isn't it wonderful what man and God can do when they work in harmony?"

"Maybe," said Fred wiping his brow. "But you should have seen this yard when God had it on his own."

* * *

WOULD you believe it? Forty-three years ago, while sunbathing in her garden, Mrs Gladys Nurkle, of 7 Paradise St, Moonee Ponds, lost her gold wedding ring.

Yesterday, while digging the garden in the very same spot, her son Clarence ruptured himself.

* * *

GRANDPA was proud of his garden, and when it was admired by visitors he would say the key to his fine crop was "manure, manure, manure."

It embarrassed his daughter. "Can't you make Dad call it fertilizer?" she asked her mother.

"It took us years to make him say manure," she replied.

* * *

OLD Jake from the Outback said his pumpkins grew so fast he kept a pack of greyhounds to round them up. And when they did it only took five to make a dozen.

* * *

"WHEN are you going to prepare the garden beds?" she asked.

"I'm thinking about it."

"You mean you're turning it over in your mind?"

* * *

THE local handyman letter-boxed his neighbours with

a handbill which read: "Don't kill yourself in the garden this spring. I will do it for you!"

*   *   *

HARRY Henpecked had been ordered by his wife to buy only organic vegetables from the market garden.

"These vegetables are for my wife," he said. "Have they been sprayed with any poisonous chemicals?"

"No," said the gardener, "you will have to do that yourself."

GOLF

FUNNY how man blames fate for all accidents, yet claims full responsibility for a hole in one.

*   *   *

QUESTION on golf etiquette: What do you do when your opponent claims to have found his ball in the rough, and you know he is a liar because you've got it in your pocket?

*   *   *

THEY called it golf because all the other four-letter words were already taken.

*   *   *

HER golf is improving. Yesterday she hit a ball in one.

*   *   *

NOW she has improved so much she misses the ball much closer than she used to.

*   *   *

A BELOW par golfer always takes two or three lumps with his tee.

*   *   *

"I GOT a set of clubs for my husband."

"Lucky you, what a swap!"

*   *   *

FRED seemed off his game. He was morose and sulky. By the fifth tee his partner said, "What the hell's the matter with you, Fred?"

174

"It's Madge, my wife. Ever since she has taken up golf she has cut my sex down to only twice a week."

"Think yourself bloomin' lucky," said his partner. "She's cut me out altogether!"

* * *

IN Africa native tribes beat the ground with clubs and utter blood-curdling screams. Anthropologisits call it the release of primitive expression. Here we call it golf.

* * *

FRED had swum through heavy seas to rescue a millionaire who fell from his yacht. The rich man was insisting that he accept some token of gratitude for saving his life. Fred said it wasn't necessary, but the millionaire persisted. "Okay," said Fred. "I'm a keen golfer. Maybe you might like to buy me a club?"

The millionaire, as good as his word, went out and bought two; Royal Melbourne and Huntingdale.

* * *

IT was a tight game in the Scottish Highlands.

"How many strokes was that?" said McTavish when they finished the fifth.

"Six," said McSporran.

"Well, I had five, so that makes it my hole."

When they finished the sixth McTavish said. "Well, how many strokes was that then?"

"Hang on," said McSporran. "It's my turn to ask."

* * *

A TOURING golf professional was having a drink at the club's bar when he was approached by a chap with a white cane and dark glasses who introduced himself as a golf champion.

"I am champion of the Blind Golfers' Association and as one champion to another, I would like to challenge you to a match which could be a fund-raiser for the blind." He said he didn't want any favors and told the pro he was keen to play for $50 a hole.

The embarrassed pro tried to avoid the challenge, but the blind man was so insistent he finally agreed.

"Okay, when will we play?" he asked.

"Any night. Any night at all."

* * *

THIS middle-aged couple had played golf together for most of their married life. One night over the evening meal she mused: "If I die before you, will you get married again?"

Although he was absorbed in the evening newspaper he muttered, "I guess so."

"Would you play golf with her?"

"I guess so," he mumbled.

"Would you take her to our club?"

"I guess so," he said.

"Surely you wouldn't let her use my clubs?"

"No, of course not. Anyway, she's left-handed!"

* * *

"I AM not playing my best game today,"

"Really, what other games do you play?"

* * *

ONE golfer was taking so much care before driving from the fifth tee that his partner asked: "Why the concentration?"

"I'm very anxious to make this shot a good one," said his partner. "My mother-in-law is down there in the club-house watching me."

"Impossible," said his mate. "You could never hit her from this distance!"

* * *

TWO businessmen took time from the office to play a round of golf during their lunch break but were hampered by two women playing ahead and slowing their game.

Finally one said, "Listen Jack, I'll go and ask if they mind if we play through."

He had only gone a hundred metres before he turned and hurried back. He was visibly shaken. "Jack, you won't believe this," he said, "but those two women... one is my wife and the other is my mistress."

Jack was a cool hand. "Listen Reg," he said. "Keep your head down while I approach them and we'll sneak past."

Jack had only gone a hundred metres when he turned back. "Listen Reg, you won't believe this ..." he began.

* * *

HIS drive from the third tee sliced to the left of the fairway and the ball ended in an impossible lie in front of the greenkeeper's tractor shed.

His wife summed up the situation. "No need to take a penalty shot darling," she said. "Just open the doors of the garage, push the tractor out, open the rear doors, and with a number three wood you could hit straight through the shed."

"Brilliant, darling," he said. He took a mighty whack but the ball hit the rear of the building, cannoned back and struck his wife, stone dead.

The following day he was playing the same hole and by sheer coincidence landed at the same place in front of the shed.

"No need to take a penalty shot," said the caddie, "we can push the tractor out and open both sets of doors. You can hit straight through the shed."

"No way," he said. "I tried that yesterday and ended up with a double bogey."

* * *

THERE were no caddies left when Fonsenby arrived at the clubhouse, but the manager said old George, sitting in the corner could do the job. "He has amazing vision. Has eyes like an eagle," said the manager.

Fonsenby had his misgivings but he gave the old bloke

the benefit of the doubt and hit his first drive a magnificent 500 metres down the fairway.

"Did you see where that went?" he asked.

"Of course I did," said the old bloke.

"Good," said Fonsenby, "Where is it?"

"I can't remember," said George.

*　　*　　*

THEY were leaning on the bar at the 19th when Fred produced a golf ball from his pocket and proudly set it on the bar. "Have a look at this," he said to his mate Charlie. "It's a digital golf ball."

Indeed, the ball was a bright irridescent orange. It had a small antennae. "It sends out beeps," explained Fred. Charlie was impressed. "Where did you buy it?"

"I didn't," said Fred. "I found it."

*　　*　　*

THEY were watching the golf classic on television when Fred entered the room and was immediately interested.

"Turn it up a bit," he called.

"Sshh. Not while Norman's putting!"

*　　*　　*

WHEN the club secretary explained to Fred that he couldn't play because the course was fully booked out, Fred was more than upset. He had been a member for 20 years too.

"Look," said Fred, "If the President of the United States lobbed here for a game today I bet you would make room for him."

The secretary admitted that he would have to.

"Well I just happen to know that he's in Washington today, so I'll take his place!"

*　　*　　*

FRED said during his last game of golf he stepped on a rake. "They were the best two balls I hit all day!"

*　　*　　*

ABE and Louie had made a pile in the rag trade and decided to take things easy and join a prestige golf club.

On the first day they went into the club bar for a pre-game drink.

"How much?" said Abe when the two whiskies were placed in front of them.

"First day at the club? New members? Well it's on the house," said the barman.

They went into the dining room and ordered lunch. "How much?" asked Louie.

"It's complimentary to new members, sir," said the waiter.

Then they wandered over to the pro shop and ordered half a dozen balls each. The pro obliged. "How much?" asked Abe.

"First day in the club?" asked the pro.

"Yes," chorused Abe and Lou.

"Well, that will be fifty-five dollars and seven cents each," said the pro.

When they finally got onto the green Abe muttered to Louie: "It sure aint by the throat that they've got you in this club."

* * *

KEVIN had made his money as a car salesman and had done so well he thought it was time to move up in society and join the golf club.

On his first day he slashed and bashed his way around the course cutting divots from fairway and the greens alike. He left a trail of disaster.

He was in the club dining room half way through dinner when he was tapped on the shoulder.

"Excuse me," said the stern official. "I am chairman of the green committee ..."

"Just the bloke I want to see," said the new member. "These brussels sprouts are hardly fresh."

GORILLAS

A GORILLA swaggered into a waterside pub, slapped a five dollar note on the bar and asked for a beer.

It quite took the barman by surprise for a moment, but ever ready to make a quid he capitalised on this unusual situation, pulling the beer, scooping up the fiver and giving the gorilla 60 cents in small change.

But as the primate sipped his beer, the phenomena of a talking gorilla aroused the barman's curiosity to the point where it could be contained no longer.

"Out for a walk, are you?" he ventured.

"Yeah," mumbled the gorilla.

"We don't get many gorillas in here," pressed the barman trying to make conversation.

"No wonder, at $4.40 a glass."

*　　*　　*

THE advertisement in "Showbiz" read: "Non-speaking part, but athletic agility a must." Paddy applied for the job and found himself being directed to Taronga Park Zoo. It was explained to him that one of the zoo's major attractions, the gorilla, had died and they needed a substitute until the real thing could be imported.

"All you have to do is don this suit for a few weeks and swing around the branches," said the zoo's director.

The few weeks turned into a month and although it was hot in the suit the pay was good. Paddy had even worked out quite a routine leaping and tumbling about.

Indeed, the crowd's applause drove him to greater heights and more daring feats until one day, while attempting a somersault he lost his grip and fell out of the tree on the wrong side of the adjacent lion's enclosure.

When he recovered his senses he saw the lion approaching and his first reaction was to let out a shriek for help.

"Shut up, you fool," said the lion.

"Do you want to get us both the sack?"

IT was a month after World War 3 had devasted the earth. Not a human being survived. Indeed a battered and dazed chimpanzee had wandered for weeks through what was left of the smouldering jungle without seeing another living thing.

One day the chimp saw something move behind the rubble. He was delighted to find it was another gorilla, and a female at that.

He rushed up and embraced her, but she pushed him away. "No. Don't let's start all that over again," she said.

HEALTH

WHEN you feel like you need more exercise, lie down until the feeling wears off.

* * *

THERE are probably better cures for a cold than three whiskies, but who cares?

* * *

FRED thought he had a club foot for forty-two years. When he died they discovered he had his boots on the wrong feet.

* * *

HE used to be an all-round athlete. Now he's just all-round.

* * *

FRED took up exercising. Now he has the energy of a man twice his age.

* * *

THE Irish are great believers in health. They are always drinking to other people's.

* * *

DOC: "Do you suffer from stress?"
    "No, but I think I'm a carrier."

* * *

DON'T tell your friends
    About your indigestion

"How are You?" is a greeting
Not a bloody question.

* * *

IT was the healthiest town in the region. They had to shoot a bloke to start a cemetery.

The only bloke to die over the last ten years was the undertaker. And he died of starvation.

* * *

PEOPLE who say they are going on a diet are just wishful shrinkers.

HISTORY

THE Magna Carta ensured that no free man could be hanged twice for the same offence.

* * *

SIR Francis Drake circumcised the world.
And did it with a 100 foot clipper.

* * *

HISTORY'S mysteries are those of the past
    Present intrigues seem worse, and are vast
    But before you condemn
    This generation, pro tem
    Remember, you're also one of the cast.

* * *

NAPOLEON came home tired and weary, wet and wounded, and went straight round to Josephine's flat. He was shocked to find a pair of large gumboots on her front doorstep.

"Josephine! Josephine!" he called out. "What are those rubber boots doing out here?"

"They're not rubber boots," said Josie. "They're Wellington's."

* * *

HISTORY records how the first union and the first timepiece occured at the same time. It was when the soldiers in Alexander the Great's army got cheesed off swinging their swords against the foe from dawn to dusk. The troops appointed the first shop steward to parly with Alexander about shorter hours. The problem was the watch had yet to be invented.

By mutual agreement it was decided that the soldiers would tie a piece of rag around the wrist of their sword arm. When it got well and truly soaked with sweat, then it was time to call it a day. They called this timing device Alexander's rag time band.

*　　*　　*

WHEN Noah was sailing his Ark there was a great accumulation of bulldust in the bull's pen and the crew wanted to know what to do with it.

"Push it over the side," said Noah.

Then in 1492 Christopher Columbus discovered it.

HORSES

THERE is nothing like horse riding, to make you feel better off.

*　　*　　*

WHAT has four legs and flies?

A dead horse!

*　　*　　*

HE named his horse Radish because he got a kick out of introducing the beast when he took it out to social functions. "This is my horse, Radish," he would say.

*　　*　　*

THE American tourist was leaning on the bar telling all and sundry about the size of things back in Texas.

"Why, I would hop on a horse and it would take three days to ride to the other side of the ranch."

"Yeah," yawned a local, "I've got a horse like that, too."

*　　*　　*

MURPHY the horse trader sold a nag to a bloke and

it dropped dead on the way home. The bloke went back to complain.

"That's funny," said Murphy, "I've had that nag for years and it's never done that before."

*　　*　　*

TRAVELLER's car broke down ten kilometres from a remote town and had the driver puzzled as he tinkered under the bonnet looking for the trouble.

"I think it's the carburettor," came a voice from behind him. The startled driver looked around. There was nobody there but a horse in a nearby paddock. "Undo the petrol lead to the carby and clean it through," insisted the horse.

Almost panic-stricken the driver did as the horse insisted. Put the carburettor together again. Pressed the starter button and the engine burst into life.

He raced to town as fast as possible and stopped at the first service station. "You won't believe it," he gasped to the attendant, "I had carburettor trouble about ten kilometres out of town and a horse told me how to fix it."

"Was it a white horse?" asked the proprietor.

"Yes," answered the amazed driver.

"Well it must be your lucky day," he said. "There is usually a black horse in that paddock and he knows bugger-all about carburettors."

*　　*　　*

A WHITE horse leant against the bar and pondered the array of drinks on the top shelf. "I feel like something different tonight," he told the barman.

The barman said: "Why not have the whisky named after you."

"Really? Okay, I'll have a double Trevor."

*　　*　　*

THE travelling parson had decided to retire from his circuit in the bush and wanted to sell his horse. Old Jack was

185

down from the high country and recognising a strong horse when he saw one soon struck a bargain with the parson.

But when Jack swung up in the saddle, the horse refused to move.

"Oh, I forgot to tell you he is a very religious horse," said the parson. "I have trained him reverently and he will only go when you say the words Jesus Christ, and he will only stop when you say Amen."

Old Jack thanked the parson, said "Jesus Christ" and the horse took off at a fast rate. They were travelling back to the high country when thunder clouds darkened the sky, and a bolt of lightning cracked to the ground.

The horse bolted in fright and a low branch struck Old Jack in the face momentarily blinding him. As the horse galloped madly through the bush he tried to think of the word to make it stop, finally yelling "Amen."

The horse skidded to a halt and when Old Jack opened his eyes he saw that his mount had stopped right on the edge of a frightening mountain precipice.

"Jesus Christ," he said.

★　　★　　★

A CITY girl arrived at the bush riding school. She said she had never been on a horse, so naturally, she wanted a horse that had never been ridden before.

HORSE RACING

DURING racing trials a trainer took the jockey aside just before the start. "I've got an option to buy this horse, but I don't know its form," he whispered. "Try him out for me, and hold it to about fourth place."

The jockey had a strong pair of arms and held him back to finish fourth as instructed.

"He's a good horse," summed up the jockey.

"Do you think he could have beaten the first three?" asked the trainer.

"Easy," said the jockey, "but I don't know about the other 12 who finished behind him."

*   *   *

A LEADING trainer was given an eye test and presented with a pair of glasses. The optician said they would cost $300.

"Too much," cried the trainer.

"They're bi-focal," said the optician.

"I don't care if they're by Phar Lap. It's too much."

*   *   *

THE secretary of the bush racing club was worried about falling attendances. On the morning of the Boxing Day Cup race meeting he got a phone call. "I'm bringing a coach-load of people," said the voice. "What time is the first race?"

"What time can you get here," replied the secretary.

*   *   *

THE drover looked over the field at the Oodnadatta Races and reckoned his nag could beat anything in the mounting yard, so he entered him for the main race.

"But what's his pedigree?" asked the steward.

"What d'yer mean, his pedigree?"

"What is he by, and what is he out of?" insisted the steward.

"He's by that bloody gum tree and out in that bloody paddock."

*   *   *

AN old hack jockey had been killed in a car crash and a leading trainer had been called to the morgue to identify him.

The trainer lifted the sheet off one body and shook his head. It wasn't his jockey. He lifted the second sheet and shook his head again. He lifted the third sheet and sadly announced: "Again, he hasn't run a place."

*   *   *

THE trainer was giving last minute instructions to the

jockey and appeared to slip something in the horse's mouth just as a steward passed by.

"What was that?" inquired the steward.

"Oh, nothing," said the trainer, "just a Mintie. He offered one to the steward. "Here, have one. And I'll have one myself."

After the suspicious steward left the scene the trainer continued with his riding instructions. "Just keep the horse on the rails. You are on a certainty. The only thing that could possibly pass you down the straight is either the steward or me."

* * *

IT was the Grand National Steeplechase and there was a terrible pile up at the third fence. Horses and jockies everywhere.

Despite two broken ribs one jockey managed to remount and with agonising pain and great applause from the crowd he was the only one to finish the course.

The trainer greeted him with a kick in the bum. "You re-mounted the wrong horse, you dopey drongo!"

* * *

THREE horses were in the pub talking about their racing days; about the times they were pipped at the post.

"Just missed the Melbourne Cup by a nose," said one.

"Same thing happened to me at Randwick," said another.

A greyhound sipping whisky at the bar moved over to their table.

"I couldn't help overhearing," he said, "but the same thing happened to me at Sandown."

The horses looked at each other. "Crikey Moses," said one, "that's amazing... a talking dog!"

* * *

A HORSE was looking over the fence watching a game of cricket.

"Any chance of a game?" he asked the captain.

At first the cricketer was taken aback by the talking

horse, but when it insisted it was keen to play the skipper thought it might be a bit of a lark if he sent the horse in as opening bat.

The horse shaped up to the first ball and slammed it over the boundary for a six. He did the same with the second and third, indeed every ball he hit for six until the over ended.

He had been partnered by the captain, and when the bowler ran in from the other end and the captain managed his first hit for a meagre single he called for the horse to run.

But the horse stood there. Frantic calls by the captain to run were ignored and in the confusion the skipper was stumped out.

"Why didn't you run?" roared the angry captain.

"Listen mate," said the horse, "if I could run I would be at the racetrack today, not messing around with this cricket game."

*   *   *

IT had started as an odds-on favourite, but by the home turn it had run out of puff and was going through the field backwards.

The irate trainer approached the jockey: "What the hell was going on?"

"The horse simply wasn't good enough," explained the jockey.

"Rubbish," roared the trainer. "You could have done much better."

"Maybe I could," said the jockey, "but you know as well as I do the rules state I must stay on the horse's back."

*   *   *

THE tipster said this horse would walk it in. It did, but all the others galloped.

*   *   *

IN the old days when tick-tackers were the stars of race

track relaying the prices and trends with hand signals one of the best, Paddy O'Reily, died.

"I can't believe Paddy's dead," said his mate at the funeral service, just as the priest blessed the coffin.

"He's dead alright," said Moloney, "He's just drifted out to 33s."

* * *

CATHOLIC priests are often at the races, but Pete the Punter was surprised to see the priest sprinkle holy water over one nag which duly went out and won by half a street.

Pete followed him closely and witnessed another holy water sprinkle and another win, at ten-to-one.

Next time he had the money ready and as soon as the priest annointed yet a third horse, albeit a skinny nag, Pete was off to the bookies.

After the horse had dropped dead on the home turn Pete tackled the priest for an explanation.

"If you were a Catholic," said the priest, "you would have known the difference between a blessing and the last rites."

* * *

PADDY the Punter cleaned out the bookies and his friends were soon pressing him to divulge his system.

"I'm superstitious, and I watch for omens," said Paddy. "On my way to the races I took a Number 5 tram. It made five stops on the way and it cost me $5 to get into the track.

"It was three fives telling me something. So I added them up, three fives are 16 so I backed Number 16 and it won by a street."

HOSPITALS
See DOCTORS

A MINOR operation is one performed on somebody else.

190

A HOSPITAL is a place where people who are run down generally wind up.

*　　*　　*

A HOSPITAL is a place where they wake you at five o'clock in the morning to give you a sleeping pill.

*　　*　　*

FRED was in hospital. At the end of his bed was a chart with lots of complaints listed on it. All the nurses had written something.

*　　*　　*

FRED was in hospital for a complicated operation. In fact, while he was in there the surgeon took his wife out.

*　　*　　*

RECOVERING from an operation in a bush hospital Farmer Brown asked why the blinds were drawn.

"Well," explained the doc. "There's a bushfire outside, and I didn't want you to wake up and think the operation was a failure."

*　　*　　*

A GIRL from the country called at the hospital. "I'd like to see an out-turn, please," she said.

"You mean an intern," said the nurse.

"Whatever you call him, I want a contamination," she insisted.

"You mean an examination," said the nurse.

"Yes, I need to see the fraternity ward."

"You mean the maternity ward."

"Call it what you will," said the girl with annoyance, "but I certainly know I haven't demonstrated for two months and I think I'm stagnant."

*　　*　　*

THE indignant patient complained: "Why did you put me in a ward with this bloke?"

"Why, is he giving you trouble?"

"He's a lunatic," said the patient. "He keeps raving on about getting rid of the monkeys in this ward and look, the ruddy room is full of them."

191

MATRON at a large hospital answered a phone call in her office.

"Could you tell me how Paddy Murphy is getting on in ward three?" asked the caller.

"Paddy Murphy," repeated the matron consulting her list. "Oh yes. He had his operation last night. It was a complete success and he will probably go home in two days. Who is this speaking?"

"It's Paddy Murphy in ward three. They tell you nothing in here."

* * *

SURGEON to his assistant as he begins an operation: "How's that for openers?"

* * *

OLD Jock was sitting up in bed when the matron approached him. "I want you to pass a urine specimen in that bottle on the trolley at the foot of your bed."

"What, from here?" said Jock.

* * *

TWO Indian doctors were having an animated discussion. "I say it's spelt W-H-O-O-M," said one. "No, it is W-H-O-M-B," said the other. A nurse passing by said "Excuse me, you are both wrong. It is spelt W-O-M-B."

"Thanks nurse," said one, "but we prefer to settle this argument ourselves, besides, we don't think you are in a position to describe the sound of an elephant passing wind under water."

* * *

TWO nurses were climbing back into the dormitory window, trying to sneak in as quietly as possible when one said, "This makes me feel like a burglar."

"Me too," said the other, "but where would we find two burglars at this time of night?"

HOTELS
See PUBS

"DO you want the porter to call you in the morning, sir?"

"No. I always wake promptly at seven."

"In that case, would you mind waking the porter?"

* * *

AN American business tycoon had just arrived at his Australian hotel. "I am a man of few words," he said to the porter. "If I beckon with my finger that means come."

"I'm a man of few words myself," said the porter. "If I shakes me head that means I aint coming."

* * *

THEY spent their honeymoon in two hotels. He didn't like the manager in the first place, and in the second place the first place was too expensive.

* * *

THE drunk in the lobby declared he could fight anybody in the entire hotel.

The elevator man took him up.

* * *

LIKE most travel writers he headed for the bar first before checking in at the hotel's reception desk. After his second drink he got the eye from a blonde drinking alone. Quick off the mark he bought her a drink and started to chat. By the third whisky he suggested going up to his room. "Look, I haven't booked in yet, so why don't I register us as man and wife?"

The blonde saw the logic in this and they had a wonderful night together.

Next morning when the writer was checking out he was presented with a bill for $1500. "Hey, I was only here one night," he protested.

"Yes," said the clerk, "but your wife has been here for a week!"

* * *

ON his first holiday to the Gold Coast the oldtimer from the bush settled at the bar and ordered a beer. The barman served him and asked for $5.

"Blimey, a fiver for one beer?"

The barman explained that the charge included the piped music, the lush drapes on the wall and the magnificent view... etc.

Next day the oldtimer fronted the bar for his usual beer and once again protested at the exorbitant price.

The barman began to repeat his routine about the carpets, the music, the view ...

"Hang on," said the oldtimer. "I paid for them yesterday."

* * *

WHEN Fred was given the bill for an overnight stay in a French hotel he thought the $500 charge was a tad excessive and raised it with the manager.

"If you remember Sir," said the manager, "you and your wife had a room with a bath."

"But we didn't take a bath," complained Fred.

"I can't help zat," said the manager. "Eet was there if you wanted it."

Fred thought about this for a moment then scribbled some words on a piece of paper and slapped it down on the counter with a $100 note.

"What eez this?" asked the manager.

Fred explained that the $100 was fair tarif for the room and that the piece of paper was an account for $400 to the manager for sleeping with Fred's wife.

"But I didn't sleep with your wife," protested the manager.

"I can't help that," said Fred, "She was there if you wanted her."

* * *

"DID you sleep well, sir?"

"No. There was a gorgeous blonde banging on my door for most of the night. I finally had to get up and let her out."

* * *

THE guest approached the hotel porter. "I know it is four in the morning, but could you let me have a glass of whisky?"

"What on earth would you be wanting with whisky at this hour?" said the porter.

"Soda?"

* * *

IN a very respectable hotel the old bloke in charge of the cloak room had been in the job for years and never bothered to give a ticket when coats were handed over to him.

A reporter got interested in him and asked the manager how the old geezer kept track of so many coats without dockets.

"Oh, don't worry about old Ted. He's been doing the job for years. Never had a complaint," said the manager.

The reporter decided to put him to the test on the next busy Saturday night. When leaving he asked for his coat and when he received one said, "How do you know if this is my coat?"

"I don't," replied Ted.

"Then why did you give it to me?" said the reporter with a hint of triumph.

"Because that's the coat you gave to me, sir," said Ted.

* * *

THE hotel manager told the elderly couple that the only room available was the bridal suite.

"But we've been married for forty years," grumbled the husband. "What the heck do I want with the bridal suite."

The manager smiled and answered, "Well, if I gave you the ballroom you wouldn't have to dance all night, would you?"

* * *

AT a party a man introduced himself, "Hello, my name is John Smith."

The other replied: "Please don't talk shop. I'm the night clerk at the motel."

* * *

THE manager of a large chain of hotels liked to travel incognito to check on the staff. After he booked in he seated himself in the dining room and when the waiter handed him the menu he tossed it aside. "Just bring me a good dinner," he ordered.

He did this at every meal during his stay and at the end of the week revealed his identity to the waiter and expressed himself highly satisfied with the food and service.

"That's alright mate," said the waiter. Then leaning over the table he added quietly, "When you or any of your mates who can't read come to town, tell 'em to stay here and ask for 'Arry."

*   *   *

FRED booked into a small country hotel and the proprietor's pretty daughter showed him to his room. He asked what the rates were.

"Fifty dollars," she said.

"That's great. I'll pay fifty dollars with pleasure."

"With pleasure it will be another twenty-five," she said.

*   *   *

"YOU won't find a single flea in this hotel, madam."

"That's what I'm afraid of," she replied. "Probably all married with children."

*   *   *

OVER dinner one evening Fred turned to a fellow diner and said, "They call this the Palms Hotel. I've been here three days and haven't seen a palm within miles."

"Wait until you are leaving, when the staff line up at the door," said his new friend.

*   *   *

THE rodeo at the Outback Hotel had put a strain on accommodation, but the American tourist was at least glad to know they had reserved his room.

"But we're short of staff," said the proprietor. "Do you mind making your own bed?"

"Not at all," said the Yank.

And he was given a hammer, a saw and some timber.

HUSBANDS
See WIVES

WOMEN's faults are many
  Men have only two
  Everything they say
  And everything they do!

*   *   *

SOME husbands come in handy round the house. Others come in unexpectedly.

*   *   *

THE smart husband thinks twice before saying nothing.

*   *   *

EVERY married man knows that the most perfect husband in the world belongs to the woman next door.

*   *   *

"A HUSBAND like yours is hard to find."
  "He still is."

*   *   *

"IF you were my husband I would give you poison."
  "If I was your husband I'd take it."

*   *   *

THE first time Ethel saw her husband he was outside a junk shop picking his teeth. Then he went in and bought them.

*   *   *

HUSBANDS regard themselves as the head of the household, and pedestrians know they have right of way. Both are safe until they try to prove it.

*   *   *

FRED described the bump on his head as a glancing blow.
  "The wife caught me glancing at a blonde," he said.

*   *   *

IT was tough luck for Ernie. He missed two maintenance payments last month and his wife repossessed him.

THE couple were on their way to a cocktail party.

"Now listen," she said, "if it's a dull party, then leave it that way."

* * *

"I DON'T think I look 35, do you?" she asked her husband.

"No, I don't," he said, "but you used to."

* * *

FRED told his mate at the bar, "I can't stay long. My wife thinks I'm in the bath."

* * *

THE drinker turned to Fred and said: "You are a typical hen-pecked weak-spined husband."

Fred replied, "You wouldn't have the guts to say that if my missus was here."

* * *

MEN have two reasons for staying at the pub all night. Either they've got no wives to go home to; or they have.

* * *

"ARE you married, Albert?"

"No, I was hit by a car."

* * *

"I WILL say this for Madge," said the henpecked husband. "Spending money is her only extravagance."

* * *

THE two women met in the supermarket. "I thought I'd lost 560 kgms of ugly fat. Then Fred came home again."

* * *

"HOW long have you been wearing that corset, Fred?"

"Ever since the wife found it in the car," he replied.

* * *

FRED was hammering away at some woodwork in his back yard when his mate Charlie looked over the fence. "Aren't you coming to work today?" he asked.

Fred said no. He had to stay home and mind his wife who was sick with a sore throat and the flu.

Hearing a strange gurgling noise coming from the house Charlie asked: "Is that her coughing?"

"Don't be stupid," said Fred, "she'd never fit into this. She's 17 stone. This is a cage for the cocky!"

* * *

TWO husbands leaning on the bar. "Did you give your wife a lecture on economy like I told you?"

"Yes, I certainly did."

"And what was the result?"

"I've got to give up smoking."

* * *

THE henpecked husband reached the end of his tether. "Money, Money, Money. Those are the only three things you are interested in."

* * *

ANOTHER henpecked husband decided to revolt. "I'm fed up. I'm leaving you and going to join the Foreign Legion."

"Well, don't come back traipsing sand through the house," she said.

* * *

GIVE a husband enough rope, and he'll skip.

* * *

FUNNY how a wife can spot a blonde hair on a chap's coat, yet miss the garage doors.

* * *

"TODAY is the wife's birthday."

"What are your getting for her?"

"What are you offering?"

* * *

HE said he hasn't spoken to his missus for a month. "I've been unable to interrupt her," he said.

* * *

"MY Missus always has her own way. Why, she even writes her diary a month ahead."

HE had a problem about the future. He was getting married in a month and he still had not found her a job.

*   *   *

THEY were leaning on the bar. "I can't understand it," said one. "The wife asks for twenty dollars every Monday, says she needs another twenty by Tuesday. Has her hand out for another twenty on Wednesday. Every week it is the same."

"What does she do with all that money," said his mate.

"I don't know. I never give her any."

*   *   *

HE used to sit on the front door step and whistle at every young woman that went by. "Why do you let him get away with that?" asked the woman next door.

"It's no problem," said his wife. "I've seen dogs chase cars, but they can't drive."

*   *   *

ALBERT had a long session at the pub. He arrived home late and was ready for trouble.

"Is that you, Albert?" called his wife as he stumbled up the stairs.

"It had flamin' well better be," replied Albert.

*   *   *

A RATHER demanding wife returning home after a long trip abroad was met at the airport by her husband. Her first question was: "How's the cat?"

"Dead," replied the husband.

His wife erupted angrily. "What a way to break the news," she said. "Why couldn't you tell me something like, well, the cat was playing on the roof, say, and it slipped off and injured itself, and although you took it to the vet it eventually passed away quietly. Why not break the news that way and not be so brutal about it. Mother always said you were brutal. By the way, how is mother?"

"Well," said her husband slowly. "She was playing on the roof ..."

HYPOCHONDRIACS

THE hypochondriac had only four words on his tomb stone: "See, I told you!"

*   *   *

SHE visited the doctor for the fifth time that week: "It's awful," she said. "The pain comes every 20 minutes and lasts for an hour."

*   *   *

THEY were the perfect pair. She was a hypochondriac, and he was a pill.

*   *   *

MRS Kelly rang the doctor. "Will you come round please. My husband says he is ill."

But the doctor replies, "Mrs Kelly, I'm not coming round again. He only things he is ill."

Next day Mrs Kelly rings again. "What is it this time," says the doctor tersely. "Does your husband think he is ill again?"

"Worse," she said. "He thinks he's dead."

I

INDIANS

GENERAL Custer's last words: "I can't make these Indians out. Just a minute ago they were singing and dancing!"

★　★　★

THE Lone Ranger and Tonto had been inseparable. Suddenly their path was blocked by a Navajo war party. To the left was a hundred Apache. To the right an equal number of Souix. And behind them they heard the blood-curdling cry of the dreaded Blackfeet.

"Looks like we're done for, Tonto."

"What d'yer mean, 'we', paleface?"

★　★　★

AN Australian travel writer touring Canada was checking out of the Spokane Hilton and as he paid his bill said to the manager, "By the way, what's with the Indian chief sitting in the lobby. He has been there ever since I arrived?"

"Oh that's Big Chief Forget-me-Not," said the manager. "The hotel is built on an Indian reservation and part of the agreement is to allow the chief free use of the premises for the rest of his life. He is known as Big Chief Forget-me-Not because of his phenomenal memory. He is 92 and can remember the slightest detail of his life."

The travel writer took this in and as he was waiting for his cab decided to put the chief's memory to the test.

"What did you have for breakfast on your 21st birthday?" said the Aussie.

"Eggs," was the instant reply, and indeed the Aussie was impressed.

He went off on his travel writing itinerary, right across to the east coast and on his return to the Spokane Hilton six months later was surprised to see the Indian chief still sitting in the lobby whittling away on a stick.

"How", said the Aussie.

"Scrambled," said the chief.

*　　*　　*

A RED Indian wishing to convert to Judaism was told by the rabbi that he would have to be circumcised.

"How much?" he asked.

"$100," replied the rabbi.

"Too much," said the Indian and he began to shop around.

Another rabbi offered $90.

"Too much," said the Indian.

Finally the medicine man said he would do it for nothing and wielded his tomahawk with one swift stroke.

The Indian looked at the result. "Too much," he said.

INFIDELITY
See WARDROBES

THERE was an almighty row when Fred discovered his best friend, Bert, had been having an affair with his wife.

"But you mustn't blame her," said Bert. "It is all my fault. I was the one who answered her advert in the Truth."

*　　*　　*

OF course high fidelity is a drunk who always goes home to his wife.

A LAWYER and his wife were out walking when a blonde on the other side of the street waved and blew him a kiss. The wife demanded to know who she was.

"Oh, I just met her recently. Professionally of course," he said.

"Whose profession, yours or hers?" said the wife.

* * *

WITH good reason she was always suspicious of her husband's philanderings and each night there would be a row when she would discover a blonde or a brunette hair on his lapel.

One night she was really puzzled as she studied his coat for ten minutes.

"Okay, who's this bald-headed tart you are flirting with now," she said.

* * *

THE parish priest made his way to the front door of the farmhouse through a swarm of fighting kids. He knocked on the door repeatedly but there was no answer. He moved along to the bedroom window, looked in and was shocked to see them in a passionate embrace on the bed.

The priest made a discreet retreat through the fighting kids and went to the next property where the farmer met him at the gate.

The priest said: "Your neighbour sure likes making babies."

"He sure does," said the farmer. "His wife is in hospital having her tenth, and my wife is over there helping him out."

* * *

THE lovers were entwined in a passionate embrace on the loungeroom floor when suddenly a car was heard coming up the driveway. "Quick!" the woman shrieked. "That will be my husband. He's a policeman and he's twice as big as you."

204

Her companion hopped about frantically and said, "Where's the back door?"

"We haven't got one," she replied.

"Well, tell me quickly," he said, "where would you like one?"

* * *

A RATHER fat woman was puffing away in the aerobics class with a worried look on her face.

"What's up?" said the instructor.

"I work out here every night because my husband says he wants to make love to a woman with a trim figure," she said, "and I'm just beginning to figure out what he means."

* * *

SHE had her suspicions about her husband, Fred, so when they had an invitation to a fancy dress party at the Smithson's she conceived a plan to catch him.

When Fred was dressed in his gorilla suit ready to leave she feigned a headache, said she would stay home, but insisted Fred should go on without her.

Later she donned her own disguise and arrived at the party to see him flirting with every floosie at the party.

In her own masked outfit she approached him, whispered a seductive phrase in his ear and was surprised at the immediate response. He rushed her outside and made passionate love to her. She resisted declaring who she was in an effort to get all the evidence possible.

Just before the unmasking at midnight she left the party and drove home, and next morning was all set to confront Fred with his infidelity.

"How was it at the Smithson's?" she asked at breakfast.

"Dullsville. Boring without you, darling," he said. "When I arrived I saw Ben and the Murphy brothers without partners so we went upstairs and played poker. I lent my gorilla suit to Harry Forbes, and he said he had a wow of a time."

INSECTS

THE fly walked almost to the top of the window pane, then had to go back. He left his specs behind.

* * *

THE last thing to go through a grasshopper's mind, as it slams into a sports car's radiator grill at 100-kmh, is its bum.

* * *

"NO! no!" cried the lady centipede, crossing her legs, "A thousand times no!"

* * *

LITTLE Johnny was watching two lanky-legged spiders.
"Hey, Dad," he said. "Is there such a thing as a Mummy Long-legs?"
"No, Son."
"I thought so," said the boy slamming his fist on the spiders. "Bloody queers."

* * *

A SINGLE gnat lays per day
A hundred thousand eggs, they say
It makes one gasp
And wonder, too
Just what a married one would do.

INSURANCE

THIS policy guarantees absolute security in the event of any fatal accident.

* * *

WHEN Fred's house burned down he went off to the insurance company and demanded his compensation money. But he was soon to learn that the company didn't operate that way.

"It is our policy to replace your house and anything else you lost exactly in the same style and condition," said the manager.

"Hell," said Fred. "In that case I would like to cancel the policy I took out on my mother-in-law."

*　　*　　*

SITTING beside her old husband in his hospital bed she had to crane forward to listen to him.

"I am worried about the cost of this treatment," he wheezed. His voice was hardly a whisper: "How will we ever pay the bills for the specialists, the hospital, the operations," he wheezed.

"Don't worry about it," said his wife. "It's all taken care of. I have had a talk with the hospital and they say I can pay as soon as I've collected your insurance!"

*　　*　　*

THE pub was sending him bankrupt so Fred decided to burn it down and collect the insurance. But not without a master plan.

After he set it ablaze he called the police and told them a gorilla had done it.

"Would you be able to recognise him again?" asked the cop.

"It would be difficult," said Fred. "He was wearing a mask!"

*　　*　　*

THE insurance company noted with suspicion that Fred's premises were burnt down the very day he took out the insurance policy. Suspecting fraud the company sent him the following message: "Sir. You took out a policy with us at 11-am, and the fire didn't break out until five the same evening. Will you please explain the delay?"

*　　*　　*

ROZENBROCK and Solzberg met on a cruise ship, got to talking and found that they were both retired from the rag trade.

"Yes," said Rozenbrock, "when I got the settlement from the insurance company after the fire, me and Rachel decided to retire."

"Same here," said Solzberg. "The floods wiped us out, but the insurance company settled quickly."

Rozenbrock looked puzzled. "Tell me, Solzberg," he whispered, "how do you start a flood?"

*   *   *

HE left the court in his wheelchair, and a compensation payment for half a million dollars. But the insurance detectives followed him down the street. "You won't get away with this fraud," said one. "We will be watching you for the rest of your life," said another.

"No worries," he replied. "You can watch all you like. You can watch me go on my world trip and you can watch me go to Lourdes and you can watch, with your own eyes, one hell of a miracle."

INVENTIONS

ONE of the greatest inventors was Pat Pending. He sure came up with a lot of gadgets, but the man who invented the convertible sofa should have been one of the richest men in the world. Millions have been made on it.

*   *   *

DID you know Alexander Graham Bell invented TWO telephones?

*   *   *

HE discovered a cure for amnesia, but forgot what it was.

*   *   *

AN Israeli chemist invented a new laxative and patented the brand name: 'Let My People Go.'

*   *   *

IT was the Irish who invented the helicopter ejection seat and the solar-powered torch while the Irish medical team developed the appendix transplant.

*   *   *

MY Old Dad was an inventor and among his accomplishments were:

Water-proof tea bags. Peddle wheelchairs. Parachutes which open on impact. L-shaped mobile homes.

The one-piece jigsaw puzzle.

An inflatable dartboard for campers.

An index for a dictionary.

Beer glasses with square bases that don't leave rings on the bar or tables.

* * *

HE invented a marvellous appliance for speeding up production in factories. He called it a whip.

IRISH

THE reason there are so many Irish jokes is because the Irish have a quaint way with words. Like the Irish patient who hobbled into the surgery's waiting room: "I hope to God the doctor finds something wrong with me because I'd hate to feel like this if I was well."

* * *

ANOTHER example of Irish logic: "Hey Paddy, here's the five dollars I borrowed last week."

"Thanks, Mick, I had forgotten all about it."

"Then why the bloody hell didn't yer say so?"

* * *

THE O'Flaherty family were small. They were all small. Even the smallest was no bigger than the rest, and what's more they never went anywhere alone unless they were together.

* * *

MURPHY dropped dead the day he arrived back from a vacation in the tropics. He was laid out in the coffin for friends and neighbours to pay their last respects.

"He's got a great tan," mused Mrs Doolan from next door. "The holiday did him the world of good."

"And he looks so calm and serene," said Mrs McGinty.

"That's because he died in his sleep," explained Mrs

Murphy, "and he doesn't know he's dead yet. But when he wakes up and finds out, the shock will kill him."

*   *   *

THERE was a power failure in a Dublin department store. Thousands of shoppers were stranded on the escalators for hours.

*   *   *

"YOUR glass is empty O'Flaherty, will you be having another?"

"And why would I be wanting two empty glasses?" replied O'Flaherty.

*   *   *

THEY were two of the IRA's top men and the lay in ambush for the Chief Provost of the Ulster Brigade. "Okay," says Paddy, "let's go through the schedule once more.

"At 4.45 he leaves his office. At 4.50 his car leaves police headquarters with an escort through peak hour traffic. At 5 pm the first of his bodyguard turn this corner and we keep low and let them pass. At 5.10 the provost himself comes by in his disguised car and we let him have it. Is that all clear?"

"Clear as a bell," says Shaun looking at his watch. "But it is 5.15 now. I hope nothing terrible has happened to him."

*   *   *

MURPHY arrived home late from the pub, well oiled and ready for trouble. As he stumbled up the stairs his wife called out: "Is that you, Murphy?"

"Be Crikey it darned well better be!"

*   *   *

McTAVISH knew he was in an Irish pub, but nevertheless, when he had a few under his belt it always made him feel boisterous.

"Down with the Pope," he roared for his fifth toast. And Paddy O'Reilly stepped forward and flattened him.

When he came to his friends asked McTavish, "Didn't ya know O'Reilly was a Catholic?"

"Of course I did," he said. "But why didn't somebody tell me the Pope was?"

* * *

TWO tough union men were working on a building site when Murphy fell from the second floor scaffolding.

"Are ya dead?" cried Gallagher calling from above.

"To be sure I am," replied Murphy.

"You are such a liar Murphy that I don't know whether to believe you or not," called Gallagher.

"That proves I'm dead," said Murphy's voice from the rubble below, "because if I was alive you wouldn't be game to call me a liar!"

* * *

PADDY was coming through customs at the airport carrying a large bottle.

"What have you there?" asked the suspicious officer.

"Tis Lourdes holy water. I am bringing it home with me," said Paddy.

The officer took the bottle and tried some. "Why, it's Irish whisky," he spluttered.

"Lord bless me," said Paddy. "Another bloomin' miracle."

* * *

PADDY had just become the proud father of twins and he was asked if they were identical.

"The boy is but the girl's not," he said.

* * *

YOUNG Teresa came home and related the awesome news to her parents. She was pregnant.

"How do you know it's yours?" asked her dad.

* * *

"TERESA has just had twins," roared Murphy angrily. "Wait till I get my hands on the other fellow."

* * *

PADDY: "Hey Shaun, what's Mick's surname?"

Shaun: "Mick who?"

ON his way home one night Paddy dropped in to the pub. The barman poured him a beer and asked if he wanted to be in a raffle.

"What's it for?" asked Paddy.

"It's for a poor widow with 13 kids," said the barman.

Paddy shook his head. "No good to me. I'd never be able to keep them."

*　　*　　*

DUBLIN'S contestant in the international quiz was waiting for his first question.

"First, what's your name and occupation?" the compere asked.

"Pass," came the reply.

*　　*　　*

PADDY had been stranded on the deserted island for two years. Then one afternoon a lifeboat drifted close enough for him to swim to it and drag it to the beach, where he knocked it to bits and made himself a raft.

*　　*　　*

SHAMUS asked Paddy how he got his black eye.

"You'd never believe it," said Paddy, "but I got it in church."

He said he had been sitting behind a fat lady and when they all stood for a hymn he noticed her dress was creased into the cheeks of her bum.

"All I did was lean forward and pull it out and she turned round an hit me," said Paddy.

It was a week later and Shamus was surprised to see Paddy had another black eye. "I got it in church," he began to explain.

He said he found himself behind the same fat woman and when they stood for the hymn her dress was once again creased into the cheeks of her bum.

"My little nephew reached forward and pulled it out. But I knew she didn't like that, so I leaned over and tucked it back!"

PADDY and Shamus were hitch-hiking.

"It's best if we split up," said Paddy. "I will meet you in the next city under the town hall clock."

Later that night Shamus was waiting at the appointed place when Paddy drove up in a swank car.

"Where the hell did you get that?"

Paddy explained that he had just walked a little way when a beautiful woman picked him up. She drove to the wood, got out and took all her clothes off.

"She said I could have anything I wanted, so I took the car," said Paddy.

"Good choice too," said Shamus. "You'd look ridiculous in her clothes."

*   *   *

PADDY: "If you can guess how many chooks I have in this bag you can have both of them."

"Three?" suggested Shaun.

*   *   *

PADDY was intent on saving the man on the edge of the cliff. "Don't jump," he said. "Think of your wife and kids."

"I have no wife and I have no kids," replied the man.

"Then think of your family."

"I have no family."

"Then think of St Patrick."

"Who is St Patrick?" said the man.

"Jump ya bastard," said Paddy.

INSULTS

"CAN I have this dance?"

"Sure, if you can find someone to dance with."

*   *   *

IF there is ever a price on your head, take it.

HE told her he was a self-made man.

She said she would accept that as an apology.

* * *

YOU are the kind of person Dr Spooner would have called a shining wit.

* * *

"I WROTE that song myself," he announced.

"It's nice of you to take the blame," they replied.

* * *

SHE said their neighbour must have taken offence at something as she hadn't been over for days.

"Be sure to find out what it was," he said, "and we'll try it on her again."

* * *

THE barmaid complained that it was only an hour to closing time and two improper suggestions had been made to her. She was quite upset about it. Normally she has nine or ten.

* * *

ONE night Fred took his mother-in-law to the pub and a stranger, a little the worse for wear, leaned over and offered her a double gin and tonic. Fred said she was affronted, but she managed to swallow the insult.

* * *

"I WOULD like to buy my girlfriend a ring but I don't know what she'd like."

"Does she like you?"

"Of course."

"Then she'd like anything."

* * *

"THAT'S a nice suit you are wearing. I wonder if the style will ever come back?"

* * *

"I WENT by your place yesterday."

"Thanks!"

AN Englishman boarded a train with a large shaggy dog and sat opposite an Irishman. Paddy looked at the dog awhile then said, "And what type of dog would that be?"

The surly Englishman replied: "It's a cross between an ape and an Irishman."

Paddy was quick with his reply: "You mean its related to both of us!"

* * *

BERT had just been fired and told his boss: "You are nothing but a miserable rogue and blackguard, and I've got a darned mind to tell you so."

* * *

IT was in the outer at the cricket match when Fred returned with two beers only to find his mate, Bert, laying flat on his back. Worse, he was dismayed to find Bert's face swollen with bruises, a cut lip and a black eye.

"Which rotten so-and-so did it?" asked Fred, all fired up. "Can you describe him?"

"That's exactly what I was doing when the whacker hit me," said Bert.

* * *

HE: "I've got an idea"

She: "Beginner's luck."

He: "Are you trying to make a monkey out of me?"

She: "No. Why should I take the credit?"

He: "So this is a battle of wits between us?"

She: "No. I never pick on a man that's unarmed."

He: "I manage to keep my head above water."

She: "That's because wood floats."

He: "I won't stand these insults. I've gots lots of backbone."

She: "Yes, but the bone is all at the top."

He: "Intelligence reigns supreme in our family."

She: "Well, you must have been born during a dry spell."

He: "I'm nobody's fool."
She: "Perhaps you can get someone to adopt you."
He: "My mother thinks I'm a great wit."
She: "She's half right."
He: "You are going to drive me out of my mind."
She: "That's not a drive, it's a putt."

J

JAIL

THE prisoner was banging on the bars making a heck of the racket. "What do yer want?" said the warder.

"I want to know the time," said the prisoner.

"It's 1992," said the warder.

*   *   *

JOE was in for the term of his natural. He was given the job of organising the social events, because he was usually the lifer of the party.

*   *   *

IN prisoner of war camps it is tougher. One day the commandant marshalled all the inmates together and announced he had good news.

"For the first time in five years we are changing the sheets," he said. "Those in Hut A will change them with those in Hut B."

*   *   *

AFTER years in a high security jail Pat devised a way of communicating with his mate Mick. It was an ingenious ploy using a secret code to tap out messages on pipes.

However the scheme was eventually thwarted when they were transferred to separate cells.

JEEVES

JEEVES said as a hostess, Lady Entwhistle was hopeless. She couldn't even entertain a doubt.

* * *

THE lady of the manor was becoming increasingly alarmed at Jeeves' practice of walking in to her bedroom without knocking. Finally she took him to task.

"It could be very embarrassing if I was in a state of undress," she admonished.

"No need to worry about that, m'lady," said Jeeves. "I always take a peek through the keyhole first!"

* * *

SHE called Jeeves into her bedroom. "Jeeves, please unzip my dress." With a great deal of embarrassment he did so.

"Now Jeeves," she said. "Take off my stockings."

Jeeves was now in a sweat.

"And now take off my underwear ... and if I ever catch you wearing them again you will be instantly dismissed."

* * *

JEEVES was interviewing a prospective maid for the household and asked the girl for her references.

She began rumaging around in her handbag. "I am afraid I've lost my reference from the Dorchester," she said, "but I've got these two spoons with the Dorchester crest to prove I worked there."

* * *

WHEN the squire announced that he was to get married Jeeves was alarmed about his future at the manor. And although the squire assured him that his position was safe, Jeeves still worried while they were away on their honeymoon.

"Jeeves, how many times do I have to tell you it's business as usual," said the squire on his return.

Sure enough, next morning, the squire was up at dawn for his breakfast, promptly at 6-30 his horse was ready, and at seven Jeeves went into the bedroom slapped the bride on the bottom and said: "Okay, back to the village my lass!"

*   *   *

JEEVES was called by Lord Ponsonby. "Jeeves, could you ride down to the village and fetch a bottle of whisky, a box of cigars and a few ounces of snuff. That free-loading bishop will be calling in this afternoon."

Jeeves mounted his trusty bicycle and was off on his errand. It was not until the return trip and he had pedalled up the long hill to the manor gates that he realised he had forgotten the snuff.

What to do? It was too hot and too far to ride back down to the village. By chance the problem was solved, right there on the nature strip was a barker's nest with three of those white eggs dogs leave in neat little clumps. When dried in the sun and ground back to powder it looks for all the world like snuff.

Did he dare take the chance?

Jeeves quickly bent down, snatched up three portions and put them in his pocket.

"Did you get the whisky, Jeeves?"

"Yes, M'lord."

"And the cigars, and the snuff?"

"Yes M'lord," said Jeeves as he prepared to leave the room.

"I say, Jeeves," said Lord Ponsonby sniffing the air. "You didn't by any chance stand in something down in the village?"

"No M'lord."

The bishop arrived soon after and headed for the Scotch. "You don't mind if I have a drink, Ponsonby old boy?"

"Not at all, Bishop, go for your life," but Ponsonby was pre-occupied with the pervading odour.

"I say bishop, can you smell dog's doings in here?"

"Can't say as I can dear boy," said the bishop. "I happen to have a heavy head cold."

"In that case, take a pinch of snuff," said Ponsonby.

The bishop responded by taking two pinches and sniffing it up both nostrils.

"Gracious me," he said. "You always get the best snuff. That's cleared my head completely and I can smell that dog's stuff now!"

*   *   *

THE lady of the manor decided to dismiss the parlour maid and dressed her down with some sarcastic remarks about her unsatisfactory service as a cook and general housekeeper.

But the fiery parlour maid took the opportunity for a parting shot. "Your husband happens to think I am a better cook and a better housekeeper than you are," she retorted. "And what's more I am a damn sight better in bed than you are."

"Oh, and my husband told you that too?"

"No, Jeeves told me that!"

*   *   *

LADY Fontigue-Smythe took more than the usual care of her staff. So when her butler was hurt in an accident she was quick to attend the hospital.

"Sorry," said the nurse. "No visitors except family. Are you his wife?"

"Indeed not," said her ladyship. "I'm his mistress."

*   *   *

HIGH society couple were making love.

She: "Darling, do poor people do this?"

He: "I believe so, my sweet."

She: "It's much too good for them, don't you think?"

*   *   *

THE squire of the manor awoke with a raging erection one morning and immediately called his valet.

"Congratulations sir," said Jeeves. "Shall I awaken madam?"

"No, Jeeves. Get me my baggy shorts and we'll smuggle this one down to the village."

JEWISH

PREP school son was studying his arithmetic and asked for help from his dad. "What's two and two, Dad?"

"Depends, son. Are we buying or selling?"

*　　*　　*

"PAPPA," said the lad. "What's Yiddish for a hundred per cent?"

"Izzy, my son, a hundred per cent is Yiddish."

*　　*　　*

OLD Abraham Cohen is knocked down by a tram and is laid gently on the median strip. A lady gets a pillow from her car and places it under his head.

"Are you comfortable?" she asks.

"Ah well," he says, "I make a living."

*　　*　　*

A JEWISH mother gave her son two ties for his birthday, a striped one and a spotted one. Next day she saw him wearing the striped one.

"So what's the matter with the spotted one? You don't like it?"

*　　*　　*

THE reporter was interviewing the socialite who had organised the charity ball and couldn't take his eyes off a massive diamond on her left hand.

"Oh, that," she said. "It's the famous Guggenheimer diamond."

The reporter was dazzled by it.

"Unfortunately it has a curse attached to it," said the socialite.

"A curse?" gasped the reporter. "What curse?"

"Mr Guggenheimer," she said.

* * *

ABRAHAM wandered into Sam's pawnshop and placed a leather coat on the counter. "How much will you give me for this jacket?"

Sam checked it over. "$20, and that's the best."

"But that jacket is worth $100."

Sam was adamant. "$20 or nothing."

"Are you sure that's all it's worth?" pressed Abe.

"Positive."

"Okay," said Abe. "Here's your $20. The jacket was hanging in your doorway and I was wondering how much it was worth."

* * *

IN a small school in Dublin the teacher told the class she would give 50 pence to whoever could name the holiest man in history.

Only one hand went up, that of little Izzy O'Cohen. "That would be St Patrick, Miss," he said.

Teacher handed over the money and said to Izzy, "How come the only boy to know the answer was Jewish?"

To which Izzy replied: "In my heart of hearts I know it was Moses, but business is business."

* * *

THE aircraft was flying into Honolulu when the man in the window seat spoke to his fellow passenger for the first time.

"How do you pronounce it, Hawaii or HaVaii?"

"HaVaii." said the passenger.

"Thanks."

"You're Velcome."

* * *

MRS Goldberg was heartbroken when young Moishe told her he was getting married to Rosie McEvoy.

"Oh, why are you not marrying a lovely Jewish girl? Why are you marrying a shikseh?"

222

"Jewish girls are terrible, Momma," said Moishe, "they grow fat and get varicose veins."

"So do all the shiksehs," cried his mother.

"Yes, but who cares about shiksehs?" said Moishe.

* * *

MRS Plotkin was waiting for an appointment with Dr Goldstein and the only other person in the waiting room was a young businessman reading the Financial Review.

"Excuse me young man," she said. "Are you Jewish?"

"No I'm not," he replied.

A little later she repeated the question: "Are you sure you are not Jewish?"

"Definitely not," he said without looking up from his newspaper.

But she kept her eyes on him, and a little later: "Are you really certain you are not Jewish?"

The young man threw his paper aside. "Okay," he said in utter exasperation, "I am Jewish."

Another five minutes went by. "That's funny," she said. "You don't look Jewish."

* * *

A JEWISH man went into Izzy's corner shop and asked for some ice-cream.

"We don't sell ice-cream to Jews," said Izzy.

"But you are Jewish yourself. This is disgraceful."

"Have you tasted our ice-cream?" said Izzy.

* * *

IZZY entered the room all agitated.

"There is a new Nazi party and their manifesto states they intend to kill a million Jews and five postmen."

"Why five postmen?" somebody asked.

"That's typical," cried Izzy in despair. "Nobody ever cares about the Jews."

* * *

IZZY and Rachel went to Switzerland for a holiday and

223

while in the mountains Izzy decided to try his hand at skiing. Down the slope he went and disappeared with a scream over a crevasse. When he didn't return that night a Red Cross rescue team was despatched to the area.

They searched all night and most of the next day until they discovered some tracks.

"Mr Guggenheim, Mr Guggenheim," they kept shouting. "It's the Red Cross."

And finally a feeble voice was heard in reply. "I've given already."

* * *

IT was interval at the opera when Mrs Sternberg rose from her seat and called: "Is there a doctor in the house. Is there a doctor in the house?"

A man in a tuxedo pushed his way towards her. "I'm a doctor," he said.

"Oh doctor," she said, "Have I got just the loveliest daughter for you!"

* * *

THE rabbi was hit by a bus and first on the spot was his old friend the Catholic priest who thought it was an excellent opportunity for conversion.

"Do you believe in the Father, Son and the Holy Ghost?" whispered the priest.

The rabbi opened his eyes. "I'm dying and he asks me riddles!"

* * *

MOISHE was on his death bed and raised his head gently. "Moira, are you there?"

"Yes, Moishe, I am here."

A moment later Moishe said, "Izzi, are you there?"

His son, Izzi assured him he was by his side.

"Joshua," said the ailing Moishe, "Are you there?"

"I'm here poppa," said Joshua taking his hand.

Moishe raised himself on his elbow, "Then who the hell is minding the shop?"

GOLDSTEIN and Plotkin had spent a lifetime in competition climbing the social ladder, but Izzi Goldstein's barmitzvah was to be the calendar event of the year. It began at the London Ritz where guests were delivered in white Rolls Royces. The cabaret featured Liza Minelli and Barbara Striezand accompanied by the London Philharmonic Orchestra. The food was flown in from Vienna. Then the 100 guests were flown first class to Kenya where they set out on safari riding a team of elephants.

Two hours out from the village there was an elephant jam and the safari came to a halt.

"What's the hold-up?" demanded Mr Goldstein of the lead elephant boy.

A runner came back with the message: "There appears to be another barmizvah up ahead, by the name of Plotkin," he said.

* * *

IT was with much wringing of the hands that Rachael discovered her husband, Hymie, had a mistress. Rachael, however, was not the sort to kill the goose that lays golden eggs, rather, she decided to find out what the mistress had that she didn't.

After long interrogation Hymie finally relented. "Well to tell you the truth, Rachael, you are too cold. When we make love you don't do anything. You just lay there, whereas she moans and groans with feeling."

"Is that all," thought Rachael. "Is that all there is to it?"

That night she dressed in her most alluring lingerie, slipped Hymie a shot of his favourite cognac and got him into bed.

Half way through the business she decided to give her most passionate moans and groans.

"Oh Hymie, darling," she began. "I've had the most terrible day. Our shares have dropped two points. The washing machine broke down. You don't give me enough housekeeping money..."

A TOURIST asked a Jewish gent where Plotkin's jewellery store was located.

The Jew was loaded with parcels and began handing them over until the tourist was holding them all.

When his arms were completely free he shrugged his shoulders: "How should I know?" he said.

* * *

MOISHE is on his death-bed and and finally realises that he is about to cash in his worldly chips.

He calls for his wife, Beckie and says, "I want to leave the business to Izzi."

"No, not Izzi, he's too much of a gambler. Leave it to Abie," said his wife.

"Okay, the Rolls I will leave to Michael."

"Na, not Michael. He has smashed up three cars this year," said Beckie.

"Okay," said Moishe, "Then the summer house I will leave to Rachael and her husband."

"Na, don't let that schmuck get his hands on that property, leave it to Rachael herself."

Moishe raised himself on his elbow. "Listen Beckie. Tell me who's dying here?"

* * *

MR GOLDBERG ran a clothing factory and had the reputation of wringing a full day's work from his employees. Abe had worked there for 30 years and had never been late... until today.

He limped in an hour late on crutches with his head bandaged. Mr Goldberg pointed to the clock and asked him to explain.

Abe said he was on his way to work when he stepped on his son's skate and crashed down seven flights of stairs. He tumbled out into a laneway only to be hit by a truck.

Goldberg listened to the story and then said: "And this takes an hour?"

THE eldest son took his father aside and said he had a problem. "I have had a bit of a fling Dad and unless I come up with a thousand dollars she will sue me."

Dad reluctantly wrote a cheque to save the family name.

A week later his second son approached him. "Father I have had a bit of a fling and unless I pay a thousand dollars she will sue me."

Dad coughed up another cheque to save the family name.

A week later his daughter approached him. "Father, I am ashamed to say that I have had a bit of a fling and..."

Her father interrupted, and rubbing his hands said, "At last. We make a collection this time."

* * *

A JEWISH man boarded an overnight train and found himself sharing a sleeping compartment. As they were preparing for bed the Jew said: "Excuse me, I wonder if I could borrow a towel." The man lent him a towel.

"Excuse me," said the Jew again, "I appear to have left my pyjamas at home." The man lent him a tracksuit.

"Excuse me," said the Jew yet again, "Will you lend me your tooth brush?"

This time the man refused.

When he was met by his son at Central Station he was asked if he enjoyed the journey.

"No, I had to share with an anti-semite," he replied.

* * *

WHILE Abe Rosenberg waited at the Pearly Gates, St Peter thumbed through his lengthy personal file with an ever darkening frown. Finally, he said, "I am afraid you can't come in Mr Rosenberg."

"Look at this file," said St Peter, "it's nothing but good deeds, practically every day. The problem is Abe, we've got popes, archbishops and rabbis up here and if we let you in with this impecable record it would cause great embarrassment to the social order, not to mention putting a few pontifical noses out of joint. We can't have a mere tailor coming up here with a clean slate."

Old Rosenberg didn't protest. He was that type of bloke.

"Tell you what," said St Peter leaning forward on the counter in a confiding manner. "I'll zap you back to earth for the afternoon. You've got six hours to blot your copy book with a little sin. Do you think you could commit just one minor infringement? Then we could let you in without disturbing the heirarchy up here."

Rosenberg said he would do his best, and in a flash he found himself sitting in his lounge chair by the fire-place in his flat.

The mantelpiece clock chimed 12 noon and he began thinking. "What sin could I commit?"

He didn't smoke. He didn't like strong drink and no way would he risk a dollar on a horse.

He spent the first three hours racking his brain before he remembered the middle-aged spinster in the flat above, Miss Leonski. Yes, it was definitely a sin to make love to a woman to whom you were not married. And hadn't Miss Leonski gone out of her way at the last Body Corporate social function by deliberately sitting beside him and offering him tea and biscuits?

"That's what I'll do," he thought, and putting on his hat and coat he made his way up to her flat and knocked on the door.

"Oh, Mr Rosenberg," she said, "This is a surprise. Last thing I am hearing of you is that you are very sick, maybe dying. Will you come in for a glass of tea?"

Rosenberg sat there sipping tea, checking his watch and mentally noting that his life was fast ticking away while he was wasting time with small talk. By five o'clock he was beginning to panic as he realised there was no tactful way to dive into sin.

So suddenly he jumped up, grabbed Miss Leonski,

pushed her into the bedroom, ripped off her clothes and threw her onto the bed.

Then he sinned.

And while he was at it, he thought that if this was to be the only sin in his life he might as well give it all he had.

About five-to-six he began to feel life slipping away and he got out of bed to reach for his clothes. He turned to smile down at Miss Leonski and said: "Miss Leonski, I want to thank you. This afternoon you have shown me the way to heaven."

Miss Leonski looked up with a tired little smile. "Mr Rosenberg," she said. "You shouldn't mention it. Only me and the good Lord will know what a good deed you have done for me today!"

JOBS

MOST young blokes stop looking for work the moment they get a job.

* * *

MY father works as a blacksmith in a butcher shop. He shoos flies.

* * *

MY uncle works as an espionage agent at the Mint.

He's a Mint Spy.

* * *

I ONCE worked at factory that made fire hydrants, but there was nowhere to park.

* * *

"ARE you looking for work, my man?"

"No. But I wouldn't mind a job."

* * *

BOSS: "How many times have I reprimanded you about being late?"

"I don't know. I thought you were keeping score."

BOSS: "You should have been here at nine o'clock."

"Why, what happened?"

* * *

BOSS: "It distinctly says on the notice out front that we have no vacancies."

"Yes, I saw that. But take a chance. The bit of work I do would make no difference."

* * *

THE boss told the applicant there was a vacancy for a responsible worker. "Are you responsible?"

"I'm the right bloke alright," said Fred. "Every job I've had, when anything happened, everybody said I was responsible!"

* * *

HE started as an office boy on January 1. By February he was a salesman. Two months later he was regional manager. By mid year he was assistant general manager, and by November he was general manager.

On the first anniversary of his start with the firm he took over as chairman of the board. As he met the outgoing chairman at the office door he shook his hand and said, "Thanks Dad."

* * *

THE teenager was complaining that his job was menial and boring. His father reminded him that digging holes was the only job you can get where you start at the top.

* * *

HE saw the sign "Handyman Wanted" outside the convent and immediately applied. Mother Superior gave him a quick approval and asked if he could mend the fuse.

"Oh, I'm no good at electical matters," he said.

"Well, the front fence needs painting," said the nun.

"Oh, I'm no good at painting," he said.

"Well, we need a new door on the kitchen," she said.

"Oh, I'm no good at carpentry, sister," he said.

"Well tell me," she said. "What makes you think you are a handyman?"

"Oh, I just live around the next corner," he said.

* * *

HIS new job is touting for a doctor. He goes around making people sick.

* * *

FRED said if the foreman didn't take back what he said that morning he was leaving the job.

"What did he say?"

"He gave me a week's notice," said Fred.

* * *

"WHAT are you working at now?"

"Nothing, but it's steady."

* * *

THE young man was having a very loud argument with his girlfriend. "That's it. I am going to end it all," he cried and climbed on the the parapet of the bridge.

"I'm going to jump and I don't want anybody to save me," he said as he leapt into the water.

A young bloke who had witnessed this dived in after him.

"I told you I don't want to be saved," cried the young man.

"That's okay," said the other bloke, "I don't want to save you. Just tell me where you work."

* * *

THE manager was giving the applicant the job.

"I think you will be very happy with us," he said. "We have a bonus scheme, a non-contributory pension scheme, special medical and hospital insurance schemes, free training and recreational facilities and a profit-sharing plan."

"Sounds wonderful," said the applicant, "and what are the wages?"

"Wages?" said the manager. "Hell, with all that we can't afford wages!"

THE man at the employment centre said there was indeed a job.

"What does it involve?" asked Fred.

"It is a photographer's assistant. Seems he wants a bikini-line shaver to ensure there are no pubic hairs showing when he photographs models in the latest swim gear."

"I'll take it," said Fred.

"Then you will have to go to Bachus Marsh."

"Why Bachus Marsh?"

"Because that's the end of the queue!"

* * *

THEY were arguing about which was the oldest profession.

The surgeon rose to his feet and said: "When God created Eve he took a rib from Adam in the first surgical operation."

The architect made his claim: "In order to restore order from chaos, God must have needed the services of an architect."

The civil servant came in with the clincher: "Ah, but who created the chaos?"

JOGGERS

FRED joined Joggers Anonymous. Whenever he feels like a run they send someone round with a dozen bottles to talk him out of it.

* * *

FATHER: "Why don't you go for a run around the block?"

Son: "Why? I'm already here."

* * *

FRED was told that he should exercise and that jogging would add years to his life.

"How do you feel?" asked his wife when he staggered once around the block.

"They're right. I feel ten years older," he said.

WHEN the husband came home unexpectedly, Larry the lover had to leap from the bedroom window. Spotting some joggers running by he quickly joined them.

"Do you usually jog in the nude?" asked one of the runners after a while.

"Oh yes," said Larry. "It's very stimulating."

"And do you usually jog with a condom on?"

Larry kept his cool. "Well, to tell you the truth, it was raining when I set out."

* * *

HAVING trouble with his sex life, Fred was advised by the doctor to take up jogging.

"Take it easy to start with, just two miles a day," said the Doctor, "and give me a call this time next week."

Fred did so. "And how is your sex life now?" asked the Doc.

"Worse," said Fred. "I'm 14 miles from home."

* * *

AFTER a very heavy night he left the nightclub at dawn and being in no condition to drive he stopped the car in the first recreation reserve and tried to sleep it off.

He had just settled down when a jogger tapped on the window and asked for the time.

"It's 5.30," he grumbled.

He snuggled down again, but only a few minutes passed before another jogger rapped on the window and asked the time. "It's 5.35," he roared.

In desperation he scribbled a note in large letters and stuck it against the window. It read: "I haven't a watch and I don't know the time."

Five minutes later a jogger stopped to rap on the window and told him it was 5.40.

JOKES

THE only catch in telling a good story, is that it usually reminds the other bloke of a bad one.

* * *

"I'VE got a million jokes," he said.

"Then why did you tell us that one," they said.

* * *

HE always wanted to be a comedian, but he was afraid people might laugh at him.

* * *

A MAN who says his wife can't take a joke forgets himself.

* * *

HE who laughs last doesn't get the joke.

* * *

"DID you hear my last joke?"

"I hope so."

* * *

THE comedian's first professional engagement was at the Oodnadatta Social Club and his first performance was greeted with stony silence.

He was sitting in his dressing room drowning his sorrows while the bingo session was in full swing and he heard the MC trying to call the crowd to order.

"Now then," said the MC. "If you don't shut the noise while we're running the bingo I'll get that comedian on again!"

* * *

THE travelling salesman's car broke down and he wandered across the paddock to the farmhouse and asked if he could sleep the night.

"You're most welcome," said the farmer, "but I must warn you that I don't have daughters, I am a bachelor and you will have to share the only bed with me."

"Oh hell," said the salesman, "I'm in the wrong bloomin' joke."

THE Taxation Department is putting jokes and cartoons on the back of the income tax form now, so that taxpayers can see the funny side.

*　　*　　*

FRED was often the butt of office jokes. "Have you heard the story of the dirty window, Fred?" they said.

When he said no, they said: "It's no use telling you. You wouldn't see through it."

Fred could hardly wait until he got home. "Darling," he said. "Have you heard the story of the window you couldn't see through?"

"No," she said.

"Well I can't tell you. It's too dirty."

*　　*　　*

"THE trouble with you, Mabel, is that you have no sense of humour," he said.

She thought about it for a moment. "Well, I don't think that's funny."

*　　*　　*

WHEN the little man came home, his rather formidable wife gave him such a wallop on the head with a rolling pin that his knees buckled and he fell to the floor.

Shaking his head groggily he said: "Was that a joke, or did you mean it?"

"I bloody-well meant it," she said.

"That's okay then. Because I don't appreciate jokes like that."

*　　*　　*

DON'T worry if your life's a joke
And your successes are but few
Remember that the mighty oak
Was once a nut like you.

*　　*　　*

WE editors may dig and toil
Till our fingertips are sore

235

But still a few are bound to say
"I've heard that joke before."

* * *

EVERYBODY'S idea of a joke is different. Like the fellow who hit his mate on the head with a dead chicken.

"Hey," said the victim, "are you having a go at me, or was that a joke?"

"I'm having a go at you," was the reply.

"Well that's okay then. 'Cos I don't like that kind of joke."

* * *

A WISE man never laughs at his wife's old clothes.

* * *

HE is convinced women don't have a sense of humour. He asked one to his room and she said: "Don't make me laugh."

* * *

HE who laughs last usually has a tooth missing.

* * *

HISTORY records that when Churchill met Stalin at the famous Yalta conference they discussed their hobbies.

Churchill said he collected jokes people told about him.

Stalin said he collected people who told jokes about him.

K

KIDS

CHILDREN, what a comfort in old age. And how soon they bring it on.

* * *

PRIDE is something you feel when your kids run a garage sale and raise a few hundred dollars.

Panic is when you go to get your car, and find it gone.

* * *

YOUNG Billy brought a note home from school. His Dad read it and announced to his wife: "They want a written excuse for his presence."

* * *

THE little boy in the crowded showgrounds was obviously distressed. "I've lost my Dad," he sobbed when the policeman approached him.

"What's your Dad like?" said the cop.

"Beer, women and the odd bet," said the lad.

* * *

LITTLE Mary stuck her head around the kitchen door, "Hey Mum. Can an eight-year-old girl get pregnant?"

"Of course not," said her mother.

Mary turned round. "It's okay fellas, we can keep playing the game."

THE RSPCA inspector stopped three kids in a billy-cart. It was being pulled by a big mongrel dog they had harnessed to the cart. He accused the kids of cruelty.

"Rubbish," chorused the kids. "Bonzo loves it, he has been doing it for years. He doesn't look unhappy does he?"

The officer had to admit that the big dog seemed to be enjoying himself.

"Okay," he conceded, "but that piece of string hanging from his testicles will have to come off. That could hurt him."

"Arr hell," said one of the kids. "There goes our brakes!"

* * *

"ARE you a gardening expert?" asked the small girl when the visiting neighbour was seated in the lounge.

"No Mary I'm not. What makes you think that?"

"Mum says if there is any dirt about you'll dig it up!"

* * *

LITTLE Johnny was having a lot of trouble with his arithmetic and when teacher asked him what two plus two was he counted on his fingers and said, "four."

"And how much is three and three?"

Again Johnny counted on his fingers and came up with "six."

"Johnny," stormed the teacher, "it is cheating to use your fingers. Now put your hands in your pockets and tell me what is five and five."

There was a fumble and a pause before the answer came up. "Eleven," he said.

* * *

WHEN young Billie returned from his first time at church they asked him how he liked it. He said the music and singing was good, but he didn't think much of the news.

* * *

HIS dad asked what he had learned in Sunday school that morning.

"I learned about a cross-eyed bear whose name was Gladly," replied the youngster.

Dad was puzzled and had to press the point further to finally discover it was a hymn: "Gladly, the Cross I'd Bear."

* * *

A COP saw a little boy standing in the pub smoking a cigarette and drinking a pot of beer.

"Why aren't you in school?" he asked.

"Because I'm only four years old," replied the kid.

* * *

"MUM," said the little boy, "where did I come from?"

"The stork brought you, dear," was the reply.

"And where did you come from, Mum?"

"The stork brought me too."

"And what about grandma?"

"The stork brought her too."

"Gee," said the little lad, "Doesn't it ever worry you to think that there have been no natural births in our family for three generations?"

* * *

"HEY Mum, where do babies come from?"

"From the stork of course."

"But who gets the stork pregnant?"

* * *

SMALL boy watching his Mum do the washing. "Mum, where did you work before you got this job here with us?"

* * *

LITTLE Tommy, aged eight, marched into the living room with an important announcement for his father. "Dad," he said with great seriousness, "I'm gonna get married."

His Dad grinned indulgently, "Who to, son?"

"My girlfriend, Mary, next door."

Mary was also eight and his Dad decided to carry the joke along. "Found a place to live yet?" he asked.

"Well, she gets 50 cents pocket money and you give me a dollar. So if she moves in with me, we can manage," said Tommy seriously.

His Dad nodded. "Well, $1-50 a week is okay for now, but what will you do when the kids start to arrive?"

"Don't worry," said Tommy confidently. "We've been lucky so far."

* * *

GRANDMA was spending a few days with the family, and on the fourth morning when everybody was seated around the breakfast table little Freddy said: "When are you going to do your trick, Dad?"

"What trick is that, son?"

"You know. You said if Grandma stayed more than three days you would climb the wall."

* * *

YOUNG Basil had moved to town from the country and had settled in at the suburban primary school fairly well; except for his constant swearing. It was "bloody" this and "bloody" that until he was sent home with a note: "If this boy won't stop swearing he will not be allowed to school anymore."

His father gave him a bloody hiding and sent him back next day with a note to say he wouldn't bloody-well swear again.

The teacher was impressed and sent home another note. "Basil has been so good he can come to the school picnic on Saturday week."

When the big day came, little Basil set off for the picnic, with a caution and yet another note. "If he swears again, please send the little blighter straight home."

In less than an hour Basil was back, weeping his eyes out, and copped another hiding from his father for swearing.

"I didn't swear," he protested. "You sent me off on the wrong bloody Saturday. The bloody picnic is not until next bloody week!"

240

TWO young brothers were sent home from their country school with a note to say they had been suspended for the afternoon for swearing.

Their father gave them a hiding, a lecture and sent them to bed without dinner.

Next morning as they sat down for breakfast their father, in a more conciliatory mood, asked what they would like for breakfast.

The first one said: "I'll have some of those bloody cornflakes." He received an immediate thrashing from his father and was sent back to bed for the day.

The father then asked the second boy what he would like for breakfast. "I don't know," he said. "But it won't be bloody cornflakes, that's for sure."

*   *   *

BECAUSE he had been heard swearing, young Billie had been put across his father's knee and given a few good whacks. "Now son," said his Dad, "tell me why I punished you."

The kid threw up his hands in despair. "That does it. First you belt hell out of me and now you don't know why you bloody-well did it!"

*   *   *

"DAD, all the kids at school hit me and call me Pansy."

"That's all right son," said his father. "Next time they do that, whack them over the head with your handbag."

*   *   *

LITTLE Johnny had just met the new kid at playgroup.

"How old are you?"

"I don't know," said the new kid.

"Do women bother you?"

"No."

"Then you are five."

*   *   *

A YOUNG boy was approached by the young housewife who had just moved into the flat next door. "Sonny, I need some bread at the corner store. Do you think you could go for me?"

"No," said the lad, "but I've heard Dad say he could."

* * *

DAD had just settled down with a book when young Johnny came home from school and asked the question he had dreaded to hear: "Where did I come from, Dad?"

Wiping the sweat from his collar Dad began the lengthy explanation beginning with the birds and the bees right through to sexual intercourse, and after an agonising half hour summed it all up with, "Now, do you understand, son?"

"Not really, Dad," said the lad. "Luigi says he comes from Italy and Ng VanDong says he comes from Vietnam. Where do I come from?"

* * *

WHEN his wife said she was going to change the baby, he said: "Well get a quieter one!"

* * *

SHE married a sailor because she wanted to have children and rear admirals.

* * *

"I HEAR you have finally cured little Tommy of biting his nails?"

"Yeah, we pulled his teeth out!"

* * *

LITTLE Agatha was crying bitterly because her father drowned the three new kittens. He had promised her she could do it.

* * *

"MUMMY, you know the vase you were always worried I would break?"

"Yes."

"Well, your worries are over."

242

KIWIS

A BLOKE went into the fish shop and asked for some "Fush 'n chups."

"Ar! You're a Kiwi, eh?" said the proprietor.

The Enzedder got sick and tired of this so he spent the next three months at an elocution class.

He finally returned to the shop and asked, in perfect English for some "Fish and Chips."

"Ar, you're a Kiwi, eh?"

"How the hell did you know that?"

"Because this has been a hardware shop for the last two weeks."

* * *

THE potato farmer had recently arrived from Rotorua and had taken up a farm in Gembrook. "You look worried," said his mates in the pub, "what's bothering you?"

"Sex!" he replied.

They gathered around for more information.

"Well," explained the Kiwi, "as you know this is my first harvest here. I've got a wonderful crop of spuds, but not enough sex to put them in."

* * *

THREE couples went into a restaurant in Auckland and asked for a table for sex.

"And three pillows," they added.

L

LAW
See POLICE

IT'S illegal to make liquor privately, and to make water publicly.

* * *

THE lag in the dock said: "As God is my judge I am not guilty."

The magistrate replied: "He's not. I am. You are. Three years."

* * *

THE judge called the court to order to make a serious announcement. He said he had been bribed $2000 by the defendant and $3000 by the plaintiff.

"This is a serious matter and I have given it earnest consideration," he said. "I've decided to return $1000 to the plaintiff, and judge the case on its merits!"

* * *

THE judge, he populates
  The city jails
  By grave decisions
  Heads or tails

* * *

DAN Murphy was a popular bloke in the one-horse town, but he was charged with stealing cattle. After the bush jury of his peers heard the evidence the foreman stood up and said: "Not guilty. So long as he returns the cattle."

The circuit magistrate was infuriated with the finding and demanded they go back and reconsider their verdict.

After a short wrangle among themselves the foreman stood once more. "Okay, not guilty, and he can keep the bloomin' cattle."

*　　*　　*

"YOU seem to have more than an average share of intelligence for a man of your background," sneered the lawyer at the witness stand.

"Thank you," said the witness. "If I wasn't under oath I'd return the compliment."

*　　*　　*

FRED knew that a former partner owed him $500 but he was unable to legally prove it. He asked his solicitor what to do about it.

"Easy," replied the legal eagle. "We will send him a letter demanding payment of the $1000 within seven days and ...

"But it is only $500," said Fred.

"And that's exactly what he will reply in his letter, and then we have the proof."

*　　*　　*

THE clerk turned to the little bloke in the dock. "Prisoner at the bar," he said, "do you wish to challenge the jury?"

Fred eyed the jury. "Not all of them at once," he said, "but I think I could go a few rounds with the little fat geezer in the middle."

*　　*　　*

A BLOKE due to appear in court was talking about the case in the bar and was advised by his drinking mate: "If you want to get off, just send the judge a case of whisky."

The defendant discussed this with his solicitor next morning. "On no account do anything like that," said the legal man. "We've got a thin argument already without complicating it with a bribe."

To the solicitor's astonishment our bloke won his case. "We would have lost if you sent that case of whisky."

"Oh, but I did," said our bloke, "but I put the other party's name on the card."

*   *   *

JUDGE: "Can't you settle this out of court?"

"That's what we were doing when the police interferred."

*   *   *

"THIS pen leaks," said the prisoner as the rain came through the roof.

*   *   *

THE Melbourne lawyer received a fax from his partner representing a client in Sydney. It read "Justice has prevailed."

The Melbourne man faxed back a message; "Appeal at once!"

*   *   *

McTAVISH was as shrewd as they come and when he sat down with the lawyer he said: "I'm not into throwing money about, but I will certainly pay if you can give me an undertaking that you can win my case."

The lawyer said that was fair enough and told McTavish to outline the story.

McTavish launched into a terrible tale of breach of contract, lying, cheating and fraudulent business practices.

"That's an open and shut case," said the lawyer. "I will cheerfully accept such a brief."

"Oh that's bad news," said McTavish.

"Why?" asked the lawyer.

"That was my opponent's side of the story."

*   *   *

THE defendant had just been convicted and fined and was asked by the judge if he could pay anything at all towards the penalty and costs.

"Not a brass razoo," he replied. "All the money I had has gone to my lawyer and five of the jurors."

* * *

CHARGED with stealing a barrel of beer from the back of the pub the old defendant was not familiar with legal jargon. So when the judge said he would have to dismiss the case due to insufficient evidence the old lag scratched his head and said "What d'yer mean?"

The clerk explained: "It means you are let off."

"And does it mean I can keep the grog?" he asked.

* * *

DAD is very popular in prison. He's the lifer of the party.

* * *

"YOUNG man, you are accused of stealing a petticoat."

"It was my first slip."

* * *

"HAVE you ever been cross-examined before?"

"Yes, your honour, I'm a married man."

* * *

"DO you plead guilty or not guilty?"

"What else have you got?"

* * *

"DO you plead guilty or not guilty?"

"How do I know. I haven't heard the evidence yet."

* * *

"HAVE you anything to offer before judgement is passed?"

"No, judge, my lawyer has left me skint."

* * *

"GUILTY. Ten days or two hundred dollars."

"I'll take the two hundred thanks, judge."

* * *

"ORDER, order in the court."

"Whisky, on the rocks for me thanks."

* * *

JUDGE: you are charged with habitual drunkeness, what is your excuse?"

"Habitual thirst, yer worship!"

BOSS to pretty secretary: "Just because I made love to you last night, who said you could come in late?"

Secretary: "My solicitor."

* * *

JUDGE, to jury: "What possible reason could you have for acquitting this man?"

"Insanity," said the foreman.

"What, all of you?"

* * *

FRED consulted his lawyer. "I've been receiving threatening letters," he said.

"That's terrible," said the legal eagle. "We'll put a stop to that. Who are they from?"

"The Taxation Department," said Fred.

* * *

TWO tramps were hauled before the court and charged with vagrancy.

"And where do you live?" asked the judge.

"Nowhere," said the first tramp.

"And where do you live," he asked the second tramp.

Indicating his mate he replied, "Next door to him!"

* * *

SHE was seeking maintenance for her baby.

"Do you know who the father is?" asked the solicitor.

"Yes," she sobbed. "It was Tommy."

"But we can't sue Tommy. Don't you know his surname?"

"No. You see I didn't know him personally."

* * *

TWO magistrates were rolling home from a reunion, arms around each other, singing Sweet Adeline.

"Hey," said one. "I think we're drunk."

"You're right. And according to law I will have to charge you with being drunk and disorderly," said his mate.

"And you will have to appear before me at 10 tomorrow," said the first.

Next morning in court the first pleaded guilty to the charge and was fined $10. They then changed places.

"Drunk and disorderly, eh, fined $20."

"Hey," protested the first. "When I was in the chair I only fined you $10."

"Yes," said the second magistrate. "But the offence is getting too prevalent. You are the second drunk to appear before this court this morning!"

*　　*　　*

JUDGE to habitual defendant: "Is this the first time you have been up before me?"

"I dunno yer honour. What time do you get up?"

*　　*　　*

THE solicitor told Paddy that if he wanted to be defended in court tomorrow he would need money, but Paddy was broke.

"All I've got is an antique gold watch," he said.

Solicitor: "Well that's okay, you can raise cash on that. Now what are you accused of stealing?"

Paddy: "An antique gold watch!"

*　　*　　*

"HAVE you got anything to say for yourself?" said the judge sternly after hearing the case.

"Stuff all," muttered the defendant.

"What did he say?" asked the judge learning forward to the clerk.

The clerk stood up, turned, and whispered quietly to the judge: "He said 'stuff all' your worship."

"That's funny," said the judge, "I'm sure I saw his lips move."

*　　*　　*

WHEN the stranger entered the bar the publican said, "Good evening, Sir, would you like a drink?"

"Yes," he replied, "I will have a double Scotch."

It was plonked in front of him and the publican said, "That'll be five dollars, thanks."

"No," said the stranger, "It's your treat. I clearly heard you invite me to have a drink."

Another gent at the bar who heard the argument said to the publican. "He's right you know. I am a solicitor and I distinctly heard you invite him to have a drink."

The angry publican told the stranger to drink his whisky and leave and never come back.

Ten minutes later the stranger returned. "I thought I told you never to come back," roared the publican."

The stranger protested. "I've never been here before in my life."

The publican grudgingly conceded, "Well you must have a double."

"Thanks very much," said the stranger, "and one for my solicitor friend."

*   *   *

TWO workers entered the same pub, pulled their stools up to the bar and opened their cut lunches.

"Hey," said the barman, "You can't eat your own sandwiches here."

So they swapped.

LAZINESS

HE was so lazy he married a pregnant woman.

*   *   *

HE was so lazy he had his window box concreted over.

*   *   *

HE was so lazy he used to ride the underground in peak hours just to press his clothes.

*   *   *

THE only thing he ever took up at school was space.

*   *   *

HE called her Baseball because she would never play without a diamond.

*   *   *

THE lazy German lived by the sweat of his frau.

LETTERS

HE got a letter from his wife: "Fred, I missed you yesterday. Come home and let me have another shot. — Beatrice."

* * *

SMOOTH Sam was confiding to Fred over a beer that he had a problem. "I'm worried, Fred," he said. "This letter came the other day and it said if I didn't stop making love to this bloke's wife he was going to kill me."

"So what's the problem?" said Fred.

"It wasn't signed," said Sam.

* * *

FRED was always coming home from the pub in the early hours of the morning, and eventually found this note from his missus:

"The day before yesterday you came home yesterday morning. Yesterday you came home this morning. So if today you come home tomorrow morning you will find that I left you yesterday."

* * *

"DEAR Sir. Please find enclosed $10.50 for one of your razors as advertised. — Billy Bong. PS: I forgot to enclose the money, but no doubt a firm of your reputable standing will send the razor anyway.

Dear Mr Bong. Thank you for your order and we have pleasure enclosing the razor as requested.

PS: We forgot to enclose the razor, but no doubt a man with your cheek doesn't need one."

* * *

"DEAR John. I have been unable to sleep since I broke off our engagement. Won't you forget and forgive? Your absence is breaking my heart. I was a fool, nobody can take your place. I love you. I love you. — Marsha.

PS: Congratulations on winning the lottery."

* * *

THE university chancellor discovered that one of his

professors had been messing about with his wife. So he sent him a letter demanding his presence in the office on Tuesday morning.

The offending professor sent the following reply: "I received your circular letter. I regret that I cannot attend, but rest assured that I will accept the majority vote."

* * *

LETTER from a travel agent: "Dear Sir, in reference to your proposed trip to London, the flight you requested is completely full, but we will keep in contact and inform you immediately somebody falls out, as is often the case."

* * *

LETTER FROM AN IRISH MOTHER
DEAR SON. Just a few lines to let you know I'm still alive. I'm writing this letter slowly because I know you can't read fast. You won't know the house when you get home because we have moved.

About your father. He has a lovely new job. He has 500 men under him; he cuts grass at the cemetery. There was a washing machine in the new house when we moved in but it hasn't been working too good. Last week I put Dad's shirt in, pulled the chain and haven't seen it since.

Your sister Mary had a baby this morning but I haven't found out if it is a boy or a girl yet, so I don't know if you are an auntie or an uncle.

Your Uncle Patrick drowned last week in a vat of whisky at the Dublin Brewery. Some of his workmates tried to save him but he fought them off bravely. They cremated him and it took five days to put out the fire.

I went to the doctor last Thursday and your father came with me. The doctor put a small glass tube in my mouth and told me not to talk for ten minutes. Your father offered to buy it off him.

It only rained twice this week, first for three days and then for four.

We had a letter from the undertaker. He said if the last payment on your grandfather's plot isn't paid within seven days, up he comes.

— Your loving mother.

PS: I was going to send you $10 but I had already sealed up the envelope.

*   *   *

WHY I FIRED MY SECRETARY

TWO weeks ago it was my 45th birthday. I didn't feel too well that morning, but I knew that when I went to breakfast my wife would be pleasant and say "Happy Birthday". But she didn't even say "Good Morning".

I thought, that's wives for you. At least the children will remember. But the kids came in for breakfast and didn't say a word, so when I started for the office I was feeling pretty low and despondent.

As I walked into the office, Janet said "Good Morning, boss. Happy Birthday." I immediately felt better because somebody remembered.

About noon she knocked on my door and said that it was such a lovely day we should go out to lunch. It was the best news I had all day.

We went to lunch. We didn't go where we normally go. Janet said she knew a little private place out in the country. We had two martinis and enjoyed lunch tremendously.

On the way back to the office she said, "You know, it's such a beautiful day it would be a shame to go back to the office." When I agreed she said: "Let's go to my apartment and I will fix you another martini."

We did just that, in fact she fixed two martinis which put me in a very pleasant mood. Then she said, "Boss, if you don't mind, I think I will go into the bedroom and slip into something more comfortable." I assured her I didn't mind at all.

She went into the bedroom and in about six minutes

she came out carrying a big birthday cake followed by my wife and children, all singing Happy Birthday, and there I sat with nothing on except my socks!

* * *

AUSTRALIAN EXPORT
MEIN Tear Herren.

Der last two pecketches ve got from you off coffee vas mitt rattschidtten mixt. Ve did not see any rattschidtten in der samples vich you sent us. It takes much valuable time to pick de ratten durden from der coffee. Ve order der coffee clean but you schipt schidt mixt mit it.

Ve like you schip us der coffee in vun sek, und der rattenschidtten in an udder sek. Und zen ve can mix it to suit der customer. Write please if we should schip der schidt bek und keep der coffee, or should ve chip bek der coffee und keep der shidt, or should ve schip bek der whole schidtten vurks?

We remain at your conwenience...

LIARS

THE lie is an abomination to the Lord; but damned helpful in getting out of trouble.

* * *

SHE said she can tell by looking at your husband's face if he is lying.

"Yes," she said. "If his lips are moving, he's lying."

* * *

DOES your husband lie awake at night?

Yes, and he lies in his sleep, too.

* * *

THEY say the first lie detector was made out of the rib of a man. And they have been unable to improve on that model ever since.

* * *

THE vicar from the pulpit announced that his sermon

that day would be on the sin of perjury. "How many of you have read the 25th chapter?"

All in the congregation raised their hands.

"That's good," said the vicar. "There is no 25th chapter so you are exactly the people I want to talk to."

* * *

THERE are two kinds of people who live in Sydney. Those who admit they have cockroaches and the others who lie about it.

* * *

THERE is only one thing that stops him from being a bare-faced liar.

What's that?

His moustache.

* * *

MADGE fixed her eye on her husband Fred and said: "So, where are you going today?"

"I'm going to the pub."

"Ha, when you tell me you are going to the pub I know that you think that I'll think you are going to the races, but this time I know you are really going to the pub, so why are you lying?"

* * *

HE described his wife as having a keen sense of rumour.

* * *

HE's not really a liar. He just arranges the truth in his favour.

LIFE

THE best way to face life is with a stiff upper lip, a firm chin, your feet planted firmly on the ground your head high in the air, your nose to the grindstone, an ear to the ground and a shoulder to the wheel... and you'll find it's damned uncomfortable.

IF I had my life to live over again, I'd start making the same mistakes earlier.

* * *

NEVER let life get you down. Remember, when one door closes, another slams in your face.

* * *

ABOUT the time you are financial enough to eat, drink and be merry, the doctor limits you to a glass of milk.

* * *

THE only certain way to reduce the cost of living is to drop dead.

* * *

LIFE is to be enjoyed. We will never get out of it alive.

* * *

LIFE. The first half is ruined by your parents. The second half is ruined by your kids.

* * *

IF you want to remember, tie a short string around your finger.

If you want to forget, tie a long rope around your neck.

* * *

LIFE begins at 40, but you could miss a lot if you wait till then.

* * *

LIFE is like a shower. One wrong turn and you are in hot water.

* * *

WHAT is the reason women live longer than men?
Because they have no wives.
(And of course the reverse applies.)

* * *

HE was asked if he ever realised any of his childhood dreams.
"Yes. When I was young and my mother kept insisting on combing my hair I often wished I didn't have any."

LIFE can be hard, but some hearts can be harder as the tramp found out when he knocked on the back door of the inn looking for a hand-out.

The landlady fixed him with a steely glare. "Would you eat yesterday's stew?"

"Yes," he said eagerly.

"Well, come back tomorrow," she said.

LITERATURE

SHE went to Stratford-on-Avon to see her first play, A Midsummer Night's Dream, and was so moved by it that on the final curtain she stood and called: "Author! Author!"

* * *

A CRITIC, said Kenneth Tynan, is a man who knows the way but can't drive a car.

* * *

A CRITIC is a legless man who teaches running.

* * *

AND the critic's response. "I can't lay an egg either, but I am a better judge of an omelette than any hen."

* * *

"WHAT do you think of Kipling?"

"Don't know. I've never tried it."

* * *

THE English teacher looked dejected. "I have just given that class a lecture on Keats, and I doubt if any of them know what a keat is."

LOCAL GOVERNMENT

A TEDDY Bear got a job on a council road gang. Monday went well, Tuesday likewise, but on Wednesday when he returned from his lunch break he discovered his pick had been stolen.

He complained to the foreman who was undismayed and had the obvious answer.

"It's Wednesday," he said. "That's the day the Teddy Bears have their picks nicked!"

* * *

SOCIETY matron was crowing over her husband's re-election on the municipal council. "Yes. My John got elected for his third time and got in unexposed!"

* * *

WHEN the municipal council decided to build a fountain outside the town hall they put the project to tender and got three quotes, from contractors in Brisbane, Sydney and Melbourne.

The town clerk interviewed the Brisbane builder and asked his price. "$3000," was the reply.

"And how do you break that down?" asked the clerk.

"That's $1000 for the material, $1000 for the workers and $1000 for me."

The town clerk called in the Sydney contractor who quoted a price of $6000. "And how do you break that down?" asked the clerk.

"That's $2000 for materials, $2000 for the workers and $2000 for me."

The clerk called in the Melbourne bloke, whose price was $9000.

"And how do you break that down?" asked the clerk.

The bloke from Melbourne said, "$3000 for you, $3000 for me, and we give the job to the bloke from Brisbane."

* * *

THEY had never had a woman on the town council before and newly elected Cr Flossie Firebrand intended to make her mark.

The first item on the engineer's agenda was the cost of constructing a urinal.

"What's a urinal?" she asked.

When it was fully explained to her she immediately demanded that the funds be doubled.

"If we are gonna have a urinal I insist that we have an arsenal too."

      ★   ★   ★

PAYING his parking fine at the town hall the commercial traveller complained to the clerk that the town didn't have enough parking spaces.

"We're a small country town with lots of expenses," said the clerk. "If we can't catch you blokes for speeding, then we rip a little bit off for standing still."

      ★   ★   ★

HE was mayor of the town, and a justice of the peace which meant he sat on the bench on court days. He glared over his glasses at the tramp charged with vagrancy.

"Have you ever earned a dollar in your life?" he sneered.

"Yes, yer honour," answered the defendant. "It was a tenner remember, for voting for you at the last election."

LOGIC

TWO Catholic women were enjoying a cup of coffee opposite a house owned by a notorious call girl when they saw a protestant minister go in.

"Disgraceful," whispered one to the other.

Later they saw the local rabbi emerge from the same door and they shook their heads in despair.

"What's the world coming to?"

They were on their second cup of coffee when they saw Father O'Kelly knock on the door and enter.

"Dear, the poor woman must be awfully sick," they agreed.

      ★   ★   ★

TWO travellers, one with years of experience, found themselves in a strange town without lodgings. It was a warm night so they decided to sleep out in what appeared to be a quiet lane.

The older of the two elected to lay in the middle of the road. His younger companion, declaring his mate a fool, settled down on the side of the road.

As they were sleeping a truck came down the road and the driver, seeing the old bloke in his path, swerved to avoid him and ran over the young man on the pavement.

* * *

SOCIETY Sally said to the good-looking stranger: "Gee you look like my fifth husband."

The stranger was taken aback. "How many times have you been married?" he asked.

"Four," she replied.

* * *

THE club's fund-raiser approached the born loser.

"Will you buy a raffle ticket for a keg of beer?"

"I don't like beer," he said.

"Not to worry," she said. "There are too many in it already. You haven't a chance of winning."

"Good," he said. "I'll take two."

* * *

AFTER catching a stranger in bed with his wife the irate husband reaches for his gun.

"Wait!" cries his wife. "Remember the world cruise we went on after I told you I won the lottery. Well, Lionel paid for it. Remember the strange circumstances which caused our mortgage to be paid off. Well, Lionel actually paid it. Remember the diamond ring I found. Well, again, Lionel paid for it..."

The husband lowers his gun.

"For goodness sake, woman. Cover him up he'll catch a chill."

M

MAGIC

AN old magician was working the Titanic on its last fateful voyage. He used to put a rabbit in his top hat and pull a hair out of his bum. (No, that's not the joke).

The old-timer had been down on his luck and couldn't afford one of those attractive leggy blonde assistants. On the Titanic he had to make do with a parrot, but to give it credit, the parrot had developed repartee and would squawk to the audience: "It's up his sleeve", or "It's under his cloak, folks."

They were half way through their act when the Titanic hit the iceberg and sank.

The magician swam all night while the parrot fluttered overhead. He swam all next day and the parrot still fluttered overhead. It was evening of the second day when the parrot finally alighted on the magician's head.

"Okay, I give up. What have you done with the bloomin' ship?"

*   *   *

AFTER the leggy blonde had flagged him down on the country road he asked her what she did for a living.

"I'm a magician," she said.

"Get away, prove it then."

And with that she touched him on the knee and turned him into a motel.

THE party had been very entertaining and now it was Paddy's turn to do a magic trick. He stretches his arms forward, thumbs up, and says to the person opposite: "Pick a thumb, any thumb at all will do."

The volunteer makes his choice and Paddy quickly whips his arms behind himself and fumbles for a moment. Then, holding his clenched fists forward he says: "Okay, okay. Which hand is it in?"

MARRIAGE
See WEDDINGS, NEWLY-WEDS

REMEMBER, Socrates died from an overdose of wedlock.

* * *

MOST marriages are happy. It is trying to live together afterwards that causes the tension.

* * *

MARRIAGES are made uneven.

* * *

MARRIAGE is the price men pay for sex and sex is the price women pay for marriage.

* * *

MARRIAGE has its good side. It teaches you loyalty, forebearance, self-restraint, and many other qualities you wouldn't need if you stayed single.

* * *

MARRIAGE is not a word, it is a sentence.

* * *

MARRIAGE is not a lottery. In a lottery you have a chance.

* * *

MARRIAGE is like a three ring circus. First the engagement ring, second the wedding ring and third the suffer-ring.

* * *

THERE'S a lot to be said about marriage. But try not to say it in front of the children.

262

STATISTICS prove that at least 50% of all people who get married at Easter are women.

* * *

IF a woman does household chores for $250 a week, that's domestic science. If she does it for nothing, that's marriage.

* * *

LAUGH, and the world laughs with you. Quarrel with your wife and you sleep alone.

MARRIAGE COUNSELLING

COUNSELLOR: "Are your relations pleasant?"
   "Mine are, his are horrible."

* * *

THE marriage counsellor asked the wife: "Did you shrink from love-making?"
   "No," she replied, "I've always been tiny like this."

* * *

"OF course we are incompatible," she said, "but he's far more incompatible than I am."

MARRIEDS

DARLING is the wife's maiden name.

* * *

THEY got off to a bad start at the altar.
   When he said "I do," she replied, "Oh no you don't," and they have been arguing ever since.

* * *

ONE month after the wedding Arthur began to wonder if he has made the right decision. Every evening meal had consisted of wedding cake and chips.

* * *

"I SHOULD never have got married, Fred."
   "Why not, Harry?"

"Because the wife hates me when I'm drunk and I can't stand the sight of her when I'm sober."

* * *

"MONEY, money, money, they are the only three words you know!"

* * *

HE said his wife doesn't understand him, but it is his own fault. He shouldn't have married a Chinese girl.

* * *

"I'VE been married five years, and believe me, when it comes to making money you've just got to hand it to Madge."

* * *

"TELL me dear, before we were married did you say you were oversexed, or over sex?"

* * *

"DOES your wife pick your clothes?"

"No, only the pockets."

* * *

"I HAVE a clever wife."

"Mine always finds out, too."

* * *

"TELL me Charles," she said. "If I died before you, would you still go to our golf club on week-ends?"

"Oh, I suppose so, dear."

"I guess, after a time, you would take up with another partner?"

"Oh, I suppose so, dear."

"Tell me Charles, would you let her use my clubs?"

"No dear, she's left-handed."

* * *

SHE nudged her husband awake when she thought she heard a burglar, but he refused to get out and investigate.

"What's happened?" she whispered. "You were brave when you married me."

"Yes, that's what all my mates said," he replied.

SHE arrived at the breakfast table in an old chenille dressing gown and her hair in rollers.

"Why can't you look like you did when I married you?" he grumbled.

"Because I'm not pregnant now," she said.

*　　*　　*

IT was another domestic that had reached the stage where they were not talking to each other. Notes were in vogue.

She found a note pinned to her pillow: "I have to be at the office early. Wake me at seven."

When he woke at 9-30, there was a note pinned to his pillow which said: "It's seven o'clock, wake up!"

*　　*　　*

THE old couple sat on the porch, as they had for many years. "I was just thinking," said the old lady, "we've had such a grand life together, but sooner or later one of us will pass on."

"Yes, but don't worry about that now," he said.

"Well I was just thinking," she said, "when it does happen, I'd like to go and live in Queensland."

*　　*　　*

REMEMBER that your wife is a romantic and still enjoys chocolates and flowers. So show her that you too remember, by speaking of them occasionally.

*　　*　　*

"WHAT'S your husband's average income?"

"About midnight."

*　　*　　*

THEY say he married her because her aunt left her a fortune.

He hotly denies it, and says he would have married her whoever left her the fortune.

*　　*　　*

MR and Mrs Offenbloo had been married for 20 years and they were still in love. She with the doctor and he with his secretary.

BLOKE came home to find his wife in bed with the next door neighbour.

"What the hell do you think you're doing?" demanded the husband.

The wife said to her bedmate: "There you are, I told you he was stupid."

* * *

THE wife was nervous as she got behind the wheel of their new car for the first time. "I hardly know what to do," she said.

"Just imagine I'm driving," he said.

* * *

"THERE must be something, even one thing," he said in a heated argument "that my family scores over your family."

She pondered for a while. "Yes. Your in-laws are better than my in-laws."

* * *

WIFE: "Before we were married you told me you were well off."

"Yes, but I didn't know it at the time."

* * *

THEY had been married for ten years. She looked up from her sewing and said: "Darling, why don't we go out tonight?"

He put his book aside and said, "What a splendid idea. And if I get home before you I will leave the light on."

MECHANICS

WHEN her date, a young mechanic, arrived to take her out she was surprised to see a set of jumper leads around his neck with the clips holding up his trousers. "My braces broke," he explained.

She gave the jumper leads a dubious look and said: "Well okay, I will come out with you. But don't start anything."

266

THE mechanic itemised the bill for the woman driver: "$100 repairs to fender, $150 repairs to the tail-light fixture, $50 for not telling your husband and $50 for running over Pete, the petrol pump attendant."

* * *

THE car mechanic went to the psychiatrist and laid down under the couch.

MISTRESSES

FRED has got so many mistresses that when he takes his wife for a drive she has to hide under the dash when they pass a woman in the street.

* * *

IZZY's wife became piqued when a woman passing their table gave Izzy the eye.

"Who's that?" she wanted to know.

"Actually, it's my mistress," explained Izzy. "She is vital for business. Got essential connections in the trade. You know how it is."

This didn't exactly calm Mrs Izzy but at that moment Mr Rozenbloom walked past with a rather brassy tart on his arm.

"Who's that woman?" demanded Mrs Izzy.

"That's Rozenbloom's mistress," explained her husband.

She pondered for a moment and then said, "Izzy, I think our mistress is much better than Rozenbloom's."

MOTHERS-IN-LAW
See FATHERS-IN-LAW

MY mother-in-law thinks I'm effeminate. But compared to her I probably am.

* * *

ONE mother-in-law to another: "I have never made a

fool of my son-in-law. I always allow him the opportunity to develop his natural capacities."

*   *   *

I NEVER forget a face. But in my mother-in-law's case, I am willing to make an exception.

*   *   *

THE local Peeping Tom knocked on the door the other night and asked if the mother-in-law would mind closing her bedroom curtains.

*   *   *

WONDERFUL woman my mother-in-law, 75 years old and never uses glasses. Drinks straight from the bottle.

*   *   *

FOR 20 years my mother-in-law and me were happy.
Then we met.

*   *   *

MY mother-in-law is musical and does a bit of singing. Yesterday she was practising and three factories knocked off for lunch.

*   *   *

MY mother-in-law has a speech impediment. Now and then she has to pause for breath.

*   *   *

FRED rented a little cottage by the sea and wired his wife that the holiday was arranged and to come and join him. But he got a shock to see both wife and mother arrive with luggage.

First chance he got he took his wife aside and whispered: "Didn't you get the telegram not to bring your mother?"

"Yes," she replied, "that's what she wants to talk to you about."

*   *   *

MARRIAGE Anonymous is a club for bachelors. If any member is tempted to get married they send over a mother-in-law in a dressing gown and hair curlers.

268

FRED was explaining to his mate at the bar that he had yet another fight with his mother-in-law.

"But at least she came crawling to me on her hands and knees this time," he said.

His mate was impressed: "Why, what did she say?"

"Come out from under the bed you pathetic, snivelling little coward and I'll clobber you again!"

* * *

BLOKE on a caravan holiday in Far North Queensland with his wife and mother-in-law was wakened one morning. His wife said her mother hadn't returned from her morning walk and she was alarmed. They searched along the river bank for a while before the wife let out a scream when she saw her mother paddling in the shallows and a large crocodile stalking her from behind.

"Oh my Gawd," screamed the wife, "Do something, quick!"

The man considered the situation for a moment and said: "The croc got himself into this trouble, let him get himself out of it."

* * *

THE same mother-in-law was kidnapped when they returned from their holiday. After three days they got a note from the kidnappers saying that if they didn't send the ransom money immediately, they would send her back.

* * *

HE complained to the doctor that he was worried about his mother-in-law. "She keeps blowing smoke rings through her nose when she talks to me."

"Nothing unusual about that," said the Doc. "Lots of people blow rings when they are smoking."

"Yeah, but my mother-in-law doesn't smoke," he said.

MOTORING

THE freeway is where drivers under 25 do over 90, and drivers over 90 do 25.

THE motorist on tour stopped his car at Oodnadatta and asked a local how to get to Tennant Creek.

"Well, I certainly wouldn't start from here," he said.

*　　*　　*

THE garage mechanic lifted the bonnet. "If I was you, sir, I'd keep the oil and change the car."

*　　*　　*

THE best thing to say for the advent of motoring, is that it has certainly stamped out horse-stealing.

*　　*　　*

CITY couple were driving in the country and stopped in a one-horse town to ask a local how to get back on the highway.

He scratched his head and said. "I don't think you can get there from here."

"It's no use asking him," said the woman to her husband. "He's stupid."

"Me? Stupid?" exclaimed the local. "I'm not the one that's lost. You two are."

*　　*　　*

COP stopped a motorist one night. "How long have you been driving without a tail light?" he asked.

The driver jumped out and went to the rear of the car and began to moan and groan. "Oh hell," he lamented.

His distress was so genuine the cop was sympathetic. "Oh c'mon Sir, it is not that serious an offence."

"Isn't it?" moaned the driver. "What about the wife and kids and the whole bloomin' caravan?"

*　　*　　*

IRISH cop stopped a motorist. "Would you be having a driver's licence?" he asked.

"Indeed I have," said the driver.

"Well that's good. Because if you didn't I'd have to see it."

*　　*　　*

SHE took her car to the service station. "What's wrong with it?" said the mechanic.

"It's got an indifferent horn," she said.

"What d'yer mean?"

"It doesn't give a hoot."

*　　*　　*

THE police stopped him because he looked as if he was a bit under the weather. He was approached with the breathalyser bag.

"What's that?" he asked.

"It tells you if you have had too much to drink," said the cop.

"Amazing. I'm married to one of them."

*　　*　　*

FRED drove his car back to the second-hand dealer.

"You remember you sold me this car last week and said its sole previous owner was a little old woman, quiet and reserved and only used the car to go to church on Sundays?"

"Yes," said the salesman a little cautiously.

"Well can you give me her name," said Fred. "I have cleaned out the boot and the glove box and I want to return her cigar butts, two empty gin bottles, a pair of silk garters with spangles on them and a pair of red knickers."

*　　*　　*

HE was parking his battered old jalopy in the main street when a policeman stopped beside him and asked if he had reported the accident.

*　　*　　*

SHE was explaining the damage to the side of their new car to her husband.

"An old man in a Ford ran into me," she said.

"Yeah, but how many times?"

*　　*　　*

"I GOT rid of that rear noise in the car."

"How?"

"I made her sit in the front with me."

MIDDLE-AGED couple were driving along when the traffic cop pulled them over. "You were travelling at 90," said the cop.

"Rubbish," said the husband, "It was only 60."

The cop insisted on 90 and the driver was getting angry, at which point his wife leaned over. "Don't argue with him officer. He's always pig-headed when he's had a few drinks."

* * *

TRAFFIC Cop: "Hey, you are blocking traffic, can't you go any faster?"

"Yes, but I don't want to leave the car."

* * *

TRAFFIC Cop: "Do you know you were doing over 100 kilometres an hour?"

"Impossible," she said. "I only left home twenty minutes ago."

* * *

HIS wife was waiting for him when he got home. "Darling," she sobbed. "I'm afraid I dented the front bumper of your new car today."

"Oh that's okay darling," he said. "Where is it?"

"In the back seat."

* * *

FRED was driving his van slowly and with great caution, but what attracted the traffic cop was the frequent stops when Fred would dash to the rear of the van and kick the back doors.

The cop stopped him and asked for an explanation.

"Well officer," he began, "I have three tonnes of budgerigars on board and if they all land at once the van's springs will collapse."

* * *

IT was Saturday and the traffic cop signalled the bloke driving the horse float to pull over.

"What's your hurry?" he said.

The trainer looked at his watch. "I have to be at the track for the first race at 1.30," he said.

The cop did a slow circumnavigation of the vehicles, looked in the float, and finally re-appeared at the driver's window.

"You've got no horses on board," he said.

"I know, I know," said the trainer. "I'm taking the non-starters aren't I?"

* * *

FOR some learner drivers, L-plates are more like destination boards.

* * *

THE distinguished old gent driving the Rolls had finally spotted a parking space and was sedately reversing into the kerb when a flash little sports car zipped in, skidded to a halt and stole the space from under his nose.

The cheeky driver hopped out and said, "You've got to be young and nippy to do that, Pops."

The old gent ignored him and the Rolls continued reversing until there was the sound of breaking glass and crunching metal and the sports car was reduced to a crumpled heap.

When he got out the old gent said: "You've got to be old and rich to do that, Sport!"

* * *

HIS car was veering from one side of the road to the other. He nearly ran off the road, when the cop pulled him up.

"You are drunk," said the cop.

"Thank goodnesh for that offisher. I thought my steering had gone."

* * *

PADDY was leaning on the bar enjoying a "point" when somebody yelled, "Hey Paddy, there's a bloke stealing your car!"

Paddy dashed from the pub but came back five minutes later all puffed out.

"Did you get him?" pressed his mates.

"No, I got close," puffed Paddy. "But it's okay, I took the number."

*   *   *

TWO Aussie tourists were motoring in England along one of those tight country lanes when the squire, in his Rolls, approached from the opposite direction. As the cars drew close the squire wound down the window, looked the Aussies in the eye and shouted, "Pigs!"

Our lads were taken aback and were still getting over the shock when, right around the next bend, they ran into a herd of pigs.

MOVIES

HE said he saw a good film last night. It was called Moby Dick.

"I don't like sex films," she replied.

He said it wasn't about sex. "It was about whales."

"I don't like the Welsh either," she said.

*   *   *

WHEN the matron's eyes got accustomed to the dark she realised a young lad was sitting beside her.

"Why aren't you at school?" she said.

"Because I've got chicken pox," he replied.

*   *   *

A WOMAN rushed from the front stalls to tell the manager she had been molested. He tried to calm her down but when two more complained about the same thing he thought he had better investigate. In the second row he found a man on his hands and knees.

"I've lost my toupé," said the luckless patron. "I had my hand on it three times but it got away."

*   *   *

A MOVIE star is a person who strives for years to be well-known, then goes down side streets with dark glasses to avoid being recognised.

A HOLLYWOOD marriage is a great way to spend a weekend.

* * *

HE was only six years old, but he decided to take his girlfriend to the movies.

"How much is it?" he asked at the box office.

"Well, sonny, for grown ups in long pants it is eight dollars, but as you are only wearing short pants it is four dollars."

"Well in that case," piped up his girlfriend, "I should get in for nothing!"

* * *

THEY snuggled down in the stalls at the movies, but the woman in front was wearing a large hat which obstructed their view. He tapped her on the shoulder. She turned round and it was his wife.

MULTI-NATIONAL

THE author just happens to be multi-national. He's part Irish and part Italian. That's Irish from his mother's side, and Italian by a friend of his father's.

* * *

BEFORE this country became multi-cultural a traditional Australian seven-course meal consisted of a six-pack and a pie.

* * *

AN Englishman, an Australian and a Scotsman were invited to a party. The Englishman took six bottles of Guiness, the Aussie took six cans of beer, and the Scotsman took six of his friends.

* * *

THREE soldiers met in the pub. The Australian stood a round, the Englishman stood a round and the Scotsman stood six feet tall.

"I'M Murphy, Irish, and proud of it."

"I'm McTavish, Scotch, and fond of it!"

* * *

IF a paddock full of Irishmen is a Paddy Field, then a paddock full of Ockers must be a vacant lot.

* * *

WHEN Paddy emigrated from Ireland to Australia, it lifted the IQ of both countries.

* * *

YOU can tell a Pommie, but you can't tell him much.

* * *

A LAZY German lives by the sweat of his frau.

* * *

BRITONS have an infinite capacity for churning themselves up into a terrific calmness.

* * *

A SCOTSMAN had been playing the pools and eventually won £500,000.

"We've made it at last," he told his wife.

"What are you going to do about the begging letters?" she asked.

"Keep sending them I suppose," he replied.

* * *

AN Irishman went for a job and was told he would have to pass an IQ test. When he asked what an IQ was the employer explained that anyone with an IQ of 150 would be admitted to university, but a bloke with an IQ of 50 would have trouble tying his shoe laces.

"Oh," said the Irishman, "So that's why so many Australians wear thongs."

* * *

IT was the bad old days and an Englishman, an Irishman and a Jew were sentenced to 50 lashes. The commandant said the rules allowed for oil or ointment on their backs.

"Then I will have olive oil, please," said the Englishman.

The Irishman was defiant. "I despise the English. I'll have nothing on my back, because I'm tough."

Then the Jew was asked what he wanted on his back.

"The Irishman," he said.

*　　*　　*

THREE different nationalities were discussing the meaning of 'savoir faire'.

The American said, "It means that if you came home and found your wife in bed with another man and you refrained from killing the son of a bitch, that's 'savoir faire'."

The Englishman said: "Hardly chaps. If you found your wife in bed with another man and excused yourself for interrupting and invited them to carry on, well that's 'savoir faire'."

The Frenchman had a different view: "If you came home and found your wife in bed with another man and you said 'Please continue, monsieur' and he was able to, then HE'S got 'savoir faire'."

*　　*　　*

IT was Luigi's first day on the job, high on the scaffolding of the 51st level of a sky scraper when the hook of a crane knocked him off balance.

He fell into the rubbish shoot, and for the next five minutes he crashed, banged and walloped his way to the ground until he was discharged in a cloud of dust on the footpath.

"Where the hell did you come from?" asked the surprised foreman.

"Italy," said Luigi.

*　　*　　*

PADDY got into a fight at the pub and was knocked down five times.

"Well, have you had enough?" said his much bigger opponent.

"Don't know," said Paddy. "This is my first fight."

THE Scottish publican picked up the phone to hear a voice say that there was a bomb planted under the pub and it would go off in ten minutes.

He put the phone down and called: "Last orders, gents!"

* * *

AND what's the difference between a Scotsman and a coconut?

You can get a drink out of a coconut.

* * *

TWO Scots met in Collins Street. They hadn't seen each other since they migrated from Edinburgh together 25 years ago. They hugged and slapped each other on the shoulder.

"Let's have a drink, like we did in the old times," said Jock.

"Aye, and don't forget, it's your shout," said the other.

* * *

THE Greek businessman went to his favorite taverna and was surprised to be served by a Vietnamese waiter who spoke perfect Greek.

When paying his bill to Con the proprietor he raised the point. "How come the waiter speaks perfect Greek?" he asked Con.

"Ssh! Don't mention it. He thinks it's English."

* * *

NEW Zealanders get the mickey taken out of them because of their funny accents when ordering "fush and chups." But we know of a chap in Auckland, when out with his girlfriend and two other couples, who went into a restaurant and ordered "a table for sex," and then added, "and three pillows."

* * *

THE Chinese take-away and the Greek fruit shop were side by side, and each Friday morning the two owners would sweep the pavement.

Con the Greek would take the opportunity to have his little joke: "What day is it today, Charlie?"

"It's Fliday," the Chinaman would reply, and Con would roll about laughing.

Each week it was the same and Con would even get some friends to come along and listen to Charlie say "Fliday."

It got on Charlie's wick. So he went along for elocution lessons and concentrated on "Friday, Friday, Friday."

Next morning he was waiting for the big showdown, sweeping a clean pavement for ten minutes before Con appeared. "What day is it today, Charlie," grinned Con.

"It's Friday … you Gleek plick!"

*   *   *

RED Adair's fame in quelling oil rig fires stretches around the globe, so when a well in the middle of the Sahara Desert spewed smoke and flame the alert went out: "Get Red Adair."

But Red had his hands full with a fire crisis on the other side of the world, and nobody can be in two places at the same time. The Exon magnates were frantic. Without the famous Red Adair they were in heaps of trouble.

"Why not try Green Adair?" suggested a lackey.

"Who?" But as the flames roared higher in the sky, why not try Green Adair indeed.

Green Adair was contacted in the Limerick Arms in Belfast and offered one million pounds to do the job.

Within a few hours the oil engineers were amazed to see an air transport land in the desert. They gasped as the nose of the aircraft opened and a truck, bearing Green Adair and his crew sped towards the fire. They watched in amazement as the truck approached the wall of flames and disappeared into the very heart of the fire. They could see Green Adair and his men leaping about, jumping and stamping out the flames.

Finally, all charred, singed and blackened they emerged from the smoke to the cheers of their incredulous admirers.

"What will you do with the million pounds?" asked the first reporter on the scene.

"The first thing I do," said Green Adair, "will be to get some brakes for that bloomin' truck!"

*　　*　　*

IN a pub Harry the car dealer was trying to flog a heap of junk parked outside to a Chinese student.

"It's a reliable car," said Harry. "It is yours for five hundred dollars, but if you have the cash I will take off 20%."

The student was too shrewd to admit he didn't understand the discount and said he would think it over.

When he got the chance he asked the barmaid quietly, "If I give you five hundred dollars, how much you take off?"

"Everything except my earrings, honey. No worries."

*　　*　　*

THREE men answered an advertisement to join a mining survey expedition into the Outback. They were a Scotsman, a German, and a Chinaman. The boss said the Scotsman would be in charge of the engineers, the German would be in charge of the mechanics, and the Chinaman, well, they are all good cooks, so he said the Chinaman could be in charge of supplies. "But we leave promptly at eight tomorrow," he said.

Next morning, the Scot and the German showed up, but there was no sign of the Chinaman. They waited for half an hour before the boss gave a curse and ordered that they set off without him.

The party had travelled only a few hundred metres up the road when the Chinaman jumped out from behind a tree and shouted: "Supplies, supplies!"

AN Englishman, American and an Irishman were arrested in South America for smuggling. "We'll give you gringos a fair trial and shoot you tomorrow," said the "capitan" of the guard.

The three spent a restless night. "But not to worry, chaps," said the Englishman. "I shall invoke the natural disaster plan. These South Americans are terrified of natural disaster. Just watch me."

So at dawn the Englishman said he would face the firing squad first and the other two watched from their cell as the capitan said "Ready ... Aim ..."

"Earthquake! Earthquake!" roared the Englishman at the top of his voice. The South Americans panicked and in the confusion the Pommie escaped.

Later the American was led to the stake and the capitan said: "Ready ... Aim..."

"Flood! Flood!" roared the Yank and in the confusion he escaped too.

The Irishman had picked up the drift of the plot. It was all a matter of timing, so he listened as the capitan ordered, "Ready... Aim..."

"Fire!" yelled the Irishman.

★   ★   ★

JILL, she was a pretty girl,
and Jack, an ardent male
He praised her shapely beauty
In English, French,
And Braille.

MUSIC

THE serious music lover is the bloke who, hearing a soprano in the bathroom, puts his ear to the keyhole.

★   ★   ★

AN earnest young man with a violin case under his arm asked a London Bobby: "How do I get to the Albert Hall?"

The bobby replied: "Practice, practice, practice."

THE old lady asked the busker: "Do you always play by ear?"

"No, Ma'am, sometimes I play over there."

* * *

"WHY do you play the same piece all the time?"

"It haunts me."

"So it should. You've murdered it often enough."

* * *

"I AM always breaking into song."

"Well, if you found the right key you wouldn't have to break in."

* * *

"CAN you sing opera?"

"Yes."

"Can you sing Faust?"

"Faust or slow, any way you like."

* * *

PADDY Murphy thought the Guinness Book of Records was an LP of Irish drinking songs.

* * *

AFTER the concert she said, "My word, that soprano had a wonderful repertoire."

"Yes," he said, "and that tight dress showed it off well."

* * *

THE Scotsman said his singing voice was a natural gift.

We all agreed, it would have to be.

* * *

HE was a short-sighted musician, and one day he fell over a clef.

* * *

SHE went out with a musician once, and has never been composed since.

* * *

I CAN'T sing. So I am looking for a ravishing blonde accompanist who can't play the piano.

INTRIGUED by the complications in trying to fold road maps while seated in a Mini Minor, Arthur persevered until he became a celebrated accordian player.

* * *

HE had just landed on English shores from Dublin and went straight to a pub and bought a round of beers.

"Will an Irish tenner be alright?" he asked the barman.

When the barman replied, "no problem" he broke out in the chorus of "Oh Danny Boy..."

* * *

FRED played the trombone and eventually got a gig in Las Vegas. Tired from the long flight he booked into the swank hotel and turned in early but was awakened by a knock on the door about midnight.

"Hello there," said a ravishing brunette. "Are you Frank Sinatra?"

"No Miss, I'm Fred Nerd from Moonee Ponds, Melbourne," and he shut the door and climbed back into bed.

An hour later there was another knock. Fred wearily opened the door to see a lovely redhead. "Hi there, are you Frank Sinatra?"

"No," he said, "I'm Fred Nerd," and slammed the door and dived back into the blankets.

You've guessed it, there was yet another knock on the door. This time a ravishing blonde wearing a see-through negligee says: "Hello, are you Frank Sinatra?"

"Am I Frankie, baby?" And throwing his arms out wide Fred starts singing at the top of his voice, "Strangers in the night ... New York, New York ..."

* * *

THE old maestro had fallen on hard times, mainly due to tippling the whisky bottle. He had been a concert pianist of great renown in his time and his drinking pals at the Pig and Whistle decided they should be responsible for putting him back on the concert circuit.

They chipped in and bought an old tuxedo from the Opportunity Shop, not knowing that the trousers had a split in the crotch.

They booked him for the next benefit concert at the Mechanics' Hall and lined the front row on the opening night. When the maestro came on stage, bowed and sat on his chair at the piano there was a gasp of concern from the front row, and one of his friends was so bold as to leap onto the stage and whisper.

"Do you know your old flannel shirt is flapping through a hole in your tuxedo?"

"No," said the maestro thoughtfully, "But if you hum the tune I will soon pick up the melody!"

* * *

A SAILOR who had been six months at sea was hunting the waterfront looking for a bar where he could have a quiet drink. He inspected a few, but the one that took his fancy had a South Sea Island motif, a monkey swinging around the chandelier and a pianist tinkling out a tune in the corner.

He went in and ordered a martini. As the barman put the drink on the counter the monkey swung down from the rafters, spun around and dunked his feet in the glass.

Naturally, the sailor reacted with loud abuse at the barman.

"Did you see that!" he roared. "Get me another drink."

The barman dutifully delivered another martini and set it on the bar, but before the sailor could reach for the glass the monkey dropped from the roof again, spun round and once more dunked his feet in the drink.

The sailor was furious. He gripped the barman by the shirt-front and lifted him across the bar.

"It's not my monkey. Not my monkey," protested the barman. "It belongs to the pianist over there."

The sailor dropped the bartender on the floor and strode over to the pianist.

"Do you know your monkey is paddling his feet in my martini,?" he roared.

"No," replied the pianist thoughtfully, "But if you hum the tune I'll soon pick up the melody!"

* * *

THE guest had heard the strains of classical music but when he entered the drawing room he was amazed to see a large tomcat playing the piano.

"And there is no music," he noted with further astonishment.

"No," said the proud owner. "He writes his own music, and the piece he is playing now is one of my favourites."

"You should have it orchestrated," said the guest.

The cat leapt out of the window and has never been seen since.

* * *

THE busker was repeating the same old tune on the corner of the street until the lady shopkeeper came out and said: "Do you play the refrain?"

"Yes Ma'am," he said.

"Then would you please refrain from playing it here," she said.

* * *

THE vicar's sermon was again interrupted by the arrival of yet another late straggler. "There have been more late entries than an Irish orchestra," he said.

* * *

HE is an original player. He makes a lot of mistakes, but they are always different each time.

* * *

AN Indian psychiatrist from New Delhi visiting Salt Lake City called at the local asylum and heard the inmates singing. Investigating further he saw a large group of choristers holding an apple and tapping the apple with the other hand. "Are they inmates?' he asked.

"No, that's the Moron Tap-an-Apple Choir," he was told.

So he hot-footed it back to India and told Indira Ghandi that there was a lot of money to be made with choirs.

Hadn't the Vienna Boys Choir been successful?

So they got 500 young boys together and trained them for weeks until they were ready for their first audition before a visiting Italian maestro. He listened to their first rendition with eyes averted and then said "terrible, terrible. They are not castrata." Indira Ghandi was told they had to have that little operation that made all the difference. They did and they were ultimicimo, and began their world tour as the Indian Nackerless 500.

*   *   *

THE band had just finished its first bracket when the master of ceremonies came on stage. "Ladies and gentlemen. I have wonderful news. Our band leader's wife has just presented him with a fine bouncing baby boy. I would like the proud father to stand and take a bow.

As the leader stood and bowed, so did the entire band behind him.

*   *   *

IN the orchestra he plays piano. At home he plays second fiddle.

*   *   *

MY brother was known as the Van Gogh of the violin. He had no ear for it.

*   *   *

MY sister used to play the banjo until she married. Now she picks on her husband.

*   *   *

THE young musician with a violin case under his arm was boasting of his prowess.

"The director of the National Symphony Orchestra was trying to get me for months."

"Who were you playing with at the time?"

"His wife!"

286

IT was amateur night down at the local and Fred stood on the table and rendered "An Irish Lullaby."

He noticed one young lady reach for a handkerchief and wipe a tear from her eye. Thinking she was overcome with emotion he later approached her.

"Are you Irish then?"

"No," she said with a sob. "I'm a music teacher."

* * *

THE professor had a theory that music would sooth the savage beast so he took his violin and trekked deep into the jungle of darkest Africa. All around were the roars and screams of ferocious animals.

When he came to a little clearing he opened the violin case and began playing classical music. One by one the animals came out to listen, and soon, sitting quietly in a circle, was an elephant, a gorilla, three buffalo, a few snakes and a pair of tigers.

They were listening enraptured, when with a loud roar a lion sprang into the clearing and bit off the professor's head.

"What did you do that for?" chorused the other animals. "First time we get to hear lovely music and you spoil it," they said.

The lion cupped a paw to his ear and said "Eh?"

* * *

FRED has a musical nature
He can yodel, whistle and hum
He goes out fit as a fiddle
And comes home tight as a drum.

N

NAMES

RUTH is stranger than fiction.

* * *

I WAS born on the first of the month, so they called me Bill.

* * *

ARE you chewing gum?
  No, I'm Harry McGillicardy.

* * *

"I LOVE men who are frank."
  "Bad luck. My name's Algernon.

* * *

"WHAT are the names of your parents?"
  "Mum and Dad."

* * *

THE new vicar in town even entered the country pub in a bid to introduce himself and approached an old-timer at the bar with outstretched hand.
  "My name is Paul," he said.
  The old-timer studied him for a moment and then said: "Did those Thessalonians ever write back to you?"

* * *

THE track official approached the new athlete. "Are you a pole vaulter?"

"Yes," he replied, "I am from Gdansk. But how did you know my name vas Valter?"

* * *

AS the MC said when introducing the prime minister: "I am keen on genealogy. I've made a study of names and I can tell you that Keating means bright and intelligent.

Unfortunately, Paul means 'Not Very'."

(Change name to suit guest of honour).

NEIGHBOURS

EVER since we put the "Neighbourhood Watch" sign on our gate every nosey neighbour comes in and wants to know the time.

* * *

IT'S been tough keeping up with the Jones. Especially since Tom moved next door.

* * *

DON'T keep trying to keep up with the Joneses. Drag them down to your level.

* * *

BERT stuck his head over the fence and asked Fred if he could borrow his mower.

"Sorry, Bert," said Fred. "The neighbour on the other side has had it for a week. I've just got it back and I've got to cut my own lawn. It will take me all day."

"In that case then," said Bert, "you won't mind if I borrow your golf clubs?"

* * *

THE easiest way to meet your new neighbours is to play the stereo full blast at 2 a.m.

* * *

A NEIGHBOUR is a person who listens to you attentively, through a wall.

A GOOD neighbour is the one who, when borrowing a corkscrew, says bring it over.

NEWLY-WEDS

HERE today, gone home to-momma.

* * *

HE has a problem about the future. He's getting married in a month and he hasn't found a job for his wife.

* * *

A YOUNG bride was explaining her problem to her long-married friend. "How can I keep my husband in line?" she asked.

Her older and wiser friend didn't hesitate: "My dear," she said, "your husband shouldn't have to wait in line!"

* * *

THE newly-weds had been married for a month and some of the novelty appeared to be wearing off.

"Well I'm getting sick of the same meal morning noon and night," he complained. "Nothing but wedding cake and chips."

* * *

SHE had served him so many burnt offerings that on their first anniversary he bought her an altar cloth.

* * *

THE new husband sat down at the table after his young bride had just cooked her first chicken.

"What did you stuff it with?" he asked in hungry anticipation.

"I didn't stuff it," she said. "It wasn't hollow!"

* * *

BILL and Beryl had been married only a few weeks when Bill had to travel interstate on a job. While he was away, Beryl's sister Betty moved in to keep her company.

Bill finished the job sooner than expected and was

quickly on a plane home. When he arrived at the airport he dashed to a phone.

Betty answered the call.

"Is Beryl there?" he asked.

"No, she's having a bath," said Betty.

"Don't disturb her then. Just tell her to put a couple of stubbies in the fridge and I will be home about midnight. Tell her to put on her sheerest nightie and a dab of perfume and I will sneak in and wake her with a kiss."

"Okay, and who will I say called?" asked Betty.

*　　*　　*

HE had only been married six months when he confided to his mate: "I've just had a terrible shock. I have just discovered my wife is a liar."

"How do you know?" asked his mate.

"She said she was out with Betty last night. But I was out with Betty last night!"

*　　*　　*

THE newlyweds had just settled on their farm and she brought his lunch out to the home paddock. As he was finishing his last sandwich a little red hen dashed by being chased by a rooster. He threw the rooster a piece of crust and it stopped dead in its tracks and began to peck the bread.

"I hope you never get that hungry," mused the bride.

*　　*　　*

"HOUSEWORK, it's so boring," said the first-year bride. "You make the beds, clean the floors and do the dishes. Then three months later you have to do it all again."

*　　*　　*

(R) THE new bride was too embarrassed to talk about sex, so the groom explained it as delicately as he could.

"No need to talk about it," he said. "Whenever we are in bed and you want it, just pull it once. If you don't want it, just pull it about 350 times."

NEWSPAPERS

NEWSPAPERS are still credible, provided you read between the lies.

* * *

YOU should never tell a journalist what you don't want to read in the papers.

* * *

LIKE a dead wombat, a good journalist always keeps his ear to the ground.

* * *

THE reporter was pressing the old gent on his 100th birthday as to why he had lived so long.

"Two reasons," said the old-timer, "The first is my life-long practice of having two whiskies a day."

"And second?" asked the reporter eagerly.

"Cancelling my voyage on the Titanic," said the old gent.

* * *

NEWS Flash! A helicopter crashed into the cemetery of an Irish village this afternoon. At last count, 705 bodies had been recovered.

* * *

THE Free Press: Where three men impose their prejudices on 15 million.

* * *

SHE was only the newsagent's daughter, but she loved her Daily Mail.

* * *

MY dad was an old newspaper man. He went broke. Nobody wanted old newspapers.

* * *

AS a reporter he was trained to ask Who? What? Where? When? and Why? Then his first assignment turned out to be a wedding.

"PAPER, paper, gigantic fraud!" roared the newsboy. "Fifty-six victims in gigantic fraud!"

Chap stopped to buy a paper and quickly scanned the front page.

"Just a minute," he said. "This is yesterday's and there's nothing about a fraud."

"Paper, paper! Fifty-seven victims in gigantic fraud," roared the paperboy.

* * *

THE advertisement in the local newspaper read: "Editor urgently needs poof reader."

* * *

LETTER to the advertising manager. "Last Friday I lost a gold watch which was a valuable heirloom. I advertised in the Lost and Found column of your Saturday edition with almost immediate results. Yesterday I found the watch in the pocket of another suit in my wardrobe. Congratulations."

* * *

A FRONT page panel on the newspaper read: The Daily Bugle was the first to report the death of Cr Grabalot, and was the first to announce that this report was untrue. The Daily Bugle is always first with the news.

* * *

CORRECTION: The China Seafood Restaurant advertisement in Saturday's edition was incorrect. It read #/ @%**%#. It should have read !**&/#@*&##. We regret any inconvenience this may have caused.

* * *

THE businessman stopped by the newsboy. "Anything new in the paper today?" he asked.

"Naw," said the lad. "Just the same things happening to different people."

* * *

THE country newspaper was prospering so well with advertising it couldn't cater for all the news. The pointer on the front page explained it all: "On account of lack of space this week, 15 births and three deaths have been held over until next issue."

* * *

IT was rare for the Archbishop of Canterbury to visit a small town so at the press conference the local reporter desperately wanted to scoop his metropolitan rivals. He managed to get the first question away: "Will you be visiting the nightclubs?"

The archbishop was a little surprised. "Are there nightclubs in this small town?" he said.

The newspaper had its headline. "ARCHBISHOP'S FIRST WORDS: ARE THERE ANY NIGHTCLUBS IN THIS TOWN?"

* * *

IT had been a slow day, so when a bloke got hit by a bus, reporters from both rival newspapers were on the scene. One was a seasoned journo, the other was a cadet.

Next day the cadet's editor called him in to show that the old scribe had gleaned a more interesting item from a routine event. It happened to be the victim's birthday.

"Ask more questions," roared the editor.

The lad was a quick learner and at his very next accident he crawled under an overturned bus to reach a moaning victim to ask, with notebook in hand: "Don't suppose it's your birthday today?"

* * *

HE was sent to cover the earthquake and began his first bulletin with "God has caused tremendous devastation ..."

He received an urgent message from his editor: "Forget the earthquake. Interview God."

* * *

AT the press conference the boring politician groaned along on his dreary speech, ad nauseum, until one reporter, a little the worse for drink, actually threw a bottle at him.

Unfortunately it missed the politician and hit another journalist a glancing blow on the head, to which his immediate response was: "Hit me again, I can still hear the bludger."

* * *

THE cadet had been assigned to do the annual story on Colonel Frobisher. "He has the reputation of being England's bravest soldier," said the editor. "The story has been done before, but if you can get a new angle, then you are well on the way m'lad."

The cadet went off to the Old Soldier's Home with the advice of his chief still ringing in his ears. "If only there was a time Frobisher had been scared ..."

He found the colonel sitting in his wheelchair and soon came to the point. "Surely, Sir, surely there was a time when you were frightened?"

The colonel looked thoughtful for a while. "Well there was the time I was with the fusiliers in India and this rogue tiger had eaten two or three of the native chaps," he began.

"I remember tracking the beast through the jungle, followed his tracks and got a glimpse of him hiding behind some tall grass.

"I cocked my gun and crept right up to the grassy patch and I was about to peep through when the monster leapt straight at me and roared 'Aaaarrgh!' My God, I shit myself."

The cadet whipped out his notebook. "When was that?" he asked eagerly, "when was that?"

"Just then when I went 'Aaaarrgh'," said the colonel.

* * *

A SUB-EDITOR had doubts about a cadet's story on a farmer who had lost 2025 pigs from a small farm in the outer suburbs. It seemed too many pigs, so the sub rang the farmer.

"Is it true that you owned two thousand and twenty-five pigs?"

"Yeth," lisped the pig farmer. "That wath the thituation."

The sub said thanks, hung up and corrected the copy to read: Two sows and 25 pigs.

*　　*　　*

THE businessman was testifying that advertising got results. "We advertised for a nightwatchman, and that very same night our safe was robbed," he said.

*　　*　　*

A SHARK alarm at Bondi sent everyone rushing from the surf, except three young boys who didn't hear the siren. Those on the beach were aghast to see the dorsel fin moving towards them.

A tall, blonde, bronzed young man took a deep breath and plunged into the surf, swam right past the shark and brought in two of the boys.

He took another deep breath and plunged through the surf again to snatch the third boy from the jaws of the monster.

When all three were safe on the beach he took yet another deep breath and with a knife between his teeth, swam out for a third time to tackle the shark in a struggle to its death.

When he finally staggered up the beach a reporter who had witnessed it all ran up to him. "That's the most heroic feat I have ever witnessed. What's yer name? This is bound to make the front page tomorrow. I can just see the headlines: AUSSIE HERO KILLS SHARK, SAVES THREE!"

The young man interrupted him. "Thanks, that's nice of you, but I must correct you on one point. I am not Australian. I am an Englishman out here on holidays."

The reporter looked a bit crestfallen but said, "No worries, it's still a great story."

The headlines next day read: "POMMIE BASTARD KILLS KIDS' PET!"

HEADLINES:

"DON'T PRINT STORY OF MY DIVORCE" sobs Actress. See sensational exclusive, page 7.

WOMAN RECOVERING AFTER FATAL CRASH

POLICE MOVE IN BOOK CASE

BISHOP TURNS SOD

*   *   *

AFTER a man escaped from an asylum, raping a washer-woman as he fled, the headline that afternoon read: NUT SCREWS WASHER AND BOLTS.

*   *   *

THE sub was handling a sports report from the local cricket club secretary who spelt bowling, b-o-e-l-i-n-g. "That," said the sub, "is the worst spell of bowling I have seen."

*   *   *

AND full credit to American journalist William Safire for this advice on, How to Write Good:

Avoid run-on sentences they are hard to read.

No sentence fragments.

It behoves us to avoid archaisms.

Also, avoid awkward or affected alliteration.

Don't use no double negatives.

If I've told you once, I've told you a thousand times: resist hyperbole.

Avoid commas, that are not necessary.

Verbs has to agree with their subjects.

Avoid trendy locutions that sound flaky.

Writing carefully, dangling participles should not be used.

Kill all exclamation marks!!!

Never use a long word when a diminutive one will do.

Poofread carefully to see if you any words out.

Take the bull by the hand, and don't mix metaphors.

Don't verb nouns.

297

Never, ever use repetitive redundancies.
Last but not least, avoid cliches like the plague.

*   *   *

THERE was a young lady from Stawell
  Wore a newspaper dress to a ball
  But her garb caught on fire
  And burned her entire
  Front page, sports section and all.

O

OCKERS ABROAD

KEVIN and Bruce had overstayed their English holiday and were in desperate need of a job, so the advertisement they saw in the "Times" was most appropriate. It read: "Two butlers needed for Scottish country manor. References a must."

The references were an initial problem, but was solved with simple Aussie ingenuity. Keven wrote Bruce's reference and Bruce gave Kevin a splendid wrap.

When they were ushered before the lady of the manor they proffered their references but she waved them aside. "Later," she said, "First, I'd like to check your knees. Formal wear here means wearing kilts so if you would be so kind as to drop the tweeds ..." The lads thought it a little strange, but they did so.

"Not bad," she said. "Now you can show me your testimonials."

When they picked themselves up from the gravel driveway, Kevin said: "With a little more education we would have got that job."

*   *   *

TWO Ockers from the same town met in London. "Fancy meeting you over here," said Bruce to Merv. "Listen mate, you've got to come over to my flat tomorrow night. We're having a small gathering."

Merv said he'd be in like Flynn.

"Get the tube to Earl's Court, straight down the High Street, second on the right, number 35 and you can ring the bell with your elbows."

"What's with the elbows bit?" said Merv.

"Well you're not coming without bottles are ya?"

*   *   *

AT the Ockers picnic they were selling coffee at 50 cents a mug. The queue of mugs stretched back around the corner.

*   *   *

THE pretty fraulein approached the Ocker at the Munich beer hall and invited him to her flat. She gave him a nice meal and he stayed the night.

In the morning after a hearty breakfast he was about to leave and made a little speech about the outstanding hospitality he had received.

"Ja, the words are nice," she said, "but what about marks?"

"Bloomin' oath, nine out of ten I reckon," he said.

ODDS

I KNOW a woman who has got more brains in her head than I've got in my little finger.

*   *   *

"DO you know a bloke with one leg called Moloney?"

"No. What's the name of his other leg?"

*   *   *

"HEY Fred, what's Billie's other name?"

"Billie who?"

*   *   *

ETHYL says her husband is a man of few words, and every one of them unprintable.

*   *   *

"FRED'S taken up meditation."

"Well, that's better than sitting around doing nothing."

HE spent a fortune on deodorant before he realised that people didn't like him anyway.

* * *

"WHAT'S that mark on your shoulder?"
  "A birthmark."
  "Had it long?"

* * *

A SNAIL got rich and fulfilled a lifelong dream by buying a racing car and lodging an entry in the Grand Prix. He painted the letter "S" for snail on the side of his speedy machine and when he raced down the straight the crowd roared: "Look at that "S" car go."

* * *

THE nun who always slept with her clothes on just couldn't get out of the habit.

OFFICE

THE boss is the bloke in the office who is late when you are early, and early when you are late.

* * *

HE nervously faced the boss: "My wife told me to ask you for a rise."
  "Okay. I will ask my wife if you can have one."

* * *

TESTY boss: "Answer that phone."
  "It hasn't rung yet."
  "Well, why do you have to wait until the last minute?"
  And to the latecomer: "You should have been here at nine o"clock."
  "Why, what happened?"

* * *

HE advertised for a secretary: "Wanted. Young lady assistant who can type. One who has no bad habits and is willing to learn."

301

THE boss's secretary had been hired for her legs and figure, but her sloppy arithmetic was getting too much to bear.

Finally, the boss said, "Next time you deliver the day's figures make sure you add up the column at least three times."

She went one better the very next day. "Mister Smithers, I have added these figures ten times," she said dropping the papers on his desk with a dazzling smile, "and here are my ten answers."

* * *

"WHAT do you think of our new boss?"

"He dresses smartly."

"And quickly too!"

* * *

THE salesman set the computer up on the executive's desk at W.F. Fotheringham & Son. "This is the latest technology, Mr Fotheringham," he said. "Ask it any question. Even personal questions."

The executive was sceptical. "Okay," he said, and typed in: "Where is my father?"

The answer came back instantly: "Your father is playing golf at Royal Melbourne."

"There you are," said the boss. "It's wrong. My father died five years ago."

The salesman was surprised, but not flustered. "He typed in: "Where, exactly, is Mr Fotheringham senior?"

The answer was just as prompt. "Mr Fotheringham senior died five years ago, but Bill Fotheringham's dad is still at the seventh green at Royal Melbourne!"

* * *

SOME couldn't spell, others couldn't type, few could do shorthand. The businessman who wanted a private secretary was about to despair when the employment agency phoned to say they were sending round a girl who had a number of things going for her.

302

She turned out to be a ravishing long-legged blonde, and the business executive was immediately entranced.

"I'll pay you $500 a week, with pleasure," he said.

"With pleasure, will be $1000 a week," she said.

* * *

NOTICE in the office: In an effort to spread the work more evenly would all staff take advantage of the stenographers earlier in the day!

* * *

GLOSSARY of Management terms:

Delegate: Pass the buck.

Pending: Haven't figured it out yet.

Delayed: Forgotten.

Urgency: Panic.

Extreme urgency: Blind panic.

Frank discussion: Bloody argument.

Analytical projection: Guess.

Forecast: Guess.

Long-range forecast: Wild guess.

Scheduled: Hoped for.

Deficiency analysis: Search for scapegoat.

Ambitious: Ruthless.

Strategy: Low cunning.

Shrewd: Devious.

Profit: Profit.

Profit before tax: Loss.

Deficit: Staggering loss.

Industrial by-product: Waste.

Environmental pollution: Other people's waste.

Pilfering: Theft by employee.

Fringe benefit: Theft by executive.

Terminal payment: Golden handshake.

Supplementary statistical information: Padding.

OLD CODGERS

DO not complain about growing old. Many are denied the privilege.

* * *

FRED was determined to keep healthy in his old age, and when he turned 60 he decided to walk five kilometres every day. He has now reached Adelaide.

* * *

BY the time you reach 75 years of age you've learnt everything. All you have to do is to try and remember it.

* * *

A GERIATRIC is a German cricketer who captures three successive wickets.

* * *

EVEN the parish priest was a welcome visitor for short-sighted Mrs Flannigan. "But that wasn't the priest," said her daughter after the man had left, "that was the doctor."

"Oh was it?" she exclaimed with relief, "I thought Father O'Reilly was getting rather familiar."

* * *

MRS Flannigan described herself as a sprightly old girl. "Actually I see seven gentlemen a day," she said. "I get out of bed with Will Power, then I go to my John, next it's breakfast with Uncle Toby, followed by Billy T.

Then the rest of the day is spent with either Arthur Ritis or Al Zymer until I finally go to bed with Johnny Walker.

* * *

OLD Fred fronted up to the Sperm Bank and insisted on making a donation. The matron looked at him doubtfully. He was 83. But Fred would not be denied and protested that he was as fit as a prize bull.

Finally she gave Fred a little jar, ushered him towards

304

a cubicle and closed the door. For the next few minutes all she could hear was much grunting and puffing and it went on for so long she got worried. She knocked on the door.

"Are you okay?" she called

"No. I need some help," said Fred. "I can't get the lid off this bloody jar."

* * *

THE old gent was backing his Rolls into the last available parking space when a zippy red sports car whipped in behind him to take the spot. The young man jumped out and said: "Sorry Pops, but you've got to be young and smart to do that."

The old man ignored the remark and kept reversing until the Rolls had crunched the sportscar into a crumpled heap. "Sorry son, you've got to be old and rich to do that!"

* * *

AN old bloke was sitting at the bar sobbing with the odd tear dropping in his beer. "I got married to a lovely young widow last week," he explained to the barman. "She is a great cook, keeps my clothes in great nick and is insatiable in bed," he said.

"Then why the hell are your crying?" said the barman.

"Because I can't remember where I live," sobbed the old codger.

* * *

OLD Jake went for his annual medical check-up. "Your hearing is getting worse," said the Doc. "And you will have to cut out drinking, smoking and sex."

"What?" cried Jake in alarm, "Just so I can hear better?"

* * *

A YOUNG social worker used to call on Old Jake to cut up his steak and help with his meals. She noticed a bowl of almonds beside his tray. "They were given to me as a present, but I don't want them," he explained. "You can have them."

She said thanks and began to nibble away on them. "Funny present to give a man with no teeth," she remarked when she had eaten most of them.

"Oh no," he said. "They had chocolate on them then."

*　　*　　*

THE doctor had examined Old Jake's heart and summed up his advice with "No smoking, no drinking and no sex."

After much protesting by Jake the doctor relented: "Okay, one cigarette only after meals, and no more than two glasses of light beer a day.

"What about sex?" pressed Jake.

"Very occasionally," said the doctor, "and only with your wife because it is important you avoid any excitement."

*　　*　　*

AN old chap in his seventies was concerned about the lack of his sex drive and consulted his doctor.

"Well, what would you expect at your age?" said the medic.

The old geezer was still worried, "But my nextdoor neighbour is over eighty and he says he gets it every night."

The doc thought for a moment. "Well, why don't you say it too?"

*　　*　　*

A COUPLE of old timers were discussing their sexual situation. "You know Jack," said one, "I understand that drinking stout will put lead in your pencil. Why don't we try a bottle?"

"I don't know about you," replied Jack, "but I don't have that many women to write to."

*　　*　　*

ON his morning round the doctor stopped beside the little old lady he had been treating for asthma. He checked her over, asked a few questions and listened to her croaky replies.

"What about the wheeze?" he said.

"Oh, fine," she replied. "I went three times last night!"

* * *

THREE old codgers had been playing cards for a few days when one noticed that they had run out of beer. They pooled their money, drew straws and Old Jake was sent for the beer.

An hour passed. Three hours passed and there was no sign of Jake's return. One said, "I think the old bugger has run off with the money."

Jake's voice was heard from near the door. "One more smart comment like that and I won't go at all."

* * *

THE old farmer had married a comely young wench of 18 years and after a month of wedded bliss he visited his doctor for some advice.

"It's so tiring, Doc," he said. "I am still working the farm, and when I am out in the field and get the urge I have to run back to the house, jump in to bed, and afterwards, I have to walk back to the job again. It's knocking me out."

"No wonder," said the doctor. "You are 82 and she is only 18. She should be running out to you," he said.

He solved the problem by suggesting that the farmer take a shot-gun out into the field, and every time he got the urge he could fire a shot to signal that his young wife should come running.

A month later the doctor bumped into the old man down the main street and out of curiosity asked him how the shot-gun scheme was working.

"Oh it worked well for the first two weeks, but then the duck season opened and I haven't seen her since!"

* * *

THE vicar called on the rich 80-year-old grazier who had recently married a 20-year-old bride to see how he was coping.

307

"Can't keep my hands off her," he said.

The vicar mumbled his approval and went on his way. He called back in a week. "How's the bride?" he enquired.

"Can't keep my hands off her," repeated the old farmer. "Worse, now she has run off with one of them."

* * *

THE old codger came to see the doctor for a check up. "I'm getting married next week," he said.

The doctor was surprised for he knew the old gent was 84.

"Why would you want to get married?" he asked.

"I don't want to, I have to," said the old codger.

* * *

OLD Jake came back from the doctor's anxious to show his missus his new $3000 silicon chip hearing aid.

"It looks fine," she said.

"Half past seven," he replied.

* * *

WHEN Old Jake returned to the doctor he was given a bottle of medicine. "This is potent stuff," said the doc, "don't take it every day." The doctor wanted to make sure Old Jake understood. "So take it on alternate days, do you know what I mean? Take it tomorrow, then skip a day, then take it the next day and skip another day, and so on."

A month later the doctor saw Jake's wife in the street and enquired after the old codger.

"Oh, he's dead," she said.

The doctor was aghast.

"No, the medicine wasn't that strong," she said. "It was all that skipping!"

* * *

"WHAT'S the matter little boy," said the old codger when he saw the lad sitting on the kerb crying.

"I'm crying because I can't do what the big boys do," he said.

The old man sat on the kerb and started crying too.

OLD Jake tottered into the clinic. "Doc," he said, "you've got to do something to lower my sex drive."

"C'mon Jake," said the doctor. "Your sex drive is all in your head."

"That's what I mean. You've got to do something to lower it!"

*   *   *

THE old codger came to the doctor with the exciting news that he was going to marry a 20-year-old bride. "Well, I think at your age you should take things easy. In fact I think you should take in a lodger," said the doctor.

A year later he bumped into the old codger and asked how was married life.

"The wife's pregnant, I am happy to say," said the old man, and with a wink and a nudge he added, "thanks for that advice about taking in a boarder. She's pregnant too."

*   *   *

OLD Jake was reminiscing. "I can remember the time I gave up both booze and sex at the same time. Crikey, in all of my life that was the worst half hour I've ever spent!"

*   *   *

THE exhausted bush-walker stumbled into a drover's hut high in the Southern Alps and was immediately welcomed by its lone inhabitant, a tough old mountain man.

The visitor was offered food and invited to sit by the log fire.

After the meal the old man pulled down an unlabelled bottle from a shelf and offered the visitor a drink. The bush-walker accepted, but when he pulled the cork and sniffed the evil home-brew he graciously declined and attempted to return the bottle.

"Drink it!" insisted the old-timer. When the lad declined again the old man reached for his rifle, cocked it and pointed it at the lad's head.

There was no other alternative but to take a swig of the vile firewater that had a kick like a mule. When the bush-walker gasped his way to recovery he handed the bottle back, and the old man handed him the rifle.

"Now you hold the gun on me while I have a drink," he said.

OLD SOLDIERS

IT was a regimental dinner testimonial:

"Today we honour a man who doesn't know the meaning of fear; a man who doesn't know the meaning of defeat, quit or surrender.

"So we have all chipped in and bought him a dictionary."

* * *

TWO old blokes in the Returned Servicemen's Club were talking. "Do you remember those pills they used to give us in the army to keep our minds off girls?" said one.

"Vaguely," said the other.

"Well," said the first, "I think they are beginning to work."

* * *

WHEN old Fred went to join the Returned Servicemen's Club they asked him if he had a war record: "Bloody oath I have," he said, "I've got Vera Lynn singing the White Cliffs of Dover."

ONE-LINERS
See PROFOUND STATEMENTS

A STRING of one-liners unashamedly woven into a yarn on a single topic can reduce listeners to tears. While they are short and punchy in themselves, they have far more effect queued up in the same story. Sure, it requires a good memory and a little practice for delivery, but with a prompt card in your hand ready for the occasional glance to find the key word, the story line should flow with each one-liner bolstering the next.

One of the easiest forms of monologue is your own "biography." We all find it easy to talk about ourselves, so it is comparatively simple to deliver your own preposterous life story around a dinner table of strangers or friends, or even from the rostrum.

Here's an example, but remember it is an overloaded version. It can be ready to be released at the drop of several trigger questions which are bound to crop up in such groups; like what do you do for a living, how long have you lived in these parts, or where do you come from?

Where do I come from? Actually, I am part Irish and part Italian. (If you have their attention with this line, follow with): I'm Irish by my mother's side, and Italian by a friend of my father!

The family was in iron and steel. My mother ironed and my father stole.

(Now ramble on)

I was born at an early age. Premature actually. I am a man before my time.

I am really only 25.

My birth was a surprise to my Mum

... and everyone else in the Tankerville Arms at the time.

It was during the Depression, and they were tough times.

I was abandoned on a doorstep.

I wasn't found there. No, the door opened out.

I was found two somersaults out on the roadway.

There was a note pinned to my shawl.

It read: "Keep your head down. The door opens out." It was signed, "Mum!"

Years later when Mum had enough coupons to get me out of the orphanage, I met my brothers.

That's when the tough times really started.

We were so poor the woman next door had my brother.

He was a Caesarian birth. It didn't effect him, but I noticed he always left the house through the front window.

We lived in a tough neighbourhood.

You could walk ten blocks without leaving the scene of the crime.

Any kid in our street with two ears was a sissy.

Any cat with a tail in our neighbourhood was a tourist.

We used to call the nuns the Little Sisters of the Rich.

Our school still retained capital punishment.

And when we went to school my Dad used to paint the house a different colour and change the number on the front gate.

When I was seven, my Dad took me aside. And left me there.

He was tough on us. He made us run two miles every night.

By the end of the week we were 14 miles from home.

His swimming training was tougher.

He threw us off the deep end of the pier.

Swimming to shore wasn't so bad. Getting out of the bag was the hard part.

Tough? We used to have bread and pullet most nights.

Except Saturdays. On Saturday night we always had Windmill Pie. (What's Windmill Pie?) You get a bit if it goes round!

Before our Mum and Dad ran away from home Dad gave me some serious advice about getting a job. I will never forget it. He had taken me aside one day and said, "Fred!" (he was hopeless with names).

He said: "Fred. There are three kinds of people in this world; those who can count and those who can't."

I knew he was in the latter category when he used to read us nursery rhymes: "One, two, three, buckle my shoe. Three, four, five, open the door."

I got the message to dodge accountancy and took my first job which determined my destiny as a travel writer. I became a proof reader for a sky writing firm.

P

PARROTS

THE young woman got out of bed, slipped on a silk gown, drew back the curtains, switched on the coffee percolator and uncovered the parrot.

Then the phone rang and a man's voice announced he had just arrived on the morning flight and would be there in ten minutes.

The young woman switched off the coffee percolator, covered the parrot, drew the curtains, took off her silk gown and got back into bed.

And the parrot muttered: "Jeez, that must've been the shortest day of the year!"

      *   *   *

HE refused to buy her a pair of budgerigars. He said one could cheep as lively as two.

      *   *   *

WOMAN goes into a pet shop. "I'd like a parrot for my husband."

Proprietor: "Sorry, we don't do swaps!"

      *   *   *

OUTSIDE the petshop in the pouring rain was a galah in a raincoat.

"He's poly unsaturated," explained the proprietor.

AFTER buying a pair of talking parrots Miss Prim wanted to name them but found she couldn't tell Joey from Polly. She phoned the pet shop proprietor for advice. "Simple," he said. "Wait until you see them mating, then fasten something around the male's neck so that you can identify him."

Miss Prim watched and watched. One day she heard flutters and squawks and dashed in to tie a white ribbon around the male's neck.

A few day's later Miss Prim threw an afternoon tea party for the church. Joey spotted the vicar and said: "Ha, so she caught you at it too!"

*　　*　　*

(This is an action joke, best told with a loud squawk when imitating the parrot)
THE lady of the manor had called the plumber weeks ago, but the leeking pipe was far from her mind when she set off early one morning for a day's shopping.

No sooner had she left when the plumber arrived and knocked on the tradesmen's door.

"Squawk! Who is it?" came the raucous voice of the parrot on the enclosed rear porch.

"Tis plumber, come to fix pipes," said the man knocking again.

"Squawk! Who is it?" came the response.

"Tis plumber, come to fix pipes."

"Squawk! Who is it?"

"Tis plumber come to fix pipes."

To cut a long story short, this went on all day until late in the afternoon the frustrating repetition caused the plumber to have a seizure. He collapsed and died on the back steps.

The lady of the manor arrived home and was confronted with the shocking scene. She let out a squawk and cried: "Who is it?"

"Tis plumber come to fix pipes," replied the parrot.

CHAP said he wanted a canary that was a good singer. "Then listen to this one," said the proprietor and he produced a great little whistler that delighted the customer's ears.

"Yes, he's good alright," said the customer, "but I notice he only has one leg."

"Make up your mind," said the proprietor, "D'yer want a singer or a dancer?"

* * *

THE lady with the blue rinse entered the pet shop and said she wanted a parrot, provided it could talk.

"Got just the model for you, madam," gushed the proprietor leading her to a cage. "This little chap is in training," he said. The proprietor explained if madam pulled the string on the parrot's right leg it would say "Pretty Polly," and if she pulled the string on his left leg he would say "Polly wants a cracker," and he successfully demonstrated the exercise.

Madam was impressed. "What if I pull both strings together?" she asked.

"I'll fall off the bloomin' perch ya stupid old bag," said the parrot.

* * *

THE priest had two parrots and taught them religiously to say the rosary. He even had two sets of rosary beads made and after a year of rigorous training he was delighted to have them perform at fetes and country fairs.

The priest was so pleased he decided to teach another parrot the rosary and bought a new bird from the pet shop.

When he put it into the cage one of the originals said to the other. "Throw away your beads Fred, our prayers have been answered. It's a sheila!"

* * *

TALL bloke entered the pet shop and said he wanted a parrot. "It has to be a big red and green one, exactly

315

like the one in Treasure Island," said the customer explaining that he was going to the Arts Fancy Dress Ball as Long John Silver.

The proprietor said he could get such a parrot if he called back on Wednesday.

"Oh, not Wednesday. That's the day I'm having my leg off!"

* * *

HERBIE operated his SP bookie business in a pub and had a pet parrot called Percival who became a perceptive talker. Always looking for the chance to make some money on the side Herbie taught the parrot to sing Advance Australia Fair and when he was word perfect took him down the pub to clean up on a wager or two.

At the bar Herbie turned the conversation round to the fact that not too many Australians knew the words of the national anthem.

"It's a disgrace," said Herbie. "Why even my parrot knows it."

That brought in the suckers. They were queuing up to place their fivers, tenners and hundred dollar notes at 25-to-one against Percival singing the national anthem.

When Herbie had scraped in all the money on offer he gave the parrot the nod. But not a word.

He cajoled, begged, threatened and swore at the parrot, but not one squawk.

After a disastrous payout Herbie stormed off home and threw the cage into the corner.

"Hang on," said Percival. "Don't get upset. Think of the odds we will get tomorrow night!"

PEARLY GATES

AN elderly spinster approached the pearly gates and knocked.

"Who is it?" asked St Peter.

"It is I," came the reply.

"Oh no," muttered St Peter. "Not another school teacher."

* * *

ST PETER: "How did you get up here?"
New arrival: "Flu."

* * *

TWO Rotarians died and arrived at the Pearly Gates. St Peter asked the first if he had ever been unfaithful to his wife. "Once," was the reply.

"That's not bad," said St Peter, and he gave him the keys of a Rolls Royce. "You can drive around Heaven in that," he said.

St Peter put it to the second Rotarian: "Have you ever been unfaithful to your spouse?"

"No more than a dozen times," he replied. "Okay," said St Peter. "That's your battered old Holden. Fix the tyres and you can drive around Heaven in that."

The very next day when the Holden was repaired he was chugging along Celestial Way when he saw the Rolls parked on the side of the road and his friend crying his eyes out.

"Why the grief?" he said. "You got the best deal. Look at the heap I've got to get around in."

"It's not that," said the Rolls owner, "I just saw my wife go past on a skate-board!"

* * *

TWO Kiwis in black singlets, shorts and thongs arrived at the Pearly Gates. St Peter took one look at them and said, "Nick off. You look like wharfies. We know all about you thieving Kiwis. Pinch anything that wasn't nailed down. Nick off."

St Peter informed God he had just got rid of two Kiwis. God went berserk. "You can't do that. Everyone is entitled to get to heaven. Go and get them back."

317

St Peter went off to do his bidding but soon returned. "They've gone," he said.

"Who? The Kiwis?"

"No, the bloomin' Pearly Gates," said St Peter.

* * *

THERE was an orderly queue outside the Pearly Gates as people waited patiently to get into Heaven. But suddenly there was commotion along the line as a man, muttering and grumbling, began pushing people aside and barging his way up to the gates. He went straight in, past St Peter.

"What a cheek," said some.

"Who was that?" enquired others.

St Peter replied. "Oh, that was God. He sometimes likes to think he is a journalist!" (Or a lawyer, an accountant, a doctor, a politician, the Member for Somewhere... whatever the audience)

* * *

THERE were two signs outside the Pearly Gates. A long line of men were queued at the first sign which said: "Hen-Pecked Husbands Report Here."

At the other sign which read: "Liberated Men Report Here," there was only one small timid man.

St Peter said to him: "Why are you standing here?"

He said: "Because my wife told me to."

* * *

THREE nuns died at the same time, arrived at the Pearly Gates simultaneously and intended to go straight in, but St Peter barred their way.

"Just because you are nuns," he said, "doesn't mean you barge straight in without the religious test."

"You," he said to the first one. "What was the name of the first man?"

"Er, Adam?" she answered, and the bells clanged and the trumpets blew and in she went.

"You," said St Peter addressing the second, "What was the name of the first woman?"

"Er, Eve?" she ventured, and the bells clanged and the trumpets blew and in she went.

"You," he said to the quaking third nun, "What were the first words Eve said to Adam?"

"Oh, gee. That's a hard one." And the bells clanged and the trumpets blew and in she went.

* * *

NOTICE came to St Peter at the Pearly Gates that the Devil and his mob had challenged Heaven in a football match.

St Peter was quickly on the phone to accept. "By the way," he told Satan, "you haven't much of a chance, all the best footballers are up here."

"Maybe," said Satan, "but we've got all the umpires down here."

* * *

ST PETER was interviewing a new arrival:

"While on earth, did you ever drink?"

"Good gracious no."

"Ever go with women?"

"Indeed I did not, no sir."

"Gamble then?"

"No, no, never."

Said St Peter, "Well, what took you so long?"

* * *

AN old farmer died at the age of 90 and arrived at the Pearly Gates. "Now I will have my reward, thanks," he said to St Peter.

"What reward is that?" asked the saintly gate-keeper.

"When I was a lad," said the farmer, "my old Dad took me out of school and put me on the ploughs. When I constantly complained that I wanted an education he said I would get my reward in heaven. Now I am here and I want my reward. I want an education."

St Peter said he was a fair-minded bloke but told the farmer he would have to mark time for a while and sent him off on a heavenly tour for a hundred years.

When he returned a century later the old farmer once more demanded his education.

"Sorry, not ready yet," said St Peter, and put him on yet another 100-year heavenly tour.

When he returned from the second trip the old man was adamant. "No more procrastination. (which is a big word for an uneducated farmer) I want my education," he insisted.

"Okay," said St Peter. "I'm sorry Pops, I will have to level with you. As soon as a teacher arrives up here you will get your education as promised. In the meantime, take another trip."

* * *

ST PETER was in a sour disposition when the young and handsome negro rapped on the Pearly Gates.

"I am not letting anybody in today unless you have done something really extraordinary."

"Well I can meet that criteria," said the young negro. "I once made love to a ravishing white woman against the wall of a hall where the Ku Klux Klan was meeting."

"Well, I am impressed," said St Peter. "When was that?"

"About three minutes ago," said the negro.

PETS
See DOGS, CATS

PETS come in all shapes and forms.

A bloke was walking up High St with a crocodile on a lead when a concerned policeman said: "Where are you going with that beast?"

"I am taking him to the zoo," replied the bloke, which satisfied the cop.

Next day the same cop saw the same bloke with the same crocodile on the same lead.

"I thought you were taking that thing to the zoo?"

"Aye, I did, and he had a great time. Today I'm taking him to the pictures."

* * *

THE same bloke went into the pub and said: "Do you serve Catholics?"

The barman said he did.

"Well, I'll be having a pot of stout, and two Catholics for my crocodile!"

* * *

FRED had two monkeys as pets, but when they both died on the same day he was heart-broken. He took them to a taxidermist in the hope that they could be restored as near to life as possible.

The taxidermist said Fred would hardly know the difference and asked if he wanted them mounted.

"No, just shaking hands will do," said Fred.

PHARMACISTS

CHAP went into the chemist and bought some phensic. He was three doors from the shop when the chemist came running after him. "Stop. Stop," he cried, and when he drew level said, "There's been a dreadful mistake. Instead of phensic I have given you arsenic."

The customer said, "is there any difference?"

"Of course," said the chemist in alarm, "it's another fifteen cents."

* * *

CHAP went into the chemist shop and asked for a packet of condoms.

"That will be $3.50 with tax," said the chemist.

"Forget the tax, I'll tie them on."

* * *

"DO you sell condoms, Miss?"

"Yes."

"Well wash your hands, I want a bag of jellybeans."

THE young couple had been cuddling in the back seat of his car and he was eager to go on with it. "Not here," she said. "Come around tomorrow. It's Sunday and my parents go to Evensong. We can have the house to ourselves. Oh, and don't forget the condom."

Next evening the lad arrived at the front door just as her father announced that they were off to church.

"I'll come with you," said the lad smartly.

At the first opportunity the young girl whispered, "Why the change of plan and how long have you been religious?"

To which the lad whispered in reply: "How long has your father been a chemist?"

* * *

YOUNG socialite was advised that her miniature show dog would never win a prize because its hair was too long. It was supposed to be a smooth hair breed.

So she went to the chemist for some hair remover.

The chemist handed her the latest product. "When you slap this on, it is best to keep your arms up for at least three minutes," he said.

"Oh, you misunderstand," she said, rather embarrassed. "It is not for my underarms, it is for my chihuahua."

"Well, in that case," said the chemist, "don't ride a bike for half an hour."

* * *

THE irate young man entered the pharmacy.

"That ointment you sold me to increase the size of my penis doesn't work. I want my money back."

He assured the chemist he applied it according to the instructions on the packet which said 'Rub it in'.

"Ah, but you didn't read the small print," said the chemist. "By a woman between 16 and 25."

PHILOSOPHY

AN optimist says the bottle is half full. The pessimist says it is half empty.

THEY were watching a television soap opera and he became irritated by the way his wife was taking it so seriously.

"How can you sit there and cry about made-up troubles of people you have never met?" he demanded.

"The same way you can jump and scream when some bloke you have never met kicks a goal," she replied.

* * *

IF you are looking for a helping hand, there's one on the end of your arm.

* * *

FRED had been contemplating the world's population. "It's amazing, Ethel," he said. "Every time I breathe in and out, someone dies."

"Have you tried mouthwash?" said Ethel.

* * *

"THE trouble with the human race," thundered the pub's philosopher, "is that the world is full of ignorant and apathetic people." And nudging the drinker beside him said: "Don't you agree?"

"I don't know and I don't care" was the reply.

PHONES

OF course it should always be remembered that Alexander Graham Bell invented TWO phones.

* * *

"PARDON me Miss. I am writing a phone book, may I have your number?"

* * *

CAN you telephone from a submarine?

Of course, anybody can tell a phone from a submarine.

* * *

I RANG Madge and told her I was at St Alban's.

She wanted to know what I was doing at his place.

WHEN the vicar heard that the mayor's pretty wife had been ill he told the mayor he would call round and see her next morning.

When he was shown into her room the vicar said: "I prayed for you last night."

"Silly man," she replied. "You know I'm on the phone."

* * *

THE father of a teenage girl answered the phone.

"Is that Dreamboat?" enquired a voice.

"No," replied the father, "it's Supply Ship."

* * *

HE phoned his wife from the pub to say he had been delayed at the office, but before he got a word in he heard her voice at the other end: "A damned likely story. Never heard such rubbish. Get out of that pub this minute and come straight home. This is a recorded announcement."

* * *

BARMAN on the phone: "You will have to give me a better description than that lady, this pub is full of hopeless layabouts who should be home."

* * *

FRED finally sobered up from his lost week-end and, terror-stricken, realised he had to explain it to his wife. He reached for the phone: "Hilda darling. I have escaped. Whatever you do, don't pay the ransom money!"

* * *

FRED rang the wrong number at two o'clock in the morning.

When he realised his mistake he said, "Oh I am sorry to wake you in the middle of the night."

"Oh, that's alright," said the other party, "I had to get up and answer the phone anyway."

* * *

THE second time Fred made the mistake the other party wasn't so happy.

"Well, if you are telling me it is the wrong number," said Fred, "why the hell did you answer it?"

THE voice said: "Young Tommy won't be at school today. He is very sick."

The school principal asked: "Who is speaking?"

"My father," said the caller.

* * *

HE rang his wife to tell her the good news that he had the rest of the day off, but a small boy's voice answered. "G'day son, where's Mum?"

"She's in bed, Dad," said the boy.

"Is she sick?"

"No Dad, she's in bed with the butcher and I can hear her giggling. She's not sick."

There was a poignant silence while he figured out the gravity of the situation. "Are you still there, son?"

"Yes, Dad."

"Go and get my shotgun from the garage. Load it like I told you and give them both barrels."

He listened for an interminable five minutes or more until he finally heard two loud blasts, then the boy's voice again: "I did it, Dad."

"Okay, son, now drag them out and drop them in that big hole I dug for the compost pit."

There was another long silence before the boy, still puffing, came back to the phone and said "I've done it Dad, but I've got a bit of blood on my arms."

"Then jump in the pool and swim around for a bit."

"What pool, Dad. We don't have a pool."

After a few seconds silence Dad said: "Is that 584-8400?"

* * *

"IS that the motor pool?" asked a posh voice.

"Yus."

"Tell me, my man, what vehicles are operational at the moment?"

"Five trucks, three utilities, two staff cars and the Bentley that pompous old colonel swans around in."

325

There was a few seconds silence.

"Do you know who this is?"

"No."

"It is the so-called pompous old colonel you so insubordinately referred to."

There was another short silence.

"Do you know who this is?"

"No."

"Well you can go and jump in the lake," and the phone was slammed down.

* * *

THE little old spinster rang Telecom's complaint department.

"The cord on my phone is toolong. Could you pull it back a bit on your end?" she asked.

* * *

PEDANTIC boss; "Answer that phone."

"But it isn't ringing."

"Why do you have to wait until the last minute!"

* * *

IT was six in the morning when the phone rang at the reception desk of the hotel. The night porter picked it up to hear a slurred voice say: "Excoosh me, my fren, hic. What time dush the bar open?"

The porter replied, "It doesn't open until ten, but by the sound of your condition you won't be allowed in."

"Allowed in?" shouted the drunk. "I've been waiting all night to get out!"

* * *

THE drunk phones the police station: "I've been driving along the (hic) highway and I think itsh my duty to tell you I have knocked down two signposts, and a (hic) telephone box."

"Indeed, sir," says the cop. "And where are you?"

"Wouldn't yoush like to know?"

326

SHE answered the phone to hear a very repentent voice.

"I'm sorry darling," he said. "I have thought it over and decided that you can have the Rolls as a wedding present and we will move to the Gold Coast immediately, and, okay, your mother can come with us. Will you marry me?"

"Of course I will," she said, "who's speaking?"

* * *

HE answered the phone only to hear heavy breathing and the occasional obscene suggestion.

"It's for you dear," he said.

* * *

THE phone rings and Joe answers to hear a voice enquire: "Could I speak to Bobby Bonkbrake, please?"

"I don't know anybody by that name," said Joe, "but hang on a moment and I'll ask." Do we have Bonkbrake here?" shouts Joe.

"No, it's all we can do to get a coffee break," was the answer.

* * *

A MATHEMATICIAN named Paul
Has a hexahedronical ball
And the cube of its weight
Times his pecker, plus eight
Is his phone number,
Give him a call.

PILOTS

AIR Traffic Control to Aer Lingus: "Identify yourself, and what is your height and position?"

"I'm Captain Paddy Murphy, I'm five-feet-two, and I'd be sitting up the front."

* * *

THE passengers were shocked to see a nude man dash up the aisle of the aircraft and into the flight deck, but then it was fully explained with the announcement: "This is your captain streaking."

* * *

THE airline pilot was having his regular medical check.

"When did you last have sex?" asked the doctor as a routine question.

"Nineteen fifty-eight," said the pilot.

"Hell, that was along time ago."

The pilot looked at his watch. "It's only twenty-two fifteen now," he said.

* * *

THE captain made an announcement.

"Does anybody on this aircraft know how to pray?"

The clergyman put his hand up.

"Good," said the captain. "You start praying. The rest of us will don our parachutes. We are one short."

* * *

THE aircraft was on its final approach and the intercom was still switched on when passengers heard the captain's comment to his co-pilot.

"First thing after we land I'll have a couple of beers, then I intend to make love to that blonde stewardess."

The stewardess turned red with embarrassment and dashed down the aisle intending to alert the pilots that the intercom was still on. But she tripped over a case.

A little old lady passenger helped her to her feet.

"It's alright miss," she said. "Plenty of time. He said he was going to have a beer first."

* * *

THE co-pilot had an unfortunate name, and he was late. When he finally stepped aboard the captain called: "Hi, Jack!" and most of the passengers tried to jump out.

* * *

IT looked like an Irish hijack. Paddy used one of those airline sleeping masks with no eye holes. He jumped up, with the gun pointing the wrong way and roared: "Hands down this is a stuff up."

"One move out of you and you'll be geography," he said.

"Er, don't you mean history?" ventured a passenger.

"Don't change the subject," roared Paddy.

POEMS

SAID the young man to his new fiancee: "Have you told your folks that I am a poet?"

"Not yet," she said, "I've mentioned your police record, and that you smoked, drank, were presently bankrupt because of your gambling habit, but I thought we'd wait until we were married first."

* * *

A MAGAZINE ran a poetry contest setting out three rules for submissions: The poem had to rhyme, be brief and appeal to most people.

The winner is printed below:
Pay Day.

* * *

BEWARE of strong drink, my dear
And only have two, at the most.
Three, and you're under the table,
Four and you're under the host.

* * *

"DON'T drink nought but water,"
Was Mum's word to her daughter,
"Say no to men,
"Be home by ten,
"And behave just like you oughta!"

* * *

ROSES are reddish
Violets are bluish
If it wasn't for Jesus
We'd all be Jewish.

GOD is good,
Yet all his peoples
Put lightening rods
On top of steeples.

*   *   *

"AND what'll have?"
Said the waiter, idly picking his nose.
"I'll have two boiled eggs, ya drongo.
Ya can't stick yer fingers in those."

*   *   *

THE difference between prose and poetry is clearly illus-
trated by this sample of prose:
The young maiden entered the water
   First time away from her mum
   All her clothing was strewed
   So she stood there quite nude
   While the tide lapped up round her knees.
Now, had she gone in a little deeper it would be poetry.

*   *   *

WITH the police still hot on his trail
He was tempted by fanny for sale
So the crook went to bed
With a price on his head
With a girl with a price on her tail

*   *   *

THIS is the story of Signwriter Joe
While painting a sign he fell through the 'O'
No need to cry "shame"
What end could be better
He went as he came, through a hole in a letter.

*   *   *

MOST poets will tell you that rhyme doesn't pay.

*   *   *

SAY it with flowers
Or say it with sweets,
Boxes of chocolates

330

Or plush theatre seats,
Say it with diamonds,
Or say it with mink
But whatever you do
Don't say it in ink.

* * *

THE limerick packs laughs anatomical
Into space that is quite economical
But the good ones I've seen
So seldom are clean
And the clean ones are so seldom comical

POLICE
See LAW

"OFFICER," said the Sweet Young Thing coming into the police station, "where do I apologise for shooting my husband?"

* * *

ROBBERS broke into a Dublin bank and stole half a million pounds and a quantity of gold bullion. Baffled police are trying to figure out a motive for the crime.

* * *

POLICE are looking for a three-fingered pick-pocket who specialises in stealing bowling balls.

* * *

THE detective wanted to know what the dead body was doing in the living room.

* * *

MADGE always wanted to be a policewoman. Now she's on the beat. "It's not much of a job, but it's better than walking the streets," she said.

* * *

A FRIENDLY cop found two young women crying their eyes out at the Railway Station and was unable to console them until he took them to a nearby cafe and ordered a pot of tea and a plate of cakes. They dried their tears and smiled.

Then he plonked the teapot in the middle of the table and said: "Now who's going to be mother?"

And they both burst into tears again.

* * *

A POLICE sergeant in the bush doubled as the local vet and late one night his wife answered the phone. "Is your husband there?" queried the voice.

"Do you need the services of the police or the vet?" she enquired.

"Both," said the caller, "we can't get our dog's jaws open and there's a burglar in them."

* * *

TRAFFIC cop stopped a very fast car and approached the driver with note-book in hand.

"You were doing 100 kilometres an hour in a 60 zone. What's your name?"

Driver: "Mickhaelovic Dubroevscnzkics."

Cop, flipping his note book shut: "Okay, don't do it again."

POLITICS

POLITICIANS are ubiquitous. Everybody knows one, which makes them legitimate targets for lampooning in speeches or yarns. Jokes on politicians are perennial, only the names have to be changed to make them current, or switched to suit your own political bias.

* * *

NO matter who you vote for, a darned politician always wins. And the only thing wrong with political jokes is, they get elected.

* * *

MAKE your MP work — Don't re-elect him.

POLITICIANS are people who have to mind their appease and accuse.

* * *

WHAT's the difference between a flattened politician and a flattened kangaroo on the road to Canberra?

There are skid marks to the kangaroo.

* * *

NEVER believe anything about a politician, until he has made an official denial.

* * *

BOB Hawke died and went to heaven. As he approached the celestial chair God said: "Who are you?"

"I'm Bob Hawke and that's my chair you are sitting in."

* * *

"MR MINISTER!" boomed the back-bencher, "What are you going to do about the Abortion Bill?"

"Shhh, not so loud," said the Minister, "I'm paying it tomorrow."

* * *

PAUL Keating was asked if he had heard the latest political jokes.

"Heard them?" he said. "I work with the bludgers."

* * *

CABINET decided to adjourn business for a dinner break and they trouped into the parliamentary restaurant.

The prime minister ordered a mixed grill.

"And what about your vegetables?" asked the waiter.

"Oh they can order what they like," he replied.

* * *

WHILE on safari in cannibal country a traveller came across a cafe in a clearing in the jungle. The sign out front advertised: Fried Missionary $5, Boiled Hunter $4.50, Grilled Safari Guide $5, Stuffed Politician $15.

333

When the traveller asked why so much for the politician the chef replied, "Have you ever tried to clean one?"

*   *   *

THE election campaign had become fairly bitter and when the two opponents met at a social gathering it was a chance to make a pact to stop insulting each other.

"Let's make a clean fight of it," said Smith. "I promise to stop telling lies about you."

"That's fair," said Brown, "and I will stop telling the truth about you."

*   *   *

HE had listened to the politician's speech for a solid hour before going outside for a breath of fresh air.

"Is he still talking?" asked his mate outside.

"Yeah."

"What's he talking about?"

"He didn't say."

*   *   *

THE commercial traveller was leaning on the bar in a country pub chatting to the locals when the subject turned to politics. "I can't stand Bob Hawke. He's got a face like a sheep's head," he said.

He was immediately thrown through the swinging doors into the dust of the main street.

"What was that for?" he asked in a daze. "I didn't think anyone would feel so strongly for Bob Hawke in the bush. Is this Hawke territory or what?"

"No," said a farmer. "This is sheep territory."

*   *   *

HE walked into the general store of a country town and bought all the rotten fruit, tomatoes and eggs available. The greengrocer beamed: "I bet you are going to hear the visiting MP at the Mechanics' Hall tonight."

"No," he replied. "I AM the visiting MP!"

HOW come there is only one Monopolies Commission?

* * *

ON the headstone of a grave in the Cemetery is the most unusual epitaph: "Here lies the body of a great politician, an honest man and the Member for Wills."

It is unusual because it is not often they bury three men in one grave.

* * *

ONE thing about our local MP. He's an honest politician. When he's bought he stays bought.

* * *

THE Leader of the Opposition was walking along the banks of a river when he slipped and fell in and was soon in difficulties. The Prime Minister dived in, swam to his aid and hauled him ashore.

The Opposition Leader thanked him and said. "Can you do me one favour. Don't tell my party that I can't swim?"

"That's okay," said the Prime Minister, "provided you don't tell my mob I can't walk on water."

* * *

LATE at night the Prime Minister was walking by the lake and preoccupied by affairs of State, slipped and fell in.

A youth heard his cries for help and at great risk to himself dived in and saved him.

When he recovered the great man said to the lad: "Boy, you saved my life. Anything you can name you can have."

"I don't want anything," said the lad. "Just don't tell my Dad."

* * *

THE Prime Minister had gathered caucus about him to outline the strategy of the next campaign. "I am going to describe the tactics in the simplest possible terms, so if there are any idiots in the room will they stand up now."

After a pause one politician got to his feet. "So you are an idiot are you?" said the P.M.

"Not exactly, P.M., I just didn't like to see you standing alone!"

* * *

THE proposition to put a king-sized statue of the Prime Minister in central park has been well supported. It will give shelter when its raining, shade in the summer, and the pigeons a chance to speak for us all.

* * *

"AND as for the problem of the pigeons around the town hall," said the mayor, "it's no use trying to dodge the issue."

* * *

GOD called the world's three greatest leaders up to heaven for a special caucus meeting. George Bush, Mikhail Gorbachev and Bob Hawke were told that the world would end in three days and to go back and prepare their communities.

George Bush went on television: "My fellow Americans, I have good news and bad news. The good news is that God exists, as we all believed. The bad news is that the world will end in three days."

Mikhail Gorbachev told the Soviet Union: "Bad news and worse news. God exists and the world will end in three days."

Bob Hawke went nationwide: "Good news and better news. God exists, I am no longer an agnostic. And in three days, no Australian child shall live in poverty!"

* * *

OUR local Member of Parliament says at the forthcoming election he will stand on his record.

That's the only way he can stop people examining it.

* * *

DON'T Vote. It only encourages the bastards.

DURING the pilots' strike a charter flight was carrying four passengers. One was a businessman, one was a priest, one was a back-packing tourist and the fourth was none other than the Prime Minister.

Somewhere over the alps the pilot made the shocking announcement that the aircraft would shortly run out of fuel. He said there were only four parachutes on board and apologising for being a coward he threw three into the cabin and jumped out with his own.

The priest said he was an important man with a large diocese to look after so he grabbed one of the three parachutes and jumped out.

The Prime Minister said he was the most important leader in history and must have a parachute, and so saying he made a grab and jumped out.

The businessman said to the hiker, "That leaves one parachute between us."

"Not so," said the back-packer. "We have a parachute each. The most important leader in history has leapt out with my haversack."

*   *   *

POLITICAL definitions:

Capitalism: You possess two cows. You sell one and buy a bull.

Socialism: You possess two cows. You give one of them to your neighbour.

Communism: You possess two cows. The government confiscates them and provides you with milk.

Nazism: You possess two cows. The government confiscates them and shoots you.

European Common Market: You possess two cows. The government confiscates them, shoots one, milks the other and pours it down the drain.

PRAYER

AN MP, noticing his colleague on his knees asked if he was praying for the House.

"No," was the reply. "I've looked at the House. I was praying for the country."

* * *

THE gambler was praying for a win.

"Oh God. Let me win the pools."

And God answered his prayer with a thundering reply: "Meet me halfway, and fill in the coupon."

* * *

A JEWISH mother was standing with her toddler son in the shallows at the beach when a freak wave crashed ashore, knocked the little boy off his feet and dragged him into the surf and out to sea.

The distraught mother fell on her knees and prayed that God would take her life instead, so that her son should live.

In answer to her prayer the very next wave washed the boy ashore.

Again she fell to her knees. "Lord, thank you, thank you, this is truly a miracle. How can I ever repay you?"

Then taking a second look at her child she added: "Excuse me Lord, before you go, there's just one thing. He did have a hat!"

* * *

TWO mates who had been out fishing all day couldn't get the motor started. Night had fallen and a strong offshore wind was carrying the frail boat further out to an increasingly stormy ocean.

Jack fell to his knees in prayer. "Oh Lord, get us out of this and I promise to change my life. I promise to pay my debts, I promise to be faithful to my wife. I promise to give up the booze. I promise..."

He was interrupted by his mate. "Hang on Jack. Don't go too far. I think I can see a light coming towards us."

PREGNANCY

A YOUNG woman looking as if she was in photo finish with the stork staggered into the maternity ward and grabbed a nursing sister. She said she needed immediate attention.

"Ah," said the sister, "due are you?"

"No, Church of England."

* * *

OLD Mrs Gerrarty staggered into the doctor's surgery and complained of stomach pains.

After an examination the doctor declared, "You're pregnant."

"But I can't be," she said in shock. "I'm 83."

The doctor said he was positive and when he calmed her down said, "You had better ring your husband."

"Brace yourself Fred," she said on the phone. "I'm pregnant."

"Crikey Moses," said Fred. "And who is speaking?"

* * *

THE unwed Irish girl settles down in the confessional and begins: "It's a shameful thing I have to confess. I am pregnant."

"Are you sure it's yours?" says the priest.

* * *

ON a crowded bus the young woman asked the gent: "Do you mind if I sit down, I'm pregnant?"

He stood up and gave her his seat, but then took a second look.

"You don't look pregnant. How long have you been pregnant?" he asked.

"Oh, about 15 minutes," she said, "but doesn't it make you tired!"

* * *

THE young woman looked at the beer gut on the Ocker with disgust. "If that stomach was on a woman, she would be pregnant," she said.

"It was and she is," replied the Ocker.

339

FRED was stunned by the news of his wife's pregnancy. "It's impossible," he lamented. "I'm always so careful. How could it possibly happen?"

"There, there," she consoled him. "Who says it was your fault?"

* * *

SIGN in a maternity shop: We supply the accessories after the fact.

PROFOUND STATEMENTS
See ONE-LINERS

HERE is a most important segment of the book.

The Master of Ceremonies constantly has cause to make an announcement or introduce somebody, and claim attention over and above the clatter and buzz of conversation.

Sometimes, one can say "Excuse me ladies and gentlemen, can I have your attention please?" And you can repeat it ad nauseum while banging champagne glasses together. Let's face it, "Ladies and gentlemen can I have your attention?" is a pretty dull statement and grabs nobody's attention.

On the other hand, step to the microphone and say: "You can always tell a happy motorcyclist by the insects on his teeth." Someone will hear it.

Follow with a number of the throw-aways listed below and eventually there is dead silence while they strain to catch these profound statements.

Some are so profound they should be dropped into the middle of your address whether you have lost your place or not, in case the audience has drifted away. Here are a few which should recapture their attention.

* * *

TIMING is the essential factor in the success of any rain dance.

SMOKING shortens your cigarettes.

LOCKJAW means never having to say you're sorry.

MONOGAMY leaves a lot to be desired.

NO woman has ever shot her husband while he was doing the dishes.

IF you feel strongly about graffiti, sign a partition.

THERE is no alcohol in Iran, but you can get stoned anytime.

AN optimist is one who thinks the future is uncertain.

ABSTINENCE is the thin edge of the pledge.

A CHRYSANTHEMUM by any other name would be easier to spell.

NEVER play leapfrog with a unicorn.

LET him among us to run the fastest cast the first stone.

CRIME doesn't pay, but the hours are optional.

ONE-legged girls are a push-over.

YOU can lead a horse to water but you can't lead a whore to culture.

A MAN is known by the company he floats.

ALL is fair in love and the war which follows.

ANY port in a storm is better than no rum.

ANYTHING for a quiet wife.

IF I'd known she'd take offence so easily I would have entered her in the Grand National.

PUNCTUALITY is something that, if you've got it, there is few to share it with.

THIN yaks leave light tracks.

NO leg is too short to reach the ground.

PORNOGRAPHY is in the groin of the beholder.

OBSCENITY is anything that gives the judge an erection.

WHEN God created man, She was only joking.

BEGGARS can't be boozers.

CONTRACEPTIVES should be used on all conceivable occasions.

CANNIBALS are not vegetarians. They are humanitarians.

W.C. FIELDS is alive and drunk in Alburqueque.

CIRCUMCISIONS alter cases.

STATISTICS prove that 50% of all people who get married at Easter are women.

DON'T put all your bags in one exit.

HALF a loaf is better than no tea-break at all.

342

HERE today, gone home to Momma.

IF you like home cooking, stay home.

GOING steady only means you've sobered up.

IF Labor is the answer, it must have been a bloody stupid question.

ONE good turn gets most of the bedclothes.

ONE door closes, another slams in your face.

PROCRASTINATION is the thief of time, especially if you can't spell it.

SEX is bad for one, but it is good for two.

RUTH is stranger than fiction.

THE opera's never over until the fat lady sings.

IF the epileptic fits, wear it.

HE who laughs last doesn't get the joke.

TWO can live as cheaply as one, but for half as long.

CONFUCIUS, he say too much.

A FRIEND in need is a pest indeed.

THERE is nothing like horse riding to make a person feel better off.

THERE are three kinds of women, the beautiful, the intelligent and the majority.

THERE are three kinds of men, the handsome, the caring and the majority.

THERE are three kinds of mathematicians, those who can count, and those who can't.

SOME girls are like flowers. They grow wild in the woods.

NOT to mention the monkeys.

THE man who goes into the bar optimistically, usually leaves misty optically.

HE may drink to forget, but he never forgets to drink.

YOU don't get a second chance to make a first impression.

TIME wounds all heels.

TIME is nature's way of stopping everything from happening at once.

DEATH is nature's way of telling you to slow down.

NEVER leave a turn unstoned.

NEVER put off till tomorrow what you can avoid altogether.

BETTER to be a coward for a minute than dead for the rest of your life.

SHE was only the horse trainers daughter, but all the horse manure.

THERE were more late entries than an Irish orchestra.

HE had an ego bigger than the outdoors.

DON'T come the raw prawn.

DON'T try to keep up with the Joneses. Drag them down to your level. It's cheaper.

A CULT is a group too small to be a minority.

IF you don't go to your friends' funerals, they certainly won't come to yours.

THE number of people at your funeral can depend on the weather.

I KEEP fit by wrestling, with my conscience.

MY wife keeps fit by jumping, to conclusions.

I LOVE women so much I think I'm a lesbian.

MY carma run over your dogma.

LIVE every day as if it is your last. One day you'll be right.

ALL babies are subject to change without notice.

ALL my life I have been doubtful. Now I'm not so sure.

A CLOSED mouth gathers no feet.

THEY were so progressive they tried to adopt a gay baby.

SHE had more chins than the Singapore phone book.

SHE was only a newsagent's daughter, but she loved her Daily Mail.

SHE was only a cab driver's daughter, but you sure auto meter.

SHE used to be married to a trapeze artist, but she caught him in the act.

HE'S very broad minded. He thinks of little else.

THEY were thicker than mourners at a brewer's wake.

SHE was so mean she used to heat the knives so the family would use less butter.

HE'D steal the harness off a nightmare.

I AM so miserable, it is as if you hadn't left.

NEVER go round with another man's wife, unless you can go a round with her husband.

SILENCE isn't always golden... sometimes it's guilt.

DIPLOMACY is the art of saying "nice doggie" until you can find a rock.

PROPOSALS

YOUNG Jock McTavish got down on his knees to propose to her when a 25-cent coin dropped from his pocket and rolled under the sofa. In the 20 minutes it took him to find it she had lost interest.

★　★　★

BLOKE walked up to a lovely blonde on the corner. "I'm

sorry to bother you," he said, "but I am a stranger in town and I don't know my way around. Could you tell me where you live?"

PSYCHIATRISTS

ANYBODY who goes to a psychiatrist needs their head read, but read on.

* * *

PSYCHIATRY is the care of the id by the odd.

* * *

NEUROTICS build castles in the air. Psychotics live in them, and psychiatrists collect the rent.

* * *

YOU go to a psychiatrist when you feel slightly cracked and keep going until you're completely broke.

* * *

"DOCTOR, doctor," said the patient as he burst into the psychiatrist's room, "I feel invisible."

Doctor: "I'm sorry, I can't see you now."

* * *

HE stopped going to his psychiatrist. He asked too many personal questions.

* * *

"NOW that I have cured you of your gambling addiction," said the psychiatrist, "I can present you with your bill."

"Thanks doc. Toss you double or nothing."

* * *

PATIENT: "How do I know if you can help me?"

Doc: "I can guarantee a sure cure, or your mania back."

* * *

THE friendly psychiatrist is the one who lies on the couch with you.

* * *

GOING to the psychiatrist didn't cure Fred's drinking problem. He kept falling off the couch.

DID you hear about the psychiatrist who kept his wife under the bed because he thought she was a little potty?

* * *

A FELLOW phoned his psychiatrist. "Doctor, my wife needs help. She thinks she's a horse."

The doctor heard a few more details and said, "Mmmm, it seems serious. It could be a long and costly treatment."

"Money is no object," came the reply. "She's won her last three starts!"

* * *

"MY doctor insisted that I come and see you," said the patient to the eminent psychiatrist. "Goodness knows why, because I'm happily married, I like my job, got lots of friends and no worries..."

"Hmmm..." said the psychiatrist reaching for his notebook, "How long have you been like this?"

* * *

I TOLD my girlfriend the truth, that I was seeing a psychiatrist.

She told me the truth, that she was seeing a psychiatrist, a plumber and two barmen.

* * *

PATIENT: "Why do you think so many people take an instant dislike to me?"

Psychiatrist: "Saves time."

* * *

PATIENT: "Everybody hates me."

Psychiatrist: "Don't be silly. Everyone hasn't met you yet."

* * *

"DOC, my wife is a kleptomaniac."

"Is she taking anything for it?"

* * *

"I THINK I am going mad, doctor. Every time I ask someone the time I get a different answer."

"I USED to suffer from a split personality, Doc, but now we're both okay!"

* * *

SHE took her husband to the psychiatrist. "He says he is suffering from hallucinations, but I'm sure he is only imagining it," she said.

* * *

"NOW tell me," said the psychiatrist, "have you had any more of those sexually erotic dreams?"

"No," said the patient.

"Tough luck, I've had some beauties."

* * *

HE asked her to explain her dreams.

"I haven't had any this week, doctor," she said.

"Well how the hell can I help you if you don't do your homework?"

* * *

THE shapely blonde entered the psychiatrist's office. She stood nervously by his desk as he told her to lie on the couch. She hesitated.

"Come, come, now," said the psychiatrist, "how can I help you unless you lie down on the couch?"

Finally, she walked over and stretched out on the couch.

"Now then," he said, "tell me how your troubles began."

She looked him straight in the eye, "Just like this," she said.

* * *

PSYCHIATRIST: "So, you think you are a dog, eh? That's no problem. Just hop up on the couch."

Patient. "I can't. I'm not allowed."

* * *

HE helped cure my phone phobia. I was always scared of answering it. Now I answer it all the time, whether it rings or not.

* * *

THE patient explained to the psychiatrist: "Every time

I go to sleep I dream of cricket. It's the most important match of the year and every time I get a duck. Doc. it's driving me mad."

Doctor: "Well, when you go to bed tonight try thinking of something else."

"What, and miss my turn to bat?"

* * *

HE briskly entered the psychiatrist's rooms and settled himself down on the couch with his brief case. "Let's talk business," he said. "I want to rent advertising space on your ceiling."

* * *

HOW many psychiatrists does it take to change a light bulb?

Only one. But the bulb must want to be changed.

* * *

A PSYCHIATRIST on holiday became fascinated by the antics of an apparent simpleton who had set up a sign on the beach which stated "Seagulls for sale."

"That's why we are needed," he said to his wife. "I think I will humour him."

"How much are the seagulls?" asked the psychiatrist.

"Only a fiver each," the jolly hawker replied.

"Okay," said the psychiatrist, "I'll buy one."

The man took the note, and pointing skywards said: "That's your one, up there."

* * *

THE psychiatrist treated Bazza for two hours and finally solved the problem. "You've got a split personality. You are really two different people struggling for supremacy of yourself."

The doc then handed him a bill for $100. Bazza produced $50. "There's my half. Why should I pay for the other bloke's troubles?"

* * *

THE psychiatrist had listened for ten minutes while his patient insisted he had turned into a bell.

"Take these pills. If they don't work, give me a ring!"

350

THE middle-aged woman settled herself on the couch. "It's about my son, doctor. He keeps making mud pies."

"I wouldn't worry about it," said the doctor, "It's quite normal really."

"Well I don't like it," she said, "and neither does his wife!"

* * *

ONE psychiatrist to another: "All day long I have to listen to stories of pain and suffering, raw deals, persecution complexes, husbands complaining about wives, wives complaining about husbands, family feuds, everybody's problems, the world's troubles. It's getting me down.

"But tell me Dr Entwhistle, how come you look so serene after listening to everybody's troubles?"

"So, who listens?"

* * *

THE psychiatrist told Fred he was going to drop some ink on a blotter and he wanted Fred to explain what the random designs meant to him.

"That's Marilyn Munro in the nude," said Fred deciphering the first blotch.

"That's Jayne Mansfield taking a bath," he described the second.

He said the third spattering of ink was the Luton Girls Choir all singing in the nude.

"The trouble with you Fred," said the doctor with some satisfaction, "you are obsessed with sex."

"What, me?" exclaimed Fred. "It's you who's drawing the filthy pictures."

* * *

TWO psychiatrists met in the hospital corridor. One said: "You're feeling good. How am I?"

* * *

A PSYCHIATRIST spent two hours listening to a young woman pour out the details of her anxieties and emotional problems.

Finally he said there was nothing wrong with her, she was coping well, and she was quite normal.

"Normal?" she repeated. "But what about these caterpillars crawling all over me. I can't stand it any longer."

The psychiatrist jumped up and backed away. "Well, don't flick the damn things over me."

PSYCHOLOGY

THE psychologist put it to Fred: "If you had to give up wine or women, which would you choose?"

Fred thought for a moment. "That would rather depend on the vintage of each," he said.

*   *   *

AN attractive woman was sitting alone in a bar when a young man approached her. "Excuse me," he said, "may I buy you a drink?"

"What, to a motel?" she screamed.

"No, no," protested the man, "You misunderstood. I just asked if I could buy you a drink."

"You are asking me to go to a motel?" she screamed, even louder.

Completely bewildered the young man retreated to a corner table while everybody glared at him indignantly.

After ten minutes the young woman came over to explain. "I'm, sorry to have created such a scene," she said. "I am a psychology student studying human behaviour in unexpected situations."

The young man looked at her and shouted, "What? A hundred dollars?"

*   *   *

OLD Jacob lived in a small side street in Fitzroy and was being annoyed by a group of kids who would play cricket in this alley, using a tin can as a ball.

The noise would irritate him and sleep was hopeless, so he decided to put an old business principle to work.

He called the boys together and explained that he was an old pensioner, and that nothing gave more pleasure than to see young lads playing cricket with a tin can. He said if they would come there every night and play cricket he would pay them fifty cents each, per night.

The kids thought this was great and turned up the following evening to make their usual noise and were duly paid fifty cents each.

The second night old Jacob explained to the boys that he was an old-age pensioner and would they mind copping 40 cents because he was a little short. The lads accepted the money.

The third night he told the boys that he had suffered some unexpected expenses and would they mind taking just 30 cents.

The fourth night he explained that his pension cheque hadn't arrived and the best he could do was five cents each.

The news wasn't taken gladly. The boys looked at each other and finally one said. "To hell with this. I'm not wasting my time playing cricket with a tin can for a measley five cents. I'm off."

The rest followed, and he has never seen them again.

* * *

HE had suffered from insomnia for years and at last the psychologist was giving him some sound advice.

"Next time you are in bed relax your body bit by bit, starting from the toes," said the psycho.

"Go to sleep toes," he said that night. "Go to sleep feet, go to sleep ankles, go to sleep knees, go to sleep thighs..."

Just then his wife walked in to the bedroom in a sheer negligee.

"Wake up everybody," he yelled.

* * *

FRED had been out with the boys. And as the night

developed he found himself among the girls, and one of them, a buxom blonde, eventually took him home to her flat.

It was three a.m. when he was set to leave and he was overtaken by remorse. "What will I tell the missus?" he muttered.

"No worries," said the blonde, "Here's the plan and put this bit of chalk behind your ear."

At four a.m. he was tip-toeing across the bedroom when the light flashed on. "Where have you been?" demanded his wife.

"I've been in bed with a big buxom blonde who wouldn't let me come home until I satisfied her five times," he began.

"You bloody liar," said his wife. "You've been out playing pool. You've still got a bit of chalk behind your ear!"

PUBLIC RELATIONS

HYMIE was the world's first public relations officer and worked with Moses on the flight of the Israelites. When they reached the shores of the Red Sea, hotly pursued by Pharaoh's army, Moses sent for his PR man.

"Where are the boats? You forgot the boats," Moses roared at Hymie.

"When were boats in the contract?" asks Hymie.

Moses was in a rage. "I must have boats. Do you want me to part the sea and walk across it?"

"Great thinking Moses," said Hymie. "If you do that I will get you two whole pages in the Old Testament!"

PUBLIC SPEAKING

VETERAN guest speaker: "I don't mind them looking at the time when I'm talking. But when they take their watches off and shake them to see if they are still going, then I find it disconcerting."

HE was pacing up and down when the young lady approached and asked if he was the guest speaker. He replied that he was.

"Do you get nervous before you speak?" she enquired.

"No," he lied.

"Then what are you doing in the ladies' loo?"

* * *

HE lacked confidence as a public speaker. "I'm afraid I'm not good at it," he admitted. "Last time I even stuffed up the minute's silence."

* * *

AFTER he addressed the Chamber of Commerce, the guest speaker stayed on for a while but was looking despondent.

"What's bothering you?" asked the chairman.

"Well, one of your members, that chap there, just told me that it was the most boring speech he had ever heard."

"Oh, don't worry about Smithers," said the chairman. "He's the type of chap who just goes round repeating what everybody else says."

* * *

"HAVE you ever spoken before a large audience before?"

"Yes. And I said Not Guilty."

* * *

"I HEARD your wife was an after-dinner speaker."

"Don't be silly. She couldn't wait that long."

* * *

AN ideal response from the guest of honour: "I really don't deserve this award. But then, I've got arthritis and I didn't deserve that either."

* * *

OPENING remark for a public speaker:

"The prime minister would have been here tonight but for a conflict of interest. He didn't want to come."

PUBS
See HOTELS

ON the chest of the barmaid in Sale
  Were tattooed the prices of ale,
  And on her behind,
  For the sake of the blind,
  Was the same information in Braille.

*   *   *

THINGS are so tough at this pub that they employ a chucker-in! Patrons are frisked for weapons. If they don't have any they are given some.

*   *   *

SOME of the pubs around Sydney are the toughest in Australia. The drinkers can fight at the drop of a hat, have muscles like knotted wire, covered in tatts and swear like troupers. The men are just as wild.

*   *   *

"WHY do you throw your drinks down so fast, one after the other?"
  "Cos I once had one stolen."

*   *   *

IT was in a pub where unattended beers were unsafe and Jake had a need to go to the loo. So he left a note beside his beer, reading: "I've spat in this."
  When he returned there was an addendum to his note: "So have I."

*   *   *

YOU can always tell the stranger in our local pub.
  He's the one who puts his drink down on the bar.

*   *   *

A VENTRILOQUIST asked the barmaid for a gottle of gear and then drank it without moving his lips.

*   *   *

"DO you serve women in this bar?"
  "No, you have to bring your own."

THE barman gave me a nasty look. I didn't need it. I already had one.

* * *

HE wanted to go to a topless bar.

So they took him to a pub without a roof.

* * *

THE barman at the bush pub was one of the toughest he had ever seen; muscles, tatts, unshaven, sweaty and pulling beers in a black singlet.

The shearer couldn't take his eyes off him. "What the hell d'yer think yer staring at?" said the barman eventually.

"I just can't get over the likeness. It's a truly remarkable resemblance," said the shearer. "You are a dead-ringer for my wife. In fact if it wasn't for the moustache..."

"I haven't got a moustache," interrupted the barman.

"No, but my wife has!"

* * *

THE barmaid wondered where the voice came from, before she saw the little lad in short pants with his nose just reaching the bar.

"Hey, you. I said I'll have a glass of beer and a packet of fags," insisted the brat.

The barmaid saw that he was a lad of about 13.

"Do you want to get me into trouble?" she said.

"Forget the sex, just give me the beer and fags," he said.

* * *

ALTHOUGH it was a tough Outback pub, Dick the barman could cope with the evening rush because everyone drank beer. Well, everyone except the town's doctor who, as regular as clockwork, would dash in at 6.30 each evening and order an almond dacquiri.

One night, at the peak of the rush hour, Dick saw the good medic pushing his way through the crowd and realised he had run out of almonds.

357

Like any good barman he was equal to the task, snatched up some hickory nuts, crushed them, and had the drink ready by the time the doctor breasted the bar.

The doctor tasted it, tried it again, and said: "This is not an almond dacquiri Dick!"

"No, it's a hickory dacquiri, Doc!"

* * *

THE guest complained to the proprietor of an Outback pub that the outhouse was full of flies.

"What time did you go down there?"

"Oh, about noon," said the guest.

The licensee nodded his understanding. "You should go down about one o'clock," he said "They are all in the dining room then!"

* * *

"THE flies are thick," said a drinker.

"Well what would you expect out here," said the barman, "educated ones?"

* * *

BLOKE fronted the bar with a newt perched on his shoulder and after serving his fifth beer the barman could contain his curiosity no longer.

"You've got a newt on your shoulder," he said.

"I know," said the drinker. "His name is Tiny."

"Why Tiny?" asked the barman.

"Because he's my newt!" was the obvious answer.

* * *

PADDY rushed into the bar and said: "Quick, a beer before the fight starts, quick."

The barman pulled a beer and Paddy gulped it down.

"Quick, another beer before the trouble starts," he said.

The barman watched him quaff the second pot and said: "Righto, when is this row supposed to start?"

"Right now," burped Paddy, "I'm broke!"

PADDY ordered a pot of stout, but as soon as it was placed before him he cancelled the order and asked the barman for a pot of lager instead.

When he drank it the barman asked for the money.

Paddy was indignant. "I gave you a pot of stout for it."

"But you didn't pay for that either."

"Well I didn't drink it, did I!"

* * *

THE travelling salesman arrived at the one-pub three-dog town and fronted the bar. After a couple of drinks he said to the barman: "Is there any night life hereabouts?"

"You just missed it by a few days. She's gone to the city for a holiday."

* * *

THEN there's the Scot who drinks Scotch and Horlicks. When it is his turn to shout he is fast asleep.

* * *

A SCOT pushes his way to the bar. "I've had an attack of the Yaws," he says to the barman.

"What's Yaws?" he says.

"Double whisky," says the canny Scot.

* * *

A SCOT ordered a pot of beer and as the barman handed it over he said, "D'yer think yer canna fit a nip o' whisky in it too?"

"Certainly," said the barman.

"Then fill it ta the top wi' beer."

* * *

THERE is a pub in town that has a fifty cent entrance fee. It's to keep out the riff-raff.

* * *

BLOKE went into a pub and had a ploughman's lunch. The ploughman became quite agitated.

* * *

PADDY fronted the bar and said: "Drinks all round, barman, and have one yourself."

Paddy was immediately the toast of the pub and after all pots were quaffed the barman gave him the bill.

"But I haven't got a cent," he said.

The angry barman grabbed him by the scruff of the neck and hurled him straight through the swinging doors onto the pavement outside.

It was a few moments before Paddy managed to stand himself up and dust himself down. He staggered back into the pub.

"Drinks all round," he proudly declared for a second time, "but not you, barman. One drink and you go bloody mad."

* * *

AFTER a long overseas assignment Charlie returned to the pub he liked to call his local.

"You know," he said nostalgically to the barmaid, "it's all of ten months since I've had a drink here."

"Look," she replied, "this is my first night and I'm serving as fast as I can!"

* * *

TWO brothers were leaning on the bar enjoying a drink when one pushed two bottle-tops across to the barman as payment for a round.

In response to the puzzled look on the barman's face the elder of the brothers beckoned him close and whispered: "My brother is not the full two-bob. He always pays in bottle-tops. If you can humour him for a while I will settle up before we leave."

The barman wasn't entirely happy with this arrangement, but went along with it for the rest of the afternoon.

When both brothers went to stagger out that evening he said "Hoy," and indicating the great heap of bottle-tops said: "What about settling up?"

"No worries," said the elder brother turning back and throwing a garbage bin lid on the counter. "Here, take it out of this and keep the change!"

HE was about to enter the Pig & Whistle when he was accosted by a nun who began berating him on the evils of strong drink.

He was equal to the challenge. "Unless you've tried a drop yourself, Sister, you don't know what the hell you're talking about. Don't knock it unless you've tried it."

He ranted on until he convinced her to have a taste.

"Well, only for the purpose of argument, mind. What do ladies drink?"

"Try a gin and tonic," he said.

"Okay, but I'm not going into that evil place, and I'm not drinking from their glasses." She unhooked a tin mug from her belt. "Get me some in this."

When he fronted the bar for a beer and a pannikin of gin the barman said: "Don't tell me that nun is still out there!"

* * *

THE conversation stopped as the old bloke entered the pub. He was in his pyjamas, slippers and with the aid of a walking frame shuffled towards the bar.

"I'll have three double Scotches," he whispered to the barman.

The drinks were placed in front of him. He gulped down two and just before he quaffed the third he said: "Shouldn't be drinking these really, with what I've got."

"Why?" asked the barman. "What've you got?"

"Just 15 cents," replied the old-timer.

* * *

A BLOKE with a pig under his arm approached the bar.

"Where did you get that?" asked the barman.

"I won it in a raffle," replied the pig.

QUESTIONS

SHOULD single crabs have nippers?

CAN a cross-eyed teacher control her pupils?

IS it cruel to sew buttons on flies?

IF a light sleeper sleeps with the light on, does a hard sleeper sleep with the window open?

COULD a drinking lizard be any flatter?

COULD a half-wit work part time for intelligence?

INSTEAD of having ballet girls prancing around on tip-toe why don't they hire taller showgirls?

IF the answer is "9W" what was the question?

The question is: "Hey Fritz. Do you spell Wagner with a V?"

IF the answer is "Washington Irvine"

The question is: Who was the first president of the United States, Fred?"

   ★ ★ ★

WHY is 'abbreviation' such a long word?

R

RADIO ANNOUNCERS

THE radio announcer was delighted to hear the way in which his little son said his prayers, concluding with: "And here again, Dear God, are the headlines."

* * *

AN Aussie on a flight to Rome got talking to the fellow seated beside him and couldn't help noticing he had one heck of a stutter. He was even more astonished when his new acquaintance told him, with difficulty, that he was going for an audition as an announcer for Radio Vatican.

"How do you rate your chances?" asked the Aussie.

"Ner, ner, ner, not too good," he replied. "They will per-per probably ger-ger give the job ter-ter some ber-bloomin' Catholic!"

* * *

A RADIO announcer is one who works for the love of mike.

* * *

THE longest word in the English language is announced by disc jockeys as "Now a word from our sponsor."

RELIGION

THE trouble with born-again Christians is that they are a worse pain in the neck the second time around.

THE meek had a meeting today and decided they don't want to inherit the earth.

* * *

PEOPLE who use the rhythm method of contraception are usually called Parents.

* * *

FROM the pulpit the vicar announced that one of his flock, Miss Helen Hunt, had found a purse containing money, a variety of personal items and what he believed to be a small packet of white balloons. "So whoever has lost this purse, go to Helen Hunt for it!"

* * *

AS the proud father handed the baby to the vicar at the christening font the cleric said: "And what will we call this little chap?"

"It's a girl," whispered the father. "You've got hold of my thumb!"

* * *

THERE was a knock on the door and Fred found himself being asked to become a Jehovah's Witness.

Quick on his feet, Fred replied: "I didn't even see the accident," and shut the door.

* * *

THE priest took Paddy aside. "I've been told that you went to a football match last Sunday morning instead of coming to Mass."

"No father, not true, and what's more, I've got the fish to prove it."

* * *

THE protestant minister met his friend the priest and said he dreamed about a Catholic heaven last night.

"It looked like a nice place, with plenty of pubs, bright music and people dancing about," he said.

"That's funny," said the priest. "Only last night I dreamt about a Protestant heaven. It looked nice with lots of flower beds, pretty trees and gardens."

"And what were the people doing?" asked the vicar.

"What people?" replied the priest.

* * *

THE vicar's term at the parish was up and he was about to be transferred. The regular parishioners had gathered at a tea party in his honour.

"We'll really miss you," said one little old lady. "No matter who they send as a replacement he will never be as good as you."

The vicar was flattered, but he assured her his successor would be an adequate and caring pastor.

"No, no," the old-timer insisted, "it's always the same. We've had six ministers here in my time and I can assure you each one has been worse than the one before!"

* * *

THE not-too-successful minister was asked by the bishop why he had entered the clergy.

"I was called," he replied.

"Are you sure," pondered the bishop, "it wasn't some other noise you heard?"

* * *

A BISHOP had fallen seriously ill and was told by his doctor not to have too many visitors. But when his long-time agnostic friend called he was ushered in to the bishop's bedside.

"My Lord," said the unbeliever, "I do appreciate you seeing me when your friends have not been admitted."

"It's like this," said the bishop, "I feel confident of seeing my friends in the next life, but I was concerned that this might be my last chance of seeing you."

* * *

PADDY crept around the back of the country parish presbytery and nicked one of the priest's chooks. He then promptly went to confession.

"I stole a chook, father," he began. "I know it was very wrong and I am sorry. Can I give it to you for repentence?"

365

"Certainly not," said the priest. "I don't want it. Return it to the man you stole it from."

"Oh, he says he doesn't want it," said Paddy.

"In that case you might as well keep it and say ten Hail Mary's."

* * *

AS Rabbi Rozenbloom was passing St Patrick's, Fr O'Calleghan rushed out in an agitated state. "Izzi, you're just the man," said the priest. "Can you help me out of a tight spot?"

The priest explained that he was double booked. He had to officiate at the funeral of the local bishop but couldn't find another priest to take over the confession session.

"Surely you can stand in for me. It's only an hour."

The rabbi said he didn't know anything about confession. Jews were not into confessing anything.

"There's nothing to it," insisted the priest. "Come with me now and listen to the first few, then you can take over."

When they got to the dark confessional the rabbi sat behind the priest and listened to the procedure.

A woman came in: "Father I have sinned."

"What have you done my child?"

"I have committed adultery."

"How many times?"

"Four times father, and I sincerely repent."

"Put $2 in the poor box and say ten Hail Marys and you will receive absolution," said the priest.

Then a second woman came in.

"Father I have sinned."

"What have you done my child?"

"I have committed adultery."

"How many times?"

"Twice, Father."

"Put $1 in the poor box and say five Hail Marys, and you will be forgiven," said the priest.

366

As soon as the woman had left the priest whispered to the rabbi, "You have got the hang of it now, quick, take my place, I have to rush."

The rabbi settled down in the priest's position and soon enough another woman knelt at the other side of the grill.

"Father, I have sinned," she said.

"What have you done my child?"

"I have committed adultery."

"How many times?"

"Just the once, father."

"Well, you had better go and do it again. It's two for a dollar this week."

*　　*　　*

"FORGIVE me Father, but I have had an obsession about stealing wood from the timber mill where I work. I have suffered with this problem for years. What shall I do?"

"That's alright my son," said the priest. "But because this sin has been perpetuated for so long I must ask you to make a novena."

"If you've got the plans Father, I've got the timber."

*　　*　　*

TERESA went to confession and told the priest she had sinned three times that week. She said she had slept with Shaun on Tuesday, Paddy on Wednesday and Shamus on Friday night. "Oh Father what should I do?"

"On your way home, my child," he said. "Call in at Con the Fruiterer's, buy a lemon and suck it."

"Oh Father, will that cleanse me of my sins?"

"No. But it should take that damn smile off your face."

*　　*　　*

ON Saturday nights the three lads always went out on the town together, but Shamus always made a point of going past the church first so he could duck into confession while the other two waited outside.

"It's been a week since my last confession father," said

Shamus, "and I'm sorry to say that I have sinned of the flesh once again."

"Was it that O'Flannagan hussey from the dairy?"

"No father."

"Was it the cheeky Costanzo girls in the fruit shop?"

"No father."

"Don't tell me it was the widow Murphy flauntin' her wares again?"

"No father."

"Well do your usual penance and be off with you then," said the priest.

Shamus rushed out of the church to his waiting mates. "Got at least three good tips for tonight," he said.

* * *

"FATHER, yesterday I made love to my wife."

The priest explained that there was nothing wrong with that.

"But Father, I did it with... lust."

Again the priest re-assured the man that it was no sin.

"But Father, it was the middle of the day."

The priest was growing uncomfortable with the description but assured his parishioner that it was a natural act for man and wife.

"But Father, it was sheer passion. As she leant over the deep freeze I just jumped on her and we did it on the floor. Am I banned from the church?"

"Of course not," said the exasperated priest.

"Oh good. We're both banned from Safeways."

* * *

LITTLE Patrick to little Isaac: "Our parish priest knows more than your rabbi."

Isaac: "That's because you tell him everything."

* * *

THE vicar, the priest and the rabbi were always arguing about which was the true religion. But they were friends

368

enough to make a pact that whoever died first the other two would each put $300 in the coffin to ensure admittance to the Pearly Gates.

It came to pass that the vicar died first. The other two attended the funeral service and as good as his word the priest approached the coffin and put in his $300. The rabbi followed, wrote a cheque for $600, put it in beside the vicar and took his $300 change.

* * *

MY wife converted me to religion. I never believed in hell until I married her.

* * *

IT all started in the Garden of Eden, and one day Adam was intrigued by the antics of a buck rabbit. "What's he doing?" he asked God, and was told that the rabbits were simply making love.

He saw two birds doing something similar, and upon enquiry from on high was told they were also making love.

"Why I haven't I got anybody to do that with?" he asked God, who replied that he would fix it first thing next morning.

Sure enough, when Adam awoke, there was Eve laying beside him. He took her by the hand and they ran into the bushes.

Ten minutes later Adam emerged from the bushes. "Hey God, what's a headache?"

* * *

HELL is multi-cultural.

The Germans are the police force, the Italians the defence force, the Indonesians are in charge of housing, and the Indians run the railways. The Irish make the laws, the English are the cooks and the common language is Dutch.

* * *

A MINOR religious sect in India worships the Goddess of the Harvest, Kali. Every morning they visit Kali's temple and make an offering; a watermelon.

They present the offering and then sing their sacred song: "Here's another melon Kali baby!"

*   *   *

A NUN raced in to mother superior's office screaming and waving her hands. "Oh, mother," she cried "we seem to have a case of hepatitis!"

"Well, my dear, bring it in," said mother superior. "I'm sick to death of Bernie Smith's Bodega."

*   *   *

SATURDAY night is confession night but Father O'Riley stopped Pat as he entered the church. "Pat, the church is full. Can you come back tomorrow night? You haven't committed murder since last time have you?"

"Indeed I haven't," said Pat and he turned to leave.

On the way out he met Shamus. "Go home Shamus and come back tomorrow. They are only hearing murders tonight!"

*   *   *

THE monastery was in financial trouble and decided to go into the fish and chip business. One night a customer rapped on the door which was opened by a monk.

"Are you the fish friar?"

"No," replied the robed figure, "I'm the chip monk!"

*   *   *

"I DON'T like the look of the new missionary," said one cannibal to the other.

"That's alright," said the other, "just eat the potatoes."

*   *   *

ISRAELI prime minister Rabin invited the Pope to a game of golf. Since the Pope had no idea of the game he convened the college of cardinals and asked their advice.

"Call Greg Norman, make him a cardinal, tell Rabin you're sick and send Cardinal Norman in your place."

Honoured by the Pope's request Greg Norman agreed to represent him.

When he returned from the game the Pope asked how he had done. "I came in second," said Norman.

"You mean Rabin beat you?"

"No, Your Holiness, Rabbi Nicklaus did."

       ★   ★   ★

THE sermon for the evening was "Christian Perfection," and the minister was quick to point out that this was an ideal state of grace unattainable by the sinners as constituted the nondescript congregation before him. Nevertheless, in the course of his sermon he challenged anyone present to stand and proclaim they were perfect. To his astonishment a bloke in the fifth pew got to his feet.

"Do you dare claim you are perfect?" thundered the cleric.

"No, not me," replied the man, "I am standing proxy for my wife's first husband!"

       ★   ★   ★

A COUPLE who went to the movies found themselves sitting directly behind two nuns; the ones with the large headgear.

Trying to see the screen past these obstacles the girl muttered to her boyfriend: "It would be nice to go to Scotland, there are not so many nuns there."

The boyfriend replied audibly: "What about Sweden, there were even fewer there."

One of the nuns turned around, gave the couple a sweet smile and said: "Why don't you both go to hell, you won't find any there!"

       ★   ★   ★

THE two men dressed in black were the only occupants in a compartment on a long train journey. After a time one said, "Excuse me, but would I be right in thinking you are a Catholic priest?"

"Yes. And would you be a rabbi?"

"I am," said the first.

They had a lot of time to kill and eventually the rabbi said: "Have you ever broken a commandment?"

The priest admitted that he had "taken a woman."

After a while the priest said: "Have you ever eaten pork?"

The rabbi looked around as if to check nobody else was in the compartment, then nodded his head, "yes," he whispered.

The long silence was broken by the priest. "Sex is much better than pork isn't it!"

*　　*　　*

A JEWISH tailor was troubled the way his son had turned out and went to see his rabbi about it. "I brought him up in the faith, gave him a very expensive bar mitzvah, cost me a fortune to educate him. Then he tells me last week he has decided to be a Christian. Rabbi, can you help me, what will I do?"

"Funny thing you should bring that problem to me," said the rabbi. "Like you I brought my boy up in the faith, put him through university, cost me a fortune, then one day he comes and tells me he has decided to become a Christian."

"What did you do?" asked the tailor.

"I went to the synagogue and prayed to Almighty God for an answer."

"And what happened," pressed the tailor.

God's voice came into the synagogue as clear as a bell: "Funny thing you should bring that problem to me," he said.

*　　*　　*

OF course it was a certainty that Jesus was Jewish. He lived at home until he was 30, he went into his father's business, his mother thought he was divine, and he thought she was a virgin.

*　　*　　*

WHY wasn't Christ born in Australia?

Well, where would you find a virgin, and where would you find three wise men?

*　　*　　*

ACTUALLY there were four wise men. While following the star on the way to the manger, one of them said he knew a short cut.

THE city council had just taken delivery of the new mayoral car and called on the three denominations to consecrate it at a special ceremony.

The priest chanted a blessing and sprinkled it with holy water. The parson chanted a blessing and waved the cross over it. The rabbi chanted a blessing, went round the back and cut an inch off the exhaust pipe.

*　　*　　*

THE minister pranged his brand new car when a woman stopped to check her make-up in the rear-vision mirror. It was only the car's first time on the road and the minister got really angry.

He got out and roared at the woman: "Why don't you go forth and multiply!"

*　　*　　*

THE priest called on the village belle Mary O'Shaunessy who was in hospital after falling off the stage during her dance act for the church fete. "I prayed for you last night," he said.

"No need," she replied, "I'm in the phone book."

*　　*　　*

MOTHER Superior rapped the desk with her cane and asked the Grade IV girls what they wanted to be when they grew up.

One 13-year-old put up her hand and said: "I want to be a prostitute."

Mother Superior fainted with shock. When she was revived and had composed herself she asked the same girl: "What did you say you wanted to be?"

"A prostitute," affirmed the youngster.

"Oh, thank goodness, I thought for a moment you said you wanted to be a Protestant."

*　　*　　*

THE vicar walked around to the back of the church and saw three boys sitting on the ground with a handful of coins at their feet. "What might you boys be doing?" he enquired.

"We're having a competition," explained one. "Whoever tells the biggest lie gets the money."

The vicar was visibly shocked. "When I was a boy," he said, "I never told untruths."

They said "Okay, you win," and gave him the money.

* * *

IT was one of those silent orders where the only utterances allowed were the morning and evening rituals to greet the head monk. "Good Morning Head Monk" they would chant at breakfast and "Good Evening Head Monk" just before retiring.

After 15 years this ritual was getting on Brother Paddy's wick and causing rebellion to swell within him. Finally he planned a revolt.

Next day, when the brethren chanted "Good Morning Head Monk," he would deliberately chant "Evening!"

The prospect nearly sent his rocks off. He was all of a tremble at the breakfast table and when the head monk entered he stood with the rest of them and in the chorus of "Good Morning Head Monk" Paddy threw in his rebellious "Evening!"

The head monk was very perceptive. There was an awesome silence until his monotone baritone loudly proclaimed: "Someone Chanted Evening!"

* * *

AGAIN it was one of those monastic orders where the monks were silent, except on the day of their patron saint, St Titus. The first year Brother Basil asked for another blanket. The second year he asked if he could have porridge instead of wheaties. The third year he asked if he could have sugar in his tea. The fourth year he asked if he could leave the order.

"You might as well," said the head monk, "You've done nothing but winge since you've been here."

* * *

GOD spent a lot of time hacking out the commandments on one tablet of stone then he offered it to the first tribe he saw. They happened to be Germans, and after studying the bit about "Thou Shalt Not Kill," decided it was not their cup of tea. God offered them to the French. They took one look and said "What's all this ban on adultery. That's not for us," so they refused.

God then offered them to the Jews.

"How much?" said Moses.

"They are free," said God.

"Okay, we'll take two."

* * *

TRAVEL seems to induce confession, so when three priests found themselves in the same compartment of a train on a long journey to a eucharistic council, they began to bare their souls and admit to certain sins.

"It's women with me," said the first. "I find them very hard to resist and I have fallen several times."

"It's the grog with me," said the second. "Struggle as I may there have been times when the proceeds of the poor box have gone on Demon Drink."

The third priest was quiet. "I suppose you succumb to gambling," prompted his colleagues.

"No," he said. "My problem is gossip. I am a blabber-mouth and I can hardly wait to get off this train."

* * *

A DRUNK sat opposite a priest on the train and studied him for ten minutes. Finally he said, "Tell me, yer worship. Why do you wear your collar back to front?"

"Because I am a father," said the priest.

"But I'm a father too," said the drunk.

"No, I am a father to hundreds in my parish."

"Then maybe it's your trousers you should be wearing back to front," said the drunk.

* * *

LEANING on the bar, two drinkers were arguing about religion. "What do you know about the Lord's Prayer," said one. "I'll bet you ten cents you don't know the first line."

"You're on," said the other, and put his ten cents on the line.

"Now I lay me down to sleep," proudly recited the first.

"You win," said his mate. "I didn't think you knew it!"

* * *

A SWAGGIE happened to call at the vicarage, on the bite for a hand-out.

"I want to ask you one question," said the vicar when he had heard the man's hardluck story. "Do you take alcoholic drinks?"

"Before I answer that," said the swaggie thoughtfully, "is that in the nature of an enquiry or an invitation."

* * *

THE vicar had not seen young Johnny at Sunday school, so when he found the lad beside a country road minding his dad's cattle he thought it an appropriate time to deliver an impromptu sermon. "They are fine bullocks, Johnny, do you know who made them?"

"Dad did," replied Johnny.

"Oh no," the vicar smiled, "God made those bullocks."

Johnny shook his head. "God made them bulls. Dad made them bullocks."

* * *

AN Aussie on holiday in Ireland was given a piece of advice by his Irish wife before the aircraft landed at Shannon Airport. She told him not to tell religious jokes or to be critical of Catholics.

He was in a pub the very next night playing a darts match with the locals when a television bulletin reported that the Pope was sick, and near death. The locals all gathered around the television set.

"C'mon you fellas, to heck with the Pope let's get on with the game," he said.

When he woke up in hospital with his wife sitting beside him he said, "Nobody told me the Pope was a Catholic."

376

THE priest, the vicar and the rabbi were discussing how they divided the collection between God's work and themselves.

"We lean more towards the fundamentalist side," said the rabbi. "I take the money outside and literally fling it up to heaven and what God wants he keeps, what falls back on the ground, I keep."

* * *

THE district inspector of Catholic Primary Schools called at St Patrick's and decided to put Grade V to the test with some basic questions on the faith.

When he came to young Johnny he asked: "Who knocked down the Walls of Jericho?"

"It wasn't me," was the instant reply.

The inspector was taken aback. Johnny's parents obviously needed a word about their responsibility in religious instruction so he noted the address and knocked on the door that evening.

When Johnny's Mum opened the door the inspector introduced himself and said: "When I asked your boy who knocked down the Walls of Jericho, his answer was that it wasn't him." he said.

In a defiant pose she answered: "If my Johnny said he didn't do it then he didn't do it."

This was too much for the inspector and he asked to see the man of the house. Paddy was in bed, looking for work, but when the inspector revealed the purpose of his visit Paddy reached for his trousers. "Okay, okay, how much did this bloomin' wall cost anyway?"

* * *

PUZZLED about his first lesson on evolution young Joey arrived home and said: "Mum, is it really true that I am a descendant of apes, monkeys and gorillas?"

"I don't really know, darling," she replied, "I never knew any of your father's family."

377

A RICH tourist who had come to Vatican in hope of seeing the Pope was estatic when the Pontif came into the crowd near him and placed his hands on the shoulders of a derelict. The tourist was amazed to see the Pope do the same thing the following day, so he approached the tramp and offered him $100 to swap clothes, to which the down-and-outer eagerly agreed.

Next day, dressed in the tramp's smelly rags the tourist was delighted to see the Pope turn and approach him. With both hands on his shoulders the Pope bent forward and whispered: "I've told you to push off twice. Now beat it!"

* * *

THERE was a young lady called Alice
  Who peed in the presbytery's chalice
  The padre agreed
  'Twas done out of need
  And not out of Protestant malice.

* * *

A RENOWNED archaeologist named Nostle
  Discovered a fantastic fossil
  He knew from its bend
  And the knob on the end
  'Twas the peter of Paul the Apostle.

* * *

THE eternal question was being argued by a theologian and a philosopher.

The theologian defined a philosopher as being like a blind man in a darkened room looking for a black cat that wasn't there.

"That's as may be," said the philosopher, "but the theologian would have found it."

* * *

THE vicar was the lone survivor of a shipwreck and as he staggered ashore he found himself surrounded by hundreds of spear-wielding warriors.

"Oh God! I'm finished," he cried.

"No you are not," thundered a voice from on high.

"Who's that?" asked the vicar.

"It's God. Now listen carefully. Grab that spear from the thin native next to you and plunge it into the heart of the chief."

Although terrified the vicar did exactly as he was told, and as the chief collapsed to the ground the voice boomed out once more: "NOW you are finished."

RESTAURANTS
See WAITERS

THE couple had just finished dinner and the waiter was pouring a third glass of port when he noticed the gentleman slide off his chair and disappear.

"Excuse me madam," he said. "Your husband is under the table."

"No he's not," she replied white-faced. "My husband has just come through the door!"

* * *

THERE were only two restaurants in the little tourist village, one opposite the other. The visitor stopped a local and asked which served the best meals.

"Let me put it this way," he replied. "Whichever one you go into, you will have wished you had gone to the other."

* * *

THE diner called the waiter: "I would like to report this meal to the Bureau of Missing Portions."

* * *

THE food was so bad at this place the mice used to send out for take-away.

* * *

THE estate agent said it was not the right location for a Chinese restaurant.

"They'd be flogging a dead horse."

HE was in a hurry. "I'll have a crocodile sandwich. And make it snappy."

* * *

"A GLASS of vin rouge, please Ethel."

"Certainly sir, red or white?"

* * *

"WHAT'S that?" said the stuffy matron looking at the morsel on the plate set before her.

"It's pressed tongue," said the waiter.

"Yuk! I could never eat anything that came out of a beast's mouth," she said. "Bring me a boiled egg!"

* * *

FRED got into trouble when he took his girlfriend to a restaurant. They ordered soup, and when the waiter brought it his girlfriend spotted a bug in it. She screamed and said: "Waiter, remove this insect."

The waiter threw Fred down the front stairs.

* * *

SOUP du jour, $2.

Soup de yesterday, $1.

Swiss cheese with holes, 50 cents.

Extra serve of holes, 25 cents.

* * *

SIGN: Customers who pay for their meal then leave without eating will be prosecuted.

* * *

THUMP and thump the old sauce bottle

First none'l come, And then the lott'l.

* * *

"I'LL have some Spinoti Vertimicelli."

"Where did you see that?"

"On the menu."

"Oh, that's the name of the proprietor."

* * *

SHE was such a noisy eater that when she started on her soup three couples got up to dance.

* * *

THE fat lady had an enormous steak on her plate. Her

husband took one look at it and said. "Surely you are not going to eat that alone?"

"Of course not. I've just ordered some potatoes."

* * *

FRED was the type of bloke who always let his friends pick up the dinner bill. He had an impediment in his reach.

* * *

TWO crayfish were in the restaurant's aquarium. It seemed this would be their last night so the male cray put the hard word on the female.

She said: "Okay, but will you still respect me in the mornay?"

* * *

SIGN in a restaurant window: "Kitchen hand wanted, to wash dishes, and two waitresses."

* * *

THE commercial traveller entered the dining room of the hotel and gave the waiter a complicated order.

"I want two fried eggs so over-done they would chew like tennis balls, two slices of burnt toast, some charred bacon and a cup of cold coffee that tastes like dishwater and don't forget to slop it into the saucer."

The waiter scratched his head. "That's a tall order, I don't know if I can manage that."

"Oh?" said the traveller. "You didn't seem to have any trouble yesterday."

(There is another punchline to this. The traveller says he is homesick and misses his wife's cooking).

* * *

IT was a roadside cafe and the traveller asked for the menu. It read: Ham sandwiches, bacon, roast pork, pigs feet, pork chops or pork sausage."

"Could I have a glass of water first?" he asked.

"Sure," said the proprietor, "but we only have bore water out here."

"Blimey, you don't waste much of that pig do you," said the traveller.

TWO society dames settled down for a cup of coffee and when the waitress delivered the drinks she also brought a plate with two cakes; one was large, the other small.

"After you," said one socialite offering her friend the plate.

"No, after you."

"No, but I insist," said the first.

"No, you take first pick," said the other.

Eventually, one broke the stalemate by taking one of the cakes. The big one.

The other was upset. "Oh, you helped yourself first and took the big cake," she pouted.

"So, and if you had chosen first, which one would you have taken?"

"The smaller one of course."

"Well, what are you complaining about, that's what you've got!"

* * *

IT was such a high class restaurant they could provide gravy that would match your vest.

* * *

WHAT'S worse than eating shepherd's pie in a restaurant where you don't know what's gone into it?

Eating it at home where you do know what's gone into it.

* * *

THIS restaurant boasted that it could provide any dish the customer could order, no matter how alien or rare. If the chef couldn't produce the dish, then an alternative meal was on the house.

Consequently they did good business with smart alecs ordering filleted bee's knees marinated in port sauce, or roast goanna tails in curry, surrounded by Tibetan cabbage on rice.

But one evening the order was for braised elephant's kidneys on toast. A simple demand, but as ten minutes stretched to 20 the chef finally came out to apologise.

Due to an earlier rush on crocodile knuckle sandwiches they were completely out of bread.

*   *   *

MARY had a little lamb
A lobster and some prunes
A glass of wine, a piece of pie
A plate of macaroons
She gobbled down a sponge cake
And what else we don't know
But when they carried Mary out
Her face was white as snow.

ROMANCE

WHEN she asked him why he had suddenly stopped loving her, he said he had a train to catch.

*   *   *

EVE: "Do you love me?"
ADAM: "Who else?"

*   *   *

HE told his girl of course he knew where the erogenous zone was. He got booked for parking in one yesterday.

*   *   *

ON their wedding night he declared his love for her. He said he would swim the deepest river, cross the widest desert and climb the tallest mountain.

She divorced him. He was never home.

*   *   *

IN the warm summer night the young couple lay in close embrace in the canoe as it gently drifted out on the shimmering lake. She looked up at him and asked: "Will you love me always?"

"Of course my darling, which way will we try first?"

*   *   *

IT was only their second night out but he had fallen deeply in love with her after they spent the entire night in his flat. To him it was the real thing.

"Am I the first man you ever made love with?" he asked.

She studied him reflectively. "You might be. Although, you're face looks rather familiar!"

* * *

IT was one of those enchanting evenings when the lights were dim and the music softly sentimental. They sat in a corner and he gazed into her eyes.

"Drink does a lot for you," he murmured. "It makes you look beautiful, appealing, divine..."

"But I haven't been drinking," she protested.

"I know," he whispered, "but I have."

* * *

HE noticed her bedroom was stacked high with teddy bears and other toy animals, but he was more intent on the job in hand.

After they had made love he asked how it had been for her.

"Yeah, you were alright," she said. "You can have anything on the bottom shelf."

ROYALS

WHEN Prince Philip visited Korumburra to open a butter factory he looked resplendent in his naval uniform, except for the fur hat.

A local reporter, suspecting there might be a story attached to it, waited for the appropriate moment and asked: "Why the fur hat?"

"Well, I phoned Mummy last night," began the Prince, "and she asked me what I was doing today. I said I was going to Korumburra and she said "Where the fox hat?"

S

SALES

SALES resistance, of course, is the triumph of mind over patter.

* * *

"THERE'S a salesman outside with a young lady."

"Tell him I'll take one."

* * *

"HOW did the new salesman go today?"

"He got two orders. One to get out, and one to stay out."

* * *

FROM the For Sale section of the newspaper: "Home Computer, as new. Never been figured out."

* * *

A MELBOURNE youth wanted to buy a motor cycle. "It must be the fastest machine you've got," he demanded.

The salesman said he had just the bike, but its true speed could only be demonstrated at night when the roads were clear. "Come back tonight, at midnight, and I'll guarantee we can be in Geelong in 45 minutes," he said.

The youth thought for a minute. "No thanks."

"Why not. It's very fast."

"It may be, but who wants to be in Geelong at a quarter-to-one in the morning?"

"DON'T you know you can't sell second-hand cars without a licence?" said the inspector.

"Thanks, I knew I wasn't selling any, but I didn't know the reason."

* * *

AN attractive salesgirl approached a young man in a department store and said: "What would you like, sir?"

"What would I like?" he repeated. "Why I would like to take you out of here, take you to my pad, mix a nice cocktail, take you in my arms and make passionate love to you. That's what I'd like. But what I NEED is a pair of socks."

* * *

A TRAVELLER noted that the small corner store in the country town had large bags of salt stacked high around the verandah. When he went in to buy some cigarettes he saw more bags of salt stacked so high they reached the ceiling. After he paid for his cigarettes he said, "You must sell a lot of salt."

"To tell you the truth, I hardly sell any," said the storekeeper. "But the wholesale rep who calls here, boy can he sell salt."

* * *

SID was told if he didn't sell more toothbrushes he would be fired. One month later his sales record had soared and the manager called him in to explain the dramatic turnaround.

Sid explained that he got sick of calling on pharmacies. He said he set up a little table at Flinders St Station with some dry biscuits and a new dip.

"Try my dip," he would say, and a constant stream of people did so. When they enquired about the ingredients of the dip Sid told them: "Garlic and chook shit!"

They would go "Aaaargh!" and spit it out.

Then Sid would say: "Would you like to buy a toothbrush?"

IT was the old story of a salesman finding himself stranded in the country and knocking on the door of the only pub in town.

"Well, we don't have a spare room," said the proprietor, "but you are welcome to share with the little red-headed school teacher if you like."

The salesman could hardly contain his excitement. "Oh thanks. I will be a real gentleman."

"That's good," said the farmer. "So's the little red-headed school teacher!"

*   *   *

ONCE again the salesman found himself knocking on a farmhouse door seeking a bed for the night.

"Sure," said the farmer, "but we only have one spare bed and you will have to share that with Cecil, my son."

The salesman turned and headed for his car. "Crikey, how did I get into the wrong joke?"

*   *   *

HARRY and Sam were travelling together when their car broke down in the country. They approached the farmhouse and were well received by Widow Mary who fed them well and put them up for the night.

It was about nine months later when Harry rang Sam.

"Remember the night the car broke down out in the country?" he asked. "You didn't by any chance slip into the widow's bedroom did you?"

Sam admitted he did. "And you didn't by any chance use my name did you?"

Sam admitted that he did, and said he was sorry.

"Don't worry about it Sam," said Harry. "I've just got a letter from a legal firm that says she has died and left me the farm."

*   *   *

THIS salesman was travelling late at night when his car blew a tyre and he realised he didn't have a jack. It was miles from anywhere, but across the field he could see a farmhouse in silhouette against the rising moon.

"He could lend me a jack," mused the salesman as he set off towards the farm.

As he stumbled across the paddocks in the dark he wondered if farmers still had the hospitality for which they were renowned.

"It's late," he thought. "He probably won't be too pleased about being woken up. He has probably had a hard day in the field and was looking forward to a bit of rest."

He approached the farmhouse and knocked on the door.

While he waited his thoughts continued: "The poor bloke is most likely getting out of bed now. His wife could be nagging him. The jack's probably out in the cold garage. He will be upset. He could even put the dogs onto me."

When the farmer opened the door the traveller said: "To hell with your jack!"

* * *

TOLD to accompany the firm's top salesman on his round to learn the ropes the rookie noticed that before entering a prospective client's office the super salesman would always make the sign of the cross, and inevitably make a sale.

"I didn't know you had to be a Catholic," said the rookie.

"I'm not," replied his mentor. "But never tackle a client without checking your glasses, your wallet, your pen, and your zipper!"

* * *

THE travelling salesman sent a telegram to his wife: "Coming home Friday."

When he arrived home he was alarmed to find a man in bed with his wife. He went berserk, but was restrained by his mother-in-law. She urged him to keep calm and not to commit any violent and hasty action he would, in time, regret. "Leave it to me," she said. "There must be an explanation."

Next day she had her explanation. "I have gone into the matter thoroughly, and like I told you, there is a reason for your wife's behaviour. There was a postal strike on Friday and she didn't get the telegram!"

* * *

THEY just buried a salesman named Cripps
He married, on one of his trips
A widow named Block
Then died of the shock
When he found there were nine little chips.

SCHOOLS
See EDUCATION, TEACHERS

JOHNNY told his dad: "There's going to be a small meeting of the Parent Teacher Association at the school tomorrow morning.

"What's a small meeting?" asked his dad.

"Just you, me and the headmaster," said the lad.

* * *

TEACHER: "Name two pronouns?"

Johnny: "Who? Me?"

* * *

WHEN I was a kid I went to an immoral school. It had no principle and it had no class.

* * *

"STAND up all the little boys and girls who want to go to heaven," said the Sunday School teacher.

They all stood except little Fred.

"Don't you want to go to heaven," she asked Fred.

"Not yet, Miss," he said.

* * *

THE six-year-old was a study of concentration as she laboured over her drawing. "What will your picture be, Angela?" said the teacher.

"I'm drawing God," she said.

"That's a difficult subject," said teacher. "Nobody knows what he looks like."

"They will when I'm finished," said the youngster.

* * *

IT was Monday morning and Mum was having a tough time preparing a rebellious son for another week at school.

"Nobody likes me," he groaned. "Teachers don't like me. The kids don't like me. I just don't want to go anymore," he complained.

"Pull yourself together," said his mother. "School can be tough, but at 40 years of age and as principal of the school you've just got to go."

* * *

THE demure co-ed said to her tutor: "I would do anything to pass my exams."

"Anything?" he queried.

"Yes, anything."

"Well try studying," he said.

* * *

"DO you know your alphabet?"

"Yes."

"What comes after G?"

"Whizz."

"Right, and what comes after whizz?"

"Bang."

"Good boy."

* * *

ONCE I won a prize for arithmetic. The teacher asked what was 20 multiplied by four. I put up my hand first and said "thirty-four." I got the prize for being closest.

* * *

"JOHNNY, how much is three times three?"

"Nine, Miss."

"That's pretty good."

"Pretty good. It's bloody perfect."

"THAT essay on the dog is exactly word for word, the same as your brother's."

"Of course sir, it's the same dog."

*　*　*

O'GRADY was asked how many honours he received in his leaving certificate.

"Three," he said proudly. "Pure mathematics, and applied mathematics."

*　*　*

THERE are three kinds of people in this world: Those who can count and those who can't.

*　*　*

THE kids at our school were so tough the teacher used to play hookey.

*　*　*

THE voice over the phone said; "Young Tommy won't be at school today, he is very sick."

"Who is speaking?" said the principal.

"My father," said the caller.

*　*　*

YOUNG Freddy was on his feet as soon as the teacher entered the room. "Do you think it is right to punish people for things they haven't done?" he asked her.

"Certainly not," she replied.

"That's good. Because I haven't done my homework."

*　*　*

TEACHER: "What is a comet?"

Johnny: "A star with a tail."

Teacher: "Name one."

Johnny: "Mickey Mouse."

*　*　*

TEACHER: "Which month has 28 days?"

Johnny: "They all have."

*　*　*

OVER a row of hooks in the cloakroom was a sign which said: "These hooks are for teachers only."

Underneath, some bright spark had added: "They may also be used for hats and coats."

* * *

THE young schoolteacher had been assigned to a country school for three years before her mother had a chance to visit her.

Mum noticed that most of the men in town seemed to know her daughter.

"Oh they are probably fathers of some of my children," explained the teacher.

* * *

THE school inspector was sent out into the country to check on the standard of education in the bush school.

His first question to the class, "Who knocked down the Walls of Jericho?" was met with an embarrassing and fidgety silence.

"Can't you tell me?" he said pointing to young Murphy.

"It wasn't me, honest sir," was the only response.

Disappointed at the low standard of the class the inspector went to the headmaster. "I asked a young lad in your school who knocked down the Walls of Jericho and he said it wasn't him."

"The little scally-wag," said the headmaster. "I'll bet it was him all the time."

Staggered at this response the inspector sought out the president of the Parents and Teachers' Association to report the sad state of affairs.

"Well," said the president, "young Murphy comes from an honest family and you can take it from me that if he says he didn't knock them down, then he is bloody-well telling the truth."

Finally, in despair the inspector reported the matter to the Department of Education and a week later received the following reply:

"Dear Sir. With regard to your letter regarding the Walls of Jericho, we are obliged to inform you that this matter does not come within our jurisdiction. We suggest you contact the Board of Works."

* * *

THE teacher was getting to know the kids.

"What does your father do, Johnny?"

"He's a train driver, Miss."

And what does your father do, Sammy?"

"He's a policeman, Miss."

"And what about your father, Freddy?"

"He's dead, Miss."

"Oh. And what did he do before he died?"

"He clutched his throat, let out a groan and fell on the floor."

SEDUCTION

HE wined and dined her before they went to the theatre.

"Thanks for a beautiful evening," she said when he had driven her home.

"Ah, but the night's not over," he said, pouring her a glass of champagne. And as she sipped the drink he pushed two white tablets towards her.

"Aren't these aspirins?" she asked.

"Indeed they are," he replied.

"But I haven't got a headache."

"Good," he said. "Then let's go to bed."

SHEPHERDS

THE locals in the village pub watched the stranger with suspicion because it was rumoured he was a taxman. Finally, they elected one of their number to check him out.

The appointed one moved along the bar and engaged him in conversation. "You're not from these parts?" he began.

"No," said the stranger.

The local continued with the small talk for a time and then asked what the stranger did for a living.

"I'm a taxidermist," he said.

"Oh yeah," said the local. "And what have you been doing around here?"

"Had a marvellous time really," said the stranger. "Yesterday I stuffed a prize sheep dog, this morning I mounted Farmer Brown's goat and tomorrow I am going to have a go at his sow."

At this the local retreated slowly along the bar to where his mates were eager for his report.

"He tried to tell me he was a taxi driver, but I've figured him out. He's really a shepherd like us, on holiday."

SHOPPERS

FRED was talking to his mate in the pub.

"The wife is shopping crazy. She will buy absolutely anything marked down. Yesterday she came home with an escalator."

* * *

HIS wife was a kleptomaniac. But her sister was worse. She used to walk into stores backwards and leave things on the counter.

* * *

"WHERE can I get some talcum powder?" she asked the supervisor.

"Walk this way, madam" he said.

"If I could walk that way I wouldn't need the talcum powder," she answered.

* * *

WHEN he claimed his money back under their "satisfaction or money refunded guarantee," they said they were perfectly satisfied with his money.

MISS Lottzabazooma bought a dress. It was marked down 50%, and that's how she wears it.

* * *

THE advertisement for a kitchen gadget said it was so marvellous it would cut the housework in half. So she bought two.

* * *

"THANKS for your patience in showing me all that linen, but I am not buying anything myself. I am looking for my neighbour."

"Well, do you think she may be in that last bolt of pink on the top shelf?"

* * *

SHE walked into the delicatessen and selected a chicken. She prodded and poked it. She lifted one wing and sniffed underneath, lifted the other wing and did the same. Finally she looked at the chicken's rear end and gave it another sniff. "This chicken is not fresh," she declared.

"Lady," said the shopkeeper, "do you think you could pass the same test?"

SHOWBIZ

IT has been attributed to the great actress Katherine Hepburn that there wasn't much to acting. "After all," she said, "Shirley Temple could do it at the age of four."

* * *

TWO sailors spent the evening getting drunk then decided to go to a variety show. Half way through the program one sailor needed to go to the toilet. On asking directions from the usherette she told him, "Go left, then to the end of the passage on the right, left again and straight ahead."

A little the worse for wear the sailor followed the directions with some difficulty, relieved himself and eventually found his way back to his seat.

"You missed the best act," whispered his mate.

"While you were out a sailor came on stage and pissed into the orchestra pit."

* * *

A VENTRILOQUIST with the usual dummy on his lap was making several offensive jokes at the expense of the Irish. Finally, Paddy could take it no longer.

"Hey, you!" he shouted. "I object to you making fun of my countrymen."

"I'm sorry," said the ventriloquist. "I meant no offence."

"I'm not talking to you," said Paddy. "I'm talking to that cheeky little bastard on your lap."

* * *

HE will never forget his first Royal Command performance. The Queen told him to shut up.

* * *

"YOU can't resign," said the circus manager to the human cannonball. "Where would I get another man of your calibre?"

* * *

OLD actors never die, they just get smaller parts.

* * *

THE ventriloquist was so bad his lips were moving when he wasn't saying anything.

* * *

THE ventriloquist went into a pub and asked for a gottle of gear. Then he drank it without moving his lips.

* * *

CONCEITED actor: "Have you seen my latest show?"

"I never miss it. I've never seen it and I never miss it."

* * *

"DID the new show have a happy ending?"

"Sure, everybody was delighted it was over."

* * *

THE show closed after its first night. A foul play was suspected.

"THIS is an education show," said the comic. "When you leave you will say: 'That taught me a lesson'!"

*　　*　　*

IT was a sneak preview. After 15 minutes everybody sneaked out.

*　　*　　*

HOLLYWOOD is the only place where the brides keep the bouquets and throw away the grooms.

*　　*　　*

HER adoration of the actor was obvious. "When will your life story be published," she asked, "I would love to read it."

"Oh, not yet," he said, "My life story will be written posthumously."

"Well, I do hope it is soon," she gushed.

*　　*　　*

THE actor had a hard time deciding whether to marry the chorus girl, who was very pretty, but a little scatty, or his leading lady, who was not so beautiful, but had a magnificent singing voice.

It was a close decision, but he went for quality and married the soprano.

The morning after the honeymoon he took a good hard look at his bride. Then he nudged her and said, "For Goodness sake, sing!"

*　　*　　*

IN Hollywood parents have to edit the fairytales they tell their children: "Once upon a time there were three bears. Daddy Bear, Mummy Bear, and a baby bear by a previous marriage."

*　　*　　*

WHEN the much married actress finally died her friends clubbed together for a fitting funeral and a tomb stone with the fitting epitaph: "At last she sleeps alone."

*　　*　　*

THIS week's movie trailer: "You yelled when you saw

397

"Psycho," you screamed when you saw "Cape Fear," and you literally shrieked when you saw "Vampire Wolves." So now a word from the manager: Why do you make so much bloody noise at the pictures?"

* * *

A PEDANTIC theatrical producer decided to direct his own wedding. He insisted on two rehearsals, and after the second he called for someone to replace the leading female role.

* * *

A GROUP of showgirls had been entertaining the troops at a remote army camp. After their performance the major asked: "Would you girls prefer to mess with the officers or the troops?"

"Makes no difference to us," said one shapely blonde, "but we've just got to have something to eat first."

* * *

TWO nuns had gone to the circus, but after the show they were dismayed to find heavy rain had created a deep puddle between the bigtop and their bus stop. They didn't want to get their habits or their shoes wet.

Two clowns came to their rescue and offered to piggy-back them across the water.

Halfway across one clown stopped and said to his mate: "Do you realise that this is virgin on the ridiculous?"

* * *

PADDY dragged a shaggy mongrel into the talent scout's office and announced, "This is the best dog act you're ever likely t' see. This dog can count, and I trained him m'self."

The agent gave the pair a dubious stare.

"Okay, I'll prove it," said Paddy, and holding a commanding finger to the dog said, "Right Nigel, what's two and two?"

The dog went "woof, woof." Then there was a pause until Paddy said, "C'mon Nigel, you can do it." There was another "woof" then a long pause and another "woof."

"C'mon Nigel," said Paddy. "Just one more."

*　　*　　*

BERT said he had two tickets for the Elton John show.

"Don't want to go, he's awful," said Fred.

"But you've never heard him."

"I have heard a bloke at the pub imitate him," said Fred, "and he's damned awful."

*　　*　　*

ONE actress complained to her friend that she was so tired. "I didn't get to sleep until after three," she said.

"No wonder you are tired," said her friend, "two is all I need."

*　　*　　*

THE young actor was excited at getting a job and rushed home to tell his father: "Guess what, Dad, I play a man who has been married for 30 years."

"No matter, son. Let's hope you will eventually get a speaking part!"

*　　*　　*

HE had been the clumsiest dancer in the chorus line and when he fell into the orchestra pit he was carted off to hospital.

Like everybody in show business he was worried about being replaced in his absence. "Oh don't worry about that," said his mate on a visit to the ward. "Everybody has been talking about you. Why only yesterday the director said, 'Whatever happened to old whats-is-name'!"

*　　*　　*

AT the reunion of Actors Equity members one old thespian who had the reputation of being an utter bore looked around the room and said, "How many great actors do you think there are in this room?"

"One less than you think," came the reply.

THEY were dancing together at the Arts Fancy Dress Ball. "Can I drive you home?" he leered.

"Of course," she said. "What kind of a car have you got?"

"I don't have a car," he said. "But I've got a whip."

* * *

A YOUNG trapeze artist well stacked
Is faced by a very sad fact
Imagine the pain
When time and again
He catches his wife in the act.

* * *

PADDY had a good repertoire of jokes and was always making his mates roar with mirth.

"You should go on the stage, Paddy," they said.

"No way," said Paddy. "People would laugh at me."

* * *

ACTORS' Equity's surveillance officer had been following Dan Duo's Dog Show around the country circuit for some time. He suspected there was something phoney about a cocker spaniel playing the piano while a fox terrier sang assorted excerpts from Gilbert and Sullivan.

And sure enough he caught them out.

At the next show he rushed onto the stage to expose them. "The fox terrier can't sing a damned note," he told the audience, "the cocker spaniel is a ventriloquist!"

* * *

INSTEAD of getting ballet dancers to prance around on tiptoe, why don't they get taller showgirls?

* * *

THE man had sought an audition with a prominent theatrical agent who was pressed for time and when the newcomer said he was a bird impersonator he dismissed him with some irritation.

"Bird imitators are more common than pop singers," said the agent. "I've got no time to hear you now. Just give me your name and leave your number."

The man said his name was Willie Warbler, took a numbered ring off his left leg and dropped it on the desk, laid an egg, cacked on the window sill and flew away.

* * *

SHE had egged him on to be an actor, and his very first audience egged him off.

* * *

HIS mother would be most upset if she knew he was an actor. She still thinks he is running dope from Bangkok.

* * *

THE definition of a Shakespearean actor is tall, dark and some ham.

Definition of a conceited actor is Ham and Ego.

* * *

THERE was a young actor named Bates
Who danced the fandango on skates
But he fell on his cutlass
Which rendered him nutless
And practically useless on dates.

SIGNS

ENGLISH speaking travellers, particularly travel writers, should forgive the well-meaning attempts to anglicise official notices in foreign lands. Instead, I've chuckled and written them down. Indians have produced more than their share of wonderful signs and are the source of the majority listed below:

* * *

NOTICE on a Kashmir houseboat, where drinking water is always regarded with suspicion: "Clients should disregard worries about the water on this boat. It has been personally passed by the proprietor."

* * *

SIGN in an Indian maternity hospital: "Visitors. Husbands only. One per patient."

SIGN in a Bombay beauty parlour: EARS PIERCED WHILE YOU WAIT.

* * *

SIGN on an Irish pub door: "Gone to lunch, back in an hour. PS: Already gone 15 minutes!"

* * *

SIGN on a Melbourne pub: "Good clean entertainment, every night except Monday."

* * *

PLAYERS picked for the darts team will be pinned to the notice board on Thursday.

* * *

SIGN beside the sandwiches on the bar said: "Do not touch the food."

* * *

"TRY our home-made pies. You'll never get better."

* * *

IN several pubs: "We have an agreement with the bank. They don't serve beer and we don't cash cheques."

* * *

IN a Scottish pub: Happy Hour, 5-30 pm until 6 pm.

* * *

LADIES are requested not to have children in the bar.

* * *

DON'T drink if you're driving. There's no cure for the mourning after.

* * *

IF you are driving, be sure you have a car.

* * *

DON'T drive yourself to drink. Get a chauffeur.

* * *

ONE for the road could be the pint of no return.

* * *

PLEASE do not leave while the bar is in motion.

* * *

THIRST come. Thirst served.

OUTSIDE the Registry Office: Marry Now, Pay Later!

* * *

SIGN outside the church: "Next week's preacher will be pinned on the notice board."

* * *

DIRECTIONS on a jam jar: "To open lid, pierce with knife to release vacuum, then push off."

* * *

PATRONS WHO CONSIDER OUR STAFF UNCIVIL SHOULD SEE MANAGER. — New Delhi restaurant.

* * *

CUSTOMERS GIVING ORDERS WILL BE PROMPTLY EXECUTED. — New Delhi restaurant.

* * *

The Germans have theirs too: PATRONS WHO REQUIRE BATHING, PLEASE NOTICE THE CHAMBERMAID.

* * *

IN CASE OF FIRE, PLEASE DO YOUR BEST TO ALARM THE PORTER.

* * *

AND one from a British tourist brochure: These self-contained apartments are excellently situated near the Torquay sea front. Practically on the level.

* * *

THE Houses of Parliament in Budapest are magnificent structures fronting the Danube, but as our Hungarian guide put it: "The buildings are best viewed from the backside."

* * *

TO avoid burning your hands with hot water feel the water first before putting your hands in.

* * *

"INSTANT hot water, in two minutes."

* * *

PASSENGERS HIT BY CANCELLED TRAINS — Leader Newspapers, Victoria.

403

FROM Flinders Street railway station, Melbourne: TOILETS OUT OF ORDER, please use platform 7–8.

* * *

PADDY had a sign under his arm which read LONG VEHICLE. A cop stopped him and asked him where he got it. Paddy replied: "It fell off the back of a truck."

* * *

SIGN in a Fitzroy fruit shop: "God help those who help themselves!"

* * *

SIGN in a book shop read: "Browsers welcome, both high browse and low browse."

* * *

SIGN in an Albury Returned Servicemen's Club says: "Don't thump the machines, look for an attendant!"

* * *

SIGN on a photocopy machine: "The typists' reproduction equipment is not to be interferred with without prior permission of the manager."

* * *

ON the barber shop window: HAIR CUT, WHILE YOU WAIT.

* * *

LARGE sign on the door of an Australian church: "This is the House of God, and these are the Gates of Heaven." And below in smaller print: "This door is locked between the hours of 6 pm and 10 am."

* * *

"BOAT for sale, one owner, green in colour."

* * *

OUT to lunch. If not back by five, out to dinner also.

* * *

SIGN outside a funeral parlour: "Parking for clients only!"

* * *

WANTED. Man to wash dishes and two waitresses.

PRICES subject to change, according to customer's attitude.

* * *

SIGN at a creek: "When this sign is under water the crossing is dangerous."

* * *

SIGN in a pub: "If you are drinking to forget, please pay for your drinks in advance."

* * *

PLEASE do not insult our bartenders. Customers we can get.

SMOKING

CANCER cures smoking.

* * *

SMOKING shortens your cigarettes.

* * *

HE has read so much about the effects of smoking that he has finally given up reading.

* * *

IT took a lot of will power, but finally he has given up trying to give up smoking.

* * *

"WILL you give up smoking for me?" she said.
   "Who says I've been smoking for you?" he said.

* * *

"GIVE me a cigarette, Fred."
   "But I thought you had given up smoking."
   "Well, I've reached the first stage. I've stopped buying them."

* * *

"HOW many fags do you smoke a day?"
   "Any given amount."

* * *

ASKED why he smoked 100 cigarettes a day, Fred replied: "Coughing is the only exercise I get."

FRED and Harry formed Smokers Anonymous. When one of them feels like a cigarette he rings the other and they get drunk instead.

* * *

DON'T smoke in bed, for the ashes which fall on the floor may be your own.

* * *

AND one for the smokers: And old bloke from the bush settled himself into the train compartment and began to light up his pipe, much to the obvious disgust of the only other occupant, an elderly woman.

"Do you know," she said, with all the disapproval she could muster, "my husband is 65 and he has never once put a pipe in his mouth."

The old-timer pondered this for a moment and replied, "I'm just on 70, and I've never put it anywhere else."

SONGS

SHE used to go out with the landlord, but now she goes with the lease.

* * *

YOU can lead a horse to water, but you can't lead a whore to culture.

* * *

SHE wore a string of love beads and I knew I could count on her.

* * *

THE volcano song: "Larva Come Back to Me."

* * *

DRINK to me Only with Thine Eyes, cos I need all the Scotch myself.

* * *

I'LL be Seizing You, in all the old familiar places.

IF you were the only girl in the world, well okay, but as you're not, forget it.

SPEECHES

THE MC is the bloke who introduces people who need no introduction.

*　　*　　*

HE was testing the microphone. "Can you hear me in that back corner?"

"Yes," came a reply, "and I will gladly change places with somebody who can't."

*　　*　　*

I DON'T mind people looking at their watches when I'm making a speech, but it is damned disconcerting to see them shaking them to see if they are still going.

*　　*　　*

SO many people start with the words, "I am not really a speech-maker." Then they spend the next half hour proving it.

*　　*　　*

THE vicar asked the pert young widow to give a little talk to the Temperance Society because he said the men liked her short addresses.

*　　*　　*

EVERY rose has its thorn
  That's the catch life teaches
  There hasn't been a free lunch yet
  Without those boring speeches.

SPINSTERS

SHE called at the police station to complain about the young man next door. "It's not safe to go out on the street," she said. "He's always sitting on his front porch whistling dirty songs!"

MISS Prim had phoned the local police station several times to complain about the man next door who walked around his apartment completely nude. Finally the sergeant called around. "But you can't even see his window from here," he said.

"Try standing on that kitchen chair and looking through the skylight," she said.

* * *

TWO elderly spinsters were sitting on the front porch of their country house convincing each other they had made the right choice in life when a rooster chased a flurried hen past them. The hen took evasive action, running around the house three times, then dashed onto the road, straight into the path of an oncoming car.

"See that," said one spinster, "she'd prefer to die."

* * *

SPINSTER Brown rang the police to say she had captured a man climbing into her bedroom window, and that they could call around for him next morning.

SPORT
See FOOTBALL, TENNIS, CRICKET

"I'M a little stiff from Badminton."

"I don't care where you come from."

* * *

SHE thought lacrosse was something you found in la church.

* * *

BOXING is like marriage. The preliminaries are often better than the main event.

* * *

AN Englishman, an Irishman and a Scot were sentenced to share a prison cell. The Englishman produced a pack of cards.

"At least we can pass the time playing poker."

The Scot said he liked music and would while away the time playing his mouth organ.

The Irishman smiled and said he had something better than either of his mates and produced a packet of Tampax. "It says on the packet that you can go riding, swimming, skiing, and play tennis with these."

SQUELCH

WHEN a reporter asked New Zealand's ex-prime minster David Lange if he was concerned about the exodus of New Zealanders to Australia the PM replied, "Not at all. I think it is bound to raise the IQ of both countries."

* * *

HE saw himself as a maker and shaker, but he was having trouble clinching the deal with two executives he had tried to impress over lunch.

He saw Bob Ansett pass by on the way to the gents, and quickly excused himself to follow. He lined up beside Bob and introduced himself. "My name's Peter. I have been a fan of yours for a long time, Bob. I admire your corporate image. Could you do me one great favour, little cost to you, but forever appreciated by me, if you just say hello to me as you pass my table. It would help me clinch the deal."

"Not at all," said Bob Ansett.

Sure enough, our yuppie had got settled and had resumed his spiel when Bob Ansett came by and said, "Hi Peter, how's it going?"

"Push off, Bob. Can't you see I'm talking business!"

* * *

THE local State School decided to challenge the toffs at the Grammar School to a game of football. The date was arranged and the State School boys decided to adopt a gentlemanly stance and send the college a telegram which read: "May the best team win."

The college sent a telegram in reply which read: "May the better team win."

* * *

THE train was rattling towards a long tunnel and in one compartment sat an Englishman, an Irishman, a pretty young woman and a little old lady.

The train entered the tunnel and all went black. There was a loud kiss followed at once by an even louder smack.

When the train emerged from the tunnel the four occupants were still in their seats and busy with their own thoughts about what happened.

The pretty young woman was thinking: "Why would that Irishman want to kiss an old lady?"

The old lady was thinking: "What a hussy sitting there as if nothing had happened when I know that Englishman kissed her."

The Englishman was thinking: "I didn't do a damned thing, so why should I get my face slapped?"

And the Irishman was thinking: "How about that! I kiss my own hand, smack an Englishman in the mouth and get away with it!"

* * *

PADDY O'Leary boarded a train and found himself sharing a compartment with a snobby Englishman and his large dog.

"And what koind o' dog be that?" he asked the Pommie.

"It's a cross between an ape and an Irishman," was the surly reply.

"You mean it's related to both of us," said Paddy.

* * *

THE drunk boards the train and plonks himself down beside a priest and begins to read the paper.

He looks up after a bit and says: "Tell me father, what causes arthritis?"

It was just the opening the priest wanted. "I will tell you what causes arthritis my man," he said with passion.

"It's immoral living, too much drinking and smoking and no doubt sins of the flesh. How long have you had it?"

"Oh it's not me, father," said the drunk. "It says here the Pope's got it."

* * *

A NEWLY commissioned army lieutenant was standing outside a public phone box sorting through some coins. He stopped a passing soldier to ask if he had change of a dollar.

"I think so, mate," said the trooper diving his hand into his pocket.

"Just a minute, that's no way to address an officer," snapped the young lieutenant. "Let's try that again shall we. Do you have change of a dollar?"

The trooper snapped to attention and saluted. "No, sir!"

* * *

SHE was the self-appointed supervisor of village morals and accused a workman of having reverted to drink because with her own eyes she had seen his car parked outside the local pub.

The accused made no defence, but that night he parked his car outside her house, and left it there all night.

* * *

AS he arrived home from the pub he noticed his wife ironing her bra and couldn't refrain from commenting, "I don't know why you bother with that, dear, you've nothing to put in it."

She continued ironing and casually remarked, "I often think the same thing when I'm ironing your underpants."

* * *

AFTER 25 years of marriage a couple decided on an amicable divorce. To celebrate the granting of the decree they had dinner together. After the third glass of champagne the husband said, "There's something I have always wanted to ask you, but I didn't have the nerve. Now it can't possibly worry me."

"What's that?" said his immediate ex-wife.

"Why is it that five out of our six children have black hair and Tommy is so blonde."

She didn't answer. "Come on, you can tell me now," he insisted. "Whose child is Tommy?"

Finally she acquiesced. "Well, if you really want to know, Tommy is your child."

* * *

A NUN had just beaten three young men to the last table in the railway cafeteria. They sat down beside her and decided to embarrass her with a conversation which would force her to leave.

"Your Mum and Dad get married yet?" said one to his mate.

"No. What about yours?"

"No. Not interested in that church stuff."

This went on for awhile until the nun said: "Excuse me, would one of you bastards pass me the salt?"

STINGY
AS IN CHEAP, MEAN OR PARSIMONIOUS

JOCK McTavish went to the Op Shop to buy a suitcase for his holiday. He found one at a reduced price. The manager asked if he wanted it wrapped. "Nae mon. Just put the brown paper and string inside."

* * *

HE took all his money out of the bank for a holiday. After it rested in his pocket for a week he put it all back.

* * *

WHEN the police put a price on his head he gave himself up.

* * *

IF Jock and Sandy were alone in a bar together they would die of thirst.

THE first time Jock used the free air at the service station he blew out four tyres.

*   *   *

HE wouldn't shout if a shark bit him.

*   *   *

SHE said she would never go to a restaurant with Jock again. "He reads the menu from right to left," she said.

*   *   *

HER husband seldom bought her anything. He was a man of rare gifts.

*   *   *

HE took his kids to the beach and bought them an ice-cream, but they still squabbled and fought. They wanted one each.

   ... or, JOCK had promised to buy his mates a beer. Eventually he did, but they were still dissatisfied. They wanted one each.

*   *   *

JOCK was so mean that when he found a bottle of indigestion mixture, he ate a jar of pickles.

*   *   *

JOCK was down in the dumps and his office mate wondered why, because he left the pub the previous evening with a lovely blonde on his arm.

   "What happened?"

   Jock said he took the blonde to dinner, bought her chocolates and champagne and they went back to his flat for the night.

   "Well why so gloomy?"

   "I spent a fortune," said Jock, "and another bloke has just told me I could have got the same result with a couple of beers and a packet of potato chips."

*   *   *

NEXT night he hailed a cab to go home with his new girlfriend. She was so ravishingly beautiful he could hardly keep his eyes on the meter.

413

THE Salvation Army lass approached Jock and asked him for a dollar for the Lord.

"How old are ye?" said Jock.

"I'm nineteen," said the lass.

"Well, I'm 75 and I'll be seeing the Lord before you do, so I will slip him the dollar myself."

* * *

HE had been mean and stingy all his life so when he finally arrived at the Pearly Gates St Peter asked for his report card. "I once gave a dollar to a widow who was turned out of her house, and I once gave two dollars to an orphan who had just lost his parents."

God overheard it and said to St Peter: "Give him his three dollars back and tell him to go to Hell."

* * *

AN old farmer and his son had scratched out a living on their farm for 30 years. One day the son came home yelling for joy that he had won the $500,000 first prize in the lottery.

"Here Dad, here's your share," and he slapped a hundred dollar note on the table.

The old man looked at it a while. "When I was young," he said, "I never had time to smoke, drink or gamble because working this farm took all my time. In fact, I never had time to marry your Ma."

The young man considered this. "Well that's a nice state of affairs," he complained. "Of course you know what that makes me?"

"Yeah," said the old man, "and a bloody mean one at that."

* * *

TWO Scots established a business and at the end of the financial year they tried to balance the books, but no matter how many times they went through the accounts and receipts they were constantly $23.50 short.

Finally Jock confronted his partner: "Tell me the truth Angus. Have you been keeping a woman?"

PADDY had two stingy mates, Jock and Isaac. So he was surprised when they reluctantly agreed to take him out for his birthday. At the end of the meal he waited with some anxiety to see which one offered to pay.

"I'll take care of the bill," piped up Jock when the waiter approached.

Paddy went home that night amazed at Jock's generosity, until he read the newspaper headline next morning: Jewish Ventriloquist Strangled by Crazed Scotsman.

* * *

WE went round to a party at Jock's place where the water flowed like champagne.

SWEARING

WHEN he boarded the country train he explained he was tired and asked the conductor if he could be woken at Junction Town.

"Don't worry if I swear a lot," said the passenger. "I am a notorious grump when I get woken up."

"No worries," said the conductor.

It was dark when the train stopped and the conductor finally gave the passenger a shake.

"What the hell's this?" roared the passenger realising he was at the terminus. "I told you to wake me at Junction Town you godforsaken son of a no-good bastard."

The conductor listened to the long string of abuse and finally muttered: "Yes, you can sure swear a lot. But not as much as the bloke we put off at Junction Town."

* * *

YOUNG Basil had moved to town from the country and had settled in at the suburban primary school fairly well; except for his constant swearing. It was "bloody" this and "bloody" that until he was sent home with a note:

"If this boy won't stop swearing he will not be allowed to school anymore."

His father gave him a bloody hiding and sent him back next day with a note to say he wouldn't bloody well swear again.

The teacher was impressed and sent home another note. "Basil has been so good he can come to the school picnic on Saturday week."

When the big day came, little Basil set off for the picnic, with a caution and yet another note. "If he swears again, please send the little bugger straight home."

In less than an hour Basil was back, weeping his eyes out, and copped another hiding from his father for swearing.

"I didn't swear," he protested. "You sent me off on the wrong bloody Saturday. The bloody picnic is not until next bloody week!"

★　　★　　★

TWO young brothers were sent home from their country school with a note to say they had been suspended for the afternoon for swearing.

Their father gave them a hiding, a lecture and sent them to bed without dinner.

Next morning as they sat down for breakfast their father, in a more conciliatory mood, asked what they would like for breakfast.

The first one said: "I'll have some of those bloody cornflakes." He received an immediate thrashing from his father and was sent back to bed for the day.

The father then asked the second boy what he would like for breakfast.

"I don't know," he said. "But it won't be bloody cornflakes, that's for sure."

★　　★　　★

BECAUSE he had been heard swearing, young Billie had been put across his father's knee and given a few good whacks. "Now son," said his Dad, "tell me why I punished you."

The kid threw up his hands in despair. "That does it. First you belt shit out of me and now you don't know why you bloody-well did it!"

T

TACT

TACT is the ability to describe others as they see themselves.

* * *

A SALESMAN with a phenomenal record finally revealed his secret to the new sales recruits. He said he put it down to the first seven words he invariably uttered when a woman answered his knock on a door: "Miss, may I speak to your mother?"

* * *

THE patient told his psychiatrist, "I don't seem to be able to mix with people. I have no friends. When I talk to people they soon walk away. Do you think you can help me you money-grabbing parasite and incompetent shrink?"

* * *

"HERE is a photo of my new bride."
  "Gosh. She must be very wealthy."

TAXATION

WHOEVER said you couldn't be wounded by a blank obviously hasn't received a taxation form.

* * *

A CLOUDFUL of clergymen arrived at the Pearly Gates

and were gathered around the reception desk booking in when suddenly a fanfare of trumpets signalled a late arrival and St Peter called for the clergy to stand aside.

The new arrival was the taxman and he was ushered straight in on the red carpet.

The clergy were amazed and demanded to know why the preferred treatment.

"Because that bloke," said St Peter, "has put the fear of God into more people than the lot of you put together."

* * *

THE new tax inspector was intrigued to find that for many years Mr Abraham Finklestein had consistently claimed deductions for substantial amounts to charity.

The inspector became downright suspicious when he found that these annual donations were being made to St Mary's Catholic Church, and that Mr Finklestein could produce hundreds of cancelled cheques going back for years, all made out to the church, and each endorsed by the priest.

The inspector decided to question Fr. O'Malley over Mr Finklestein's generosity.

"Generosity?" said the priest. "Yes I know Finklestein well, but he is hardly generous."

"But we have his cancelled cheques going back over years," said the tax man.

"Oh those," said the priest. "Indeed he helps us there. We take up a big collection each mass, and as the banks are closed on Sundays, Mr Finklestein will always give us a cheque for it to save us worrying about the cash over the weekend."

TAXIS

"IT's not so much the work I enjoy," said the cabbie, "it's the people I run into."

THE pompous English colonel arrived in New York and hailed a cab. "Take me to Christ's Church," he said.

About ten minutes' later the cab stopped outside St Patrick's cathedral.

"That's not Christ's Church," protested the colonel.

"If He's in town He's in that one," said O'Flaherty.

* * *

THE surly businessman jumped into the cab.

"Where to?" said the cabbie.

"Mind your own business," he replied.

* * *

SHE was only a cab driver's daughter but you sure auto meter.

* * *

BUT he finally gave the job up. He didn't like people talking behind his back.

* * *

FRED took a cab to the drive-in. The movie cost him $120.

* * *

THERE were no serious injuries in an accident on the highway when a car collided with a taxi. The couple in the car escaped unhurt, but the 16 Scotsmen in the taxi were treated for shock, as they had paid for the trip in advance.

* * *

JOCK picked up a lovely young woman in the pub and hailed a cab to take her home. He was so infatuated with her he could hardly keep his eyes on the meter.

* * *

CHAP phoned the taxi company to complain that a cab he ordered had not arrived at the specific time.

"I told you when I made the booking that I had to be at the airport at a certain time," he complained.

420

"Don't worry, it will be there soon," said the girl. "Anyway, your plane is bound to be a few minutes late."

"You're damned right it will," complained the man. "I'm the pilot!"

* * *

THE passenger got a hell of a shock when the cab driver accelerated and raced through an intersection against the red lights. "Hey, go easy, where the heck did you get your licence?"

"Relax," said the cabbie. "My brother taught me to drive and he taught me how to run red lights."

The lights were red at the next intersection and to the passenger's horror he raced through again. It was not until he approached the fifth set of lights that they suddenly turned green and the cabbie nearly stood the taxi on end as it screeched to a stop.

"I don't understand, that's a green light," said the passenger.

"I know that, mate," said the cabbie looking both ways, "but my brother drives around this neighbourhood."

* * *

THE cabbie's careless driving was a worry to the expectant mother. "Be careful," she said, "I'm expecting my fifth child."

"And you're telling ME to be careful?" he asked.

* * *

IN a taxi on the way to the maternity hospital the 19-year-old wife complained she was in pain and terrified. Her 20-year-old husband put a comforting arm around her and asked: "Darling, are you sure you want to go through with this?"

* * *

HE lay under the cab tinkering with the motor and groping for spanners and tools when his attractive fare said: "Do you want a screwdriver?"

"Not now, Miss, but as soon as I fix this I'll be in it."

TEACHERS
See EDUCATION, SCHOOLS

A STRAPPING young farm hand was sent to the station to pick up the new school teacher who turned out to be an attractive young woman.

On the way back to the farm she noticed a stallion mounting a mare. "How do they know when to do that?" she enquired.

The young man explained that it was a sense of smell.

In the very next paddock a bull was enjoying himself on a cow.

"Again, it is a sense of smell," explained the country boy, "just like that ram and ewe over there."

He unloaded her luggage at the farmhouse and turned to go. "See you later," he said.

"Thanks," she replied, "And do come over when your cold gets better."

TEENAGERS

"MY son is going through one of those awkward stages, changing from a hooligan to a layabout."

*　　*　　*

ADOLESENCE is that stage between infancy and adultery.

*　　*　　*

TEENAGERS are very much alike in many disrespects.

*　　*　　*

TEENAGE girls are between pigtails and cocktails.

*　　*　　*

TEENAGE boys complain there is nothing to do and then stay out all night doing it.

*　　*　　*

TEENAGERS express a burning desire to be different from anyone else, then dress exactly alike.

TEENAGERS think curbing their emotions means parking by the roadside.

* * *

WHEN he knocked on the door for his first date her father opened it and shouted back into the house, "Joanne, there's something here to see you."

* * *

MUM heard her daughter come home an hour ago, but she hadn't heard the new boyfriend leave, so she tiptoed down the stairs. She heard a giggle in the darkened lounge room. She switched on the light to find the couple in a passionate embrace on the couch.

"Well I never," she gasped.

"Oh, c'mon Mum, you must have," said the daughter.

TENNIS

TENNIS was the trendy thing to do, so the Yuppie fronted the local sports store and asked to be kitted up. The proprietor sold him tennis shoes for $300 a pair, shorts for $200 a pair, a can of balls for $60 and shirts at $150 each.

"Oh, and I'll need a racquet," said the Yuppie.

So the proprietor sold him a half share in the store.

TIME

TODAY is Tomorrow's Yesterday.

* * *

TIME is nature's way of preventing everything happening at once.

* * *

THINGS are getting so bad so quickly that the Good Old Days seem only a week old.

* * *

"WHEN I am with my girlfriend, time stands still."

"No wonder. She's got a face that would stop a clock."

DON'T give me a watch for Christmas. I've already got one. And I can assure you a man with one watch knows what time it is, while a man with two would never be sure.

* * *

MABEL told him: "Your father can stay longer in an hour than others can stay in a bloomin' fortnight."

TOASTS

THE purpose of most public speaking is to propose a toast. While the speech is designed to put everyone at ease and remind those who started drinking early why they are present, the patter merely paves the way towards the toast. So always have a few up your sleeve.

Toasts are also a wonderful ploy for having another drink and most of the Irish examples listed here are the result of a memorable night in a Dublin pub called the Limerick Arms.

A starter to claim the attention of those present is to stand and pronounce in a loud voice: "Fornication." And when that stops the conversation, continue with "Fornication like this we need champagne for the toast..."

* * *

HERE'S to abstinence — provided it's in moderation.

* * *

MAY we all get to heaven half an hour before the devil knows we're dead.

* * *

MAY the skin of your bum never cover a drum.

* * *

MAY you live as long as you want, and may you never want as long as you live.

* * *

MAY you live a hundred years, and another month to repent.

MAY we never put our finger in another man's pie.

*   *   *

MAY you never have to eat your hat.

*   *   *

May the frost never afflict your spuds.

*   *   *

MAY the Blue Bird of Happiness crap down your chimney.

*   *   *

MAY we drink to the thirst which is yet to come.

*   *   *

MAY we all be alive this time, twelve months.

*   *   *

MAY you slide down the bannister of life, with nary a splinter.

*   *   *

MAY your luck be like the capital of Ireland, always Dublin!

*   *   *

MAY the fleas of a thousand camels infest the underpants of our enemies.

*   *   *

MAY their chooks turn into emus and kick down their dunny door.

*   *   *

HERE'S to the wowsers, whose abstinence gives us all the more to drink.

*   *   *

THERE'S many a toast, if I could think of it
    Damned if I can, so let's drink to it.

*   *   *

TO our wives and sweethearts. May they never meet.

*   *   *

LET'S drink to the soup. May it be seen and not heard.

*   *   *

HERE'S to the girl who lives on the hill
    She won't be in it, but her sister will
    Here's to her sister, then.

425

HERE'S to the happiest days of my life,
   Spent in the arms of another man's wife,
   My mother's.

*   *   *

HERE'S to your eyes, and mine
   Here's to your lips, and mine
   The former have met
   The latter not yet
   So here's to that moment, sublime.

*   *   *

HERE'S to us
   May we live a long life
   And here's mud in your eye
   While I wink at your wife.

*   *   *

HERE'S to Miss Prim
   For her life held no terrors
   Born a virgin, died a virgin
   No hits, no runs, no errors.

*   *   *

TO the office bore: May he give us a few brilliant flashes
of silence.

*   *   *

REMEMBER the poor. It costs nothing.

*   *   *

MUSICIANS' TOAST: May your organ never quit while
you are half way through your favourite piece.

*   *   *

I DRINK to your health when I'm with you
   I drink to your health when alone
   I drink to your health so often
   I'm becoming concerned at my own.

*   *   *

MAY you live as long as you want to
   And want to, as long as you live.

MAY we kiss who we please
And please who we kiss.

* * *

IF I'm asleep when you want me. Wake me.
And if I don't want to. Make me.

* * *

HERE'S to the bloke down the lane
He courted a girl, all in vain
She swore when he kissed her
So he slept with her sister
Again and again and again.

* * *

AND one to the author: May he live to be as old as his jokes.

* * *

A SURPRISE toast at a wedding goes this way:
"And finally, may the happy couple lie, steal and cheat. (Pause, then explain). May they lie in each other's arms, may they steal away for a blissful honeymoon, adn may they cheat time to live as long as possible."

TOUGH TIMES

IT'S tough when you call Suicide Prevention and they put you on hold.

* * *

IT'S tough luck when your car horn accidentally blasts off and remains jammed, while you're driving behind a group of Hell's Angels.

* * *

TIMES are so tough the local council has created a job for a painter. Signs that read "Keep off the grass" are to be re-painted, "Don't eat the grass."

* * *

MISTER, will you give me a dollar for my sick wife?
Sorry old man, but I've already got one.

COULD you give a poor bloke a bite?

Sorry my man, I don't bite myself, but I'll call the dog.

* * *

HERE'S fifty cents then. How did you get so destitute in the first place?

Like you sir, giving away vast sums to the poor and needy.

* * *

WILL you give me a dollar for a sandwich?

Let's see the sandwich.

* * *

THE cook came to the door of the country pub: "Aren't you the same bloke I gave a pie to yesterday?"

"Yes, but I hardly expected to find the same cook here today."

* * *

THINGS were so tough in our family my parents couldn't afford to have children. Our neighbours had to have me.

We were so poor I didn't have my 21st birthday until I was 35.

* * *

THINGS get so bad so fast in these times, it seems the good old days were only a week ago.

TRADESMEN

MANY electricians make light work.

* * *

JAKE signed on as a builder's labourer and set to work with a pick and shovel. After three days' toil he fronted the boss and asked for his week's wages in advance.

"Hang on, you've only done half a week's work," protested the boss.

But Jake had the answer. "I trusted you for the first half, now you trust me for the other!"

428

AFTER announcing his retirement, it was the postman's last day in the neighbourhood and most householders were giving him little presents. But he got the shock of his life when Mrs Smith took him upstairs, stripped off and took him to bed.

Afterwards she made him a cup of coffee, a hot breakfast and then pressed a dollar into his hand. The postman couldn't believe it and upon leaving asked for an explanation.

"It was my husband's idea, although he was a little preoccupied at the time," she said. "I told him you were retiring and I insisted we do something for you. He said, 'Oh, stuff the postman. Give him a dollar and a cup of coffee'."

"The breakfast was my own idea," she said.

* * *

AN Irish handyman went down to the hardware store for some bolts.

"How long do you want them?" enquired the salesman.

"Well, to tell you the truth," replied the handyman, "I was sort of hoping to keep them."

* * *

THE plumber finally arrived. "How have you managed?"

"Not too badly," said the housewife, "while we were waiting for you I've taught the kids how to swim."

* * *

TWO plumbers were working in the street trying to unblock a drain when an angry gent came out of the house opposite.

"Go easy with that long wire you're poking about with, boys," he said. "You've had my missus leap off the toilet seat three times!"

* * *

IT was many years ago since the embarrassing day that a young woman, with a baby in her arms, entered his butcher shop and confronted him with the news that the baby was his, and what was he going to do about it?

Finally, he capitulated. He promised to provide her with free meat until the boy was 16. She agreed.

He had been ticking the years off on his calendar and one day, the teenager who had been collecting the meat each week, came in to the shop and said: "I'll be sixteen tomorrow."

"I know," said the butcher with a smile, "I've been counting too, and tell your mother when you take this parcel of meat home that it is the last free meat she will get, and watch the expression on her face."

When the boy arrived home he told his mother. The woman nodded and said, "Son, go back to the butcher and tell him I have also had free bread, free milk and free groceries for the past 16 years and watch the expression on his face!"

* * *

THE apprentice draftsman had just drawn his first construction plan and laid it out before his boss. "I think that's near enough," he said.

"Near enough is not good enough," said the boss pushing the plans away. "It's got to be perfect. Do it again."

The apprentice knuckled down at the drawing board for another two hours and finally presented them to the boss again.

"It's perfect now," said the lad.

"Well that's near enough," said the boss.

* * *

IT was the day Fred was released from prison and they handed back his suit. He put his hand in the pocket and found a ticket for his shoe repairs. Although he thought the shoes would be out of style he decided on a whim to pick them up.

"It's been ten years and you may not remember them," said Fred producing the ticket, "but they were brown brogues to be half-soled and heeled."

430

"No worries, I remember them," said the shoe-repairer. "They will be ready on Tuesday."

* * *

THE lawyer's brand-new television set was on the blink so he called for the maintenance man who duly arrived, pulled the set away from the wall replaced a fuse and put his hand out for $72.

"What," said the lawyer. "That's outrageous. $72 for five minutes' work? I am a lawyer and I don't get that much money."

"Neither did I when I was a lawyer," said the maintenance man.

* * *

THEY called the maintenance man when the washing machine broke down. He duly arrived, pulled the machine out from the wall, studied it a few minutes, then got a large hammer and gave it a mighty whack.

It started straight away.

He then handed the couple a bill for $50.

"Fifty bucks?" said the husband. "All you did was whack it with a hammer."

"It is all itemised on the bill," said the tradesman. "Hitting the machine with the hammer is $2. Knowing exactly where to hit it is $48."

* * *

WHEN the doctor rang the plumber to complain that the toilet cistern had developed a fault the weary plumber reminded him that it was 2.30 in the morning.

"So what," said the doctor. "I get called out at all hours. I have a problem which needs fixing, so what does the time of day or night have to do with it?"

Ten minutes later the plumber arrived on the doorstep and was shown to the bathroom. He lifted the lid of the toilet, threw in two aspirins and flushed it.

"If it hasn't improved by the morning ring me again," he said.

431

TRAINS

A GROUP of people on the train were discussing why the railway was losing money.

"Hopeless management," said one old gent.

"Too many lazy employees," said the woman by the window.

"It's the union," said another.

A fourth was about to give his opinion as the train stopped at a station and an inspector got on board, and they all jumped out.

* * *

OLD Fred and his son were down from the bush and enjoying a ride on a train when a priest hobbled into their compartment on crutches.

"Slipped in the bathtub," he explained.

When the priest got out at the next station the son said: "What's a bathtub, Dad?"

"Dunno," said Fred, "I'm not a Catholic."

* * *

THE middle-aged couple had just settled in the compartment for a long rail journey. As the train pulled out of the station he asked: "Comfortable dear, is the seat soft?"

"Yes," she said.

"Not feeling any draught?"

"No."

"No vibrations or shaking?"

"No."

"Right then," he said, "let's change places."

* * *

EACH time the train stopped at a station the little old man would get up, walk to the door, look out and say "Oh Damn!"

Every station it was the same until the bloke opposite, exasperated by this behaviour asked him what was wrong.

"I'm on the wrong damned train!"

FOUR people were in the same compartment on a long train journey; a young woman, a priest, a businessman and a drunk.

All had been quiet for an hour or two until the young woman suddenly began to sob. The priest bent over to console her. "Tell me why you are crying," he said.

The girl sniffed and said: "I have just learnt that I am illegitimate."

The priest replied, "That's no sin. As a matter of fact I am illegitimate myself."

Then the businessman spoke up. "Excuse me, I couldn't help overhearing, but I must tell you that I am a self-made man. I own several businesses, in fact I am a millionaire, yet I am illegitimate too."

The drunk took out a cigarette and asked: "Any of you bastards got a light?"

* * *

IT was the new Very Fast Train and halfway through the journey there was a violent vibration. "What was the trouble back there?" asked a passenger, "I thought this was supposed to be a smooth ride."

"Sorry sir," said the porter. "We ran over a politician."

"Goodness. What was he doing on the tracks?"

"Oh, he wasn't on the tracks Sir, but we got him."

TRAVEL

SOME people travel for a change and a rest; only to find the hotel takes the change and the taxi takes the rest.

* * *

TRAVEL advice: Don't put all your bags in one exit.

* * *

"MR Wong! Mr Wong!" cried the distraught tourist, "the monkeys have run away with my travellers' cheques!"

"Ah, what sort were they?"

"Brown ones with red backsides!"

THE best time to visit Paris is between your 18th and 25th birthdays.

*   *   *

TRAVEL advice: Take twice the money you've got and unpack half the clothes.

*   *   *

I'VE just come back from a pleasure trip. I drove the in-laws to the airport.

*   *   *

"CARRY your bag, sir?"
"No, let her walk."

*   *   *

THE woman was booking a holiday for her husband. The travel agent asked her if she had any destination in mind.
"Anywhere in the Bermuda Triangle," she said.

*   *   *

SEASONED couple at the airlines reservations counter: "Two tickets to wherever our luggage is going."

*   *   *

YOUNG bloke went to the doctor for a check-up. "You need to relax more," said the doc. "You need to get away from it all for a while. Could you go abroad?"
"Sure could," replied the patient. "What's she like?"

*   *   *

FIRST snob: "I understand you are not going to Paris this year?"
Second snob: "No, it is London we are not going to this year."

*   *   *

EUROPE is so wonderful. If you ever go there, don't miss it.

*   *   *

REMEMBER, it is easier to find a travelling companion than to get rid of one.

*   *   *

I MET my wife in Acapulco. She was looking for a vacation and I was the last resort.

A RESORT is where the locals live off your holiday until next summer.

* * *

I WENT to a travel agent and asked where I could go for $50. He told me.

* * *

"WHEN you sailed around Italy, did you touch Florence?"

"No, her husband never let her out of his sight."

* * *

MURPHY opened a pub on the moon. But it had no atmosphere.

* * *

JOCK thought Niagara Falls was a terrible waste of water.

* * *

SHE was on the phone from the Riviera. "The holiday is wonderful darling, I feel like a new woman."

"So do I. Stay there another week."

* * *

A YOUNG Aussie was enjoying his first night in Rome drinking cappuccino at a pavement cafe when a pretty girl sat beside him.

"Hello," he said. "Do you understand English?"

"Only a little," she answered.

"How much?" he asked.

"Fifty dollars," she replied.

* * *

AN older Aussie, a wealthy man who had made his money in the furniture business, was also in Rome, and alone at the same cappuccino bar, when a young woman smiled at him, and naturally he returned the smile.

She was soon by his side. He said hullo, but she shrugged her shoulders to indicate she couldn't speak English.

He took a pen and paper from his pocket and drew a glass of wine with a question mark. She nodded and they had a drink. He drew a taxi with a question mark. She nodded and they soon had a tour of the city by cab.

He then drew a table for two which had the desired result, and after a splendid meal with two bottles of vino she reached for the pen and paper. She drew a four poster bed with a question mark.

"How perceptive of you," laughed our hero. "I am astounded. How did you know I was in the furniture business?"

* * *

SHE insisted on taking innumerable outfits with her, and they arrived at the airport loaded with luggage.

"I wish," said the husband thoughtfully, "we had bought the piano."

"No need to be sarcastic," said the wife, "it's not a bit funny."

"I'm not trying to be funny," he said, "I've left the tickets on it."

* * *

THE American was bumping about in the rear of the bus. "How far is it to Alice Springs then?" he asked.

"About a thousand kilometres as the crow flies."

"Hell. Why do we have to follow a dog-gone crow?"

* * *

FRED says travel broadens the mind. A trip to the Holy Land taught him a lot about the bible. "They took me to see Dan and Beersheeba, and I found they were two villages," he said.

"I always thought they were man and wife, like Sodom and Gomorrah."

* * *

THE coach was travelling through Dublin when the guide announced: "We are now passing the biggest pub in Ireland."

An Aussie voice at the back of the bus said: "Why?"

HE had a bent for pornographic literature, and he was in a taxi leaving Hongkong for the airport when the cab stopped outside a bookshop. There it was, a large volume in the window titled "How to Woo."

He told the cab driver to wait, dashed into the shop, asked the attendant to wrap it in brown paper, and bought it.

Not until he was comfortably seated on the flight home did he tentatively open the wrapper and learn that he had bought volume two of the Hongkong phone directory.

* * *

YOUNG chap boarded the Ansett flight at Cairns and the hostess noticed a newspaper parcel under his arm. "Mudcrabs," he explained. "I'm taking them back to Melbourne for a gourmet meal tonight."

"Then in that case they would be best placed in the fridge," said the hostess, stowing them away appropriately.

The flight landed on time and as the aircraft taxied across the tarmac the passengers were welcomed to Melbourne, told to remain seated until the aircraft came to a halt ... "And would the gentleman who gave me the crabs in Cairns please identify himself?"

* * *

PADDY, the left-handed barman had been pulling beers for 25 years in the same pub. "Why don't you travel and broaden your mind?" he was told repeatedly.

Finally he took the advice and booked a week's holiday in the Canary Islands.

When he returned he was a changed and knowledge-able man. "Well what did you learn?" asked the regulars. "I can tell you this," he said as they all leaned forward for his pearl of wisdom.

"There are no canaries in the Canary Islands."

A year passed and Paddy once more took his annual

leave abroad. This time his travel agent suggested the Virgin Islands.

"Well what did you learn this time, Paddy?" asked the regulars when he returned from his second world odyssey.

"I can tell you this," he said as they all leaned forward. "There are no canaries on the Virgin Islands, either!"

  ★ ★ ★

DEAR diary. This is day one of my first holiday on a cruise ship.

Day two. While the cruise is nice there is an awful lot of men, including the stewards, making passes at me.

Day three. I have been invited to sit at the captain's table.

Day four. The captain made an improper suggestion last night. I refused.

Day five. The captain says that unless I agree, he will sink the ship.

Day six. Last night I saved the lives of 965 people.

  ★ ★ ★

"THEY say that London is the foggiest place in the world, but I have been to a town where the fog was much thicker."

"Where was that?"

"Don't know. It was too foggy to tell."

  ★ ★ ★

HE is a mental traveller. His mind wanders.

  ★ ★ ★

SIAMESE twins were having a terrible argument about where to go for their next holidays. "We're going to America," stamped the one on the left. "I want to drive for a change!"

  ★ ★ ★

"I WOULDN'T go to America if you paid me," said Fred.
 "Why?"
 "Cos they drive on the wrong side of the road."

"What's wrong with that?"

"I tried it the other night," said Fred. "It's bloody dangerous!"

* * *

TOURIST: "Have you lived here all your life?"

Local: "Not yet!"

* * *

A HUNGRY back-packer in a youth hostel complained about the sandwich he just bought.

"I haven't found any ham in this sandwich yet," he said.

Manager: "Try another bite."

The back-packer did so. "No, nothing at all."

Manager: "Heck, you must have passed it."

* * *

TWO professional hitch-hikers travelling through Europe were sitting by the roadside. One was poking his tongue out at passing cars. He even gave some motorists the raspberry.

"You will never get a lift doing that," said his mate.

"I know that. Who cares. I'm on my lunch break!"

* * *

THE lad from Australia got quite a buzz walking down Fifth Avenue in the heart of the Big Apple. He was looking up at the skyscrapers when he felt somebody bump him slightly.

With a jolt he remembered he was in New York and reached for his wallet. It was gone. And the youth who bumped him was hurrying down the street.

Our lad sprinted after him, grabbed him by the shirt-front and backed him against the wall. "Okay pal. You've met your match. You're dealing with an Aussie. Hand over that wallet."

The youth produced the wallet, ducked out of the grip and ran. It wasn't until our Ocker got back to his room that he saw his wallet where he had left it beside the bed.

SOME of the famous duty-free airports of the world are Schipol at Amsterdam, Singapore and Dubai. But for the most unusual items, try Shannon Airport. Here you can get water-proof tea bags, one-piece jigsaw puzzles, inflatable dartboards for campers and solar powered torches.

*   *   *

A TRAVEL agent looked up from his desk to notice an old lady and an old gent peering in the shop window at the posters showing the glamorous destinations around the world. The agent had had a good week and the dejected couple looking in the window gave him a rare feeling of generosity.

He called them in. "I know that on your pension you could never hope to have a holiday, so I am sending you off to a fabulous resort at my expense, and I won't take no for an answer," he said.

He took them inside and asked his secretary to write two flight tickets and book a room in a five-star hotel. They gladly accepted and were off.

About a month later the little old lady came in to his shop. "And how did you like the holiday?" he asked eagerly.

"The flight was exciting and the room was lovely," she said. "I've come to thank you. But one thing has puzzled me. Who was that old bloke I had to share the room with?"

*   *   *

BACHELOR Joe had led a quiet life. But for years he had been dreaming of a cruise in the South Pacific and when he received his superannuation he had enough money to make his dream come true.

When he boarded the ship, he had no friends to wave him goodbye so he went below to look for his cabin. He went down to C-deck, then down to D-deck, then down once more where he was suddenly grabbed by two burly seamen, rushed down more flights of stairs, stripped of his clothes on the way and finally thrown into a large space down in the bilge of the ship.

In darkness and confusion he was shoved onto a long bench and felt the chains go around his ankles and a rough oar was thrust into his hands.

In the dim light he could see he was one of many.

Suddenly, he heard a drum beat and could just make out a large muscular negroid man beating a drum to an ever increasing rhythm. With the crack of a whip a raucous voice yelled "Row you Scum, Row."

Shackled to the oar Joe could do nothing else. In fact, to the monotonous beat of the drum Joe did nothing else for the next two weeks until they arrived somewhere and the drummer stopped the tedious beat. The reprieve lasted only two days. The drum started again and under the crack of the whip they began to row back home.

As the ship tied up Joe slumped on his oar and turned to the emaciated figure beside him which had been his companion for the voyage.

Joe addressed him for the first time. "Excuse me," he said. "I've never been on a cruise before. How much should I tip the drummer?"

"Don't know really," said his gaunt companion. "I gave him $20 when I did this cruise last year!"

* * *

KIWI tourist driving around the UK got himself lost along the south-east coast of England. He saw a local and said: "Excuse me, can you tell me where I am?"

The local said: "Great Yarmouth."

"Same to you, fish-face," was the Kiwi's retort.

* * *

AN American tourist on a trip to Ayers Rock suddenly yelled "Stop the Bus" and scrambled to the front to get off. He had spotted an aboriginal with his ear to the ground on a track which turned off the main road. "He must be one of your famous black-trackers you have out here," he said as he ran back to the aboriginal.

"Can you tell me about the last people to pass this way?" enquired the Yank.

"Yeah," answered the aboriginal, and pointing to the wheel tracks he said "It was a Ford utility."

This didn't impress the Yank much. "Anything else?" he said.

"Yeah. There was ten people in it. Three in the front and seven in the back."

Now the yank was impressed. "Anything else?"

"Yeah. The three in the front were blokes with four women and three kids in the back and the truck has yellow wheel caps."

This amazed the Yank. "And you can tell all that just by putting your ear to the ground?"

"Not really," said the aboriginal. "I just fell off the plurry thing!"

*   *   *

VISITOR to the city could not decide whether to spend his last day at the football finals or at the massage parlours in the 'Red Light' district. He finally opted for the football.

"Sorry sir," said the attendant, "the only seats left are the higher priced ones at $30."

"What?" said the visitor. "I could have gone to a brothel and got a woman for that."

"Ah, yes," said the attendant, "but you wouldn't have had 100 minutes of action-packed play and a brass band at interval would you?"

*   *   *

GUIDE on a conducted tour of Rome: "And this ancient monument dates back over 2000 years."

"Don't be ridiculous," said one little old lady. "It's only 1990 now."

*   *   *

AT the airport Trevor the Traveller abused the luggage handler. His case comes up next week.

HE told the travel agent: "I want a round world ticket."
"One way?" she asked.

★ ★ ★

AN Australian and Irishman were waiting in the travel agent's office.

"How much to South America?" asked the Australian.

"That will cost you $1000," said the travel agent.

"But I only have $500," said the Aussie.

The agent thought for a moment.

"That's okay, just go into the next office and you will be attended to."

The Irishman said he also wanted to go to South America, and observing what happened said he also only had $500.

"Could I have the same deal?"

"Okay," said the agent. "Step inside the next office."

Paddy goes through the door and is immediately hit on the head with a club. He wakes up chained to an oar beside the Aussie and a hundred others rowing to the beat of the drum master.

"I wonder if they will fly us home?" mutters the Irishman.

"They didn't last year," replied the Australian.

U

UNIONS

HALF a loaf is better than no tea-break at all.

       ★   ★   ★

THE politicians were host to a United States business delegation and at the height of the dinner one of the Americans at the head table asked the waiter for some more butter.

"Sorry, just one pat of butter per person," said the waiter.

The chamber president was embarrassed to overhear this and called the waiter aside.

"Do you know who that man is?" he said angrily. "He is in charge of the American delegation."

"And do you know who I am?" said the waiter. "I am in charge of the butter."

       ★   ★   ★

WHEN Harry Bloggs arrived at the building site he was told "no ticket, no start." But Harry said it was against his principles to join the union.

They argued with him, the union organiser was called, even the boss who didn't want trouble on the site tried to cajole him to join the union. Harry wouldn't have it.

He was working on the scaffolding on the 52nd level, high over the street, when the man from the union arrived.

"I will only tell you once, Harry," he said. "If you don't join the union I will pick up that piece of timber, wrap it around your neck and throw you right off this platform onto the tram tracks below."

Later, when they asked Harry why he joined, he said, "I had never had it explained so succinctly before."

*　　*　　*

THE waterside workers were having a break on the wharf when a leading hand said to his boss, "Hey, that new bloke you hired this morning; he's not a spy is he?"

"No, I think he checked out okay, why?"

"Well, he just stubbed his toe on a crate of pig-iron and said, 'Oh, the perversity of inanimate objects!' "

*　　*　　*

A MOTORIST had been picked up on a traffic infringement and had given his name as Fred Shagbreak and his place of employment. When the cop arrived to deliver the brief he asked the girl at the enquiry desk: "Have you got a Shagbreak here?"

She replied: "You must be joking, the union has battled for two years just to get a coffee break."

*　　*　　*

SHOP-STEWARD: "From now on all wages are doubled, holidays extended to six months and we shall only work on Fridays."

From the back of the hall: "What, every bloody Friday?"

*　　*　　*

MANAGER to boss: "The workers are demanding shorter hours."

"Right, we'll cut their lunch hour to 30 minutes!"

*　　*　　*

THE unionist on holiday sent a postcard home: Having a lovely time-and-a-half.

V

VETS
See DOGS

THE German tourist dived into the river, dragged the apparently drowned dog ashore and revived it.

"Are you a vet?" asked an impressed bystander.

"Ya, I'm bloody soaking," he replied.

* * *

HE entered the vet's clinic with a cat under his arm. "It's been as sick as a dog," he said.

* * *

THE vet was in the middle of a tricky operation on a dog when the phone rang.

"How long should I leave a rooster in with a hen?" enquired the voice at the other end.

"Just a minute," said the busy vet.

"Thank you," said the caller, and hung up.

* * *

THE elderly spinster told the vet her dog had become so old it had forgotten its house training. "I'm sorry," said the vet, "but the only thing I can suggest, is the lethal chamber."

"Yes, but will the old fleabag use it," she said.

* * *

FRED the farmer told the vet that he had just purchased a very expensive prize stud bull, but it wasn't the slightest bit interested in the cows. "I've done my dough," he moaned.

The vet said it wasn't a problem and gave him some tablets to include in the bull's feed. Next day the bull began performing with great passion and stamina.

Fred was telling his neighbour about the potency of the tablets. "Flamin' marvellous," he said. "What's more, they don't taste too bad either."

*   *   *

(R) TWO women were sitting in the waiting room with their dogs, one a fox terrier, the other a Great Dane. The foxie's owner said she was there because her pooch had a shocking habit of humping anything that went past, even visitor's legs.

"I know," said the other woman. She said her Great Dane had the same embarrassing habit.

"So you are here to have him de-sexed too?"

"No," she replied, "I'm getting his toenails cut."

WAITERS
See RESTAURANTS

"AND what'll you have?"
    Said the waiter, idly picking his nose.
    "I'll have two boiled eggs, ya mongrel,
    "You can't put your fingers in those!"

                *   *   *

WAITER: "How did you find the meat Sir?"
    "I just lifted a potato chip and there it was."

                *   *   *

"WAITER! What is this fly doing in my soup?"
    Waiter studies it for a while.
    "Backstroke, I believe Sir."

                *   *   *

"WAITER! Bring me a smaller cheque!"

                *   *   *

"WAITER, what's the difference between the steak and
the hamburger?"
    "About one day, sir."

                *   *   *

"WAITER! This food is terrible. I demand to see the
manager."
    "Sorry, sir. He is out to lunch."

"WAITER! There's a fly in my soup."

"Well, don't complain to me, mate, it's the chef that was once a tailor!"

* * *

"WAITER, what's with this chicken soup?"

"I dunno, what's with the chicken soup?"

"It tastes funny."

"Well, start laughing!"

* * *

"WAITER! Your thumb is on my steak."

"Well, you don't want it to drop on the floor again, do you?"

* * *

"WAITER, this plate is wet."

"That's your soup sir."

* * *

"WAITER, why does this chicken have one leg missing?"

"It was in a fight."

"Well take it away and bring me the winner."

* * *

"WAITER, what's the special on the menu today?"

"I'll call the chef."

"I don't want him. I'm not a cannibal."

* * *

"WAITER, this soup isn't fit for a pig."

"I will take it back sir and bring you some that is."

* * *

"WAITER, what's the best dish in the place?"

"That blonde sitting at table three."

* * *

"WAITER, can I have a salad sandwich without cucumbers?"

"Sorry, we are out of cucumbers. Can you take it without tomatoes?"

* * *

"WAITER, what time is it?"

"Sorry sir, this is not my table."

"WAITER, what's the soup du jour?"

"It's off. We ran out if it yesterday."

* * *

"WAITER, I would like a stew that will give me indigestion immediately, instead of three o'clock in the morning."

* * *

"WAITER, is there lots of juice in this grapefruit?"

"More than meets the eye, sir."

* * *

THE waiter approached the diner. "Why are you eating those olives on a string, sir?"

"Because I may not like them."

* * *

"YOU are not eating your fish," said the waiter, "what's wrong with it?"

"Long time no sea," said the diner.

* * *

"WAITER, are you sure this lobster is fresh?"

"Yes Sir, it walked here from the beach this morning."

The customer gave it another sniff. "Well I think it must have trodden in something on the way!"

* * *

IF you think the service is bad, wait until you taste the food.

* * *

ENGRAVED on the Maitre d's tombstone: "Bye and by, God caught his eye."

* * *

ON his first date with her he decided to impress her. He took her to a posh restaurant and ordered the whole meal in French.

Even the waiter was surprised. It was a Chinese restaurant.

* * *

THE irate diner had complained to the waitress about the unsatisfactory pastries. She in turn got the manager.

"I don't see why you should complain about our pastrycook," said the manager, "she has been making pastry since before you were born."

"As maybe," said the diner, "but why wait until now to sell them?"

* * *

THE bachelor finished his meal and placed his tip on the table as he finished his coffee. The waitress took one look at the three single cents and said. "Thank you for your generosity. You can always tell the character of a diner by the way he tips."

"Oh really," he said, "and what does that tell you about me?"

"Well you put the three cents in a row," said the waitress. "That tells me you are tidy for starters. The first cent tells me you are frugal. The second cent tells me you are a bachelor."

"That's true," he said, "but what does the third cent tell you?"

"That tells me your father was a bachelor too."

* * *

THE waiter brought the cheque and the diner studied it, then sorted through his money. "By golly," he said, "I have exactly that amount, but I'm afraid I haven't got enough for a tip."

"Let me add up that bill again, sir," said the waiter.

* * *

THE two women from the blue-rinse set ordered their meal. "And we will have two glasses of wine," said one. "And make sure I get a clean glass. The one you gave me last week was filthy."

After a while the waiter brought the food and wine, "And which of you ordered the clean glass?" he said.

CUSTOMER in a French restaurant. "Waiter, do you have frogs legs?"

"Oui monsieur."

"Then hop across the road and get me a packet of cigarettes."

★ ★ ★

"WILL you have pie sir?"

"Is it customary?"

"No, it's apple."

★ ★ ★

MOISHE settled down in his favourite kosher restaurant. "Oi waiter, do you have matzo balls?"

"No," he said, "I always walk like this!"

★ ★ ★

"WHAT do you think of that brandy, sir?" said the waiter showing him the bottle. "It's 1856."

"What? Just for one bottle?"

★ ★ ★

WHEN he ordered a plate of oysters he noticed that the waitress was quite pretty. When she delivered the meal he said: "How about a smile and a few kind words, darling?"

The girl obliged with a beaming smile and turned to walk away.

"Hang on," he said, "I've got the oysters and the smile, but where's the few kind words?"

She bent down, put her lips close to his ear and whispered: "Don't eat the oysters."

WARDROBES
See INFIDELITY

HE was in bed with a married woman when he heard the back door slam. "Hell. It's my husband," she cried. "Quick, hide in that wardrobe." He gathered up his clothes and dived from the bed to the wardrobe in a flash. After a few moments another voice in the wardrobe said "It's dark as a dog's belly in here isn't it?"

The man, shivering in the nude, was shocked. "Who is it?" he whispered. It was a little boy's voice and it said: "I know who you are and it will cost you. Give me $50 or I will yell for my Dad."

He was in no position to argue, he grudgingly paid up, and when the crisis was over made a quick exit from the bedroom window. Next day the little boy and his mother were down town and he said he was going to buy a brand new skateboad. "What with?" asked his mother.

"I've got $50" said the boy.

"Where did you get that kind of money," said his mother, but the lad refused to tell. "You must have done something wrong," she persisted and after slapping him about the ears dragged him across the street to the church.

"Confession is the thing for you my lad. If you won't tell me, then you will have to tell the parish priest," and she shoved him into the confessional box and shut the door.

"Gawd. It's dark as a dog's belly in here," said the boy.

"Now don't you start that again," said the priest.

*　　*　　*

HUSBAND came home unexpectedly and found his wife in bed. But when he went to hang his suit in the wardrobe he was surprised to see a man in there, busily snatching at things in the air.

"What the heck are you doing?" asked the husband.

"I am a moth catcher," said the stranger, still snatching at imaginary insects as if they were flying around his head.

"Then why are you doing it in the nude?" asked the suspicious husband.

With that, the moth catcher looked down and noticed

his absence of clothes. "Crikey, they're worse than I thought," he said.

(Another explanation for the man in the wardrobe comes from the husband's wife: "Oh, he's just a nudist who came in to use the phone.")

* * *

HE arrived home from work earlier than usual and found his wife in bed. There was a long whisp of smoke coming from a cigar in the ashtray on the bedside table.

"Where did that cigar come from?" he roared.

A timid male voice from the wardrobe said, "Cuba."

* * *

PADDY fell into a terrible state of remorse when he discovered his wife's lover in the wardrobe. They had a frightful argument, then he reached in a drawer and pulled out a gun. He cocked the trigger and held it to his head.

"For God's sake, Paddy, put that gun down," cried Teresa.

"Shut yer mouth and say your prayers woman. You two are next," said Paddy.

* * *

IN the long queue waiting at the Pearly Gates were three men, all from the same town. "How come?" asked St Peter.

The first said he had suspicions his wife was having an affair so he left for the office as usual, but doubled back to their penthouse apartment in a bid to catch her. He rushed into the bedroom, sure enough, she had gone back to bed, but a search of the wardrobe revealed no trace of her lover.

But when he looked out of the kitchen window he saw a bloke putting his clothes on behind a bush in the garden. He got so angry he picked up the refrigerator with superhuman strength and hurled it down at him. "The strain gave me a heart attack and that's why I am here," he told St Peter.

The second man said: "That's funny, I am a landscape gardener and I was just getting changed for work, putting my overalls on, when I was hit with a fridge. That's why I'm here."

"That's funny," said the third man. "I was hiding in this fridge ...!"

* * *

PADDY O'Flaherty came home early one Friday afternoon and found his wife lying naked on the bed and crying.

"Whatever is the matter?" asked Paddy.

"We're invited to a wedding tomorrow," sobbed Teresa, "and I have nothing to wear."

"That's ridiculous," said Paddy. Going over to the wardrobe he said, "Look in here. Here's a red dress, a green dress, a pink dress... Hello Father, a yellow dress..."

WEATHER

IT was so cold last week that the local flasher was spotted describing himself to a group of women.

* * *

IT was so cold on the Antarctic Expedition that when he returned she broke it off.

* * *

IT was as cold as a barmaid's heart.

* * *

IT was so dry the frogs were taking swimming lessons.

* * *

IT was so dry the Council closed two lanes of the municipal swimming pool.

* * *

AFTER he answered the phone yet again he said to his saucy young wife. "That's funny. We must have a number similar to the Weather Bureau. That's the third bloke to ring and ask if the coast was clear."

SITTING on the pub's verandah one farmer looked at the threatening sky and said: "D'yer think it'll rain?"

"I hope so," said the other. "Not for myself, mind you, but for the sake of my two sons. They haven't seen rain."

* * *

THE farmer had a rope hanging from a dead tree at his back door.

"What's it for?" asked a visitor.

"It's my weather guide," the old farmer replied. "If its swinging back and forth, its windy, and if its wet, its been raining."

* * *

IT rained cats and dogs. Poodles everywhere.

* * *

THE wind blew so hard...

it blew three dogs off their chains... a chook facing east laid the same egg three times...

it blew the pricks off a barbed wire fence.

* * *

"HOW did you find the weather on your holiday?"

"I just opened the door and there is was, everywhere."

* * *

"THEY say London is the foggiest place in the world, but I have been to a place where the fog was much thicker."

"Where was that?"

"Don't know. It was too foggy to tell."

* * *

UNCLE Fred worked in the Weather Bureau for years, but when he was promoted to the main office he only lasted a month. The weather didn't agree with him.

* * *

THE BBC announcer said: Today it will be muggy, followed by Tuggy, Weggy, Thurggy and Fruggy.

* * *

HE went to Mexico where the weather was more predictable: Chili today, hot-tamale.

456

WEDDINGS
See MARRIAGE, MARRIEDS, NEWLY-WEDS

HAPPY is the bride that the sun of a tycoon takes a shine to today.

* * *

THERE is so much permissiveness in the world today that the only way to stop having sex is to get married.

* * *

THE relative from out of town arrived late. "Who gave the bride away?" he asked.

"Any one of us could, but we all agreed to keep our mouths shut."

* * *

SHE had turned 30 and had been difficult to unload, so when her father finally gave her away at the altar he demanded a receipt.

* * *

AFTER a few champagnes the tipsy young bride stood up to thank the guests for the presents. "... and I'd like to thank my parents-in-law for giving me such a perky copulator."

* * *

EVEN these days there are a few four-letter words which can still shock most brides, like cook, wash, dust and iron.

* * *

"DO you like big weddings or little ones?"

"Without big weddings you shouldn't have little ones."

* * *

USHER at the wedding reception: "Are you a friend of the groom's?"

Woman: "Indeed I am not. I am the bride's mother."

* * *

I WILL never forget my wedding. God knows I've tried.

THE bride wept, the bridesmaids wept, even the wedding cake was in tiers.

* * *

THE minister reached that part of the ceremony where the congregation is asked if anybody knows why this man and woman should not be joined together in holy matrimony.

A thin voice replied, hesitantly, "... er, yes. I'd like to say something."

The minister looked at him sternly. "Shut up. You are not part of the congregation. You're the groom!"

* * *

THE MC at the wedding reception stood up and roared: "Fornication!" "Fornication like this," he continued, "we should toast the happy couple in champagne."

* * *

A WAG who was known as a practical joker and who had played the most diabolical tricks on his friends was about to be married himself and was therefore very nervous. Would his friends get their revenge?

He was in a sweat when the vicar announced: "Is there any reason why this couple should not be joined together?" and despite his constant fear the ceremony and the wedding reception went without water pistols or rude telegrams. They even got to their hotel without incident.

Next morning the groom called room service. "This is Mr Smith in room 13, I'd like to order breakfast for two."

At this point a voice from under the bed said: "Make that five!"

* * *

BEN and Betty decided to get married in the Registry Office.

When filling in the appropriate forms the clerk queried Ben's name. "That's a nickname, surely," he said. "Go upstairs to the Birth, Deaths and Marriages Department and check your christened name."

Ben did so and came back to sign as Benjamin.

Betty met the same problem. "Go upstairs and check the records," said the clerk. "Betty can't be your right name."

Sure enough, she returned to sign her name as Elizabeth.

"Lucky I was here," said the clerk. "Otherwise this marriage wouldn't be legal and any kids you had would be technical bastards."

"That's funny," said Elizabeth, "that's what the bloke upstairs said about you."

* * *

"CONGRATULATIONS, my boy," said the groom's uncle. "I'm sure you will look back on today as the happiest day of your life."

"But I'm not getting married until tomorrow," protested the lad.

"I know," said the uncle.

* * *

THE ardent groom had exhausted his young bride on their honeymoon and one morning, while he was having a shave, she dressed and staggered down to the coffee shop. "What's the matter dear?" asked the waitress. "You look all-in. Aren't you the bride with the older husband?"

"Indeed I am," she confessed. "He is 75, but he has double-crossed me," complained the bride. "When he told me had saved up for 60 years I thought he was talking about money!"

* * *

COMPLETE in her wedding gown the tearful young woman confronted her cricket-mad fiance.

"How could you do it? There I was on Saturday waiting at the church with all my relatives and where were you? Playing cricket. You left me in the lurch."

He tried to calm her down. "I distinctly said 'If it rained'."

THE Matron of Honour confided to the bride that if she wanted an unforgettable wedding night she should ensure that her groom should eat a dozen oysters at the marriage ceremony.

Next day the bride thanked her friend, but added dolefully, "Only eight of them worked!"

*　　*　　*

THE bride and groom sat up all night waiting for their sexual relations to arrive.

*　　*　　*

SHE married a sailor because she wanted to have children and rear admirals.

*　　*　　*

THE father was giving advice to his son just before his marriage. "Son, in the beginning it will be tri-weekly. After ten years it will be try weekly, and after 20 years it will be try weakly."

*　　*　　*

THE bridegroom was enjoying his last night of freedom at the buck's night when his mate confided, "Surely you can't be serious about marrying Wendy. She's been out with every bloke in town."

The bridegroom thought this over for a while. "Yeah, but it's not really a big town."

*　　*　　*

THERE was a little man
　And he had a little gun
　And his bullets were made of lead
He stood close by
　With a fatherly eye
　While me and my girl were wed.

*　　*　　*

IT was a typical Outback Australian wedding and the reception party was in full swing by the time Jack arrived and parked his car outside the shearing shed.

He was about to go in when he met Fred coming out shaking his head.

"It's all over," said Fred. "Don't bother going in. It's a total disaster. They've run out of beer and the best man has just stuffed the bride."

The news was enough to turn Jack back towards his car. They were about to leave when another guest came out of the hall and began shouting: "Don't go you blokes. Everything is okay. They have found another keg and the best man has apologised."

WEDDING TELEGRAMS

TO the groom: "Congratulations Gerald. It was better to have loved and lost, than never to have loved at all." — Mary, Terese, Wendy, Karen, Julie, Barbara, Estelle and Agatha.

* * *

TO the bride: "Congratulations from your loving mother. 22 years ago I sent you to bed with a dummy. Tonight history repeats itself."

* * *

TO the bride: "Congratulations Mabel. It was better to have loved and lost, than never to have loved at all." — Southside Football Club, and coach.

* * *

TO the groom: "Congratulations Gerald, and welcome to the family from the delighted father of the bride. Now that I have given the bride away, can I have a receipt?"

* * *

TO the groom. "Congratulations Gerald from your new in-laws. Be warned, she likes to spend money, but that's her only extravagance."

* * *

TO the bride: "Congratulations from all your friends at the family Planning Centre. PS: The test is positive."

461

TO the groom. "Congratulations from the local feminist movement. And remember, no woman has ever shot her husband while he was doing the dishes."

* * *

TO the groom: "Congratulations from the Maffioso. We have just kidnapped your new mother-in-law. If you don't pay the ransom money we will send her back."

* * *

TO the groom: "Laugh and the world laughs with you. Quarrel with Mabel and you sleep alone."

TO the groom: "Congratulations and all the best. But remember, Socrates died from an overdose of wedlock."

* * *

TO the groom: "Congratulations Gerald and all the best for the future. From all your mates at Alcoholics Anonymous.

* * *

TO the groom: "Congratulations from the best man. Can I have first option on your little black book?"

* * *

TO the groom: "Congratulations from your new family. We assure you your bride has led a sheltered life. She thinks Good Housekeeping is a women's magazine. She never uses four letter words like Work, Shop, Bake, Dust. And she believes intercourse is a ticket to the races."

WIDOWS

WHAT would you call a woman who always knows where her husband is?

A widow!

* * *

"SO you are going to marry Widow Brown. I wouldn't like to be the second husband of a widow."

"It's better than being the first."

"WHERE did you get that black eye?"

"You know that pretty little woman who said she was a widow? Well she isn't."

* * *

HER husband didn't leave her much when he died. But he left her a lot while he was living.

* * *

A NOSEY neighbour chided Widow Watkins. She said she didn't think it proper for the widow to entertain the grocer boy for hours each evening.

"It's only platonic," she said.

"What do you mean, platonic?" persisted the nosey neighbour.

"It's play for him and a tonic for me," said the widow.

* * *

TWO mates were leaning on the bar. "The problem is," confided Bill, "I can marry a widow with heaps of money who I don't love, or I can marry a girl on the dole who I love very much."

"Follow your heart," was Fred's advice. "True love is best."

After a few minutes' silence Bill agreed: "You're right, I will."

"Good." said Fred, "And by the way, what's the widow's address?"

WIVES
See HUSBANDS

HERE'S to the man who takes a wife
But let him make no mistake
For it makes a lot of difference
Whose wife it is you take.

* * *

WIFE, to woman next door: "I can only tell you this once, Bronwyn, I promised not to repeat it."

JAKE lamented to his mate: "How come my wife can spot a blonde hair on my shoulder, yet miss the garage doors?"

* * *

FRED is darn lucky. He has got a wife and a transistor, and they both work.

* * *

OVERHEARD at the bar: "Is it possible for a man to make a fool of himself without knowing it?"

"Not if he has a wife," counselled his wise friend.

* * *

"MY husband wears the pants in our family. But I tell him which pair to wear."

* * *

WIFE: "You certainly made a fool of yourself tonight. I only hope nobody realised you were sober."

* * *

"NO. I don't wake up sleepy and irritable," she said. "I let him sleep in."

* * *

SHE had always been a bossy wife and he had always taken the easy way out and never complained.

But when their South American tour went wrong and the bandits put them both before the firing squad he decided to make a stand.

When he was offered a blindfold he refused it and shouted, "You can stick the blindfold ya dirty rotten bastards."

"Gerald," she said. "Stop making trouble!"

* * *

HE reckons his wife is an outspoken woman. And having met her we would be mighty interested to know who outspoke her.

* * *

"WE were married in secret," she said. "Even my husband didn't know until he sobered up."

"MY husband is a man of rare gifts. I haven't received one for years."

* * *

HE introduces his missus as the awful wedded wife.

* * *

SHE was the kind of wife who spends her evenings dining and whining.

* * *

"MY mother says I should never have married you," said the young wife during a tiff. "She thinks you're effeminate."

"Well," he said, "compared to her I probably am."

* * *

A BLOKE comes home and starts to tell his wife some jokes he just heard at the pub. She interrupts and tells him to stop. "You," she says severely, "have got a dirty mind."

"Well..." he shrugged. "I suppose that's because I don't change mine as often as you do."

* * *

A COUPLE got married and the wife put a wooden box under the bed and told her husband he wasn't allowed to look inside it until after she died.

After 20 years of marriage her husband couldn't resist his curiousity any longer. While his wife was out he opened the box and found three eggs and $25,000.

He looked at it so long in puzzled amazement that his wife caught him.

"Well, what are the eggs for?" asked the husband.

"Every time I've been unfaithful to you, I put an egg in the box," she explained.

The husband said, "Only three times in 20 years, well, that's not bad. I can live with that. But what's the money for?"

The wife replied, "Every time I got a dozen I sold them!"

* * *

A COUPLE were having a heated argument about family

finances. Finally the wife exploded: "If it wasn't for my money we wouldn't have that television set. And if it wasn't for my money we wouldn't have any furniture. And if it wasn't for my money this house wouldn't be here."

"Listen," snorted her husband. "If it wasn't for your money I wouldn't be here."

* * *

CHAP met his ex-wife at a party and after a few drinks he suggested they go to bed.

"Over my dead body," she sneered.

He downed his drink and replied, "I see you haven't changed."

* * *

AS the old stockman lay dying she sat beside him wiping his fevered brow. Raising himself up on one elbow he turned to her and spoke:

"Ethel, you've been with me through it all. Remember the time when I got trampled in the stampede? You were there.

"And when I lost all that money at the cattle sale. You were at my side.

"And now I've been shot by a rustler, here you are again. You know, Ethel, I'm beginning to think you're bad luck!"

* * *

"HOW'S your wife?"

"Compared to what?"

* * *

"OUR marriage is based on trust and understanding. She doesn't trust me, and I don't understand her."

* * *

"EVERY night my wife covers her face in mud and puts her hair in rollers."

"Does it help?"

"A little. But I can still tell it's her."

* * *

"IF you're fed up with your marriage, why don't you leave him?"

"I would, if I could find a way of doing it without making him happy."

* * *

SHE said she married one of the world's greatest lovers. "And one day I'm going to catch him at it."

* * *

TWO young housewives were having their regular cuppa but one was very depressed. "What's up?" said her friend.

"I caught my husband making love," she explained.

"So what? Don't let that bother you. I got mine the same way!"

* * *

"MY husband is an angel."

"You're lucky. Mine's still alive!"

* * *

HE got a telegram from his wife: "Harry, I missed you yesterday. Come home and let me have another shot."

* * *

HE joined the Foreign Legion to try and forget his wife, but at least six of the legionaires looked like her.

* * *

WIFE, to woman next door: "My husband has just run off with my best friend."

"Oh, gracious me, who was it?"

"Don't know, never met her."

* * *

"THERE was a phone call for you while you were out," said the wife to her husband.

"Oh, who was it?"

"It was one of those trouts you were fishing for last week."

* * *

FRED was staggering home from a bucks party when the milkman picked him up. "Where do you live?" asked the milkman.

"Robinson St," muttered Fred.

"Oh, Robinson St," said the milko. "Know it well. I have a great time on collection days in that street. Have a wonderful time with every woman except one," he laughed.

This news disturbed Fred and he woke his wife as soon as he got home and relayed the story. "Every woman except one, that's what the milkman said."

His sleepy wife thought for a while. "Oh that would be that stuck-up bitch at number 10," she said.

* * *

HARRY Henpecked stepped on the weighing machine and was about to read his horoscope when his domineering wife snatched the card from him.

"Strong leader of men, Ha," she read aloud. "Master of your own destiny." She turned the card over. "It's even got your weight wrong."

* * *

HARRY Henpecked finally had enough. He declared that he was going to commit suicide and stormed out of the house. She called after him that she had heard that story all too often before. About an hour later she went down the main street to do her shopping and saw a crowd gathered outside a very high building. The crowd was hushed and horrified, for there was Harry balancing on the highest parapet.

She screamed: "That's my husband! Save him! Somebody save him!"

A cop looked round and gave the woman a long hard stare. "Is that man really your husband?" he asked.

"Of course he is," she snapped.

"Oh, that's okay then," said the cop. "For a while we thought he was crazy and didn't know what he was doing."

* * *

HE came home in a state of utter despair and sat with his head in his hands. "I have just been sacked," he told his wife.

"After 40 years of doing the same job week after week I have been replaced by an electronic gadget about the size of a torch," he lamented. "What's more it can do everything I can do, and do it better and never wear out," he moaned.

But nobody was listening. She had gone out to buy one.

* * *

EIGHT kids were too many and the cost of rising prices was getting Fred down. He told his wife if they had any more kids he would go out of his mind with worry.

A week later his wife announced that she was pregnant.

"That's the end," lamented Fred. He opened the drawer beneath his desk and pulled out a revolver and held it to his head.

"Stop!" cried his wife. "You'll be killing an innocent man!"

* * *

MRS Murphy said: "Oi don't think my husband has been completely fait'ful t' me."

"Why, what makes you so suspicious?"

"My last child doesn't resemble him in the least."

* * *

CHAP watering his front garden saw a taxi leave the house next door and his neighbour waving his visitors farewell.

"Goodbye. Your wife is great in bed," he shouted as the cab drove off. "She's fantastic in the cot."

He could hardly believe it and when the cab had gone he called his neighbour over to the fence.

"Did I hear right?" he said. "Did I hear you say that bloke's wife was good in bed?"

"Well it isn't really true," said his neighbour, "but I didn't want to hurt his feelings."

* * *

SHE had been married so long she even faked the foreplay.

A MAN never knows the value of a woman's love until he pays maintenance.

* * *

IF your wife wants to learn to drive, don't stand in her way.

* * *

IF you don't like the way women drive, then get off the footpath.

* * *

MY wife has been booked so many times the cops have now given her a season ticket.

* * *

"IS your wife outspoken?"

"Not by anyone I know of."

* * *

WHEN a woman is looking for a husband she is either single or married.

* * *

MARIA Lotzabazooma has had eight husbands. Three of them were her own.

* * *

THE upkeep of a wife is often the downfall of a husband.

* * *

OLD Minnie was complaining to the doctor about the antics of her husband. "He's always looking at pretty girls and wandering off after them," she complained.

"Well, its hard to stop men admiring pretty girls," said the doctor.

"But my husband is 82 years of age," persisted Minnie.

The doctor considered this for a minute and said: "Let me put it this way. I have a little fox terrier that chases motor cars. What would happen if he ever caught one?"

* * *

THE brewery manager called around, hat in hand, to solemnly announce that her husband, Fred, had suffered

470

a tragic and fatal accident at work. He had fallen into a vat of beer and drowned.

"Oh dear. Did he suffer much?" asked the bereaved wife.

"I don't think so," said the manager. "He got out twice to go to the loo."

* * *

HARRY stopped off at the pub and was soon chatting up a blonde at the bar. Near closing time she suggested going to her place. They did and after a few more drinks they had a wonderful time.

It was three in the morning when Harry got out of bed and began to dress. And with a worried frown said "How will I explain this to the wife?"

"No problem," said the blonde, "and by the way, put this bit of chalk behind your ear."

Harry was creeping up the stairs when the light was flicked on, and there was his fuming wife waiting with folded arms.

"And where the hell have you been?" she demanded.

Harry remembered the blonde's advice and told the truth. "I've been tumbling in bed with a lovely blonde I picked up in the pub," he said.

"Liar!" she roared. "You have been playing billiards all night with those hopeless mates of yours. I can tell by the chalk behind your ear."

* * *

THE wife was understandably annoyed when her husband came in drunk at midnight.

"I could forgive you if it was the first time," she said. "but you came home in the same condition on March 15, 1958."

* * *

"HOW'S your headache, Fred?"

"Out doing the shopping."

* * *

"YOU haven't nagged me all evening. Is there someone else?"

"ONE more word," she said, "and I'll go back to my mother."
"Taxi!"

THE doctor asked her: "Has there been any insanity in the family?"
"Yes, Doc," she said. "My husband thinks he's the boss."

* * *

SHE has a tongue that jaywalks over every conversation.

* * *

SHE gives me a 'Going Away Party' every time I take the garbage out.

* * *

GOING to a party with your wife is like going fishing with a game keeper.

* * *

IF you want your wife to listen, then talk to another woman.

WOMEN
See WIVES

GENERALLY speaking, women are generally speaking.

* * *

FOUR women, one English, one American, one German and one French, were all asked the same question: "What would you do if you were shipwrecked on an island with a regiment of soldiers?"

The Englishwoman said she would hide. The American said she would seek the protection of the commanding officer. The German woman said she would be out marching and it wouldn't bother her.

The French woman thought for a moment; "I understand ze question, but what seems to be ze problem?"

* * *

WHEN a woman is looking for a husband she is either single or married.

TWO psychiatrists were in a restaurant. One said, "See that man over there, well, he claims to understand women."

"Really," said his friend, "and he's a professional colleague?"

"No. He's a patient."

WORDS

WORDS are the means by which we confuse each other as three New Australians discovered. One was lamenting the fact that he and his wife had no children. "My wife is unbearable," he explained.

"No, you mean she is inconceivable," said the second.

"You are both wrong," said the third. "He means his wife is impregnable."

* * *

THE longest word in the English language is the one following the phrase: "And now a word from our sponsor."

* * *

FRED always called a spade a spade, until the night he fell over one.

* * *

HE was going to have a few words with his wife, but he found she had cornered the market.

* * *

ONE word of censure makes Dad hold his tongue; and Mum's the word.

* * *

PROCRASTINATION is the thief of time, especially if you can't spell it.

* * *

WHEN a politician says a meeting was meaningful; it means that it was meaningless.

* * *

COULD-Be-Better-Put Dept: A woman on a crowded train thought she recognised her husband in the crush.

She pushed through, came up behind him and kissed him on the neck. When he turned round she was shocked to find it wasn't him at all.

"Terribly sorry," she blushed, "but your head looks just like my husband's behind."

* * *

TO awaken a student sleeping in his class the English professor threw a book at him.

"What hit me?" spluttered the student.

"That, my lad," replied the professor, "was a flying Chaucer."

* * *

LETTERS can be as confusing as words. Following a lesson on genetics one student asked of his colleague what DNA stood for.

"That's simple," said his friend. "It stands for the National Association of Dyslectics."

* * *

THE Maharaja of an Indian province once decreed that no wild animals were to be killed. Soon his realm was overrun with tigers. When the people could stand it no longer they gave the Maharaja the heave-ho.

It was the first time on record where the reign was cancelled because of the game.

* * *

ON the anniversary of Shakespeare's birth a BBC announcer achieved this vintage spoonerism: "The usual festivities were held in Stratford today to celebrate the Bird's bathday!"

* * *

THE flying instructor had just delivered a lesson on parachute jumping. "And if it doesn't open?" asked a student.

"Well, you are jumping to a conclusion," he replied.

* * *

SHE said she had started a new diet: "No more eating my own words, swallowing my pride, or putting my foot in my mouth," she said.

WHEN Joe Bloggs scooped the agricultural show with all prizes for his vegetables he was invited on television.

"And what is the secret of growing prize vegetables?" asked the compere.

"Manure," answered Joe. "Manure for tomatoes, manure for pumpkins, manure for cabbages..." and he went on extolling the virtues of manure.

A very embarrassed daughter was watching at home. "Oh Mum, why can't Dad say fertilizer instead of manure?"

"Count your blessings," said Mrs Bloggs. "It took me 30 years to get him to call it manure!"

*　　*　　*

THE Archbishop of Canterbury was a distinguished guest at the mayoral dinner. As the first course was being served a waiter slipped and dropped a bowl of hot soup upside down in the Archbishop's lap.

The Archbishop looked depairingly around the table and said: "Is there any layman present who will be good enough to express my feelings?"

*　　*　　*

WHEN it came to writing up the log book Captain Squiggs was a stickler for accuracy, so when the first mate received news that he was the father of twins and celebrated in his cabin the captain noted in the logbook: "The first mate was drunk last night."

When the mate saw it he argued that it should be struck from the record but the pedantic captain was resolute. "You were drunk last night. I can't change that fact, so it must stay in the log."

Next day the mate was on watch and it was his duty to keep the log. In the morning the captain was aghast to read: "The captain was sober last night."

*　　*　　*

YOU have heard of the TATE family? They're everywhere.

There is Dick Tate who wants to control everybody. Ro Tate who tries to turn things around. Agi Tate who stirs up trouble and Irri Tate who helps. Hesi Tate and Vege Tate always procrastinate. Imi Tate mimics everybody. Devas Tate likes to destroy things and Poten Tate wants to be a big shot, but it's Facili Tate, Cogi Tate and Medi Tate who save the day.

*   *   *

THE Aussie had just taken up a job in the wildlife sanctuary and was explaining to some American tourists the difference between an echidna and a porcupine. "The echidnas' pricks are longer," he said.

This caused great embarrassment amongst the mixed group and later the supervisor took him aside to reprimand the Aussie on his choice of words.

"It's quills. Use a bit of decorum," he said. "It's quills."

The next group of Yanks raised the same question. "That's a doggone porcupine," said one.

"Different animal altogether," said our Aussie with authority. "The echidna is smaller, lighter in colour and its quills are longer ... but their pricks are about the same size."

The
Seriously
Rude
Joke Book

The
Seriously
Rude
Joke Book

George Coote

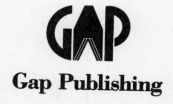

Gap Publishing

Contents

G

H

I

J

K

L

M

Q

R

S

T

Introduction

In the previous volume, The Serious Joke Book, we banned the rude, the racist and the blasphemous due to a false notion of sensitivity. In a blow for free speech they are resurrected in this volume.

You have heard the stories about the Englishman, the Scotsman and the Irishman; and you always will, for these jokes are as old as the language itself. Now we have listed the best to include the Greeks, Germans, French, Italians, Turks, Russians, Chinese, Japanese, Vietnamese, New Zealanders, English and the Australians.

It seems all nations have their fall guys, and usually the butt of their jokes is the inhabitants of the country next door. In the United States a few years ago a Pole gained notoriety by entering bookshops and ripping out pages of Polish jokes from a magazine. He left the Jewish, Irish and Italian sections because they didnt offend him; a statement in itself. This author takes the view that nationalism, like patriotism, is the last refuge of scoundrels and therefore should not be protected. The best way to break down ethnic barriers is to laugh at ourselves and anyone else who takes jingoistic nationalism too far. So read them while you can. And if you are a Scot then you are quite at liberty to re-tell the joke and call Jock an Irishman.

Jokes can heal as well as wound. In Australia Greek and Italian migrants are accepted. The last wave of arrivals to bear the brunt of discrimination are Vietnamese boat people. A Vietnamese comedian, Hung Le, is smashing through this prejudice by telling jokes and is the most unlikely comedian for the pub circuit. He tells his audience he was excited to find a hot dog stand when he arrived in Australia, but his elation turned to disgust when he took a closer look.

"Thats the only bit of the dog we dont eat," he said.

Religion gets a belting in this edition too. In earlier times when blasphemy was a capital offence, most of the jokes in this volume would have had the authors balls burned at the stake. Today one can get away with it. Thanks to the English church and its notorious proclivity for extra-mural activities such as bishops dropping their breeches, deans dressing in drag, transvestite vicars and other eccentric ecclesiastics, the church has become a legitimate butt of ridicule.

"I'll be buggered if I'll be a bishop," said the curate.

The Roman Catholic church is also in disarray with a legion of priests and brothers following their carnal calling. Meanwhile the succession of American television evangelists and fundamentalists who have embezzled profits to pursue sins of the flesh have evidently checked the dictionary to learn that fundament means buttocks. It is hoped that the ribald jokes deflate the pompous and cause the Church to suffer in dignified silence.

As for the ribald jokes that are just plain rude, the Kama Sutra has been around for centuries, proving that sex is here to stay, and while there are many ways of doing it, there are also many ways of laughing at it.

A

ACCIDENTS

FRED pulled out to avoid a child, fell off the sofa and strained his ankle.

* * *

REMEMBER, ninety per cent of the population was caused by accident.

* * *

SIGN in the Family Planning Agency's car park: "Be Careful when Pulling Out."

* * *

THE inspector at the bus terminal was checking schedules with the drivers: "What time did you pull out this morning?"

Murphy: "I didn't. And I'm worried about it."

* * *

THE Hare Krishna rushed in to tell the priest:

"My karma has run over your dogma."

* * *

ONE car had stopped at the lights, the second ran into its rear with the tinkle of broken headlights. The odd thing was that the first car was driven by a vicar and the second by a priest. They were arguing about the blame when the police arrived on the scene.

"How fast would you say he was going," interjected Sergeant O'Flaherty, "when he backed into you, Father?"

THE truck driver couldn't believe his eyes. When he rounded the bend there, at the bottom of the hill, was a couple making love in the middle of the road.

He blew the horn. They didn't stop screwing.

The truck finally screeched to a halt barely a hair's breadth from the humping couple.

The driver got out and demanded an explanation: "What the bloody hell is going on?"

When the young man recovered he stood up. "I was coming. She was coming. You were coming," he said, "and you were the only one that had brakes."

* * *

FARMER Brown lost control of his jalopy on the bend and ended up in the river. He managed to climb out and scramble on top of the car to await rescue.

He heard one car stop. It was his neighbours, Mr and Mrs Jones. Then a second car arrived with more neighbours, Mr and Mrs Ball.

As Bill Jones pulled him to safety Farmer Brown said: "I'm glad you got here first Bill. I'd hate to be pulled out by the balls."

* * *

IN a factory accident a worker lost two fingers. But he didn't notice the loss until he was saying goodnight to the boss.

* * *

A SCOT bought a round of drinks at the pub the other night. He has asked police to appeal for witnesses to the accident.

* * *

THE cop arrived at the scene of the accident to find a couple bonking their heart out on the nature strip.

"My fault," said the blonde when the cop pulled her off the recovering victim.

' "I was giving him mouth to mouth resuscitation when we both got carried away."

2

AFTER the car skidded into the tree the first man on the scene found the driver still behind the wheel, dazed and bleeding.

"How badly are you hurt?" he enquired.

"How the hell should I know," muttered the driver. "I'm a doctor not a lawyer."

* * *

TEN per cent of all accidents are caused by drivers affected by alcohol.

Which is another way of saying 90 per cent of accidents are caused by non-drinkers.

* * *

A BUSINESSMAN returned to his parked car to find the headlights broken and damage to the front end. Stuck under the windscreen wiper he found a note which read:

"Hey, man. I just backed into your car. The folks that saw the accident are nodding in approval because they think I am writing down my name and other particulars, but I aint."

* * *

IT was a nasty accident. A woman who swallowed a razor blade was rushed to the emergency ward. After an X-ray the doctors decided to let it take its natural course.

A few months later she eventually passed the razor blade, but in the meantime she had not only given herself a tonsillectomy, an appendectomy and a hysterectomy but had also castrated her husband, circumcised his best friend, given the vicar a hare lip and cut the finger of a passing acquaintance.

* * *

THE woman at the cocktail party was intent on making the acquaintance of the young medical officer.

"Do you deal with many accidents?" she asked.

"I really don't know," he replied.

"But you are a doctor, what do you mean you don't know?"

"How could I," he said. "My field is obstetrics."

ADVERTISEMENTS

BY-SEXUAL man aged 40 seeks young married couple.

* * *

LOST. Antique cameo brooch depicting Adam and Eve in St Killed Saturday night.

* * *

ADVERTISEMENT in a tourist guide: Accommodation, Bed & Breakfast, $60. Mrs Frampton, $80.

* * *

FOR Sale: Complete set of Encyclopaedia Britannica. Never been opened. Wife knows everything.

* * *

LOST dog. Has three legs, blind in left eye, right ear missing, broken tail, no teeth, recently castrated. Answers to Lucky.

* * *

GIRL wanted for petrol pump attendant.

* * *

IT pays to advertise. A salesman found himself in a country town overnight where the only excitement appeared to be watching the clothes go round in the laundromat.

Out of sheer boredom he opened the Gideon Bible supplied in all motel rooms.

On the flyleaf was the message: "If thou art bored and lonely and desireth some warm comfort, ring Lulu, 580-6683.

ADVICE

THE doctor told the young man the reason for his depression was stress. "Take life easier," was the doc's advice. "Do you drink?"

"No," said the young man, "never have."

"There is no harm in a quiet drink," said the doctor, "even

4

a smoke to relax, and sex at least once a week. In fact, in your case it is essential."

Two months later the patient returned and was evidently in much better health. He told the doctor he enjoyed a glass of beer each night and had taken up the pipe.

"And sex?" asked the doctor.

"Hard to find it every week," admitted the patient, "especially for a parish priest in a small country town like this."

* * *

MURIEL was in a serious mood and asked her mother for advice. She was about to be married and the groom had come to stay with the family for the weekend during which time she had blundered into the bathroom and saw him naked.

"Mother," she said, "what was that thing hanging down between his legs?"

"They call it a penis my dear, nothing to worry about."

"And the knob on the end, like a fireman's helmet."

"Just the glans," said Mother.

"And there are two round things about 13 inches back from this glans. What are they?"

"For your sake, my dear," said Mum, "I hope they are the cheeks of his arse."

* * *

FRED had a problem and he confided in Jed because he was a little older.

"Problem is," said Fred, "I have a choice of two women. One is young and beautiful and I love her dearly. But she is broke. The other is an older woman, a widow and quite plain, but she is a millionaire. What should I do?"

It was no problem for Jed.

"Follow your heart," he said. "Marry the young girl you love. And give me the address of the widow."

ALCOHOLICS

AN alcoholic is a man who goes in to a topless bar for a drink.

* * *

THE difference between being a drunk and being an alcoholic is that the drunk doesn't have to bother attending all those boring meetings.

* * *

"WHY was alcohol invented?" asked one wino of another.

"So that ugly women could get laid too," said his mate.

ANIMALS

"ARE you an animal lover?"

"Well, my wife thinks so."

* * *

THE tortoise told the police she had been raped by two snails.

"Can you describe them?" asked the cop.

"No," she said, "it all happened so fast."

* * *

THE bi-sexual donkey had a hee in the morning and a haw at night.

* * *

A BEAR and a rabbit were sitting side by side having a crap in the woods.

The bear said, "Do you have any trouble with shit sticking to your fur?"

"No," said the rabbit.

With that the bear promptly picked up the rabbit and wiped his arse with him.

* * *

MIKE the Monk was having a quiet drink in the Animals

Bar when Mick the Mouse climbed up on the stool beside him.

"How did you go with that giraffe last night?" enquired the monk.

"What a night!" said the mouse, "I'll never take her out again. She's a nymphomaniac, and what with kissing her and screwing her I must have run a hundred miles last night."

*　*　*

LEO the lion was drinking from a stream with his bum in the air, just as a big chimp was passing. From the chimp's viewpoint it looked like Lily the lion so he crept up quietly and planted the sausage with a wallop.

The lion let out a mighty roar and the chimp took off like greased lightning. He sped through the jungle with the outraged lion in hot pursuit.

The chimp dashed into a hunter's camp, quickly donned a safari suit, snatched on a pith helmet, dived into a chair, grabbed a copy of The Times and hid behind it as if were reading.

The lion screeched into the clearing and as soon as the dust settled asked the "hunter."

"Have you seen a chimp dash past here?"

"Not the chimp that rooted the lion down by the stream?"

"Hell," said the lion, "don't tell me it's in the papers already."

ANNIVERSARIES

"I'M afraid I can't make the darts match tomorrow night, Fred. I promised to take Thingummy out for our silver anniversary."

*　*　*

ANNIVERSARIES are like toilet seats.

Men usually miss both.

ARMY

THE colonel was a rare drinker, but at the annual regimental dinner he ate too much food, drank too much wine and got the fright of his life when he was challenged to a duel.

His colleagues were quickly to the rescue and sent him home in a cab.

Next morning he had to explain to his batman why there was such a mess on his jacket. "Some bounder bumped into me and was sick all over my tunic. I'll give him a month's detention when I find him," he said.

The batman gathered up the clothes. "I'd make it two months, sir. The bastard has shit in your trousers, too,"

* * *

THE seat-belt sign switched off and the three men seated together settled down for a long flight.

The distinguished man in the middle began the introductions with himself: "General, Australian Army, married, two sons, both lawyers."

The second took the cue: "General, Artillery, married, two sons, one a surgeon the other a judge."

There was an embarrassing silence until the third responded, "Petty Officer, Australian Navy, never married, two sons, both generals."

* * *

A POSTING to the Far East was a plum reward for officers during the height of the British Empire so when Ponsonby won such a posting and had been established there for several months his wife eventually came out to join him.

With servants on hand the wife decided to sleep in on her very first morning, but around 9-30 the Chinese valet came in, whipped off the bedclothes, slapped her on the bum and said: "All light Missy, get your bleakfast then go home."

PRIVATE Murphy was on patrol in the jungle when he discovered a quiet pool by the edge of the river. He stripped off for a swim and was standing by the bank when a shot rang out.

He woke up in hospital.

"What happened?" he said to the medical team around him.

"Actually, to come to the point old man," said the chief medic, "a sniper's bullet has shot your balls off. Neatly off I might add. We just had to sew up the wound."

Murphy surveyed the damage.

"Could of been worse," he said. "Lucky I was thinking of me wife's younger sister when it happened."

* * *

IN the same hospital one of the soldiers had his head so swathed in bandages he could only be fed rectally, through a tube.

The nurse had just served his morning coffee when he began waving his arms around.

"What's up?" she said, "too hot?"

She bent down to hear his muffled response: "Too much sugar."

* * *

NEXT day the wife of the soldier with his head in bandages called to see how he was recovering.

"How is his appetite?" she asked.

"Terrific," said the orderly. "It would have done your heart good, ma'am, to see his arse snap at a piece of toast this morning."

* * *

THE young officer arrived at the India regiment and reported that he was eager for active service to defend the empire.

"Oh no, all that skirmishing stuff is over," said the colonel, "we have a different program now, old chap. Tomorrow is Tuesday, which means we play tennis."

"Oh, I don't play tennis," said the officer.

"Well then, Wednesday we play polo. You do play polo?"

"No sir."

"Hmmm," said the colonel, "Then Thursday we enjoy the regimental dance."

"I'm afraid I don't dance at all, sir."

"Then you will enjoy Fridays," said the colonel. "That's wife-swapping night. Lot's of sex and fun."

"Sir, I'm afraid I couldn't be part of anything like that," said the officer.

"Good gracious man," said the colonel. "You must be some kind of homosexual?"

"No, I certainly am not," replied the officer.

"Then you probably won't like Saturday nights either," said the colonel.

*   *   *

"DEAR Dad," said the letter from his soldier son, "I can't tell you where I am, but yesterday I shot a polar bear."

Two months later another letter arrived: "Dear Dad," it began. "I can't tell you where I am but yesterday I danced with a native girl."

Another month passed before the third letter: "Dear Dad. The doctor tells me I should have danced with the polar bear and shot the native girl."

*   *   *

FRED decided to dodge the call-up by being medically unfit. The easiest way, he decided, was to pull the last of his remaining teeth out. They wouldn't take a bloke with a completely gummy mouth.

Fred was third in line when a tough sergeant major began the examination.

"What's wrong with you?" he demanded of the first man.

"No teeth at all," was the reply.

The sergeant stuck his finger in the man's mouth and felt around. "You're right. You are no good to us."

Fred's spirits brightened when he heard that decision.

"And what's wrong with you?" said the sergeant to the second man.

"Piles, sir."

The sergeant stuck his finger up the man's bum, felt around and said: "Yes. You are no bloody good to us."

Turning to Fred he said: "And what's wrong with you?"

"Nothing at all," said Fred.

ARTS

A RENOWNED art critic named Flo
Was accosted a fortnight ago
When the flasher unzipped
She allegedly quipped
"An exhibit well hung sir, Good show."

* * *

THE celebrated eye surgeon had operated on the eyes of the ageing artist and fully restored his sight. In his everlasting gratitude the artist insisted on painting a large mural across the front of the hospital to honour the doctor.

When the surgeon saw the massive work depicting a large eyeball and massive lashes he was asked for his opinion of the work.

"I'd just like to say thank God I decided against being a gynaecologist," he said.

* * *

CURLY had a way with words which made him a winner with women. So when he scored the loveliest girl at the party his two mates followed and pressed their ears to the bedroom door.

"You've got a magnificent body," they heard him say. "It is so lovely that it should be captured on canvas and painted by a master."

Just then there was a knock on the door.

"Who's there?" asked Curly.

"Rembrandt and Reubens," came the reply.

"GOOD news," said the promotor to the artist. "I told a guy that paintings appreciate in value after the artist's death and he bought all your works."

"Who was it?" asked the artist.

"Your doctor," replied the promotor.

ASTRONAUTS

THE first Jewish astronaut was Nose Cohen.

* * *

THE first male and female astronauts landed on Mars and made scientific contact with the locals. The Martians showed how they made little Martians, by shaping little boys and girls out of plastic, putting them on a conveyor belt which went through an oven and produced little children at the other end.

"How do you make humans?" asked the Martian.

The astronauts removed their clothes and gave a perfect performance of sexual intercourse.

When they had finished the Martian said: "Well, where are the babies?"

"Oh, it takes nine months," said the Earthlings.

"Well why were you in such a hurry at the end?"

ATHEISTS

THE Atheists organised a dial-a-prayer service.

When you phone up, nobody answers.

* * *

A SINCERE Atheist is one who eats pork on Good Friday and wipes his bum with his right hand.

It's the only way he can insult three religions at once.

AUSTRALIANS

HE couldn't believe it himself, but there he was, ship-wrecked with Miss Australia.

There would be no hanky-panky of course because he was a married man and she was too famous to have her reputation damaged. So they made a pact.

He said: "You stay this side of the island and I will keep to the other. We will meet in a week to check on provisions and rescue prospects." She agreed. But of course when they met a week later they were as horny as hell.

"We might never be rescued," he said, "so why don't we do it?"

They virtually tore each others clothes off and went at it hammer and tongs. In fact it was so good they promised each other to meet the next night, same time, same place.

"But could you do me a favour," said the Aussie.

"What's that?"

"Could you dress up as a man?" he said. "I have salvaged some shirts and trousers."

Miss Australia looked at him askance. "You're not kinky are you?"

"No. Nothing like that."

She reluctantly agreed. And next evening she was walking along the beach looking for all the world like a bloke when he fell into step beside her.

"G'day mate," he said slapping an arm around her shoulder. "You'll never guess who I fucked last night!"

* * *

A LION in the London Zoo was lazing in the sun and licking its arse when a visitor turned to the keeper and said, "that's a docile old thing isn't it?"

"No way," said the keeper, "it is the most ferocious beast in the zoo. Why just an hour ago it dragged an Australian tourist into the cage and completely devoured him."

"Hardly seems possible," said the astonished visitor, "but why is he lying there licking his arse?"

"The poor thing is trying to get the taste out of his mouth," said the keeper.

AN Englishman, a Scotsman and an Australian went for a job. The boss asked them all the same question: What is the capital of Ireland?"

"New York," said the Scot.

"No. It's Vancouver," said the Englishman.

"Fools," said the Australian, "anybody knows the capital of Ireland is Brussels."

The Australian got the job because he was closest.

* * *

WHEN their car broke down a Jew, an Indian and an Australian knocked on a farmer's door to ask for accommodation for the night.

"One will have to sleep in the barn," said the farmer.

"I will," said the Jew.

But five minutes later there was a knock on the door.

"There's a pig in the barn," said the Jew.

"Okay, I'll go," said the Indian.

Five minutes later there was a knock on the door.

"There is an un-sacred cow in the barn," he said.

"I'll go," said the Australian.

Five minutes later there was yet another knock on the door. It was the pig and the cow.

* * *

THERE was a young man from Australia
  Who painted his arse like a dahlia
  The drawing was fine, the colour divine
  But the scent? Ar, that was a failure.

* * *

IN Sydney she was Rhonda
  She was Patsy out in Perth
  In Brisbane she was Brenda,
  The sweetest girl on earth.
  In Wagga she was Wendy
  The pick of all the bunch,
  But down on his expenses
  She was petrol, oil and lunch.

14

THREE men and a woman were in the lift of Australias tallest building when the cable broke and they began plummeting towards certain death. The woman was a quick thinker . She looked at the three men and said: "Is there one more chance of being a woman?"

Only one had the presence of mind to whip his trousers off. He flung them at her and said:

"Here, iron these."

AVIATION

THE pilot's girlfriend hung on every word he said, and when he spotted an aircraft flying high overhead, he made the idle comment, "thats the mailplane."

She said: "Marvellous how you can tell from this distance."

* * *

IT had been an all-night flight and with the sun beginning to rise the crew switched on the cabin lights for breakfast.

"Who switched on those fucking lights?" said a male passenger who had made a constant nuisance of himself.

The hostess had had enough.

"These are the breakfast lights, sir," she said. "The fucking lights are much dimmer and you snored right through them."

* * *

THE aircraft was just about to take off when the door of the flight deck opened and the stark naked pilot dashed down the aisle with a microphone in his hand.

"This is your captian streaking," he said.

* * *

THE aircraft was on its final approach and the captain had announced landing time. However he left the PA system on and the next statement surprised the passengers.

"As soon as I clock off I'm going to have a nice cool beer and then screw the arse off that red-headed hostess."

The hostess was shocked and began a hurried dash to the flight deck but tripped over a suitcase.

A little old lady leant down. "No need to hurry dear," she advised, "he said he was going to have a beer first."

* * *

IT was the first time Harry had flown the modern wide-bodied jets equipped with the latest facilities. Even separate ladies' and gents' loos.

Finding the men's room occupied during a quiet section of the flight he thought he would slip into the Ladies. While sitting on the seat he noticed the array of buttons and pushed the one marked "WW". Immediately warm water was squirted on his bum. He pushed "PP" and was delighted to feel a powder puff gently tapping him dry.

Thrilled at the service he pushed the button marked "ATR". And and that's the last thing he remembered.

He woke up back in his seat looking up at the smiling faces of the hostesses.

"Christ, what happened?" he said.

"You pressed the Automatic Tampon Remover," said the hostess, "when you are able to walk you will find your penis waiting for you with the purser."

B

BACHELORS

EVERY man should have a girl for love, companionship and sympathy, said a wise and mature bachelor, "and preferably at three different addresses," he added.

BAKERS

PETE the Pastrycook was preparing apple pies and crimping the edges down a set of false teeth when the health inspector made a visit.

"Hey, haven't you a tool for that?"

"Yes," said Pete, "but I use it for putting the holes in the doughnuts."

* * *

THE sign out front declared it was the Hygiene Bakery, and indeed, Mrs Grump was delighted to be offered her loaf of bread on a long toasting fork.

"Untouched by human hands," said the baker.

Mrs Grump was impressed, but she noticed a piece of string hanging from the baker's trouser fly.

"What's that?" she asked.

"Part of the hygiene program," said the baker, "when I go for a leak I pull it out with the string, untouched by human hands."

"But how do you get it back?" asked Mrs Grump.

"With the fork," said the baker.

BALLS

THERE was a young Scot named McIvers
Whose knackers were two different sizes
One was so small
'Twas no ball at all
But the other won several first prizes.

* * *

TWO inquisistive old maids approached the giraffe enclosure at the zoo and were intrigued to find a pair of balls at eye-level.

"They're testicles alright," said one "and I reckon I could touch them from here." She reached through and squeezed one of the giraffe's coconuts.

The animal reacted in the normal manner, by jumping 20 metres into the air, clearing the enclosure fence and galloping out of the zoo.

The keeper dashed out and asked the startled old maids what had happened. When they explained he dropped his dacks.

"Here," he said, "you'd better squeeze mine because I have to catch the bastard."

* * *

A TOURIST went into a Madrid restaurant and asked for the speciality of the house. He was served a magnificent plate bearing two king-sized rissoles.

The tourist tucked in, found them to be delicious and called the waiter to express his appreciation.

"What do you call that dish?" asked the tourist wiping his lips with the napkin.

"They are gonads," said the Spanish waiter. He went on to explain that the gonads were the testicles of the bull killed in the adjoining bull ring that very day.

"Always fresh, senor," said the waiter.

It was quite a shock for the tourist, but he had to admit they were tasty, satisfying and cheap.

In fact, the very next evening he returned and asked for the same dish. When they were served he called the waiter back to complain about the size of the two miserable rissoles which sat forlorn and lonely in the centre of the plate.

"Yes, senor," agreed the waiter, "they are much smaller than yesterday, but today, the bull wins."

* * *

THERE are fancy dressed balls too, and dusky Rita went to such an event stark naked. But the doorman refused to let her in.

"You have to represent something," he said.

Rita returned wearing black gloves and shoes.

"I'm the five of spades," she said.

* * *

IT was a fancy dress ball with scores of lavish costumes but Lulu arrived stark naked.

"What do you represent?" asked the host.

"I'm Adam," she said.

He took a close look and said, "But you don't have a cock."

"I'll soon find one," she said.

* * *

NEXT to be admitted to the fancy dress ball was a stunning brunette in red stockings, thigh length boots, red suspenders and matching bra and panties.

"And what are you?" asked the host.

"I am Dying Embers," she said, "and if I don't get a poke soon I'm going out."

* * *

FRED got up to join the parade at the fancy dress ball wearing nothing but his underpants.

"What's this?" said the MC with his notebook, "You've got to represent something."

19

Fred insisted he did. He was Premature Ejaculation. After several attempts the MC admitted he was unable to spell it.

"Just say I came in my underpants," said Fred.

* * *

IF you have a green ball in your right hand and a green ball in your left, then you have Kermit the Frog's undivided attention.

* * *

WHY do dogs lick their balls?
Because they can.

BANANAS

DOCTOR Watson was amazed to be told by Sherlock Holmes that the three women eating bananas in the park were a spinster, a hooker and a newly-wed.

"Amazing," said Watson, "but how can you tell?"

"Elementary, my dear Watson," replied Holmes. "You see how the spinster breaks the banana into little pieces before delicately popping them into her mouth, while the prostitute, the one in the middle, holds the banana in both hands."

"Yes, Holmes, but how can you tell the third is a bride?"

"See how she holds the banana in one hand and thumps herself on the back of the head with the other?" explained the detective.

* * *

"WHAT are you shaking for?" said the banana to the vibrator, "I'm the one she's going to eat."

BARBERS

BOB the barber broke his leg in a skiing accident.
Now he can only cut hair on crutches.

SUPPORT your local barber and help get rid of the lunatic fringe.

* * *

A CASANOVA type entered the barber shop. " How many before me?" he asked.

"Three haircuts and two shaves, sir," replied the barber.

The young man left and didn't come back.

Next day he reappeared. "How many before me today, barber?"

"Two haircuts, one shave and one trim."

The young man left and didn't return until the following day for the same routine.

Finally the barber sought an explanation of such behaviour and sent his apprentice to follow him.

"I'm none the wiser," said the lad. "He just goes round to your place, Boss."

* * *

IT was an Italian barber shop and Guiseppe had always promised his son Luigi that he would teach him the trade.

So on the boy's 21st birthday Guiseppe took him to the shop for the first time and presented him with a white coat and a brand new razor.

"Here comes a man for a shave Dad, please let me practise on him."

"Okay," said Guiseppe, "but be careful and don't cut yourself."

* * *

BOB the barber had a secret formula for hair restorer and used to pass it on to special customers. One day a completely bald man pressed $500 in his hand for the remedy.

Bob relented. "It's simple. All you do is apply female secretions to the bald patch. It stimulates hair," he said.

"How do I know it works?" said the punter. "I notice you have a bald spot yourself."

"Yes," said Bob, "and did you notice my one hell of a moustache?"

21

THE customer was complaining about the price of the haircut. "I've just been to Italy," he said. "Over there you can get a haircut for five dollars."

"Maybe," said the barber, "but what about the bloody fare!"

* * *

JAKE and Fred were getting their hair cut and when the barber started to sprinkle Eau de Cologne on his hair Jake protested. "Don't put that stinky stuff on me. My wife will think I smell like a whore-house."

In the next chair Fred chirped up. "You can sprinkle it on me. My wife doesn't know what a whore-house smells like."

BARS

IT is the ultimate in singles bars.

Girls have to show their IUDs to be admitted.

* * *

EVERY night the bloke in the corner was attracting all the girls.

The rest of the fellows couldn't understand it. The barman couldn't explain it. "He's not that handsome," he said, "he's not a flashy dresser and he hardly says a word. Just sits there licking his eyebrows."

* * *

A BLOKE sidles up to a long-legged blonde in the singles bar and says: "Would you like a Harvey Wallbanger?"

"Yes," she says, "but can we have a drink first?"

* * *

A CAR salesman appeared dejected as he leant on the bar.

"What's the trouble?" asked a blonde who sat beside him.

"If I don't sell more cars this month I'll lose my arse."

"I know the feeling," she said. "If I don't sell more arse this month I'll lose my car."

22

A BLOKE went in to a bar with a chequered flag.

The barman said: "I hope you're not going to start anything."

* * *

TWO middle-aged blokes were leaning on the bar.

"Ya know Kev, we should be grateful we are not young anymore. Sex is such an accepted thing to the younger generation today that it has almost become meaningless to the lucky bastards."

BIKIES

IT was after closing time at the country pub yet the local cop noticed two motorbikes still parked out front.

He walked round the back of the hotel and found the two bikies, one with his pants down, the other with his finger up his friend's bum.

"Hullo, hullo, hullo," said the cop. "What's going on?"

"My mate's had too much to drink, I'm trying to make him sick."

"Well you don't put your finger in there. You put it down his throat," said the cop.

"Yeah, I'm just about to."

* * *

FLASH the bikie told his gang that he was divorcing his wife because of her disgusting habits.

"I went to piss in the sink this morning, only to find it was full of dirty dishes," he said.

BIRDS

A SMALL boy told his mother that he was surprised to learn that birds had spare parts.

"What do you mean, son?"

"Well, I just heard Dad tell Uncle Ron that he would like to screw the arse off the bird next door."

"SEEN any unusual birds lately," said the ornithologist to Fred at the bar.

"Well, apart from a double-breasted seersucker, a morning pee-wee, an extramarital lark and a pink-titted bedthrasher, no. Nothing to crow about."

* * *

NEVER cross a disobedient dog with a rooster.

You will only get a cock that doesn't come.

* * *

WHILE on the long migratory flight one crow said to the other: "Have you bred any good rooks lately?"

* * *

MY wife does bird imitations. She watches me like a hawk.

* * *

WHAT'S the difference between a canary with two wings and a canary with one.

A difference of a pinion.

* * *

IF a bird craps on your car, never take her out again.

* * *

DONALD Duck split with Daisy and soon found his way to the brothel.

"I'm down for a good time," he said, "and you can stick it on my bill."

* * *

A BLOKE at the singles bar was making headway with a bird and thought he would put the hard word on her.

"How do you like your eggs in the morning?" he said.

"Unfertilized, thanks," she replied.

* * *

A BLONDE and a brunette were walking along a country path when the brunette stopped and said: "Oh dear, look, a dead bird."

The blonde looked up in the sky and said: "Where? Where?"

A BLOKE tried to take his pet duck to the movies but was told in no uncertain manner that ducks were not allowed in the stalls. Like a true duck owner he went to the Gents, stuffed the duck down the front of his trousers and in a defiant mood bought his ticket and entered the theatre.

Unfortunately, half way through the movie the duck became fidgety through lack of air so our man opened his fly and let the duck stick its head out.

The woman seated next to him nudged her husband and whispered: "The bloke next to me has his thing sticking out."

Her husband, absorbed in the film, said not to worry about it.

"Don't worry about it?" she said. "The bloody thing is eating my popcorn."

* * *

TWO naked statues, male and female, had graced a park for centuries. One day a bolt of lightning struck them and the booming voice of the Almighty said: "Statues. In recognition of your long service you can come alive for an hour."

They jumped down from their pedestals, held hands and rushed into the bushes where, for the next hour there came sounds and strains of grunting and moaning.

"Look at the time," said the man, "we've only two minutes to go. Shall we do it one more time?"

"Yes," she said with enthusiasm, "this time I will hold the pigeon and you shit on it."

BIRTHS

THE baby was born on their first wedding anniversary and the proud mother told the husband to lodge a birth notice in the newspaper.

"Gawd they know how to charge," said the husband on his return. "The girl at the newspaper office asked me how many insertions. I said twice a day for 12 months and I didn't get much change from $200."

* * *

JACK and Jill were ecstatic. After five girls the new baby turned out to be boy.

Jill rang her mother to tell her the good news.

"That's wonderful," said her mother. "Who does he look like, you or Jack?"

"Don't know yet, Mum. We haven't looked at his face."

* * *

AN oil rigger setting off for another month on the platform told his pregnant wife: "When the baby arrives send me a telegram. But say 'bicycle arrived' and that will save me buying a round of drinks for everyone."

She said she would, "And I'm sure we are going to have a boy," she said.

A week later he received a telegram: "Bicycle arrived. Punctured back and front."

BONKS

MAN cannot live on bread alone.

He needs a bit of crumpet.

* * *

THEY we adjusting their clothes after a quickie in the back seat. "Gee," he said. "If I knew you were a virgin I would have taken more time."

"If I knew you had more time," she said, "I would have taken off my panty hose."

* * *

THE frustration the first time you can't make it the second time is nothing compared to the second time you can't make it the first time.

* * *

PUT some excitement into your sex life and try riding your wife Rodeo Style.

That's when you mount her from behind then whisper in her ear: "This is how I do it with your sister."

Then try to stay on for ten seconds.

* * *

WHAT I like to hear most of all,
  And I am sure that you'll say that I'm right,
  Is a girl who says, "I shouldn't,
  But for you I will tonight."

* * *

FRED was saying that sex with his wife was like New Year's Eve.

"You mean bells, whistles and fireworks?"

"No. Once a year."

* * *

"WHY are you taking so long?" demanded his wife.

"I'm trying," he said, "but I just can't think of anyone."

* * *

KEENLY in need of feminine company the salesman struck up a conversation with the barman who suggested the blonde in the corner was a good chance.

The salesman quickly made contact and she accepted his offer of dinner at the hotel's expensive restaurant where she ordered practically everything on the menu.

"Do you always eat this much?" asked the salesman, thinking of the bill.

"Only when I've got my period," she said.

* * *

AFTER their first night bonk she said, "Well I figured you were a doctor, but I didn't know you were an anaesthetist."

"How did you know?"

"You washed you hands before and after the event," she said, "and through the entire performance I didn't feel a thing."

* * *

AFTER a week on board the new bosun asked, "What do you do for sex on this ship?"

27

He was told "On Friday nights we fuck the Chinese cook for $23."

"Why does it cost so much?"

"Well the captain doesn't like it, so we slip him $10, the padre doesn't approve so we slip him $5 and the cook doesn't like it so we slip $2 each for four blokes to hold him down."

* * *

A COP walking along the foreshore at night stepped on a bloke's bare bum. A woman's voice said, "Sock it to me again, Sam."

* * *

A COP discovered a couple bonking away on the foreshore.

"Hullo, hullo, hullo," he said, but the steamy scene before him nudged his primeval urge and he recognised the woman as one of the more attractive pros.

He checked to see nobody else was about and said to the bloke. "Hey, do you reckon I could be next?"

"Dunno," he replied, "I've never screwed a copper before."

* * *

ON the river bank in Alabama he found some soft grass then took off his trousers and hung them on a tree.

"You must be from the north," she said.

"Right on, babe, but how could you tell?"

"A southern boy wouldn't hang up his clothes," said Lulu Belle, "because when we've finished we're gonna be miles from here."

* * *

THE Irishman was bonking a Scottish lass in the park and she wasn't impressed with his performance.

"I thought Irishmen were supposed to be big and thick," she grumbled.

"And I thought the Scots were tight," he replied.

* * *

"LET'S make love a different way tonight, dear," he said.

"Lovely. What way do you propose, darling," she replied.

"Back to back," he said.

"How do we do that?"

"I've invited another couple," he said.

* * *

A WOMAN was gazing into the window of a shoe store admiring a pair of red shoes when a suave middle-aged man sidled up beside her.

Coming to the point he said: "I'll buy those shoes if you will come to bed with me."

She really wanted the shoes and after a moment's thought said: "Okay. But I have to tell you that I am not very keen on sex."

He bought the shoes and soon had her back in his apartment where they went to bed. Just as she had told him she was very passive and he was getting a little bored himself humping away in the missionary position while she lay so still.

Then suddenly she threw her legs up in the air and sighed: "Wow, lovely, bee-yooti-ful."

"I thought you said you didn't like sex," he said.

"I don't," she replied, "I'm just admiring these beaut new shoes."

* * *

IT was after their first night bonk and the egotistical stud, lying back on the pillow, said: "On a scale of one to ten, how would rate that performance?"

"Three," was the quick answer that shocked him. "But you still have seven more chances to notch the perfect score," she said.

BOOBS

THE Pop Concert was about to start when a female streaker raced down the aisle.

She was caught by the bouncers and chucked out.

* * *

DOLLY Parton has just had a single come out.

* * *

A YOUNG husband watched his flat-chested wife try on her new brassiere.

"Why did you buy that for?" he said. "You've nothing to put in it."

"Listen," she said, "I don't complain about you buying underpants."

* * *

SIGN on Fred's door:

"Knock firmly. I like firm knockers."

* * *

SHE was always trying to enlarge her breasts. "I might try silicon implants," she said.

"Costs too much," said her laconic husband.

"Just get some tissue and rub it along your cleavage."

"Will that make them larger?"

"It did a good job on your arse," he said.

* * *

HER cynical husband asked why she was so bright and cheerful.

"I saw my doctor today and he said I had firm breasts like an 18-year-old."

"Yes," said the husband, "but what did he say about your 45-year-old arse?"

"Your name wasn't mentioned," she said.

* * *

A TABLE top dancer called Valerie
Started to count every calorie
Said her boss in disgust
If you lose half your bust
Then you'll be getting just half of your salary.

* * *

THE foundation garmet store unveiled its latest model

30

brassier called the Sheepdog. It rounds them up and points them in the right direction.

*　*　*

"DID she blush when her shoulder straps broke?"

"I didn't notice."

*　*　*

IT was such a hot day Miss Prim took a cold shower and was relaxing on the sofa in the nude when there was a knock on the door.

"Who is it?" she said in alarm, frantically looking for a gown.

"Just the blind man," said the voice outside.

Relieved at the news she opened the door slightly with one hand while reaching for her purse with the other. It was enough for Fred to barge in.

"Great set of norks, lady," he said, "but where do you want these venetians hung?"

*　*　*

THERE was once a maid from Assizes
Whose boobs were two different sizes
One was so small
It was nothing at all
While the other was large and won prizes.

*　*　*

MUM arrived at the function looking the best she had for years. "You look great," said her husband. "You should always leave your bras at home."

"How did you know?" she asked.

"Because you've lost all the wrinkles from your face," he said.

*　*　*

WHILE they were cuddling under the trees
She said to her boyfriend: "Oh please,
It would give me such bliss
If you play more with this
And give less attention to these.

31

SHE was a buxom young woman with a baby in her arms and when she walked into the clinic the doctor asked what the problem was.

"It's the baby," she said, "he seems under-nourished."

The doc carried out an extensive examination of the baby but could find nothing wrong.

"Is he bottle or breast fed?" asked the doc.

"Breast fed," she replied.

"Then I'd better check you too. Strip off to the waist please."

She looked rather embarrassed but did as she was told to reveal a perfect pair of norks. The doctor weighed each one lightly in his hand, then gave the nipples a gentle squeeze and a tug.

"That's the problem." he said. "You are not giving any milk."

"I'm not expected to," she said, "I'm the baby's aunt, but it's been very nice to meet you."

*　*　*

AFTER years in a seminary three priests were assigned to parishes in Tottenham. At the railway station the girl in the ticket box proved to be a buxom wench boasting a pair of very disturbing norks. It brought the priests out in a sweat.

"Three tickets to Titterton," stammered the first before retreating in embarrassment.

"Here, give me the money, I'll have a go," said the second priest approaching the window: "Three titties to Tockerton," he muttered.

"Here, you are making a mess of it," said the third, snatching the money and getting a grip on himself.

"Three tickets to Tottenham, Miss," he said sternly, "and unless you dress more demurely St Finger will point his Peter at you."

*　*　*

EXPERTS were called in from all over the world to diagnose the Pope's illness. Finally, it was agreed that his long life of celibacy had built up such a store of seminal fluid it was choking his arteries.

The only cure was to have intercourse with a woman.

The Pope was aghast. He wouldn't hear of it. Vows and all that.

His physician was convincing: "Your Holiness," he said, "if you persist in celibacy you will be condemning yourself to death. That's suicide, which is also a mortal sin."

The Pope was in great anquish. "I will retire to my room for three days of prayer to help me make a decision," he said.

On the third day the physician was waiting when the Pope emerged. "My decision has been made," he announced. "I will be guided by your advice, but please be sure that she has big tits."

* * *

SHEILA the feminist insisted on attending the church hatless and in a see-through blouse.

"You can't enter the church like that," said the priest.

"I have a divine right," persisted Sheila.

"By what I can see your left is divine too, but you still can't come in."

* * *

PERCY the 'Perv was a short bloke and used to enjoy riding home on the subway in peak hour when, more often than not, his head would be jammed between the breasts of so many buxom office girls.

Once he was nose to nipples with a tall tough blonde.

"Listen, Joe," she sneered, "how would you like a bust in the gob?"

"Oh, you mind-reader you," said our Perce.

* * *

THERE was a young woman called Clair
  Who possessed a magnificent pair
  Or that's what we thought
  Til we saw one get caught

On a thorn and begin losing air.

* * *

AT a city hotel a waiter was dismissed for having his thumb in the soup and a topless waitress was dismissed for two similar offences.

* * *

THERE was an argument at the topless bar when the president of the Beer Appreciators' Society complained that the beer was okay but his waitress was flat.

* * *

A TAXI driver who undid his lady passenger's bra was charged with exceeding the limits in a built up area.

* * *

TO his bride said the sharp-eyed detective
    "Can it be that my eyesight's defective?
    Has your east tit the least bit
    The best of the west tit?
    Or is it a trick of perspective?"

* * *

MISS Lottsabazooma was so proud of her boobs she always chose a dress to show them off to best advantage.

Trying on a low cut dress she checked it in the mirror and then asked the supervisor if she thought it was cut too low.

"Do you have hair on your chest?" asked the supervisor.

"Of course not."

"Then this dress is too low," she said.

* * *

HE placed his stethoscope on the young women's chest and said, "Big breaths my dear."

"Yeth," she said, "and I'm only thixteen."

* * *

A MOUSE dashed up a girl's leg, passed her navel and came to rest snugly in her cleavage.

She looked down and said: "You must be a titmouse."

"No," he replied, "I'm a Mickey Mouse. I just overshot the mark."

* * *

TWO blokes entered a noisy pub and were surprised to see a buxom waitress bouncing from table to table and getting her boobs felt at each stop.

"Looks like a friendly pub," said one, so they sat down and waited until she reached their table.

"Can I have a feel?" said one.

"Certainly not," she replied.,

"But those other blokes did."

"They didn't ask," she replied.

* * *

AN old man was the only other occupant of the train compartment and he had fallen asleep, so the young mother had no qualms about breastfeeding her baby.

However, he woke halfway through the process.

"What a lovely child," he said, "what do you feed him on?"

"Just milk and orange juice," she replied.

The old man thought about this for a moment. "Which one is the orange juice?" he asked.

* * *

THE two gossips noticed Miss Lottzabazooma in the park.

"Is that hussy breastfeeding again, right out in public?"

"It's her right enough," said the other sticky-nose, "and look, the boy is at least 25 and not even her son."

* * *

A BUXOM young miss from Valetta
Loved to parade in a sweater
Three reasons she had
To keep warm was not bad
But the other two reasons were better.

* * *

AND lastly, as all parents well know, a baby is someone who must have a bottle or bust.

BRITISH

WHY is British beer like making love in a canoe?

Theyre both fucking close to water.

* * *

WHEN Britain was an empire it was ruled by an emperor.

When it was a kingdom it was ruled by a king.

When it became a country it was ruled by Maggie Thatcher.

* * *

WHY do British bulldogs have flat faces?

From chasing parked cars.

BROTHELS

AFTER months at sea the sailor asked the cab driver to take him to the nearest knocking shop. When he got out and rapped on the door a small panel opened and a female asked what he wanted.

"I want to come in," said the sailor.

"Well, this is a private club and you will have to slip a $50 membership fee through the mail slot."

He did. Minutes passed and nothing happened.

"Hey," he roared, "I want to be screwed."

"What," said the woman's voice through the door. "Again?"

* * *

THE businessman arrived at the brothel at midday only to find a sign on the door: "Out to Lunch. Go Fuck yourself."

So he decided to go to the whorehouse next door only to be greeted by another sign: "Out to lunch. Beat it!"

* * *

WHEN there are clients more than a few

A cunning old madam called Lou

Will establish a line

By displaying a sign

That informs new arrivals: "Fuck Queue."

36

IT was peak hour on Saturday night and the sign on the brothel door said: "Last butt not leased."

* * *

THE young man was very fit. Indeed he gave his hired lady the best workout she ever had. "Listen," she said, "If you can repeat that I will give it to you for nothing."

"No worries," he said. "But I will need a rest for ten minutes to recharge my batteries and you will have to hang on to my cock."

"I understand why you need a rest," she said, "and you want me to hold your cock to keep it interested?"

"No, it's not that," he replied. "The last prostitute I was with stole my wallet."

* * *

"I'VE never bothered with drawers"
    Said one of the prominent whores.
    "There isn't much doubt
    I do better without
    In handling my everyday chores."

* * *

HE was eight-feet tall and he asked the Madam if she had a girl his height.

"No," she replied, "the only two girls unengaged are only around four feet tall."

"Good," he said, "I'll screw them together."

* * *

THE madam brought her girls in for inspection. "This is Susan," she said, "for $200 you may join her in the bath with champagne on the side. This is Lulu. For $250 she will entertain you on a trapeze. And this is Carmen who offers unlimited delights on a chandelier over a water bed for $300 ..."

"Excuse me," said the punter, "got anybody that still does it in the missionary position?"

* * *

A CULTURED young lad from the bush was taken by taxi

cab to a house of ill-repute. He was impressed by the manners of the young woman who called her mother "Madam".

In the morning he dressed and was about to leave when the young woman who had been so nice to him said: "What about some money?"

"Oh I couldn't," he said. "You've been so nice to me already."

* * *

I have no aversions
    To mergins with virgins
    Though it's more fun to pet
    With a well-seasoned vet.

* * *

HE was knocking on the door of the brothel at three in the morning. Madam opened the door to find him with both arms and legs in plaster casts.

"I want a woman," he said.

"Go away," she said. "We're closed."

"I want a woman," he insisted.

"Go away," she repeated. "Anyway, what could you do with a woman in that condition?"

"I knocked on the door didn't I?"

* * *

PAT and Mick were digging up the road outside the local knocking shop when they noticed the vicar approaching furtively before he ducked into the entrance.

"Did yer see that?" said Pat. "The dirty Protestant minister sneaking in for his share o' sin. What a hypocrite."

After further denouncement of the vicar they began digging again until Mick spotted a rabbi make a tentative but swift entry into the brothel.

"Didja see that?" said Mick. "The Jews are no better."

About an hour went by before they spotted Father McGuire hurry in to the whorehouse.

"Mick," said Pat, "take off your hat. One of those poor girls must be dying in there."

* * *

WHEN he entered the high-class brothel he couldn't help but notice an extremely homely woman, hair in curlers and sitting in a shabby chenille dressing gown.

"Oh, that's Madeline," said the Madam, "She's our answer for our clients who suffer from premature ejaculation."

* * *

ISAAC was the first to admit he was a little kinky. "I'm a monster," he told the madam, "I like to beat women and I've got my own whip. Have you got anybody for a wild pervert like me?"

"Olga's just the ticket," said the madam, "but whipping comes pretty high. It will cost you $500."

Olga insisted on the money up front. Once the cash was handed over Isaac went to work with his whip.

After ten minutes an exhausted Olga gasped: "I can't take much more. When are you going to stop?"

"When?" roared Isaac between frenzied strokes. "When you give me my money back."

BUSES

A MAN with eight kids boarded a bus. When they were all seated there was no place for him, so he clung, swaying to a strap.

An alert drunk had sized up the situation and finally leaned across the aisle to tap him on the shoulder. "Fucked yourself out of a seat, didn't you!" he said.

* * *

ALL the team was aboard the bus but it wouldn't leave the hotel. They were waiting for their groupie.

They were waiting for her to get on so that they could all get off.

HEADS turned as the buxom young blonde innocently enquired of the bus driver that she would like to get off on the end of his route.

* * *

PADDY, his wife and their seven kids were waiting at the bus-stop when they were joined by a blind man. When the bus arrived it was almost full and the conductor said only eight could board.

"Okay Teresa," said Paddy to his wife, "You take the kids on board and me and the blind man will walk."

Without giving the blind man an option in the matter Paddy helped his family scramble aboard and the bus took off.

He and the blind man then set off walking down the road and all went well until the constant tap-tap-tap of the blindman's cane began to irritate Paddy.

"Tap-tap-tap, that bloody tapping is driving me crazy. "Can't you put a bit of rubber on the end of it," he complained irritably.

The blindman was quick to respond. "If you had've stuck a bit of rubber on your own stick we would be on that bloody bus."

* * *

THE pretty stenographer left the office and was on her way home in a very tight mini-skirt. She tried to board the high step on a bus but her skirt was too tight. She reached round and loosened the zip, but still couldn't get her leg up on the step.

She reached behind and unzipped it a bit further, but again the skirt was too restrictive.

Then she was suddenly lifted on board by two strong hands on her bottom.

She turned round to the young man responsible and said, "How dare you."

"Well I thought you wouldn't mind after you opened my fly twice," he said.

BUSINESS

AS the hooker said to her client: "It's a business doing pleasure with you."

* * *

THE business partners were at the bar for their usual Friday night drink. Suddenly one of them said: "Heck. I will have to go back to the office. I forgot to lock the safe."

His partner, well into his third drink replied, "Take it easy, John. Nothing to worry about. We're both here."

* * *

YOUNG Isaac was learning economics and asked his father for advice on business ethics.

"Ethics?" repeated his father. "Well it's like this my lovely boy. Let me put it this way. Suppose a woman comes in and buys a garment for $95 and pays with a $100 note. She is very excited while I wrap the garment, and as she leaves with the parcel under her arm I notice she has left her $5 change on the counter. This is where the big question of ethics comes in my son. Do I tell my partner or not?"

* * *

IT was Saturday morning and the suave Romeo walked into the jewellery store with a gorgeous blonde on his arm. "Choose any ring you want, darling," he said.

She chose a whopper and the Romeo asked if he could pay the $50,000 by cheque.

"Of course sir," said the manager, "but you will understand that I will have to keep the ring in the safe for you until the cheque is cleared on Monday morning."

It was Tuesday when the Romeo returned.

"Oh, it's you sir," said the manager with a frown. "I'm afraid your cheque bounced."

"That's okay," said the Romeo, "I just wanted to thank you for best weekend I've ever had."

* * *

BUSINESS is business, so when a high-class call girl

refused an all night stand with Isaac Goldstein he wanted to know why.

"For everyone else it is one hundred dollars," she said, "But for you it would be two hundred because, frankly, I don't like Jews."

When Isaac put his money down she reluctantly agreed, "on condition the lights are off all night so that I don't have to look at your nose," she said.

However, half way through the night she had to admit that the Jew could certainly ride. He had screwed her 15 times before midnight with only a quick dash to the toilet between each session to make a quick recovery.

Finally, half way through another vigorous session, she had to comment. "My gawd, Isaac, I must admit you are much raunchier than I expected."

"Ah ain't no Isaac, maam," said a black man's voice, "Isaac is in der toilet selling tickets."

BUTCHERS

IT was Friday evening and Bill the butcher went out on his rounds to collect some bad debts.

Miss Lottsabazooma had owed $7-50 for some time and he meant to collect it. She opened the door wearing a short flimsy nightie and invited him in.

She apologised for not having the money, claiming she hadn't been able to get to the bank. "Maybe there is some other way I can square the account?" she said suggestively.

"Okay, but can I borrow your lipstick for a moment?" said Bill. He then drew a circular line around his donger half-way between his knackers and the nob. "You're not getting all of this for $7-50," he said.

IT was many years ago since the embarrassing day when a young woman, with a baby in her arms, entered his butcher shop and confronted him with the news that the baby was his, and what was he going to do about it?

Finally, he capitulated. He promised to provide her with free meat until the boy was 16. She agreed.

He had been ticking the years off on his calander and one day, the teenager who had been collecting the meat each week, came in to the shop and said: "I'll be sixteen tomorrow."

"I know," said the butcher with a smile, "I've been counting too, and tell your mother when you take this parcel of meat home that it is the last free meat she will get, and watch the expression on her face."

When the boy arrived home he told his mother. The woman nodded and said, "Son, go back to the butcher and tell him I have also had free bread, free milk and free groceries for the past 16 years and watch the expression on his face!"

C

CAMELS

A BABY camel said to its mother one day: "Why do I have such long eyelashes?"

"Because they shield your eyes in desert dust storms."

"And why," said the little camel, "do I have such big feet?"

"That's so you won't sink down in the sand."

"And why do I have a hump on my back?"

"That's so you can carry a large quantity of water so you can survive for a month in the desert."

"Well Mummy, what the bloody hell am I doing in the zoo?"

* * *

ACHMED the camel driver had piles of gold, which are just as uncomfortable as any other kind. Piles are an occupational hazard for camel drivers and it was folk-lore tradition to treat the complaint by shoving a handful of cold tea leaves up where the sun don't shine.

Achmed did this ritual night and morning, but to no avail. So when the camel train eventually reached Cairo he took the opportunity to see an English doctor.

Dropping his dacks he bent over while the doctor spread his cheeks apart and began to mutter to himself: "Hmm, yes, hmmm."

"Something wrong?" asked Achmed.

"No, quite the contrary," said the doc. "You are going to take a long trip...you will meet a tall, dark romantic stranger..."

*　　*　　*

IN the serene atmosphere of the club's reading room one gent leaned over to the other and whispered: "I say, old boy, did you hear Ponsonby has been drummed out of the Royal Hussars in India?"

"Indeed I did not," replied his companion. "What for, ol' man?"

"Rooting camels I believe," said the first.

The second pondered over this for a while, then leaned over, tapped his friend on the shoulder and asked: "Male or female camels?"

"Females of course. There's nothing queer about Ponsonby."

*　　*　　*

AN old Arabian classic:
　　The sexual urge of a camel
　　Is stronger than anyone thinks
　　He's lived for years on the desert
　　And tried to seduce the Sphinx
　　But the Sphinx's centre of pleasure
　　Lies buried deep in the Nile
　　Which accounts for the hump on the camel
　　And the Sphinx's inscrutable smile.

CARS

See MOTORING

WHAT'S the difference between a sheep and a Honda?

You don't mind being seen getting out of the back of a Honda.

*　　*　　*

OUTSIDE the pub two Volkswagen beetles had their

bumpers locked together and the owners were having difficulty disengaging them.

A drunk took stock of the situation and said: "Throw a bucket of water over them."

* * *

HE stumbled into the bar and after several drinks confided to his mate. "The next time I give her the ultimatum 'Screw or Walk' I must remember to be in my own car and not hers."

* * *

WHEN Henry Ford went to heaven he started to reorganise the place with a production line on harps and angel wings.

God got his nose out of joint over the pushy entrepreneur. "Listen," said God, "you are talking to the inventor of the human female, the most efficient machine ever made."

"Her bodywork might be great," said Ford, "but her input valve is too close to her exhaust and men often get them mixed up."

"Even so," said God, "there are more men riding my machine than anything you ever made."

CATS

LARGE cats can be dangerous,
   but a little pussy never hurt anyone.

* * *

SIMPLE Simon was accosted by a cheeky street-walker.

"Can you help me, love?" she said, "I've got an itchy pussy."

"Sorry," said Simon, "I don't know a thing about Japanese motorbikes."

CHINESE

BLOKE in a Chinese restaurant shouts to the manager:

"This chicken is bloody rubbery," to which the manager smilingly replies, "Thank you very much."

* * *

WHEN visiting the local hospital Fred felt sorry for a Chinese patient who appeared to have no visitors. When he approached the bed in a friendly manner the Chinese mumbled something, went red in the face and then grasped his throat.

Fred asked if he could help, maybe get a doctor.

The Chinese reached for pen and paper and scribbled some Chinese characters, then gave a last gasp and died.

A week later after ordering his usual Chinese takaway he produced the note for Charlie the Chow to interpret.

Charlie squinted at it and said: "Get off. You are standing on my fukin oxygen supply."

* * *

WHAT do you call a Shanghai woman who wins ten million dollars?

A Chinese fortunate cookie.

* * *

ACUPUNCTURE fees in China are so cheap it is called pin money.

* * *

MISTER Wong rushed his wife to the hospital where Mrs Wong gave birth to a bouncing baby boy. All white.

"It must have been the milkman," said Mr Wong sadly. "Two wongs don't make a white."

The doctor consoled him: "Occidents do happen," he said.

* * *

SAID the Chinese maid when she received her marriage licence: "It won't be wrong now."

* * *

CRITICAL about the lack of democracy the western reporter asked the Chinese General: "Well, when did you have your last election?"

"Just before blekfast this morning," he replied.

* * *

THE Chinese cook had been teased unmercifully by the shearers who had put snakes in his bed and mice in his boots. Finally they relented and said enough was enough and assured him they would torment him no more.

"No more spiders under pillow?"

"No," they assured him.

"No more flighten me?"

"No, no more tricks," they said.

"Glood, then I stop pissee in soup."

* * *

CHINESE Proverb: Man who goes to bed with sex problem on mind wake up with solution in hand.

* * *

CHARLIE ran a take-away in the red light district. Indeed the girls would often eat there and relate stories about their trade and some of the tricks they got up to.

It got him so horny one night he closed the shop and went home early.

He tapped his wife on the bum and said: "What about a little 69?"

"Why the hell would I want chicken and almonds at this time of night?" she said.

* * *

THE phone rang at the Chinese Laundry.

"Can I speak to Half-in?"

"No. Half-in's out."

"Is that Half-out?"

"No. Half-out's not in."

"Who's that?"

"I'm Half-up, the secretary."

"Sorry, I'll call back when you're not busy."

* * *

THE boss said the expedition was to set forth at dawn next morning. The Italian was to drive the truck, the German

48

was to bring the tent and the Chinaman was put in charge of supplies.

Next morning the Italian and the German were punctual at dawn, but there was no sign of the Chinaman. After waiting an hour the boss ordered the expedition to start. The truck had gone only a few hundred metres when the Chinaman jumped out from behind a tree yelling: "Surplise! Surplise!"

* * *

LEE Pung used to eat regularly at a Greek restaurant and always ordered fried rice as a side dish. Each night Con the Greek used to fall about laughing when Lee would order his "flied lice."

Sometimes Con would have two or three friends gather around to hear Lee say "flied lice."

Lee got sick and tired of the taunting and took a month off for an intensified course in Oxford English.

When he returned he ordered, loud and clear, "and a large serve of fried rice."

"What did you say?" said a very surprised Con.

"I said fried rice, you fluckin' Gleek."

CHRISTMAS

WHEN the garbage cart entered the street of a posh suburb on Christmas Eve the eager housewife was waiting at the front gate. One by one she took the garbos by the hand upstairs to her bedroom. When the driver thought it was his turn he was very disappointed to be handed a five dollar note.

"Whats this?" he asked.

"For Christmas," she replied. "My husband said give the driver a fiver and fuck the rest."

* * *

WHEN the three wise men reached the stable and stooped

to bob through the small stable door one of them banged his head on the low lintel. "Jesus Christ!" he said.

"Now that's a better name," said Mary. "We were going to call him Fred."

* * *

RUDOLPH the Red Nosed Reindeer always led the sled team, while Rudolph the Brown Nosed Reindeer always brought up the rear.

* * *

ACTUALLY Rudolph the Brown Nosed Reindeer rides in the sleigh with Santa.

* * *

SANTA doesn't have any children of his own.

He only comes once a year, and then it is down a chimney.

CLAIRVOYANTS

ROGER the pharmacy clerk fancied himself as a mind-reader. He would study facial expressions as customers came in.

"Wait," he said to the blonde before she could order. "I know what you want."

He handed her a packet of Kotex.

"No," she replied. "I want a roll of toilet paper."

"Darn," said Roger. "Missed it by a whisker."

* * *

WHEN a midget fortune teller escaped from jail the newspaper headline read: "Small Medium at Large."

* * *

GYPSIES are good at predicting the future because their fathers had crystal balls.

* * *

IN court last week a clairvoyant sued for divorce on the grounds of her husband's adultery next week.

THE local Society for the Investigation of Psychic Phenomena was meeting in the village hall and being addressed by a leading spiritualist.

At the conclusion of a quite spooky address the spiritualist asked: "Now I am quite sure some of you have had quite intimate relationships with a ghost. Don't be shy, come tell us about it."

From the back of the hall came a voice, "Well, actually I have, but I'd rather not talk about it."

While the speaker cajoled him to come forward there was applause and encouragement from the audience.

The timid man eventually approached the stage. "And now," said the chairman, "Mr Smithers will tell us of his intimate relationship with a ghost."

"Ghost?" said Smithers turning on his heel and heading back to the stalls, "I thought you said goat."

* * *

HE asked Madame Celeste to look into her crystal ball.

"I fear I am going to die," he said.

"Rubbish," she said confidently, "That's the last thing you'll do."

She took his palm, gazed into it for some time and said: "You will live to be ninety."

"But I am ninety."

"Well there you are then, what did I bloody well tell you."

CLUBS

WUTHERING-Smith was reminiscing. "Remember that lovely barmaid, Belle, who served here for so long?"

Frobisher remembered. "She used to wear a black garter."

"Indeed she did, Frobisher, why was that?"

"It was in memory of all the chaps who passed beyond!"

IT was at a gentleman's club. "Sorry, old boy, to hear you had to bury your wife yesterday."

"Had to," replied the other gent. "Dead you know."

CONDOMS

THE condom vending machine in the pub carried the notice: "If machine is out of order, see publican."

And scribbled below: "If the machine is in order, see the barmaid."

* * *

BUY condoms and avoid the issue.

* * *

BUY one for fun.

Buy 144 and be gross.

* * *

IF the cap fits, wear it.

* * *

IN case of malfunction, marry.

* * *

McTAVISH bought a packet of condoms.

"That will be $5.50, with tax," said the clerk.

"Forget the tacks. I'll tie 'em on with string."

* * *

THEY were having their post coital cigarette when she asked: "If I am pregnant and we have a baby what will we call him?"

He ripped off his condom, tied it in a knot and flung it out the window. "If he gets out of that we'll call him Houdini."

* * *

"HAVE you seen the printed warning on condoms?"

"No."

"Don't you roll them right down?"

* * *

WHAT do Scotsmen do with their old condoms?

They keep rooting with them.

* * *

THE priest gathered everybody into the village hall for the Pope's latest decree. "The men must not use condoms and the women must not use the pill."

A shapely young woman stood up at the rear of the hall and replied: "If you don't play the game you don't make the rules."

* * *

WE know a bloke who put a condom on inside out, and went.

* * *

ON a sure thing he hurried to the gent's room at the pub only to find a drunk at the condom vending machine. The drunk was feeding coins into the machine and thrusting the packets of condoms into his coat pocket.

Afraid the drunk would empty the machine the young man tapped him on the shoulder and asked if he could use it just once.

"No way," replied the drunk, "not when I'm on a winning streak."

* * *

LOUIS Lane noticed that Superman fitted a condom before he got down to the business.

"How nice," she said, "Is that for safe sex?"

"No," replied Superman, "it's to protect my dick of steel from rust."

* * *

LUIGI's wife was having too many children so the doctor advised him to use a condom. "Wear this sheath and as long as you wear it your wife cannot conceive," instructed the medic.

Three months later when his wife became pregnant again the doctor called Luigi to explain.

"I swear I no take it off," he told the doctor. "It's still on now. But every morning I needa piss so I cut the end off it."

* * *

WHEN Fred said he was getting married the boys at the factory took up a collection and bought him a 13-piece bedroom set; a dozen condoms and a sleeping bag.

* * *

AN entrepreneur is distributing his own brand of condom and has called his product Planned Parent Hood.

* * *

WHEN Gino brought Gina into the clinic to tell the doctor that she was once more in the family way the doctor exploded. "Didn't you use the condom as I instructed?"

"Si, Doc," said Gino, "but we haven't got an organ so I stuck it over the tamborine. It's the only musical instrument I've got."

* * *

A DUCK had been such a regular customer at the local pharmacy that he had his own private account.

One day he waddled in to buy a condom.

"Will I stick it on your bill?" said the chemist.

"What d'yer think I am, a dick-head?" said the duck.

* * *

THE little girl said to her mum, "Daddy must be going to buy a very small car."

"Why is that, dear."

"Because," said the girl, "I just found this very small inner tube in his pocket."

* * *

THE young teenagers met in the back stalls of the theatre and after a hot petting session he wanted to go on with it.

"Not here," she said. "Come around tomorrow. It's Sunday and my parents go to Evensong. We can have the house to ourselves. Oh, and don't forget the condom."

Next evening the lad arrived at the front door just as her father announced that they were off to church.

"I'll come with you," said the lad smartly.

At the first opportunity the young girl whispered, "Why the change of plan and how long have you been religious?"

To which the lad whispered in reply: "How long has your father been a chemist?"

CONFESSION

IT is hard to envisage the torture of a man giving up his sex life only to have people come in and tell him the highlights of theirs. But here we go:

* * *

THERE is so much sin around these days that the local church has put in two more confessionals.

And a sign over one reads: "Eight items or less."

* * *

WHILE on an athletics camp Gina the gymnast had her first sexual encounter with Pete the pole vaulter. Next morning she felt shame and couldn't get to her local church and confession quickly enough.

The priest was sympathetic and gave her absolution. Gina was so elated she did spontaneous cartwheels down the aisle.

Mrs O'Flaherty witnessed it. "Oh Gawd, is that today's penance? The very day I've forgotten to wear my drawers?"

* * *

MURPHY nicked round to the priest's house and stole one of his chickens. He then went straight to confession.

"Forgive me father, for I have sinned. I have stolen a chook and I'm very sorry. Can I give it to you for repentance?"

"Certainly not," said the priest. "You must give it back to the person you stole it from."

"I have offered it to him, father, but he doesn't want it."

"Oh well, then you'd best keep it. Say 10 Hail Mary's."

* * *

PRIEST: "Are you troubled by improper thoughts?"

Fred: "No. I rather enjoy them."

* * *

WHEN the sliding door opened in the confessional box he started: "Father, I had sex with a pair of lovely 18 year-old nymphomaniac twins five times last week."

"What kind of Catholic are you?" demanded the priest.

"I am not a Catholic," he replied.

"Then why are you telling me this?"

"I am telling everyone!"

* * *

GOING to confession the young man confessed that he had committed sins of the flesh with a new woman in town. "Her name is Pussy Pink and she is a seductive, voluptuous redhead, and if you saw her father you would understand."

The priest granted absolution but was intrigued about the description of the town's new vamp.

The following Sunday he saw a well-built redhead sway down the aisle all the way to the front pew.

Nudging the organist he said: "Hey, Reynolds, is that Pussy Pink?"

Reynolds turned and squinted at the woman as she crossed her legs. "No, Father," he said. "It's just the sunlight coming through the stained-glass windows."

* * *

O'FLAHERTY was in confession and the priest asked: "Now tell me son, did you ever sleep with a woman?"

"No, not me, Father."

"Now son, I'll ask you again," said the priest, "did you ever sleep with a woman?"

"No, er, well, no, Father."

"Now son, there's just me and God listening. I will ask you for the last time, did you ever sleep with a woman?"

"Well, come to think if it, Father," said O'Flaherty, "I believe I did doze off once or twice."

"FATHER," said Murphy, "I feel I don't need forgiveness for the various adulteries I have scored this month."

"And why not?" asked the astonished priest.

"'Cos all the married women I slept with were Jews," he said.

"Ar, you're right me son," said the priest. "That's the only way to screw the Jews."

* * *

BRIGID was still a new bride and sought some advice from Father McGinty in the confessional box.

"Father," she whispered, with a little embarrassment, "is it alright to have intercourse before receiving communion?"

"Certainly, my lass," he replied, "just as long as you don't block the aisle."

* * *

A DRUNK staggered into the church, bumped his way down the aisle, entered the confessional took a seat and promptly went to sleep.

A short time later he was rudely woken by the priest rapping on the partition.

"It's no use banging," said the drunk, "There's no paper in here either."

* * *

EVERY Saturday night the three lads went out on the town together, but Shamus always made a point of going past the church first so he could duck into confession while the other two waited outside.

"It's been a week since my last confession, Father," said Shamus, "and I'm sorry to say that I have sinned of the flesh once again."

"Was it that O'Flannagan hussy from the dairy?"

"No Father."

"Was it the cheeky Costanzo girls in the fruit shop?"

"No Father."

"Don't tell me it was the widow Murphy flauntin' her wares again?"

"No Father."

"Well do your usual penance and be off with you then," said the priest.

Shamus rushed out of the church to his waiting mates. "Got three certainties for tonight," he said.

* * *

"FATHER, yesterday I made love to my wife,"

The priest explained that there was nothing wrong with that.

"But Father, I did it with...lust."

Again the priest re-assured the man that it was no sin.

"But Father, it was the middle of the day."

The priest was growing uncomfortable with the description but assured his parishioner that it was a natural act for man and wife.

"But Father, it was sheer passion. As she leant over the deep freeze I just jumped on her and we did it on the floor. Am I banned from the church?"

"Of course not," said the exasperated priest.

"Oh good. We're both banned from Safeways."

* * *

WHEN the priest finally noticed the little boy sitting close to the confessional box he grabbed him by the ear. "You young rascal," he said, "have you been listening to confessions all evening?"

"No Father," said the kid, "I've only been here since Mrs Murphy told you about doing it with the baker."

* * *

MISS Lottsabazooma went to confession and told the priest that she had been having an affair with a married man.

"But this is the fifth time you have told me this week," said the priest.

"I know," she said, "I like to talk about it."

THERE was a young lady called Tessa
  A quite unrepentant transgressor
  When sent to the priest
  The rude little piece
  Would try to undress her confessor

CONMEN

LARRY was the slickest talker in the world. He even made his wife feel sorry for the hitch-hiker who lost her bra and panties in his car.

* * *

THE debutante was learning to swim and was being held by the handsome swimming instructor, Ron the Con. While he displayed a benign smile there was a look of puzzlement on her face.

"Will I really sink if you take your finger out?" she asked.

* * *

AT the City Magistrate's Court today Slippery Samuel, the world's greatest confidence trickster, sentenced the chief magistrate to two year's hard labour.

* * *

IT was one of those swinging house-parties. He sidled up to the newly arrived blonde and said: "Why don't we pop into the bedroom while its empty. We've got the rest of the evening to get acquainted."

* * *

RON the con had it all sussed out. His millionaire father was terminally ill, only had a month to live. He could hardly wait to get his hands on the money and start living it up with wine, women and fast cars.

In the bar that night he saw a ravishingly beautiful woman and with the confidence of his impending wealth decided on the bold approach.

"I might be an ordinary clerk at the moment," he said,

"but within one month I will inherit five million dollars. Interested?"

Indeed she was. She even went home with Ron that night. Next day she became his stepmother.

* * *

McTAVISH was the meanest of Scottish conmen. When he had need to write a letter to his brother Hamish he would use the post office pen, then seal the letter in an envelope addressed to himself and post it without a stamp.

When it was duly delivered to his address McTavish refused to pay the duty and refused to accept the letter. It was therefore returned to sender whose name was on the back.

* * *

A YOUNG woman was walking along the street when she saw a ladder with a notice attached to the bottom rungs. It said CLIMB THE LADDER TO SUCCESS.

It so intrigued her she climbed to the top of a flat roof where she found a naked man.

"Who are you?" she asked.

"I'm Cess," he replied.

* * *

RON the Con has some advice for husbands too.

Always have a packet of aspirin on hand, he says. Then when you get randy you simply hand two tablets to the Missus.

When she says: "What's that for?" you say, "for your headache."

"But I haven't got a headache."

"Good, then lets screw."

* * *

FOR months now he had noticed a very attractive nurse travelling on the same tram he caught every night and he would seek a seat where he could quietly admire her.

He was enjoying some lecherous fantasies when he was

startled by the tram conductor's first words: "She does it yer know!"

The tram conductor continued. "I can read your thoughts. You would like to get off with that nurse. She's a nympho and kinky you know."

It was a shock to hear the tram conductor's next statement. "She turns it on for the tram conductors every Friday night behind the depot."

When he got off the tram his mind was full of visions of the nurse and his ears were ringing with the tram conductor's words.

Next morning was Friday, so as soon as dusk had settled into night he made his way to the park behind the tram depot.

Sure enough, there she was in the park. Worse, as he came up behind her he knew she heard him approaching, yet she hiked up her skirt so that he could make out the two white orbs of her bum. The temptation was too much. He virtually jumped on her and went at it like a jack hammer.

He was lying back having a quiet smoke when he began to chuckle.

"What are you laughing at," she said.

"I am not really a tram conductor," he confessed.

"That's okay," came the reply, "I'm not really a nurse. Actually I'm a tram conductor."

COURT

See LAWYERS

"HAVE you got anything to say for yourself?" said the judge sternly after hearing the case.

"Fuck all," muttered the defendant.

"What did he say?" asked the judge learning forward to the clerk.

The clerk stood up, turned, and whispered quietly to the judge: "He said 'fuck all' your worship."

"That's funny," said the judge, "I'm sure I saw his lips move."

* * *

THE young woman, accusing her boss of sexual harassment, told the court that she was too embarrassed to repeat the words he said to her. The judge suggested she write them down and that the words be passed to himself and the jury.

Fred was a member of the jury. When the note was passed to him he read: "Get your pants off and have a drink with me tonight." Fred passed it on to fellow jury person, elderly Miss Smithers, who unfortunately had nodded off. He had to nudge her. She woke, read the note, smiled at Fred and put it in her handbag.

* * *

RASTUS was giving evidence in a rape case but was reprimanded by the judge for openly using the magic word.

He began the second time. "Yes, yer Honour, on the night of the thirteenth I seen them on the beach and they was fucken..."

The judge was aghast at the frank language and rapped the bench with his gavel again.

"I will adjourn the case for five minutes to allow time for this witness to come up with a more palatable description," he announced.

After the break, Rastus resumed his evidence:
"Her pants were down
His arse was bare
His balls were flying in the air
His you-know-what
Was you-know-where
And if that ain't fucking
Then I wasn't there!"

* * *

IN a small country town the farmer was asked to testify about the character of a woman defendant.

"What about her veracity?" he was asked.

The farmer thought for a moment and said:

"Some says she does, some says she doesn't."

* * *

A MOTHER of three filed paternity charges on a prominent test cricketer.

"On what grounds?" she was asked.

"Lords, Old Trafford and the MCG," she replied.

* * *

THE company director who had just been found responsible in a paternity case was told by the judge: "There is no such thing as a free lunge."

* * *

IN the dock was a 13 year-old boy on a paternity charge.

To emphasise the ridiculousness of the case the defence counsel asked the boy to stand up then unzipped his fly and took out the alleged weapon.

Taking the limp tool in his hand he began: "Ladies and gentlemen of the jury, I ask you to study this undeveloped penis."

Emphasising his point by rattling the flacid dick around he continued: "Ask yourself, is it possible he could have fathered a baby with this?"

The defendant tapped him on the shoulder and whispered, "If you don't let go we are going to lose this case."

* * *

THE judge called the court to order to make a serious announcement. He said he had been bribed $2000 by the defendant and $3000 by the plaintiff.

"This is a serious matter and I have given it earnest consideration" he said. "I've decided to return $1000 to the plaintiff, and judge the case on its merits!"

* * *

DAN Murphy was charged with stealing cattle. After the bush jury heard the evidence the foreman stood up and said: "Not guilty. So long as he returns the cattle."

The circuit magistrate was infuriated with that finding and demanded that they go back and reconsider their verdict.

After a short wrangle among themselves the foreman stood once more. "Okay, not guilty, and he can keep the bloody cattle."

* * *

"YOU seem to have more than an average share of intelligence for a man of your background," sneered the lawyer at the witness stand.

"Thank you," said the witness. "If I wasn't under oath I'd return the compliment."

* * *

THE clerk turned to the little bloke in the dock. "Prisoner at the bar," he said, "do you wish to challenge the jury?"

Fred eyed the jury. "Not all of them at once," he said, "but I think I could go a few rounds with the little fat geezer in the middle."

* * *

A BLOKE due to appear in court was talking about the case in the bar and was advised by his drinking mate: "If you want to get off, just send the judge a case of whisky."

The defendant discussed this with his solicitor next morning. "On no account do anything like that," said the legal man. "We've got a thin argument already without complicating it with a bribe."

To the solicitor's astonishment our bloke won his case. "We would have lost if you sent that case of whisky."

"Oh, but I did," said our bloke, "but I put the other party's name on the card."

* * *

JUDGE: "Can't you settle this out of court?"

"That's what we were doing when the police interfered."

* * *

THE defendant had just been convicted and fined and was

asked by the judge if he could pay anything at all towards the penalty and costs.

"Not a brass razoo," he replied. "All the money I had has gone to my lawyer and five of the jurors."

*　*　*

CHARGED with stealing a barrel of beer from the back of the pub the old defendant was not familiar with legal jargon. So when the judge said he would have to dismiss the case due to insufficient evidence the old lag scratched his head and said "What d'yer mean?"

The clerk explained: "It means you are let off."

"And does it mean I can keep the grog?"

*　*　*

"HAVE you ever been cross-examined before?"

"Yes, your honour, I'm a married man."

*　*　*

"DO you plead guilty or not guilty?"

"WHAT else have you got?"

*　*　*

"DO you plead guilty or not guilty?"

"How do I know. I haven't heard the evidence yet."

*　*　*

"HAVE you anything to offer before judgement is passed?"

"No, judge, my lawyer has left me skint."

*　*　*

"GUILTY. Ten days or two hundred dollars."

"I'll take the two hundred thanks, judge."

*　*　*

"ORDER, order in the court."

"Whisky on the rocks for me thanks."

*　*　*

JUDGE: you are charged with habitual drunkeness, what is your excuse?"

"Habitual thirst, yer worship!"

JUDGE, to jury: "What possible reason could you have for acquitting this man?"

"Insanity," said the foreman.

"What, all of you?"

* * *

TWO tramps were hauled before the court and charged with vagrancy.

"And where do you live?" asked the judge.

"Nowhere," said the first tramp.

"And where do you live," he asked the second tramp.

"Next door to him!"

* * *

TWO magistrates were rolling home from a reunion, arms around each other, singing *Sweet Adeline*.

"Hey," said one. "I think we're drunk."

"You're right. And according to law I will have to charge you with being drunk and disorderly," said his mate.

"And you will have to appear before me at 10 tomorrow," said the first.

Next morning in court the first pleaded guilty to the charge and was fined $10. They then changed places.

"Drunk and disorderly, eh, fined $20."

"Hey," protested the first. "When I was in the chair I only fined you $10."

"Yes," said the second magistrate. "But the offence is getting too prevalent. You are the second drunk to appear before this court this morning!"

* * *

JUDGE to habitual defendant: "Is this the first time you have been up before me?"

"I dunno yer Honour. What time do you get up?"

* * *

ON his second murder charge the accused decided that the only way to avoid a life sentence was to bribe a juror to reduce the conviction to manslaughter.

His hopes were raised when the jury was out for three

days. Then they finally announced the verdict was guilty of manslaughter.

"Thanks," said the accused later. "How did you manage it?"

"It was bloody difficult, I can tell you," he replied. "The others were hell-bent on acquitting you."

* * *

THE judge, he populates
    The city jails
    By grave decisions
    Heads or tails

COURTING

See ENGAGEMENTS, NEWLY-WEDS

WHEN asked to explain why the relationship was over she told him straight:

"Because you are no good in bed."

He was miffed. "But how can you tell after 15 seconds?"

* * *

HE: "Don't the stars look lovely tonight?"

She: "Can't tell. I'm in no position to say."

* * *

THEY were both nervous on their first night together. When he parked the car in a shady lane he summoned up the courage to say: "Would you like to get in the back seat?"

"No," she said. "I'd rather stay in the front with you."

* * *

THEY were cuddled up in the back seat of the car when he proffered it to her.

"But if I do perform oral sex on you," she said squinting at the monster in front of her, "won't you lose respect for me in the morning?"

"Of course not," he said, "provided you are good at it."

* * *

SOME joy rides can extend from here to maternity.

THINGS were not going too well in the motel bed.

"Maybe I am not the greatest lover," he said, "but things would improve if you would grind your arse instead of your teeth."

* * *

"DARLING," he said, "am I the first man to make love to you?"

"Of course you are. Why do you men ask the same stupid question?"

* * *

THE couple were having a heavy petting session in the park.

"Gee, I wish I had a torch," he said.

"So do I," she said, "You've been eating grass for the last ten minutes."

* * *

OUT on her first date her mother's words were ringing in her ears: "Say no to everything he suggests."

So as she got into his car he said: "I suppose a root is out of the question?"

* * *

HE was a man of few words.

"What about a root?" he said.

"Your place or mine?" she replied.

"If you are going to argue about it, forget it," he said.

* * *

FRED was making a timid advance. "What would you say, sweetheart, if I stole a kiss?"

"The same thing I'd say to any dickhead who had the chance to steal a car and only took the hub caps," she said.

* * *

THEY were sitting in his car when she took the initiative and slid her hand down inside his trousers and grabbed his dong.

"What are you doing?" he enquired tentatively.

"Oh, nothing," she said. "For a moment I thought this might be the start of something big."

* * *

IT was their first date and her stern father was intent on having the last word:

"Young man. I want Beryl to be home early tonight."

"Don't worry," said the young suitor, "I'll have her in bed by ten."

* * *

THEY were fondling in the back seat of the car.

"Oh," she said. "Don't do that or I'll go to pieces."

"Go ahead," he panted, "I've got hold of the bit I want."

* * *

AFTER two hours of struggling in a parked car she managed to protest to her date:

"Do you know what good clean fun is?"

"No," he said, "what good is it?"

* * *

THERE was a young woman named Gloria
Whose new man said: "May I explore ya?"
She replied to the chap:
"I'll draw you a map
Of where others have been to before ya."

* * *

SHE finally got fed up with her boyfriend's fumbling advances and decided to put him in her place.

* * *

HE: "It's so dark I can't see my hand in front of my face."

She: "Don't worry, I know where it is."

* * *

JAKE said "How about a good night kiss?"

She refused. "I don't do that sort of thing on my first date."

"Well," replied Jake, "how about your last?"

IT was their first date and as he delivered her to her front door she gave him a lingering kiss.

"Is there anything else I can do for you?" he asked hopefully.

She leaned close to his ear and whispered: "I want you to weigh me."

Anxious to impress, he drove her back to town and found a pharmacy which had a pair of scales.

When she finally got home her mother asked if she had a nice time.

"Absowoutwy wousy," she said.

* * *

HE told his doctor that he had just met the love of his life but was very worried. He didn't know if she had VD or TB.

The doctor listened to the symptoms the young man had observed and then gave his diagnosis.

"If she coughs you can screw her," he said.

* * *

AFTER their first date and a wild night together he lay back enjoying an after-coitus cigarette.

"Do you tell your mother everything you do?" he asked.

"Of course," she said. "My mother couldn't care less. It's my husband who is so damned inquisitive."

* * *

HE sidled up to the bar beside the brunette and struck up a conversation.

"Before we go too far," she said, "I think you should know I am a lesbian."

"That's okay. I've got a cousin in Beirut," he said.

* * *

ON their first date they were getting to know each other.

"Are you a virgin?" he asked.

"Yes," she replied, "but I'm not a fanatic about it."

"BUT John," she said, "why did you park here where there are so many nicer spots down the road?"

"I believe in love at first site."

* * *

SHE cuddled up to him and said: "Do you think of me when you're away?"

He replied: "I always bare you in mind."

* * *

HE begged and pleaded for more
But she said: "You've already had four
And I'm sure that you've heard
Although it's absurd,
That Eros spelt backwards is Sore."

* * *

"I don't believe we've met. I'm Mr Right."

* * *

HE had been watching the blonde at the other end of the bar for some time before he got sufficient courage to approach her.

"Would you like a Harvey Wallbanger?" he asked.

"Love one," she said. "But let's have a drink first."

* * *

HE snuggled up to her and said: "I'm yours for the asking."

She snuggled back and said: "I'm asking fifty bucks!"

* * *

IT was love at first sight and they had taken the big step and slept together for the first time. They were still in bed when the phone rang next morning.

He reached out and picked up the receiver, listened for a moment, then gave her a shake.

"It's for a Miss Sheila Kelly," he said. "Is that you?"

* * *

WHEN Myrtle finally brought a bloke home her parents were relieved that this might be the Mr Right who would take her off their hands. But when they took a closer look they took Myrtle aside.

"He's not exactly a young man," whispered Mum to her daughter. "He's fat, he's bald and he's pretty old isn't he?"

"There's no need to whisper, Mum," said Myrtle, "he's bloody deaf too."

*   *   *

IT was only three weeks after Fred got engaged to the circus contortionist that she broke it off.

*   *   *

CUDDLING on the couch he was using his best lines and favourite moves. But he was getting nowhere. When she yawned and a light shone out of her mouth he knew it was time to go.

CRICKET

SHE was only a cricketer's daughter,
  but she could take a full toss in the crease.

*   *   *

THE district cricket secretary was preparing the match reports to send on to the local newspaper when he noticed the scribe from Wonga Creek had written "boeling."

"That's the worst spell of bowling I've seen for a long time," he mused.

*   *   *

THE club's best batsman was on the phone to his captain trying to explain why he couldn't play next day.

"No, I can't let you off the game," said the captain who was made of stern stuff. "If I did, then I would have to do the same for any other player whose wife dies."

*   *   *

THEIR marriage had been shaky and it was one of those embarrassing truces while they washed the dishes in silence. But when she passed him a plate and he dropped it, crash, on the floor, her nerve broke.

"And where do you go Tuesday and Thursday nights?" she blurted out.

72

"Down to the brothel, like I told you," he said. "I just go down for a bit of extra sex."

"I don't believe you," she said spitefully. "And what about Saturday afternoons. Where do you go then?"

"Just looking for the odd root, to pick up a tart or two. I promise."

"Are you sure you haven't been playing cricket?"

"Of course not," he said, putting his arm around her.

This seemed to settle her down. She continued with the dishes and handed him a plate.

He reached for it, fumbled, took a second grab, missed, and it crashed to the floor.

"You bastard," she roared. "You've been playing with the English Eleven* all this time."

(* or any other team, cricket or football, currently on the bottom of the ladder).

CROCODILES

TARZAN lumbered home after a hard day's work just in time to see a crocodile snap one of his 15 kids off the river bank.

"Hey Jane," he complained, "did you see that?"

"Oh come to bed and let's make another one," said Jane.

The very next day as he was coming home it happened again. A croc took another kid in the shallows.

He complained to Jane but she merely replied: "Oh let's go to bed and make another one."

Tarzan put his foot down. "I'm not working all day and rooting all night just to feed the bloody crocodiles," he said.

* * *

TARZAN rushed into the Jungle Fast Food outlet: "I'll have a crocodile sandwich. And make it snappy," he said.

* * *

THE crocodile sauntered into the men's wear shop.

"Do you have any shirts with little men on the pockets?" he asked.

CUSTOMS

BLOKE carrying two heavy suitcases is stopped by customs.

"What's in the bags, sir?"

"Chook food," he says.

When the bloke was asked to open the cases the customs agents found radios, calculators, gold wrist watches, miniature computers, and a range of electrical gadgets.

"Okay," he says. "I feed it to the chooks, but if they don't like it I try to sell it."

* * *

CUSTOMS officer was inspecting a sweet young thing's suitcase and discovered six pair of French knickers. "What are these for?" he asked.

"Sunday, Monday, Tuesday, Wednesday, Thursday and Friday," she replied.

"And what about Saturday?" he asked.

"I dont wear any on Saturday," she replied with a smile and a wink and minced by.

Next was a big German frau who flung her suitcase onto the counter.

"And what are these for?" asked the customs officer discovering 12 pairs of thick flannel bloomers.

She replied: "January, February, March, April........."

* * *

AN importer lost a trunkful of pornographic books due to luggage mishandling but the authorities eventually found them.

His trunk came up on Thursday and his case comes up on Friday.

LONG John decided to smuggle five gold watches into the country, but the trick was how to sneak them past Customs.

Wearing his most nonchalent expression he approached the officer he thought looked most amiable and friendly.

"G'day," said the officer, "got the time on yer dick?"

"Damn. You bastards know everything."

* * *

A MARRIED couple, Freda and Fred, had been successfully smuggling native birds out of Australia to the United States for years.

Fred suggested they could double their earnings by smuggling some American wildlife on the return trips.

"For example," he said. "I've got a squirrel here and I am going to hide it by stuffing it down the front of my pants."

"And this is for you," he said, handing Freda a skunk. "That will bring big money in Australia. Stuff it down the front of your panties."

Freda protested: "What about the smell?"

Fred shrugged his shoulders. "If it dies ... it dies."

CYCLISTS

TWO gays were arrested for riding a bisexual built for two.

* * *

TWO young women were riding their bicycles off the beaten track.

Admiring the scenery one said: "I've never come this way before."

"Neither have I," said her friend, "it must be the cobblestones."

* * *

THE Vaseline and Malvern Star classic:

MR and Mrs Coddle lived with their daughter Molly in a neat little suburban street next to a lad called Albert.

For years Molly had romantic designs on Albert, after all he was The Boy Next Door.

But Albert was oblivious to these overtures and more obsessed with his Malvern Star bicycle which he cared for with a passion.

One day he was polishing his bike as usual when Molly looked over the fence and asked if he would like to come to tea next Saturday night.

"Can I bring my bike?" was Albert's immediate reply.

"I guess so," said Molly.

Saturday night came around and sure enough Albert arrived at the front step with his Malvern Star. "Can I bring my bike inside?" he asked.

"No. Leave it on the porch," said Mr Coddle from inside the house.

"Okay," said Albert. "But if it is staying out in the moist air I need to give it another rub with Vaseline to keep the rust away. I do this every day," he said as he began busily polishing.

It was a lovely meal, but as they pushed away the empty plates from the third course, Mrs Coddle said: "Well, that was nice, but I'm not doing the dishes."

"Well I'm not," said Molly.

"And I'm not," said the father.

"And I am certainly not," said Albert. "It looks like rain outside and I want to polish my bike."

"Well I cooked the meal and I'm not doing the dishes," insisted Mrs Coddle.

"Enough!" roared Mr Coddle. "No more argument. Not another word. In fact, whoever utters the next word will do the dishes."

They all sat there, tight-lipped. Silence.

Outside there were some storm clouds gathering and Albert became agitated about the possible dampness on his bike. He desperately wanted to get the Vaseline jar and rub the frame over.

But grim silence persisted.

Another look at the threatening clouds and Albert decided he would be forced to make somebody speak.

He leapt on Molly, wrestled her to the floor and deflowered her.

Mr and Mrs Coddle were aghast; but not a word was uttered.

Another period of grim silence ensued.

Albert took his second desperate action. He jumped on Mrs Coddle wrestled her to the floor and gave her one too.

Father's jaw dropped open but he gritted his teeth again and nary a word escaped.

What else could Albert do? He was defeated for it began to sprinkle rain and there was a distinct chance his bike was not fully under cover on the porch.

"Okay, I've got to get the Vaseline," he said.

"I'll do the dishes. I'll do the dishes," said Mr Coddle jumping up and running into the kitchen.

D

DANCING

A BUCK rabbit went to the square dance but was soon asked to leave. He kept doing the dozy doe in the corner.

* * *

FRED has been barred from the hokey cokey dancing class.

He was putting it in when he should have been shaking it all about.

* * *

THE chorus girl said her left leg wasn't bad, her right was a little better, and between the two she could make a fortune.

* * *

DISCO dancing is for jerks.

* * *

SHE said she didn't like dancing.

"It's just screwing set to music," she said.

"Well what's wrong with that?" he said.

"It's the music," she said.

* * *

STAR acts at the Dancing Society's Annual Review were Miss Lottzabazooma who performed the Dance of the Virgin entirely from memory, partnered by Alfonso who danced the fandango with his fan in one hand and his dango in the other.

* * *

FRED went to the annual dance at the Deaf and Dumb

Institute and was impressed by the way the members were able to feel the vibration, the rhythm and beat of the music.

He spotted an attractive girl and with gestures and signs asked her to dance. She nodded and they were soon whirling around the floor.

After a bracket of numbers he made signs of drinking. She nodded and he took her arm and they headed for the bar.

On the way a young man tapped the woman on the shoulder. "What's this?" he said, "I thought you were going to have a drink with me?"

"I intend to," she answered, "as soon as I can get rid of this deaf and dumb bastard."

* * *

THE director of entertainment walked into the hotel's dance hall. "What's going on?" he said.

The choreographer replied: "The chorus girls are rehearsing the Dance of the Virgins."

"That's tough," said the MC. "They would all be doing it from memory."

* * *

TO overcome an embarrassing shyness Charles was advised to take up dancing. He plucked up courage to ask a buxom young wench to waltz when halfway through the number her necklace became unfastened and slid down the back of her dress.

"Be a darling and reach down and get it," she said.

His first fumbling attempt failed.

"Further down, further down," she said.

Aware that he was being watched he said, "I feel a perfect arse."

"My tits aren't bad either," she said, "but just get the necklace."

* * *

TWO old ladies were discussing the good old dancing days.

"Remember the Pride of Erin," said one, "and the barn dance?"

"Yes, great old times," said the other, "And what about the Minuet?"

"What? You expect me to remember the men I eat. I can hardly remember the men I fucked."

DEFINITIONS

ABSENTEE: A missing golfing accessory.

ABUNDANCE: A local hop usually staged in a barn.

ACME: Pimples on the face running towards the top.

ADAMANT: The very first insect.

ADIEU: Hymie Finklestein.

ADORN: What comes after the darkest hour.

ADVERTISEMENT: Something that makes you think you've longed for it for years, but never heard of it before.

ALIMONY: A mistake by two people paid for by one.

ALPHABET: Not quite the complete wager.

ANTI-FREEZE: When you don't talk to your uncle's wife.

APEX: The female of the gorilla species.

AROMATIC: An automatic longbow.

ARTFUL: A painting exhibition.

AUTOBIOGRAPHY: The car's logbook.

AUTOMATIC SHIFT: When the driver moves closer to his girlfriend.

AVAIL: Helpful for ugly women.

AWE-STRUCK: Being hit with a paddle.

BACTERIA: A modern self-service TAB.

BADMINTON: The reason the lamb tasted off.

BALANCE: Something you lose if the bank pushes you.

BARBARIAN: The man who cuts your hair.

BIGAMIST: A fog over Italy.

BIGOTRY: An Italian redwood.

BLUNDERBUSS: A coach which goes from Melbourne to Sydney, via Port Augusta.

BOOKCASE: Litigation about a novel which ensures wide sales.

BOXER: A bloke who stands up for the other fellow's rights.

BRAZIER: Something to warm your hands on.

BRUSSELS-SPROUTS: A world famous statue found in that city.

BURLESQUE SHOW: Where attendance falls off if nothing else does.

CABBAGE: The fare you pay a taxi driver.

CLIMATE: The best thing to do with a ladder.

CONDOM: An item to be worn on every conceivable occasion.

CONDOM: A sock in the puss.

CONDOMS: Homes for Retired Semen.

CONSCIENCE: The thing that aches when everything else feels good.

COPULATE: What an Italian police chief says to an officer who doesn't get to work on time.

COWARD: A man who thinks with his legs.

DETEST: The West Indies playing India.

DIAPHRAGMS: Trampolines for dickheads.

DUCK DICK: A game warden.

ECSTACY: It's the feeling you feel when you feel you are going to feel a feeling you have never felt before.

ELECTRICIAN: A switch doctor.

ENGLISH GENT: One who gets out of the bath to piss in the sink.

EUNUCH: Massive vassel with a passive tassel.

FASTIDIOUS: A girl who is fast and hideous.

FAUCET: What you have to do if the tap won't turn.

FELLATIO: The French Connection.

FETE: A boring picnic worse than death.

FLOOZIE: A sweet girl with the gift of the grab.

GALLERY: A hostel for young women.

GAY MILKMAN: Dairy Queen.

GRANARY: A home for senior female citizens.

HEBREW: a male teabag.

HEN'S Party: A bunch of birds cackling about who is laying whom.

HIGH FIDELITY: A drunk who always goes home to his wife.

HORIZON: Callgirl getting up in the morning.

HUMBUG: A singing cockroach.

HYACINTH: A yank greeting a gal called Cynthia.

IDOLISE: Eyes that refuse to look at anything.

INCOME: What you have to make first, because you can't make it last.

INNUENDO: An Italian suppository.

JEALOUSY: The friendship one woman shares with another.

JEWISH DILEMMA: Free Pork.

LACTIC: A grandfather clock which doesn't work.

LIBERAL: A Conservative who's been arrested.

LESBIAN COCKTAIL LOUNGE: Her-She Bar.

LESBIANS: Insurmountable odds.

LESBIAN: A manic depressive with illusions of gender.

MADAM: One who offers vice to the lovelorn.

MARCONI: The first man to send a message through a length of spaghetti without it touching the sides.

MINE SHAFT: What a German calls his dick.

MONOLOGUE: A discussion between man and wife.

NONDESCRIPT: A television play.

ODIOUS: Not very good poetry.

ORGY: Grope therapy.

PARENTS: Couples who practise the Rythym Method.

PEDESTRIAN: A motorist with teenage sons.

PIMP: Nookie Bookie.

PIMP: Public relations man for a public relations girl.

PORNOGRAPHY: Cliterature.

PREMATURE Ejaculation: The come before the scorn.

RACIAL DISPUTE: When the course judge calls for a photo.

RED RIDING HOOD: A Russian condom.

REFLECTION: What a girl looks at, but is not given to.

SAGE: A bloke who knows his onions.

SITTING Pretty: Sitting Bull's gay brother.

SNOW JOB: How a woman defrosts her man.

SNUFF: Sufficient unto the day.

SONATA: A song sung by Frank.

SPECIMEN: An Italian astronaut.

STALEMATE: A husband who has lost his ardour.

TEAR JERKER: A bloke who cries while wanking.

TRUE LOVE: An injection with affection to the midsection from a projection without objection.

VICE SQUAD: The pussy posse.

VICE VERSA: Dirty poetry from Italy.

VIRGIN: A girl who whispers sweet nothing doings.

VIRGIN: A girl who won't take in what a guy takes out.

VIRGIN: Any Hicksville girl who can outrun her brothers.

VIRGIN SQUAW: Wouldn't Indian.

WELSH RAREBIT: A Cardiff virgin.

WET DREAM: A snorgasm.

ANTI-CLIMAX: Bore-gasm.

CORPORATE VIRGIN: New girl in the office.

DESPERATE Straights: Sex-starved heterosexuals.

GAELIC: An Irish Lesbian.

INCEST: Relatively boring.

LUBRICATED CONDOMS: Bedroom slippers.

MASTURBATION: I-balling.

SELF-DECEPTION: Faking an organism during masturbation.

DENTISTS

JOE wasn't keen on having his tooth pulled out. In fact

every time the dentist tried to get the pliers near the tooth Joe would clamp his mouth shut.

The dentist whispered an instruction to his nurse, then got his pliers ready and gave the nurse the nod.

She took a firm grasp of Joe's balls and gave them a sharp twist. When he let out a yell the dentist swiftly siezed the tooth and yanked it out.

"That wasn't so bad?" said the dentist.

"No," said Joe. "But by Jeeze the roots went down a long way."

* * *

OLD Fred had always feared the dentist and had delayed making a visit until the last of his aching teeth forced the issue. The dentist took one look and declared they all needed root canal work.

"No way," protested the old man, "I am too much of a coward. I can't stand pain."

"Who said anything about pain. I am the painless dentist."

But the old man could not be convinced.

"Listen," said the dentist, "I did a multi-tooth replacement on a rabbit trapper up north. He will vouch for me. Here, I'll phone him now."

The dentist dialed, then handed Fred the phone.

"You don't know me," Fred began, "but I am in the office of your dentist. He told me he did a job on your teeth and it didn't hurt. Is that true?"

"Well, put it this way," said the gruff voice on the other end of the phone. "I'm a rabbit trapper by trade. I was trudging through the scrub a few days ago and I had a sudden urge to have a crap. I moved in behind a bush, dropped my trousers and squatted down ..."

"Yes," said Fred, "but about your teeth ..."

"I'm getting to it. I was just about to have this crap when my foot trips the trigger of a rabbit trap I set on that exact spot a week before. The steel jaws snap shut, right on my balls. I let out a scream and try to make a mighty leap only to find the trap is on a very short chain to the steel anchor peg. To get to the point, it was the first time in months that my teeth didn't hurt."

* * *

A DASHING young dentist, Malone
    Attends all the nice women alone
    And tries, from depravity
    To fill the wrong cavity
    It's the reason his practice has grown.

* * *

THERE was a young lady called Billing
    Who went to a dentist for drilling
    Out of depravity
    He filled the wrong cavity
    And now Billing's nursing her filling.

DESERT ISLANDS

A SAILOR stranded on a desert island for years had only a pig and an Alsatian for company. He formed a romantic attachment for the pig, and rightly so, because Porky was female. But every time he tried to root the pig the dog would snap at his heels.

One day a beautiful blonde waded ashore. She was the answer to his prayer. His problem was solved.

She thanked him for the fresh food: "I owe my life to you," she said, and noticing his tanned nude body and his rising endowment added, "is there any way I can repay you?"

The sailor got straight to the point with the vital question: "Would ya mind taking the dog for a walk while I fuck this pig?"

* * *

SEVEN survivors staggered ashore from the shipwreck, six women and a man. They were civilised about it. The women decided they would each have the bloke for one night each and he could rest on Sundays. The bloke agreed with relish, but as the weeks went on he realised what a physical commitment he had undertaken.

Then one day he spotted a raft with a lone figure paddling toward the island. It was a man.

Elated at finding unexpected help the bloke ran into the shallows to help him ashore.

The guy on the raft waved a handkerchief to him and said: "Oh, Hello Big Boy!"

"Oh shit," said the rescuer, "there goes my Sundays."

* * *

A GOLFER fell overboard from a Sitmar cruise and finally drifted ashore on a tropical island. He was eventually revived by a beautiful bare-breasted native girl.

She took him to her hut where she supplied him with food.

Then she produced a bottle of Scotch from a crate which had also drifted onto the beach.

Then she said: "Would you like to play around with me?"

The golfer was frankly astonished. "Don't tell me you've got a set of golf clubs too?"

* * *

BLOKE walking along a deserted beach picks up a bottle and rubs it. Sure enough, out pops a genie and offers him two wishes.

"I wish I was always hard, and I wish I could get all the arse I wanted."

"Whatever turns you on," said the genie and turned him into a toilet seat.

DICKS AND DONGERS

AN erection is like the Theory of Relativity;
the more you think about it the harder it gets.

A YOUNG mother took her five-year-old son to the doctor because she was concerned at the small size of his penis.

The doctor said size was not important. She was unconvinced so he placated her with a line that plenty of Vegemite would do the trick. "Give it to him on toast," he said.

Next morning little Johnny was surprised to see 16 slices of toast and Vegemite on the table.

"I can't eat all that, Mum," he complained.

"Shut up," she said, giving him a clip over the ear, "Two slices are for you. The rest are for your father!"

*   *   *

FRED dropped his dacks to show the doctor the damage to his donger.

With embarrassment he explained that he was climbing out the bedroom window when the husband fired an accurate shotgun blast that hit him in the privates.

The doctor looked closely then reached for his pad and scribbled a name.

"Is he a specialist?" asked Fred.

"No," replied the doc. "He's a a top piccolo player. He will show you where to put your fingers next time you want a leak."

*   *   *

"HEY Mum," he said as he rushed in from school. "I've got the biggest dick in grade five."

"Well so you should, ya dickhead," she said, "you'll be 21 next August."

*   *   *

HE rushed in to the clinic. "Can you take a look at my dick, doctor."

"Of course," said the doctor, and after examining it for five minutes said: "There's nothing wrong with that."

"I know," said the man, "but it's a fucken beauty isn't it!"

HE then went into a chiropodist and plonked his donger on the counter.

"Why, that's not a foot," said the doctor.

"I know, but it's a good ten inches."

* * *

JAKE and Fred went behind a fence for a leak. While they stood side by side Jake said: "I wish I had a big one like my brother. It's so big he has to hold it with all five fingers."

Fred looked down. "But you are holding yours with all five fingers."

"Yes, but I'm pissing on three of them."

* * *

HOWEVER hard you shake your peg

At least one drop goes down your leg.

* * *

ON their wedding night he dropped his trousers and climbed in beside her.

"Oh, what a nice pee-wee," she said.

"My dear," he said, mustering all the authority of a new husband. "The first thing you must learn is that it isn't called a pee-wee. It's a cock."

"Oh, no," she said. "A cock is long, black and fat. That's a pee-wee."

* * *

THE girls were comparing notes, "I hear your new boy friend is very well hung?"

"You bet. You should see his fiveskin."

* * *

WE know a bloke who has five dicks.

His underpants fit him like a glove.

* * *

HE complained to his psychiatrist that he had an inferiority complex because of the diminutive size of his penis.

The shrink looked at it for a moment and said: "Oh, I wouldn't let a little thing like that worry you."

DID you know that former US Vice President Spiro Agnew was an anagram for "Grow a Penis?"

*   *   *

A POLICEMAN from North Bondi Junction
Whose organ had long ceased to function
Deceived his poor wife
For the rest of her life
With intelligent use of his truncheon.

*   *   *

HE picked her up in the singles bar and they had walked to his apartment in silence. "You are not the communicative type," she said as they were undressing.

"No," he replied, and lapsed back into silence until he dropped his underpants.

"I do all my talking with this," he said.

The girl leant forward, squinted, and said, "Gawd. Don't tell me that's all you've got to say?"

*   *   *

ALTHOUGH it was their first date she was anything but shy and soon had his donger in her hand.

"What's your pet name for it?" she asked. "I know some fellows call it Dick, their Willie or their Peter. What do you call yours?"

"I don't call mine anything," he said. "It always comes without being called."

*   *   *

OF course men give their dicks names because they don't want a stranger making 99 per cent of their decisions for them.

*   *   *

SHE said her current boyfriend said he had no need to call his organ Willie, Peter or Dick. "He calls it Confidence," she confided to her girlfriend.

"Is that because he has no trouble getting it up?"

"No," she replied, "it's because he likes instilling it in me."

A BLOKE went to a country dunny and got bitten on the donger by a spider under the toilet seat. He spent a week in hospital and the circumstances of his injury soon became the talk of the town.

On his first return visit to the pub one of the regulars, Spinster Sal, said she heard about his injury but insisted to know where he was bitten.

"Well Sal," he replied. "If you got bit where I got bit you wouldn't have been bitten at all."

*   *   *

A HORNY young man named Fats Wallow
    Told a maid as they kissed in a hollow
    "Did you know that my dick
    "Is three inches thick?"
    She said. "Gee, that's a hard one to swallow."

*   *   *

ADOPTING the metric system was the best thing that ever happened to Fred. He claims he has 18 centimetres instead of seven inches.

*   *   *

AN elephant and a rat had become good mates and while wandering through the jungle together the elephant fell into a deep hole. The rat rushed out to a nearby highway, flagged down a Mercedes Benz and with the elephant hanging on to a rope the car pulled him out.

A year later the rat fell down and it was the elephant's turn to rescue him. The elephant simply dropped his dick down for the rat to climb up.

The moral of this story is: If you've got a big dick you don't need a Mercedes Benz.

*   *   *

THE upwardly mobile manager finally arranged a dirty weekend with his secretary. Despite champagne, silk sheets, her alluring lingerie and suggestive poses he was unable to raise an erection for the entire weekend.

When he arrived home he took a shower and entered his

bedroom to find his wife, hair in curlers, in a crumpled flannel housecoat lying on the bed reading.

He looked down to find he was sporting a spectacular erection. "You bloody confused thing," he said. "No wonder they call you a prick."

* * *

IN the deep south Rastus was rambling along the road and almost stumbled over a $20 note. His sore feet prompted him to say: "Feet. At last I can buy you a comfy pair of shoes."

A little further, with the hot sun on his forehead he said. "And Head, we'll get a nice shady hat."

A bit further and the pangs of hunger prompted another promise. "Okay Belly, "we'll get ourselves some soul food."

Then he looked down and noticed he had an erection. "Okay Big Dick. Who told you we come into money?"

* * *

UNBEKNOWN to Fred the zip on his fly was broken. The woman sitting opposite on the train could stand it no longer.

"Young man," she protested, "your member is sticking out."

Fred looked down: "Don't flatter yourself. It's only hanging out."

* * *

THEY were camping in the outback and enjoying a few beers when Kev got up to go for a leak. When he returned he had forgotten to do up the fly in his shorts and as he sat down Dave told him that a big snake had just wriggled through the camp.

"It was one of the biggest I've seen," enthused Dave. "It was right near your chair. Heck! There it is, I can see the head there now," and reaching for a beer bottle said, "hold still, I'll kill it."

Dave brought the bottle crashing down and Kev let out a wail.

"Hit it again," screamed Kev. "It just bit me."

* * *

THE salesman was put up for the night by an old farmer who only had one bed. Just before dawn the old man woke and began shouting: "Bring me a woman! Look at that erection, I haven't had an erection like that for years. I need a woman."

The traveller told him to calm down. "It's an erection alright," he said, "but it's not yours, it's mine."

* * *

THE politician went to Harley St, London, for a dick transplant. It rejected him.

* * *

NORMAN had to summon up considerable courage to go to the clinic. "You promise not to laugh?" he tentatively asked the doctor.

"Of course not. I'm a professional. Now come along, what's the problem?"

"It's like this. I'm worried about the size of my penis," said Norman.

"Understandable," said the doctor. "It is a common problem. Now drop your trousers and we'll check it out."

Norman did so and the astonished doctor had to struggle to contain a burst of laughter as he found himself looking at a tiny button, the smallest dick he had ever seen.

Choking back a tear the doctor said: "How long has it been like that?"

Norman replied: "It's been swelling up like that for weeks."

* * *

WITH his ten-gallon hat and his high heeled boots the big man leaning on the bar was obviously a Texan. And he soon had a woman by his side.

"Tell me," she said. "Is it true that everything is big in Texas?"

"Yes, Ma'am."

One thing led to another and they were soon back at her her flat where he took off his big Texas hat, and his big Texas boots. He took of his Big Texas pants to reveal that indeed, everything was big in Texas.

They were having their post-bonk cigarette when he said: "By the way, Ma'am. What part of Texas do you come from?"

*   *   *

ON business in Hong Kong he had been playing around too much and one day noticed his dick had turned yellow.

He went to an expatriate doctor who quickly diagnosed the trouble as Hong Kong Dong and told him that his dick would have to be amputated.

Shocked he sought a second opinion, only to receive the same advice on amputation.

As a last resort he went to a Chinese doctor who confirmed that the complaint was Hong Kong Dong, but there was no need for amputation.

"Oh, I'm so relieved," said the businessman.

"Yes, no need to cut off dick," said the Chinese medic, "in few days it fall off by itself."

*   *   *

OCKER had just taken up the job as a guide at an Outback wildlife sanctuary and was explaining the difference between an echidna and a porcupine to a group of American tourists. "The echidna is a different colour, different size and anyway," said Ocker with authority, "their pricks are longer."

This caused some embarrassment among the mixed group which quickly dispersed to look at the kangaroos, giving a chance for the supervisor to reprimand Ocker on his choice of words.

"Quills," he said. "Use a bit of decorum. They are quills," and he stood by to listen as Ocker guided the next group through.

"Is that a dog'gone porcupine?" drawled a yank when he saw the echidna.

"Different animal altogether," said Ocker authoritively. "The echidna is smaller, lighter in colour and its quills are longer, but their pricks are about the same size!"

* * *

THERE was a young stud called Sir Lancelot
Women would glance him askance a lot.
For whenever he'd pass
A presentable arse
The front of his pants would advance a lot.

* * *

AN old archeologist named Tossel
Discovered a marvelous fossil
He knew from its bend
And the knob on the end
'Twas the peter of Paul the apostle.

* * *

FOUR blokes had been playing golf together each week for years. At the end of the game three would have a shower and a few drinks at the bar while the fourth would always dash away.

Finally they asked him why he didn't join in the social hour. "To tell you the truth," he admitted. "I don't shower at the club because my penis is so small and I would be embarrassed."

"Does it work?" asked one of his mates.

"Of course it works."

"Well how would you like to swap it for one that looks good in the shower?"

* * *

THE young body builder was proud of his physique and when he took his new girlfriend home she was surprised to see NIKE tattooed on his biceps. "I've won an advertising contract," he explained, "$1000 for each arm."

Then he took off his shirt to display SLAZENGER tattooed across his chest. "I got $5000 for that one," he said.

When he removed his shoes and socks she saw PUMA on his calf muscles. But she was aghast to see AIDS tattooed on his most prized possession.

"No, no. don't go," he said, as she attempted to leave. "If you hang on a bit you will see why I got another $5000 from Adidas."

* * *

THEY had been having a few beers at the bar together recounting old times when the call of nature caused them to line up at the same time, still deep in conversation. But Fred could hardly ignore the fact that Chas was very well endowed.

"I say, that's a remarkable donger you have there old boy," Fred was prompted to remark.

"Wasn't always that way," replied Chas. "Medical science can do wonders with transplants these days," he said. "I got this done over in Harley St, England. Cost a thousand bucks, but as you can see, well worth every cent."

Fred was envious. In fact, he packed his bag that night and flew off to the Old Dart first thing.

It was a good six months later before he ran into his old cobber once again and Fred could hardly wait to tell him that he had taken his advice and was well pleased with the result.

"But Chas, I will tell you something else," said Fred. "You were diddled. I got mine for $500, not a thousand."

Chas couldn't believe it. Same address in Harley St, same doctor. Complaining that he had been ripped off, he asked Fred if he could have a look.

Once more they lined up at the porcelain and when Chas took a peek over the partition the worried frown which had creased his face disappeared.

"No wonder," he laughed. "That's my old one!"

95

A YOUNG bloke was infatuated with his new girlfriend, but the problem was, he was ashamed of his small penis.

One dark night in the back seat of his car he finally took his courage in hand and put it in her hand.

"No thanks," she said, "I don't smoke."

* * *

FRED had dropped his dacks and the doctor had taken a long hard look before announcing the bad news. "I'm afraid it's got to come off," he said.

Fred was terrified. "Not to worry," said the doc. "We live in the age of transplants. We can get a new one on order."

"How much," asked Fred timidly.

"$500 for the standard model, $1000 for the super model and $1,500 for Every Woman's Delight," said the doctor.

Fred pondered this for a moment. "Do you mind if I talk it over with the wife?"

Fred returned next day. "We've decided to have a new kitchen," he said.

DIPLOMACY

SCHULTZ from the CIA had finally got invited to the diplomatic corp dinner where he intended to make some valuable contacts. However the pre-dinner cocktails had the effect of getting him in a randy mood and he made sure he sat next to the long-legged blonde.

When his hand wandered under the table and came to rest on her knee he was encouraged by the lack of resistence. He moved a little further up her thigh. Again no rejection. He moved further, to her stocking tops.

His heart quickened as he saw her write a note and pass it to him.

It read: "Don't give the show away when you reach my balls. Smithers from MI5."

* * *

LATE one dark night a secret operative disguised as an

Arab slipped into the entrance of a Tel Aviv apartment and crept up to the stairs to the fifth floor.

He counted the doors until he arrived at No.7 where he knocked quietly; two loud knocks, a pause then three soft.

The door opened and an old man said: "I'm Goldstein the pawnbroker, what do you want?"

The shadowy visitor said: "Wet pigeons never fly at night."

"What?" said Goldstein who had been disturbed from his favourite television program.

"Wet pigeons never fly ..."

"Oh no," said the old man, "I'm Goldstein the pawnbroker. You want Goldstein the spy, No.7 down on the fifth floor," said the old man.

* * *

A YOUNG bloke had just become engaged and met his fiancee's mother for the first time. "How old do you think I am?" she asked the lad.

"Well," he said after a moment's thought, "I am wondering whether to make you ten years younger to fit with your looks and figure, or ten years older on account of your wise intelligence."

* * *

THE white missionary had lived with the Bullabukanki tribe for 18 months when the chief took him aside and said the reverend was in big heaps of trouble.

"Yesterday a white baby was born to my sister, and you are the only white man in this village," said the chief, sharpening his axe.

The missionary broke out in a sweat. "Look, old man, I know it looks bad, but see your flock of sheep down by the river?"

"Yeah, I see them," said the chief.

"Well can you see the black sheep in the flock. There is only one and ..."

"Okay, okay," said the chief, "I'll keep quiet if you'll keep quiet."

DISCRIMINATION

WHEN their car broke down a Jew, an Indian and an Australian knocked on a farmer's door to ask for accommodation for the night.

"One will have to sleep in the barn," said the farmer.

"I will," said the Jew.

But five minutes later there was a knock on the door.

"There's a pig in the barn," said the Jew.

"Okay, I'll go," said the Indian.

Five minutes later there was a knock on the door.

"There is an un-sacred cow in the barn," he said.

"I'll go," said the Australian.

Five minutes later there was yet another knock on the door. It was the pig and the cow.

* * *

WHAT is a nigger?

A black man who has just left the room.

* * *

WHEN does a Pommie become a Briton?

When he marries your daughter.

* * *

THE notice outside the Lion Safari Park read: Coaches $50, private cars $5, Pommies on bikes, free."

* * *

THE new migrant was getting familiar with filling in official forms.

Where it said, "Name?" he wrote: Chizkinsky, Boris.

Where it said "Nickname?" he wrote: Hole Arse.

* * *

LUIGI was a recent migrant to the country and they asked him how he was settling in.

"I dunno understand," he said. "They call a bald man

98

Curly, they call a man with red hair Bluey, they call a big man Tiny, and me who has been here for a year with no girl friend they call a Fucking Wog."

* * *

MOISHE Isaacson was walking down a street in Belfast when he suddenly felt a pistol in his back.

"Catholic or Protestant?" demanded the voice behind him.

"Jewish," replied Moishe.

"Well then. I am surely the luckiest Arab in the whole of Ireland."

* * *

AN Englishman, a Scotsman and an Australian went for a job. The boss asked them all the same question: What is the capital of Ireland?"

"New York," said the Scot.

"No. It's Vancouver," said the Englishman.

"Fools," said the Australian, "anybody knows the capital of Ireland is Brussels."

The Australian got the job because he was closest.

* * *

A JEW had settled in a train compartment when an American negro entered and sat opposite. The blackman opened a bag and took out a Yiddish newspaper and began to read it.

The Jew was intrigued. He watched for ten minutes before he leant over and said: "Being black isn't enough?"

* * *

A LION in the London Zoo was lazing in the sun and licking its arse when a visitor turned to the keeper and said, "that's a docile old thing isn't it?"

"No way," said the keeper, "it is the most ferocious beast in the zoo. Why just an hour ago it dragged an Australian tourist into the cage and completely devoured him."

"Hardly seems possible," said the astonished visitor, "but why is he lying there licking his arse?"

"The poor thing is trying to get the taste out of his mouth," said the keeper.

* * *

AN UPPER-class Pom went into a butcher shop in Dublin and with a haughty accent said: "I'd like a sheep's head, my man. And make sure it is an English sheep."

So the butcher shouted to his apprentice; "One sheep's head, O'Reilly, and take the brains out."

* * *

MURPHY was on his death bed. "Teresa, call the vicar," he said.

"Don't you mean the priest?"

"No, the vicar. I want to become a Protestant," said Murphy, "better one of them bastards die instead of one of ours."

* * *

A CIVIL Rights official phoned the State Library and told the chief librarian that there were 15,000 books with the word "nigger" in them and that the books would have to be removed within a month.

"What?" said the librarian, "but there are fifty thousand volumes with the word bastard in them."

"I know," said the Civil Rights man, "but you bastards aren't organised."

DIVORCE

ALTHOUGH she divorced him on the grounds that he couldn't consummate the marriage he had no hard feelings.

* * *

MICKEY Mouse had separated from Minnie and told his lawyer he wanted a divorce.

"But Daisy's not insane," said the mouse's brief.

"I didn't say she was insane," protested Mickey. "I said she was fucking Goofy."

THE judge asked Fred's wife to explain her grounds for wanting a divorce. "You say it's due to poor health and exhaustion. What do you mean?" asked the judge.

"I'm sick and tired of the little bastard," she said.

* * *

SHE told the Family Law judge that she wanted a divorce on the grounds that her husband was wrecking her life with his unbridled lust.

"How often?" asked the judge.

"Twice a week," she replied.

"Good God," said the judge. "Women have stood where you are standing now and called twice a week desertion."

* * *

SHE was suing for divorce. She told the judge that every time she and her husband drove past one of his girlfriends, he made her duck her head.

* * *

BE warned. Fred Nurk failed to keep up his maintenance payments and was repossessed by his wife.

* * *

VINNIE and Louie were whiling away a few hours at the new singles bar and starring into their drinks.

"Ever seen an ice cube with a hole in it?" said Vinnie.

"I was married to one," said Lou.

* * *

"DOCTOR, I have a small, embarrassing wart."

"Divorce him."

* * *

HER lawyer asked her what ground she had for wanting a divorce.

"Well he wants sex every night and he is as big as a horse. It hurts unbearably," she said.

The lawyer said: "In that case I will file your petition."

"File my partition? No, no, let the bastard sandpaper his."

IT was an amicable divorce. They parted good friends. Indeed a few years later when he broke his arm he rang her and asked if he could stay at her apartment for a time. He was having trouble cooking and caring for himself.

She readily agreed and even helped him into the bath one night. While scrubbing his back she noticed he was beginning to get an erection.

"Now isn't that sweet," she said. "Look John, it still recognises me."

* * *

CHAP met his ex-wife at a party and after a few drinks he suggested they go to bed.

"Over my dead body," she sneered.

He downed his drink and replied, "I see you haven't changed."

DOCTORS
See HOSPITALS, HEALTH

BRUNO told the doctor he felt weak and run-down.

When questioned about his sex life Bruno admitted he had sex with five, sometimes six, different girls every night.

"Well," said the medic, "that's obviously the cause of your trouble."

"I'm glad to hear that, doc," said the hot-blooded youth, "I was afraid it might be the masturbation."

* * *

FRED visited his doctor. He was tired and run down.

"How's your sex life?" asked the doc.

"Every Monday, Wednesday and Friday, without fail."

"That might be too much, why not cut out Wednesdays?"

"I can't Doc. That's the only night I'm home."

* * *

FRED's wife went to see her doctor and after an examination he diagnosed her condition as run-down.

"Can you stop having sex with your husband for a month?"

"Sure," she said, "I've got a couple of boyfriends who could stand in for that long."

* * *

THE doctor's phone rang. "Doc, I gotta see you. I think I've got the clap."

"Okay, but first you will have to make date with my nurse."

"I did. That's how I got it."

* * *

AN old Frenchman told his doctor he was worried about his libido and his sexual ability.

"Then show me your sex organs," said le doc.

The aged rogue presented his index finger and stuck out his tongue.

* * *

MRS Lottsabazooma was complaining to the doctor in a very deep voice. "I think you have over-prescribed the hormone pills."

"Don't worry," said the Doc, "a baritone voice is a natural development. It won't last long."

"But I also have hair on my chest," she protested.

"Show me," he said, surprised, "how far down does it reach?"

"All the way to my balls," she said.

* * *

"THERE is something wrong with my aviaries," she said.

"You mean ovaries," said the doc.

She insisted it was "aviaries," so rather than continue the argument he said okay, lift your dress.

"By cripes, you're right," he said. "Looks like there's been a cock-a-too up there!"

* * *

A DOCTOR is a man who gets women to take off their their clothes, then bills their husbands for it.

"OH, Doctor," she said coyly, "Where will I put my clothes?"

"Put them over there, next to mine!"

* * *

THE doctor scratched his head as he studied two reports.

"What's up, Doc," asked the patient.

"It appears the test results are mixed up with those of another patient," the doc said with a frown. "Either you've got Alzheimer's disease, or AIDS."

"That's terrible," said the patient. "What shall I do?"

"All I can suggest at this stage," said the doc, "is if you can find your way home, don't screw your wife."

* * *

TWO doctors were seated on a park bench when one noticed an old man approaching. His knees were pressed together and his fists were tightly clenched and bent inwards.

One doctor nudged the other. "You still reckon you can diagnose on sight?"

"Sure, why?"

"Take a look at this chap."

"Arthritis, no doubt about it," said the first doctor.

"Cerebral palsy. I'll bet on it," said the second.

They were about to ask when the man shuffled right up to them and said through gritted teeth: "Pardon me, do you know where the shithouse is?"

* * *

HE went to the doctor with stomach trouble.

"Are your bowel movements regular?"

"Yes, Doc, every morning at eight o'clock."

"Then what's your problem?"

"I don't get up till nine."

* * *

THE aging playboy was having his annual medical check.

"Sex?" asked the doctor.

"Infrequently," came the reply.

"Hmmm," said the doctor, "is that one word or two?"

* * *

DOC: "Have you ever been incontinent?"

Patient: "Nope. Never been interstate for that matter."

* * *

EXAMINING Luigi for constipation the doctor gave him three suppositories. "You put them up the back passage, do you understand what I mean?" said the doc.

"No worries," said Luigi.

A week later Luigi was back, to complain he still had the constipation. "The pills were useless," he said. "I did what you told me, but for all the good they were I might as well have stuck them up my arse!"

* * *

THE doctor told him he had good news and bad news. Which did he want first.

The patient opted for the bad news first and the doc told him he had three weeks to live. "Hell, what's the bloody good news then?" he asked.

The doctor leaned close and whispered. "See that blonde nurse with the big tits. I'm screwing the arse off her tonight."

* * *

AFTER a lengthy examination the doctor came out of the surgery and said to the patient's wife, "I don't like the look of your husband."

"Neither do I, but he's nice to the kids," she said.

* * *

SHE told the doctor that every time she sneezed she had an orgasm.

"What have you been taking for it?" he asked.

"Pepper," she replied.

* * *

"DOCTOR, is it okay to file my nails?"

"Of course, but why don't you throw them out like everybody else?"

PENSIONER patient was told to bring a specimen to the clinic. He arrives next day with a full jerry pot.

"God, man, did you walk down here with that?"

"No, I took the tram!"

* * *

A DEAF pensioner was told that the doctor wanted a stool specimen, a urine specimen and a sperm specimen.

"What's he talking about?" said the deaf pensioner to his wife.

"He wants you to leave your underpants here," she said.

* * *

WITH great embarrassment the woman had to explain how she had the skin off her knees and elbows. "It's because we have sex doggie fashion in the garage on the concrete floor," she said.

The doctor was a little surprised.

"Goodness, madam, why don't you do it in the conventional fashion?"

"I'd like to, but my dog's quite ugly and I can't stand his breath."

DOGS

A MAN came home early one day and found his wife in bed with his best friend.

He shot the wife, but decided to give the dog another chance.

* * *

TWO drovers stood on the veranda of the bush pub with pots in their hands. Nearby a kelpie sheepdog was sitting in the shade licking its balls.

"You know Jake," said one of the drovers watching the dog, "I'd like to be able to do that."

"Well why don't ya," said his mate. "It's your dog."

* * *

A FOX terrier went in to a post office and took down a blank form and wrote, "woof, woof, woof, woof-woof, woof, woof, woof-woof, woof, woof-woof."

He handed it to the clerk who studied it for a while.

"You have nine words here. You can have another word for the same price."

"Yeah," said the fox terrier, "but it wouldn't make any bloody sense, would it."

* * *

WHEN Mrs Murphy bought a dozen cans of dog food the grocer said he didn't know she had a dog.

"I haven't," she said. "I feed it to my husband. It's cheap and he doesn't know the difference."

The grocer was aghast. "Oh, you shouldn't do that," he cautioned, "It could kill him."

Mrs Murphy took no notice and bought a dozen cans a week until she entered the shop one day dressed in black.

The grocer, fearing the worst, asked about her husband.

"He's dead," she said.

"I told you," said the grocer, "I told you it would kill him."

"Oh no. It wasn't the dog food at all," she said. "He sat down on the road to lick his balls and a truck ran over him."

* * *

FRED's lovelife had waned. "The wife doesn't seem interested anymore," he confided to his neighbour.

"Probably because you've been doing it the same way for years," said his neighbour. "You've got to vary your technique. You've got to try new positions. Just then the neighbour spotted two dogs at it on the front lawn.

"There," he said, "have you tried that?"

Fred said he would think about it.

A few weeks later the neighbour enquired if things had improved.

"Yeah," said Fred, "I love it doggie fashion, but by gee it's costly. It takes a full bottle of whisky before she will get out on the lawn."

THE workmates were chatting at the bar.

"So, have you talked your wife into doing it doggie style?" asked one.

"Actually, she's the one that started the doggie tricks," replied the other. "Every night I have to sit up and beg for it, then she rolls over and plays dead."

*   *   *

LITTLE Johnny was waiting at the gate for his dad with a tear in his eye. He couldn't wait to tell that his new pup had died. There it was, on its back, legs in the air, stone dead.

"It's gone to heaven," consoled his dad. "Don't worry. I'll buy you another one."

A week later Little Johnny was at the gate waiting for Dad again.

"Gee Dad," he began, "we nearly lost Mum today. When I came home she was lying on her back, legs in the air calling out 'Gawd, I'm coming' and if it wasn't for Uncle Fred holding her down we could have lost her."

*   *   *

THEY sat in the vet's waiting room together, the shapely Miss Trim and prudent Miss Prim.

Miss Prim confided that her miniature poodle had the embarrassing habit of humping her ankles. In fact, it would try to hump everything in sight.

"That's funny," said the shapely Miss Trim, "my Great Dane, Roger, has the same behavioural pattern."

"So you are here to have your dog desexed too?" said Miss Prim.

"No. I'm getting his nails clipped," said Miss Trim.

*   *   *

THE sign outside the pet shop said: "Special dog for spinsters," and sure enough, it soon attracted a well-dressed woman in her mid-forties who pretended to browse around the shop before she got to the point.

"And what does this dog do?" she asked.

"He's a big boy. A Great Dane," said Charlie the conman.

"He does little tricks for lonely women, if you get my meaning, nudge, nudge, wink, wink."

"I don't know what you mean, but I'll buy him," she said.

A week later Charlie received a phone call. It was to complain that the so-called special dog was a non-performer. It hadn't done a thing.

"Are you in bed?" asked Charlie.

"Yes," she replied.

"Hmmm, I can't understand it. I'll come right over."

When Charlie arrived the woman was indeed in bed and the dog was sitting on a chair peering out the window.

"Damn it, Roger," said Charlie taking off his clothes, "I'm going to show you this trick just one more time."

* * *

IT was the day the kids brought their pets to school.

Little Mary told the class her poodle was called Mitzi, "because poodles are French and Mitzi is a French name."

Little Jean told the class her Pomeranian was called Puff because it was dainty and had fluffy hair like a lady's powder puff.

Little Fred said his dog was called Porky because it fucks pigs.

* * *

THE barman was quick to act when he saw an old bushman and his dog walk into the bar. "Dogs not allowed in here," he said gruffly.

It was the dog that stopped and said to his master: "Ar, c'mon, let's go somewhere else."

The barman was shocked. "Did that dog talk?" he said incredulously.

"Of course," said the bushie. "He's been talking for years. He's been my only companion."

The barman settled them in the corner and each time he served the old timer with a beer he couldn't resist having a chat to the dog.

It was when the old man went to the loo that the barman

said to the dog. "My brother runs the pub across the road. It would be a great wheeze if you could go over and ask for a beer. He would get the shock of his life."

The barman gave the dog a $20 note and away it went.

When the old timer came back he was alarmed to find the dog missing, and was all the more worried when the barman explained his errand.

"He's a bush dog. He doesn't know city traffic. He could be killed," he said. The old-timer rushed to the door, but his faithful dog hadn't crossed the road. In fact he was humping a cocker spaniel on the footpath.

The old man was shocked.

"I've never seen you do that before," he said.

"I've never had the money before," said the dog.

* * *

A BLIND man had been at the bar drinking all afternoon with his faithful Labrador at his feet. Finally the dog got up, cocked its leg, and pissed on the blind man's trousers.

The man felt the warmth on his leg and began slapping his pockets until he produced a dog biscuit and lowered it to the dog.

A chap who had observed all this said: "Excuse me mate. I wouldn't reward that dog. He just pissed on your leg."

"I know, I know," replied the blind man. "When I find which end his head is, I am going to sink my boot into his knackers!"

* * *

A BLIND man went into the department store and suddenly began swinging his dog around and around above his head.

The superintendent rushed over and ducking each time the dog passed overhead said: "Sir, can I help you?"

"No, I'm just looking around!"

* * *

WHENEVER two drovers get together there is the inevitable argument about who has the best kelpie sheep dog. So the merits of their respective dogs was the subject of the debate at the bar.

"My dog's so smart," said one, "I can give him five instructions at the same time and he will carry them out to perfection."

"That's nothing," said his mate. "I only whistle and point and Bluey anticipates the whole exercise."

Finally they decided to put their dogs to the test. The first drover whistled his dog and told him to dash to the saleyards, select the oldest ram, bring him back into town and load it into the ute which was parked outside the pub.

The dog sped off in a cloud of dust and ten minutes later was seen bringing a large ram down the main street. He jumped into the ute, dropped the tail gate and hunted the ram in.

"Well that's not bad," conceded the second drover. "But watch this."

"Bluey, what about some tucker?"

In a cloud of dust Bluey streaked down the main street to a farm five kilometres out of town. The dog raced into the chook house, nudged a hen off the nest and gently picked up an egg.

The dog then sped back to town and gently placed the egg at his master's feet. But without waiting for a pat on the head the dog gathered a few sticks and lit a fire, grabbed a billy in his teeth and dashed to the creek, set the billy on the fire and dropped the egg into the simmering water.

After exactly three minutes, Bluey rolled the billy off the fire, laid the boiled egg at his master's feet and stood on his head.

"Well, that beats all," conceded the first drover, "but why is he standing on his head?"

"Well he knows I haven't got an egg cup," said the proud owner.

USUALLY, anyone who has a dog calls him Rover or Spot

or some such name. I called mine Sex, and it got me into constant trouble.

One day when he was young I took Sex for a walk and he slipped his collar and ran away. I spent hours looking for him. A policeman came along and aked me what I was doing in an alley at midnight. I told him I was looking for Sex.

That was my first court appearance.

One day I went to the town hall to get my dog registered. I told the clerk I wanted a licence for Sex. He said he would like one too.

When I said he didn't understand, that it was a dog. He said he didn't care what she looked like.

Again I said he didn't understand and that I had had Sex since I was five years old. He said I must have been a strong boy.

When I decided to get married I told the minister that I wanted to have Sex at the wedding. He told me to wait until after the ceremony.

I said that Sex had played a big part in my life and my whole lifestyle revolved around Sex. He said he didn't want to hear about it and he would not allow us to have Sex in the church.

I told him all my friends and relatives coming to the church would enjoy having Sex there. He barred the lot of us and we had to get married in the Registry Office.

Of course, my wife and I took the dog along with us on our honeymoon and when I checked into the motel I told the clerk we wanted an extra room for Sex. The clerk said every room was for sex.

I said you don't understand, Sex keeps me awake at night, and the clerk said "Me too."

When my wife and I divorced we went to court to fight for custody of the dog. I said: "Your honour, I had Sex before I was married," and he replied, "Me too."

Well, now I have been thrown in jail, been married,

divorced, and had more darn troubles with that dog than I ever bargained on.

Why, just the other day when I went for my first session with my psychiatrist she asked me what seemed to be the trouble. I replied that Sex had died and left my life. It was like losing my best friend.

She said: "You should buy yourself a dog."

* * *

A WEE little dog
    Passed a wee little tree
    Said the wee little tree
    "Won't you have one on me?"
    "No," said the little dog
    No bigger than a mouse
    "I've just had one.
    And I had it on the house."

DROVERS

IT was the end of the financial year when Jake and Bill, two drovers who spent most of their life on the Outback stock routes, rode into Stumpy Gully for a beer and to lodge their tax return.

They had been given the drum that a tax agent had set up in the town. Indeed, Jake noticed the sign on his shop as they rode by. "Taxidermist" it said.

After several rounds Jake declared he would go and see to the tax business and was soon told by the taxidermist that he was barking up the wrong tree.

"Well, what do you do then?"

"I preserve animals," said the taxidermist. "Like all those you can see around this shop."

"Can you stuff sheep?"

"Yes," was the reply.

"Can you stuff kangaroos and emus?"

"Of course."

When Jake went back to the pub he told Bill that the bloke in the shop wasn't a tax agent at all.

"What is he then?" said Bill.

"Oh he's just another drover," said Jake.

DRINKERS

MY Dad was known as a light drinker.

As soon as it was light he would start to drink.

* * *

A PROSPEROUS man was accosted by a disreputable looking bloke who asked for some money for a meal.

"Here, have a cigarette," said the businessman.

"No, I don't smoke," replied the tramp.

"Then let me buy you a drink."

"No, I don't drink."

"Then let me give you this lottery ticket,"

"No thanks, I never gamble. Couldn't you spare some money for a decent meal?"

The businessman looked at him. "I can do better than that," he said. "You come home with me and I'll cook you the biggest meal you ever saw."

"Wouldn't it be easier if you just gave me the money?"

"Easier, yes," replied the businessman, "but I want to show my wife what happens to a man who doesn't drink, smoke or gamble."

DRUNKS

SITTING in the corner of the pub one drunk said to his alcoholic mate: "I'll never forget the day I turned to the bottle as a substitute for women."

"Why, what happened?"

"I got my dick stuck in one."

STUMBLING onto the bus just as it was leaving the drunk staggered down the aisle, trod on a passengers foot, tripped over a shopping bag and flopped into a seat next to a very disapproving woman.

She said: "You, my man, are going straight to hell."

"Oh Christ," said the drunk trying to stand up, "don't tell me I'm on the wrong bus again."

* * *

A DRUNK tottered into the police station to report his car stolen.

"Where did you leave it?" asked the constable.

"It was right on the end of this key," said the drunk, showing the cop his ignition key. "Right on the end of this key," he repeated, holding the key out in front of him.

The cop wasn't impressed. "You should be ashamed of yourself coming into the police station at this time of night in that condition. Look at yourself, why even your fly is open."

The drunk looked down.

"Strewth, they've stolen my girlfriend too!"

* * *

THE cops had been instructed to clean up the neighbourhood so it was dead easy when one drunk staggered towards a constable and said: "Excuse me offisher, what time is it?"

The cop replied, "One o'clock," and hit him once over the head with his baton.

"Jeezus," said the drunk, "I'm glad I didn't ask you an hour ago."

* * *

TOM, Dick and Harry would often drink together. After a long session one night Harry's elbow slipped off the bar and he fell flat on his face.

"That's one thing about Harry," said Tom. "He always knows when he's had enough."

TWO drunks were coming home when they saw a young couple screwing in the park.

"I didn't have sex with my wife before I was married, did you?"

"Don't know," said his mate, "What was her maiden name?"

* * *

THE policeman became suspicious as he watched O'Flaherty cursing and fumbling with the front door lock on a house. When O'Flaherty forced a window and was half way through the cop put the heavy hand on his collar.

"But it's my house, offisher," protested O'Flaherty and invited the cop inside to prove it.

"Look offisher, that's my cat, that's my armchair, this is my bedroom, that's my wife in bed, and that bloke with her, that's me."

* * *

FRED woke his wife. "It's a miracle," he said. "You wouldn't believe it, Muriel. I just went for a leak and the light came on by itself. Didn't touch the switch. Had a leak and as soon as I left the light went out. Untouched by human hands. It's a miracle."

His wife gave an understanding sigh. "For goodness sake go to bed, Fred. "It wasn't a miracle. You've pissed in the fridge again."

DUMB

DUMB Duncan was telling the barman the big city was too expensive. "There's a pub back home where you can get a pot of beer, a ham sandwich and a fuck, all for a tenner."

"Sounds great," said the barman. "How often do you go?"

"Well I haven't been there yet," admitted Duncan, "but my wife goes there regularly."

DUMB Duncan was chuckling to himself at the bar.

"What's the joke?" asked the barman.

Duncan said the joke was on his rival, Fred.

"I have just learned that Fred is paying my Missus $20 for her to sleep with him. She sleeps with me for nothing."

* * *

"WHAT can you tell me about current affairs?"

"Not a lot," said the blonde, "I've never had an affair with a currant."

* * *

"WHAT can you tell me about Kipling?"

"Not a lot," said the blonde, "I've never kipled."

E

ECONOMY

IT was tough times and the husband was going through the household receipts. "You should clean the house yourself," he said, "and that will save on the cleaning lady."

"You should also learn to cook and that will save on the catering," he said.

"And you should learn to do the ironing so we won't need to pay the ironing woman," he said.

"And you should learn to fuck," she said, "then we could get rid of the gardener."

* * *

ECONOMY is a factor in all decisions.

"How much are the bananas?" asked Jean and Jan of the fruiterer.

"Seventy five cents each, or three for a dollar," he replied.

The girls thought it over for a moment. "Oh, lets buy three," said Jan, "we can always eat the other one."

EDUCATION

See Teachers, Schools

THE difference between a university lecturer and a proctologist is that the proctologist only has to deal with one arsehole at a time.

THE professor was giving a lecture on anatomy, but for one prim and proper miss he had dwelt too long on the physiology of the male genitalia.

He continued: "The Mongu tribe in Southern Africa are known to have the longest ..."

It was too much for Miss Prim and she got up to leave the lecture hall.

As she neared the door the professor fired one more shot. "There is no need to hurry, madam, the next plane to Southern Africa doesn't leave until Friday."

ELEPHANTS

WHAT'S grey and comes in buckets?
An elephant.

*   *   *

AS the elephant said when he saw the naked man:
"How the hell does he eat with that thing?"

*   *   *

MY first job was a responsible position in the circus. I used to circumcise elephants. The pay wasn't much but the tips were enormous!

*   *   *

IT is common knowledge that an elephant's genitals are in its feet.

If they step on you, then you're fucked.

*   *   *

AND male elephants have four feet because six inches would never satisfy a female elephant.

*   *   *

AFTER a wild night on the town a blonde woke to find an elephant in bed with her.

"Gracious," she said. "What a drinking spree. I must have been tight last night."

"I've had tighter," mumbled the elephant.

THE cub reporter rushed into the office with the news that while the circus was moving to the next town a catastrophe occurred. Seven elephants were lumbering along the road, each hanging on to the other's tail as is their habit.

"When crossing the trainline," said the reporter, "the last one failed to get clear and was struck by the goods train."

"What was the damage?" asked the editor.

"One elephant killed instantly and the arseholes ripped out of the other six."

*   *   *

AN elephant was drinking from the Zambezi when he noticed a turtle asleep on a log. He ambled over and kicked it clear across the river.

"What did you do that for?" asked a passing giraffe.

"Because I recognised it as the same turtle which took a nip out of my trunk 53 years ago."

"What a memory," exclaimed the giraffe.

"Yes," said the elephant, "turtle recall."

*   *   *

WHEN young Freddie visited the zoo with his parents he was intrigued by the elephant. He had never seen one before.

"What's that thing hanging down between its legs, Mum?" he asked.

"That's its trunk," said mother with some embarrassment.

"Nar, I mean the other end, at the back."

"That's nothing," said Mum, giving the boy a clip over the ear.

Freddie moved closer to his Dad. "What's that thing hanging down there between his back legs, Dad?"

"That's his donger," said Dad frankly.

"Mum said it's nothing," said young Freddie.

"Yes, your mother's been spoilt," said Dad smugly.

AN elephant escaped from a circus and no trace had been found until a lady who had never seen an elephant before rang the police. She was panic-stricken.

"There is a weird monster is in my back yard," she said. "It is pulling up the cabbages with its tail. But what is worse...I cannot describe what it is doing with them!"

* * *

ALBERT had been engaged to three young women, but when they got to the pre-marital petting stage and the debutantes discovered the diminutive diameter of Albert's willie, they had called the whole thing off.

It was this sad story that Albert confided to his local GP, who could hardly contain his excitement as he referred the matter to Dr Doodlelittle, the eminent transplant surgeon, currently in town on a lecture tour.

"Albert," said the excited GP, "there is also a circus in town and you are certainly the man who could do with a smidgen of elephant's trunk and help us all in the advancement of medical science."

So to make a short story feasible, Albert made medical history by having a smidgen of elephant trunk implanted, and sure enough, his next engagement went through the pre-marital test with flying colours and was running right up to the wedding.

That is, until the night of the bride's kitchen tea. Albert thought he would help out by playing the role of waiter, but as he moved close to the table, something shot out of his trousers and whisked off a small plate of sandwiches.

He stepped back in amazement and hoped nobody saw what he could hardly believe himself. He cautiously approached the table again. It flashed from his fly once more scooping up a Boston bun, three cream cakes and a lamington. It proved to be a show-stopper. Nobody missed it that time.

"Albert!" screamed his would-be mother-in-law. "What are you doing? You are embarrassing us all."

"Embarrassing you?" said Albert. "Where the hell do you think it is stuffing all these goodies?"

ENGAGEMENTS
See COURTING, HONEYMOONS

THE young man was so nervous when he approached his highly formal prospective father-in-law that he blurted out the words: "I am asking for your daughter's hole in handy matrimony!"

* * *

THE suitor had been shown into the lounge room to wait for his date while she got ready. Then her little brother came in.

"Is Jean your oldest sister?" the suitor said to make small talk.

"Yep," said the kid.

"And who comes after her?"

"You and two other blokes."

* * *

THEY got engaged on the eve of his departure for a three month stint with the Antarctic Expedition.

As soon as he returned she broke it off.

* * *

IT was hardly three weeks after Fred got engaged to the circus contortionist that she broke it off.

* * *

THE French maid announced that she was leaving service now that she was engaged.

"Congratulations," said her mistress, "you will have it much easier now that you are getting married."

"Yes, madam, and more frequently as well."

ETIQUETTE
SIR Reginald Snodgrass was the epitome of British eti-

quette, so when he came home unexpectedly and found his young wife entertaining the young duke on the floor it was just too much.

"Sarah," he roared, "arch your back this instant and lift that gentleman's balls off the cold floor."

* * *

WHEN Lady Ponsonby decided to impress the local society by staging a candle-light dinner she hired a maid.

"Don't forget the sugar tongs," ordered her ladyship, but when the girl looked puzzled she had to explain: "When the male guests go to the loo they hold their member with their fingers so we can't have them handling lumps of sugar too can we?"

The explanation didn't entirely satisfy the maid but she went about her business.

Half way through the evening her ladyship summoned the poor girl: "Where are the tongs?" she demanded.

"Hanging in the toilet," she replied.

* * *

THE feuding neighbours had decided to patch up their differences with a few drinks. All was going well until the host broke wind.

"How dare you fart in front of my wife," roared the husband.

"How was I to know it was her bloody turn," he replied.

F

FAIRY TALES

SNOW White gave a sigh, "Gee fellas, I had always dreamed of having seven inches, but not one inch at a time."

* * *

HE had lost all his money. He had lost his job and his wife had left him. In utter despair he climbed onto the bridge railing and was about to end it all in the murky river below.

"John! Don't jump!" cried a womans voice.

He turned to see a scrawny woman behind him.

"How did you know my name?" he said.

The scrawny one waved her arm in a wide arc, there was a flash of light and a flutter of confetti glitter.

"There are five hundred thousand dollars in your bank account this instant," she said with authority.

"Who are you?" said John.

There was another flash and a shower of confetti glitter. "All your problems are solved," she said.

He climbed down from the railing. "Who are you?" he repeated, "and what about my job?"

"You have been reinstated, at a better position and double the salary." There was another flash and John was impressed.

"I am the good fairy," explained the scrawny one, " but I look like this because of a spell cast on me by the wicked fairy, which will remain until I have sex with a man. I have solved your problems, can you help me solve mine?"

"Fair enough," he said.

She took him to a secluded place on the river bank where he humped his heart out until he fell off exhausted. "That's the best I can do," he muttered.

She raised herself on one elbow and dragged on her after-coitus cigarette. "That's alright John," she said, "although it's rare that I get the name right. Anyway, aren't you too old to believe in fairies?"

* * *

BETSY was walking through the woods one day when a large frog jumped into her path.

"Pretty maiden," said the frog, "please save me. I am really a tall prince with blonde hair and broad shoulders but a witch has cast a spell on me. If you take me home and hold me to your bosom all night the spell will be broken by morning."

Betsy gathered up the frog and took it home. She held it to her bosom all night, and sure enough, lying beside her in the morning was her prince, with blonde hair and broad shoulders.

Until this day Betsy's mother has never believed that story.

* * *

THE Big Bad Wolf had hurried through the woods before Little Red Riding Hood could get to her Granny's house.

He burst into the cottage and said: "Okay Granny, out you get. I'm going to lock you in the wardrobe."

But Granny pulled a shotgun from under the blanket with one hand and lifted her nightie with the other.

"Oh no you don't, Mr Wolf. You do like the story says!"

* * *

THE handsome prince had finally come of age and was to meet his promised princess. With great pageantry she was ushered before the throne, but when she was unveiled the prince flinched in terror. She was fat, ugly, nearly bald, cross-eyed and had three teeth missing.

The prince leaned towards the king and noted all her defects. "How could you do this to me father?" he whispered.

"No need to whisper son," said the king, "she's bloody-well deaf too."

* * *

TWO young women were walking along a country lane when a large green frog jumped out before them and said: "Please dear maidens. One of you kiss me and I will turn into a handsome prince."

One girl quickly scooped up the frog and put it in her handbag.

"Aren't you going to restore him to a prince?" asked her friend.

"No. Princes are a dime a dozen. But a talking frog, now there is potential for making a dollar."

* * *

CINDERELLA was really a nymphomaniac. She was always at it. One day her Fairy Godmother appeared and told her that if she didn't stop screwing she would not be allowed to go to the ball where she would meet the Prince.

Only the next day the Fairy Godmother found her in bed with the chimney sweep.

"That's the last straw," said Fairy Godmother. "I can't stop you going to the ball because it is in the script but at least I can stop you screwing the Prince." And she waved her wand and changed Cinderella's pussy into a pumpkin.

Cinderella returned from the ball with a big smile and a new boyfriend. "Hello Fairy Godmother," she said, "meet Peter Peter."

FAMILIES

"WHATS an orgasm, Mum?"

"I dont know. Ask your Father."

* * *

MOTHER was scolding her daughter. "I don't like that boy you are going with. He's too dumb."

"No momma," she said. "He is going to be a doctor and already he has cured me of that little illness I used to get every month."

* * *

IT was one of those small towns, and when young Nigel announced he was going to marry Jenny Bloom his dad got all agitated and took him aside.

"You can't my son," he said. "It's difficult to explain. Don't tell your mother, but Jenny is your half-sister." He gave the boy a wink and said, "Er, I used to get around a bit on my bike."

The following year he got really dejected when his dad told him the same story about Rosie O'Grady.

The boy looked so down in the dumps that he spilled the beans to his mother.

"It's no problem," she said."You can marry either of them. Your Dad is not the only one who had a bike, and for that matter, he's no relation of yours at all."

* * *

BEFORE Susie was allowed to move out on her own her mother wanted an assurance that she wouldn't bring her boyfriends back to her flat. "It would worry me too much," she said.

Six months later she phoned her daughter. "This new boyfriend of yours, you haven't brought him home to your place?"

"No, Mum," she said, "we went to his flat and let his mother worry."

FANNIES

THE first fanny was made as an afterthought.

God had made Adam and Eve. He looked at his handy-work and thought they looked too much alike. So he split the difference.

* * *

A VAGINA that talks back to you
is called an Answering Cervix.

* * *

AND if Eve wore a fig leaf what did Adam wear?
A hole in it.

* * *

COMPUTERS were already in the Garden of Eden.
Eve had an Apple and Adam had a Wang.

* * *

HE put his head under her skirt and said: "Wow. What a big one. Wow, What a big one."

"Okay," she said self-consciously, "you don't have to repeat it."

"I didn't" he said, "that was an echo."

* * *

CONCERNED that her love-life had quietened down somewhat Miss Lottsabazooma went to the doctor who asked her to strip off.

He noted that she was overweight.

"Why don't you diet?' he said.

She looked down. "What colour do you suggest? she said.

* * *

FRED said to his mate, "Did you know my wife is a wrestler?"

"No, why do you ask?"

"I thought you might have seen her wrestle."

"No. But I've seen her box a few times."

* * *

IT was a first night stand and it wasn't working.

She pushed him back. "It's your organ. It's not big enough."

"Sorry," he said. "It wasn't meant to be played in a cathedral."

* * *

AN Irish lad was making a love to a Scottish lass and she wasn't impressed.

"I thought you Irishmen were supposed to be big and thick," she said.

He replied: "I thought you Scots were supposed to be tight."

* * *

HE stood beside the blonde at the bar for a while and then said: "Can I smell your fanny?"

"Certainly not," she replied.

"Must be your feet then," he said.

* * *

RASTUS and Lulu Belle were walking home across a long low bridge when Lulu desperately needed a leak.

"Rastus, Rastus," she said, "I must do it. There's no-one about so hold me over the rail."

She hitched up her skirt, lowered her drawers and strong Rastus held her over the lake.

Suddenly Lulu looked down and became agitated. "Quick, Rastus, lift me back. There's a man down there in a canoe."

Rastus looked over the rail.

"Silly girl," he said. "That's your darn reflection."

* * *

A WOMAN goes in to a sex shop and browses for a while at the dildo counter.

"I'll have that one there, the tartan one with the big white top."

"That's not for sale," said the manager, "That's my thermos flask."

FARMERS

TWO wheat farmers finally sold their properties and decided to retire from the land. They surprised each other by buying a four-wheel-drive each and announcing that they intended to drive around Australia.

"What route are you taking?" said one.

"Ar, I think I'll take the missus. She stuck to me through the drought."

* * *

DAVE was courting Mabel who lived on a neighbouring farm.

They were watching a bull humping a cow and Dave took the cue to put the hard word on Mabel.

"I'd sure like to be doing what that bull is doing," he whispered.

"Well why don't you," she whispered back, "it's your cow."

* * *

THE best way to make a bull sweat is to give him a tight jersey.

* * *

WHEN the farmer's daughter responded to a knock on the door she found a neighbouring farmer looking very angry.

"Where's your father?" said the visitor sternly.

"If you've come about the bull it is a hundred dollars, and we have the pedigree papers," she began.

"Miss. I want to see your father," he insisted.

"We have another bull. We don't have papers for him but he is very well bred."

"Young lady. I don't want to talk about any bulls. Your brother Frank has got our daughter pregnant. Where's your father?"

"Oh," she said, "I don't think there is any charge for Frank."

* * *

BREEDING season is a crucial time on the farm so it was

natural that the farmer's son rushed in and said, "Dad, come quick, the bull is fucking the brown cow."

The farmer shook him by the collar. "The vicar is coming this afternoon so watch your language. If it happens again just say the bull is playing one of his dirty tricks, right?" And he gave the boy a clip over the ear for good measure.

Indeed, the vicar was sipping tea with the farmer and his wife that afternoon when the lad rushed in again.

"Dad, the bull has played a dirty trick on the brown cow," he said.

"Really?" said the farmer.

"Yes," said the lad, "he's just fucked the white cow."

* * *

TWO cows were talking in a paddock.

"Aren't you worried about this Crazy Cow disease that's going about?"

"No," said the other, "I'm a goat."

* * *

AT the National Agricultural Conference it was easy to pick the dairy milking champion. He was the bloke who shook hands with everybody, one finger at a time.

* * *

FARMER Snodd called the vet because he though his prize bull was a fairy. "He's not interested in the heiffers," he said. The vet prescribed a special mixture.

A week later Snodd's neighbour commented on the vigour with which the bull was mounting anything that moved.

"What was the mixture the vet prescribed?" he said.

"Don't know," said a very happy Farmer Snodd, "it's brown in colour and tastes like aniseed."

* * *

THE travelling salesman was driving along a country road when he skittled a rooster which ran across the path of his car.

Feeling guilty about killing such a fine bird he approached the farm house and knocked on the door.

A demure young farmer's wife answered.

"Excuse me, missus, I have just killed your rooster, and I would like to replace it."

"Please yourself," said the lady. "The chooks are around the back."

* * *

IT was the night of the school concert and all the kids had their poems, songs and recitations at the ready; except little Charlie had just come down from the country and had started school that day.

"C'mon Charlie," said the teacher. "Surely you can do something for the concert."

It took much cajoling, but finally Charlie agreed to do some farmyard impressions.

The instant applause gave Charlie a boost of confidence and he strode to centre stage."Farmyard noises," he announced.

Then cupping his hands to his face like a megaphone he yelled at the top of his voice: "Get off that f'ckn tractor. Shut that f'ckn gate. Get that f'ckn bull out of that yard .....!"

* * *

THE mayor and mayoress were leading the inspection around the agricultural show when the mayoress stopped beside a prize bull. "My word, what a fine beast," she said.

"Yes, he's a champion," said the lad attending it, "he stood to stud five hundred times last year."

The mayoress was impressed. "Five hundred times you say. Would you mind telling my husband that when he comes along?"

The lad did so. "Very interesting," said the mayor, "five hundred times you say. Always with the same cow of course."

"Oh no sir. Five hundred different cows."

"Would you mind telling that to the mayoress when she comes past?"

FARTS

THE reason farts smell like they do,
   is so that the deaf can enjoy them too.

* * *

SHE was delighted when the most eligible bachelor asked her to dance but while they glided around the floor doing the cha-cha-cha the effort caused him to let go a few whoofers.

"Oh what an original way to keep time," she said.

* * *

WHAT do you get when you've been eating onions and beans?

Tear Gas.

* * *

AT the Galloping Gourmet's annual feast Fred Flabby set a new record of 35 plates of baked beans. However the record was not counted due to a following wind.

* * *

PADDY the Irish cook was famous for his bean soup.

"I use exactly 239 beans," he said. "One more and it would be too farty."

* * *

STEPPING into the elevator the businessman quickly detected an offensive odour. The only other occupant was a little old lady. "Excuse me," he addressed her, "did you happen to pass wind?"

"Of course I did," she replied. "You don't think I stink like this all the time do you?"

* * *

IT was so cold in the mountains that Old Jake woke one morning to find two ice cubes in his sleeping bag.

When he threw them on the fire they went: Phartsst! Pharsst!

*   *   *

IT is her first date with her supervisor from the office and she is edgy. They are going to a charity concert but she is gripped with nerves and a tightening of the stomach. Just as she hears the doorbell ring she is taken by a great desire to fart.

In great discomfort she stifles it.

Outside in the dark street the young man ushers her into the front seat of the car but does not get in himself. "I'll just nip over to the shop and get some cigarettes," he says.

Immediately she takes the opportunity to let go a rip-snorter of a fart, lifting one cheek of her bum off the seat to let the blast go free. A few seconds later her date returns, settles behind the wheel and says: "Oh, I'm sorry. I forgot to introduce you to my parents," and turning round he indicates the two people sitting in the gloom of the rear seat.

*   *   *

MADAM was quite the old stager
   Who as the result of a wager
   Consented to fart the complete oboe part
   Of Mozart's Quartet in F major.

*   *   *

BUT the violinst was just a bit smarter
   For he was a magnificent farter
   He could play anything, from God Save the King
   To Beethoven's Moonlight Sonata.

*   *   *

AN embarrassed young woman was farting uncontrollably when her date was due to arrive. She was an accomplished pianist so to drown the noise she offered to play the Storm Scene from the William Tell Overture.

She had concluded the piece when she felt another fart attack on its way and quickly asked him if he would like another tune on the piano.

134

"Well if it is that storm scene again," he said, "can you leave out the bit where the lightning strikes the shithouse?"

* * *

HER marriage into high society was an excuse for Lady Upstart to inveigle princes and diplomats to her candlelit suppers and to put on airs and graces above her station.

It all got up the butler's nose.

But it turned out that on one of these society occasions her stomach was suffering a little internal turbulence and during an unfortunate lull in the conversation she let forth an audible fart.

Without batting an eyelid she turned briskly on the butler and said "Jeeves, stop that."

Jeeves was up to the mark, "Certainly madam, which way did it go?"

* * *

HE sat next to the duchess at tea
It was just as he feared it would be
Her rumblings abdominal were simply phenomenal
And everyone thought it was he.

* * *

AT the Twilight Home old Jake was dozing in his chair. Every time he leaned too far to one side a nurse would gently push him straight. Bert, a new arrival, asked how he liked the rest home just as a nurse pushed Jake up straight again.

"Oh the home is alright," said Jake, leaning to the left again, "It's just that they make it bloody difficult to fart."

* * *

THE sex surrogate had been hired by the rich farmer to teach the son the intracacies of love and she was delighted to find he was a fine strapping lad.

She even skipped some of the basics and advanced to the sophisticated *soixante-neuf* position.

Unfortunately, she got so excited and carried away she let go a little whoofer.

135

"Crikey, what d'yer call that?" said the country lad.

"Sorry, just an accident," she said. "It's called the 69 position."

They got back to work but again she got so excited another puff of wind escaped her buttocks.

The boy scrambled out from underneath. "That enough," he declared. "Damned if I can stand another 67 of them."

*　*　*

ELI MUSTAFA was in the Arab bazaar one day when he felt terrible stomach cramps. He couldn't control the thunderous fart which followed. Stall holders and customers alike were startled.

It was so embarrassing for Eli that he ran home, packed his bags on his trusty camel and wandered the Middle East for the rest of his business life.

At last, a weary old man, he yearned to return to the town of his boyhood. He reasoned that most of those who had witnessed his embarrassment would be dead by now. He had grown a long white beard and he was so aged he was sure nobody would recognise him. His heart longed for the old familiar streets of his boyhood.

Once in town he headed for the bazaar and found that the power had been connected and there were bright lights.

He turned to a stallholder and asked when were such improvements carried out.

"Oh that," said the man. "That was done 15 years and 5 months to the day Eli Mustafa farted in the bazaar."

*　*　*

THERE was a young man from Australia
Who painted his arse like a dahlia
The drawing was fine, the colour divine
But the scent? Ar, that was a failure.

*　*　*

THE Scot was so mean the only way he would take a bubble bath on Saturday morning was to eat baked beans for his supper on Friday night.

TWO old maids were discussing the merits of pantyhose.

"Don't like them at all," said one. "Every time I fart it blows my slippers off."

* * *

IT was the season's diplomatic dinner and at the head of the table sat Madam Lottzabazooma, society matron and matriarch of the diplomatic corp. On her right was the British Consul and on her left was the French Consul.

Suddenly, in an unfortunate lull in the conversation the Madam let go a loud and reverberating fart.

The Briton leapt to his feet and apologised profusely to the startled diners. "I crave your indulgence," he said, "a serious war wound makes me particularly susceptible to flatulence and in stimulating conversation such as this, with excitement and laughter, I sometimes lose control. My humblest apologies. I hope you will forgive me." He sat down.

The French consul was puzzled. He knew it was Madam Lottzabazooma who had unleashed the whoofer, yet the Briton had taken the blame.

Twice more the Madam let farts rumble by and twice more the Briton jumped to his feet and apologised.

It was only when the Madam left for the powder room that the Frenchman leaned across and asked for an explanation.

"Well, old chap, we can't let her get embarrassed about it can we. It is my duty as a British gentleman to take the rap. It's a matter of honour," he said.

The conversation was cut short with Madam's return. A few moments later she discharged a rip-snorting fart that shook the chandeliers.

This time both consuls jumped to their feet at the same instant. The Frenchman waggled his finger at the Briton: "Oh, no my friend. The honour of France is at stake. This one is on me."

THE Queen was showing the Archbishop of Canterbury around her new stables when a stallion nearby let go such a resounding fart it rattled the windows and couldn't be ignored.

"Oh dear," said the Queen, blushing, "I'm frightfully sorry about that."

"Think nothing of it, Madam," said the archbishop, "it's a perfectly natural function. Anyway, I thought it was the horse!"

FASHION

HER jeans were so tight she was making a fashion statement without words; you could read her lips.

* * *

MISS Lotzabazooma was very fashion conscious. When she went walking she wore walking clothes. When she went riding she wore riding clothes, and going out for evenings she wore evening clothes.

Which is why her boy friend could hardly wait for her birthday.

* * *

BESSIE was picked up in a singles bar and the following night flounced back to the bar wearing a very expensive fur coat.

"Wow, what an expensive coat," said her friend. "What did you have to do for it?"

"Not much, just shorten the sleeves and raise the hem a little," she said.

FATHERS AND SONS

HIS father was alarmed when he announced that he was going to marry Miss Lottsabazooma.

"But son," he said, "Everybody in town has been to bed with her."

The son thought this over for a moment.

"Yeah, but it's not a very big town is it."

* * *

ESTABLISHED at university the son was always writing home for more money. He needed money for football gear, for tennis, for excursions and for an extravagant social life.

Finally he wrote to say he had a part in the college's Gilbert & Sullivan show and he needed money for the costume. Father was annoyed, but mother sent the money.

A month later he wrote home to say thanks for the costume. "Everybody agreed I looked a proper count," he said.

"All that money," said the father "and he still can't spell."

* * *

THE farmer decided to send his son into the world to learn about commerce and life. "You are now 18, son. Here is a duck. Go to town and see what you can exchange it for."

The lad soon found the town's knocking shop and wandered in. "It's my 18th birthday. What can I get for my duck?"

The madam said she was sentimental about birthdays and said she would handle the lad herself.

Actually she enjoyed the vigour of the youngster and said: "If you can do it again, I'll give you back the duck."

After the lad had completed his pleasant assignment he was walking home with the duck when a passing truck flattened it. The driver said he was sorry and gave the lad two dollars.

When he got home his father wanted a full report on the day's transactions.

The son said: "I got a fuck for a duck, then a duck for a fuck, then two bucks for a fucked duck."

* * *

HE was a young father, wheeling the pram through the gardens while the baby was screaming its head off. "Take it easy Jason," he said calmly. "There's nothing to fuss about."

A middle-aged woman noticed his soothing manner and marvelled at the new breed of young husbands.

When the baby screamed even louder she heard him say: "Cool it, Jason, don't get excited, lad, cool it son."

Touched by his gentle manner the woman leaned into the pram and cooed: "There, there Jason, what's bothering you?"

"Excuse me, lady," said the father, "that's Jeremy, I'm Jason."

* * *

LADY Muck finally confronted the Major and said it was about time their son Cecil was told about the birds and bees.

At the appropriate time that evening the Major did so.

"See here, Cecil," he said. "You remember that time I caught you rooting the maid? Well you mother wants you to know that the birds and bees do it too."

FEMINISTS

THE difference between a clitoris and a pub is simple: Most men know where to find a pub.

* * *

DO you know what you call that useless piece of skin on the end of a penis?

A man!

* * *

THE reason Australian men come so fast is they can't wait to get down the pub and tell their mates about it.

* * *

SHE said her boyfriend wasn't a Sensitive New Age Guy (SNAG). "He's more a Caring Understanding Nineties Type," she said.

* * *

THE feminists were hailing a miracle birth.

The baby had both, a dick AND a brain.

* * *

AUSSIE men don't suffer from piles because they are perfect arseholes.

* * *

MALE Chauvinist Pig's motto:
  Put Womens Libbers behind bras.

* * *

SUPPORT Women's Lib. Get out from under.

* * *

A DISCERNING feminist called Ida
  Said to her bloke as he slipped it insider
  "I'd much rather be
  Underneath as 'ridee'
  Than on top in the role of the rider.

* * *

A MAN wrapped up in himself makes a very small parcel.

* * *

BETTER to have loved and lost than spend your whole damned life with him.

* * *

GERMAN men live by the sweat of their fraus.

* * *

WHEN all that's stiff is his socks,
  take the money and run.

* * *

ONE man's Sunday lunch is one woman's Sunday gone.

* * *

A WOMAN who thinks the way to a man's heart is through his stomach is aiming a little too high.

* * *

IF you want a chick, go buy an egg.

* * *

A WOMAN who calls herself a bird deserves the worms she gets.

* * *

A HARD man is good to find.

NO man has ever stuck his hand up a skirt looking for a tram ticket.

* * *

A MAN who has lost 90 per cent of his brain is called a widower.

* * *

IF a woman does household chores for $300 a week, that's domestic science.

If she does it for nothing, that's marriage.

* * *

SHE said she wouldn't mind having a baby. "But unfortunately," she said, "you have to marry one to get one."

* * *

THERE are three kinds of men in this world; the caring, the sensitive and the majority.

* * *

A WOMAN who strives to be like a man lacks ambition.

* * *

WHEN the boss put the hard word on the lively new employee she had the answer. "No way, Bozo," she said, "you've got the words 'liberated' and 'free' mixed up."

* * *

LOVE is the delusion that one man is different from the rest.

* * *

WHEN a woman makes a fool of a man it is usually an improvement.

* * *

IT is said that the wisest of men can become foolish over woman; and the most foolish of women is wise to man.

* * *

THE only difference between men and pigs is that when pigs drink they don't make men of themselves.

* * *

MEN are like pigeons. They should never be looked up to.

THE only things wives have in common with their husbands is that they were married on the same day.

* * *

SHE wanted a husband and put an advertisement in the Personal Column.

She got a hundred replies saying; "You can have mine."

* * *

WOMEN are called birds because of all the worms they pick up.

* * *

FRED was a window cleaner and he couldn't believe his eyes when he saw a young woman get out of the bath and start drying off right in front of him.

She was a feminist and instead of screaming she stared straight back at him in an effort to shame him.

Their eyes locked in confrontation for an interminable minute. Neither would budge.

Fred finally roared: "What are you staring at? Haven't you ever seen a window cleaner before?"

* * *

THE young couple had a knee-trembler against a paling fence and got so excited they knocked it down. The commotion aroused the householder who grabbed the young man and collected a hundred dollars on the spot for repairs to the fence.

Later the young bloke said, "Listen Mabel. You are a feminist and you are always shouting about equal rights. Here's your chance. You owe me fifty dollars for half the cost of the fence."

"No way," she said, "it was you who did all the pushing."

* * *

"WHERE have you been all my life?" sleazed the middle-aged Casanova.

She looked up and said coyly, "Well, for the first half of it, I wasn't born."

CUCUMBERS are better than men because:
Cucumbers stay hard for weeks.
Cucumbers never suffer performance anxiety.
Cucumbers are there when you want them.
Cucumbers will always respect you next morning.
Cucumbers are eaten only when YOU fancy it.
Cucumbers never need a round of applause.
Cucumbers can stay up all night.
Cucumbers don't mind hiding in the fridge
when mother calls.

FINANCE

WHAT'S the difference between a wanker and a banker?
The wanker knows what he is doing.

* * *

THE Irish call their basic currency the punt,
because it rhymes with bank manager.

* * *

THE Chinese businessman pressed the teller to explain why his interest rate had increased two points from the previous day.

"Fluctuations," said the teller.

"And fluck you too, ya bloody ocker," said the Chinaman.

* * *

MORE often than not, bankruptcy is due to a lack and a lass.

* * *

THE bank manager and his wife were walking down the street when a buxom blonde in a red convertible waved to him as she passed by.

The wife glared and said: "Who the hell was that?"

"Just someone I know professionally," he said.

"Whose profession?" she said sternly. "Yours or hers?"

A FINANCIALLY astute prostitute who works around the stock exchange is known as Cash Flo.

* * *

PADDY fronted the bank teller and whispered gruffly: "This is a cock up."

The startled teller said, "Don't you mean a stick-up?"

"No," said Paddy, "I've left me bloody gun at home."

* * *

TREASURER'S report: "Last year we we were poised on the edge of a precipice. This year we have made a great leap forward!"

* * *

THE wealthy financier took a tumble for a blonde and lost his balance at the bank.

* * *

THE bank manager managed to get his pretty bank teller to bed. As they slid under the sheets he said: "Aren't you going to warn me that there will be a substantial penalty for early withdrawal?"

"That's not likely as your interest begins to peak," she replied.

* * *

A YOUNG woman approached the bank teller with a large bag of cash and said she wanted to open an account.

The teller was surprised at the amount of money she pushed across the counter.

"Did you hoard all this money yourself?"

"Don't be silly, my sister whored half of it."

* * *

THE bank manager noticed the new clerk was adroit at counting money and adding up figures.

"Where did you get your finance education?" he asked.

"Yale," replied the lad.

"And what's your name?" asked the manager.

"Yim Yohnston," he replied.

A BLOKE recently discharged from bankruptcy went down to see the manager of his local bank.

"I'm sorry sir, the manager died last week," said the clerk.

The bloke came in next day and said he would like to see the manager.

"I told you yesterday, sir. He is dead."

When the bloke came in on the third day the clerk said: "How many times do I have to tell you. He is dead, dead, dead."

"I know," said the former bankrupt. "I just like to hear it confirmed."

* * *

TIMES were hard so Fred suggested to his wife that every time they went to bed for a nookie he would put a dollar in the jar.

A few months later he happened to empty the jar and found it contained a bunch of dollar notes, mixed with fivers, tens and twenties.

"Where did all this money come from?" he asked his wife. "Each time we screwed I only gave a dollar."

"So?" she said, "Do you think everyone is as miserable as you?"

* * *

ANOTHER bloke who put his wife on the streets grabbed her money bag at the end of the week and tipped out the cash. It amounted to $75 dollars and fifty cents.

"What miserable bastard gave you 50 cents?" he said.

"They all did," she replied.

* * *

AFTER a political meeting one of the candidates approached the rostrum to announce that he had lost his wallet with $500 in it. "I will pay $50 to anybody who returns it," he said.

"And I'll give $100," said Moishe Isaac.

IT might be the age of the computer and the calculator but some of us can remember the constipated accountant who had to work it out with a pencil.

* * *

PATRICK Whack was promoted to Loan Arranger at the local bank, but the manager made it clear that he would be on trial.

His first customer was an Italian who wanted a loan of $100,000, and of course Paddy asked if he had any collateral.

"I have this miniature elephant carved out of ivory with some precious stones implanted in it?" said the Italian. "It's out in the car."

Patrick didn't think it was good enough, but asked the Italian to bring it in for inspection.

"What did he want, Paddy?" asked the bank manager when he had left.

"Oh, he wanted a loan for $100,000, but all he had for collateral was some knick-knack. He's gone to the car to get it."

The Italian returned with a bundle under his arm and proceeded to unwrap it on Paddy's table. It proved to hold a large ivory carving of an elephant with dazzling diamonds studded all down its back.

The bank manager saw it from his adjoining office and burst in: "What a knick-knack, Paddy Whack, give the wog a loan."

* * *

IN Sydney she was Rhonda
   She was Patsy out in Perth
   In Brisbane she was Brenda,
   The sweetest girl on earth.
   In Wagga she was Wendy
   The pick of all the bunch,
   But down on his expenses
   She was petrol, oil and lunch.

147

AN Indian squaw was elated
  She knew she was to be mated
  Asked how she knew
  That her brave's love was true;
  "Because," she said, "the buck is inflated."

* * *

TWO female bankers were talking. "My neighbour threatened to take me to court because her husband gets an erection when he sees me sunbathing nude in my yard."

"What did you do?"

"I put up a hedge against inflation," she replied.

FISHERMEN

SHE went out fishing with five blokes and came home with a red snapper.

* * *

WE know a nurse who hates fishing.

But she doesn't mind going down on the Docs.

* * *

WHEN the boat sank, Gerry knew they were in trouble because Fred couldn't swim.

"Get on my back and we'll do our best," said Gerry as he struck out for the shore.

But after an hour Gerry was getting exhausted. "Try a few strokes," he told Fred.

"But if I take my hands off your shoulders I'll drown," spluttered Fred.

They struggled on and Gerry was encouraged to see Fred making a better effort with his arms.

Eventually they staggered ashore where Gerry collapsed on the beach. "I'm fucked," he said.

"I'm sorry," said Fred, "It was the only way I could hang on."

HE had been away for a dirty weekend with the floozie from the office but had told his wife that he had gone on a fishing trip with the boys.

"How was it?" she enquired when he arrived home.

"Great. But you forgot to pack my shaving gear," he said.

"I put it in your tackle box," she said coldly.

* * *

"THERE was a phone call for you while you were out," said the wife to her husband.

"Oh, who was it?"

"It was one of those trouts you were fishing for last week."

* * *

O'FLAHERTY was fishing when he hauled up a small stone jar. He looked at it, rubbed it and Whoooosh! Out came a small genie.

"I've been there ten thousand years," it said, "you know the rules, I owe you three wishes," and so saying it disappeared.

O'Flaherty rushed home to tell Brigid. Then they decided to go to town and see what the shops had to wish for.

First Brigid said they would have a quick dinner and she reached for a can of beans but couldn't find the can opener.

"I wish I could find that can opener," she muttered, and Kerzaam! The opener appeared in her hand.

"Christ. You've wasted one wish on that bloody can opener," roared an angry O'Flaherty, "I wish it was up your arse."

It took the third wish to get it out again.

* * *

SHE was only a fishermans daughter,
   but she knew her plaice and to fillet.

149

FLASHERS

FLASHER'S motto: Grin and bare it.

* * *

FLASHER'S theme song: Whistle while you lurk.

* * *

IT was Fred the Flasher's most humiliating experience.

A woman charged him before the Small Claims Tribunal.

* * *

STANDING in a crowded train the pervert squeezed his body against the buxom woman and she could feel something like a coke bottle in his pocket pressed against her thigh.

She said: "I have only three words to say to you; You Filthy Beast."

Later, as the train approached his station he said: "I have only three words to say to you; Let Go Now."

* * *

A gent in a long flowing cloak
  Unzipped his fly for a joke
  An old man gave a shout
  A nun almost passed out
And a lady close by had a stroke.

* * *

AS the female conductor came along the train checking tickets the kinky passenger opened his raincoat with a flourish and exposed himself.

"I'm sorry," she said, "but you'll have to show me your ticket, not your stub."

* * *

SHE had a dick-shrivelling approach to flashers.

"Why have you taken that thing out of your trousers?" she demanded.

"It likes the fresh air," he taunted.

"Yes, it needs some," she said, "It strikes me as being considerably short of breadth."

ON the crowded train she turned to the man behind her.

"For God's sake will you stop pushing that thing at me?"

"It's only my pay packet," he said.

"Well, you must have a good job," she retorted, "You've had three rises since we left Central Station."

*   *   *

THREE old maids were on a seat in a park when a member of the raincoat brigade flashed at them.

Two had a stroke. The third was too slow.

*   *   *

HE had a sign hanging on the lowest button of his closed overcoat: "Next session, 4pm".

*   *   *

AS she walked throught the park at Exeter

Men whistled and craned their necks at her,

But some more depraved,

Went further and waved

The distinguishing mark of their sex at her.

FLOOZIES

A FLOOZIE is a girl who has been tried and found wanton.

*   *   *

THE richest floozie on Park Avenue wears mink all day and fox all night.

*   *   *

FLOOZIE failed her driving test.

When the car stalled she got over into the back seat from force of habit.

*   *   *

THE store attendant said: "I'm, awfully sorry, Miss, this fifty dollar note is counterfeit."

"Damn. Call the police," she said, "I've been raped."

*   *   *

THE blonde sat at the bar beside Fred and ordered a gin and tonic and swallowed it in one gulp. Then she ordered another and did the same. Fascinated by her capacity to drink Fred watched a third and fourth go down. "Would five make you dizzy?" he asked her.

"The price is alright," she replied, "but the name is Daisy."

* * *

SHE had told the court the defendant had robbed her.

"Yes," said the judge. "You claim this man stole a hundred dollars you had pinned inside your knickers?"

"Yes, judge, that's him."

"But why didn't you put up a fight, scream or kick?"

"Your Honour, at the time I didn't know he was after my money."

* * *

FLOSSIE the floozie said she was off to the Middle East.

She had just read that the favourite pastime for Arabs on Saturday nights was to sit beneath palm trees eating their dates.

* * *

INTERVIEWER: "How many husbands have you had?"
Movie Floozie: "Should I count my own?"

* * *

MANY a starlet trying to make it to the top often wears clothes that don't.

* * *

SHE has an impediment in her speech. She can't say no.

* * *

WHEN he whispered something in her ear she indignantly raised herself to her full height and angrily exclaimed: "Really! Do I look like the sort of girl who would tell a perfect stranger that she lives alone in her own apartment just five minutes from here?"

* * *

A SALESMAN went to a singles bar and fronted the first woman he saw. "I'm only in town for one night and I'm afraid I can't waste time. Do you fuck or don't you?"

"Well," she replied shyly, "I don't usually, but you've talked me into it."

* * *

ONE actress complained to her friend that she was tired. "I didn't get to sleep until after three," she said.

"No wonder you are tired," said her friend, "two is all I need."

* * *

SHE sauntered into the singles bar wearing the tightest pair of jeans the regulars had seen. One bloke quickly sat beside her and said: "Heck, honey. How do you get into those pants?"

"A gin and tonic could well be the first move," she said.

* * *

THERE was a young floozie from Kent
Who said she knew what it meant
When men asked her to dine
Gave her cocktails and wine
She knew what it meant ...But she went.

FOOTBALL

THE football star from the bush was not all he was cracked up to be so the runner was sent out with a message.

"The coach says he will pull you off at half time."

"That's great," replied the country lad. "We only get oranges at Snake Gully."

* * *

THEN the coach got the shock of his life when the team filed on to the ground, dropped their shorts and started wanking.

"But you told us to," said the players. "You said go out and pull yourselves together."

* * *

THE English football team was examined by a medical panel and pronouced fit for FA.

FOOTY FANS

ACCORDING to a survey taken on the state of origin of all football umpires in the Football League, not one of them was born in the state of wedlock.

* * *

TWO factory workers were discussing next Saturday's football match. "I would love to go, but the wife wouldn't let me," said one.

"There's nothing to it," said his mate. "On Saturday morning, buy her a bunch of flowers, then sweep her up in your arms, take her to bed, give her your best and when its finished just tell her your are now going to the footy."

The following Monday the first one said, "What happened? I didn't see you at the game."

His mate said: "Well, I did as you suggested. I bought the flowers, carried her to the bedroom, and flung her onto the bed.

"Then as I dropped my trousers I thought to myself, what the hell, the team hasn't been playing that well lately."

* * *

AT the last grand final the stadium was packed, every seat was sold, except one. It was noticed by the television broadcaster who sent a reporter down to sniff out the story.

"How come this seat is empty?" he asked the man sitting beside it.

"It's my wife's seat," he replied.

"Then why isn't she here?"

"She died," he said, "I'm on my own now."

"Sorry to hear it," said the reporter, "but couldn't you find a friend who could use the seat?"

"No," he replied, "they are all at the funeral."

FRENCH

A FRENCHMAN is a man who kisses other men on cheeks, and girls on all fours.

THERE will never be a French astronaut.

Who ever hears of a Frenchman going up?

* * *

THE French groom was so exhausted by the day's wedding events, the reception, and the celebrations, he went to sleep the moment his feet hit the pillow.

* * *

A FRENCH politician was pleading for legislation giving more equality to women.

"After all," he told the House, "there is very little difference between men and women."

The Chamber rose as a body and shouted: *"Vive la différence!"*

* * *

THE difference between a madam and a mademoiselle, is a monsieur.

* * *

FRENCH kissing is like a toothpick.

You can use it either end.

* * *

FRENCH girls are good at holding their liquor. "First get a good grip of his ears," said Fifi.

* * *

A FRENCH Square Dance is a Go Down Hoedown.

* * *

THE new French Consul was being shown around the city.

"And that is our tallest building," said his guide, "what do you think of it?"

"It reminds me of sex," said the French dignitary.

"That's strange," said his guide, "how can a building remind you of sex?"

"Everything does," replied the Frenchman.

* * *

THE restaurant was not doing so well so the proprietor decided to hire a French chef to stimulate business. But the Frenchman proved to be a hopeless cook, and worse, the proprietor discovered him performing cunnilingus on his wife.

"Look at that," he said. "First he screws up my eating, and now he's eating up my screwing."

* * *

THE difference between French women and those in the rest of the world is simple: All women know what men like, but the French girl doesn't mind.

* * *

IN fact, a French girl went to live in London for a time, but she missed her native tongue.

* * *

A LONDON society couple advertised for help. They had five daughters and desperately wanted advice on how to conceive a son. Advice came from around the world.

Americans suggested apple pie.

An Irishman sent a bottle of whisky.

A German offered a collection of whips.

An Indian suggested yoga.

A Frenchman wrote: "May I be of service?"

* * *

AN angry young man who discovered Pierre had been screwing his fiancee sent a letter challenging Pierre to a duel at an appointed place and time.

Pierre wrote back: "I have received you circular letter. I will be present at the gathering."

* * *

PIERRE passed away at 69
    And we all miss him so
    Pierre passed away at 69
    Boy, what a way to go!

FUNERALS

SOME of the greatest followers of the medical profession are Funeral Directors.

ALL her life she had been a good-time girl.

In fact they had to bury her in a Y-shaped coffin.

* * *

ON an old maid's tombstone:

"Who said you can't take it with you?"

* * *

THE tombstone read: "Here lies the body of Sir Roger Limp, an Englishman and a gentleman."

"Never," said Paddy O'Reilly, "no gentleman would agree to be buried with a Pommie."

* * *

UNCLE Fred died of asbestosis. It took six weeks to cremate the bugger.

* * *

THE Hollywood starlet with the reputation of a steamy sex life had finally died.

"Together at last," said one mourner.

"You mean with her late husbands? asked another.

"I mean her legs," said the first.

* * *

AMONG the funeral and death notices was this little advertisement: For Sale. Second-hand tombstone. Bargain for anybody named McDougal. Owner going abroad."

* * *

ONE mourner said: "I believe Isaac left just on a million dollars."

"No," replied the second mouner, "he didn't leave the money. He was taken from it."

* * *

PADDY O'Flaherty had been ill for some time and he knew he was not long for this world. But one morning the smell of corned beef and cabbage reached his nostrils and quite perked him up.

Feebly, he called his son. "As one of my last requests please fetch me a plate of that lovely corned beef I can smell your mother cooking."

The lad was back in a trice. "Mum says you can't have any. It's for the wake."

* * *

PAT and Mick were working together on the 25th floor when Mick fell to his death. The foreman gave Pat the responsibility of breaking the news to his wife.

"But do it gently," said the foreman.

That afternoon Pat knocked on the door and said, "Does the Widow Gilligan live here?"

"I'm Mrs Gilligan, but I'm certainly no widow."

"That's what you think," said Pat. "Wait till you see what the boys are dragging up the stairs."

* * *

THE Aussie had just laid a wreath of flowers on a work-mate's grave. On the way out of the cemetery he was intrigued to see a Chinese sprinkling rice around a head-stone.

"When do you expect your relative to come and eat the rice," he chuckled.

"The same time your friend pops up to smell the flow-ers," replied the Chinese.

* * *

BENEATH this stone lies Kierly
   They buried him today
   He lived the life of Riley
   While Riley was away.

* * *

IF you don't go to people's funerals...they won't come to yours.

* * *

THE deceased, Frederick, had always been so mean and nasty to her that it was a surprise to relatives and friends when the widow asked for his ashes and carefully cradled the urn on the journey back to their home.

She then took the lid off. "Look at this diamond ring,

Fred," she said, holding the glittering bauble near the ashes, "it's the ring I always wanted."

Then she carried the urn to her wardrobe. "And look at that fur coat, Fred. It's the one I always wanted."

Then she took the ashes over to the window. "And see that Mercedes Sports in the drive-way. It's the one I always wanted."

"And Fred," she said, coming closer to her departed husband's ashes. "You know that blow job you always wanted. Well here it is ...whooosh!"

* * *

BRIDGET took one look of her late husband, laying in his coffin with a smile on his face.

"Look at him now," she said. "He's smiling because he died in his sleep and he doesn't know he's dead yet. He is dreaming he is still alive, so when he wakes up and finds that he is dead, begorrah, the shock will kill him."

* * *

WHEN Isaac's wife died he was told it was the usual thing to place a bereavement notice in the newspaper.

He went down and lodged the notice: "Rachael died."

The clerk pointed out that the minimum charge allowed for five words. So Isaac added three more words: "Holden for sale."

* * *

THE widow placed the death notice in paper but added the line that her husband had died from gonorrhoea.

The family was horrified and quickly pointed out that it was diarrhoea that caused his demise.

The widow said there was no mistake: "I would rather have him remembered as great lover than the great shit he really was."

* * *

AT the funeral service the vicar and the undertaker had never seen a husband so grieved. Fred was sobbing his heart out and beating his breast.

He was so distraught that the vicar took him aside in a bid to comfort him.

"It's tough, I know," said the vicar, "but believe me you will eventually get over it. And dare I say it," he paused, "in three or six months you might well meet another woman and ..."

"Yeah!" wailed Fred, "but where will I get a fuck tonight?"

* * *

A GOURMET writer called Brereton
Took some liver pate and spread it on
A savoy cracker biscuit
Then muttered, Ill risk it."
His tomb bears the date he said it on.

G

GAMBLERS

AN orthodox jew who was worried about his son's gambling sent him a message to remind him of his religious commitments. "And don't forget Yom Kippur starts on Sunday."

"Put $50 on it for me, Pops," replied the son.

*   *   *

A PUNTER would bank $500 every Monday morning so regularly that finally the bank manager's curiosity got the better of him. Where did he get the money?

"I am a punter," explained the customer, "but I only bet on sure things."

Intrigued, the banker pressed him for an example of a sure thing.

"No worries," said the punter. "I'll bet you $500 that you've got red jocks. That's a sure bet for a start."

The banker could hardly believe his ears, and slapping the money on the counter he said: "You're on."

"Okay, drop your trousers so I can check," said the punter.

"Not here," said the banker, "come into my office."

Once inside the banker said, "there you are, they are definitely not red."

"Not good enough," said the punter, "they look red to me, but I will take an unbiased opinion. Your friend Charlie

161

Smithers is out in the lobby. Call him in and I'll accept his opinion."

When Charlie came in the punter asked, "what d'yer think, Charlie?" But Charlie had fainted.

"What's up with him?" asked the manager.

"Oh, I bet him $1000 I'd have your trousers off before 10 this morning."

* * *

CHARLIE the conman was usually broke so the barman was wary. "You don't get a drink until I see the money on the bar," he said.

"But I know you to be a sporting man," said Charlie. "I'll bet you the price of a pint that my dick's longer than your cat's tail."

The barman couldn't resist a winning bet and quickly accepted. He also whipped out a measuring rule and checked both items.

"You lose, Charlie, by a good two inches, now beat it."

"Hang on," said the conman, "tell me, from where did you begin measuring the cat's tail?"

"From its arse of course," said the barman.

"Well, would you mind giving me the same courtesy?"

* * *

SHE was an attractive barmaid so he slapped a fiver on the bar and said: "Betcha I can keep an eye on my beer while I go to the loo." She knew the loo was outside and around the corner, so she slapped down a fiver and said. "You're on."

He took out his glass eye, placed it beside the glass and went outside. When he came back he collected the money.

"Betcha I can bite my own ear," he said, thumping another fiver on the bar.

"You're on," she said.

He took out his false teeth, nipped his ear lobe and once again scooped up the money.

He made a circle with the thumb and index finger of his left hand. "Betcha I can poke my head through this."

She looked at the size of hole, shook her head and slammed another fiver on the bar.

With his right index finger he poked his forehead, through the hole made by his left hand, and collected.

"Okay, a chance to get your money back," he said. "Betcha I can make love to you so tenderly that you won't even feel it."

Now that's one thing she did know about. "You're on," she said, and down went another fiver.

He jumped the bar, moved behind her and lifted her skirt.

"I can feel that. I tell you I can feel it," she said.

"Oh well," he mumbled as he shrugged his shoulders and humped away, "win some...lose some."

* * *

A VARIATION on the same joke goes through the glass eye and false teeth routine with the gambler taking the money from, this time, a barman.

"Now I'll give you a chance to win some money back," he says. "Betcha I can pee into the neck of a beer bottle while its rolling along the bar. Betcha a fiver."

The barman could hardly believe the bet but the gambler insisted he could do it, provided the neck of the bottle faced him as it rolled along the bar.

"You're on," said the barman, and laid a bottle on the bar.

"Hang on," said the gambler, "let me get ready," and he lined up opposite the bottle, unzipped his fly, took his weapon in both hands and said, "okay, let it roll."

The barman gave the bottle a push and as it rolled along the bar the gambler shuffled sideways, keeping pace, but with lamentable aim failed to get a single drop in the bottle and ended up piddling along the entire length of the bar.

"Hopeless," said the barman, "the fiver's mine."

"Yes," said the gambler, "five for you, but I collect fifty

each from those three blokes who bet I couldn't piss all over your bar and get away with it."

* * *

PUNTER Pete had won $500 at the trots and went straight to the pub with his mates. He woke next afternoon with a hangover and less than a fiver in his pockets.

He went back to the same pub that evening.

"Tell me," he asked the barman, "was I in here last night?"

"You sure were," he replied. "You shouted drinks all round and we had a hell of a time."

"Thank goodness for that," said Punter Pete, "I thought I'd squandered it."

* * *

THE doctor told the gambler he had some bad news and some good news.

"The bad news is that you have a disease which kills nine out of ten."

"Hell," said the gambler, "then what's the good news?"

"The past nine patients I have treated have all died," said the doc.

* * *

THE big gamblers in the casino had gathered around a rather large dice game. An attractive woman in a long fur coat picked the precise time to flash it open to reveal she was nude, at the same time shouting, "I've won, I've won!"

She scooped up the chips and walked away leaving everybody dumbfounded by this sensational event.

"What was her score?" asked the manager later.

"I don't know," said the croupier, "I wasn't looking at the dice."

* * *

WHEN he got to the tote window a little voice in his ear said: "Put it all on number six."

He did, and it came in at 100 to one.

When he fronted the window for the second race a little voice in his ear said: "Put the lot on number 13."

He did and it romped home by a street.

When he pushed ten thousand over the counter at the tote window for the third race a little voice said: "Put it all on number nine."

He did and it ran stone motherless last, and the little voice in his ear said: "Oh well. Win some, lose some."

GARDENERS

GERALD the gardener was surprised when the lady of the house called him in one morning. He was even more astonished when she took him by the hand up the stairs and into her bedroom where she dropped her housegown and took the startled man to bed.

After a delightful session she took him downstairs, gave him a five dollar note and made him a cup of coffee.

When the shock had eased and Gerald was half way through his coffee he summoned the gumption to ask why.

"Oh, it's Christmas you know," said her ladyship. "I asked my grumpy husband last night what should we give the gardener and he replied: 'Oh fuck him. Give him a fiver.' The coffee was my own idea," she said.

* * *

"ARE you a gardening expert?" asked the small girl when the visiting neighbour was seated in the lounge.

"No Mary I'm not. What makes you think that?"

"Mum says if there is any dirt about you'll dig it up!"

* * *

THE gardener had taken on a new apprentice who was told to mow the lawn. The lad gave a yank on the starter cord and it roared off across the green, through a garden bed and straight into the swimming pool with the lad hanging on like grim death.

The apprentice failed to surface.

After a while the gardener ambled over to the pool and looked in. There was the lad on the bottom pulling at the starter cord over and over again.

"What a fuck-wit," said the gardener, then cupping his hands he shouted at the top of his voice: "More choke! More choke!"

* * *

WHEN the Minister for Prisons visited the low security prison he was impressed by the farm and gardens.

"Oh, that's Old Tom's work." explained the governor. "He's an expert gardener, makes the farm self-sufficient, and his flowers always win first prizes at the horticultural shows."

The Minister was intrigued and sought Tom out. He found him in the gardener's shed which Tom had built himself and which was stocked with books on horticulture, literature and art.

"You really shouldn't be in here, Tom," said the Minister.

"That's what I've been telling them for years," said Tom. He explained that the loss of legal papers concerning his case was the only complication keeping him there.

"First thing on Monday morning I will start the process to get your immediate release," said the Minister. He shook his hand and turned to leave.

That's when he was hit fair square on the back of the head with half a red brick. Tom had thrown it. "You won't forget, will you?" he asked.

GAYS

CECIL said it was true. Your entire life flashes before your eyes when you have gone down on for the third time.

* * *

I'LL be buggered if I'll join the British Conservative Party.

THE definition of an Aussie queer is a bloke who prefers girls to beer.

* * *

AT prison muster one lag said: "I think my cell mate is becoming a queer."

"How can you tell?"

"He shuts his eyes when I kiss him goodnight."

* * *

THEY were leaning on the bar. "Have you ever slept with a gay?"

"Certainly not. But I once slept with a bloke who had."

* * *

PUT the anal back into analysis.

* * *

A HUSBAND and wife were having a rowdy domestic argument in the pub. Observing the disturbance one gay said to his partner, "See. I told you those mixed marriages were no good."

* * *

WITH gay marriages being recognised in America it follows that divorces will be recognised as Gay Abandon.

* * *

GAY pride is a group of homosexual lions.

* * *

CYRIL sauntered into the Interflora shop.

"Is it true that you send flowers abroad?" he asked.

"Yes," was the reply.

"Oh goody, then send me to London, I'm a pansy."

* * *

A CHAP went to the doctor because he had a pain in the bum.

"No wonder," said the doc. "You've got a bunch of roses jammed up there."

"Really?" said the patient excitedly. "Who are they from? Can you read the card?"

DAISIES of the world unite.

You have nothing to lose but your chains.

* * *

AN alligator walked into a menswear shop.

"Do you have any shirts with little faggots on the pocket?" he said.

* * *

A GAY masochist is a sucker for punishment.

* * *

TWO very contented Irish gays were Thomas Fitzpatrick and Patrick Fitzthomas.

* * *

A NEW Gay Club in the Italian quarter of the city is called Innuendo.

* * *

THE new card game at the Gay Club is called camp poker.

Queens are wild and straights don't count.

* * *

OVER the years a lawyer became concerned that his son was doing poorly at university. Each year his marks seemed to be worse so the lawyer eventually rang the dean.

"Well, I have good news and I have bad news," said the dean. "Your son has failed most of his exams because he is a blatant homosexual."

"Good God," said the lawyer, "then what is the good news?"

"He's been voted Queen of the May," said the dean.

* * *

THERE was an airline steward whose colleagues considered him a sexual pervert. He went out with women.

* * *

IF horseracing is the sport of kings,

drag-racing is the sport of queens.

* * *

AS a football coach Cecil was in great demand by teams who wanted to know how to win by coming from behind.

THERE was a gay guy who was so ugly he had to go out with girls.

* * *

WHY are there so many queers in the British aristocracy?
Have you seen their women?

* * *

CECIL the ballet star was relating the day's exciting event to his room mate. A society matron had stopped her car, offered him a lift and driven him to her apartment.

"Then she took all her clothes off and said I could have anything I wanted."

"How exciting, what did you do?"

"I took the car. None of her clothes suited me."

* * *

OLD fairies never die. They merely blow away.

* * *

A JEWISH lawyer looked so despondent that his close friend asked him why. "I have just learned that my son is homosexual," he said. But then he added, "but the situation could be worse. He is in love with a Harley St doctor."

* * *

HOW did it feel when you first discovered you were a homosexual?

It was quite a blow.

* * *

DID you hear about the girl whose bloke didn't drink, didn't swear and never made a pass at her?

He also made his own dresses.

* * *

FRED says he loves women so much he thinks he must be a lesbian.

* * *

BI-SEXUALS have twice as many friends.

And it doubles your chance of a date on Saturday night.

WHEN we drink to the Dear Old Queen
   Save a drop for the Queer Old Dean

                    *   *   *

UP before the court on a charge of sodomy it was mentioned in evidence that the more passive of the partners was a member of town's philharmonic orchestra.

"Case dismissed," said the judge.

"Why?" asked the prosecutor.

"I have heard them play," said the judge "and I can tell you they all need fucking."

                    *   *   *

WHEN two judges found they were gay they decided to try each other.

                    *   *   *

HE told his psychiatrist he suffered from anxiety because he thought he was gay.

"What makes you think that?"

"Because my father was a poof."

"Well the condition is not hereditary," said the shrink.

"My brother is a poof," insisted the patient.

"Well that doesn't mean you are."

"And my Uncle Cecil...and my cousin Walter."

"Heck," said the doctor, "doesn't anyone in your family have sexual contact with women?"

"Yes," said the patient, "My sister does."

                    *   *   *

TWO words that will clear the gent's room, even at the interval break at the theatre.

"N-i-i-ice dick!"

                    *   *   *

THE old actor said the queers in town were the ugliest he had ever encountered. "But then, buggers can't be choosers," he said.

                    *   *   *

TWO old boys met at the club after years apart. "How's your son making out in life?" asked one.

"Oh he's the top car salesman of a nationwide franchise. Going so well he topped the sales chart and they gave him a brand new Mercedes," said the proud father. "But he gave it away. Can you imagine that, gave it away."

"That's amazing," said the other old chap. "My son's in real estate and development. Clinched the biggest deal on the Gold Coast and they gave him a penthouse, but he gave it away. Can you imagine that?"

Right then a third old boy came in. "How's your son?" they asked him.

"Bit disappointing really," he said. "He's turned out to be a raving poofter. But still, he's managing quite well. One of his best friends gave him a Mercedes last week, and another gave him a penthouse."

* * *

THE publican was considering hiring a barman who had just been sacked from the pub next door. He was fired because he had his hand in the till, was often late and was suspected of being gay.

"I'll take you on," said the publican, "but you had better not be one cent short and never late. Now give me a kiss and get to work."

* * *

THE Odd Couple, Cecil and Cyril, went to Sydney for a holiday and saw all the boats in Circular Quay.

"What are they?" asked Cyril.

"They are ferry boats," he said.

"Gracious. Don't tell me we have our own Navy now?"

* * *

THE Odd Couple, Cecil and Cyril, had lived together for years and were fixed in their ways.

"Has the newsboy come yet?" called Cyril one evening.

"No, but his eyes are glazing over," came the reply.

* * *

THE travelling salesman's car had broken down and he had

staggered for miles to the proverbial farmhouse. He finally stuggled to the porch and knocked on the door.

The farmer said the salesman was welcome to food and water and he could stay the night. "But I must warn you, I don't have any daughters for I am a bachelor," he said.

"Oh gawd," said the salesman, "how far to the next farm?"

*   *   *

THEN there was the Scottish gay, Ben Doon.

He was found in the bush with nothing but an old Mackintosh on him.

*   *   *

AND the Greek soldier who re-enlisted because he didn't want to leave his mate's behind.

*   *   *

IN the days of the Roman Empire many Romans thought that sex was a pain in the arse.

*   *   *

WHY are there so many gays in Italy?

If you were brought up with so many ugly woman what else could you be?

*   *   *

TWO fellows in a gay bar had a misunderstanding.

They went outside and exchanged blows.

*   *   *

DARREN was in the mood for the Gay Mardi Gras.

"I want to eat, drink and be Mary," he said.

*   *   *

THE Gay Lib recruiting vehicle was seen patrolling the red light district. One couldn't miss it. It was mauve in colour with registration plate: RU 1-2.

*   *   *

A GAY lad who came from Yeppoon

Took a lesbian up to his room.

They argued a lot
About who would do what
And how and with which and to whom.

GERMANS

NEAR the conclusion of World War 2 Hitler's valet told him that the gossip around the ranks was that he should make an appearance at the front line.

"I have laid out your red tunic," said the valet, "because Napoleon used to wear red in battle so that nobody knew if he was wounded and bleeding."

"Indeed," said Hitler. "In that case get my brown trousers."

* * *

HITLER was depressed and consulted his clairvoyant about his future. The mystic studied her crystal ball for some time without a word, for all the prospects were grim.

Finally, she said: "At least you will die on a Jewish holiday."

"Which Jewish holiday?"

"No matter. Any day you die will be a Jewish holiday."

* * *

IT is odd that the German police have been unable to catch the Nazis, particularly when they were so efficient when they were the Nazis.

* * *

THE Lufthansa flight was about to take off and the captain's voice was heard:

"You vill now fasten your safety belts. And I vant to hear just vun click. Not clickety-clickety click."

GOLF

A WOMAN golfer staggered in to the pro shop to complain she had been stung by a wasp.

The pro looked concerned, "Where?" he asked.

"Between the first and second hole," she said.

"Gawd, you must have a wide stance," he said.

*   *   *

FRED seemed off his game. He was morose and sulky. By the fifth tee his partner said, "What the hell's the matter with you, Fred?"

"It's Madge, my wife. Ever since she has taken up golf she has cut my sex down to only twice a week."

"Think yourself bloody lucky," said his partner. "I know some blokes she has cut out altogether!"

*   *   *

THE pro was teaching the young woman the proper stance. He moved behind her and reached around to show her the right grip but the movement of a few practice swings hooked the zipper of his fly to the rear zipper of her skirt. They were stuck fast in a very embarrassing position.

They were moving together towards the clubhouse when a large sheep dog threw a bucket of water over them.

*   *   *

TWO golfers were enjoying a drink at the 19th when one confided in the other that his wife was making it difficult for him to get to the course every Saturday.

"Nothing to it, old boy," said his mate.

"Every Saturday morning I roll back the bedclothes and say, 'intercourse, or golf course'? It works like a charm."

*   *   *

THE club officials were called to the fifth tee where three men were fighting. A fourth lay dead in a bunker.

When they quietened them down they got an explanation.

"That's my partner there in the bunker," said one man. "He had a stroke and these two bastards want to add it to my score."

GOLF was invented in Scotland and there are still clubs there that have signs on the course which read: Members will Refrain from Picking Up Lost Balls Until they have Stopped Rolling."

* * *

THE blonde secretary noticed a couple of golf balls on the boss's desk. "What are those things?" she asked.

"They're golf balls," he said.

The following Monday she noticed two more golf balls on his desk.

"Oh I see you shot another golf over the weekend," she said.

* * *

TWO businessmen took time from the office to play a round of golf during their lunch break but were hampered by two women playing ahead and slowing up their game.

Finally one said, "Listen Jack, I"ll go and ask them if they mind if we play through."

He had only gone a hundred metres before he turned and hurried back. He was visibly shaken. "Jack, you won't believe this," he said, "but those two women...one is my wife and the other is my mistress."

Jack was a cool hand. "Listen Reg," he said. "Keep your head down while I approach them and we'll sneak past."

Jack had only gone a hundred metres when he turned back. "Listen Reg, you won't believe this ..." he began.

* * *

HE was a pro with a great ability to teach the game but some argued that he over-corrected faults. Like the young woman who wanted tuition in correcting a terrific slice she had developed. He worked on her for two weeks, now she's the biggest hooker in the club.

* * *

FRED said during his last game of golf he stepped on a rake.

"They were the best two balls I hit all day!"

ONE of the club officials, a stickler for the rules, noted a golfer shaping up to drive off at least half a metre the wrong side of the tee marker.

"Excuse me," he said, "in this club we frown on anyone trying to gain advantage by not driving off from behind the tee marker."

"So do I," said the golfer. "But this is my second shot."

* * *

OLD Ponsonby arrived at the club to find the only person present was a leggy blonde. "I wouldn't mind playing a round with her," he thought (but that's not the joke).

They teamed up together and as he hit the first drive down the fairway she said: "That's terrific, considering your handicap."

"Oh, there's more to it than that, love," said Ponsonby. "I've got a wooden arm."

"Get away, I don't believe it," she said.

And straight away he proved it by rolling up his sleeve and screwing his arm off.

At the next fine drive she said: "That's terrific considering your handicap."

"More to it than that, love," he said. "I've got a wooden leg."

"Get away," she said in disbelief, but to demonstrate, he rolled up his trouser leg and screwed his leg off.

The next driving shot was equally splendid and she said: "That's terrific considering your handicaps."

"There's more to it than that, love," said Ponsonby, "I've got a wooden heart."

She gasped incredulously. "Nobody has a wooden heart," she said.

He began to unbutton his shirt, had second thoughts, then said: "Just come behind this bush and I'll show you."

It was the foursome playing behind who caught up, looked over the bush, and saw Ponsonby screwing his heart out!

FUNNY how man blames fate for all accidents, yet claims full responsibility for a hole in one.

* * *

QUESTION on golf etiquette: What do you do when your opponent claims to have found his ball in the rough, and you know he is a liar because you've got it in your pocket?

* * *

THEY called it golf because all the other four-letter words were already taken.

SHE always wears two pair of pants to golf, in case she gets a hole in one.

* * *

HIS drive from the third tee sliced to the left of the fairway and the ball ended in an impossible lie in front of the greenkeeper's tractor shed.

His wife summed up the situation. "No need to take a penalty shot, darling," she said. "Just open the doors of the garage, push the tractor out, open the rear doors, and with a number three wood you could hit straight through the shed."

"Brilliant, darling," he said.

He took a mighty whack but the ball hit the rear of the building, cannoned back and struck his wife stone dead.

The following day he was playing the same hole and by sheer coincidence landed at the same place in front of the shed.

"No need to take a penalty shot," said the caddie, "we can push the tractor out and open both sets of doors. You can hit straight through the shed."

"No way," he said. "I tried that yesterday and ended up with a double bogey."

GORILLAS

A GORILLA left the zoo's reading room quite confused.

He had read the Bible and Charles Darwin's Origin of the Species and didn't know if he was his brother's keeper or his keeper's brother.

*   *   *

SISTER Anastasia wandered away from her party at the zoo to take a second look at the gorilla. Actually, she leant too close to read his name and the brute reached out, grabbed her by the habit, pulled her through the bars and had his wicked way with her.

She was in such a state of shock that it was seven days before the other nuns could visit her in hospital.

"How do you feel?" they asked in chorus.

"How do you think I feel?" she replied. "It's been a week and he hasn't written, he hasn't phoned ..."

*   *   *

AFTER contacting every other zoo in the world Taronga Park realised that it possessed the last of a species; a female gorilla. It called for desperate measures as an international search for a male mate had failed. So as a last resort an advertisement was lodged for a surrogate to do the job for the sum of $5000.

Paddy was the only applicant.

"Oi'll be taking t' job on t'ree conditions," he said.

"Foist, oi be wanting a curtain across the cage for proivacy, loik.

"Second, Oill be wanting any off-spring raised in t' true faith.

"And t'oid, about the money. Can Oi be paying it off in instalments?"

*   *   *

IT was a month after World War 3 had devastated the earth. Not a human being survived. Indeed a battered and dazed chimpanzee had wandered for weeks through what was left of the smouldering jungle without seeing another living thing.

178

One day the chimp saw something move behind the rubble. He was delighted to find it was another chimp, and a female at that.

He rushed up and embraced her, but she pushed him away. "No. Don't let's start all that over again," she said.

GRAFFITI

GRAFFITI should be obscene and not heard.

* * *

AYATOLLAH Khomeini is a Shiite.

* * *

ORAL sex is a matter of taste.

* * *

EUNUCHS Unite! You have nothing to lose.

* * *

YOU can tell the sex of a chromosome by taking down its genes.

* * *

ROSES are red, Violets are blue and Jean isn't wearing any.

* * *

SADO-Masochism means not having to say you are sorry.

* * *

IF you feel strongly about graffiti, sign a partition.

* * *

LIFE is a sexually transmitted disease.

* * *

I CHOKED Linda Lovelace.

* * *

UNTIL I discovered women I thought love was a pain in the arse.

* * *

LOWER the age of puberty.

* * *

WAKE up to insomnia.

GREEKS

WHEN a Greek kid asked his dad what an IQ meant, Nick explained: "When your IQ is over 120 you are very intelligent, when it's around 100 your are average, when it is down below 50 you are bloody stupid. You wouldn't be able to tie your show laces."

"Is this why Australians wear thongs?" asked the kid.

* * *

THE Greek businessman went to his favourite taverna in Carlton and was surprised to be served by a Vietnamese waiter who spoke perfect Greek.

When paying his bill to Con the proprietor he raised the point. "How come the waiter speaks perfect Greek?" he asked Con.

"Ssh! Don't mention it. He thinks it's English."

* * *

THE Greek taverna and the Chinese take-away were side by side and each Friday morning the two owners would sweep the pavement.

Con the Greek would take the opportunity to have his little joke: "What day is it today, Charlie?"

"It's Fliday," the Chinaman would reply, and Con would roll about laughing.

Each week it was the same and Con would even get some friends to come along and listen to Charlie say "Fliday."

It got on Charlie's wick. So he went along for elocution lessons and concentrated on "Friday, Friday, Friday."

Next morning he was waiting for the big showdown, sweeping a clean pavement for ten minutes before Con appeared.

"What day is it today, Charlie," grinned Con.

"It's Friday ... you Gleek plick!"

* * *

WHEN near-sighted Doreen saw Papadopoulos she thought he was a Greek God.

Now that she's had her eyes fixed he lookes like a Goddamned Greek.

* * *

A GREEK truck-driver had just carried a large sack of potatoes up six flights of stairs.

"That will be seven bucks, lady," he said.

Smiling, the woman let her robe slip open. "Wouldn't you like some of this instead?" she said.

"I'll have to see my partner," said the driver, "already this morning we have screwed away ten cases of bananas, 20 kilograms of tomatoes and seven sacks of potatoes."

GYNAECOLOGISTS

THEY called him the conscientious gynaecologist.

Even on his holidays he looked up his old girlfriends.

* * *

THE gallant gynaecologist liked to keep his patients happy: "I'll be at your cervix, madam," he would quip as he invited them to lie on the couch.

And his regular patients would reply: "I am dilated for you to see me."

* * *

THE gynaecologist was also a home handyman. He not only wall-papered the hallway, but he did it through the front door letter box.

* * *

AFTER many years in the practice he described himself as a spreader of old wives' tails.

* * *

AND the deaf gynaeocologist was able to read lips.

H

HEALTH

THERE is a clear difference between cholesterol and fat.

You can hardly wake up in the morning with half a cholesterol.

* * *

THE hypochondriac lift driver was a worrier.

He kept thinking he was coming down with something.

* * *

SHE asked the doctor: "What's the best thing to take when you are run down?"

"The number of the bastard who hit you," he said.

* * *

AT the clinic the nurse asked Lulu, "When did you have your last check-up?"

"Never have," said Lulu. "A Pole and a Ukranian, but never a Czech."

* * *

A MAN went to the health clinic with green balls.

The doctor examined the emerald knackers and said, "Have you ever heard of cauliflower ears?"

"Yes," said the patient.

"Well you have got brothel sprouts."

HISTORY

SIR FRANCIS Drake circumcised the world and did it with a hundred-foot clipper.

* * *

NAPOLEON came home tired and weary, wet and wounded, and went straight round to Josephine's flat. He was shocked to find a pair of large gum boots on her front doorstep.

"Josephine! Josephine!" he called out. "What are those rubber boots doing out here?"

"They're not rubber boots," said Josie. "They're Wellington's"

HONEYMOONS
See NEWLY-WEDS

THE new bride was a little embarrassed to bring up the matter of sex, so the groom explained it delicately, yet with authority.

"No need to talk about it, Muriel,"he said. "These are the rules. When you need it just give it a tug three times. When you dont need it just give it a tug 395 times."

* * *

THE morning after their first night he awoke to find his bride crying.

"What's up darling?" he said. "Didn't you enjoy our bridal night?"

"Yes," she sobbed, "but look at it. We've used it all up in one night."

* * *

MISS Fauntleroy-Jones was nearing her use-by date and was finally unloaded from the aristocratic but bankrupt family. On her wedding night she entered the bedroom wearing a sheer nightgown and long white gloves.

"You look lovely dear," said the groom. "but why the white gloves?"

"Because I understand that on these occasions one is expected to handle the filthy thing," she said.

* * *

RUSHING naked from the bathroom to the bedroom, Fred tripped on the rug and pole-vaulted out the window.

* * *

THE honeymoon couple was playing deck quoits on the cruise ship when they suddenly got the urge and rushed to their cabin.

A case of quoitus interruptus.

* * *

THEY began to undress and she got the shock of her life to see he had no toes on his right foot. She thought it was a shocking deformity and grabbed her clothes, jumped in her car and fled home.

In tears she rushed into her mother's kitchen.

"But I told you about the birds and the bees," said her mother. "You knew what to expect. Couldn't he get it up?"

"Oh, it's not that," she sobbed, "when he stripped off he only had half a foot."

Mum chucked the tea towel at her. "That's much better than your father's. Here, you finish the dishes. I'll be back in the morning."

* * *

IT was the first night of their honeymoon and they had booked sleepers on a night train. But somehow they had been assigned top bunks on opposite sides of the corridor.

During the night the bridegoom whispered, "Come on over."

"I can't reach," she said.

"Here, look at this," he said, "poking a very erect donger through the curtains, "grab it and haul yourself over."

A voice from the lower bunk piped up: "And how the hell will she get back?"

HORSES

A HORSE was playing his first cricket match and was slogging sixes all over the ground. Then his partner took the strike, hit a single and dashed up the wicket but the horse just stood there.

"Run," he yelled, "run you bastard," he yelled at the horse.

"If I could run I wouldn't be playing bloody cricket," said the horse, "I'd be at the race track."

* * *

THE trainer was giving last minute instructions to the jockey and appeared to slip something in the horse's mouth just as a steward passed by.

"What was that?" inquired the steward.

"Oh, nothing," said the trainer, "just a Mintie." He offered one to the steward. "Here, have one. And I'll have one myself."

After the suspicious steward left the scene the trainer continued with his riding instructions. "Just keep the horse on the rails. You are on a certainty. The only thing that could possibly pass you down the straight is either the steward or me."

HOSPITALS

See DOCTORS

THERE is a sign in the toilet of the Sex Change Clinic.

It reads "We may never piss this way again."

* * *

THE young intern said to the nurse, "That bloke in bed 15. He's got WOG tattooed on his penis. True, take a look if you get the chance."

Meeting her later in the day he said "Did you see that tattoo?"

"Yes," said the nurse. "But it's not WOG, it's Woollongong!"

*   *   *

DID you hear about the clumsy surgeon who was performing a vasectomy? He missed and got the sack.

*   *   *

TWO nurses were climbing back into the dormitory window, trying to sneak in as quietly as possible when one said, "This makes me feel like a burglar."

"Me too," said the other, "but where would we find two burglars at this time of night?"

*   *   *

THEN there was the time the nurses' dormitory caught fire. It took the firemen 15 minutes to put the fire out. And it took the nurses three hours to put the firemen out.

*   *   *

DOCTOR: "How's that man who swallowed the fifty cent piece?"

Nurse: "Still no change."

HOTELS
See PUBS

IT was a small hotel like Fawlty Towers and Fred was half way through his meal when he called the manager.

"Look at this spaghetti," he complained, "there is a hair in it. So I am not paying for it." He left the table.

Later that night the manager found Fred with his head down between the legs of one of the hotel house maids and couldn't resist the jibe: "I see you don't mind a bit of hair now."

Fred lifted his head. "No I don't. But if I find any spaghetti down here I'm not paying for it either."

*   *   *

ALL hotel rooms have a copy of the Gideon Bible as a comfort to travellers and it was natural for the tub-thumping evangelist to reach for it and thumb through a few pages before going downstairs for a nightcap before retiring.

He soon engaged the barmaid in conversation and was still chatting her up at closing time when she even agreed to come to his room where, after another drink, they adjourned to the cot.

"Should we be doing this?" she giggled as she undressed, "after all, you are a man of the cloth."

"I assure you it is alright. It is written in the Bible," he said, dropping his trousers.

During her post-coitus cigarette, a very reflective time for women, she said to the Bible-basher: "Show me the passage which it says we should have done what we did?"

The evangelist picked up the Bible and turned to the fly-leaf to show her the quote: "The barmaid downstairs is a certainty."

* * *

NEXT at the reception desk was a newly married couple.

"Bridal suite?" he asked discreetly.

"No," she giggled, "I'll just hang on to your ears."

* * *

YOU can tell what kind of a hotel it was.

I left a call for seven in the morning; and woke up with seven blondes in my room.

HUNTERS

EACH day on safari the two hunters pulled on their heavy boots for trekking through the jungle. But there came a day when one bloke pulled on a pair of running shoes.

"What for?" asked his mate in the heavy boots.

"There is a man-eating tiger in these parts."

"But you won't out run a tiger in those."

"Don't have to," said the smartie. "I just have to be faster than you."

A HUNTER had been tracking a huge bear and finally had him in his sights. He fired a shot and then bounded through the bush to where he expected to find the carcase. To his dismay there was no dead bear. To his horror he was tapped on the shoulder by a very live one.

"I am sick of being shot at by you bloody hunters," said the bear. "I'm going to teach you a lesson. So get down on your knees and give me a blow job. Now!"

The terrified hunter did as he was told.

But next day the hunter returned with a bigger gun and spent hours waiting to ambush the bear. Finally he sighted him again, blasted away and dashed forward to where the dead bear should have been. Nothing.

Once more he received the terrifying tap on the shoulder. "You know the ritual," said the bear. "Down you go."

The infuriated hunter returned the following day with yet a bigger and more accurate gun. This time he stalked closer and let go with both barrels.

He ran into the clearing only to find the very alive bear waiting for him once more.

"Okay, let's have the truth," said the bear, "you are not in this for the hunting are you?"

* * *

MURPHY knew nothing about the wild when he went on his first hunting trip. He walked into a clearing and was surprised to find a young woman lying there in the nude.

"Pardon me," said Murphy, "are you game?"

She looked him up and down and said, "Yes."

So he shot her.

* * *

THE major came home from a hunting trip to spot his wife being humped by a bounder under the oak tree on the front lawn.

In a rage he asked his batman for his rifle and took steady aim.

"Do the sporting thing, sir," said the batman, "shoot him on the rise."

HUSBANDS

A HUSBAND? That's what's left of a lover after the name has been extracted.

* * *

A HUSBAND? That's a gardener who gets to sleep with the boss of the manor.

* * *

USUALLY the husband regards himself as the head of the household, and the pedestrian knows he has the right of way. Both of them are safe until they try to prove it.

* * *

FRED was admitting his great blunder of the previous night. "I must have been legless. So drunk I don't remember leaving here," he confided to Charlie at the bar.

"But I woke up in a bed, with a woman next to me, so I automatically gave her twenty bucks."

"And you don't remember getting your money's worth? Is that why you're sad?" ventured Charlie.

"No," said Fred. "It was my wife and she automatically gave me ten bucks change!"

* * *

TWO blokes were discussing their sex life in the pub.

"We've gone stale on it," said one, "my wife doesn't move and to tell you the truth it has become boring."

His mate gave him some advice. "I went through that stage," he said. "But you have to jazz it up. I buy my wife a bottle of champagne and supply her with some sexy gear then rip it off her every night. Then we screw on the lounge room floor. You ought to try that."

Next week they met again.

"Did you take my advice?"

189

"Sure did. Sex is great now, and I just love your lounge room carpet."

HYGIENE

WHEN Fred asked for two pies and some dimsims at the local take-away he was impressed to see Luigi using tongs to place the food in the bag.

"Yes, sir," said Luigi responding to Fred's comments, "we are very clean here. Always use tongs. No hands ever touch the food."

As Fred turned to leave he noticed a piece of string hanging from Luigi's fly and asked its purpose.

"All part of the hygiene program," said Luigi. "When I go to the toilet I simply pull it out with the string. Not touched with human hands."

Fred was about to leave when the obvious question prompted him. "How do you get it back?"

"With the tongs," said Luigi.

* * *

THE health inspector was aghast to see the pastrycook crimping the edge of the apple pie pastry with his set of false teeth.

"Haven't you got a tool for that?"

"Yes, but I save it for putting holes in the donuts," replied the pastrycook.

I

IMMIGRATION

LUIGI hadn't been long in the country, but urged on by his friends and family he made an application for citizenship and presented himself before the tribunal.

He was nervous. "Yer honor, I not speeka good Eenglish cos I no beena in this country not long. Maybe I no getta my papers because I talka like theese?"

The judge said: Donjoo worry, yousa gonna get yousa papers."

* * *

LUIGI was digging a trench by himself on one side of the street while the rest of the road gang worked together on the other.

He finally asked the foreman why he was alone.

"You've got bad breath," was the answer.

"And so would you if you kissed as many politicians' arses as I had to to emmigrate here."

* * *

AN enterprising young woman working the docks in New York established her own immigration office in the back seat of her car where she would give newcomers a hand job.

She was officially the Yanker and for $10 her clients became the Yankees.

191

INDIANS

GENERAL Custer's last words: "I'll never understand these bloody Indians. Just a minute ago they were singing and dancing!"

* * *

THE little Navajo brave asked his father why the members of his tribe had such unusual names like Running Deer, Brown Eagle, Red Wolf and Flying Cloud.

"You see son," began his dad. "We Navajos name our children after the first thing we see after conception. Why do you ask, Broken Rubber?"

* * *

BIG Chief Sitting Bull had a daughter he called Ninety-nine Cents because she was always just under a buck.

* * *

WHILE driving through outback America a woman's car ran out of petrol. However she was delighted when a strong young Indian offered her a lift to the gas station on his horse.

She sat behind him and was intrigued with his habit of letting out a wild yell every so often. Must be one of those Indian whoops, she thought.

When she alighted at the gas station he rode off with yet another "Ya-hoo!"

"What were you two doing?" asked the gas station owner.

"Nothing," she said. "I simply rode behind him with my arms around his sides hanging on to the saddle horn," she said.

"Don't you know Indians ride bareback," he said.

* * *

BIG Chief Running Bear's warriors were soundly defeated by General Custer's army and after the council of war the chief had to report to his tribe.

"Good news and bad news," he said. "The bad news is that the paleface army have routed our warriors, wrecked our camps and destroyed our crops and buffalo herds. We will have nothing to eat through the winter but buffalo turds."

"Hell, what's the good news," piped up one brave.

"We have great stacks of buffalo turds," said the chief.

* * *

IN the same valley lived the Fuk-ar-wee tribe.

They were a tribe of indians with very short legs who persisted in making camp in very tall grass and were noted for doing standing jumps and yelling: "We're the Fuk-ar-wee?"

INFIDELITY
See WARDROBES

"DO you cheat on your wife?"

"Who else?"

* * *

A SAILOR returned home to find his wife had been unfaithful.

"Damn it," he said, "was it Tom?"

"No," she said.

"Was it Dick?" he persisted.

"No."

"Was it my best friend, Harry?"

"No," she yelled, "don't you think I've got any friends of my own?"

* * *

"I WANT to divorce my husband," said the shapely blonde to her lawyer.

"On what grounds?" he asked.

"Infidelity," she said, "I don't think he's the father of my child."

* * *

FRED was relating the amazing experience to his mates at the bar. "Muriel was not too well this morning so I told her that instead of going to work I would stay and care for her.

"So I threw on Muriel's chenille bathrobe and was standing at the stove when the milkman comes in the backdoor behind me, slides his hand under the bathrobe and squeezes my bum.

"Can you imagine the coincidence," said Fred. "The milkman's wife has a chenille bathrobe exactly the same as Muriel's!"

* * *

"THIS suit was a surprise from my wife," said Fred.

"Really?" said his drinking mate.

"Yes, I came home unexpectedly one night and there it was, hanging on the end of the bed."

* * *

WHILE a husband and wife were asleep she had a big smile on her face because of an erotic dream involving another man. It was so real she began to murmer and said: "Look out darling, my husband is coming."

He leapt from the bed and jumped out the window.

* * *

THEY snuggled down in the stalls at the movies, but the woman in front was wearing a large hat which obstructed their view. He tapped her on the shoulder. She turned round and it was his wife.

* * *

AFTER an extremely wild party the hung-over couple were having a late breakfast.

"This is a little embarrassing," he said, "but was it you I made love to in the garden last night?"

"About what time?" she replied.

* * *

The husband came home and found his wife in bed with a strange man. The stranger was exhausted and was sprawled, nude and asleep.

The husband was outraged by the sight and reached into the wardrobe for his gun.

"Wait, darling," she said. "You know the red sports car

194

I drive? This man gave it to me. You know that brand new set of golf clubs I gave you last week? This man gave me the money. You know we have paid off the mortgage. This man supplied the finance..."

"For Chri'sake woman," said the husband, "cover him up so he doesn't catch cold."

* * *

FRED was trying to console his mate who had just found his wife in bed with another man.

"C'mon, Bert," he said, "it's not the end of the world."

"All right for you to say," said Bert, "but what if you came home one night and caught another man in bed with your wife?"

Fred pondered for a moment. "I'd break his white cane and kick his dog."

* * *

JOCK was in the habit of handing over his sealed pay envelope each week to his wife. But for the last three weeks she noticed that it had been opened and two dollars was missing.

Finally she confronted him: "Right, Jock, tell me straight," she said. "Who's the bit o' skirt you've been taking out these past three weeks?"

* * *

PADDY divulged the sad news to his mates at the bar. He already had eight kids and his sexy wife was once again in the puddin' club. "I swear I'll hang myself if this happens again," he said.

But it was no surprise, one year later, when Paddy announced that his wife was once again pregnant.

"You said you were going to hang yourself," one of his mates reminded him.

"Indeed I did," said Paddy, "indeed I got the rope and threw a loop over the branch of the apple tree. Then I thought, maybe I was hanging the wrong man."

FRED and Joe were talking over their old schooldays with a few drinks. Unfortunately, time got away and Fred had missed the last train.

Joe and his wife insisted he stay the night, but there was no spare bed and Fred would have to bunk in with the married couple.

As soon as Joe was snoring his wife tapped Fred on the shoulder and whispered an invitation.

"No way," said Fred. "Joe would kill me."

"When he has had a few beers like tonight nothing will wake him," the wife insisted.

Fred was still unconvinced.

"Look, pull a hair out of his bum. I'll bet he won't move."

Fred tentatively plucked a hair and, indeed, Joe never stirred.

So Fred threw the leg and enjoyed a quiet screw.

About 15 minutes later the wife tapped him on the shoulder again and whispered the same invitation. And once more Fred was scared about waking the sleeping husband. But again he pulled a hair to test if his old friend was asleep, then did the job.

This went on for much of the night until Joe finally raised himself on one elbow and muttered: "Listen Fred, I don't mind you screwing my wife, but for Chris'sake stop using my arse as a scoreboard."

*　*　*

WHEN Rachel found Isaac had a mistress she demanded to know why, and gave him hell until he explained.

"It's not that I don't love you, my dearest," said Isaac.

"What then?" pressed Rachel.

Finally Isaac admitted that Rachel had always been passive. "This woman moves. She expresses passion. She moans and groans with ecstasy," he said.

With Isaac's fortune in mind Rachel decided to play along. The next evening she enticed him into the cot with a bottle of champagne and new seductive underwear.

While Isaac was humping away she remembered the peculiarity of his mistress and this was the time to start moaning.

"Oh Isaac, vat a day I had today," she moaned, "first the washing machine broke down, then I was short-changed at the supermarket ..."

* * *

SHE had her suspicions about her husband, Fred, so when they had an invitation to a fancy dress party at the Smithsons' she conceived a plan to catch him.

When Fred was dressed in his gorilla suit ready to leave she feigned a headache, said she would stay home, but insisted Fred should go on without her.

Later she donned her own disguise and arrived at the party to see him flirting with every floozie at the party.

In her own masked outfit she approached him, whispered a seductive phrase in his ear and was surprised at the immediate response. He rushed her outside and gave her a passionate knee-trembler against a gum tree.

She resisted declaring who she was in an effort to get all the evidence possible.

Just before the unmasking at midnight she left the party and drove home, and next morning was all set to confront Fred with his infidelity.

"How was it at the Smithsons?" she asked at breakfast.

"Dullsville. Boring without you, darling," he said. "When I arrived I saw Ben and the Murphy brothers without partners so we went upstairs and played poker. I lent my gorilla suit to Harry Forbes. He said he had a wow of a time."

* * *

BIG Rastus came home early one day to find Lulu Belle lying on the bed. She was naked, except for a small wet towel on her thigh.

"What's going on?" asked Rastus suspiciously.

"Nothing," replied Lulu Belle, "just got a fever and lying in bed."

"What's dat towel doing there?"

"I dipped it in water to put on my brow, dat's all," she said.

Rastus pulled out his razor and began stropping it.

"What yo gonna do wit dat razor, honey?" she asked.

"If that towel dries out soft," said Rastus, "I'm gonna shave."

* * *

THE businessman kissed his wife at the usual time, got into his car and headed for the office.

He was half way there when he remembered his wallet and glasses were in his other suit.

He arrived back at his home to find his wife totally nude on the bed and the plumber standing beside the bed, also totally nude.

The plumber promptly went into a squatting position. "I'm glad you are here Mr Fotheringham," he said. "I was just explaining to your wife that if she doesn't pay the outstanding monies on our account I am going to shit on this floor."

* * *

COMING home at a quarter to three
I caught my wife cheating on me
I yelled: "Who's this fink?"
She replied with a wink:
"I dunno. He's a new one on me."

INSULTS

"OF course there is nobody else," she told her doubting boyfriend, "do you think I'd be sitting here with a dick-head like you if there were?"

* * *

THE sex session was a failure. He said: "You are so

unresponsive I wouldn't be surprised if you used cold cream between your legs."

She replied: "I wouldn't be surprised if you used vanishing cream between yours."

* * *

SHE raised herself on one elbow and snapped: "You are the world's most incompetent lover."

"I couldn't be," replied the husband, "that would be just too much of a coincidence."

* * *

McTAVISH was a bad loser. When he was cleaned out in a poker game for particularly high stakes he threw down his hand and stood to leave the table.

He couldn't resist insulting Dapper Dan, the bald gambler who had cleaned him out.

As McTavish walked past he ran his hand over Dan's bald head. "And your noggin feels just like my wife's bum," he said sarcastically.

Dan put his hand to his head. "By crikey, Mac," he said, "you're right, it does."

* * *

THE politician entered the doctor's surgery with a frog on his head.

"That's nasty," said the doctor.

"Bloody oath," said the frog. "It started as a pimple on my bum."

* * *

THE housewife inspected the three small tomatoes and was told by Tony the Fruiterer that they were 55 cents each.

"Well you know what you can do with them," she said. "You can stick them up you know where."

"I can't do that, lady," said Tony. "There is already a three dollar fifty water melon there."

* * *

THE vicar, while pouring the tea
    Once asked: "Do you fart when you pee?"

I replied with some wit:

"Do you fart when you shit?"

So the score was one up for me.

* * *

AN indignant lady approached the host of the party and said she was leaving. "Your wife has insulted me," she complained. "She told me I was a woman of the streets."

"Think nothing of it my dear," said the host, "I've been retired from the army for 15 years and she still calls me Colonel."

* * *

SHE said their neighbour must have taken offence at something as she hadn't been over for days.

"Be sure to find out what it was," he said, "and we'll try it on her again."

INSURANCE

FRED was delighted with his new job. He had just sold a life insurance policy for $100,000 and slapped the papers down on the boss's desk.

"Not bad," said the boss, "but you forgot one thing. You forgot the urine specimen for our doctors to examine. That's part of the deal. Remember it next time."

Fred took the rebuke on board and the following week he staggered into the office with two buckets of yellowish fluid.

"I've just sold a big group policy," he beamed.

* * *

MOISHE Leiberwitz was driving along a country road when he came across the scene of an accident. Beside an overturned car was a man covered in blood and groaning.

"Call the ambulance," moaned the injured man.

Moishe quickly surveyed the scene.

"You mean nobody has reported this accident yet?"

"No. It just happened. Get a doctor."

"You mean the police haven't arrived, the insurance people haven't arrived?"

"No."

"Then move over," said Moishe, "let me lie down beside you."

* * *

"DOES this policy have any death benefits?"

"Sure does. When you die you pay no more dues."

* * *

CHARLIE Rippoff had a leg broken in an accident and lodged a claim with the insurance company that he was crippled for life and confined to a wheelchair.

A smart lawyer got him $500,000 compensation.

The insurance company was suspicious. In fact they told Charlie he would not get away with it and that they were assigning an insurance detective to follow his every move.

"Good," said Charlie. "Then he might like to follow us on our world trip."

Charlie said his wife would accompany him and help with the wheelchair on a tour through the United States, then across to Europe and to London, Rome, Paris, "and then to Lourdes where your detective might witness one of the greatest miracles of modern times."

INTERPRETERS

WHAT do you call a brunette with a blonde on either side?

An interpreter.

* * *

WHEN the Godfather in Sicily realised that one of the family bosses in New York was fiddling the books he decided to deal with the matter himself.

As he couldn't speak English he took Luigi as an interpreter.

In New York the first of the suspects was led in and the Godfather put a pistol to his head.

"It wasn't me," he blubbered, "I swear by my mother's heart."

Luigi interpreted: "He says it wasn't him and he swears so by his mother's heart."

The second suspect was confronted with the pistol. He also protested his innocence and invoked the Pope as his witness. Luigi interpreted his denial.

The third suspect was brought in and with the pistol at his temple said: "Okay, I'm sorry. Please be merciful. The million dollars is in a suitcase under my bed upstairs."

"What did he say?" asked the Godfather.

Luigi replied: "He says he did it. He's spent the money and he bets you haven't the balls to pull the trigger!"

* * *

LITTLE Isaac was doing his homework.

"Dad, can you tell me what a vacuum is?" he asks.

"A vacuum, my son is a void."

"I know that," said the lad, "but vat's dat void mean?"

INVENTIONS

* * *

AFTER 15 years of research Dr Schlicker finally presented the Government Scientific Bureau with a cosmetic vaginal deodorant that smelt like oranges.

He received a swift reply: "When you can produce a cosmetic compound that makes oranges smell like fannies, then we're in business."

* * *

MY Ol Dad was an inventor and among his accomplishments were:

Water-proof tea bags.

Peddle wheelchairs.

Parachutes which open on impact.

L-shaped mobile homes.

The one-piece jigsaw puzzle.

An inflatable dartboard for campers.

An index for a dictionary.

Beer glasses with square bases that don't leave rings on the bar or tables.

* * *

AN innovative young scientist at the sperm bank has packaged their product in an aerosol can and labelled it Heir Spray.

* * *

THERE is a new patent medicine called Preparation A.

It is for video-game addicts who have asteroids.

* * *

HE invented a marvellous appliance for speeding up production in factories. He called it a whip.

* * *

IT was an Irishman who invented the toilet seat.

It was a Scot who figured out how to put a hole in it.

* * *

THE professor invented the perfect love potion.

It stopped your back from pegging out

and your peg from backing out.

And you had to swallow it quick or you got a stiff neck.

* * *

IT is not commonly known that the first timepiece was not invented by the Swiss but by the troops fighting for Alexander the Great.

It was back in the days when Alexander was conquering the world and his troops were fighting Persian hordes day after day with no double-time for weekends, definitely no overtime and no holiday pay. Indeed, no holidays.

Finally they got jack of it and formed the first soldiers' trade union.

The delegation fronted Alexander and told him bluntly that eight hours a day was enough sword wielding for anybody.

Alexander saw the point and agreed. But the Swiss had

not yet invented the watch and the problem was how to measure a regular work day.

Alexander himself came up with the answer. If all the troops tied a rag around their wrist and continued to chop away at the enemy, until the rag got damp with sweat, it was time to knock off.

That time-piece became known as Alexander's Rag Time Band.

IRISH

CLEANLINESS is next to Godliness.

But only in an Irish dictionary.

* * *

PADDY thought oral sex was just talking about it.

* * *

THE Irish maiden's prayer: "And now Dear Lord, please have Murphy on me."

* * *

PADDY and Shamus were walking along the pavement when Paddy suddenly grabbed Shamus by the arm.

"Look out," he said. "Mind where you're stepping. It looks like dog shit."

Paddy bent down and pushed it with his finger. "It feels like dog shit," he said.

He put his finger to his lips. "It tastes like dog shit. Shamus my friend I think it is definitely dog shit. Lucky we didn't step in it."

* * *

PADDY entered the bar and approached his mates with a handful of dog shit.

"Look what we nearly trod in," he said.

* * *

HOW do the Irish count bank notes?

One, two, tri, four, foive, another, another, another ...

THERE was a 10pm curfew in Belfast so the sergeant in charge of the patrol got a surprise when he heard a shot ring out at 9.30.

He was alarmed when he discovered Private Murphy had shot a man.

"Why did you do that?" demanded the sergeant.

"But that's O'Flannagan," said Murphy. "I know where he lives. He would never get home by 10pm."

* * *

RED Adair's fame in quelling oil rig fires stretches around the globe, so when a well in the middle of the Sahara Desert spewed smoke and flame the alert went out: "Get Red Adair."

But Red had his hands full with a fire crisis on the other side of the world, and nobody can be in two places at the same time.

The Exxon magnates were frantic. Without the famous Red Adair they were in heaps of trouble.

"Why not try Green Adair?" suggested a lackey.

"Who?" But as the flames roared higher in the sky, why not try Green Adair indeed.

Green Adair was contacted in the Limerick Arms in Belfast and offered one million pounds to do the job.

Within a few hours the oil engineers were amazed to see an air transport land in the desert. They gasped as the nose of the aircraft opened and a truck, bearing Green Adair and his crew sped towards the fire. They watched in amazement as the truck approached the wall of flames and disappeared into the very heart of the fire. They could see Green Adair and his men leaping about, jumping and stamping out the flames.

Finally, all charred, singed and blackened they emerged from the smoke to the cheers of their incredulous admirers.

"What will you do with the million pounds?" asked the first reporter on the scene.

"The first thing Ill do," said Green Adair, "will be to get some brakes for that bloody truck!"

* * *

"DO you think if I pour you some gin again,"
    Said Finnegan, "You might care to sin again?"
    Said she with a grin
    If you want it back in
    You must pay me a fin again, Finnegan."

* * *

THERE was a young colleen named Flynn
    Who knew fornication was sin
    But when she was tight
    It seemed quite all right
    So everyone filled her with gin.

ITALIANS

LUIGI considered himself a charmer and had no qualms about heading for the prettiest blonde at the bar.
    "Hello, darling,"he said. "Are you Italian?"
    "No,"she replied.
    "You look Italian," he said.
    "Well, Im not."
    "Surely you have a bit of Italian in you?"
    "No, I dont."
    "Would you like some?"

* * *

IS an IQ of 105 considered high?
    Yes!
    For ten Italians?

* * *

WHY does an Italian have a hole in his pocket?
    So he can count to six.

* * *

THE Mafia moll dumped her boyfriend when she learned he was just a finger man.

RECTAL thermometers are banned in Italy.

They found they caused too much brain damage.

* * *

WHEN the Italian girl told her brother the astounding news that she was going to have a baby he replied:

"Well, I'll be a monkey's uncle."

* * *

THE doctor was examining Luigi.

"Have you ever committed sodomy?" he asked.

"No way. One wife is enough for me."

* * *

ITALIAN is an easy language to learn.

All you need to know is one word, *Atsa*. Then you can speak fluently, "atsa car, atsa woman, atsa church, atsa everything."

* * *

THE Italian Don was returning to Italy for a visit and had arranged two appointments, one with the Pope, the other with the Mafia boss.

"Who should I see first?" he asked his lieutenant.

"The Pope first," said his adviser, "you've only got to kiss his hand."

* * *

THE sociologist was taking a survey in the Italian quarter and approached a gentleman in a black suit.

The survey got to sex. "How many times do you do it, sir?"

"Oh, about seven or eight times a year," replied the gent.

"But you are Italian," said the sociologist, "Italians are supposed to be great lovers."

"Well, I'm not doing too badly for a 65-year-old priest without a car."

* * *

WHEN the Italian girl had sex in the back seat of a hire car she said, "Its-a hurts."

AFTER a month's holiday in Australia Paddy returned to Ireland where the family wanted to know all about his trip.

He said Australians were the most hospital people he had ever met. "They will share their house, share everything," he said. "It's the white bastards you have to watch."

J

JAIL

THE judge had just made his routine tour of the prison and told the governor he was delighted to hear of the social event planned that evening.

"What do you mean?" said the governor.

"Well one of the prisoners wanted to sell me a ticket for the Wardens' Ball."

"That's not a dance, sir, that's a raffle."

* * *

THE padre was on his regular visit to the jail and came across three lags in the remand yard.

"What are you in for?" he asked the first.

"Murder," was the reply.

"And what did you get for that?"

"Life."

The padre asked the second man what he was in for.

"Fraud," he said. "And I got 15 years.

The padre asked the third what he was in for.

"Pouring petrol over Protestants and setting them alight."

"And what did you get for that?" asked the padre.

"About 15 to the gallon," replied the lag.

* * *

"THIS pen leaks," said the prisoner as the rain came through the roof.

DAD is very popular in prison. He's the lifer of the party.

JAPANESE
WHAT do Japanese men do when they have erections?
  Vote.
*　　*　　*
JAPANESE cunnilingus is "constluctive cliticism."
*　　*　　*
A JAPANESE orgasm is a Gland Finale.
*　　*　　*
A PELVIC examination in Japan is a "nookie lookie."
*　　*　　*
THE Japanese call girl call went broke.
  Nobody had a yen for her.
*　　*　　*
THE Japanese firm making vibrators is Genital Electric.
*　　*　　*
LACKANOOKIE is one of Japan's most dreaded diseases.
*　　*　　*
WE know a bloke who is half Japanese and half black.
Every December 7 he attacks Pearl Bailey.
*　　*　　*
THE Japanese are beginning to own so much of Queens-
land that travellers will soon have to leave their shoes at the
NSW border.
*　　*　　*
THE Japanese tourist fronted the bank teller and presented
his traveller's cheque. When he counted the cash he said:
"How come I get less money today than yesterday?"
  "Fluctuations," said the clerk.
  "And the bloody same to you," said the tourist.
*　　*　　*
THERE was a great lord in Japan
  Whose name on a Monday began
  It carried through Tuesday

Till twilight on Sunday
And sounded like stones in a can.

JEEVES

LORD Ponsonby awoke one morning with a tremendous erection and quickly called for his butler, Jeeves.

"Yes, a magnificent weapon," said Jeeves after close inspection of the member, "shall I rally her Ladyship?"

"No Jeeves," said Ponsonby. "Bring me my baggy golf trousers and I will try to smuggle it down to the village."

* * *

THE lady of the manor was becoming increasingly alarmed at Jeeves' practice of walking in to her bedroom without knocking. Finally she took him to task.

"It could be very embarrassing if I were in a state of undress," she admonished.

"No need to worry about that, m'Lady," said Jeeves. "I always take a peek through the keyhole first!"

* * *

LATER that evening her Ladyship called Jeeves into her bedroom. "Jeeves, please unzip my dress."

With a great deal of embarrassment he did so.

"Now Jeeves," she said. "Take off my stockings."

Jeeves was now in a sweat.

"And now take off my underwear ... and if I ever catch you wearing my gear again you will be instantly dismissed."

* * *

HER Ladyship called Jeeves to her bedroom and he was surprised to find her reclining on the sofa entirely nude.

"Jeeves," she asked. "Are you a good sport?"

"Er, yes, Madam, as a matter of fact I am."

"Good," she said, "and are you a good fuck?"

"Indeed I am, Madam."

"Well fuck off, it's April Fool's Day."

HER Ladyship couldn't remember a thing about her night out with the girls. All she knew when she woke up next morning was that she was totally naked and hung over.

Eventually Jeeves knocked on the door and came in with the breakfast tray.

"Just a moment, Jeeves," she said sleepily. "I can't remember a thing about last night. How did I get into bed?"

"Begging your pardon, your Ladyship, I helped you upstairs and put you to bed."

"But, my dress...?"

"It seemed a shame to crumple it, I took it off and hung it up," said Jeeves.

Looking under the bedclothes she said, "but, my underwear...?"

"I thought the elastic might stop the circulation," explained Jeeves, "I took the liberty of removing them."

"What a night," said her Ladyship, "I must have been tight."

"Only the first time your Ladyship."

* * *

JEEVES was called by Lord Ponsonby. "Jeeves, could you ride down to the village and fetch a bottle of whisky, a box of cigars and a few ounces of snuff. That free-loading bishop will be calling in this afternoon."

Jeeves mounted his trusty bicycle and was off on his errand. It was not until the return trip and he had peddled up the long hill to the manor gates that he realised he had forgotten the snuff.

What to do? It was too hot and too far to ride back down to the village. By chance the problem was solved, right there on the nature strip was some dog shit, three of those white eggs dogs leave in neat little clumps. When dried in the sun and ground back to powder it looks for all the world like snuff.

Did he dare take the chance?

Jeeves quickly bent down, snatched up the three portions and put them in his pocket.

"Did you get the whisky, Jeeves?"

"Yes, M'lord."

"And the cigars, and the snuff?"

"Yes M'lord," said Jeeves as he prepared to leave the room.

"I say, Jeeves," said Lord Ponsonby sniffing the air. "You didn't by any chance stand in something down in the village?"

"No M'lord."

The bishop arrived soon after and headed for the Scotch. "You don't mind if I have a drink, Ponsonby old boy?"

"Not at all, Bishop, go for your life," but Ponsonby was preoccupied with the pervading odour.

"I say Bishop, can you smell dog's doings in here?"

"Can't say as I can dear boy," said the bishop. "I happen to have a heavy head cold."

"In that case, take a pinch of snuff," said Ponsonby.

The bishop responded by taking two pinches and sniffing it up both nostrils.

"My God," he said. "You always get the best snuff. That's cleared my head completely and I can smell that dog's stuff now!"

* * *

EVERY time her Ladyship swoons
   Her boobs would pop out like balloons
   With nary a stare
   Jeeves would always be there
To lift them back in with warm spoons.

JEWISH

HE was a rabbi who kept a scrapbook of all his clippings.

WHAT do you call an uncircumcised Jewish baby?

A girl.

* * *

OF all the pornographic movies Jewish films are the worst. They consist of five minutes of sex and and ninety-five minutes of guilt.

* * *

THE Jews have discovered a new disease.

It is Waldheimer's Disease. People who suffer from it forget that they were ever Nazis.

* * *

THERE was a Jewish kamikaze pilot. He crashed his plane into his brother's scrap metal yard.

* * *

MOISHE and Izzy were out on the harbour when their launch struck a rock and sunk. Moishe was the stronger swimmer and took hold of Izzy with one hand as he paddled towards the shore with the other.

However Moishe soon got exhausted and asked Izzy if he could float alone for a while.

"We're in trouble like this," spluttered Izzy, "and you want to talk business?"

* * *

THE Jews are the most confident race in the world.

They cut the end off a dick before they know how long it will grow.

* * *

THE Jewish lawyer wore a worried frown. "It's my son," he confided to his rabbi, "he has come out of the closet and declared himself a homosexual. But the situation could be worse," he continued, "at least he is in love with a doctor."

* * *

The police sergeant entered the home of Mrs Bernstein to find her at the kitchen table eating her soup.

"Sorry to disturb you," he said, "but I have some terrible news."

"What is it?" she asked, slurping her soup..

"I'm afraid your husband has been killed in an accident," said the cop.

Mrs Bernstein continued to slurp her soup.

"I said," pressed the cop once more, "I said your husband has been killed."

"I know what you said, (slurp, slurp). Believe me, as soon as I finish (slurp) this soup (slurp) I am going to let out one almighty scream."

* * *

THERE was a sound reason why the Israelis did not get involved in the Gulf War. The last time they listened to a Talking Bush they wandered the desert for 40 years.

* * *

TWO Jews were lined up before the Nazi firing squad when the officer asked if they had any last requests.

One said he would like a cigarette. When the Nazi came close enough the condemned man spat in his face.

"Please, Izzie," said his mate, "don't make trouble."

* * *

MOISHE finished his business in Hong Kong early on the Friday and after many enquiries finally found the local synagogue.

Complete with his prayer shawl he attended the service and began to pray, surrounded by Chinese.

He was spotted by the rabbi who introduced himself and asked why he was there.

"Well, whenever I am in a foreign city I like to pray in the synagogue," he said.

"You are a Jew?" asked the rabbi with some surprise.

"Of course," replied Moishe.

"You don't look like a Jew," said the rabbi.

* * *

SAM Goldstein was at the funeral of a good friend when one of the mourners remembered he owed the deceased $10.

"I am a man of my word," he said, placing a ten dollar note in the coffin.

It reminded another of the deceaseds debtors, "I am also a man of my word," and he shuffled forward to place another $10 in the coffin.

"You two have pricked my conscience," said Sam, "for I also owe our dear departed friend $10."

So Sam came forward, wrote a cheque for $30, threw it in the coffin and took $20 change."

* * *

YOUNG Hymie went off to America and after three months he phoned his Momma from Hollywood.

"I'm married, Momma," he said.

"Oh no. You haven't married a goy have you?"

"No Momma."

"Then what's her name?"

"Goldberg, Momma."

"Oh, thank goodness for that. What's her first name?"

"Whoopie, Momma."

* * *

TWO men were standing side by side in the loo when the smaller of the two looked up and said, "You are a Jew?"

"Yes," said the taller.

"And you come from the Greensberg district?"

"Yes."

"And at your circumcision, you were cut by the cock-eyed Rabbi Finklebaum?"

"Yes. How do you know all these things?"

"Because Rabbi Finklebaum always cut with a left bias and you are pissing on my boots."

JOBS

"WHAT do you do for a crust?"

"Simple. I never wash my underpants."

HE works at a circus where he circumcises elephants.

The wages are not much, but the tips are enormous.

* * *

TWO young women renewed acquaintance after being out of touch since their school days and one asked the other what she worked at.

"I am a receptionist at a hotel and getting half my board."

"Gee," chided the other, "I work at a massage parlour and get my whole board."

* * *

FRED had been unemployed for months. One day he was browsing through the newspaper and was startled to read an item which said that men were so scarce in France that women were paying the equivalent of $50 a night to gigolos.

"I might go over there," he said.

His wife wasn't impressed. "How could you live on $50 a week?"

* * *

O'FLAHERTY saw a poster outside the police station: "Man Wanted for Armed Robbery in Dublin."

He said to Paddy, "Now if that job was in Donegal, I'd take it."

* * *

QUASIMODO, the Hunchback of Notre Dame, told the bishop he needed a holiday after ringing the bells for 15 years so they agreed to put an advertisement in the Bell Ringer's Bugle.

By strange coincidence the only applicants were a pair of identical twins, both with no arms. But they quickly dispelled Quasimodo's doubts that they could do the job.

"Just watch," said one, and he rushed at the bell and butted it with his head. The result was a loud gong.

They both proved they could ring the bells with head butts but Quasi insisted it was a job for one only and the decision was made on the toss of a coin.

Things went well the first week with Armless head-butting the bell each day, but the inevitable happened. While taking his usual run at the bell he tripped on the ropes, missed the bell, and came hurtling down, crash, on the plaza.

The crowd quickly gathered around the body. A gendarme pushed through and said: "Does anybody know his name?"

"No," said a bloke, "but his face rings a bell."

The unfortunate incident caused Quasimodo to send for the bellringer's twin who quickly took over the job.

However, on the third day exactly the same accident occurred. He tripped on the ropes and crashed to his death on the plaza below.

Again the crowd gathered round and a gendarme pushed through. "Does anybody know his name?" he asked.

"No," said a bloke, "but he's a dead ringer for his brother."

JOGGERS

WHEN they heard the back door slam she said: "Quick, that must be my husband." He jumped clean out the window, dashed across the park and merged with a group of joggers.

After he had gone three blocks he knew that he had escaped, but the jogger beside him could contain himself no longer.

"Do you always jog in the nude?" he asked.

"Only in summer," said our Romeo.

"Do you always jog with a condom on?"

"Only when it's raining," he replied.

TWO bachelors were jogging through the park when one said. "I lost my shorts here yesterday?"

"They must have been loose," said his mate.

"No, but the woman I was jogging with was."

* * *

A JOGGER picked up a tennis ball while on his regular morning run and having no pockets he put it down the front of his shorts. He was joined by a jogger friend who noticed the bulge.

"What's that?"

"Tennis ball."

"Gee, it must be painful. I had tennis elbow once."

JOKES

THE travelling salesman's car broke down and he wandered across the paddock to the farmhouse and asked if he could sleep the night.

"You're most welcome," said the farmer, "but I must warn you that I don't have daughters, I am a bachelor and you will have to share the only bed with me."

"Oh hell," said the salesman, "I'm in the wrong bloody joke."

* * *

FRED was often the butt of office jokes. "Have you heard the story of the dirty window. Fred?" they said.

When he said no, they said: "It's no use telling you. You wouldn't see through it."

Fred could hardly wait until he got home. "Darling," he said. "Have you heard the story of the window you couldn't see through?"

"No," she said.

"Well I can't tell you. It's too dirty."

K

KIDS
See SCHOOLS

THE little girl came home from school a bit distressed. In her hand was a computer print-out of her personal data which the teacher had asked her to give to her parents to check.

"And look, Mummy," she said. "Where it has got sex they have put an F and I'm damned if I can remember having one at school."

* * *

LITTLE Johnny happened to look into his big sister's bedroom and was intrigued to see her rubbing her hand between her legs and muttering "I want a man, I want a man."

He was even more surprised to look in next evening to see her in bed with a man.

He rushed to his own room rubbed himself between the legs and muttered: "I want a bike. I want a bike."

* * *

THE barmaid had to look over the bar to see where the voice came from. It was a six-year-old kid.

"Gimme a double Scotch and a packet of cigarettes," he said.

"Do you want to get me into trouble?" she asked.

"Leave the sex out of it," he said, "just get me the booze and fags."

* * *

YOUNG Billy brought a note home from school. His Dad read it and announced to his wife: "They want a written excuse for his presence."

* * *

THE little boy in the crowded showgrounds was obviously distressed. "I've lost my Dad," he sobbed when the policeman approached him.

"What's your Dad like?" said the cop.

"Beer, women and the odd bet," said the lad.

* * *

LITTLE Mary stuck her head around the kitchen door, "Hey Mum. Can an eight-year-old girl get pregnant?"

"Of course not," said her mother.

Mary turned round. "It's okay fellas, we can keep playing the game."

* * *

THREE kids are smoking behind the bike shed.

"My dad can blow smoke through his nose," said one.

"Mine can blow smoke through his ears," said the second.

"Mine can blow smoke through his arse," said the third, "I've seen the nicotine stains in his underpants."

* * *

THE English teacher asked young Johnny to give her a sentence using the word "definitely."

Johnny thought for a minute then said, "Miss, does a fart have lumps in it?"

A little shocked but outwardly unperturbed she replied. "No. Not to my knowledge, why do you ask?"

"Well, Miss," said Johnny, "I've definitely shit myself!"

* * *

TWO kids had been sent home with a note from the teacher

saying they were not to return to school until their language improved.

"You bastards been swearing again?" said the father, and he sent them to bed without their dinner.

Next morning, hoping that they had learned their lesson, the father asked what they would like for breakfast.

"I'll have a plate of those fuckin' cornflakes," said one.

His father immediately started thumping him. Gave him a hell of a hiding and sent him back to bed.

"Now what about you?" he said to the second son. "What will you have for breakfast?"

"Well, I won't be having any of those fuckin' cornflakes, that's for sure."

* * *

THE RSPCA inspector stopped three kids in a billy-cart. It was being pulled by a big mongrel dog they had harnessed to the cart. He accused the kids of cruelty.

"Rubbish," chorused the kids, "Bonzo loves it, he has been doing it for years. He doesn't look unhappy does he?"

The officer had to admit that the big dog seemed to be enjoying himself.

"Okay," he conceded, "but that piece of string hanging from his testicles will have to come off. That could hurt him."

"Arr hell," said one of the kids. "There goes our brakes!"

* * *

FIRST day at school and two eight-year-olds were assessing their new teacher.

"How old d'yer reckon she is," said little Fred.

"Dunno," said his mate. "But if we can get her knickers off we can find out."

"How can that help?"

"Well, on the back of mine it says 8-10 years."

* * *

LITTLE Johnny was having a lot of trouble with his

arithmetic and when teacher asked him what two plus two was he counted on his fingers and said, "four."

"And how much is three and three?"

Again Johnny counted on his fingers and came up with "six."

"Johnny," stormed the teacher, "it is cheating to use your fingers. Now put your hands in your pockets and tell me what is five and five."

There was a fumble and a pause before the answer came up.

"Eleven," he said.

* * *

"MUM," said the little boy, "where did I come from?"

"The stork brought you, dear," was the reply.

"And where did you come from, Mum?"

"The stork brought me too."

"And what about Grandma?"

"The stork brought her too."

"Gee," said the little lad, "doesn't it ever worry you to think that there have been no natural births in our family for three generations?"

* * *

"HEY Mum, where do babies come from?"

"From the stork of course."

"But who roots the stork?"

* * *

LITTLE Tommy, aged eight, marched into the living room with an important announcement for his father.

"Dad," he said with great seriousness, "I'm gonna get married."

His dad grinned indulgently, "Who to, son?"

"My girlfriend, Mary, next door."

Mary was also eight and his Dad decided to carry the joke along.

"Found a place to live yet?" he asked.

"Well, she gets 50 cents pocket money and you give me

a dollar. So if she moves in with me, we can manage," said Tommy seriously.

His Dad nodded. "Well, $1-50 a week is okay for now, but what will you do when the kids start to arrive?"

"Don't worry," said Tommy confidently. "We've been lucky so far."

* * *

ON Sunday morning, while giving little Nigel his breakfast, his mother asked: "Did Daddy look after you last night?"

"Daddy put me to bed," said the boy, "but I couldn't sleep so I got up and opened the door just in time to see Daddy go into the maid's room. He shut the door but I looked through the key hole and saw him get into her bed and ..."

"Don't say any more," said the angry mother. "Here comes your father now and I want you to start again and tell us both what you saw."

The boy began his story again while the wife stared daggers at her husband.

"And what were Daddy and the maid doing?" she gritted through her teeth.

"The same thing you and Uncle Tom were doing last Friday when Dad went to the football."

* * *

"DAD, all the kids at school hit me and call me Pansy."

"That's all right son," said his father. "Next time they do that, whack them over the head with your handbag."

* * *

LITTLE Johnny had just met the new kid at playgroup.

"How old are you?"

"I don't know," said the new kid.

"Do women bother you?"

"No."

"Then you are five."

A YOUNG boy was approached by the young housewife who had just moved into the flat next door. "Sonny, I need some bread at the corner store. Do you think you could go for me?"

"No," said the lad, "but I've heard Dad say he could."

*　*　*

DAD had just settled down with a book when young Johnny came home from school and asked the question he had dreaded to hear: "Where did I come from, Dad?"

Wiping the sweat from his collar Dad began the lengthy explanation beginning with the birds and the bees right through to sexual intercourse, and after an agonising half hour summed it all up with, "Now, do you understand, son?"

"Not really, Dad," said the lad. "Luigi says he comes from Italy and Ng Van Dong says he comes from Vietnam. Where do I come from?"

*　*　*

THE young mother was entertaining her neighbours when her three-year-old son burst into the room, hopping from one foot to the other. "I gotta piss, I gotta piss," he said.

She dragged him off to the toilet by the ear and told him in no uncertain terms, "Next time you want to go, don't use that word. Come in and whisper, right?"

Sure enough, two hours later the youngster interrupted the women again by rushing in, hopping from one foot to the other. "I wanna whisper. I wanna whisper," he said.

At least he was rewarded with a cake for the advance he had made.

That night he jumped out of his bed yet again and ran into his mother's room. She wasn't there, but his dad had just settled down in bed. "What is it son?" he asked.

"I wanna whisper, Daddy, I wanna whisper."

"Okay, son, come and whisper in my ear."

L

LAWYERS

WHAT'S the difference between a prostitute and a lawyer?

Not much. Except the prostitute will stop screwing you once you are dead.

* * *

A BLOKE phoned a lawyer. "I am in deep financial trouble, and I need some advice. I'm down to my last hundred dollars so I want to know if you can answer just two questions for this amount?"

"Certainly, sir," answered the lawyer, "what is the second question?"

* * *

WHAT do you call a hundred lawyers at the bottom of the harbour?

A bloody good start.

* * *

WE know a bloke who buries lawyers in holes fifty feet deep.

Because deep down they are good people.

* * *

WHAT do you call a lawyer with an IQ of 25?

"Your Honour."

* * *

WHAT'S the difference between a lawyer and a football?

You only get six points for kicking a football between the uprights.

* * *

THE lady solicitor dropped her briefs and became a lawyer.

* * *

HE introduced himself as a criminal lawyer.

"Well at least you're up front about describing yourself," said his client.

* * *

FRED knew that a former partner owed him $500 but he was unable to legally prove it. He asked his solicitor what to do about it.

"Easy," replied the legal eagle. "We will send him a letter. We will demand payment of the $1000 within seven days and ..."

"But it is only $500," said Fred.

"And that's exactly what he will reply in his letter, and then we have the proof."

* * *

THE city lawyer received a fax from his partner. It read: "Justice has prevailed."

He faxed back a message immediately: "Appeal at once!"

* * *

McTAVISH was as shrewd as they come and when he sat down with the lawyer he said: "I'm not into throwing money about, but I will certainly pay if you can give me an undertaking that you can win my case."

The lawyer said that was fair enough and told McTavish to outline the story.

McTavish launched into a terrible tale of breach of contract, lying, cheating and fraudulent business practices.

"That's an open and shut case," said the lawyer, "I will cheerfully accept such a brief."

"Oh that's bad news," said McTavish.

"Why?" asked the lawyer.

"That was my opponent's side of the story."

* * *

"YOUNG man, you are accused of stealing a petticoat."

"It was my first slip."

* * *

SHE was seeking maintenance for her baby.

"Do you know who the father is?" asked the solicitor.

"Yes," she sobbed. "It was Tommy."

"But we can't sue Tommy. Don't you know his surname?"

"No. You see I didn't know him personally."

* * *

THE solicitor told Paddy that if he wanted to be defended in court tomorrow he would need money, but Paddy was broke.

"All I've got is an antique gold watch," he said.

Solicitor: "Well that's okay, you can raise cash on that. Now what are you accused of stealing?"

Paddy: "An antique gold watch!"

LESBIANS

HE sat next to her at the singles bar, bought her a beer and began chatting her up.

"Look," she said, "I'd better tell you right from the start. I'm a lesbian."

"What's that?" he asked in all innocence.

"Well," she said, "see that blonde over there. She appeals to me. In fact, I'd love to get her into bed and get into her pants."

"Strewth," he said, "I must be a lesbian too."

* * *

AFTER the examination the gyneocologist said to her patient, "Well, everything's neat and tidy there."

"So it should be," said the lesbian, "I have a woman in twice a week."

LETTERS

JAKE was complaining that he had received a letter from an irate husband who had threatened to shoot his balls off if he didn't stop screwing his wife.

"It's got me worried," he confided to his mate.

"Well, stop screwing her and your worries are over," said his mate.

"That's not the problem," said Jake, "the letter was unsigned."

* * *

HE wanted to write a letter so he went to the post office and got side-tracked for a moment by the voluptuous young blonde behind the counter. He just couldn't help chatting her up.

"By the way, do you keep stationery?" he asked.

"I try to," she said. "Right up until the last few seconds, then I go crazy."

* * *

A SAILOR named Harold had an affair with a geisha girl in Japan. A few months later he received a letter from her:

"Dear Harry. You gone three months. Me gone three months. Should I carry Harry, or hari-kari?"

* * *

HE got a letter from his wife: "Fred, I missed you yesterday. Come home and let me have another shot. ...Beatrice."

* * *

THE university chancellor discovered that one of his professors had been messing about with his wife. So he sent him a letter demanding his presence in the office on Tuesday morning.

The offending professor sent the following reply: "I

received your circular letter. I regret that I cannot attend, but rest assured that I will accept the majority vote."

* * *

A FEW weeks before Christmas the postmaster in a small town received a letter addressed to Santa Claus. He opened it and was touched by its unusually pathetic message.

It read: "Dear Santa. Do you think you could give me fifty dollars for a bike? It is not for myself, but my mother is a widow with five children and we have hit hard times. The bike would help me deliver newspapers and get some medicine for young Johnny ..."

The postmaster was so touched that he took it along to his Masonic Lodge that night and read it aloud. It prompted a quick collection which raised $48. The postmaster slipped the money into a Masonic envelope, addressed it to the boy and posted it.

The following week he noticed another letter to Santa in the same lad's handwriting. He slipped the unopened envelope in his pocket and at the appropriate time stood up at lodge and read it aloud.

It said: "Dear Santa. Thank you for sending the money for the new bike, only next time you do this sort of thing be sure not to sent it through the Masons as the bastards took a two-dollar commission."

* * *

LETTER FROM AN IRISH MOTHER

Dear Son. Just a few lines to let you know I'm still alive. I'm writing this letter slowly because I know you can't read fast. You won't know the house when you get home because we have moved.

About your father. He has a lovely new job. He has 500 men under him; he cuts grass at the cemetery. There was a washing machine in the new house when we moved in but it hasn't been working too good. Last week I put Dad's shirt in, pulled the chain and haven't seen it since.

Your sister Mary had a baby this morning but I haven't found out if it is a boy or a girl yet, so I don't know if you are an auntie or an uncle.

Your Uncle Patrick drowned last week in a vat of whisky at the Dublin Brewery. Some of his workmates tried to save him but he fought them off bravely. They cremated him and it took five days to put out the fire.

I went to the doctor last Thursday and your father came with me. The doctor put a small glass tube in my mouth and told me not to talk for ten minutes. Your father offered to buy it off him.

It only rained twice this week, first for three days and then for four.

We had a letter from the undertaker. He said if the last payment on your grandfather's plot isn't paid within seven days, up he comes.

...Your loving Mother.

PS: I was going to send you $10 but I had already sealed up the envelope.

* * *

WHY I FIRED MY SECRETARY

Two weeks ago it was my 45th birthday. I didn't feel too well that morning, but I knew that when I went to breakfast my wife would be pleasant and say "happy birthday". But she didn't even say good morning.

I thought, that's wives for you. At least the children will remember. But the kids came in for breakfast and didn't say a word, so when I started for the office I was feeling pretty low and despondent.

As I walked into the office, Janet said, "Good morning, Boss. Happy birthday." I immediately felt better because somebody remembered.

About noon she knocked on my door and said that it was such a lovely day we should go out to lunch. It was the best news Id had all day.

We went to lunch. We didn't go where we normally go. Janet said she knew a little private place out in the country. We had two Martinis and enjoyed lunch tremendously.

On the way back to the office she said: "You know, it's such a beautiful day it would be a shame to go back to the office."

When I agreed she said: "Let's go to my apartment and I will fix you another Martini."

We did just that, in fact she fixed two Martinis which put me in a very pleasant mood. Then she said, "Boss, if you don't mind, I think I will go into the bedroom and slip into something more comfortable." I assured her I didn't mind at all.

She went into the bedroom and in about six minutes she came out carrying a big birthday cake followed by my wife and children, all singing Happy Birthday, and there I sat with nothing on except my socks!

* * *

CHAIN LETTER FOR WOMEN

Dear Sister. This letter was started by a woman in the hope of bringing relief to other tired and discontented females.

Unlike other chain letters, this one does not cost anything. Just send a copy to five of your friends who are equally tired and discontented, then bundle up your husband or boyfriend. Send him to the woman whose name is at the top of the list and add your name to the bottom of the list.

When your name comes to the top of the list you will receive 16,877 men and one of them is bound to be a heck of a lot better than the one you already have.

Do not break the chain. One woman broke this chain and got her own bastard back.

At this writing a friend of mine has already received 184 men. They buried her yesterday, but it took three undertakers 36 hours to wipe the smile off her face and three days to get her legs together so they could close the coffin. Have faith.

...Liberated Woman

* * *

AUSTRALIAN EXPORT

Mein Tear Herren.

Der last two pecketches ve got from you off coffee vas mitt rattschidtten mixt. Ve did not see any rattschidtten in der samples vich you sent us. It takes much valuable time to pick de ratten durden from der coffee. Ve order der coffee clean but you schipt schidt mixt mit it.

Ve like you schip us der coffee in vun sek, und der rattenschidtten in an udder sek. Und zen ve can mix it to suit der customer. Write please if we should schip der schidt bek und keep der coffee, or should ve chip bek der coffee und keep der shidt, or should ve schip bek der whole schidtten vurks?

We remain at your conwenience...

* * *

DEAR Sir. Please find enclosed $10.50 for one of your razors as advertised. ...Billy Bong.

PS: I forgot to enclose the money, but no doubt a firm of your reputable standing will send the razor anyway.

Dear Mr Bong. Thank you for your order and we have pleasure enclosing the razor as requested.

PS: We forgot to enclose the razor, but no doubt a man with your cheek doesn't need one.

* * *

DEAR Sir. God bless you for the beautiful radio your company donated as a prize at our recent Senior Citizen luncheon. I was the lucky one to win it.

I am 86 years old and live at the Country Home for the Aged. All my people are gone and it was nice to have someone think of me. God bless you for your kindness to an old forgotten lady.

My room mate is 95 and always had her own radio but would never let me listen to it. The other day her radio fell and broke into lots of pieces. It was just awful. She asked if she could listen to my new radio and I told her to get fucked.

Sincerely,
Elsie McEvoy

LIFE

LIFE is a sexually transmitted terminal disease.

*　*　*

LIFE can be a bed of roses...full of pricks.

*　*　*

LIFE is like a pubic hair on a toilet seat.
Eventually you get pissed off.

*　*　*

A WOMAN was walking down the street with her seven-year-old daughter when they couldn't help notice two dogs copulating right on the pavement ahead of them.

"What are those dogs doing, Mummy?" she asked.

The mother was very embarrassed but did some quick thinking to come up with an explanation.

"The dog on top has hurt its leg," she said, "the dog underneath is its friend and is trying to carry the injured one home."

"That's life," said the little girl, "try to help someone and they turn round and fuck you."

LOCAL GOVERNMENT

HE had been Shire President for 15 years and the town's benefactor for 15 before that. Now he was bemoaning the fickle attitude of the town after all those years of dedicated service.

"D'yer see that town square?" he lamented to a fellow

councillor. "I not only designed it, I put thousands of dollars into its construction. I have served this community for nigh on 30 years. Worked on the hospital committee, the sports committee, the town planning committee. You'd think I would have earned a bit of gratitude from the town. But no, fuck just one goat ..."

* * *

A TEDDY bear got a job on a council road gang. Monday went well, Tuesday likewise, but on Wednesday when he returned from his lunch break he discovered his pick had been stolen.

He complained to the foreman who was undismayed and had the obvious answer.

"It's Wednesday," he said. "That's the day the teddy bears have their picks nicked!"

* * *

A SOCIETY matron was crowing over her husband's re-election on the municipal council. "Yes. my John got elected for his third time and got in unexposed!"

* * *

WHEN the municipal council decided to build a fountain outside the town hall they put the project to tender and got three quotes, from contractors in Brisbane, Sydney and Melbourne.

The town clerk interviewed the Brisbane builder and asked his price. "$3000," was the reply.

"And how do you break that down?" asked the clerk.

"That's $1000 for the material, $1000 for the workers and $1000 for me."

The town clerk called in the Sydney contractor who quoted a price of $6000. "And how do you break that down?" asked the clerk.

"That's $2000 for materials, $2000 for the workers and $2000 for me."

The clerk called in the Melbourne bloke, whose price was $9000.

"And how do you break that down?" asked the clerk.

The bloke from Melbourne said, "$3000 for you, $3000 for me, and we give the job to the bloke from Brisbane."

* * *

BANDYWALLOP had never had a woman on the town council before and newly elected Cr Flossie Firebrand intended to make her mark.

The first item on the engineer's agenda was the cost of constructing a urinal.

"What's a urinal?" she asked.

When it was fully explained to her she immediately demanded that the funds be doubled.

"If we are gonna have a urinal I insist that we have an arsenal too."

* * *

THE headline in the local paper's society page jolted a few of the community. It read: "Mayor's Ball Comes Off To-night!"

LOVE

THREE little words, "I love you," can inflate the ego.

Three little words, "Is it in?" can deflate the ego.

* * *

TO go togehter is blessed.

To come together is divine.

M

MAGIC

AN old magician was working the Titanic on its last fateful voyage. He used to put a rabbit in his top hat and pull a hair out of his bum. (No, that's not the joke).

The old-timer had been down on his luck and couldn't afford one of those attractive leggy blonde assistants. On the Titanic he had to make do with a parrot, but to give it credit, the parrot had developed repartee and would squawk to the audience: "It's up his sleeve", or, "It's under his cloak, folks."

They were half way through their act when the Titanic hit the iceberg and sank.

The magician swam all night while the parrot fluttered overhead. He swam all next day and the parrot still fluttered overhead. It was evening of the second day when the parrot finally alighted on the magician's head.

"Okay, I give up. What have you done with the bloody ship?"

* * *

AFTER the leggy blonde had flagged him down on the country road he asked her what she did for a living.

"I'm a magician," she said.

"Get away, prove it then."

And with that she touched him on the dick and turned him into a motel.

237

MARRIAGE

SHE had been married so long she even faked the foreplay.

*   *   *

THE husband complained: "You never cry out when you have an orgasm."

"How do you know," she replied, "you are never there."

*   *   *

THEY had been married for 15 years. One night while they were making love he said: "Dear, am I hurting you?"

"No," she replied."Why?"

"I thought you moved," he said.

*   *   *

SHE: "How is it that I am always catching you rooting the cook?"

He: "It's because you are always wearing sneakers."

*   *   *

THEY were having another tiff.

"I have never had an affair, never," he said. "Can you say the same?"

"Yes," she said, "but not with such a straight face."

*   *   *

AFTER 15 years of marriage they finally achieved sexual compatibility.

They both had a headache.

*   *   *

IN bed the frustrated wife was moaning to her husband: "Why is it taking so long to come up?"

"I'm trying dear, I'm trying," he said. "I just can't think of anyone tonight."

*   *   *

THE wife said: "This room needs decorating."

The husband said: "The bloke who invented decorating needs fucking."

The wife replied: "Well, you've changed your tune. Last night you said the bloke who invented fucking needs decorating."

238

THEY had been married for ten years. She looked up from her sewing and said: "Darling, why don't we go out tonight?"

He put his book aside and said: "What a splendid idea. And if I get home before you I will leave the light on."

* * *

PADDY was asked how he managed to get along so well with his wife.

"Cos I always tell her the truth, even if I have to lie a little."

* * *

REMEMBER, Socrates died from an overdose of wedlock.

* * *

MARRIAGE is the price men pay for sex and sex is the price women pay for marriage.

* * *

MARRIAGE has its good side. It teaches you loyalty, forebearance, self-restraint, and many other qualities you wouldn't need if youd stayed single.

* * *

BRIGID had been a devout Catholic so it was a surprise to everybody when she married out of the church. But although married to a Presbyterian she always attended mass.

One Sunday morning she rose as usual and began to dress. She was conscious of her husband watching her as she slipped out of her nightie, pulled on her stockings, and hooked up her bra. She even noticed the bedsheet rising just below his navel.

She took off her bra, her stockings and pants and climbed back in to bed.

"I thought you were going to church," he said.

"The Catholic Church will stand forever," she said, "but how long can you trust a Presbyterian prick?"

THE marriage counsellor asked the wife: "Did you shrink from love-making?"

"No," she replied, "I've always been tiny like this."

* * *

DARLING is the wife's maiden name.

* * *

"TELL me dear, before we were married did you say you were oversexed, or over sex?"

* * *

THE reporter wanted to know how his marriage had lasted for fifty years.

"Simple," he said. "We decided right from the start that she would make all the minor decisions while I would decide the major issues.

"So she decided where we would live, what school the kids would attend, what investments we would make, and I made the major decisions like what to do about green-house warming, the Middle East and lifting sanctions on South Africa."

* * *

A COUPLE got married and the wife put a wooden box under the bed and told her husband he wasn't allowed to look inside it until after she died.

After 20 years of marriage her husband couldn't resist his curiosity any longer. While his wife was out he opened the box and found three eggs and $25,000.

He looked at it so long in puzzled amazement that his wife caught him.

"Well, what are the eggs for?" asked the husband.

"Every time Ive been unfaithful to you, Ive put an egg in the box," she explained.

The husband said: "Only three times in 20 years, well, that's not bad. I can live with that. But what's the money for?"

The wife replied: "Every time I got a dozen I sold them!"

THE usual scene. The husband comes home and finds a man humping his wife in bed, but she pleads with him for a chance to explain.

"He's been unemployed for months. He knocked on the door and asked for something to eat and I gave him the quiche you didn't want. He had no shoes so I gave him those slippers you threw out yesterday. Then he asked if there was anything else my husband didn't use."

* * *

WHEN they checked into the hotel the clerk said the only room available was the bridal suite.

"But we've been married for 25 years, it would be wasted on us," said the husband.

"Look," said the clerk, "if we put you in the ballroom we wouldn't expect you to dance all night."

* * *

MADGE fixed her eye on her husband Fred and said: "So, where are you going today?"

"I'm going to the pub."

"Ha, when you tell me you are going to the pub I know that you think that I'll think you are going to the races, but this time I know you are really going to the pub, so why are you lying?"

* * *

HARRY stopped off at the pub and was soon chatting up a blonde at the bar. Near closing time she suggested going to her place. They did and after a few more drinks they had a wonderful time.

It was three in the morning when Harry got out of bed and began to dress. And with a worried frown said, "how will I explain this to the wife?"

"No problem," said the blonde. "Tell the truth, and put this bit of chalk behind your ear."

Harry was creeping up the stairs when the light was

flicked on, and there was his fuming wife waiting with folded arms.

"And where the hell have you been?" she demanded.

Harry remembered the blonde's advice and said, "I've been tumbling in bed with a lovely blonde I picked up in the pub."

"Liar!" she roared. "You have been playing billiards all night with those hopeless mates of yours. I can tell by the chalk behind your ear."

* * *

THE old couple sat on the porch, as they had for many years. "I was just thinking," said the old lady, "we've had such a grand life together, but sooner or later one of us will pass on."

"Yes, but don't worry about that now," he said.

"Well I was just thinking," she said, "when it does happen, I'd like to go and live in Queensland."

* * *

REMEMBER that your wife is a romantic and still enjoys chocolates and flowers. So show her that you too remember, by speaking of them occasionally.

* * *

"WHAT'S your husband's average income?"

"About midnight."

* * *

MR and Mrs Offenbloo had been married for 20 years and they were still in love. She with the doctor and he with his secretary.

* * *

A BLOKE came home to find his wife in bed with the next door neighbour.

"What the hell do you think you're doing?" demanded the husband.

The wife said to her bedmate: "There you are, I told you he was stupid."

THE miser was berating his wife over the domestic bills.

"Look at this electricity account," he said. "It's exorbitant."

"And look at these tradesmen's bills."

He held up another document. "And look at this massive gas bill. You and your bungled suicide attempts."

* * *

THE husband was at the bedside of his dying wife. She raised herself on one elbow and in little more than a whisper said she wanted to confess.

"Darling," she said, "I am the one who informed the police about your business activities. Can you forgive me? I am the one who had your mistress deported. And I am the one who stole that $100,000 from your safe and spent it on a sexual affair with your best friend. Will you ever forgive me?"

"Of course, my dear. I am the one who poisoned your mushrooms."

MISTRESSES

FRED has got so many mistresses that when he takes his wife for a drive she has to hide under the dash when they pass a woman in the street.

* * *

THE difference between a missus and a mistress is often a mattress.

MECHANICS

IT was a cold winter's night and they were out on their first date when the car broke down. He said there was nothing to worry about. He was a mechanic and would have it fixed in no time.

After fiddling under the bonnet for a moment he jumped

back into the car and gave her quite a fright when he placed both hands up between her thighs.

"It's so cold," he explained, "I can't get my fingers to work. I just need to warm them for a moment."

After five minutes or so he got out again and continued fiddling with the motor but he was soon back to warm his fingers. Again and again he was jumping back into the car to place his hands between her thighs until finally she said: "Don't your ears ever get cold too?"

* * *

WHEN her date, a young mechanic, arrived to take her out she was surprised to see a set of jumper leads around his neck with the clips holding his trousers up. "My braces broke," he explained.

She gave the jumper leads a dubious look and said: "Well okay. But don't start anything."

* * *

THE mechanic itemized the bill for the woman driver: "$100 repairs to fender, $150 repairs to the tail-light fixture, $50 for not telling your husband and $50 for running over Pete, the petrol pump attendant."

* * *

I ONCE had a dog called Mechanic. If you gave him a kick in the nuts he made a bolt for the door.

MOTHERS-IN-LAW

MY mother-in-law broke up our marriage.

My wife came home early one evening and found me in bed with her.

* * *

MY mother-in-law thinks I'm effeminate.

Compared to her I probably am.

* * *

THE local Peeping Tom knocked on the door the other night

and asked if the mother-in-law would mind closing her bedroom curtains.

* * *

THE mother-in-law was kidnapped when they returned from their holiday. After three days they got a note from the kidnappers saying that if they didn't send the ransom money immediately, they would send her back.

MOTORING

See CARS

FRED said the local cop was persecuting him. "He pulled me up and walked around my car for ten minutes trying to find some fault. Finally he booked me."

"What for?" said his mates at the pub.

He got me for having a missing hub cap."

"What? That's not an offence," they chorused in protest.

"What was the charge?" they asked.

"Exposing my nuts!" said Fred.

* * *

WE know a bloke who changed his name by deed poll to CMH-869 so that he could have personalised number plates.

* * *

THE young Romeo and his girlfriend took the sports car for a test drive. By their flushed faces when they returned the salesman thought he had made a sale.

"It's not bad," said the Romeo, "but we would like something with a bit more headroom under the dashboard."

* * *

SOCIOLOGISTS have noticed the difference when men and women drivers use self-service fuel pumps.

The men always give the hose a few shakes when they're through.

245

THE police stopped him because he looked a bit under the weather. He was approached with the breathalyser bag.

"What's that?" he asked.

"It tells if you have had too much to drink," said the cop.

"Amazing. I'm married to one of them."

* * *

FRED drove his car back to the second-hand dealer.

"You remember you sold me this car last week and said its sole previous owner was a little old woman, quiet and reserved and only used the car to go to church on Sundays?"

"Yes," said the salesman a little cautiously.

"Well can you give me her name," said Fred. "I have cleaned out the boot and the glove box and I want to return her cigar butts, two empty gin bottles, a pair of silk garters with spangles on them and a pair of red knickers."

* * *

AFTER the usual Friday night binge at the local Harry took off up High Street, went round the roundabout three times, headed back the way he came, mounted the median strip and finished up against the door of the pub he had left minutes earlier.

"Christ, bloody lucky I didn't bring the car tonight," he said.

MULTI-NATIONALS

See AUSTRALIANS, FRENCH, GERMANS, IRISH, NEW ZEALANDERS, SCOTS, TURKS, WELSH

AT a United Nations function in New York the Norwegian Consul approached a small group of diplomats and made a bid to start small talk. "Pardon me," he said, "what is your opinion of the meat shortage?"

The American looked perplexed: "What's a shortage?"

The Pole scratched his head: "What's meat?"

The Russian shrugged: "What's an opinion?"

The Israeli asked: "What's pardon me?"

FOUR women, one English, one American, one German and one French, were all asked the same question: "What would you do if you were shipwrecked on an island with a regiment of soldiers?"

The Englishwoman said she would hide. The American said she would seek the protection of the commanding officer. The German woman said she would be out marching and it wouldn't bother her.

The French woman thought for a moment: "I understand ze question, but what seems to be ze problem?"

* * *

THE Frenchman, the Italian and the Australian were discussing who was the best lover.

"When I am in bed with my wife I prepare such foreplay and technique that she rises a foot off the bed," said the Frenchman.

Not to be outdone the Italian said he whispered love-talk to his wife and employed such sensuous procedures she moaned and rose two feet off the bed.

"That's nothing," said the Australian, "after I've finished making love to my missus and I wipe my cock on the curtains she hits the roof."

* * *

A SCOT, an Irishman and an Australian were each sentenced to five years in prison and were allowed one request.

The Scot asked for all the great books so he could study and learn.

The Irishman asked if his wife could stay with him so he could start a family.

The Australian did a quick calculation and asked the equivalent of five packets of cigarettes a day for the five years.

At the end of the term the Scot emerged as an erudite scholar. The Irishman emerged from prison with a family of five kids.

The Australian emerged looking a little frustrated. "Anybody got a match?" he asked.

* * *

HELL is multi-cultural.

The Germans are the police force, the Italians the defence force, the Indonesians are in charge of housing, and the Indians run the railways. The Irish make the laws, the English are the cooks and the common language is Dutch.

* * *

LETTER received by the Bureau of Ethnic Affairs:

"Gentlemen. I have always wanted to have an affair with an ethnic. How do I go about it?"

* * *

THE brave Dutch lad stuck his finger in the dyke.

And she punched the bejeezus out of him.

* * *

THE difference between a Jewish woman and an Italian woman is that one has fake orgasms and real diamonds while the other has vice versa.

* * *

"YOU should welcome migrants to your country," said the Jewish gentleman, "you should encourage them to come from everywhere.

"The better the mix the better the population," he continued, "why, in my veins there flows the blood of Poles, Italians, Germans, Norwegians and Greeks."

"Well," said one impressed listener, "all I can say is that your mother must have been a great sport."

* * *

A YOUNG Norwegian couple fronted up to the registry for a marriage licence.

"Name?" asked the clerk.

"Ole Olson,"

"And yours?"

"Inge Olson."

"Any connection?"

Inge blushed. "Only vunce, when he yumped me."

* * *

THREE migrants appeared to be having trouble with the English language.

One was lamenting the fact that he and his wife had no children. "She is unbearable," he explained.

"No, you mean she is inconceivable," said the second.

"You are both wrong," said the third. "He means his wife is impregnable.

* * *

A WELSHMAN and a Pom were arguing politics in the pub.

The left-wing Pommie said: "I think Margaret Thatcher has a face like a sheep's arse."

The Welshman swung his fist and punched him on the nose.

"I didn't know you were a conservative?" said the wounded Pom.

"I'm not," said the Taffy, "I'm a shepherd."

* * *

THREE builders, an Australian, an Englishman and an Irishman were working on a city sky-scraper. The Australian opened his lunch: "Not bloody Vegemite again," he said. "If I get Vegemite sandwiches tomorrow I'll ... I'll jump off this bloody building."

The Englishman opened his lunch. "Not cheese again. If I get cheese sandwiches tomorrow I'll jump off with you."

The Irishman opened his lunch., "Not jam again. If I get jam sandwiches again tomorrow I'll jump with you guys."

Tomorrow came. The Australian took one look at his Vegemite sandwiches and said: "That's it." He immediately jumped off the building.

The Englishman opened his lunch. "Cheese," he roared, and immediately followed suit.

The Irishman tentatively opened his lunch bag. "Oh no. Not jam, again." He also jumped.

At the triple funeral the Australian widow sobbed away: "Oh, if I had only known that he hated Vegemite..."

The English widow was also lamenting: "I didn't know he hated cheese so much."

The Irish widow was also perturbed. "I can't figure it out. Paddy always made his own sandwiches."

* * *

THREE different nationalities were discussing the meaning of *savoir-faire*.

The American said, "It means that if you came home and found your wife in bed with another man and you refrained from killing the son-of-a-bitch, that's *savoire-faire*."

The Englishman said: "Hardly, chaps. If you found your wife in bed with another man and excused yourself for interrupting and invited them to carry on, well that's *savoir-faire*."

The Frenchman had a different view: "If you came home and found your wife in bed with another man and you said 'Please continue, monsieur' and he was able to, then HE'S got *savoir-faire*."

MUSIC

IN a smoke-filled bar in Casablanca the piano player leant across and put his hand on the American's knee.

"Didn't I tell you I could make you forget that girl?"

"Yeah," said the American, "play with it again, Sam."

* * *

GIRLS are like pianos. When they are not upright, they're grand.

* * *

THE hi-fi expert had gone to great trouble to choose the right seductive music for his date. Just as they got down to some heavy fondling he could hear an irritating noise in one of the speakers.

Getting off the sofa he said, "I'll have that Dolby on in a flash."

"Don't worry about it," she said, "I'm on the pill."

* * *

THERE is a new Israeli group called the Fore Skins.

They are backed by Jock Strap and his Elastic Band playing "Stop that Swing."

* * *

THREE music professors were paying homage at Beethoven's grave when one said he thought he heard music. The second said he thought it was the Fifth Symphony being played backwards. The third said he thought it was Beethoven de-composing.

* * *

THE couple were at the opera in a box above the stage and she took the opportunity during interval to give her boyfriend a hand job. After the boyfriend was relieved she flung the handful over the balcony and into the orchestra pit where it hit the second violinst, splat, on his bald pate.

"Hell," he said, "I've just been hit by a flying fuck."

"And so you should be," said the first violinist. "You've been playing like a cunt all night."

* * *

THE old maestro had fallen on hard times, mainly due to tippling the whisky bottle. He had been a concert pianist of great renown in his time and his drinking pals at the Pig and Whistle decided they should be responsible for putting him back on the concert circuit.

They chipped in and bought an old tuxedo from the opportunity shop, not knowing that the trousers that went with it had a split in the crotch.

They booked him for the next benefit concert at the Mechanics' Hall and lined the front row on the opening night. When the maestro came on stage, bowed and sat on his chair at the piano there was a gasp of concern from the front row, and one of his friends was so bold as to leap onto the stage and whisper.

"Do you know your knackers are hanging through the old wicker chair?"

"No," said the maestro thoughtfully, "But if you hum the tune I will soon pick up the melody!"

*　*　*

A SAILOR who had been six months at sea was hunting the waterfront looking for a bar where he could have a quiet drink. He inspected a few, but the one that took his fancy had a South Sea Island motif, a monkey swinging around the chandelier and a pianist tinkling out a tune in the corner.

He went in and ordered a martini.

As the barman put the drink on the counter the monkey swung down from the rafters, spun around and dunked his nuts in the glass.

Naturally, the sailor reacted with loud abuse at the barman.

"Did you see that!" he roared. "Get me another drink."

The barman dutifully delivered another martini and set it on the bar, but before the sailor could reach for the glass the monkey dropped from the roof again, spun round and once more dunked his vitals in the drink.

The sailor was furious. He gripped the barman by the shirt-front and lifted him across the bar.

"It's not my monkey," protested the barman. "It belongs to the pianist over there."

The sailor dropped the bartender on the floor and strode over to the pianist.

"Do you know your monkey is dunking his balls in my martini,?" he roared.

"No," replied the pianist thoughtfully. "But if you hum the tune I'll soon pick up the melody!"

"LADIES and gentlemen. We have two bands to entertain you tonight. First we have Jock Strap and his 'Lastic Band, to play *Stop That Swing*, followed by the stars of the evening, Phil Landerer and his Oversextette.

* * *

THE flat-warming party had reached the stage where everybody was required to perform their artistic act. Some sang, others recited poems or told their favourite joke.

"What about you, Albert?" they chimed when they realised he was the only one who hadn't performed.

"Well," there is something I can do, but it is a little unusual."

Under more pressure he produced a mouth organ, dropped his dacks, put the instrument behind his bum and played *Britannia Rules the Waves*.

Amazement, wonder and applause was the instant result and Albert was pressed to play an encore.

Particularly astonished was Kevin, a talent scout for Harry M. Miller. He was convinced this act was a commercial winner.

He quickly dialled the entrepreneur who wasn't at all happy about being woken at three in the morning.

"But Harry, listen to this," and he called Albert to come closer to the phone as he played a rendition of *Waltzing Matilda*.

Harry listened for a while and gave Kevin his verdict: "It just sounds like some arse playing the mouth organ!"

* * *

TO the cellist, the lovely Miss Datchet
   Said the conductor, with a voice like a hatchet,
     "You have 'twixt your thighs
     A thing of beauty and size
   Yet you just sit there and scratch it."

N

NAMES

THE three Murphy sisters, Sandy, Mandy and Fanny were the prettiest, and tallest girls in town. They also had the largest feet in town.

One night Sandy and Mandy met two fellows at the local dance and when one noticed the size of the girls' shoes he said: "Crickey, you girls have sure got big feet."

"That's nothing," said Mandy, "you should see our Fannys."

* * *

PADDY proudly announced that his sister had just given birth to twins, a boy and a girl.

"What's their names?" asked a friend.

"The girl is called Denise," said Paddy "and the boy is called Da nephew."

* * *

A REPORTER was sent to interview a woman who had 15 children. "What do you call them?" he asked.

"Henry," she said.

"You mean they are all called Henry?" said the surprised reporter.

"Yes."

"But what if you want one in particular?"

"Oh, simple," she said. "They all have different surnames."

IT was all quiet in the stable until the three wise men arrived and one bumped his head on a low beam.

"Jesus Christ," he exclaimed.

"Now that's a better name than Fred," said Mary to Joseph.

* * *

THE Cockney family was large. "And the funny thing," said the father, 'Arold, "Orl our kids have names that begin with a haitch. "There's 'Erbert, 'Enry, 'Orace, 'Ubert, 'Ugh, 'Arriet and 'Etty. All except the last one. We called her Halice."

* * *

HE said his name was Patrick S. O'Flaherty.

"What's the S stand for?"

"Nothing," said Paddy. "My father dropped some spaghetti on my birth certificate."

* * *

THE newly-weds were relaxing after a heavy sex session. He lay back exhausted while she began talking about choosing a name for the baby.

"We don't want babies yet," he mumbled.

"No, but if we do have one we should have a name," she persisted.

With that he pulled off the condom, tied a knot in it and flung it out the window. "If he gets out of that we'll call him Houdini," he said.

NEIGHBOURS

IT was the morning after an all-night party and the bloke next door was raking his front lawn when the guests began leaving.

As one couple left he heard his neighbour call: "Goodbye, and thanks for a lend of your wife. She was terrific in bed. The best hump I've had for years."

This put a stop to the neighbour's raking and he hurried

over to the fence. "I heard that," he said, how could you possible say a thing like that?"

"Oh I had to," said the host. "She's not really that good in bed but I didn't want to hurt their feelings."

* * *

AFTER his business failed and his marriage collapsed he decided to start a new life in hillbilly country. Two lonely nights made him wonder if he had done the right thing but on the third morning he saw the dust of a small truck headed up the valley towards his shack.

"My name's Jake," said the raw-boned visitor extending a friendly hand when he arrived. "Heard you had moved into the district," he continued. "I'm kind of the welcoming committee. D'yer like parties?"

"Yes, I do," said the new settler.

"Well we are having one tomorrow night," said Jake. "It will be in your honour. It's all a bit rugged up here so there'll probably be a bit of drinking, probably a fight or two, but I'll guarantee there will be plenty of sex too."

"Sounds great," said the settler warming to the prospect. "What will I wear?" he asked.

"Oh, come as you are," said Jake. "There'll only be you and me."

* * *

WITH a stern voice the clerk of courts began reading the charge against the man in the dock.

"You are charged that on May 1 you battered your wife to death with a hammer..."

A voice at the back of the court yelled: "You bastard!"

The Clerk continued: "You are further charged that on the same day you battered your mother-in-law to death with a hammer..."

The voice at the rear shouted: "You filthy bastard!"

It was too much for the judge. He ordered a constable to bring the owner of the offensive voice forward.

Hauled before the judge the man explained: "Im his

neighbour. "Only a month ago I asked him for a loan of a hammer and the rotten bastard said he didnt have one."

NEWLY-WEDS
See HONEYMOONS

ON their wedding night the groom took off his trousers and told his new wife to try them on.

"They don't fit," she said.

"Then don't forget it," said the husband, "in this house I wear the trousers."

She threw him her knickers. Put them on," she said.

He looked at the skimpy scanties and said, "I can't get into these."

"No," she said, "and if you don't change your bloody attitude you never will."

* * *

THE newly-weds had their first argument and it was the cold shoulder in bed that night. Next day the groom sought the advice of older married men at the office on how to get out of the dog-house.

"Take home some flowers," was the consensus opinion.

That evening he arrived home and presented her with the floral offering.

It worked. She disappeared into the bedroom then called for him to follow.

When he entered the room he found her stretched out on the bed, lying naked with her legs apart.

"This is for the flowers," she said.

"Haven't we got a vase?" he replied.

* * *

THEY had been married a month and while he was reading the paper she came past and gave him a kick in the ankle.

"What's that for?" he complained.

"For being a lousy lover," she replied.

He mulled over this for a while then gave her a cuff over the ear.

"What was that for?" she said.

"For knowing the difference," he said.

* * *

THEY hadn't been married long and one day he came home early to find her on her hands and knees scrubbing the kitchen floor. Her short skirt revealed her tantalising buttocks swinging from side to side.

Without a word he unzipped his trousers, mounted her from behind and they both enjoyed a quickie.

As soon as he recovered he gave her a clip over the ear.

"Is that a nice thing to do after I just gave you so much pleasure?" she said.

"It was for not looking around to see who it was," he said.

* * *

THE vicar got married. On his wedding night he got undressed in the bathroom then entered the bedroom to find his bride already between the sheets.

"I thought I would find you on your knees," he said.

She replied: "Oh I can do it that way too, but tonight I'd like to see your face."

* * *

HENPECKED for years he had always told his son to marry a girl with less intelligence because he believed his smart wife was the reason for his henpecked condition.

"I did the right thing, Dad," said his son on return from his honeymoon.

"Boy is she dumb," he continued. "When we went to bed on our first night she was so stupid she didn't know where to put the pillow. She stuck it under her bum instead of her head."

* * *

THEY had been married a week and one morning while they were lying in bed she was idly fondling his dick and said: "Darling, didn't you say you were the only man with one of these?"

"That's right, love."

"No, you've been telling fibs," she said. "Your brother has one too."

"Oh, that was my spare one. I gave it to him."

"Silly man," she said. "You gave the best one away."

*   *   *

AFTER their marriage and bridal night in the town, Jed and his new bride set off for Jed's farm up in the hills in a wooden cart drawn by a donkey.

But the donkey wouldn't move. Jed cajoled, then swore but it wouldn't budge. He then got off the cart picked up a short log and gave the donkey a severe whack over the head.

"That's one," he said, as the beast started to move foward.

An hour later the donkey stopped again. Jed cajoled, then swore at it but it wouldn't budge. He got down from the cart and gave it an almighty biff between the eyes with the short plank.

"That's two," he said as the donkey faltered forward.

When the donkey stopped for the third time and refused to move, despite a series of whacks over the head Jed said, "Well that's three," and he pulled out a shotgun and gave the donkey both barrels between the eyes. It dropped down dead.

It was too much for his new wife who uttered her first protest. "Fancy treating an animal like that," she said, "you beat it unmercifully. You are not only a cruel man you are a stupid one. That donkey was worth a hundred dollars. You are an extravagant fool."

"That's one," he said.

NEWSPAPERS

THE reporter interviewed the oldest lady in the retirement home. Aged 100 she was sprightly and in excellent health.

"Have you ever been bedridden?" he asked.

"Of course, many times, but don't put that in the paper," she said.

* * *

WHEN the reporter visited the nudist colony for a story he introduced himself: "I'm Dick Brown, from the Sun."

* * *

THREE young businesswomen, former schoolmates, went out on the town for a reunion and ended up in a bar enjoying a few drinks.

One suggested they tell each other something they'd never told anyone else. With a giggle they agreed.

The first beckoned the others to lean forward before she whispered: "I am a lesbian. Always have been, even when I was at school."

After the shock had subsided the second said: "I am having a torrid sex affair with my boss."

The third said: "I am the secret gossip columnist for the *Daily Blab* and if you will excuse me, I must run."

* * *

BACK in Egyptian times when newspapers were carved on rock two scribes were chiselling out news of the lusty young Pharaoh who had ascended to the throne. One tapped the other on the shoulder, "How do you spell macho, one testicle or two?"

* * *

WHATS the difference between *Cosmopolitan* and *Womens Own*?

Cosmopolitan will teach a woman how to fake an orgasm, *Womens Own* will teach them how to knit one.

NEW ZEALANDERS

WHAT'S long and hard and fucks New Zealanders?
  The third year of primary school.

* * *

A KIWI farmer was counting his sheep:
  "205, 206, 207, hello darling, 209, 210 ..."

* * *

LITTLE Bo Peep has lost her sheep
And doesn't know where to find them.
But a search revealed they were in the next field
With a dirty big Kiwi behind them.

* * *

TOBY had a little lamb ...
  His case comes up next Friday.

* * *

THE New Zealand couple finally worked out a solution to
the eternal triangle.
  They ate the sheep.

* * *

THE farmer's wife gave him a plate of grass for his dinner.
  "What the hell's this?" he exploded.
  "If it's good enough for your girlfriend it's good enough
for you," she said.

* * *

IT was smoko and three shearers sat against a fence when
a flock of sheep walked by.
  "I wish that one was Miss Universe," said one.
  "I wish that one was Mister Universe," said another.
  "I wish it was dark," said the third.

* * *

WHEN a tourist coach passed through a small country town
in New Zealand one of the passengers noticed a sheep tied
to a lamp-post on the corner in the main street.
  "Oh that," said the guide. "That's the Recreation Centre."

A BLOKE went into the fish shop and asked for some "Fish 'n Chups."

"Ar! You're a Kiwi, eh?" said the proprietor.

The Enzedder was sick and tired of this so he spent the next three months at an elocution class.

He finally returned to the shop and asked, in perfect English for some "Fish and Chips."

"Ar, you're a Kiwi, eh?"

"How the hell did you know that?"

"Because this has been a hardware shop for the last two weeks."

*   *   *

THE potato farmer had recently arrived from Rotorua and had taken up a farm in Gembrook. "You look worried," said his mates in the pub, "what's bothering you?"

"Sex!" he replied.

They gathered around for more information.

"Well," explained the Kiwi, "as you know this is my first harvest here. I've got a wonderful crop of spuds, but not enough sex to put them in."

*   *   *

THREE couples went into a restaurant in Auckland and asked for a table for sex.

"And three pillows," they added.

NUDISTS

STREAKERS Beware! Your end is in sight.

*   *   *

TWO nudists stopped dating because they were seeing too much of each other.

*   *   *

PADDY Murphy caused a sensation by streaking through the nudist camp.

STREAK, or forever hold your piece.

* * *

IN the nudist camp they always sent Jake for the morning tea. He was the only man who could carry two coffees and ten donuts.

* * *

THE midget was asked to leave the nudist colony because he always had his nose in everybody's business.

But then they had a disco night and he was clubbed to death.

* * *

WHEN Jake retired he decided to realise a life-long ambition and join a nudist club. "But I don't know if I'm past it," he explained to the club treasurer.

"Well, make this a probationary day. Come in and see how you go," said the treasurer.

So Jake took a seat on a log by the river bank and, watching the nude women pass by he soon got a roaring horn. Noticing the erection, one woman stopped and gave him the greatest blow job of his life.

When he recovered he went straight into the office and paid his fees.

He was walking back to the log when he dropped his cigar. He bent over to pick it up and was tail-gated by a male member.

He rushed back to the office and demanded his money back.

"I can only manage one horn a month," he said, "but I am always dropping my cigar."

* * *

A NUDIST who picked flowers for smelling
    When stung on the dick started yelling
    "Doc, get rid of the pain
    But let the other remain,
    I refer of course to the swelling."

NUNS

HELP a nun kick the habit.

*　*　*

MOTHER Superior was engrossed in a crossword puzzle for some time and muttered that something was wrong.

"What's a four-letter word relating to women that ends in u-n-t?"

"Oh dear," said Sister Priscilla, "I think that would have to be aunt."

"Of course," said Mother Superior. "Do you have an eraser I could borrow."

*　*　*

THE Queen had a baby and they fired a 21-gun salute.

The nun had a baby and they fired the dirty old Canon.

*　*　*

THE young novice soon realised that the absence of sex in the convent was a problem. She confessed to mother superior that it was unhealthy and she was restless.

"Comfort yourself with a candle," she was advised.

"I've tried that," she said, "but you get tired of the same thing wick in and wick out."

*　*　*

BECOME a nun and feel superior.

*　*　*

THERE was once a monk from Siberia
    Whose manners were rather inferior
    He did to a nun
    What he shouldn't have done
    And now she's a Mother Superior

*　*　*

THE young novice was assigned her first job at the convent: to sweep the steps of the church and keep the entrance clean. But she was having a terrible time with the pigeons. They were flapping, cooing, and shitting all over the steps she had just cleaned.

She would wave her arms and say: "Fuck off. Fuck off."

It annoyed the priest who asked Mother Superior to have a discreet word with the novice.

"Your language is unseemly and entirely unnecessary," Mother Superior told her. "All you have to do is say shoo-shoo, and swipe them with the broom and you will find they will soon fuck off."

*　　*　　*

TWO young nuns were assigned to do the shopping and drove to the supermarket in the convent's mini minor. When they couldn't find a parking space one elected to do the shopping while the other drove around the block.

The first nun finally returned to the car park with a loaded trolley and asked a council worker: "Have you seen a nun in a red mini?"

"Not since I stopped drinking," he replied.

*　　*　　*

WHEN the novice returned from the presbytery Mother Superior said: "Why were you so long, sister?"

"Father Murphy was showing me how to blow the Horn of Plenty."

"The old villian. He told me it was the Trumpet of Gabriel."

*　　*　　*

MOTHER Superior was addressing the graduation ceremony and giving motherly advice. "In the outside world you will meet many temptations," she warned the girls. "You must remember the teachings and ideals you learned here at the convent."

She preached on at length and finally said: "There will be many a wicked man trying to take sexual liberties with you. Resist, and remember that one hour of pleasure could ruin your whole life. Any questions?"

"Yes, sister. How do you make it last an hour?"

THE old priest couldn't help noticing that the new curate sent to replace him had a large stack of luggage which included golf clubs and tennis rackets. And no sooner had the new man settled into his room when he approached the older priest to ask for a loan.

"Can you lend me $25.50?" he asked.

"What for?" asked the priest.

"A nookie," said the curate.

The old priest was puzzled by the request but reluctantly handed over the money.

Later that day, and still bothered by the incident, he met Mother Superior.

"What's a nookie?" he asked.

"$25.50," she replied.

* * *

WALKING into a liquor store Sister Genevieve asked for a bottle of whisky. "Oh it's alright. It's for Mother Superior's constipation."

Later that afternoon the licensee was shocked to see the nun in the park looking the worse for wear.

"I thought you said that whisky was for your superior's constipation," he said.

"Don't worry," slurred Sister Genevieve. "When she sees me she'll shit."

* * *

THE nun began to lecture him on the evils of drink as he tried to enter the pub. "Listen Sister," he said, "how can you knock it if you've never tried it?"

The argument continued along these lines. "If you tasted one drink you would know what you are talking about," he said.

Finally she agreed he had a point. "Just a small ladies drink then," she said, "whatever that is."

He suggested gin.

"Well I don't want to be seen drinking from a hotel glass.

Here," she said, hooking a tin mug from her belt, "can you get me some in this?"

So he went up to the bar and asked for a beer, and a gin in the mug.

The barman muttered, "Ar don't tell me that nun is still out there."

*   *   *

MOTHER Superior had listened to the parish priest ramble on for hours about the increasing number of splinter groups in religion.

Finally she blurted out: "Is that all you can think about, Sects! Sects! Sects!"

*   *   *

SISTER Priscilla was sent down to get the convent's Peugot from the service station.

"What kind of a car was it, sister?" asked the mechanic.

"Can't remember, but it starts with a P."

"Not here then," said the mechanic. "All ours start with petrol."

*   *   *

IT was Sister Priscilla's task to drive into town and pick up the mail every morning but she was showing an increasing reluctance to do the job.

"What's wrong?" asked Mother Superior, "I thought you enjoyed the daily excursion away from the convent."

"I do," said Sister Priscilla, "but lately a young policeman has taken to stopping me each morning."

Mother Superior said Priscilla had nothing to fear provided she didn't do anything wrong. She sent her on her way.

She had hardly driven for two minutes along the country lane when the motorcycle policeman signalled her to stop.

"Oh no, not the breathalyser again," muttered Sister Priscilla as the cop approached unzipping his fly.

NYMPHOMANIACS

THE definition of a nymphomaniac is a girl who trips a man and is under him before he hits the floor.

* * *

A NYMPHOMANIAC is a woman who will make love the same day she has her hair done.

* * *

FRED fell in love with the girl dancing on the table as soon as he saw her. "I want to marry her," he said.

"Don't be daft," said his mate. "Don't you know she's a nymphomaniac?"

"I don't care what she steals, I love her," said Fred.

* * *

SHE has a good job in the Nyphomaniacs' Club.

She examines prospective members.

* * *

HE was delighted his brand new girl friend agreed to come home with him so he broke out the whisky and began to pour the drinks.

"Say when," he said.

"Hey," she said, "may I have a drink first?"

* * *

SHE was confiding to the psychiatrist, "Every time I see a handsome muscular man on the beach I get a funny feeling between my toes."

"That's strange," said the doctor. "Which toes?"

"The big ones," she replied.

* * *

THERE was once an English nymphomaniac.

She simply had to have a man every six months.

* * *

A JEWISH nymphomaniac is a woman who allows her husband to make love to her after she has just returned from the beauty parlour.

* * *

IN the singles bar the nympho was checking her list.

268

"I am seeing Tom at seven, Dick at eight, Harry at nine." She looked around at the remaining men. "Tennish any-one?"

* * *

IF it wasn't for orgasms our Noreen wouldn't know when to stop screwing.

* * *

THEY called her Elevator, because everybody in the build-ing had been down on her.

* * *

HE approached the blonde at the bar and said: "Are you with anyone?"

She smiled and said, "Yes, I'm with anyone."

* * *

NYMPHO Noreen said: "I don't know how I will face my mother after being screwed three times by a total stranger?"

"What d'yer mean?" he said. "We've only done it once."

"Yes, but you are not going home yet are you?"

O

OFFICE

THE new blonde in the office is called Virginia. They called her Virgin for short, but not for long.

* * *

HEAR about the office girl who married a William so she could get a Willy of her own?

Her friend married Richard.

* * *

"WHAT do you think of our new boss?"

"He dresses smartly."

"And quickly too!"

* * *

TWO stenographers were comparing experiences after the company's Christmas party.

"Did you get laid?" said one.

"Only twice," was the reply.

"Only twice?"

"Yes, once by the band and again by the despatch department."

* * *

THE new managing director took a fancy to the buxom stenographer and finally summoned up the courage to ask her out.

He took her to the finest restaurant, lavished her with

food and wine on her, took her to the theatre and then to a luxury hotel.

In the morning she had breakfast in bed before he offered to drive her home.

"Oh, you are so kind," she said, "most of you salesmen give me $20 and put me in a taxi."

* * *

TWO businessmen were discussing the managing director's obsession with the new secretary.

"I don't get it," said one, "she's dizzy. There's nothing going on in her top floor."

"That's not the floor he's getting off on," replied his colleague.

* * *

AFTER wining and dining the new secretary all evening the executive finally got around to the moment of truth. "What about dropping around to my flat and listening to some records," he said.

"No ulterior motives, no obligations?" she queried.

"Of course not. We'll just listen to music."

"And what if I don't like the music?"

"Well, you can put your clothes on and go home!"

* * *

HE advertised for a secretary: "Wanted. Young lady assistant who can type. One who has no bad habits and is willing to learn."

* * *

THE partners hired a new secretary and after the first week one of them had taken her out.

"She was terrific," he reported. "I don't mind admitting she was better in the cot than my wife."

Next night the second partner took the secretary out and the following morning he said. "You're right. She is better than your wife."

SOME couldn't spell, others couldn't type, few could do shorthand. The businessman who wanted a private secretary was about to despair when the employment agency phoned to say they were sending round a girl who had a number of things going for her.

She turned out to be a ravishing long-legged blonde, and the business executive was immediately entranced.

"I'll pay you $500 a week, with pleasure," he said.

"With pleasure, will be $1000 a week," she said.

*   *   *

NOTICE in the office: In an effort to spread the work more evenly would all staff take advantage of the stenographers earlier in the day!

*   *   *

EVER fearful of the boss the timid clerk was at his desk with a frightful head cold. "Why don't you take the day off?" said his more forthright workmate.

"The boss wouldn't like it," snuffled the clerk.

"Go on, you won't get caught. He is never here on Wednesdays anyway."

The clerk reluctantly took the advice and went home. But as he passed his bedroom window he saw his boss in bed with his wife.

He rushed back to the office. "You and your advice," he said to his mate, "I nearly got caught."

OLD CODGERS

IT was one of those cruises for the elderly and the sprightly old geezer approached a woman reclining in a deck chair. "Guess how old I am?" he said.

She looked him up and down then put her hand up his shorts and took a firm grip of his family jewels. She felt their weight, moved them gently from side to side and then declared with authority: "You are 73 and five months."

"That's amazing," said the old geezer. "How did you know?"

She replied: "Because you told me yesterday, you silly old bugger."

* * *

THE old codger staggered into the clinic. "I'm worried, Doc," he said. "I met this nymphomaniac last week and made passionate love to her. Since then my roger has become red and itchy. It has swollen to three times its size and there is a discharge beginning to appear."

The doctor examined his donger.

"You'd better sit down," he said. "You are about to come."

* * *

AN old gent visited the doctor for his annual check-up.

"Your hearing has got worse," said the doc. "So I want you to cut out smoking, drinking and sex."

"What?" said the old geezer, "just so I can hear better?"

* * *

WHEN the family learned that Gramps was set to marry a 20-year-old they were horrified. The eldest son took him aside and said: "Frankly, Dad, we're concerned that sex with a young girl like that could be fatal."

"So what," said the old codger, "if she dies, she dies."

* * *

THEY struck up a romance at the Twilight Retirement Home and he put the hard word on her.

They were quickly in his room where they started to undress. "By the way," she said as she flung off her blouse, "I have acute angina."

"Well I hope it's better than those tits," he replied.

* * *

THEY had agreed to a secret meeting on the porch of the Twilight Home immediately after supper.

With some excitement they moved their rocking chairs close together.

Then he said: "Fuck you."

She replied: "And fuck you too."

They thought about this for awhile until he said: "I don't think much of that oral sex, do you?"

* * *

GRAMPS went to the pharmacy. "You've got to help me with a potion," he said. "I've scored a date with a lovely young lady and I need something to get it up."

The pharmacist knew Gramps was 82 and past it. Nevertheless he sold him a jar of cream and sent the old man away happy and contented.

The pharmacist wondered if he had done the right thing and later that evening rang Gramps. "Did the potion help?" he asked.

"It was great," said Gramps, "I've managed it three times already."

The pharmacist was surprised, "And what about the girl?" he asked.

"Oh, she's not here yet!"

* * *

JAKE looked a little tired as he took his usual place in the sun lounge. "I'm exhausted," he said to Fred, "I pulled a muscle in the bathroom this morning."

"That shouldn't make you tired," said Fred.

"It does if you pull it 375 times," said Jake.

* * *

WHEN he fronted at the sperm bank counter the matron looked him up and down and asked what he was there for.

"I want to make a donation," he said.

"But you look about 85," she said.

"I am," said the old codger, "but I have been a goer all my life. I can do it okay."

After further pleading the matron decided to give him the benefit of the doubt and handed him a jar. "Use that cubicle there," she said.

After ten minutes of grunting, groaning and heavy

breathing she knocked on the door. "Are you okay?" she said.

He came out with perspiration all over his face. He looked distressed and was out of breath.

"I have tried with my right hand, I have tried with my left," he said. "But I can't get the fucking lid off the jar!"

*   *   *

"NOT so much sex going on as there was in the old days, eh Bert?"

"Oh yes there is," said Bert. "It's just another crowd doing it."

*   *   *

OLD Horace complained that he couldn't do it like he used to with his young wife so the doctor advised them to sleep in separate rooms. "You will get better rest and when you go to her room you will give a better performance," said the doc.

He tried it for a month before coming back to the clinic. "Didn't it work?" asked the doc.

"Worked well," said Horace. He told the doc that he got randy twice in April but when he went to her room she said: "What, again? You were here just 15 minutes ago."

"Doc," said Horace, "I think I'm losing my memory."

*   *   *

OLD Bob had been missing from the senior citizens' club for some time and when he eventually fronted his mate said: "Gee, you look pale, where have you been?"

Bob had to admit he had been three months in jail after being charged with rape.

"But you are 84," said his mate.

"Yeah, that was the trouble," said Bob. "I pleaded guilty and the judge gave me three months for perjury!"

*   *   *

TWO old ladies at the Twilight Home were talking.

"Did you hear Old Jim Mullins had a massive stroke?"

275

"Always did," said her friend, "that's what made him so popular at our social functions."

* * *

THE old codger came to the doctor with the exciting news that he was going to marry a 20-year-old bride.

"Well, I think at your age you should take things easy. In fact I think you should take in a lodger," said the doctor.

A year later he bumped into the old codger and asked how was married life.

"The wife's pregnant, I am, happy to say," said the old man, and with a wink and a nudge he added, "thanks for that advice about taking in a boarder. She's pregnant too."

* * *

OLD Jake was reminiscing. "I can remember the time I gave up both booze and sex at the same time. Crikey, in all of my life that was the worst half hour I've ever spent!"

* * *

THE old codger wrote to his doctor:

"Dear Doc. For the past sixty years or more, I have awakened in the morning with a roaring Morning Glory, so strong I have never been able to bend it.

But this morning, on applying great pressure, I was able to force a slight bow. Doc, is my dick getting weaker, or my forearm getting stronger?"

* * *

OLD Jake was alone in his hotel room watching television when there was a knock on the door. He opened it and a buxom young girl walked in.

"Oh, I am so sorry," she said, "I must be in the wrong room."

"No love," said Jake. "It's the right room, but you are just 35 years too late."

* * *

OLD Chippendale was a millionaire. He had married a ravishing 20-year-old and it was the same old problem. He was past it.

On good advice he finally went to an audio-hypnotherapist who assured him that a simple audible signal would get it up immediately and the same audible signal repeated, would bring it down again.

"For example," said the doc, "the simple sound 'beeb' will give you a roaring horn, and 'beeb, beeb' will safely bring it down again.

"But I warn you," continued the doc, "at your advanced age three sessions is all your system could stand. Any more and it could kill you."

"Three will see me out," chirped the old man elatedly. "You mean if I go 'beeb' it will ..."

And immediately Chippendale had cracked an enormous erection.

"You can't go home like that," said the doc. "You've got to go 'beeb, beeb." And as soon as the words were uttered the erection subsided.

The old man sat there exhausted, yet delighted that it worked.

But while driving home a Morris Minor overtook him and went 'beeb, then 'beeb, beeb, and he had an erection and a subsidence that caused him to pull over for 20 minutes to recover.

"One final spurt to go," he said to himself as he mounted the stairs to his bedroom, showered and donned his dressing gown.

"Darling," he said to his young bride, "get your clothes off and get on the bed. I'm horny."

She was quick to do so. "About bloody time," she said.

He flashed open the front of his dressing gown, jumped on the bed, yelled 'beep, and presented her with a gigantic throbbing erection.

"Wow," she said. "What a beauty. But what's all this 'beep beep' shit?"

IN his dotage Old Jake had become simple. On his daily walks he would talk to the trees and flowers. Going through the park one day he said, "Hello trees, hello flowers," and when he saw a little ebony idol he said: "Hello little ebony idol."

To his surprise the idol replied: "Oh, please help me. I am, not really a little ebony idol, I am really a beautiful young woman under the spell of a witch. It only needs sexual intercourse with me to break the spell."

"Well, I am a bit beyond that sort of thing," said Jake, "but let me talk to my brother, he's an idle fucking bastard."

* * *

EVEN the parish priest was a welcome visitor for short-sighted Mrs Flanigan.

"But that wasn't the priest," said her daughter after the man had left, "that was the doctor."

"Oh was it?" she exclaimed with relief, "I thought Father O'Reilly was getting rather familiar."

* * *

MRS Flanigan described herself as a sprightly old girl. "Actually I see seven gentlemen a day," she said. "I get out of bed with Will Power, then I go to my John, next it's breakfast with Uncle Toby, followed by Billy T. Then the rest of the day is spent with either Arthur Ritis or Al Zymer until I finally go to bed with Johnny Walker."

* * *

AN old bloke was sitting at the bar sobbing with the odd tear dropping in his beer. "I got married to a lovely young widow last week," he explained to the barman. "She is a great cook, keeps my clothes in great nick and is insatiable in bed," he said.

"Then why the hell are you crying?" said the barman.

"Because I can't remember where I live," sobbed the old codger.

* * *

SHE had always been a lively lady and when she was

finally retired to the nursing home she refused to lead a boring life. She was determined to liven the place up. So she put a large sign on her door: "SEX!" And the small print read: "$20 in bed, $5 on the floor."

Nothing happened for the first few nights, but on Friday there was a timid knock and she opened the door to find Jock standing there. He handed her a $20 note.

"Hang on," she said. "I'll get the bed ready."

"To hell with the bed," said Jock. "I'm here for four on the floor!"

* * *

A YOUNG social worker used to call on Old Jake to cut up his steak and help with his meals. She noticed a bowl of almonds beside his tray.

"They were given to me as a present, but I don't want them," he explained. "You can have them."

She said thanks and began to nibble away on them.

"Funny present to give a man with no teeth," she remarked when she had eaten most of them.

"Oh no," he said. "They had chocolate on them then."

* * *

THE doctor had examined Old Jake's heart and summed up his advice with "No smoking, no drinking and no sex."

After much protesting by Jake the doctor relented: "Okay, one cigarette only after meals, and no more than two glasses of light beer a day."

"What about sex?" pressed Jake.

"Very occasionally," said the doctor, "and only with your wife because it is important you avoid any excitement."

* * *

DID you hear about the 80-year-old man who was acquitted of sexual assault because the evidence wouldn't stand up in court?

* * *

AN old chap in his seventies was concerned about his lack of sex drive and consulted his doctor.

"Well, what would you expect at your age?" said the medic.

The old geezer was still worried. "But my next door neighbour is over eighty and he says he gets it every night."

The doc thought for a moment. "Well, why don't you say it too?"

* * *

A COUPLE of old timers were discussing their sexual situation. "You know Jack," said one, "I understand that drinking stout will put lead in your pencil. Why don't we try a bottle?"

"I don't know about you," replied Jack, "but I don't have that many women to write to."

* * *

ON his morning round the doctor stopped beside the little old lady he had been treating for asthma. He checked her over, asked a few questions and listened to her croaky replies.

"What about the wheeze?" he said.

"Oh, fine," she replied. "I went three times last night!"

* * *

TWO old dons were lamenting human nature. "I was the town planner in this village," said one. "Look at all those fine buildings. I was responsible for all that architecture, but do I get any recognition? Eh? No. I donated money to the church all my life, but do I get any acknowledgement, eh? No. But fuck one single goat ..."

P

PARROTS

FRED stands on the edge of a cliff. He places a budgie on the left shoulder and another budgie on the right. Then he takes a great leap into the void and plummets to the rocks below.

"Jeezuz, Kevin," he says, "this budgie jumping is not what it's cracked up to be."

* * *

THE pet shop owner had difficulty selling a parrot. Each time a customer got interested the parrot would say: "Piss off, fuck-face."

Finally the shopkeeper decided that if it could talk so well it could be educated to say phrases other than swearing. He tied a string to each leg of the parrot, repeated a phrase constantly and tugged the string at the same time.

After six months the parrot was for sale again and a customer noticed the strings attached to the parrot's legs.

"Try pulling the one on the left leg," said the shopkeeper to an interested customer. He did and the bird responded with: "Hello, have a nice day."

The customer pulled the string on the other leg and got another pleasant response: "Hello mate, what's new?"

The customer was impressed. "What happens if I pull both strings together?"

The parrot responded: "I'd fall off the fuckin' perch ya stupid bastard."

* * *

AFTER buying a pair of talking parrots Miss Prim wanted to name them but found she couldn't tell Joey from Polly. She phoned the pet shop proprietor for advice.

"Simple," he said. "Wait until you see them mating, then fasten something around the male's neck so that you can identify him."

Miss Prim watched and watched. One day she heard flutters and squawks and dashed in to tie a white ribbon around the male's neck.

A few day's later Miss Prim threw an afternoon tea party for the church. Joey spotted the vicar and said: "Ha, so she caught you fucking around too, eh?"

* * *

THE priest had two parrots and taught them religiously to say the rosary. He even had two sets of rosary beads made and after a year of rigorous training he was delighted to have them perform at fetes and country fairs.

The priest was so pleased he decided to teach another parrot the rosary and bought a new bird from the pet shop.

When he put it into the cage one of the originals said to the other. "Throw away your beads, Fred, our prayers have been answered. It's a sheila!"

* * *

MITZI Lotzabazooma's pet parrot was beginning to embarrass her because it was learning too much and talking too much. Each night when she would bring home a gentleman friend the parrot would screech obscenities and repeatedly say: "Somebody is gonna get it tonight. Somebody is gonna get it tonight!"

Mitzi talked to the bird expert at the pet shop who assured her that the problem would be solved if only the parrot had his own female bird in the cage with him.

He ordered a parrot hen for her, but in the meantime he

offered her the only female bird in the shop, a brown owl, as a stand-in until the other parrot arrived.

That night Mitzi came home with another boyfriend and attempted to creep past the parrot cage, not wanting to interrupt anything the parrot might have going with his new friend.

But suddenly she realised nothing had changed as the parrot screeched: "Somebody is gonna get it tonight. Somebody is gonna get it tonight!"

"Whoo? Whoo?" said the owl.

"Not you, ya round-eyed bag, not you!"

* * *

THE young woman got out of bed, slipped on a silk gown, drew back the curtains, switched on the coffee percolator and uncovered the parrot.

Then the phone rang and a man's voice announced he had just arrived on the morning flight and would be there in ten minutes.

The young woman switched off the coffee percolator, covered the parrot, drew the curtains, took off her silk gown and got back into bed.

And the parrot muttered: "Jeez, that must have been the bloody shortest day of the year!"

PEARLY GATES

ST PETER was checking in new arrivals at the gates.

"Name?" he said.

"Lulu Bell," she replied.

"Cause of death?"

"The clap," she said.

"Couldn't be," said Pete, "nobody dies of the clap."

"You do when you give it to Big John."

* * *

THREE nuns who died at the same time arrived at the

Pearly Gates simultaneously and intended to go straight in, but St Peter barred their way.

"Just because you are nuns," he said, "doesn't mean you barge straight in without the religious test.

You," he said to the first one. "What was the name of the first man?"

"Er, Adam?" she answered, and the bells clanged and the trumpets blew and in she went.

"You," said St Peter addressing the second. "What was the name of the first woman?"

"Er, Eve?" she ventured, and the bells clanged and the trumpets blew and in she went.

"You," he said to the quaking third nun. "What were the first words Eve said to Adam?"

"Oh, gee. That's a hard one." And the bells clanged and the trumpets blew and in she went.

* * *

WHEN the cardinals' convention was hit by a bomb it sent 50 of them to heaven in one stroke where they all began to shuffle through the Pearly Gates as if they owned the place.

"Hang on. Just a moment," roared St Peter. "You lot have to go through the religious test like anybody else. How many of you have committed sins of the flesh?"

There was an awkward silence before, one after the other, 49 hands went up.

"Right," said St Peter. "You 49 go off to Purgatory, and take this deaf bastard with you."

* * *

NOT too many know that virgins are automatically admitted through the Pearly Gates, provided they pass the inspection test.

A beautiful young brunette presented her papers to St. Peter who checked them with a frown. "It says here that there are seven little dents in your virginity, but you have still passed," he said.

"That's right." she said.

284

"What's your name?"

"Snow White," she said.

* * *

A BLOKE died and when he regained consciousness he found himself in a big crowd floating on a cloud. There were hundreds of other crowded clouds in a traffic jam at the Pearly Gates. Heaven was closed.

"What's up?" he asked.

A bishop next to him explained that the gates had been shut for a hundred years. "It appears they are adjudicating on a question of doctrine," he said.

They floated about on the clouds for days, weeks and months before a great shout echoed through the skies. People began to jump up and down and slap each other on the back. The gates opened and the clouds began slowly drifting in.

They turned to the bishop for an explanation. "What's up?" they asked.

"Looks like they have made that decision," he said with elation. "Yes, hurrah, we're in. Fucking doesn't count."

* * *

THE Pope dies and arrives at the Pearly Gates on the same cloud as a lawyer. They are both ushered in and St Peter assigns the lawyer to a mansion with a golf course while the Pope is confined to a single room with a radio.

Even the lawyer was surprised. "How come?" he asked.

St Peter replied: "We have near on a hundred popes, but you are the first lawyer."

* * *

WHEN a bus load of nuns went over a cliff they were soon lined up at the Pearly Gates where St Peter produced a large vat of holy water for the nuns' test.

"If any of you have touched a man's genitals you will have to wash your hands before passing the gates," he said.

Three of the nuns came forward, washed their hands and passed through.

Then a fourth approached the holy water, washed her hands then sheepishly opened her habit and washed her breasts before passing through the gates.

A fifth nun approached the holy water, lifted her skirt and splashed some between her legs.

The nun next in line was heard to mutter: "Hey go easy, I've got to gargle that stuff in a minute."

* * *

THE Pope and Casanova arrived at the Pearly Gates on the same cloud. While the Pope hung around the gates meeting and greeting a few friends Casanova went straight in.

When the Pope finally entered he bumped into Casanova at the reception centre and said "I want nothing more than to kneel at the feet of the Virgin Mary. Do you know where I can find her?"

Casanova said, "Yes, but you are just too late, Father."

* * *

A SCOT arrived at the Pearly Gates.

"Name?" asked St Peter.

"Jock McTavish," replied the Scot.

"Piss off," said St. Peter, "we're not making porridge for one."

* * *

WHEN old Abe Goldstein died and fronted the Pearly Gates St Peter checked his clipboard for some time with an ever increasing frown then announced that Abe couldn't come in.

"Why?" said Abe. "I have lived according to the rules."

"That's just it," said St Peter. "You've got a perfect record. Not a blemish. A life of good deeds, always doing good deeds."

"Then what's the problem?" asked the puzzled Abe.

"You're too good," explained St Peter. "We have a score of popes up here with nowhere near your saintly record. It would cause a great stir in the heavenly hierarchy, because you would have to be placed above them."

Abe said he saw the prediciment. "Look," said St Peter, "as you are such an understanding bloke why don't we send you back for another hour. Maybe you could commit a misdemeanour in that time and, with your record, you'd still be in the upper echelon."

Abe reluctantly agreed. "You've got an hour, and no more good deeds," said St Peter.

In a flash Abe found himself slumped in his favourite armchair back in his living room with the clock striking eleven.

"Now what," he thought. "I don't drink, don't gamble, never had sex. How am I going to commit even a venial sin?"

He wasted the first 30 minutes worrying. Finally he thought of Miss Plotkin in the flat next door and the time, 25 years ago, when he momentarily entertained a rude thought about her.

With 25 minutes to go he knocked on her door. "Oh Mr Goldstein," she said, "I thought you were ill. Do come in."

He sat there in silence while he drank her tea and munched on her home-made cookies, ever conscious of the time ticking away.

Suddenly he decided to act.

He threw Miss Plotkin on the sofa, lifted her dress and whipped off her pants, sprang aboard and planted the sausage just as the clock began to strike 12.

As he slipped off the couch and the room began to blur the last thing he remembered was Miss Plotkin's voice: "Oh Mr Goldstein, only God and I will know what a wonderful deed you did for me today."

PHARMACISTS

THE clairvoyant pharmacist prided himself on knowing what each customer was about to ask for. When the blonde came in he said: "Don't tell me, don't tell me. You want a packet of tampons."

"No," she replied. "I want a roll of toilet paper."

"Damn," said the pharmacist, "missed it by a whisker."

* * *

"I'D like some deodorant, please."

"Aerosol?"

"No. It's for under me arms."

* * *

A PRIM young miss asked the pharmacy clerk: "Do you sell condoms in here?"

"Yes," he replied.

"Well wash your hands and get me some cough mixture."

* * *

TWO young lads approached the counter.

"Can we have a packet of tampons, please?"

"Are they for your mother?"

"No."

"Your sister then?"

"No, they're for us."

Asked to explain the kids said: "Well on the TV it says if you've got a packet of tampons you can swim, dive, play tennis and ride horseback."

* * *

THE sweet young thing said: "Do you happen to have multi-coloured sanitary towels?"

"Not during this recession," said the pharmacist, "they were made for brighter periods."

* * *

HE stormed into the store first thing on Monday morning and slammed a receipt on the counter.

"I asked for a gross of condoms, remember? That's 12 dozen. I found one packet only contained 11."

"Sorry sir," said the pharmacist making the cash adjustment. "Sorry to have ruined your weekend."

AN elderly couple toddle into the pharmacy and the gent asks for a packet of condoms. "We are having a weekend away," he says.

The clerk eyes them suspiciously. "You are both over 80, aren't you?" He went on to explain that with the woman well past the menopause she could not become pregnant.

"It's not that," said the old gent. "Emily here just loves the smell of burning rubber."

* * *

THE pharmacist's nurse was constantly getting things back to front and could not be trusted with responsible prescriptions, but when a sportsman came in for a blood test the pharmacist delegated her the job in the belief that it was a simple task.

When more time than was necessary had elapsed he looked in to the back room.

"No, you bimbo," he yelled, "I said prick his finger."

* * *

THE young teenagers met in the back stalls of the theatre and after a hot petting session he wanted to go on with it.

"Not here," she said. "Come around tomorrow. It's Sunday and my parents go to Evensong. We can have the house to ourselves. Oh, and don't forget the condom."

Next evening the lad arrived at the front door just as her father announced that they were off to church.

"I'll come with you," said the lad smartly.

At the first opportunity the young girl whispered, "Why the change of plan and how long have you been religious?"

To which the lad whispered in reply: "How long has your father been a chemist?"

* * *

THE young man agonised outside the pharmacy for an hour before summoning up the courage to enter, only to find a woman behind the counter.

He nervously stammered, "Could I see the pharmacist?"

"I am the pharmacist," said the woman. "My sister and I have run this business for more than 30 years and I can assure you there is no need for embarrassment. We have treated everything."

She finally calmed the young man who said, "Well, I have this insatiable urge to have sex and I suffer from a constant erection. It is driving me insane. What can you do for it?"

"Excuse me a moment," said the woman, "I will consult my sister."

She soon returned and said: "The best we can do is $300 a week, and free board."

* * *

MISS Smythe-Jones was miffed. Her pet miniature chihuahua was consistently second in dog shows throughout the country. One day she decided to tackle the judges.

It was explained to her that the true pedigree chihuahua had smooth hair while her dog, perfect in every other aspect, had a coat that was too shaggy.

"Look at the smooth hair of the champion there," said the judge. A nod is as good as a wink to a keen dog fancier and Miss Smythe-Jones was off to the pharmacy to ask for some hair remover.

The chemist handed her the latest product. "When you slap this on, its best to keep your arms up for two or three minutes," he said.

"Oh, it's not for my arms, it's for my chihuahua," she said.

"In that case," said the chemist, "don't ride a bike for 30 minutes."

PHONES

A COUPLE are in the midst of a steamy session when the phone rings.

She answers it, listens for a moment, hangs up and says to her lover that it was her husband on the phone.

"Jeez, don't tell me he's coming home," says the lover reaching for his clothes.

"Calm down," she says. "He won't be home for ages. He's playing cards with you and two other blokes."

*   *   *

FLOSSIE was washing her hair when the phone rang. Her room-mate answered it, then called out: "Flossie, it's an obscene phone call for you."

"Get his number. I'll call back," she replied.

*   *   *

THE atheists have started a Dial-a-Prayer service.

When you phone nobody answers.

*   *   *

MANY believe that the Pope's phone number is Vat 69.

It's not. It's Et Cum Spirri 2-2-0.

*   *   *

SHE was in bed with her lover when her phone rang. She reached for it and said: "I'll talk to you later. I have someone on hold."

*   *   *

TOM, Dick and Harry were in the pub drinking together when a phone rang. "Excuse me fellows," said Tom drawing his right hand from his pocket to take the call. He put his thumb in his ear and spoke into the end of his little finger.

His yuppie mates were impressed. Tom explained that he had a silicon chip inserted into his thumb and another in his finger. "Saves carrying those clumsy mobile phones around," he said.

A month later they were at the same bar and the phone rang. Dick said: "Excuse me," and took the call merely by talking away. When he 'hung up' he explained that he had a chip inserted in his ear and another in his tooth, a vast advancement on the old thumb-and-finger phone.

However, about ten minutes later Dick grimaced and complained of cramps in the stomach. He leant forward, legs slightly apart and put both hands on the bar.

"Are you okay?" asked his mates.

"Yes, I'll be alright. It's just a fax coming through."

* * *

"YOU'VE only been talking an hour," muttered the sarcastic husband, "was it the wrong number?"

* * *

THE phone rang at the motor pool and an authoritative voice demanded to know how many vehicles were operational.

Paddy answered. "We've got twelve trucks, ten utilities, three staff cars and that Bentley the fat-arsed colonel swanks around in."

There was a stony silence for a second or two. "Do you know who you are speaking to?"

"No," said Paddy.

"It is the so-called fat-arsed colonel you so insubordinately referred to."

"Well, do you know who you are talking to?"

"No," roared the colonel.

"Well thank Christ for that," said Paddy as he slammed the phone down.

* * *

"PARDON me, Miss. I am writing a phone book, may I have your number?"

* * *

THE phone rings. "Could I speak to Freddie Fukbrake, please?"

"Don't know anybody by that name, but just a moment and I'll ask. Do we have a Fukbrake here?"

"Hell, we don't even have a coffee break!"

THE Scot was visiting his psychiatrist.

"McAlister, you seem to have lost your stutter."

"Yes, Doc. I've had to phone my brother in New York quite a lot recently."

* * *

MISS Prim, the town's spinster, phoned the police around midnight to complain that two dogs were copulating on her front lawn.

Constable Plod suggested she throw a bucket of water over them.

Ten minutes later the phone rang again. Miss Prim told Constable Plod that the water didn't work. The dogs were still at it.

He told her to get two dustbin lids and clang them together and make as much noise as possible.

Another ten minutes later Miss Prim phoned again. The noise hadn't worked. In fact the dogs were still rooting furiously. "How will I stop them?" she asked the policeman.

"Why don't you tell the dogs that they are wanted on the telephone," said the cop.

"Will that stop them copulating?" she asked.

"It has certainly stopped me," replied Constable Plod.

* * *

A MATHEMATICIAN named Paul
Has a hexahedronical ball
And the cube of its weight
Times his pecker, plus eight
Is his phone number. Give him a call.

PHOTOGRAPHERS

TWO Norwegian beauties were having their picture taken and the photographer was taking some time getting the right angle.

"Vy ees he taking so long?" asked Inga.

"He's got to focus."

"No. You tell him picture first and maybe fokus after."

PIRATES

HE had a wooden leg, a hook on the end of his arm and a black patch over one eye.

"You've been in the wars, matey," said one of the crew.

"Ay, a shark bit my leg off, a cannon shot my hand clean away and a seagull shit in my eye."

"I can understand the shark and the cannon, but how could you lose an eye?"

"It was the day after the hook was attached and I wasn't used to it," said the pirate.

POEMS

THERE was a young playboy called Skinner
   Who took a young lady to dinner
   Around half past nine
   They sat down to dine
   And by quarter to ten it was in her.
   (The dinner, not Skinner).

* * *

AND another young fellow called Tupper
   Took the same young lady to supper
   At half past nine
   They sat down to dine
   And by a quarter to ten it was up her.
   (Not Tupper, some bastard called Skinner).

* * *

BEWARE of strong drink, my dear
   And only have two, at the most.
   Three, and you're under the table,
   Four and you're under the host.

"DON'T drink nought but water,"
  Was Mum's word to her daughter,
  "Say no to men,
  "Be home by ten,
  "And behave just like you orta!"
              *   *   *
"AND what'll you have?"
  Said the waiter,
  Idly picking his nose.
  "I'll have two boiled eggs,
  Ya bastard,
  Ya can't stick yer fingers in those."
              *   *   *
SAY it with flowers
  Or say it with sweets,
  Boxes of chocolates
  Or plush theatre seats,
  Say it with diamonds,
  Or say it with mink
  But whatever you do
  Don't say it in ink.

              *   *   *

THE limerick packs laughs anatomical
  Into space that is quite economical
  But the good ones I've seen
  So seldom are clean
  And the clean ones are so seldom comical.
              *   *   *
ROSES are red
  Pansies are gay
  If it wasn't for women
  We'd all be that way.

              *   *   *

A HOT tempered girl from Caracas
  Was to wed an ill-favoured jackass

When he stared to cheat her
With a dark senorita
She kicked him right in the maracas.

* * *

THERE was an old gent from Cosham
Who took out his knackers to wash 'em
But his wife said: "Now, Jack
If you don't put them back
I'll jump on the damn things and squash 'em.

* * *

FEELING rude in the nude was Miss Prim
When she went down to the river to swim
A man in a punt
Stuck an oar in her eye
And now she wears glasses.

POLICE

SHE rushed into the police station. "I was graped," she said.
"You mean raped?"
"No," she said, "there was a bunch of them."

* * *

SHE rushed into the police station. "I've just been sexually
molested by a Chinese laundryman."
"Hang on," said the sergeant, "how did you know it was
a Chinese laundryman?"
"Because he did the whole thing by hand."

* * *

MISS Lottzabazooma was explaining it to the police.
"This guy came up to my apartment with me," she said.
"He tore off my clothes and threw me onto the bed. Then
when I was naked he ran off with my purse."
"Did you scream?" asked the cop.
"Of course not." she said. "How did I know he was going
to rob me?"

THE police raided the house where a steamy orgy was in progress.

"What's the matter with you blokes?" said the hostess, "haven't you ever seen 35 people in love before?"

* * *

THE phone rang at the police station. "I want to report a burglar trapped in an old maid's bedroom."

After getting the address the cop asked: "Who am I talking to?"

"The burglar," replied the frantic voice.

POLITICS

PAUL Keating rang the Queen and said: "Make Australia a kingdom and make me the king."

Her Highness replied: "I'll make it a country and you can be what you are."

* * *

ONE politician said he wouldn't mind a bit if women were in power.

The other said he wouldn't mind a bit and he didn't give a stuff who was in power.

* * *

COME to think of it, there is no difference between politicians and bull sperm. Only one in a thousand actually work.

* * *

AT the political rally the heckler yelled:

"Clinton should be bloody well hung!"

Hillary jumped up: "He is, he is."

* * *

THE romance was off to a shaky start from the beginning because she was conservative while he was traditional labor but they decided to live together on the basis of agreeing to disagree.

It went well for a short time until a television program set off the inevitable political argument.

When they retired to bed he remained on the left and she on the extreme right.

Eventually she made an overture: "There is a split in the Tory movement and it is quite likely that if a Labor member stood he could slip in unopposed."

"Too late," he said. "There's been too much stimulation in the private sector and he has blown his deposit."

* * *

WHAT's the difference between a flattened politician and a flattened kangaroo on the road to Canberra?

There are skid marks to the kangaroo.

* * *

PAUL Keating was asked if he had heard the latest political jokes.

"Heard them?" he said. "I work with the bludgers."

* * *

WHILE on safari in cannibal country a traveller came across a cafe in a clearing in the jungle. The sign out front advertised: Fried Missionary $5, Boiled Hunter $4-50, Grilled Safari Guide $5. Stuffed Politician $15.

When the traveller asked why so much for the politician the chef replied, "Have you ever tried to clean one?"

PREGNANCY

BACK from a year at sea the sailor took his wife to the doctor and demanded an explanation for her pregnancy.

"It is a vindictive pregnancy," explained the doctor. "Somebody has had it in for you while you were away."

* * *

THE Japanese sailor demanded to know why his wife presented him with a bouncing baby boy with blue eyes and fair hair.

"Occidents will happen," she said.

AND the Chinese sailor sued for divorce when he was presented with a bundle of joy with blue eyes and blonde hair. The judge agreed: "Two wongs don't make a white," he declared.

* * *

THE State's health system is so run down that the Pregnancy Test Service now has a ten-month waiting list.

* * *

THE young woman looked at the beer gut on the Ocker with disgust. "If that stomach was on a woman, she would be pregnant," she said.

"It was and she is," replied the Ocker.

* * *

TWO women had become friends after meeting each other at various fertility clinics in their quest to become pregnant.

"And now look at you," said one, "you must be six months' gone."

"Yes," said the mother-to-be, "I finally went to a faith healer."

"Oh, we tried that," said the first women, "my husband and I went there for months."

"No," whispered the pregnant one, "You've got to go alone."

* * *

"I'M going to have a little one,"
    Said his girl so pert and frisky
    When he fainted to the floor
    She told him she meant whisky.

* * *

THERE was a young Nellie McStace
    Whose corset got too tight to lace
    Her mother said, "Nellie,
    There's more in your belly
    Than ever went in through your face."

PRIESTS

SUFFERING from depression the priest was advised by his psychiatrist to take a rest from stress with a short break in Paris. "Nobody will know you there," said the shrink.

Indeed, he got to like the sinful city and even went to a strip show. And when a gorgeous blonde danced by he leaned out to touch her.

"Oh, no you don't, Father," said the blonde.

"How did you know I was a priest?"

"Because I'm Sister Priscilla, and we've got the same shrink," she replied.

* * *

THERE once was a young priest from Kew
Who preached with his vestments askew
A lady called Morgan
Caught sight of his organ
And promptly passed out in the pew.

PRIZES

IT was the last day of the Royal Agricultural Show and the crowd had gathered for the drawing of the grand raffle. The minor prizes were to be drawn first and when the mayor reached into the bin and called out the number, 738,562, there was a delighted shriek from a woman at the rear of the crowd.

"Third prize," announced the compere, "is a three-month cruise around the world for you and your family." The woman gave another shriek of delight and the crowd applauded.

The mayor dipped into the barrel again and read out "number 509,677."

This time a gentleman responded, waving the ticket aloft. "Second prize, for you sir," announced the compere, "is a two-tiered fruit cake with white icing and pink piping."

"What?" roared the indignant holder of ticket 509,677. "How come third prize is a trip around the world and I win a bloody fruit cake?"

The compere tried to placate him. "Ah sir, this is not an ordinary fruit cake. This cake was baked by the mayoress."

"Fuck the mayoress," replied the man angrily.

"No, no," said the compere. "That's the first prize!"

PROSTITUTES

A LARGE sign outside the church read: "If you are tired of sin, come in."

Underneath, written in lipstick, was the message: "If not, ring Dulcie on 041-2468."

* * *

HE was a regular client and once again asked for credit.

"No way John," she said. "You're into me for too much already."

* * *

TWO girls were working their regular beat.

"If I'm not in bed by ten o'clock I'm going home," said one.

* * *

THE prayer of the destitute prostitute:

"And now I lay me down too cheap."

* * *

THE call girl wasn't feeling so good. The doctor told her she needed a rest and suggested she stay out of bed for a few days.

* * *

WOMEN can go out and give it away

But they'll be arrested if do it for pay.

* * *

HE was such a loser. He approached a streetwalker one day and she complained of a headache.

THE streetwalker was protesting to the police that she was certainly not selling sex.

"I am selling condoms for a hundred dollars each, and I simply give a free demonstration on how to use them," she said.

* * *

THE overworked prostitute made two appointments for the same time.

She managed to squeeze them both in.

* * *

THE madame heard the commotion in the bedroom and one of her girls came out and slammed the bedroom door.

"I'll never do it that way," she said.

"How did he want you to do it?"

"On tick," said the irate hooker.

* * *

IN a bid to make her services more entertaining a prostitute had the likeness of Mick Jagger tattooed on the cheek of one bum and Elvis Presley tattooed on the other.

She could hardly wait to show her first customer.

When Fred came in, after a few at the pub, she bent over and flipped up her skirt. "Who are they?" she said.

"Easy," said Fred. "That's Mick Jagger on the left, Elvis on the right and Rolf Harris in the middle."

* * *

VINNIE detected that there was something troubling his mate Louie. "C'mon tell me all about it," he said.

A worried Louie began by saying that they had been mates for a long time, "But I've just gotta tell ya," said Louie. "It's your wife, Beryl. I was in the local brothel the other night and there she was. Vinnie, I hate to tell ya but your wife is a prostitute."

"Oh no, you've got it wrong," said Vinnie. "She's a substitute. She's only there on weekends."

A PUNTER approached Big Bessie in Harlem.

"Ah charges ten dollars," she said.

The punter said it was too much. He even refused it at five dollars.

"Okay. My last price," said Bessie. "Yo can have it fo three dollars, but at this price ah'm losing money."

* * *

TWO pros met on the street. "How's business?" said one.

"Slim prickings," said the other.

* * *

A NOTORIOUS hooker named Hurst
In the pleasure of men was well versed
Read a sign overhead
Of her ever-warm bed:
"The customer always comes first!"

* * *

THERE was a young harlot from Kew
Who filled up her fanny with glue
She said with a grin
"If they pay to get in
They'll pay to get out of it too."

* * *

ANOTHER girl who was quite canny
Charged a penny for use of her fanny
But for half of that sum
You could fondle her bum
A source of amusement for many.

PSYCHIATRISTS

ANYBODY who goes to a psychiatrist needs their head read.

A beautiful young woman comes to see the psychiatrist. He says: "Take off your clothes and lie on the couch."

She does so and he jumps on top and makes love to her.

When he falls off onto the floor he says: "Now that's my problem solved. What's yours?"

* * *

THE friendly psychiatrist is the one who lies on the couch with you.

* * *

I TOLD my girlfriend the truth, that I was seeing a psychiatrist.

She told me the truth, that she was seeing a psychiatrist, a plumber and two barmen.

* * *

THE patient on the couch said every time he lay down he saw visions of Mickey Mouse and Pluto. If he sat up suddenly he saw visions of Donald Duck and Goofy.

"How long have you had these Disney spells?" said the shrink.

* * *

THE blonde patient on the couch whispered to her psychiatrist, "Kiss me please doctor, kiss me."

"Hardly ethical," said the shrink, "I really shouldn't be screwing you at all."

* * *

"I CAN'T cure you of your premature ejaculation problem," said the psychiatrist. "But I can put you in touch with a woman who has a short attention span."

* * *

"NOW tell me," said the psychiatrist, "have you had any more of those sexually erotic dreams?"

"No," said the patient.

"Tough luck, I've had some beauties."

* * *

"MR BROWN," said the woman psychiatrist, "you have acute paranoia".

"Thanks Doc, and your tits are not bad either!"

THE prostitute had an appointment with her psychiatrist. When she entered at his office he asked her to lie on the couch.

"If you don't mind," she said, "I've been working all say. Do you mind if I stand?"

* * *

ONE intimate question led to another and the prostitute and her psychiatrist ended up on his couch in a very sexy session.

When it was over they lay silent for a moment and then both said simultaneously, "That will be one hundred dollars, thank you."

* * *

THE businessman was on the couch. "The trouble is, Doc," he said, "I've been having an affair with my secretary and I have such a guilty feeling about it that when I am humping her I pretend it is my wife. The problem is, Doc, I am beginning to like it more and more."

* * *

"IF these pills don't stop your kleptomania," said the psychiatrist, "try and get me a video recorder."

* * *

A FEMALE psychiatrist and her nurse took an evening off to go to the movies and early in the film a man seated next to the doctor began groping in his crotch with one hand while skilfully edging his other hand under her skirt and between her thighs.

The nurse observed the activity. "For goodness sake," she said, "why don't you tell that creep he's sick?"

"Why should I?" said the lady shrink. "He's not my patient."

* * *

SHE told her shrink. "I have this constant desire to have sex with every man I meet. What do you call that, Doctor?"

"Good news," he said, carrying her to the couch.

HE told the psychiatrist he thought he was going crazy because he kept dreaming he was having sex with biscuits.

"Are they chocolate biscuits?"

"No Doc."

"Are they those wholemeal biscuits?"

"No Doc."

"Are they those dry biscuits you have with cheese?"

"Yeah, yeah, that's them," said the patient.

"Then you are fucking crackers," said the doc.

* * *

HE told the psychiatrist that before he married his wife she was a nymphomaniac. "She was insatiable," he said. "She would do it anywhere. Now that we are married she is frigid. What do you call that, Doctor?"

"In the trade," said the shrink, "we call it hell freezing over."

* * *

THE psychiatrist told Fred he was going to drop some ink on a blotter and he wanted Fred to explain what the random designs meant to him.

"That's Marilyn Munroe in the nude," said Fred deciphering the first blotch.

"That's Jayne Mansfield taking a bath," he described the second.

He said the third spattering of ink was the Luton Girls Choir all singing in the nude.

"The trouble with you, Fred," said the doctor with some satisfaction, "you are obsessed with sex."

"What, me?" exclaimed Fred. "It's you who's drawing the filthy pictures."

* * *

MOST women in the metropolis
　Are opposed to psychoanalysis
　Indeed, they're annoyed
　By the great Dr Freud
　And cling to their long-standing phalluses.

PUBLIC RELATIONS

HE is the biggest bull artist since Picasso.

* * *

A PIMP is a public relations man for a public relations girl.

* * *

SHE got a job as public relations officer in a tampon distribution centre. She would put a get well card in every packet.

PUBS

BLOKE fronted the bar and ordered ten whiskies.

"Oh, and what's the occasion?" asked the barman proceeding to line them up.

"Just had my first blow job," said the customer.

"Celebrating?"

"No," said the customer, "I'm trying to get the taste out of my mouth."

* * *

THE barmaid wondered where the voice came from, before she saw the little lad in short pants with his nose just reaching the bar.

"Hey, you. I said I'll have a glass of beer and a packet of fags," insisted the brat.

The barmaid saw that he was a lad of about 13.

"Do you want to get me into trouble?" she said.

"Forget the sex, just give me the beer and fags," he said.

* * *

THE travelling salesman arrived at the one-pub, three-dog town and fronted the bar. After a couple of drinks he said to the barman: "Is there any night-life hereabouts?"

"You just missed it by a few days. She's gone to the city for a holiday."

* * *

THEY looked an odd trio in the pub; a sailor, an ostrich and a cat.

The ostrich and the sailor would take their turn buying the drinks but the cat appeared to be on the stingy side.

It intrigued the barman. "Why doesn't the cat buy a round?" he said.

"It's a long story," said the sailor. "Suffice to say that when I let the genie out of the bottle on that desert island and he granted me one wish, all I asked for was a long-legged bird with a tight pussy."

* * *

MURPHY had been at sea for five weeks and after settling into his room at his usual waterfront pub he picked up the phone and asked reception to send up a whore.

The publican had married since Murphy was last there and the new landlady was shocked to hear Murphy's request.

She demanded that her husband go up and throw Murphy out. He tried to explain that Murphy was a regular guest but to no avail. "If you are too frightened to throw him out then I'll do it myself," she said.

She was a formidable woman and when she marched up the stairs the publican could hear the sound of furniture being thrown around, thumps, bangs and curses.

Finally Murphy came down, red-faced, puffing, face scratched and shirt torn.

"That was a rugged old bitch you sent up," he said to the publican, "it was more like a wrestle than a screw."

* * *

A KANGAROO hopped up to the bar and ordered a pot of beer. He slapped down a fiver and the barman gave him fifty cents change.

The kangaroo quaffed the beer and put the change in his pocket and was about to leave when the barman's curiosity could be contained no longer.

"Excuse me for mentioning it, but we don't get many kangaroos in here."

"No bloody wonder, at $4-50 a glass," said the kangaroo.

IT is a shabby pub in the red light district. One of the hookers walks in and says: "Gimme a glass of Smirnoff."

The barman does so and she scoffs the lot in one gulp then drops to the floor in a dead faint.

The barman appeals to the only two drinkers to help him carry her into a back room where one of them says: "Hey, let's give her a quickie while she's out."

They do so and an hour later she sits up, scratches her head, says: "Where am I?", gets her bearings and leaves.

Next evening she comes in at the same time and asks for a glass of Smirnoff, drinks it in one gulp and drops to the floor again. The same three carry her to the back room and do it again.

This goes on for a third and fourth night.

On Friday night she comes in and the bartender reaches for the Smirnoff bottle.

"No Pete," she says. "I'll have Bacardi tonight, that Smirnoff makes my cunt sore."

Q

QUESTIONS

WHICH of us is the opposite sex?

* * *

IS a lesbian a pansy without a stalk?

* * *

IS camping loitering within tent?

* * *

IS Red Riding Hood a Russian contraceptive?

* * *

IS Johnny Cash the change from a condom vending machine?

* * *

IS a castrated pig disgruntled?

* * *

DOES the lateral coital position
mean having a bit on the side?

* * *

WHAT is a Jewish dilemma?
Free pork.

* * *

WHAT do husbands have in their pants that their wives don't want on their faces?
Wrinkles.

* * *

WHAT is pink and wrinkly and hangs out your pants?
Your grandma.

WHAT'S the difference between blondes and broccoli?
    Nobody eats broccoli.

* * *

WHY do so many brides start to get crow's feet as soon as they are married?
    From squinting and saying: "Suck what?"

* * *

WHAT's six inches long, has a bald head and drives Jewish women wild?
    A Yankee hundred dollar note.

* * *

WHAT'S got 75 balls and screws old ladies?
    Bingo.

* * *

WHAT does it take to circumcise a whale?
    Fore skin divers.

* * *

WHY don't rabbits make a noise when they root?
    Because they have cotton balls.

* * *

WHY is a joke like a pussy?
    Neither is any good if you don't get it.

* * *

WHAT do light and hard have in common?
    You can't sleep with a light on either.

* * *

WHAT's the difference between a monkey and a hooker?
    One lies on its back for peanuts.
    The other lives at the zoo.

* * *

WHAT'S the difference between a pothole and a politician?
    You would swerve to avoid the pothole.

* * *

WHAT'S the difference between a counterfeit note and a very thin prostitute?
    One's a phoney buck ...

WHAT'S the difference between a magician's wand and a policeman's truncheon?

The magician's wand is for cunning stunts ...

*   *   *

WHAT'S difference between a gold fish and a mountain goat?

One mucks around the fountain ...

*   *   *

WHAT'S the difference between a woman in church and a woman in the bath?

One has a soul full of hope ...

*   *   *

WHAT'S black and white and eats like a horse?

A zebra.

*   *   *

WHAT'S the difference between erotic and kinky?

Erotic is when you use a feather.

Kinky is when you use the whole chicken.

*   *   *

WHY is pubic hair curly?

So it doesn't poke your eyes out.

*   *   *

WHAT'S the difference between a vitamin and a hormone?

You can't hear a vitamin.

*   *   *

WHAT'S the difference between a slut and a bitch.

A slut will sleep with anyone.

A bitch will sleep with anyone, but you.

*   *   *

HOW do you stop a woman giving you head?

Marry her.

*   *   *

WHAT'S better than a bird in the hand?

A hand in the bush.

WHAT'S the difference between a condom and a pork pie?
  You get more meat in a condom.

* * *

WHAT'S the difference between a milk-maid and a stripper?
  The milk-maid is fair and buxom ...

* * *

WHAT do Christmas trees and vasectomised men have in common?
  They both have balls for decoration.

* * *

HOW can you tell the sex of a chromosome?
  Take down its genes.

* * *

HOW can you tell if pancakes are male or female?
  Female pancakes are well stacked.

* * *

CAN a self-made man pull himself to pieces?

* * *

IF a light sleeper sleeps with the light on, does a hard sleeper sleep with the window open?

* * *

DO fur covered toilet seats tickle your fancy?

* * *

IS a lady barrister without briefs a solicitor?

* * *

IS the Pope's wife a Catholic?

* * *

DO bears shit in the woods?

R

RADIO ANNOUNCERS

THE disc jockey was driving along the country road when he saw a young nun trying to hitch a ride. He stopped. She explained that she had been a bit naive in trying to walk the distance to church. It was further than she anticipated.

As they drove along she asked why he was up so early in the morning. "I'm a radio announcer on the morning shift at the local regional station," he said.

"Oh," said the nun. "I would do anything to be able to send a cheerio."

The DJ took another look and noticed that she was indeed a comely wench. "Anything?" he repeated.

When she indeed confirmed that it was her major wish in life he drove off the road into a shady glade and whipped out the old John Thomas, as unscrupulous DJs are wont to do.

She bent down, grabbed it with two hands and said: "Hello Mum, Hello Dad, this is Teresa here ..."

* * *

THE ABC announcer was delighted to hear the way in which his little son said his prayers, concluding with: "And here again, Dear God, are the headlines."

REAL ESTATE AGENTS

TAKE the Real Estate Agent's advice: Get Lots While You Can."

* * *

THE real estate agent fell on hard times and was selling caravans, changing his status to a wheel estate agent.

* * *

BUSINESS was bad and the real estate agent was unloading his troubles to the blonde he had just met at the bar.

"If I don't sell more homes, I'll lose my arse," he lamented.

"Funny you should say that," she said. "If I don't sell more arse I'll lose my home."

* * *

WHEN Vietnamese Louie rolled a big win at the casino he looked around town for the finest house on the choicest piece of real estate. He found that the Rothschilds, the great financiers, owned the most palatial home. So he began building an identical mansion beside it.

When it was finished Baron Rothschild complimented Vietnamese Louie on his attention to detail. The building was identical in every respect.

"But it's worth more than yours," said Louie.

"How come? I don't see that," said the baron.

"In every way the two places are alike until you try to sell them," explained Louie. "When the prospective buyer asks me about the neighbours I tell them we live next to the famous Rothchilds. But when they ask you about the neighbours you will have to admit it's Vietnamese boat people."

RELIGION

CATHOLIC girls' prayer:
"Oh Blessed Virgin, we believe
That thou without sin did conceive,

Teach us, then, how thus believing,
We can sin without conceiving.

*   *   *

AN international conference on family planning was organised by the world's church leaders.

Unfortunately, the Catholic representative had to pull out at the last moment.

*   *   *

MURPHY lived next to McTavish, one a Catholic the other a Protestant, but they were good neighbours.

One day McTavish, looking at his five kids, said to Murphy: "You Catholics don't use birth control, yet you've got no kids and I've got five."

"We use the Safe Period," explained Murphy.

"Never heard of it," said McTavish. "What's the Safe Period?"

"Every second Tuesday when you go to Lodge," said Murphy.

*   *   *

THE vicar said to the young lad: "Tell me, who went to Mount Olive?"

"Popeye," was the quick reply.

*   *   *

ONE priest said to the other. "Do you think the Pope will ever allow priests to marry?"

"Not in our time", mused his colleague, "maybe in our children's."

*   *   *

ONE priest confided in another. "I don't know what to do to repress these feelings of sexual desire."

"Take a cold shower," said his colleague.

"But I've taken so many cold showers that when it rains I now get an erection."

*   *   *

THE priest spoke to the villagers: "You must not use the pill."

The young signorina replied: "You no play the game, you no make the rules."

* * *

TERESA Murphy had married out of her faith, nevertheless she still went to mass regularly.

One Sunday morning she was getting dressed and while fixing her stockings she noticed her husband watching with a lustful eye. She also noticed his morning glory had made a little tent of the bedsheet. She paused for a moment and then began taking her clothes off.

"I thought you were going to church?" said her husband.

Now naked, Teresa hopped back into bed and said: "The Catholic Church will stand forever, but how long can you trust a Protestant prick?"

* * *

FATHER O'Grady was preaching on the difference between knowledge and faith.

"In the front row we have Teresa and Shamus with their six children," he said. "Teresa knows they are her children. That's knowledge. Shamus believes they are his children. That's faith."

* * *

MONKS do it out of habit

While nuns were once novices at it.

* * *

FROM the pulpit the vicar announced that one of his flock, Miss Helen Hunt, had found a purse containing money, a variety of personal items and what he believed to be a small packet of white balloons.

"So whoever has lost this purse, can go to Helen Hunt for it!"

* * *

"GIRLS," said the mother superior, addressing the class which was about to graduate and leave the convent.

"You are about to go into the sinful world. I must warn you against certain men who will whisper rude suggestions to you, buy you drinks, take you to their rooms, undress you and offer you money to do rude things."

"Excuse me, Mother," piped up a rather buxom girl, "did you say these wicked men would give us money?"

"Yes, child, why do you ask?"

"Father Flanagan only gives us lollies."

* * *

AN elderly couple were watching a TV evangelist ranting away and when he said he was about to transmit some spiritual healing through the telly set he urged his listeners to place one hand on their heart and the other on the organ which needed healing.

The old lady put one hand on her heart and the other on her arthritic hip.

The old man had one hand on his heart, the other on his genitals.

"For goodness sake, Jake," said the old woman, "he aims to heal the sick, not raise the dead."

* * *

AS the proud father handed the baby to the vicar at the christening font the cleric said: "And what will we call this little chap?"

"It's a girl," whispered the father. "You've got hold of my thumb!"

* * *

A PRIEST and a nun partnered up for a game of golf. As the priest swung the first drive he missed and sent a large divot flying through the air.

"Shit, I missed," he said.

The nun was shocked.

Several holes later he missed a vital putt.

"Shit, I missed," muttered the priest.

This time the nun could not contain herself. "Father, you must watch your language."

The priest apologised. "May God strike me dead if I swear again," he said.

But on the 18th he chipped the ball into a bunker.

"Ah shit, missed again," he said.

Suddenly a bolt of lightening flashed down from a black cloud and struck the nun dead.

And a thunderous voice from above boomed: "Ah, shit, missed again."

* * *

THERE was a young lady called Alice
Who peed in the presbytery's chalice
The padre agreed
'Twas done out of need
And not out of Protestant malice.

* * *

THE notice board outside the church declared the stern warning: "What would you do if Christ returned this week?"

The graffiti scrawled underneath said: "Move McNally to full foward and have Christ at centre half."

* * *

THE priest called on the village belle Mary O'Shaunessy who was in hospital after falling off the stage during her dance act for the church fete. "I prayed for you last night," he said.

"No need," she replied, "I'm in the phone book."

* * *

WHEN the diocese finally sent an assistant to Father O'Sullivan, the old priest had some misgivings when the young curate arrived with luggage that included a bag of golf clubs and two tennis racquets.

And he had no sooner settled in when he asked Fr O'Sullivan for an advance until pay day. "Can you spare $25.50?" he asked.

"What for?" asked the old priest.

"For a nookie," replied the younger man frankly.

Not wanting to appear ignorant, the priest handed over

the money, but he pondered over it for the rest of the day until he chanced to meet Mother Superior.

"What's a nookie?" he asked her.

"$25.50" she replied.

* * *

THREE young priests had been driving interstate when they stopped at a country pub for a drink. At the bar was a pretty barmaid with a shapely set of breasts set off by a deep cleavage.

One young priest approached the bar. "Could I have three pots of titters?" he stammered.

"Cheeky lad," she said as the priest retreated.

"I'll get the drinks," said the second priest, but as he approached the bar he couldn't keep his eyes off them.

"We'll have three tits of potters," he blurted.

The third priest had to take the issue in hand. He approached the bar with confidence. "Three pots of bitter please, Miss. And you should dress more modestly, young woman, or St Finger is going to point his Peter at you."

* * *

WHAT do you get when cross a Jehovah's Witness with a bikie?

Somebody who knocks on your door and tells YOU to piss off!"

* * *

AN old archaeologist named Tossel
   Discovered a marvellous fossil
   He knew from its bend
   And the knob on the end
   'Twas the peter of Paul the Apostle.

* * *

THE Archbishop of Canterbury had found a quiet corner for his usual morning fondle and got so carried away he didn't hear a tourist approach. It was the flash of a camera that jolted himback to reality from his self amusement.

"I'll buy the film," he said. "In fact, I'll buy the camera," he insisted.

Later the Dean noticed the Archbishop's new camera. "How much did you pay for that?"

The Archbishop replied: "One thousand pounds."

"My God," said the Dean. "Somebody saw you coming?"

REPARTEE

FRED was selling raffle tickets for the Society of Retired Seafarers and knocked on the door of old Mrs Billingham.

"Would you care to support the Society for Retired Seafarers?" he asked.

"What's that?" said Mrs Billingham, "I'm hard of hearing."

"Would you care to buy a ticket?" repeated Fred.

"What's that," she answered, cupping her hand round her ear.

In disgust Fred turned and walked away.

"Don't forget to shut the gate," said Mrs Billingham.

"Fuck the gate," muttered Fred.

"And fuck the Society for Retired Seafarers," said Mrs Billingham.

*　　*　　*

WHEN Doreen wore her new bikini it brought a quick response from the lifeguards.

"Hey there," called one. "You're the best thing I've seen all day. Why don't you stop so I can look a little longer?"

"No need to," said Doreen. "You look a little longer already."

*　　*　　*

AT a wild party Fred had noticed a prim and pretty girl sitting apart from the revellers. She didn't seem to be enjoying herself. He approached her and said: "You don't appear to be having a good time. Would you like me to take you home?"

"Alright," said the girl, "where do you live?"

RESTAURANTS

THERE is a Mongolian-Jewish restaurant. It's called Genghis Cohen.

* * *

THE health inspector made one of his surprise visits to the restaurant kitchen to find the pastrycook crimping the edge of the apple pies with a set of false teeth.

"Haven't you got a tool for that?"

"Yes, but I save it for putting holes in the doughnuts!"

* * *

THE editor wanted to know why the restaurant writer had never given Fred's Diner on Main St a favourable write-up.

"Don't you like the food?" he said.

"Never eaten there," said the writer."But I did notice the alley cat out back shoving its paws down its throat."

* * *

WHILE touring Madrid, Bruce the Ocker touro discovered a tavern which served the biggest rissoles he had ever seen, for a mere fifty pesetas.

After the splendid meal he asked Manuel the waiter how come the meal was so cheap.

"Two leetle secrets," said Manuel. "As you see, we are right beside the bull-ring. We gets the meat cheep, And second, seez rissoles are really the bull's testicles, sauted in beef sauce."

That was a bit of a shock to our ocker, but nevertheless, the meal was tasty and most el cheapo.

Boasting about his find to Kevin they both returned the following night and ordered the same dish. When Manuel returned with two plates bearing one small rissole on each, Bruce predictably began moaning.

"Hey, Manuel, what the hell's this?"

"Eet is the same dish senor," said Manuel with a shrug of the shoulders. "Sometimes the bull wins!"

* * *

THE discovery of a fly in the soup can mean different responses to different diners in different countries.

In Australia the soup is sent back to the kitchen and the diner has an argument with the manager.

In England the fly is quietly and daintily removed and hidden under a serviette.

In France the soup is eaten and the fly is left high and dry on the side of the plate.

In the Orient the fly is eaten first and washed down by the soup.

In Scotland the fly is wrung out and then the soup is consumed.

And there are places where the diner stares at the fly and says: "Waiter, what's this? Only one fly?"

* * *

TWO crayfish were in the restaurant's aquarium. It seemed this would be their last night so the male cray put the hard word on the female.

She said: "Okay, but will you still respect me in the mornay?"

* * *

A RESTAURANT boasted that it could provide any dish the customer could order, no matter how alien or rare. If the chef couldn't produce the dish, then an alternative meal was on the house.

Consequently they did good business with smart alecs ordering filleted bee's dick marinated in port sauce, or roast goanna tails in curry, surrounded by Tibetan cabbage on rice.

But one evening the order was for braised elephant's balls on toast. A simple demand, but as ten minutes stretched to twenty the chef finally came out to apologise.

Due to an earlier rush on crocodile knuckle sandwiches they were completely out of bread.

ROYALS

ONE day the king took a fancy to the court jester, and from then on he was at his wit's end.

* * *

THE lecherous monarch was giving the princess the option. "Which would you prefer, my dear," he said. "A crowned head or a royal shafting?"

* * *

THE king was wandering around the palace gardens when he saw the gardener's wife with seven kids.

"Are these all yours?" he asked.

"Yes, Your Majesty, and we have another seven at home."

"Good God, your husband deserves a knighthood,"

"He's got one Sir, but he never uses it," she replied.

* * *

WHEN King Arthur rode off in search of the Holy Grail he didn't trust the motley crew of courtiers he left behind, so he devised an ingenious chastity belt for his Queen Guinevere. It contained a little guillotine.

When he came back a year later he commanded the courtiers to drop their dacks and sure enough there was hardly a dick in sight. They had all been cut off, except Sir Lancelot's.

"You are the only one to remain loyal," said the king to Sir Lancelot. "What will we do with these traitors? These blackguards? What will their punishment be? Speak up, Sir Lancelot, or have you lost your tongue?"

* * *

RICHARD the Lion Heart was about to set out on yet another Crusade. He summoned his brother, Sir Arthur, and confided that he had a premonition that this time he could be killed.

"Arthur, if I do not return by this time three years hence, I want you to take this key and release the chastity belt and give the queen her freedom to take another knight."

Arthur accepted the key and said he would do as his lord bid.

At dawn next morning the column of armored knights set forth across the drawbridge and the army began its long march east.

They had stopped for morning tea when they noted a lone horseman creating a cloud of dust as he rode furiously to catch Sir Richard's battalion. He galloped to the head of the column where he was recognised as Sir Arthur.

"Richard," he said, "thank goodness I caught you." He reached into his pocket, "you have given me the wrong key."

* * *

SIR Lancelot led his war weary troop back in to Camelot and reported to King Arthur: "I have raped and pillaged all the Saxons to the south."

"You idiot," exclaimed the king, "I told you to rape and pillage the Saxons in the north. I don't have any enemies in the south."

"You do now," said Sir Lancelot.

* * *

THE Prince of Wales looked resplendent in his naval uniform while delivering a stirring speech at the opening of the Oodnadatta Flower Show. But one astute reporter had noted he was wearing a fur hat with a tail hanging down his back.

Waiting for the right moment the journo siddled up to him and said: "Er, excuse me yer Highness. The uniform looks great, but what's with the fur hat?"

"Oh that!" said the Prince. "I was tawking to Mummy

last night. When I told her I was going to Oodnadatta she said wear the fok's 'at!"

* * *

A KNIGHT of the realm asked the royal alchemist if he had discovered something to alleviate the knight's constant erection.

"No, M'Lord," said the alchemist, "but I mentioned it to the King and he has a new post for you."

"What's that?"

"You have been named His Majesty's Sundial."

* * *

AS the young man was ushered into Queen Elizabeth's presence he explained: "I'm the Royal photographer."

"How remarkable," said the Queen. "My brother-in-law is a photographer."

"How odd," said the photographer. "My brother-in-law is a queen."

* * *

OF the Edwards 'tis thought that the First,
Although bad, was by no means the worst
The Third one is reckoned
Much worse than the Second
And the Second much worse than the First.

* * *

ONE day the Queen and the Princess were driving through the Royal Estate in the regal landrover when a gang of IRA bandits jumped out from behind the trees.

"It's just yer jewels we want. Hand 'em over," said the gang leader.

It was a quick and audacious robbery and the gang soon made off with their loot.

"What a terrible loss," said the Queen. "How will we explain it?"

"Well, I saved all my jewels," said the Princess, "I stuffed them up my you-know-what."

"Oh I wish I could think as quickly. I could have saved the crown."

* * *

QUEEN Victoria lay in bed next to Prince Albert exhausted and delighted on their first night of love.

"Oh, Albert, that was wonderful," she said, "is there a name for it?"

"Yes," he murmured, "it is called intercourse."

She sighed: "Well it is far too good for the common people. Let's prohibit it."

RUSSIANS

THE sole occupants of a compartment on the Trans Siberian Railway were a man and a woman.

On the first day he said: "Do you come from Minsk?"

She replied, "Nyet."

On the second he tried: "Do you come from Vladisvostok?"

She replied, "Nyet."

On the third day he said: "Enough of this love talk. Down with your pants."

* * *

WALKING into the empty store the Russian women said to the shopkeeper, "I see you have no vegetables today."

"No," he said. "This is a bread shop. It's bread we haven't got. The shop with no vegetables is around the corner."

* * *

SHE saw a man with one shoe walking down a Moscow street.

"Excuse me," she said, "do you realise you have lost a shoe?"

"You are mistaken," he said. "I just found one."

STUNG by world criticism that Soviet agents were behind an assassination attempt on the Pope the KGB said they would take the suspects in hand and investigate the matter.

After extensive interviews and countless viewings of video tapes it became clear that the Pope opened fire first.

*   *   *

WHAT do you call an attractive woman in Russia?

A tourist.

S

SALES

WHEN you knock on her door and her husband opens it...Sell something. For Chris'sake sell something.

* * *

SHOE salesman: "Can I interest you in a casual pump?"
  Floozie: "Why not? I can look at shoes later."

* * *

THE salesman said quietly: "Is it in?"
  "Yes," she replied.
  "Does it hurt?"
  "No," she said. "It feels wonderful."
  "Shall I wrap your old shoes?"

* * *

THE car salesman divorced his wife.
  She was giving too many demonstration rides.

* * *

THE salesman with his foot in the door had been observing the curvaceous shape of the housewife.
  "I can arrange easy credit terms, Madam," he said.
  "How easy?" she asked.
  "Nothing down but your pants," he said.

* * *

IZZI Goldstein had just returned from his monthly sales schedule and had an incredible story to tell his wife, Rachel.
  When he got to Sydney there was an airport strike and

he was delayed overnight. All the hotels were booked so he had to ask Schmidst, one of his customers, if he could put him up for the night.

Schmidst gladly offered to share his double bed and even offered Izzi a fine meal with wine.

In the middle of the night Goldstein felt a hand on his privates. Possibly his companion was dreaming. But there was no mistake when he felt an erect penis pushed against his bum.

"What did you do?" said Rachel with alarm.

"What could I do," said Goldstein, "Schmidst is my best Sydney account."

* * *

THE salesman was travelling late at night when his car blew a tyre and he realised he didn't have a jack. It was miles from anywhere, but across the field he could see a farmhouse in silhouette against the rising moon.

"He could lend me a jack," mused the salesman as he set off towards the farm.

As he stumbled across the paddocks in the dark he wondered if farmers still had the hospitality for which they were renowned.

"It's late," he thought. "He probably won't be too pleased about being woken up. He has probably had a hard day in the field and was looking forward to a bit of rest."

He approached the farmhouse and knocked on the door.

While he waited his thoughts continued: "The poor bloke is most likely getting out of bed now. His wife could be nagging him. He will be upset. He could even put the dogs onto me."

When the farmer opened the door the traveller said: "You can stick the jack up your arse!"

* * *

AN attractive salesgirl approached a young man in a department store and said: "What would you like, Sir?"

"What would I like?" he repeated. "Why I would like to

take you out of here, take you to my pad, mix a nice cocktail, take you in my arms, rip your pants off and make passionate love to you. That's what I'd like...but what I need is a pair of socks."

* * *

SID was told if he didn't sell more toothbrushes he would be fired. One month later his sales record had soared and the manager called him in to explain the dramatic turn-around.

Sid explained that he got sick of calling on pharmacies. He said he set up a little table at Flinders St Station with some dry biscuits and a new dip.

"Try my dip," he would say, and a constant stream of people did so. When they enquired about the ingredients of the dip Sid told them: "Garlic and chook shit!"

They would go "Aaaargh!" and spit it out.

Then Sid would say: "Would you like to buy a tooth-brush?"

* * *

IT was the old story of a salesman finding himself stranded in the country and knocking on the door of the only pub in town.

"Well, we don't have a spare room," said the proprietor, "but you are welcome to share with the little red-headed school teacher if you like."

The salesman could hardly contain his excitement. "Oh thanks. I will be a real gentleman."

"That's good," said the publican. "So's the little red-headed school teacher!"

* * *

ONCE again the salesman found himself knocking on a farmhouse door seeking a bed for the night.

"Sure," said the farmer, "but we only have one spare bed and you will have to share that with Cecil, my son."

The salesman turned and headed for his car. "Crikey, how did I get into the wrong joke?"

"THERE'S a salesman outside with a young lady."

"Tell him I'll take one."

* * *

THE travelling salesman sent a telegram to his wife: "Coming home Friday."

When he arrived home he was alarmed to find a man in bed with his wife. He went berserk, but was restrained by his mother-in-law. She urged him to keep calm and not to commit any violent and hasty action he would, in time, regret. "Leave it to me," she said, "there must be an explanation."

Next day she explained it all to her son-in-law. "I have gone into the matter thoroughly, and like I told you, there is a reason for your wife's behaviour. There was a postal strike on Friday and she didn't get the telegram!"

SCHOOLS

See TEACHERS

THE little bush school had the reputation of being the toughest in the region so it was with a great deal of trepidation that the new mistress took her first class.

"Give me a word beginning with A," she said.

"Arsehole!" said little Johnny as quick as a flash.

She covered her shock and moved on to B.

"Bastard," came the answer from little Mick.

She thought she would give C a miss and moved on to D.

"Dwarf," said little Fred.

And with a sigh of relief she asked Fred to explain what a dwarf was.

"A little cunt about this big," said Fred.

* * *

WHEN I was a kid I went to an immoral school. It had no principal and it had no class.

332

IT was show and tell at school and little Johnny stood up and said his Dad had two dicks.

Miss Prim the teacher said she couldn't believe it.

"Yes," said Johnny, "a little one he wears in the shower and a big one he cleans Mum's teeth with."

* * *

THE new teacher at the boys' school was Miss Franny and she was disturbed to find that even the headmaster made a mistake when he welcomed her as Miss Fanny.

"The name is Franny," she said coldly.

"Sorry," said the headmaster who made a mental note not to forget the "r".

He escorted her to her new class. "Good morning boys," he said,"I would like to introduce you to Miss Crunt."

* * *

IN order to get the kids to study the teacher devised a plan. She would ask a questions early each Friday afternoon and those who could answer could go home.

"Can anyone tell me the square root of seven?" she said.

Nobody knew the answer so they remained at their desks.

Next week she said "Can anyone tell me the capital of Pakistan?" Again no answer so no escape.

Little Ronnie came up with a plan for the following Friday. He arrived with some black marbles and to the amusement of the other kids he rolled them with a clatter along the floor.

"Okay," said the teacher. "Who's the comedian with the black balls?"

"Bill Cosbie," shouted Ronnie. "See yer Monday."

* * *

IT was the geography class and little Lulu was asked to point out Tasmania on the map. She did so.

"Now Frankie," she said, "Tell us who discovered Tasmania?"

"Lulu did," said Frankie.

WHEN the school council decided to teach a sex education program there was a deputation from the parents' association.. "We want no graphic demonstrations," said one dissenting parent, "so just make sure it's oral."

* * *

POINTING at young Fred the teacher asked him to spell 'weather.

Fred made a valiant attempt: "W-O-T-H-E-R?"

In despair the teacher said: "That's the worst spell of weather we've had in quite a time."

* * *

Sex educator Miss Best
    Told Johnny his work had regressed
    "But since learning's a tool
    If you stay after school
    I'll help you bone up for the test."

SCIENCE

DURING the next lunar eclipse get out under the stars. Face south and bend your body at the waist to form a 90 degree angle. Bend the knees at a 45 degree angle. Then get a shaving mirror and hold it between your knees. With a bit of luck, and if all the angles are correct, you should see Uranus.

* * *

ARTIFICIAL insemination is so reliable because there is no chance of a cock-up.

* * *

AT an international medical conference the Russian doctor told how they transplanted a new heart into a man and he was working within one month.

"That's nothing," said the American. "We put a heart, lungs and a new liver into a man and within one month he was up looking for work."

"That's bugger-all," said the Australian. "We put a fart

in Canberra and in no time at all he put half the population out of work."

SCOTS

THE reason Scots have blisters on their dicks is because they are such tight-fisted wankers.

* * *

WHAT do Scotsmen do with their old condoms?
They keep rooting with them.

* * *

JOCK McPerv was so mean he used to reverse charge his obscene telephone calls.

* * *

WHEN Jock had a vasectomy he asked the doctor if he was entitled to severance pay.

* * *

HOW does a Scot take a bubble bath?
He has baked beans for supper the night before.

* * *

WE have all heard about the Scotsman who found a crutch.
So he broke his wife's leg.

* * *

A SCOTTISH gentleman is one who gets out of the bath to piss in the sink.

* * *

JOCK's fiancee peered at her engagement ring.
"Oh Jock, is it a real diamond?"
"Och, if it isnae, I've been done out of a fiver," he replied.

* * *

McTAVISH stopped a young man in the street. "Aren't you the chap who hauled my son from the lake yesterday?"
"Yes," said the life saver, "but think nothing of it. It was nothing."

"Nothing indeed?" roared McTavish. "Where's the lad's bloody cap then?"

* * *

TWO Scottish migrants met in Sydney. They hadn't seen each other since they migrated from Scotland together 25 years ago. They hugged and slapped each other on the shoulder.

"Let's have a drink, like we did in the old times in Glasgow," said one.

"Aye, and don't forget, it's your shout," said the other.

* * *

A SCOT, a Jew and an Englishman were dining together in a restaurant. When the waiter cleared away the coffee the Scot was heard to ask for the bill.

Next day the newspaper headlines declared: JEWISH VENTRILOQUIST SHOT IN RESTAURANT.

* * *

WHAT is the difference between a Scotsman and a canoe?

A canoe sometimes tips.

* * *

A SCOT met a doctor on the street and hoping for some free advice asked: "What should I do for a sprained ankle?"

The doctor, also a Scot, replied: "Limp."

* * *

SERGEANT McTavish of the Highland Regiment swaggered into a pharmacy. He placed a battered condom on the counter and asked the chemist how much would it cost to repair it.

The chemist held the damaged item up to the light. "I could launder it and disinfect it, vulcanise a patch on the holes and tears on the side and insert new elastic around the top, but if you take my advice it would be almost as cheap to buy a new one."

McTavish could recognise sales talk when he heard it and said he would think it over.

He returned next morning. "You've persuaded us," he declared, "the regiment has decided to invest in a new one."

* * *

A TRUE Scot never sends his pyjamas to the laundry unless he has a pair of socks stuffed in the pocket.

* * *

McTAVISH heard about a doctor who charged $20 for the first consultation, but only $5 for subsequent visits.

So when he entered the clinic he said: "Well, here I am again, Doc."

"Good. Keep up the treatment I prescribed the first time," said the doctor who was also a Scot.

* * *

WHEN the Scot went to the clinic for a check-up the doctor told him he had too much sugar in his water.

Next morning he pissed on his porridge.

* * *

A SCOT went to London for two weeks' holiday. He took a shirt and a five pound note. When he returned he hadn't changed either of them.

* * *

McTAVISH donates a lot of money to charity but he likes to do it anonymously.

In fact, he doesn't even sign the cheques.

* * *

THE Scots even enjoy being constipated.

They hate to part with anything.

* * *

DO you know what McTavish did with his first fifty cent piece?

Married her.

* * *

DID you hear about the Scotsmen who started a squash club?

Ten of them pooled their finances and bought their own bottle.

JOCK was due for his annual medical check-up and as usual arrived with a liberal specimen in a very large bottle. After the test the doctor announced that Jock was fine. There was nothing abnormal in the specimen.

Jock happily returned home to relay the good news. "Agnes," he said, "you and I, the kids and grandpa are all in good health."

* * *

AN Englishman, a Scot and an Irishman were on the Titanic when she struck the iceberg.

As she started to sink the purser shouted: "We are about to meet our maker. We'd better do something religious."

The Englishman said a prayer. The Irishman sung a hymn. The Scot took up a collection.

* * *

IN his later years Sandy began to be a little deaf but was too mean to buy a hearing aid.

So he scrounged some thin wire and put one end in his top pocket and hooked the other end behind his ear.

It made no difference to his deafness, but it prompted people to speak to him more loudly.

* * *

JOCK walked into the fish shop and ordered two pieces of fish, two pickled onions, plenty of vinegar and salt, "and wrap the lot up in today's newspaper."

* * *

McTAVISH had kept vigil beside his dying wife for two days. Finally he had to keep an appointment at the local inn. "I'll be away for a while," he said. "I'll be back as soon as I can, however, if you feel yourself slipping away while I'm gone would you mind blowing out the candle."

* * *

THE rich Sultan of Istanbul was dying from a disease that baffled the medical world for months before they discovered that only a blood transfusion would save him. It was a rare blood group and a search throughout the globe revealed that there was only one man who could match the sultan's blood group. It was Jock McTavish from the Highlands.

Jock donated the blood. It saved the sultan's life and shortly afterwards Jock received a gift of $5000.

Two years later the sultan had a replapse and Jock was asked to supply more of his unique blood. Again the sultan recovered and soon after Jock received a gift of $2000.

When the sultan fell ill for the third time Jock once again came to the rescue with more Celtic blood. The sultan recovered and sent Jock a thank-you note.

*   *   *

JOCK was walking down the street in his kilt when a curious woman asked if there was anything worn under the tartan.

"Nothing's worn," he replied, "everything's in perfect working order."

*   *   *

THE Scotsman gave the waiter a tip.

It didn't even run a place.

*   *   *

THE chaps in the bar invited Jock to a small bore shooting club. When he got there they stood him on a box and started firing at him.

*   *   *

WHEN a Scottish millionaire in his eighties decided to marry an eighteen year old chorus girl the vicar protested.

"I don't believe in marrying for money," he said.

"Good," replied the millionaire, "then I won't insult you by offering you a fee for performing the ceremony."

*   *   *

HAVE you heard about the Scotsman who gave an Englishman, a Welshman and an Irishman ten pounds each?

Neither has anyone else.

THEN there's the Scot who drinks Scotch and Horlicks. When it is his turn to shout he is fast asleep.

* * *

A SCOT pushes his way to the bar. "I've had an attack of the yaws," he says to the barman.

"What's yaws?" says the barman.

"Double whisky," says the canny Scot.

* * *

A SCOT ordered a pot of beer and as the barman handed it over he said, "D'yer think yer canna fit a nip o whisky in it too?"

"Certainly," said the barman.

"Then fill it ta the top wi beer."

* * *

THREE Scots were in church one Sunday when the collection plate came their way. One fainted and the other two carried him out.

* * *

THE young Scotsman's delight was obvious as the train pulled in to Victoria Station.

"First time in London?" enquired the passenger opposite.

"Aye," said Scotty, "and not only that, I am on my honeymoon."

The passenger looked surprised. "Then where is your wife?"

"Oh, she's been here before," said Scotty.

* * *

LETTER to the Editor: "If you don't stop making jokes at the expense of Scotsmen I shall discontinue borrowing your newspaper."

* * *

A SCOTTISH music lover married a woman because he was charmed by her voice. So charmed that he didn't realise how ugly she was until the first morning of the honeymoon when he sat in bed looking at her without her make-up.

He stared at her for some time, then grabbed her by the shoulders and roared: "Sing ya bugger, sing. Fer Chrissake sing."

* * *

DOWN at the Edinburgh Arms the worst drunk at the bar is always Duncan Disorderly.

* * *

A SCOTTISH hotel is an establishment where they pinch the towels off the guests.

* * *

McTAVISH took all his money out of the bank for a holiday. After it rested in his pocket for a week he put it all back.

* * *

WHEN the police put a price on Jock's head he turned himself in.

* * *

SHE said she would never go to a restaurant with Jock again. "He reads the menu from right to left," she said.

SEDUCTION

OVER their fifth drink the young man asked the girl to come to his apartment to see his etchings.

She thought the excuse was so corny and so sweet she agreed.

When she got there and he opened the door and snapped on the light she was surprised to see thousands of etchings covering the walls. Not a stick of furniture, not a lounge nor a bed.

Boy was she floored.

* * *

BEING seduced is a matter of perfect timing.

The woman has to give in, just before the man gives up.

"MRS Robinson, don't you think it is wrong to have an 18-year-old boy in your flat for hours every night?"

"I assure you it's only platonic. It's play for him and its a tonic for me!"

* * *

HE asked her for a dance and while he held her close he whispered: "Would you like to have breakfast with me tomorrow morning?"

She replied tentatively: "Sounds nice."

"Will I phone you, or nudge you?" he said.

* * *

THE rich old rogue was delighted that his delightful and voluptuous young niece from the country had agreed to have dinner with him. Hed had his eye on her for some time.

But he was a little surprised that when the waiter arrived she ordered big serves of the most expensive dishes.

"Do you always eat like this at home?" he asked.

"No," she said. "Only when someone wants to get into my pants."

* * *

AN Australian had been wandering the Outback for months. He finally came to a farm where a pretty girl met him at the gate.

"D'yer root?" he said.

"No," she replied, "but you have talked me into it, you silver-tongued bastard."

* * *

IN the morning was beautiful Molly
Bemoaning her nocturnal folly
She had gone with this bloke
Just for a joke
But the joke was on Molly by golly.

SHOPKEEPERS

THE shopkeeper was giving his female assistant a knee-trembler against the counter. He was right on the gravy stroke when the front door clanger signalled a customer coming in.

There was a panic for a place to hide. She dived under the counter and he stuck his donger in the till.

The customer said: "You look pleased with yourself today, Mr Johnston."

"Yes," he said. "I've just come into money."

* * *

A MAN went into jewellers shop and when the beautiful blonde assistant said: "Can I help you?" he flopped his donger on the counter.

Unperturbed, she looked him in the eye and said: "This is not a cock shop. It's a clock shop."

Just as cool he replied, "Well, can you put two hands on it?"

* * *

SHE walked into the delicatessen and selected a chicken. She prodded and poked it. She lifted one wing and sniffed underneath. Lifted the other wing and did the same. Finally she looked at the chicken's rear end and gave it another sniff.

"This chicken is not fresh," she declared.

"Lady," said the shopkeeper, "do you think you could pass the same test?"

SHOWBIZ

HE didn't have $50 to see the Broadway musical, *Cats*, so he settled for some off-Broadway pussy for $25.

* * *

"I NEVER have sex in the morning," said the pop star. "It is bad for the voice, it's bad for the health, and besides, you never know who you might meet in the afternoon."

THE young starlet wore black scanties with the label:
"Made in Hollywood, by almost everyone."

* * *

STARRING in Hamlet, actress Amelia Hubb
Learned her lines while immersed in her tub
Using Method a bit,
She fingered her clit
To memorise, with passion, "Ah, there's the rub."

* * *

A YOUNG porno star called Sue
Was a hit when it came to a screw
Her climactic fame spread
With promotions that said:
"Coming Soon, to a Theatre Near You."

* * *

MALE porno stars get it easy.
They can get away with muffing their lines.

* * *

GOING backstage after the ballet the devoted theatre fan
realised his lifelong dream.
He kissed every ballerina in the joint.

* * *

THE chorus girl scored a date with the star of mime.
"He is one of those silent actors who relies on gestures
and facial expressions," she said. "It was a mime blowing
experience."

* * *

THE old actor's agent had a good spiel on his casting couch:
"Come to bed with me and I will make you a star, and then
you can sleep with the biggest names in Hollywood."

* * *

THE director took the young starlet aside.
"In this first scene you are supposed to look virginal."
"What do you think I am," she replied, "a character
actress?"

SID the shady director heard that one of the chorus girls doubled as a hooker and was generous with her favours. He put the hard word on her and was soon invited to her room. After the steamy session he was about to leave, then reached into his pocket and gave her two tickets for Saturday's gala performance.

The woman looked at them with disdain. "Do you expect me to buy bread with these?"

"If you are looking for bread," said Sid, "you should have fucked a baker."

*   *   *

THERE was a drum roll and the spotlight hit the Great Alfonso as he approached the growling lion. He cracked the whip and the lion opened its jaws wide. The Great Alphonso stepped closer, unzipped his fly and to the amazement of the audience, flopped it between the gaping jaws.

When he stepped back after a terrifying ten seconds there was resounding applause and the ringmaster proclaimed it the bravest act in circus history. "Indeed, anyone who can emulate that feat right here and now will readily receive the sum of one hundred thousand dollars." roared the ringmaster. "Do we have any volunteers?"

There was a timid voice of acceptance in the back row and the spotlight picked out a reluctant hero being pushed to the front of the crowd.

He finally reached the ringmaster and said: "I don't think I can open my mouth as wide as the lion, but I'm willing to give it a try!"

*   *   *

STAR of film and screen, Harry Glitter, wanted a stunt man and took advantage of the achievements in medical technology to have a clone made of himself so that he wouldn't have to play the dangerous scenes.

The amazing likeness of the actor was delivered to his

penthouse where Harry soon discovered that one of his characteristics had been developed too far.

The clone stripped off, went out on the balcony and began exposing himself to the crowd below.

Harry was shocked. In the struggle to hustle the clone inside they fell against the railing and the clone overbalanced and fell to his death.

The police were quickly on the scene to charge Harry Glitter with murder.

"Murder! Of course it's not murder," said the star.

"No doubt about it," said the sergeant. "It was you who made the obscene clone fall."

* * *

A YOUNG trapeze artist well stacked
   Is faced by a very sad fact
   Imagine the pain
   When time and again
   He catches his wife in the act.

* * *

THERE was a young actor named Bates
   Who danced the fandango on skates
   But he fell on his cutlass
   Which rendered him nutless
   And practically useless on dates.

* * *

WHEN the much married actress finally died her friends clubbed together for a fitting funeral and a tombstone with the fitting epitaph: "At last she sleeps alone."

* * *

HE was only six years old, but he decided to take his girl-friend to the movies.

"How much is it?" he asked at the box office.

"Well, Sonny, for grown ups in long pants it is eight dollars, but as you are only wearing short pants it is four dollars."

"Well in that case," piped up his girlfriend, "I should get in for nothing!"

* * *

GEORGE had taken his wife to the theatre, but half way through the first act he was busting for a leak. Then at interval he had a difficult time pushing through the crowd trying to find the Gents down one passage and around the next until he was somewhere backstage.

He was desperate, and when he discovered a fountain, surrounded by foliage, the effect of the tinkling water was the last straw. Nobody was about so he took out his willy and pissed into the fountain. It was a great relief.

He took some time finding his way back to his seat and when he sat next to his wife again he whispered, "Have I missed much of this second act?"

"Missed it?" she said. "You were the star."

* * *

IT was halfway through the movie when a woman dashed up the aisle and complained that she had been "interfered with" in the front stalls.

The manager quietened her down and ushered her to another seat, but no more than a minute passed and another woman complained to him that she had been "interfered with" in the front stalls.

This was too much, so the manager went down to the front and shone his torch along the second row. He was surprised to see a bald man crawling along on his hands and knees.

"What are you doing?" asked the manager.

The bald man looked up. "Oh, I've lost my toupee. It fell off in the dark. I had my hand on it twice but it got away!"

* * *

IT happened some time ago, when a young man walked into a theatrical agency and said he could sing and dance.

347

He backed it up with such a convincing demonstration that the agent knew he had a future star.

"You are great," he said. "What's your name?"

"Penis van Lesbian," answered the young hopeful.

"That's a shocker. We'll have to change that for a start," said the agent scratching his head. "I've got it. We'll call you Dick Van Dyke."

SMOKING

THEY were surprised to find the anti-smoking crusader had married a chain smoker.

"Yes, but I am forcing her to give it up," he said. "By strictly limiting her to an after coitus cigarette only she is down to a pack a week."

* * *

AN elderly couple killed in a car accident arrived in Heaven. St Peter took them on a tour of the facilities and showed them into their ocean-view apartment.

"Here are the buttons to press if you need food, wine, movies, trips, new cars, massage, etc. It's all there."

When St Peter had gone the husband turned to the wife and snarled: "Shit Mabel, we could have been here years ago if you hadn't made us give up smoking."

SOCIALITES

THE YOUNG socialite's Porsche was weaving from one side of the road to the other as she wended her way home from a party. She was stopped by a young traffic cop and given a breathalyser test.

The young cop studied the result and said: "Well, Miss, you've had a few stiff ones tonight."

"Gracious," replied the girl, "can it tell that as well?"

* * *

KNOWN for his ranting against the evils of drink the vicar

attended a village council meeting held at the Ponsonby Manor. After the business was over Jeeves began to pour everyone a glass of whisky. The vicar placed his hand over his glass.

"None of the evils of drink for me thank you, I'd rather commit adultery."

Fred began pouring his drink back into the neck of the bottle.

"I didn't realise we had a choice," he said.

SOCIETY

LADY Ponsonby received a letter from her son in boarding school which finished with the sentence, "Last night I had my first naughty."

She was aghast and quickly wrote back berating him and instructing him not to have another one.

Eventually she got a reply. "No mother, I haven't had one since. The first one hurt too much."

* * *

WHEN the plain daughter of a tenant farmer came home pregnant he reached for his shotgun. "But father," she said, "it was the squire of the manor."

With his shotgun cocked he headed for the manor in a rage.

"Hold on Murphy," said the squire, "I'll do the right thing by your daughter. If it's a boy I will settle $5000 for you. If it's a girl, then $3000."

"And what if it's twins?" snarled Murphy.

"Double of course," said the squire.

Murphy pondered for a moment. "And if she has a miscarriage, can she have another go?"

* * *

THE squire took his son to the library for a heart-to-heart. "Look here Cecil," he said, "you are 35 now and your mother thinks it is high time you were married. What about marrying Lady Genevieve?"

"I don't love Lady Genevieve," he said.

"Well what about Lady Cynthia?"

"I don't love Lady Cynthia. Actually I love Lord Ponsonby."

"Well you can't marry him. He's a Catholic."

SONGS

MARY had a little lamb
  So her father shot the shepherd.

* * *

I'LL be seizing you, in all the old familiar places.

* * *

IF you were the only girl in the world, well okay, but as you're not, forget it.

* * *

I CAN'T get over a girl like you,
  So answer the phone yourself.

SPINSTERS

AUNT Maud dreamt she was married.

  But when she woke up she found there was nothing in it.

* * *

AN elderly spinster sniffed with disdain when asked why she didn't marry.

  "I have a dog that growls, a parrot that swears, a fireplace that smokes and a cat that stays out all night. Why should I want a husband?"

* * *

THE spinster was coming home from evensong when a man jumped from behind a tree and said: "Don't move, this is a stick-up."

"I haven't got any money," she said, showing him her empty handbag.

"I'll see for myself," he said, and with that he began searching her. He felt around her waist, felt inside her bra, ran his hands up and down her legs and even searched her knickers.

Not finding a brass cent he turned to walk away.

"Don't stop searching," she said. "I can write you a cheque."

* * *

THE spinster approached the salesman in the furniture store. "I can't decide between the armchair or the sofa," she said.

"Believe me, Madam," said the salesman, "you won't make a mistake on the armchair."

"Right, then I'll take the sofa," she said.

* * *

MURGATROYD had noticed the spinster at the next table giving him a dirty look but he persisted with his meal. Nevertheless he was surprised when the waiter delivered a note from her. It read: "Young man, maybe you don't know it but your fly is unzipped. You should be ashamed of yourself. Exposing your person in a public place is disgusting. It's indecent. PS: I love you."

* * *

STELLA the spinster had heard that men with big feet have big pricks so when a tramp knocked on her door asking for a hand-out she was quick to notice his very large shoes stretched across the entire width of the step.

She invited him in, gave him a hearty meal, a bottle of beer and took him to bed.

When he woke alone next morning he found $50 and a brief note.

It said: "Buy yourself a pair of shoes that fit."

THE spinster had just settled into the seaside resort when she noticed the sign on the wall: "If the electric blanket doesn't work switch it off and call in a man."

* * *

SHE called at the police station to complain about the young man next door. "It's not safe to go out on the street," she said. "He's always sitting on his front porch whistling dirty songs!"

* * *

MISS Prim complained to the police that the men on the building site were using foul language.

The cop told her that builders' labourers tended to call a spade a spade.

"No they don't," she said. "They've been calling it a fucking shovel."

* * *

OLD Spinster's Prayer:
    And now I lay me down to sleep
    I wish I had a man to keep
    If there's a man beneath the bed
    I hope he heard each word I said.

* * *

YOUNG Spinster's Prayer:
    Oh Lord, I ask nothing for myself, but would you please send my dear mother a son-in-law?

* * *

SPINSTER'S advice:
    Dear girls. Be wary of Cupid
    And hark to the lines of this verse
    To let a fool kiss you is stupid
    To let a kiss fool you is worse.

SPORT

"I'M a little stiff from Badminton."

"I don't care where you come from."

NEVER fall in love with a tennis player.

To them love means nothing.

*   *   *

THE annual university boat race resulted in an exciting finish, but there was a dramatic moment when a blonde rushed through the crowd and kissed the cox of the winning crew.

*   *   *

SPIV and Nick were a little cheesed off when the gates of the sports ground were slammed shut. It was full to capacity for the grand final.

The ground was so crowded the toilet facilities could not cope and at half time many fans were forced to head for the perimeter fence and find a knot hole.

Spiv and Nick were still outside mutttering about their bad luck when Spiv noticed the odd dick being poked through the fence.

"Here's a chance to make some money," he said. He grabbed a dick and shouted: "Throw a fiver over or I'll cutcha cock off."

They were delighted to see a note flutter over the fence.

"We're on to something here," said Spiv, "you go that way and I'll meet you back here when we go right around the ground."

Ten minutes later they met. "I've got near on fifty dollars," said Spiv. "How did you go?"

"Not so good," said Nick, "I got forty-five dollars. But I've got three cocks!"

*   *   *

AN AUSTRALIAN girl phoned her boyfriend.

"Trevor, I've just been to the doctor and he tells me I'm up the duff. Trevor, if you don't marry me I will drown myself."

"Well, Sheryl, that's bloody decent of you. Not only are you a good fuck, you're a good sport too."

SQUELCH

THE blonde was having a quiet drink when Larry Loudmouth sat beside her. "Hi babe," he said. "I'd love to get into your pants."

"Why?" she replied. "There's already one arsehole there."

*   *   *

AS he arrived home from the pub he noticed his wife ironing her bra and couldn't refrain from commenting, "I don't know why you bother with that, dear, you've nothing to put in it."

She continued ironing and casually remarked, "I often think the same thing when I'm ironing your underpants."

*   *   *

THE drunk boarded the train and plonked himself down beside a priest and began to read the paper.

He looked up after a bit and said: "Tell me Father, what causes arthritis?"

It was just the opening the priest wanted. "I will tell you what causes arthritis my man," he said with passion. "It's immoral living, too much drinking and smoking and no doubt sins of the flesh. How long have you had it?"

"Oh it's not me, Father," said the drunk. "It says here the Pope's got it."

*   *   *

AFTER 25 years of marriage a couple decided on an amicable divorce. To celebrate the granting of the decree they had dinner together.

After the third glass of champagne the husband said: "There's something I have always wanted to ask you, but I didn't have the nerve. Now it can't possibly worry me."

"What's that?" said his ex-wife.

"Why is it that five out of our six children have black hair and Tommy is so blonde."

She didn't answer.

"Come on, you can tell me now," he insisted. "Whose child is Tommy?"

Finally she acquiesced. "Well, if you really want to know, Tommy is your child."

* * *

HE believed in the direct approach and even on their first date asked if she wanted to hear his sexual philosophy.

"I suppose so." she replied.

"Well, it's Get-It-Up, Get-It-In, Get-It-Off, and Get-It-Out," he said, "What do you think about that?"

"I think that's the Four-Get-It approach," she said coolly.

STATISTICS

ON the question of girls legs 19% of men said they liked fat legs, 27% said they liked slender legs and the rest said they liked something in between.

T

TAXIDERMISTS

AN old lady had two pet monkeys. They had been with her for years until one died and the second died out of sympathy.

She took them to a taxidermist.

"Do you want them mounted?" he asked.

"No, just shaking hands will do," she replied.

* * *

WE knew he was elderly because he looked much older than the blonde at the table with him.

We knew he was rich because of the amount of food and wine he was lavishing on the girl.

We knew that he was a taxidermist because he was obviously stuffing the bird before mounting her.

TAXIS

THE prostitute hailed a cab and gave directions to take her home. When the cab stopped she said:

"Oh goodness. I've forgotten my purse."

"Well how are you going to pay for the ride?" demanded the driver.

She lifted her skirt. "With this," she said.

"Haven't you got anything smaller?" he said.

THE taxi screeched to a halt.

"What's the idea of stopping here?" said the bloke in the back.

"But I heard a woman say stop," said the cabbie.

"Yes, but she wasn't talking to you. Keep going."

* * *

AFTER travelling a few blocks Miss Lottsabazooma realised she had no money and immediately informed the driver. "Youd better stop. I can't pay you and it's ten dollars already," she said.

The driver checked her out in the rear-vision mirror. "That's okay," he said. "I'll turn down the first dark street, get in the back seat and take off your knickers."

"You'd be cheating yourself," she replied. "These knickers are only worth a fiver."

* * *

THE canny Scot took a taxi to the bankruptcy court, then invited the driver inside as one of the creditors.

* * *

HE lay under the cab tinkering with the motor and groping for spanners and tools when his attractive fare said: "Do you want a screwdriver?"

"Not now, Miss, but try me as soon as I fix this motor."

* * *

LEAVING the wedding reception the honeymoon couple hailed a cab to take them to their romantic boutique hotel in the hills. The driver wasn't too sure how to get there and said he would ask directions when they got closer. Meanwhile, the lovers couldn't wait and got down to it on the back seat.

Seeing a fork in the road the driver said: "I take the next turn, right?"

"No way, get your own," said the groom, "this one's all mine."

357

SCOT McTavish was lugging a heavy suitcase. He hailed a cab. "How much to the train station?"

"Five dollars," said the driver.

"How much for my suitcase?"

"Nothing."

McTavish opened the door, slung his case in and said: "Here, take it to the station then."

* * *

A DRUNK in the back seat of the cab says to the driver: "Exchooze me. Do you have room in the front for a crayfish and half a dozen bottles?"

"Yes," said the cabbie.

The drunk leans over and throws up. (Action joke).

* * *

MOISHE had a little scheme which always seemed to work. When the taxi delivered him to his address he would fumble in his waistcoat for the money and then search around the floor of the cab claiming to have dropped a fifty dollar note.

"Stay here while I get some matches from that tobacconist's stall so I can strike a light to find it," he would say.

As soon as Moishe got out of the cab it would invariably drive away.

* * *

WHEN the taxi company lowered its rates from two dollars flagfall to a single dollar there was a protest meeting at the Celtic Club. The Scots were annoyed that in most cases they were saving around five dollars a night by walking home, now they would only save around $2-50.

* * *

TWO teenage layabouts decided to share a taxi.

One took the hub caps the other took the radio.

TAXMAN

THERE is a major difference between cheating on your wife and cheating on the taxman.

When you get caught the taxman will still want to screw you.

* * *

PADDY was walking down the street when he stumbled on a fat and unopened pay envelope.

"That's a lucky find," said his mate Shamus.

"Lucky nothing," said Paddy. "Look at the bloody tax I'm paying."

* * *

FORTUNATELY the penis is still exempt from taxation. This is because it is usually hanging around unemployed.

The rest of the time it is either hard up, pissed off or in a hole. It also has two dependants and they are both nuts.

* * *

FRED consulted his lawyer. "I've been receiving threatening letters," he said.

"That's terrible," said the legal eagle. "We'll put a stop to that. Who are they from?"

"The Taxation Department," said Fred.

* * *

THE rabbi was surprised to receive a call from the tax inspector. "The synagogue is exempt from taxes," explained the rabbi.

"Oh, it's not you we are enquiring about," said the taxman, "it's one of your community, Isaac Goldstein."

The taxman explained that on his tax return Goldstein indicated that he donated $50,000 to the synagogue.

"Is this true?" asked the taxman.

"The money hasn't arrived yet but I am sure it will be here as soon as I remind dear Isaac."

TEACHERS

THE English teacher was seeking an example of the word 'contagious' and little Billy's hand went up like a rocket.

"Only last Sunday," he said, "a big truck full of oranges nearly forced Dad's car off the road. And as it swerved around the next bend the truck lost its load and my Dad said it would take that contagious to pick up all those oranges."

* * *

A STRAPPING young farmhand was sent to the station to pick up the new school teacher who turned out to be an attractive young woman.

On the way back to the farm she noticed a stallion mounting a mare. "How do they know when to do that?" she enquired.

The young man explained that it was a sense of smell.

In the very next paddock a bull was enjoying himself on a cow.

"Again, it is a sense of smell," explained the country boy. "Just like that ram and ewe over there."

He unloaded her luggage at the farmhouse and turned to go. "See you later," he said.

"Thanks," she replied. "And do come over when your cold gets better."

* * *

SHE was a teacher in her mid-forties and a spinster until she finally allowed herself to be seduced by the school inspector.

She sat up in bed and started crying. "Oh the shame," she sobbed. "How can I stand up in front of those children tomorrow and pretend to be worthy when I've been sinful so often."

"What do you mean, often?" said the school inspector, "I thought this was the first time."

"It is," she said, "but you are going to do it again, aren't you?"

TIME

THEY are thinking of putting a clock on the Leaning Tower of Pisa. It's for those who have the inclination but not the time.

* * *

TIME is nature's way of preventing everything happening at once.

* * *

MURPHY had been in the bar for a while when his mate arrived.

"Hey Murph, what time is it?"

"Don't know," replied Murphy, "Except that it ain't foive o'clock."

"How come?"

"Because I told my missus I'd be home by foive, and here I am still here."

* * *

MY brother hates daylight saving.

He gets his early morning erection on the 8-30 train to the office.

TOASTS

"FORNICATION," roared the MC, "Fornication like this we need champagne for the toast...

* * *

HERE'S to the kisses you've snatched,
   and vice versa.

* * *

MAY all your ups and downs be in a bed..

* * *

HERE'S to your genitalia
   May it never land you in jailiya

* * *

MAY you live as long as you want to
   And want to, as long as your live.

MAY we kiss who we please
  And please who we kiss.
            *   *   *
IF I'm asleep when you want me. Wake me.
  And if I don't want to. Make me.
            *   *   *
IF I am sleeping
  and you want to wake me
  don't shake me
  just take me.
            *   *   *
MAY the fleas of a thousand camels infest the underpants
of our enemies.
            *   *   *
MAY your chooks turn into emus and kick down your
dunny door.
            *   *   *
HERE'S to the bloke down the lane
  He courted a girl, all in vain
  She swore when he kissed her
  So he slept with her sister
  Again and again and again.
            *   *   *
MUSICIANS' TOAST: May your organ never quit while
you are half way through your favourite piece.
            *   *   *
MAY we all get to heaven half an hour before the devil
knows we're dead.
            *   *   *
MAY the skin of your bum never cover a drum.
            *   *   *
MAY you live as long as you want, and may you never want
as long as you live.
            *   *   *
MAY you live a hundred years, and another month to
repent.

MAY we never put our finger in another man's pie.

*   *   *

MAY you never have to eat your hat.

*   *   *

MAY the frost never afflict your spuds.

*   *   *

MAY the Blue Bird of Happiness crap down your chimney.

*   *   *

MAY we drink to the thirst which is yet to come.

*   *   *

MAY we all be alive this time, twelve months.

*   *   *

MAY you slide down the bannister of life, with nary a splinter.

*   *   *

MAY your luck be like the capital of Ireland, always Dublin!

*   *   *

HERE'S to the wowsers, whose abstinence gives us all the more to drink.

*   *   *

THERE'S many a toast, if I could think of it Damned if I can, so let's drink to it.

*   *   *

TO our wives and sweethearts. May they never meet.

*   *   *

LET'S drink to the soup. May it be seen and not heard.

*   *   *

HERE'S to the girl who lives on the hill
    She won't be in it, but her sister will
    Here's to her sister, then.

*   *   *

HERE'S to the happiest days of my life,
    Spent in the arms of another man's wife,
    My mother's.

HERE'S to your eyes, and mine
   Here's to your lips, and mine
   The former have met
   The latter not yet
   So here's to that moment, sublime.
                    *   *   *
HERE'S to us
   May we live a long life
   And heres mud in your eye
   While I wink at your wife.
                    *   *   *
HERE'S to Miss Prim
   For her life held no terrors
   Born a virgin, died a virgin
   No hits, no runs, no errors.
                    *   *   *
I DRINK to your health when I'm with you
   I drink to your health when alone
   I drink to your health so often
   I'm becoming concerned at my own.
                    *   *   *
LONG live centenarians

TRADESMEN

TWO builders' labourers were walking home from a party.

   One said: "Basil, as soon as I get home I am going to rip
the wife's knickers off."
   "Why's that, Trevor?"
   "'Cos the bloody elastic is killing me," he said.
                    *   *   *
SHE had the decorators refurbishing the house and was
proudly showing her husband the new colour of the bedroom walls when the clumsy bugger lent on the door and
smudged the new paintwork.

Next day she interrupted the painter as he was doing some work in the kitchen.

"Excuse me, Mr Painter," she said. "Can you come up to the bedroom? I'd like to show you where my husband put his hand last night."

"If it's all the same, m'am," he replied, "I'd rather a cup of tea and a cake."

* * *

IZZI came home early one day and caught Rachel screwing with the baker.

"I'm ashamed of you," he shrieked. "Why are you screwing the baker when its to the butcher we owe money?"

* * *

PADDY was new to the carpentry game so when he called at the timber yard to pick up some two-by-fours he was corrected by the timber merchant.

"You mean four-by-twos?"

"Okay, if you say so," said Paddy.

"And how long do you want them?"

"A long time," said Paddy, "I'm building a bloody house."

* * *

PADDY was a builders' labourer and found he had been overpaid a fiver. He didn't say anything about it.

However, the following week he was underpaid a fiver and he went straight to the boss to complain about being short-changed.

"But you didn't complain last week when you were overpaid," said the boss.

"One mistake is one thing," said Paddy, "but to make two mistakes in successive weeks is very sloppy administration."

* * *

A PLUMBER knocked at the door with toolbox in hand. "I've come to fix your leaking cistern," he said to the woman who answered the door.

"But we haven't got a leaking cistern."

"Aren't you Mrs Snodsbody?"

"No. They moved away six months ago."

"Bloody typical," said the plumber. "They ring for a plumber saying it's an emergency, then piss off to another address."

* * *

A PLUMBER one night feeling free
Was plumbing his girl by the sea
Said the maid: "Quick stop plumbing
I fear someone's coming
Said the plumber, still plumbing,
"It's me!"

TRAINS

THE Vatican has taken over the railways and called it the Transportus Coitus Interuptus.

Everybody gets off one stop before their destination.

* * *

WHEN the train conductor saw the young couple screwing away in the compartment he used his radio to notify the police who boarded at the next station.

The girl was let off with a warning, but the bloke was charged with mounting and dismounting while the train was in motion and for having a first class ride while holding a second class ticket.

* * *

FOUR people were in the same compartment on a long train journey; a young woman, a priest, a businessman and a drunk.

All had been quiet for an hour or two until the young woman suddenly began to sob. The priest bent over to console her. "Tell me why you are crying," he said.

The girl sniffed and said: "I have just learnt that I am illegitimate."

The priest replied, "That's no sin. As a matter of fact I am illegitimate myself."

Then the businessman spoke up. "Excuse me, I couldn't help overhearing, but I must tell you that I am a self-made man. I own several businesses, in fact I am a millionaire, yet I am illegitimate too."

The drunk took out a cigarette and asked: "Any of you bastards got a light?"

TRAVEL

IT was their honeymoon and they told the travel agent they wanted to fly United.

She said the other passengers might object.

* * *

TWO women were side by side in deckchairs aboard the Queen Mary as it crossed the Atlantic.

"I'm so lucky to have this trip," said one. "My husband worked so hard to scrape the money together."

The other neighbour was unimpressed.

"First trip is it?" she said haughtily. "This is my 20th crossing. My husband works for Cunard."

"Well I told you mine does too," said the first woman, "but I don't swear about it."

* * *

A YOUNG man was enjoying his first night in Rome drinking cappucino at a pavement cafe when a pretty girl sat beside him.

"Hello," he said. "Do you understand English?"

"Only a little," she answered.

"How much?" he asked.

"Fifty dollars," she replied.

* * *

THERE is an American Express card holder who insists on early morning sex. He never leaves home without it.

PADDY, the left-handed barman had been pulling beers for 25 years in the same pub. "Why don't you travel and broaden your mind?" he was told repeatedly.

Finally he took the advice, and a week's holiday on the Canary Islands.

When he returned he was a changed and knowledgeable man. "Well what did you learn?" asked the regulars.

"I can tell you this," he said as they all leaned forward for his pearl of wisdom. "There are no canaries in the Canary Islands."

A year passed and Paddy once more took his annual leave abroad. This time his travel agent suggested the Virgin Islands.

"Well what did you learn this time, Paddy?" asked the regulars when he returned from his second world odyssey.

"I can tell you this," he said as they all leaned forward. "There are no canaries on the Virgin Islands, either!"

* * *

SHE was on the phone from the Gold Coast. "The holiday is wonderful darling, I feel like a new woman."

"So do I. Stay there another week."

* * *

A YOUNG chap boarded the Ansett flight at Cairns and the hostess noticed a newspaper parcel under his arm. "Mud-crabs," he explained. "I'm taking them back to Melbourne for a gourmet meal tonight."

"Then in that case they would be best placed in the fridge," said the hostess, stowing them away appropriately.

The flight landed on time and as the aircraft taxied across the tarmac the passengers were welcomed to Melbourne, and told to remain seated until the aircraft came to a halt ..."And would the gentleman who gave me the crabs in Cairns please identify himself?"

* * *

AN Australian football team took an end-of-season trip to

London where they hired a double-decker bus to see the sights. Half went upstairs.

Those down below were cheering, shouting and enjoying themselves but there was not a sound from those upstairs. The coach went up to check the reason and found them all gripping the seats with white knuckles.

"It's all right for you lot down below," one said, "you've got a driver."

* * *

DEAR diary. This is day one of my first holiday on a cruise ship.

Day two. While the cruise is nice there are an awful lot of men, including the stewards, making passes at me.

Day three. I have been invited to sit at the captain's table.

Day four. The captain made an improper suggestion last night. I refused.

Day five. The captain says that unless I agree, he will sink the ship.

Day six. Last night I saved the lives of 2,765 people.

* * *

UNCLE Fred had heard about the massage parlours in Bangkok and when he booked into his hotel was surprised to find this service offered as part of the hotel facilities.

He was on the phone in a flash.

When the girl had finished working on his back she asked him to roll over and it was evident by the state of his Onkaparinga that the rub had done him the world of good.

The girl noticed it. "Oh," she said, "by the look of that you might like wanky-wanky?"

Fred gave an eager nod.

"Okay, I'll come back as soon as you've finished," she said.

* * *

A TRAVEL agent looked up from his desk to notice an old lady and an old gent peering in the shop window at the

369

posters showing the glamorous destinations around the world.

The agent had had a good week and the dejected couple looking in the window gave him a rare feeling of generosity.

He called them in. "I know that on your pension you could never hope to have a holiday, so I am sending you off to Queensland at my expense, and I won't take no for an answer," he said.

He took them inside and asked his secretary to write two flight tickets and book a room on the Gold Coast. They gladly accepted and were off.

About a month later the little old lady came into his shop. "And how did you like the holiday?" he asked eagerly.

"The flight was exciting and the room was lovely," she said. "I've come to thank you. But one thing has puzzled me. Who was that old bloke I had to share the room with?"

* * *

THE pilot had just given the passengers the usual announcement about the estimated time of arrival and weather conditions, then forgot to switch off the public address system.

"And as soon as we get settled into our hotel I am going to have a stiff whisky and put the hard word on that curvey red-haired hostess," he said to his co-pilot.

The hostess concerned was aghast that the PA system was still turned on. She hurried towards the flight deck but tripped over a small bag which had been left in the aisle.

A little old lady leant down to help her up and said: "No need to hurry, lass. He said he was going to have a whisky first!"

* * *

LETTER from a travel agent: "Dear Sir, In reference to your proposed trip to London, the flight you requested is completely full, but we will keep in contact and inform you immediately somebody falls out, as is often the case."

A BUSLOAD of tourists stopped for the night in Kakadu. The tour leader sent his offsider down to the billabong for water. A few minutes later the offsider came running back to say hed confronted a large crocodile in the shallows.

"Never mind about the croc," said the leader. "He's more frightened of you than you are of him."

"Well in that case," said the offsider, "the water in the billabong isn't fit to drink."

* * *

THE tourists all trooped off the bus when it stopped in Kakadu, except for one little old lady. "Don't you want to see the Aboriginal carving?"

"Nup," she replied. "I've lived on a farm all my life and I've seen plenty of cows calving, so I don't suppose it would be much different."

* * *

THE coach was travelling through Dublin when the guide announced: "We are now passing the biggest pub in Ireland."

An Aussie voice at the back of the bus said: "Why?"

* * *

YOUNG Aussie tourist, first time abroad, dashed into the Gents in Trinidad and lined up beside a tall Jamacian. He could hardly fail to notice the huge donger the Jamacian held with both hands, but got the shock of his life when he saw the name 'Wendy tattooed along its length.

"Look," he said excitedly, "Me too. Our girl friends have got the same name."

"Sorry man," said the Jamacian. "Mine really says: "Welcome to Trinidad. Have a nice day!"

TRUCKIES

EVER since the hitch-hiker had climbed aboard hed noticed the lack of conversation and that the truckie was the silent type. It eventually prompted him to ask the truckie if he had a radio.

"Nup," was the stern reply.

After another long silence the hiker said: "Well what do you do to help the time pass?"

There was yet another pause before the truckie finally answered: "Well I've got my little mate," and with that he snapped his fingers and a monkey jumped from behind the cabin and landed on the driver's lap.

It sat there for ten minutes or so until the hiker said: "Well you can't talk to a monkey. What's the use of that."

"Watch this," said the truckie. He gave the monkey a belt on the head and it opened the truckie's fly and gave him a head job.

Yet another poignant silence and the relieved driver said: "What do you think of that?"

"Not bad. I'm impressed," said the hiker.

"Would you like to try one yourself?" asked the truckie.

"Well I would, if you don't mind, provided you don't hit me on the head as hard as you hit the monkey."

* * *

THE truckie couldn't believe his eyes. There in the middle of the desert was a flashing neon sign: 'Mama's Desert Diner. He had crossed this desolate stretch many times and never seen it before.

"No, we are new," said Mama. "What will ya have luv?"

"Two hamburgers and a hot dog," he ordered.

He saw Mama go the fridge, reach for two rissoles and whack them up under her armpits.

"What for?" roared the truckie.

"Everything is deep frozen out here luv," she explained, "that's the only way I can thaw them out."

"Well okay," said the reluctant diner, "but cancel the hot dog."

THE hitch-hiker lay back in the cabin and lifted her skirt. "So it's true," she said as the truckie went down on her, "you truck drivers sure know the best places to eat."

TURKS

WHEN the sultan entered his harem unexpectedly his wives let out a terrified sheik.

* * *

THE sultan had ten wives.
    Nine of them had it pretty soft.

* * *

IN the harem, a lonely girl calls
    But the guard takes no notice at alls
    When asked if he cheats
    On the sultan, he bleats,
    "Oh I would, but I ain't got the balls."

U

UNDERTAKERS

IT is an unusual profession, but somebody has to do it and the money is good. Which is why old Marmaduke assigned his son as an apprentice to the great funeral director, Turner Sod.

Each evening the proud father would ask young Marmaduke what he learned in his profession.

"Well Dad," said the lad. "We had an unusual job today. We got a phone call from the Ritz to say that a man and woman had died in the hotel. They had died side by side, lying naked on a double bed."

"Well, what happened?" pressed the father. "I am sure the great Turner Sod could handle it."

"Indeed he did, Father. We donned our mourning coats and top hats and went around in style to the hotel. We met the manager and went up to the room in dignity and silence."

"And what happened then?" said his father.

"Well we came to the room and Turner Sod pushed the door open with his brolly and we entered quietly in a solemn manner befitting the occasion, and there, on the bed was this naked couple lying on their backs.

"Mr Turner's practised eye saw what I thought would be a problem. The man had a gigantic erection. But it was no problem to the experienced Mr Turner Sod who simply turned his brolly around and gave it a mighty whack with the handle."

"And what happened then, Son?"

"A hell of a commotion, Dad. We had entered the wrong room!"

* * *

DYING aboard ship can also have its complications.

The captain told his first mate, an Irishman, that a passenger had died in cabin 23 and he wanted the mate to arrange the burial at sea.

An hour later the mate returned to report that the matter concerning cabin 25 had been attended to.

"What?" exclaimed the captain, "I said cabin 23. Who the hell was in cabin 25?"

"An Englishman, sir."

"Was he dead?"

"Well, he said he wasn't, but you know what bloody liars those Pommies are!"

* * *

WHEN Widow Bloom saw how the undertaker had laid out her dear departed Horace in his coffin she was mortified to see he was in his grey suit.

"No," she cried. "I promised him I would lay him to rest in his black suit. That's the way he wanted to go."

The undertaker said it was a problem because *rigor mortis* had set in and it would be one hell of a job to change suits.

"We don't care about the cost, just do it," ordered the widow.

Next day she returned to the mortuary to find her husband laid out in his best black suit as he had wished.

"Wasn't so hard was it," she said.

"Not really as it turned out," said the undertaker. "Actually we had another widow insisting her husband should be buried in a grey suit. So we just swapped heads!"

RON Sup was a Chinese funeral director.

On the front of his parlor was his business sign: 'People Buried. R Sup.

* * *

ALL her life she had been a good-time girl.

In fact they had to bury her in a Y-shaped coffin.

UNIONS

THE police came to the factory and asked for a suspect called Harry Fukbrake.

The foreman said he didn't know him but turned and shouted: "Do we have a Fukbrake here?"

The union steward replied: "Christ, we've just managed to get a tea brake."

* * *

UNION shop steward telling his kid a bedtime story:

"One upon a time and a half ..."

* * *

THE sign in the factory read: 'Any Italian who wishes to attend the funeral of a relative must tell the foreman on the day of the game.

* * *

A SHOP steward noticed a sign outside the local church. It said: JESUS LIVES

He hurried to the union office. "Does this mean no Easter holidays?" he asked.

* * *

JAKE the plumber was on a house job and noted that the lady of the house was quite a woman. By mid afternoon they were having a tumble in the bedroom when the phone rang.

"That's my husband," she said. "He is coming home now because he has a meeting tonight. Why don't you come back and we can continue where we left off."

"What?" said the plumber. "On my own time?"

V

VETS

FARMER McTavish had groomed the prize bull for the annual show and was confident of winning a blue ribbon, but on the very eve of the big event he was aghast to find the bull had gone cock-eyed.

He made a panic call to the vet who was quickly on the scene and summed up the problem in a professional and composed manner. He simply picked up a length of plastic pipe from the barn floor, inserted one end in the bull's rectum and blew forcefully on the other.

The bull's eyes popped straight ahead.

But next day, as McTavish unloaded the bull into his stall at the show, he was distraught to find the cock-eyed affliction had returned.

He shoved the pipe up the bull's bum and blew for all he was worth, but to no avail. In desperation he made another panic call to the vet, who once again arrived in his usual calm manner.

"I did what you did," said McTavish. "But it doesn't work."

"Show me," said the vet.

Once again McTavish shoved the pipe in and blew his best.

"No, no," said the vet. He pulled the pipe out, turned it

round, and plunged the opposite end into the beast. He gave one puff and the bull's eyes popped straight.

"Oh, so I was using the wrong end of the pipe?" said McTavish.

"No," said the vet. "It makes no difference."

"Then why did you turn it around?"

"You don't think I would use the same end you've had in your mouth do you?" said the vet.

VIETNAMESE

HUNG Le, Australia's Vietnamese comic asks: "How do you know when a Vietnamese has robbed your house?"

He says because the dog is missing and your homework's done.

* * *

A VIETNAMESE migrant got excited when he saw a hot dog stall. "You beauty," he said, until he took a closer look.

"That's disgusting," he said. "In my country we don't eat that part of the dog."

* * *

SIGN on a Vietnamese restaurant door: DOGS NOT ALLOWED...OUT

* * *

HUNG LE said he came to Australia aboard a very leaky prawn boat. "It was so leaky even the prawns were wearing life jackets," he said.

VIRGINS

"OOPS," he said, "I think I felt something break."

"Oh, it's okay," she replied.'It's only my promise to my mother."

* * *

A VIRGIN is a nice girl who whispers sweet nothing-doings in your ear.

HE said: "Do you know what virgins eat for breakfast?"

"No," she said.

"I didn't think so," he said.

* * *

THE old hillbilly wanted to know why his son had suddenly cancelled his wedding when so much preparation for a wing-ding party had taken place.

"Well, Pa," drawled the son, "I got to feeling in Betsy-Lou's pants and I found out she's a virgin. That's why I decided not to marry her."

"Quite right, son," said the old man, "if she ain't good enough fer her kinfolks, then she ain't good enough for ours neither."

* * *

GERALD had always been intent on marrying a virgin and purposely selected a bride who had attended convent school all her life.

In the lobby of the hotel in which they were to spend their wedding night they passed the bar and the bride was surprised to see so many single women in there.

"I am afraid they are prostitutes," said her husband.

Gerald was delighted to hear her next question. "What's a prostitute?" she asked.

"A prostitute," said Gerald with disdain, "is a woman who will go to bed with any man for money."

"Really," said the bride in amazement, "the priests only gave us lollies."

* * *

FARMER Brown and his wife had sacrificed all to send their daughter to a convent school for a good education and when she came home for Christmas he drove in to the railway station.

"I've got a confession to make, Dad." she said while driving back to the farm. "I ain't a virgin anymore."

"What will your mother say?" he said, "after all that money spent on your education and you still say ain't."

NO longer a virgin, but wise
    She managed a marriage disguise
    More verbal than surgical art
    She mentally refurbished the part
    By constructing a tissue of lies.

W

WAITERS

"WAITER, are you sure this lobster is fresh?"

"Yes Sir, it walked here from the beach this morning."

The customer gave it another sniff. "Well I think it must have trodden in something on the way!"

* * *

"WAITER, why have you got your thumb in my soup?"

"It's bruised, sir, the doctor told me to keep it warm."

"He should have told you to stick it up your arse."

"That's what I do in the kitchen, sir."

* * *

MOISHE settled down in his favourite kosher restaurant. "Oi waiter, do you have matzo balls?"

"No," he said, "I always walk like this!"

WANKERS

HE was a whimsical masturbator, with an offbeat sense of humour.

* * *

HE was a disfunctional male patient and the sex therapist was advising him on the release that could be obtained through masturbation.

"Oh but I do get pleasure from my organ," he replied. "I frequently grasp my penis and hold it tight. It's a habit with me."

"Well, it's a habit you'll have to shake," said the therapist.

* * *

THERE is a big difference between an egg and a wank.
You can beat an egg, but you can't beat a wank.

* * *

THERE is a big difference between wanking and clogs.
You can hear yourself coming in clogs.

* * *

HE was such a conceited wanker he would call out his own name and come.

* * *

WHY is masturbation better than intercourse?
Because you know who you are dealing with.
Because you don't have to buy flowers.
Because you know when you've had enough.
Because you don't have to be polite.
Because you don't have to make conversation.
Because you don't have to look your best.
Because you meet a better class of person.

* * *

A SHAKESPEARIAN actor was being interviewed by the press.
"Did you ever have a really embarrassing experience?"
"Well, yes. One experience I will never forget was when my mother caught me playing with myself."
"Oh we all did that when we were kids."
"Yes, but this was last night."

* * *

WANKING is very much like playing Bridge.
If you've got a good hand you don't need a partner.

* * *

LOVERS may celebrate Valentine's Day, but wankers celebrate Palm Sunday.

THE leading manufacturer of imported vibrators is a Japanese firm called Genital Electric.

* * *

FRED had been stranded on the desert island for three years and now had blisters on his hands. One day he grabbed his old binoculars and scanned the horizon.

"My God, a ship," he muttered to himself. And there, on the mast, a naked blonde, beautiful breasts, and look at those hips, wow, she is headed this way."

By now he had a roaring erection.

Suddenly he flung the binoculars away and grabbed his donk.

"Gotcha again, ya bastard. There is no bloody ship."

* * *

IT was the Yuppies turn to host the bridge club evening and although they packed their 12 year-old son off to bed early, Junior was constantly coming downstairs and interrupting the game asking for drinks of water, wanting to go to the toilet, and had one excuse after another.

Finally one of the guests, Miss Lottzabazooma, said she could sort the matter out and took the youngster upstairs.

When she returned the game ran smoothly and there wasn't another sound from the lad all night.

As the guests were leaving the young mother asked Miss Lottzabazooma what her secret was.

"Nothing really," she said, "I just taught him to masturbate."

* * *

OLD Beryl and Dave struck up a relationship in the nursing home. They would meet in the television room after the evening meal, spread a rug across their adjacent chairs and Beryl would quietly give Dave a hand job.

Then one night Beryl was alarmed to see another woman sitting next to Dave, the rug spread across their knees and tell-tale movement beneath it.

"How could you, Dave?" said Beryl.

"I'm sorry," said Dave, "but she's got Parkinson's."

* * *

GOING down to the workshed one day a father surprised his 15 year-old son masturbating. In an understanding manner the father explained that what the boy had been doing was natural enough because the urge for release was strong.

"But you must save all that energy and not waste it," he said. "That sperm is your life essence. Save it until you are a man and can use it in the normal manner."

The boy promised and the years slipped by.

He was given a great party on his 21st birthday and when the guests had left he thanked his dad. "I never forgot what you told me in shed years ago," he said. "And I saved my seed like you told me to. But now I am a man and I have three barrels full. Heck Dad, what the hell will I do with it?"

* * *

BASIL was still pulling his pud and by his 30th birthday his father took him aside and said he would have to get married.

So Basil found himself a nice girl, got married and brought her home. Yet less than a month after the wedding the father found him whacking off in the shed again.

"What's this?" he said, "I thought this would stop once you got married."

"But Dad, the poor girl's not used to it. Her little arms get so tired."

* * *

THE American tourist got the shock of his life when the Mexican, brandishing a six-shooter, jumped out from behind a cactus.

"Take my money, my car, but don't kill me," said the tourist.

"I no kill you if you do what I say," said the Mexican. "Just unzip your pants and start masturbating," he ordered.

Although shocked the traveller did what he was told.

"Right, now do it again," said the Mexican.

The Yank protested but with the gun against his nose he managed again.

"And yet again, Gringo, or I shoot you dead."

With sweat running down his brow the Yank managed a final effort and fell exhausted.

"Good," said the Mexican, "now you can give my sister a ride to the next village."

* * *

"ACCORDING to the latest survey," said the sex therapist to the reporter, "only half the population sing in the shower. The other half masturbate. And do you know what the singers sing?"

"No," said the reporter.

"No, I didn't think you did."

* * *

THE single girl told her psychiatrist: "I sometimes have 20 or so consecutive orgasms during my clitoris stimulation sessions."

"That's amazing," said the normally unflappable shrink.

"Oh, I don't know," shrugged the woman, "after 16 or so I run out of fantasies and from then on it's not much fun."

WARDROBES

THE husband came home to find his wife in bed. Then he opened the wardrobe door to discover a naked woman.

"Well," he said to the stranger in the wardrobe, "fancy finding a nice girl like you in the old proverbial situation like this?"

* * *

THE car was heard to stop in the driveway. "Jeez, that's my husband," she said. Her lover grabbed a gun from his coat and jumped into the wardrobe.

The husband came in, saw his wife in bed and yelled: "I know there is a man in here. Just wait till I find him."

He looked out on the window ledge. "He's not here," he said.

He looked under the bed. "He's not here," he said.

He looked in the wardrobe where he saw the lover with the gun. "And he's not here either."

* * *

A BUSINESSMAN arrived home unexpectedly in the afternoon to find his wife in bed and the milkman standing naked in the middle of the room.

"I'm glad you arrived Mr Sullivan," said the milkman, squatting down on his haunches. "I was just explaining to your wife that if the milk bill is not paid immediately I am going to shit on this carpet!"

* * *

THE back door slammed. "Hell, it's my husband," she cried, "quick, hide in that wardrobe."

He gathered up his clothes and dived from the bed to the wardrobe in a flash. After a few moments another voice in the wardrobe said: "It's bloody dark in here isn't it?"

The man, shivering in the nude, was shocked. "Who is it?" he whispered. It was a little boy's voice and it said: "I know who you are and it will cost you. Promise to give me $50 and I won't yell for my dad."

He was in no position to argue, he grudgingly paid up, and when the crisis was over made a quick exit from the bedroom window.

Next day the little boy and his mother were down town and he said he was going to buy a brand new skateboad. "What with?" asked his mother.

"I've got $50" said the boy.

"Where did you get that kind of money?" asked his mother, but the lad refused to tell.

"You must have done something wrong," she persisted

and after slapping him about shoved him into the nearby church.

"Confession is the thing for you, my lad. If you won't tell me, then you will have to tell the parish priest," and she shoved him into the confessional box and shut the door.

"It's bloody dark in here," said the boy.

"Now don't you start that again," said the priest.

WEATHER

COLD as the depths of a polar bear's pool,
  Cold as the tip of an Icelander's tool.

* * *

IT was so cold that Old Jake woke to find two ice cubes in his sleeping bag. When he threw them on the fire they went "Fartzzz!"

* * *

FATHER Murphy was sent to a small Eskimo village in the northern wastes of Alaska. After a year the bishop paid him a visit.

"How do you stand the weather, my son?" asked the bishop.

"Oh I don't care how cold it gets," said Father Murphy, "I have my Rosary and my vodka."

"That's good," said the bishop. "Come to mention it, I wouldn't mind a vodka right now."

"No problem," said the priest. "Hey Rosary, bring two vodkas, pronto."

* * *

IT was so cold in London last week that the local flasher on the Thames Embankment was spotted describing himself to a group of women.

* * *

IT was so cold it would freeze the walls off a bark humpy.

* * *

IT was dry as a Pommie's towel.

WHEN Mrs Lottsabazooma got caught in the rain after buying a brand new hat for the Easter Parade she hoisted her dress up over her hat and dashed for cover.

It brought a comment from a taxi driver: "Hey Missus," he said. "Your arse is sticking out in the rain."

"Don't I know it," said our heroine. "But that arse is 45 years old and this hat is brand new."

* * *

THE wind blew so hard...

it blew three dogs off their chains...

a chook facing east laid the same egg three times...

it blew the pricks off a barbed wire fence.

WEDDINGS

THE priest was partial to the whisky bottle and when the young couple stood before the altar to be married the bride noticed he was slurring the wrong words.

"Father," she said, "you are reading the burial service."

"Doesn't matter," he whispered back, "you'll be under the sod tonight either way."

* * *

THE couple at the altar had almost the same thought.

He: "All I have to do is say 'I do' and I can have sex whenever I want."

She: "All I have to do is say 'I do' and I never have to have sex again."

* * *

IT was a typical Outback wedding and the celebrations had been raging for two days before Ned finally arrived at the shearing shed with his present. It was there he encountered his mate Joe leaving the party.

"Don't go in," warned Joe. "There's bound to be strife. They've run out of beer and the best man has just rooted the bride."

Indeed that meant trouble and Ned turned back towards

his car. They were about to leave when another guest came out of the hall and shouted: "Don't go you blokes. No problems. There's another keg on the way and the best man has apologised."

* * *

THERE was a little man
 And he had a little gun
 And his bullets were made of lead
 He stood close by
 With a fatherly eye
 While me and my girl were wed.

WELSH

WHY are the Welsh always singing?
 Because they don't have doors on their dunnies.

WIDOWS

THE pretty widow went into the hardware shop. She wanted a hinge for her back door. She selected one and asked if it would do the job.

"You will need a screw," said the shopkeeper.

"You men are all the same," she replied, "but I'll give you a blow job for that toaster on the top shelf."

* * *

PRETTY Widow Winkle had been in hospital three days before the vicar learned that his favourite parishioner was ill.

"But I prayed for you last night," he said as he paid his first visit.

"Silly man," she pouted. "You know I'm on the phone."

* * *

THE lawyer informed the widow: "I'm sorry to tell you, but Fred left all he had to the Twilight Home for Destitute Women."

"But what about me?"

"You're all he had."

* * *

SID Skinflint had been as mean as a junk yard dog all his life, and had been particularly stingy to his wife. So it was with some surprise to mortuary officials when she insisted on taking his ashes home in a box.

Back at the house she placed the box on the table and began walking around the room talking aloud.

"Sid, you know the red sports car I always wanted and you would never give me? Well, there it is in the driveway."

"And Sid," she said. "You know the diamond rings I always wanted and you would never buy me? Well, here they are, all from your insurance," and she displayed some dazzlers on three fingers.

"And here are the pearls I've always wanted."

"And Sid. You know that blow job you always wanted? Well, here it is," and with that she blew his ashes to buggery.

WOMEN

WOMEN have only themselves to blame for all the lying men do.

They ask so many damned questions.

* * *

THERE is hardly a woman in this country who hasn't been asked to marry at least twice.

Once by her mother and once by her father.

* * *

A WISE woman is one who makes her husband feel as if he is master of the house, when in reality he is only chairman of the entertainment committee.

* * *

HE was a bit old to be chasing young girls so one of the neighbours alerted his wife to his disgusting habit.

"It doesn't worry me," said the wife. "He can chase girls

if he wants to. After all, dogs chase cars. I've never seen a dog catch one and I doubt if they could drive one if they did."

WOMEN'S TALK

"HOW was your blind date?" asked one girl of her flatmate.

"Boring," she replied. "He was so boring I finally agreed to sit on his face just to stop him from talking."

* * *

"WHEN I met him in the singles bar I told him I was Libra on the cusp of Scorpio. He replied that he was Taurus with penis rising."

* * *

"GOING out with Trevor is like playing draughts," she said, "I make one move and he jumps me."

* * *

"FIRST I faked chastity," she said, "then I faked orgasm. And now I fake fidelity."

* * *

"I'LL never forget the night my husband discovered my great love," she said.

"What happened?"

"He beat the shit out of him."

* * *

"WHY did you divorce that big strong bikie?"

"Beats me."

* * *

"WHAT do women desire most in a man?" she asked, "brains, wealth or appearance?"

"Appearance," was the quick reply, "and the sooner the better."

* * *

"DID you sleep with my husband last night?"

"Not a wink."

"IT was a wonderful night. I had three orgasms," she said.

"Oh, I had 50," said her friend.

"He must have been a marvellous lover,"

"Oh, you mean with just one bloke!"

* * *

"MY boyfriend has just graduated as a doctor. So he is going to practice for a few years before we get married."

* * *

"DID Noreen discover the cause of those green marks on the inside of her thighs?"

"Yes. It appears her boyfriend's earrings are not gold after all."

* * *

"WHEN my sugar daddy dies I inherit the lot. It is in his last will and testicles."

"You mean testament."

"No. I've got him by the balls."

WORDS

CUNNILINGUS is a real tongue twister.

* * *

WHAT a lot of cunning linguists you are.

* * *

'CONTAGIOUS was the word the students had to use in a sentence and little Johnny's hand was up like a rocket.

"My dad doesn't like the fruiterer next door so when he knocked over his case of oranges he said it would take that con-tages to pick them all up."

* * *

"DO you know the difference between a popular girl and an unpopular girl?"

"Yes and no."

* * *

A GIRL from the country called at the hospital.

"I'd like to see an out-turn, please," she said.

"You mean an intern?" said the nurse.

"Whatever you call him, I want a contamination," she insisted.

"You mean an examination," said the nurse.

"Yes, I need to see the fraternity ward."

"You mean the maternity ward."

"Call it what you will," said the girl with annoyance. "But I certainly know I haven't demonstrated for two months and I think I'm stagnant."

* * *

THE professor was teaching an African tribe English and took the chief through the jungle pointing out various objects and relating their names, like 'Tree, monkey, bush, river.

They came across a nude couple screwing away on the river bank.

"What's dat?" said the chief.

The embarrassed professor said, "Bike."

The chief stabbed his spear into the rider's arse.

"Why did you do that?" said the professor.

"My bike," said the chief.

* * *

WHEN it came to writing up the log book Captain Squiggs was a stickler for accuracy, so when the first mate received news that he was the father of twins and celebrated in his cabin the captain noted in the logbook: 'The first mate was drunk last night.

When the mate saw it he argued that it should be struck from the record but the pedantic captain was resolute. "You were drunk last night. I can't change that fact, so it must stay in the log."

Next day the mate was on watch and it was his duty to keep the log.

In the morning the captain was aghast to read: "The captain was sober last night."

WORDS were the big topic of the million dollar television quiz show where Professor Geewhizz challenged the audience to stump him with a word he couldn't put into a sentence.

"Garn!" shouted a bloke in the third row.

"Garn?" said the professor, "Garn? It's not a swear word is it?"

"No," said the punter in the third row, "Garn."

Time elapsed, the buzzer went and the crowd applauded.

"You've stumped him," said the MC, "How do you use the word, sir?"

"Garn get fucked," said the punter and the show was closed immediately.

It took the network 12 months to get over it. Finally they had the gumption to start it up again with the proviso that they would have to screen the audience in future.

On the opening night they scrutinised each member of the audience as they arrived before asking for the first word.

A man in the third row wearing a vicar's collar and a beard put his hand up. "Smee," he said.

"Smee?" said the professor, "Smee?" The seconds ticked away and he was forced to concede on the very first word.

After the applause had died down the MC asked the punter: "How do you use the word?"

The punter stood up, pulled his false beard off and said: "Smee again. Garn get fucked!"

Z

ZOOS

A KID at the monkey enclosure said: "Hey, Mum. How long does it take to make a baby monkey?"

"About six months," she said.

"Then why are those two in such a hurry?"

* * *

CLEANING out the aviary at a run-down zoo the keeper finds two finches have dropped dead from old age.

In the monkey cage he discovers two of the oldest chimps have also kicked the bucket.

Waste not want not so he puts them in a sack with the finches and later tips them in the lion's cage at feeding time.

"Bloody hell," roars the lion. "Not finch and chimps again."

* * *

TWO zebras were debating. Were they white with black stripes or black with white stripes? The argument went on for hours until they decided to ask the wise old lion.

"Go to the mountain and ask God," said Leo.

The zebras climbed the mountain and after bellowing out the question: "Are we black with white stripes or white with black stripes?" there was a bolt of lightning and a voice roared: "You are what you are!"

The puzzled zebras went back to the lion. "What does it mean?" they asked.

"It means that you are white with black stripes," said the lion immediately, "otherwise He would have said: "Yo is wot yo is!"

* * *

THE city zoo has been showing sex films to a male and female chimpanzee in the hope that it will prompt them to breed. So far it hasn't worked, but the zookeeper and his wife close the zoo early every day.

ZENITH

ZENITH, meaning the highest point, is a ploy to have the author's favourite joke last, The Sex-Crazed Crane Driver:

* * *

CONSTRUCTION of the 50-level city tower was behind schedule and pressure was being applied to finish it on time. Gardeners were moved in to start the landscaping at ground level while carpenters were fitting out at mid-level and the crane was still lifting on the top floor.

One day the crane driver's apprentice drew his boss's attention to the absence of a dunny on the roof and that he was busting for a leak.

Conceding the lack of a loo the crane driver said there would be no problem if the lad hopped into the crane's bucket while he swung it high over the city.

"Look, Son, it's so high that it will disintigrate into fine spray long before it hits the ground. No worries."

So the lad did just that.

By the time the crane driver retrieved the bucket and the lad climbed out the boss himself was strongly inclined to take a leak.

"Well hop in the bucket. I can drive it," said the eager apprentice.

The boss was unsure, but bladder pressure was building.

"Okay," he said with crossed legs. "The green button is for easing the bucket out, the yellow button brings it back.

But whatever you do, don't touch that red button. It opens the bottom of the bucket."

"No worries, boss," said our eager lad.

While the apprentice swung the crane over Collins St with its precious cargo and the boss began to enjoy a well-earned leak a blonde in a mini-skirt swanked by the gardeners on the ground level who gave her an appreciative whistle.

The carpenters way up on the middle level heard it and looked down. They gave her a whistle too.

The crane driver's apprentice on the roof heard it and he leaned over for a look ... and put his elbow fair and square on the red button.

It was only a matter of seconds later when one of the carpenters on the mid level said to his mate: "Those crane drivers are sex crazed."

"What makes you say that?" enquired his mate.

"Well, did you see that blonde walk past down in the street?"

"Yes,"

"Well I just saw one of the crane drivers streak past with his cock in his hand screaming "C

                              u

                               n

                                t!

          *   *   *

                      C

                       u

                        n

                         t!"